BELFAST INSTITUTE

3 7777 00154553 2

Belfast Met Libraries

658.4038011
TURB
1545532

BTT

8th Edition

Information Technology for Man...

International Student Version

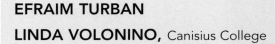

EFRAIM TURBAN

LINDA VOLONINO, Canisius College

contributing authors:

JANICE C. SIPIOR, Villanova University

GREGORY R. WOOD, Canisius College

WILEY   John Wiley & Sons, Inc.

Copyright © 2012 John Wiley & Sons (Asia) Pte Ltd

Cover Image from © ARTSILENSECOM/Shutterstock

Founded in 1807, John Wiley & Sons, Inc. has been a valued source of knowledge and understanding for more than 200 years, helping people around the world meet their needs and fulfill their aspirations. Our company is built on a foundation of principles that include responsibility to the communities we serve and where we live and work. In 2008, we launched a Corporate Citizenship Initiative, a global effort to address the environmental, social, economic, and ethical challenges we face in our business. Among the issues we are addressing are carbon impact, paper specifications and procurement, ethical conduct within our business and among our vendors, and community and charitable support. For more information, please visit our website: *www.wiley.com/go/citizenship*.

All rights reserved. This book is authorized for sale in Europe, Asia, Africa and the Middle East only and may not be exported outside of these territories. Exportation from or importation of this book to another region without the Publisher's authorization is illegal and is a violation of the Publisher's rights. The Publisher may take legal action to enforce its rights. The Publisher may recover damages and costs, including but not limited to lost profits and attorney's fees, in the event legal action is required.

No part of this publication may be reproduced, stored in a retrieval system, or transmitted in any form or by any means, electronic, mechanical, photocopying, recording, scanning, or otherwise, except as permitted under Section 107 or 108 of the 1976 United States Copyright Act, without either the prior written permission of the Publisher or authorization through payment of the appropriate per-copy fee to the Copyright Clearance Center, Inc., 222 Rosewood Drive, Danvers, MA 01923, website www.copyright.com. Requests to the Publisher for permission should be addressed to the Permissions Department, John Wiley & Sons, Inc., 111 River Street, Hoboken, NJ 07030, (201) 748-6011, fax (201) 748-6008, website *http://www.wiley.com/go/permissions*.

ISBN: 978-1-118-09225-5

Printed in Asia

10 9 8 7 6 5 4 3 2 1

BRIEF CONTENTS

CONTENTS

Students graduating today face a tough job market—making it important that they develop the expertise and critical thinking skills that give them a competitive edge. *Information Technology for Management*, 8th edition is designed to give students an edge when they face the challenges and opportunities that business careers present. This textbook covers the content that students need *to learn* and *to be able to use* for successful and sustainable management careers in any of the functional areas. For example, students learn the business value and process of actually doing mobile commerce, managing customer and supplier relationships, using business intelligence and cloud computing applications, and many other IT-centric business functions.

Each chapter reinforces important business principles: *What companies can do depends on what their information systems can do*—and what information systems can do depends on what managers understand about the latest IT, such as mobile devices, wireless networks, social media, logistic systems, interoperability, collaboration, and Internet apps. As information technologies mature and become more widespread, they add to the global IT infrastructure that support next-generation (next-gen) IT-based business strategies.

Our goal is to develop a textbook that covers meaningful foundations and trends in information systems and technology *in-depth* and *in-context;* and to provide students with a portfolio of IT skills to give them a competitive edge when competing for jobs and job advancements. We believe that providing content *in-context—i.e., within a business context*—is essential to the understanding and value of traditional and emerging information systems and technologies. Our emphasis is on both operational and strategic performance of all types of organizations—for-profit, nonprofit, healthcare, and government agencies.

Organization of the Book

The book is divided into five parts, composed of 14 chapters. On the book's Web site (*www.wiley.com/go/global/turban*) are five Technology Guides (Tech Guides), each chapter's *Link Library* with clickable links, and 23 supplemental cases. The Tech Guides cover:

1. Hardware
2. Software
3. Data and Databases
4. Telecommunications
5. A Technical View of System Analysis and Design

New and Enhanced Features of this Text

Our plan was to develop a text that prepares students in all business majors to succeed in their careers. In developing the 8th edition of *Information Technology for Management*, we have achieved our goal with the following changes in content, organization, and pedagogical features.

- **We streamlined and smoothed the flow throughout the text**, reducing the size of most chapters, as well as the number of chapters and topics covered.

- **Greater depth, simpler presentation**. We cover the most critical operational and strategic IT issues in greater depth, and have eliminated less critical topics. The 8th edition consists of fourteen chapters—all of which are in the printed book, five online Tech Guides, and 23 online cases.

- **New emphasis on *how to do things*** and explanation at both the operational and strategic levels so students are exposed to both perspectives. We discuss IT in-context so students develop a portfolio of IT skills.

- **New in-depth coverage of cutting edge topics** like IT governance, connectivity blurring public and private lives, sustainability, enterprise social media, and viral and social marketing.

- **New chapter on social networks** and the Web 2.0 environment.

- **We replaced chapter summaries with chapter previews.** Each chapter starts with a *Quick Look* to introduce students to the business issues, challenges, and IT solutions discussed in the chapter. In effect, instead of a chapter summary, we provide a chapter preview of the most valuable and interesting topics, which are explained in the chapter.

- We replaced introductory minicases with forward-thinking *For Class Discussion and Debate*, which consist of two sections. The first section, named *Scenarios for Brainstorming and Discussion,* engage students in critical thinking exercises. The second section, *Debate*, presents two conflicting scenarios to be debated by teams of students. These scenarios get students immersed and engaged in discussions and debates of

IT issues and their ethical, managerial and/or competitive implications.

- After each chapter is a **Business Case** of a for-profit enterprise and a **NEW** **Public Sector** or **Nonprofit Case.** We provide all sectors because of the sharp growth of nonprofits and government agencies.

- **NEW** *Analysis Using Spreadsheets* or *Analysis Using Simulation* activities in every chapter further engage students in research, critical thinking, analysis, problem solving, and decision making.

Hallmark Features of this Text

- *Failures and Lessons Learned.* We acknowledge the fact that many systems fail. Many chapters include discussions or examples of failures, the contributing factors, and the lessons learned from them.

- *Solid Theoretical Backing.* Throughout the book, we present the theoretical foundation necessary for understanding IT.

- *Up-to-Date Information.* Every topic in the book has been researched to find the most up-to-date information and features.

- *Economic Justification.* IT is mature enough to stand the difficult test of economic justification. It is our position that IT investments must be scrutinized like any other investment despite the difficulties of measuring technology benefits.

- *Ethics and Social Responsibility.* We take an expanded look at global warming, ecology, and managers' responsibility to individuals, society, and the environment. For example, we did extensive research to understand and then clearly explain how IT and users can reduce carbon emissions and global warming that harm the planet through green business practices and data center designs that conserve natural resources.

Pedagogical Features

We developed a number of pedagogical features to aid student learning and tie together the themes of the book.

- *Link Libraries.* Each chapter starts with a list of URLs that will be referenced in the chapter. Link Libraries with live links to the referenced URLs may be found on the book companion sites at *www.wiley.com/go/global/turban.*

- *Quick Look.* The chapter outline provides a quick indication of the major topics covered in the chapter.

- *Learning Objectives.* Learning objectives listed at the beginning of each chapter help students focus their efforts and alert them to the important concepts that will be discussed.

- *For Class Discussion and Debate.* Each chapter opens with scenarios for class discussion and team debate.

- *"IT at Work" Boxes.* The IT at Work boxes spotlight some real-world innovations and new technologies that companies are using to solve organizational dilemmas or create new business opportunities.

- *Highlighted Icons.* Icons appear throughout the text to relate the topics covered within each chapter to some major themes of the book. The icons alert students to the related functional areas, to IT failures, and to global and ethical issues.

 Ethics-related topic

 Global enterprises and issues

 Lessons to be learned from IT failures

 Accounting example

 Finance example

 Government example

 Human resources management example

 Marketing example

 Production/operations management example

 Service-company example (for example, health services, educational services, and other non-manufacturing examples)

 Material at the book's Web site: *www.wiley.com/go/global/turban*

- **Review Questions.** Each section of each chapter ends with detailed questions for review.
- *Glossary of Key Terms.* The key terms and concepts are typeset in boldface blue when first introduced in a chapter, and are defined at the end of the book.
- *Chapter Highlights.* Important concepts covered in the chapter are listed at the end of the chapter and are linked by number to the learning objectives introduced at the beginning of each chapter, to reinforce the important ideas discussed.
- *End-of-Chapter Questions and Exercises.* Different types of questions measure student comprehension and students' ability to apply knowledge. *Questions for Review* ask students to summarize the concepts introduced. Discussion Questions are intended to promote class discussion and develop critical thinking skills.
- *Exercises and Projects.* Exercises are challenging assignments that require the students to apply what they have learned in each chapter to a situation. This includes many hands-on exercises as described earlier, including the use of search engines and the Web.
- *Group Assignments.* Comprehensive group assignments, including Internet research, oral presentations to the class, and debates, are available in each chapter.
- *Internet Exercises.* Hands-on exercises send the students to interesting Web sites to explore those sites; find resources; investigate an application; compare, analyze, and summarize information; or learn about the state of the art of a topic.
- *Business Case* of a for-profit enterprise.
- *Public Sector* or *Nonprofit Case.*
- *Analysis Using Spreadsheets* or *Analysis Using Simulation.* These exercises further engage students in research, critical thinking, analysis, problem solving, and decision making.

Supplementary Materials

An extensive package of instructional materials is available to support this 8th edition.

- *Instructor's Manual.* The Instructor's Manual presents objectives from the text with additional information to make them more appropriate and useful for the instructor. The manual also includes practical applications of concepts, case study elaboration, answers to end-of-chapter questions, questions for review, questions for discussion, and Internet exercises.
- *Test Bank.* The test bank contains over 1,000 questions and problems (about 75 per chapter) consisting of multiple-choice, short answer, fill-ins, and critical thinking/essay questions.

- *PowerPoint Presentation.* A series of slides designed around the content of the text incorporates key points from the text and illustrations where appropriate.
- *Textbook Web Site.* (*wiley.com/go/global/turban*). The book's Web site extends the content and themes of the text to provide extensive support for instructors and students. Organized by chapter, it includes the Link Libraries, additional cases, PowerPoint slides and more.
- *NEW Weekly Updates* (www.wileyinformationsystems updates.com). Wiley's IS Weekly Updates keep instructors and students on top of the latest in new stories about IS and business issues. Each week we deliver several new articles, video clips, news stories and more, complete with discussion questions to spark debate in the classroom.

Acknowledgments

Janice C. Sipior (Villanova University) and Gregory R. Wood (Canisius College) are the contributing authors on the 8th edition. Janice provided her expertise on IT strategic planning. Greg developed and wrote *Chapter 7, Mobile Computing and Commerce* and *Chapter 8, Web 2.0 and Social Media* to provide the latest strategies and trends in those key cross-functional IT/marketing issues.

Faculty feedback was essential to the development of the book. Many individuals participated in focus groups and/or acted as reviewers. Several others created portions of chapters or cases, especially international cases, some of which are in the text and others on the Web site.

Our sincere thanks to the following reviewers who provided valuable feedback, insights, and suggestions that improved the quality of this text.

David Teneyuca, University of Texas San Antonio
Jerry Fjermestad, New Jersey Institute of Technology
David Bloomquist, Georgia State University
Kemal Altinkemer, Purdue University
Richard Segall, Arkansas State University
Eileen Griffin, Canisius College
Michael Mick, Purdue University Calumet
Beena George, University of St. Thomas Houston
Dan Humpert, University of Cincinnati
Greg Dawson, Arizona State University
Albert Lederer, University of Kentucky
Maureen Cass, Bellevue University
Mike Totaro, University of Southwestern Louisiana
Fiona Fui-Hoon Nah, University of Nebraska at Lincoln
Samuel Elko, Seton Hall University
Carol Jeffries-Horner, Our Lady of the Lake University
Melody N. White, University of North Texas
Susan Chinburg, Rogers State University

Barin Nag, Towson University
Jeff Miner, Rensselaer Polytechnic Institute
Werner Schenk, University of Rochester
Shimon Nof, Purdue University
Sung-Kwan Kim, University of Arkansas at Little Rock

We thank the dedicated staff of John Wiley & Sons: Chris Ruel and Mike Berlin; and the production management services of Suzanne Ingrao. A special thanks to Beth Lang Golub, who helped us to achieve this "designed for learning" 8th edition that we proudly present to you.

Linda Volonino
Efraim Turban
Janice C. Sipior
Gregory R. Wood

DR. EFRAIM TURBAN

Dr. Efraim Turban obtained his M.B.A. and Ph.D. degrees from the University of California, Berkeley. His industry experience includes eight years as an industrial engineer, three of which were spent at General Electric Transformers Plant in Oakland, California. He also has extensive consulting experience to small and large corporations as well as to governments. In his over thirty years of teaching, Professor Turban has served as Chaired Professor at Eastern Illinois University, and as Visiting Professor at City University of Hong Kong, Nanyang Technological University in Singapore, National Sun Yat-Sen University in Taiwan, and University of Science and Technology in Hong Kong. He has also taught at UCLA, USC, Simon Fraser University, Lehigh University, California State University, Long Beach, and Florida International University.

Dr. Turban was a co-recipient of the 1984/85 National Management Science Award (Artificial Intelligence in Management). In 1997, he received the Distinguished Faculty Scholarly and Creative Achievement Award at California State University, Long Beach.

Dr. Turban has published over 110 articles in leading journals, including the following: *Management Science, MIS Quarterly, Operations Research, Journal of MIS, Communications of the ACM, International Journal of Electronic Commerce, Information Systems Frontiers, Decision Support Systems, International Journal of Information Management, Heuristics,* and *Expert Systems with Applications.* He has also published 23 books, including *Decision Support Systems and Business Intelligence,* (Prentice Hall); *Expert Systems and Applied Artificial Intelligence* (MacMillan Publishing Co.), *Electronic Commerce: A Managerial Approach,* (Prentice Hall), *Introduction to Information Technology*, (Wiley), and *Introduction to Electronic Commerce,* (Prentice Hall).

DR. LINDA VOLONINO

Dr. Linda Volonino obtained her M.B.A. and Ph.D. degrees from the State University of New York at Buffalo. She is a Senior Editor of *Information Systems Management,* and Associate Editor of *Business Intelligence Journal.* She holds professional certifications as a Certified Information Systems Security Professional (CISSP) and Associate Certified Fraud Examiner (ACFE). She is a consultant for Receivable Management Services, a Dun & Bradstreet strategic partner, providing on-site seminars for senior and financial managers at large U.S. corporations. Dr. Volonino is a member of local and national organizations, including the Teradata University Network (TUN), Information Systems Audit and Control Association (ISACA), Information Systems Security Association (ISSA), the FBI's Infragard, and the Academy of Computing Machinery (ACM).

Professor Volonino developed and directed the Master of Science degree program in Telecommunications Management at Canisius College, Buffalo, NY, and has served as department chair for six years. She has taught as a visiting professor at the University of Southern California (in their overseas program in Germany), the University of Hawaii at Manoa, University of Virginia, City University of Hong Kong, University of Lyon (France), University of Hamburg (Germany), Federal University (Brazil), and Etisalat Academy (Dubai).

Dr. Volonino has coauthored five IT-related books, and has published numerous articles in IT and legal journals, including the *Journal of Data Warehousing, Journal of Management Information Systems, Erie County Bar Bulletin, Ohio Bar Bulletin, Communications of the Association for Information Systems,* and *Information Systems Management.* She has presented over a hundred seminars and workshops on cutting-edge IT topics.

Chapter

1

Information Systems in the 2010s

Learning Objectives

❶ Understand the role of information technology (IT) in optimizing performance.

❷ Explain why the business value of IT is determined by people, business processes, and organizational culture.

❸ Describe the role of IT in business performance management and the performance measurement process.

❹ Understand the strategic planning process, SWOT analysis, and competitive models.

❺ Discuss how IT impacts your career and the positive outlook for IS management careers.

Integrating *IT*

ACC

FIN

MKT

OM

HRM

IS

How to generate a Microsoft Tag *microsoft.com/tag/*

How to create a custom 2D tag *mediadl.microsoft.com/mediadl/www/t/tag/*
CreatingCustomTags.wmv

How to download a reader *gettag.mobi/*

Apple iPad *apple.com/ipad/*

iReport, a user-generated section of CNN.com *ireport.com/*

**Harvard Business Review video of Porter and the Five Competitive Forces
Model** *youtube.com/watch?v=mYF2_FBCvXw*

U.S. Bureau of Labor Statistics *bls.gov/oco/ocos258.htm*

Teradata University Network (TUN) *academicprograms.teradata.com/*

Leadership in Energy and Environmental Design (LEED) *usgbc.org/leed*

United States Central Intelligence Agency (CIA) World Factbook *cia.gov/library/publications/*
the-world-factbook/

United Kingdom National Offender Management Information System project (NOMIS)
nao.org.uk/whats_new/0708-1/0809292.aspx

QUICK LOOK at Chapter 1, Information Systems in the 2010s

This section introduces you to the business issues, challenges, and IT solutions in Chapter 1. Topics and issues mentioned in the Quick Look are explained in the chapter.

A strategically important technology trend in businesses worldwide is the growth of **interactivity applications.** Interactivity applications connect, communicate, collaborate, and do commerce on-demand, in real-time, and at a distance. The capability to "reach and respond" on-demand became technically possible thanks to the integration of broadband telecommunications, the Internet, digital communications, high-performance mobile devices, and the digitization of all media content. Integration of information technology (IT) forms the *critical infrastructure,* and that infrastructure enables the next wave of IT developments and breakthroughs.

Why does IT matter to managers? New IT capabilities (e.g., e-commerce and social networks) strongly influence competitive strategies and the efficiency of operations. Imagine the disadvantage to a traditional international retailer, like U.S.-based Walmart (*walmart.com*) or France's Galeries Lafayette (*galerieslafayette.com*), that did not sell via an e-commerce Web site. What would be the impact on a news service such as Reuters that did not add multimedia or on a network such as CNN that did not offer RSS feeds and podcasts in its media mix?

No doubt, failing to invest in IT could drive companies out of business.

New IT developments are important to all business disciplines because they trigger changes in marketing, operations, e-commerce, logistics, human resources, finance, accounting, and relationships with customers and business partners. Nothing about business or **corporate strategy** is untouched by IT. Corporate strategy is the collection of activities and actions a company chooses to invest in and perform, and those it chooses not to invest in or perform.

In Chapter 1, we provide a look at some of the latest IT developments and how companies might deploy them to improve performance. You learn about business-critical information system (IS) applications and IT solutions, most of which integrate wireless networks and social technologies, like Facebook and Twitter. We explain how IT innovations are shaking up or disrupting the ways companies do business, the jobs of managers and workers, the design of business processes, and the structure of markets. IT has evolved from narrowly focused data processing and routine reports in the mid-1970s to a function that supports business processes, manages relationships with customers and suppliers, and creates limitless possibilities in the 2010s—when out of touch means out of business.

Mobile connectivity has shown amazing growth worldwide, with China and India leading that growth. From 2010 to 2011, the number of mobile subscribers (includes feature phone and smartphone subscribers) increased from 4.6 billion to 5.3 billion, equivalent to 77 percent of the world's population.

Growth in Mobile-Only Web Access Is Leading to the "Battle for Mobiles"

According to the technology research company IDC (*idc.com*), sales of smartphone devices in 2010 totaled over 302 million units, up by 74 percent from 2009. Many of those users only access the Internet from their mobiles; that is, they do not or very rarely use a desktop, laptop, or tablet to access the Web. Such mobile-only access in Egypt is 70 percent, in India is 59 percent, and in United States is 25 percent. Now that a significant share of consumers can be reached only via their mobiles, retailers are responding with new tactics and are engaging in a *battle for mobiles*.

Being able to interact with mobile users not just at any time and place, but at the *optimal* time and place, creates many opportunities for retailers. The optimal time and place, from a marketing viewpoint, is when the customer is most likely to respond to an offer. Two-dimensional (2D) tag technology provides this capability. **2D tags**, also called **2D codes**, make it possible to interact with individuals via their mobiles when they are at their most interested and responsive.

Barcodes Are Being Replaced with 2D Codes

Barcodes that you find on products are a one-dimensional (1D) series of black and white stripes, as shown in Figure 1.1(a). Product and price data are stored in stripes that are readable by specialized scanners. New 2D codes, also known as 2D tags, consist of boxes or dots that form a matrix-like pattern, as shown in Figure 1.1(b). Tags have much greater capacity than 1D barcodes and can be designed to be colorful and visually interesting.

Each small box or dot contains data, such as a Web site address. In order to be able to read tags, a software app (application) must be downloaded to the smartphone, which gives the camera the ability to scan. When a camera snaps a 2D tag, the app can load the Web site, an instruction, or an interactive experience depending on what is coded into the tag. The camera needs to meet the code's minimum image resolution for reliable performance, which is not much of a problem because tags are designed to be snapped (scanned) by limited-performance cameras. It is relatively simple for users to find and install the software for the iPhone and Blackberry from app stores.

Japan's QR Code Spreads to Other Countries

Several types of 2D codes and readers exist. The most popular code—**QR (quick response) code**—was invented in Japan. During the 1990s, all Japanese mobile carriers agreed to include QR reading software into their phones. By the early 2000s, 2D tags had become popular in Japan. The 2D technology had spread throughout Japan, Europe, and the United States.

In Europe and America, the most common barcode types are QR and **Data Matrix**. Google's mobile **Android** operating system (OS) supports QR Codes by including the ZXing scanner on some models. Nokia's Symbian OS also has a barcode scanner that reads QR codes. iPhones can decode QR, Data Matrix, and Aztec Codes formats. The Microsoft Tag Reader is compatible with numerous mobile platforms, including the Apple iPhone; Blackberry 81xx, 83xx and Bold; J2ME based handsets; Symbian S60 3rd Edition; and Windows Mobile 5 and 6.

Figure 1.2 QR tag, code, or 2D barcode, used in tracking applications and for mobile phone users or mobile tagging. (© *Max Delson Martins Santos/iStockphoto*)

Pushing Content to Mobiles

Adopters of 2D tags were using tags to push content to mobile devices for advertising, mobile commerce, location-based commerce (l-commerce), customer service, and other

(a) 1D barcode   (b) 2D tag

Figure 1.1 Examples of 1D barcode and 2D tag. (*Wendell Franks/iStockphoto*), (© *Martin McCarthy/iStockphoto*)

revenue-generating purposes. Microsoft introduced its own 2D tag format in 2009, simply named **Tag**. Microsoft Tag uses color to increase the amount of information that can be stored.

For managers, the critical issue with any new IT is to identify and take advantage of its potential business value. To understand 2D tags' potential business value, consider the following list of interactivities that can occur by snapping a tag:

- Load a microsite on the mobile browser
- Deliver text or a message, such as an advertisement or address, to the handheld
- Start streaming a video or audio file
- Download a file
- Initiate an e-mail, instant message, phone call, fax, or other communication

Marketers are devising ways to add interactivity to their products and offline media, such as print materials. Companies can reach prospective and current customers by making their print ads immediately actionable and entertaining. Other benefits of interactivity include being able to track customers' actions. Using tracking data, analysts can evaluate what works best and what does not work in order to learn how to improve their marketing strategies. Given the huge expense of advertising campaigns, knowing what works can increase sales revenues and decrease waste. Here are a few examples showing the potential of tag-triggered interactivity:

- In Singapore, Coca-Cola launched an ad campaign, which began in June 2009, offering free downloadable content to consumers who snapped the tags on its cans. Tag technology is able to identify repeat scans and push fresh content towards the consumer. Linking physical objects to digital content is known as a **hardlink**.
- British retailer Marks and Spencer put Data Matrix 2D codes on their own brand of freshly squeezed juice, which load their 'Food to Go' mobile Web site with information about the product, and a voucher for money off their next juice purchase. The tag is printed directly onto packaging.
- Continental Airlines added QR codes to its mobile boarding pass services to London Heathrow Airport. It was the first airline to offer the convenience of paperless boarding passes on nonstop international flights.

Business Getting Dependent on Mobile IT

The use of 2D tags and readers to connect with consumers at the optimal time reinforces an important business principle: *What companies can do depends on what their information systems (ISs) can do.* And what ISs can do depends on mobile technology, wireless networks, and social media. One obvious change is in e-commerce, which is being done substantially more on mobiles. As ITs mature and become widely used, they build up the global IT infrastructure that supports next generation (next gen) IT-based strategies.

For Class Discussion and Debate

1. *Scenario for Brainstorming and Discussion:* Smartphones have innovative user interfaces and applications as well as significant processing power and storage capacity. And most owners would not ever be without their mobiles. Given those factors, consider a company that you buy products or services from that could benefit by using 2D tags. Benefits could be increased sales or improved customer loyalty.

a. Explain how the company could benefit from the "power and presence" of smartphones and 2D tag interactivity.

b. Describe where the 2D tags should be positioned or located to achieve the benefit.

c. Compare and assess your answers with others in your class.

d. Do you think that you would buy more from this company because of its use of tags? Or do you think that the IT infringes on your privacy?

2. *Debate:* The paradox is that IT advances open up many new opportunities and threaten the status quo. Assume that you work for a bank, credit union, or other financial institution whose problem is attracting new customers. Specifically, the company wants to attract recent college graduates and those in MBA programs. Your company wants to add 2D tags to postcards that are being mailed to targeted prospects (prospective customers) as part of a new marketing campaign. When tags on the postcards are snapped, the 2D tags would link to a compelling offer for customers who opened an account.

To Do: *There are two possible outcomes:* Either this proposed action will solve the problem or it won't. The latter outcome would waste most of the advertising budget. Your position, therefore, is that you're in favor of this IT solution or you're against it. Select one of these two positions and defend it. You need to make logical assumptions to support your position.

1.1 Positioning IT to Optimize Performance

Boom economic conditions typically provide companies with plenty of opportunities to improve performance. But during downturns and global financial crises, opportunities are harder to find and the risk of failure rises. As markets recover from a worldwide recession during the 2010s, managers are exploring new strategies to improve business performance, or profitability. One approach is to develop the *agility* needed to identify and capture opportunities more quickly than rivals.

| AGILITY + MOBILITY

The importance of being an **agile enterprise,** which is one that has the ability to adapt rapidly, has never been greater because of struggling economic recoveries and advances in mobile technology. Within this economic and technological context, we discuss how organizations can benefit from opportunities made possible by high-performance mobile devices and high-speed mobile telecommunication networks. Examples are the 3G (third-generation) and 4G (fourth-generation) networks of cellular service providers.

Mass migration of users from PCs to mobile devices has expanded the scope of ISs beyond traditional organizational boundaries—making *location* irrelevant for the most part. Perhaps equally significant, mobile technology has torn down the walls between our business, professional, and personal lives. We will examine the impacts of the commingling of business and personal lives in later chapters. For now, the focus is on the opportunities created by agility and mobility.

IT in the Hands of Customers. Organizations depend on IT to be able to adapt to market conditions and gain a competitive edge. That competitive advantage is short-lived if competitors quickly duplicate it. No advantage is very long-lasting. Therefore, companies need to upgrade, develop, and/or deploy new ISs to remain in the competitive game, as you will read throughout this book.

A profitable role for IT is developing ways to connect with and push content to social networks and mobile devices. During the last decade, companies were adapting to social networking. Facebook, LinkedIn, YouTube, Twitter, and blogs became extensions of businesses to reach customers, prospects, and business partners. By the start of our current decade, companies were adapting to the growing importance of being able to grab the attention of potential and current customers on their mobiles and also on customers' terms, as you will see in *IT at Work 1.1*. Making various elements of IT all work together is a huge concern because of its potentially large strategic payoff.

IT at Work 1.1

Asia-Pacific Region is PayPal's "Engine for Growth"

The online payment company PayPal (*paypal.com*) looked to the Asia-Pacific region in 2010 for many expansion opportunities. Mobile was becoming the primary access for the Internet in the Asia-Pacific. Explosive growth in mobile commerce (m-commerce)—the buying of products via wireless networks and handheld devices—also meant huge demand for secure online payments. Informa Research forecasted a 500 percent increase in the region's m-commerce between 2009 and 2012.

Rahul Shinghal, PayPal's regional head for mobile products, said: "This market is just exploding like crazy. This is the engine of growth." Much of it is still in Japan and South Korea, Asia's most electronically connected markets, but PayPal expects wider acceptance of m-commerce throughout the Asia-Pacific.

In mid-2010, PayPal signed an agreement with the Infocomm Development Authority of Singapore (*ida.gov.sg*) to stimulate m-commerce. The deal with Singapore was to make it easier for businesses and consumers to conduct transactions and make payments over mobile phones. PayPal has also entered into collaboration with Malaysia's mobile operator Maxis, which provides subscribers with secure shopping transactions.

By the end of 2010, the company doubled its number of employees in the region to more than 2,000 at its offices in Australia, China, Hong Kong, India, Japan, Taiwan and Singapore, which serves as PayPal's international base. Markets such as Australia, Singapore and Malaysia are seeing a huge jump in m-commerce, thanks to the growing popularity of smartphones that feature apps and multimedia capabilities, including fast Internet access.

Sources: Compiled from *China Post* (2010), Infocomm Development Authority of Singapore (*ida.gov.sg*; 2011), and *PayPal.com*.

Discussion Questions: What factors have contributed to, or enabled, the fast growth in m-commerce? What might deter people from making purchases over their mobiles?

IT at Work 1.2

Middle East and North Africa (MENA) Countries Engaged in Social Media

The announcement on May 24, 2010, that Facebook had more subscribers in Middle Eastern and North African (MENA) countries than the number of newspapers circulated in the region highlights how popular social media has become in the Arab world. The most popular social networks, e.g., Facebook and MXit, have exceeded the population of several nations. MXit is South Africa's largest social network that had grown to 27 million subscribers between 2003 and 2011.

Social networks are expanding into other IT functions and services. For instance, Facebook ranks first in real-time search—an area that Google had dominated for many years.

Given the sizes of their memberships, you can expect ongoing attempts to leverage social networks to influence public opinion. For example, Digital Daya (*digitaldaya.com/*), an international strategic consultancy, helps world leaders leverage social media to influence public opinion.

Sources: Compiled from Bremmen (2010), *Digitaldaya.com/*, Feuilherade (2010), and PR Newswire (2011).

Discussion Questions: Search for a recent example of how a social network is being used to influence public opinion. Identify the social network(s), the type of influence, and briefly summarize the situation and response.

In the next section, we review this IT strategic challenge. You need to understand why, for example, an e-commerce Web site designed for a large laptop screen, which is found via a search engine and transferred over fiber-optic cables, may be dangerously inadequate in the age of 3G/4G/Wi-Fi smartphones and other mobile devices.

Mobile Market Opportunities. The iPad and Que—like the iPhone, BlackBerry, Pre, Nexus One, and other smart mobile devices—quickly become gadgets that owners depend on. Mobiles are replacing computers as the primary way to connect with public and private networks, to access digital content from anywhere at any time, and to get work done. Gadgets of all kinds are starting to look and feel like proper handheld computers, able to run all sorts of software. Desktop and laptop computers are taking on more and more nontraditional duties, like streaming media to TV sets, stereos, and other household appliances. Business professionals use their mobile devices to fulfill business needs that keep their companies running at optimal levels of productivity, performance, and profitability.

This massive adoption of smart devices has created a huge base of multitasking users and a market for companies to tap and target. Touch-navigate devices running on 3G and 4G networks, combined with innovative technologies like 2D tags (as you read in the opening case), create business opportunities and threats. That is, they create opportunities for competitive advantage while destroying older ones. For example, according to Pew Research, newspapers saw ad revenue fall 26% during 2009 and 43% over the period 2007–2010 (Pew Research, 2010).

Consumers expect to be continually informed—about work, news, bank balances, credit card charges, traffic, weather—regardless of where they are. Supervisors, subordinates, friends, and family send updates through SMS (texting), tweets (microtexts), and other mobile approaches. Part of Facebook's meteoric growth has to be attributed to mobility, as 65 million members access it from mobile devices. This growth is also true for Twitter, as 80% of all Twitter interactions take place over mobile devices.

BUSINESS INNOVATION AND DISRUPTION OF THE STATUS QUO

Widespread adoption of new technology is going to disrupt the usual way business is done. Facebook outranked Google Tweets and texts can be used to influence what people do as you read in IT at Work 1.2. Apple created an entirely new market and changed the game for industries that were not its usual competitors—namely, music, media, and consumer electronics companies. With the iPod, iTouch, iTunes, iPhone, and Web apps, Apple has moved the dynamics of several industries from being technology-led to being led by customer experience. Apple then leveraged the successful *personal mobile music* business model, adapted it, and applied it in other industries (media and consumer electronics).

TABLE 1.1	Assessing the Value of Innovation

Innovation leads to profitable growth if it:

- Generates new profit pools
- Increases demand for products and services
- Attracts new customers
- Opens new markets
- Sustains the business for years to come

Here are three examples in the commercial and nonprofit sectors of innovative disruptions triggered by IT.

1. The Vancouver Winter Olympics in 2010 became the first *social media Olympics*. Twitter and Facebook were platforms used by marketers, athletes, and sports fans to share news, to get game updates, and to send and receive marketing promotions.

2. Facebook, Skype, and blogs formed critical ISs in Haiti and Chile after catastrophic earthquakes. After the January and February 2010 earthquakes hit Haiti and Chile, Facebook, Skype, and blogs were used to communicate, find missing people, and spread requests for donations to the Haitian relief.

3. Whole Foods Market attracts customers and reinforces relationships via its free iPhone app. Whole Foods' app attracts customers by providing holiday-specific and healthy recipes whose ingredients link to a Whole Foods store locator with directions on how to get there. Instead of pursuing customers with traditional advertising only, Whole Foods is attracting new and current customers via its lower-cost and more targeted iPhone app. In the fiercely competitive food market industry, Whole Foods is using the *attraction advantage* to connect with and draw customers to its stores and to beat out competitors.

Not all innovations add value. In order to improve performance, innovation needs to achieve one or more goals. Table 1.1 lists characteristics for assessing the expected value of an innovation.

Mobile marketing efforts can be invasive. As you will read in greater detail in Part III of this book, use of mobile media requires understanding best and worst practices. For example, mobile marketing strategies need to include proper tracking of customer responses to ensure that customers are drawn in, rather than turned off, by mobile messages.

It is important to recognize that some types of IT are **commodities** that do not provide a special advantage. Commodities are basic things that companies need to function, like electricity and buildings. Computers, databases, and network services are examples of commodities. In contrast, how a business applies IT to support business processes transforms those IT commodities into competitive assets. Critical business processes are those that improve employee performance and profit margins. How a company generates revenue from its assets is referred to as its business model.

BUSINESS MODELS

A **business model** is a method of doing business by which a company can generate sales revenue and profit to sustain itself. The model spells out how the company creates or adds value in terms of the goods or services the company produces. Some models are very simple. For example, Nokia makes and sells cell phones and generates profit from these sales. On the other hand, a TV station provides free broadcasting. Its survival depends on a complex model involving factors such as advertisers and content providers. Google and Yahoo also use a similarly complex business model.

According to McKay and Marshall (2004), a comprehensive business model is composed of these six elements:

1. A description of all *products* and *services* the business will offer

2. A description of the *business process* required to make and deliver the products and services

3. A description of the *customers* to be served and the company's relationships with these customers, including what constitutes value from customers' perspective (*customers' value proposition*)

4. A list of the *resources* required and the identification of which ones are available, which will be developed in-house, and which will need to be acquired

5. A description of the organization's *supply chain*, including *suppliers* and other *business partners*

6. A description of the revenues expected (*revenue model*), anticipated costs, sources of financing, and estimated profitability (*financial viability*)

Models also include a **value proposition,** which is an analysis of the benefits of using the specific model (tangible and intangible), including the customers' value proposition. We examine value propositions in detail in the later section that covers business performance management.

The next section focuses on technology issues and provides an overview of core IS and IT concepts.

Review Questions

1. What are the characteristics of an agile organization?
2. What opportunities have been created by the mass migration of users from PCs to mobile devices?
3. Describe how to assess the value of an innovation.
4. What is a business model?

1.2 Information Systems and Information Technology: Core Concepts

An **information system (IS)** collects, processes, stores, analyzes, and distributes information for a specific purpose or objective. Basic functions of an IS are shown in Figure 1.3 and described below.

• **Input.** Data and information about business transactions are captured or collected by point-of-sale (POS) scanners and Web sites and received by other input devices.

• **Processing.** Data is transformed, converted, and analyzed for storage or transfer to an output device.

• **Output.** Data, information, reports, and so on are distributed to digital screens or hardcopy (paper), sent as audio, or transferred to other ISs via communication networks.

• **Feedback.** A feedback mechanism monitors and controls operations.

The collection of computing systems used by an organization is termed **information technology (IT).** IT, in its narrow definition, refers to the technological side of an information system. Often the term *information technology* is used interchangeably with *information system*. In this book, we use the term *IT* in its broadest sense—to describe an organization's collection of information systems, their users, and the management that oversees them. For the most part, the terms *IT* and *IS* are considered to be the same thing.

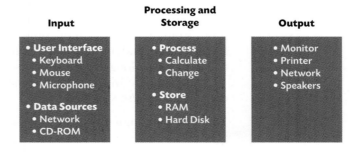

Figure 1.3 Four basic functions of an information system: Input, processing, storage, and output.

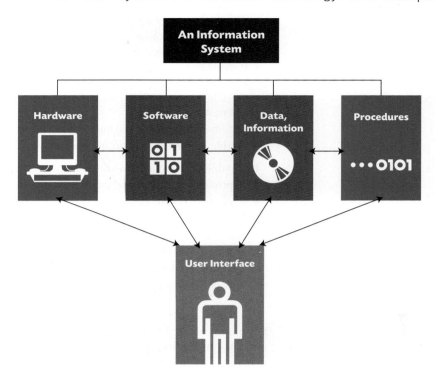

Figure 1.4 Components of information systems.

COMPONENTS OF AN INFORMATION SYSTEM

An IS uses computer technology and networks to perform some or all of its tasks. As you read in the opening section, IS can be as small as a smartphone with a software app that can snap tags to load a Web site. Or it may include several thousand computers of various types, scanners, printers, and other devices connected to databases via wired and wireless telecommunication networks. Basic components of ISs are listed next and shown in Figure 1.4. On the textbook's Web site, you find Technology Guides 1, 2, 3, 4, and 5 that contain detailed descriptions of hardware, software, data and databases, telecommunication networks, and systems analysis and design.

- *Hardware* is a set of devices such as processor, monitor, keyboard, and printer. Graphical user interfaces, which are called GUI, accept data and information that are then processed by central processing units (CPUs), stored in databases, and displayed on screens.
- *Software* is a set of applications (apps) or programs that instruct the hardware to process data or other inputs such as voice commands.
- *Data* is an essential part processed by the system and, if needed, stored in a database or other storage system.
- A *network* is a telecommunication system connecting hardware that is wired, wireless, or a combination.
- *Procedures* are the set of instructions about how to combine the above components in order to process information and generate the desired output.
- *People* are those individuals who work with the system, interface with it, or use its output.

Table 1.2 lists major capabilities of ISs and the business objectives that they support.

ISs Exist within a Culture. ISs do not exist in isolation. ISs have a purpose and a social (organizational) context. A common *purpose* is to provide a solution to a business problem. The *social context* of the system consists of the values determine what is admissible and possible within the

TABLE 1.2	Major Capabilities of ISs and Supported Business Objectives

- Perform high-speed, high-volume, numerical computations
- Provide fast, accurate communication and collaboration unrestricted by time and location
- Store huge amounts of information that is accessible via private networks and the Internet
- Automate semiautomatic business processes and manually done tasks.
- Enable automation of routine decision making and facilitate complex decision making

IS capabilities support these business objectives:
- Improve productivity (productivity is a measurement or the ratio of inputs to outputs)
- Reduce costs and waste
- Improve the ability to make informed decisions
- Facilitate collaboration
- Enhance customer relationships
- Develop new analytic capabilities
- Provide feedback on performance

people involved. For example, a company may believe that superb customer service and on-time delivery are critical success factors. This belief system influences IT investments, among other things.

The business value of IT is determined by the people who use it, the business processes it supports, and the culture of the organization. That is, IS value is determined by the relationships among ISs, people, and business processes—all of which are influenced strongly by organizational culture, as shown in Figure 1.5.

The IS building blocks that support business performance are high-performance devices (hardware); their apps (software and processing); connectivity (networks) to data; shared content, contact lists, and so on (information); and users (people). Many of today's ISs run on wireless networks, social media, and high-performance devices, making it faster and easier to reach others and to get work done with minimal downtime and effort. In Chapters 2 through 16, you will read about enterprise-wide and business-critical IS applications and IT solutions, many of which integrate mobile and social technologies.

ISs Extend Organizations and Disrupt Ways of Doing Business. The mass migration of users from PCs to mobile devices has expanded ISs beyond the organization and made *location* practically irrelevant. Perhaps equally significant, mobile technology has torn down the walls between our business lives and our personal lives.

IT innovations are shaking up or disrupting the ways companies do business, the jobs of managers and workers, the design of business processes, and the structure of markets. *IT at Work 1.3* describes how a new IS that provided feedback to operators

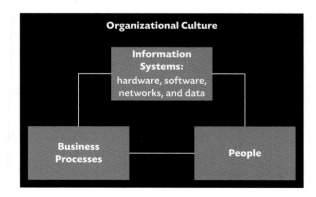

Figure 1.5 Information systems function within a ...ture.

IT at Work 1.3

Dashboards Give Operators and Managers Access in Accurate Data

MKT   HRM

1-800-CONTACTS is a leading worldwide contact lens retailer that sells directly to consumers through its Web site and call center. The company maintains an inventory of 20 million contact lenses and sells an average of 150,000 replacement contact lenses per day. Maintaining a large inventory is critical to their business strategy, which is to provide customers with a greater selection of contact lenses at better prices than retail stores.

In the past, the company's reporting systems could not provide managers and business analysts with quick and easy access to real-time (up-to-date) sales data. For example, when business analysts wanted to review the average number of contact lens boxes shipped per order, they had to get the data from the IT department. Response time for data reports often took several days. Managers faced an information bottleneck that created *blindspots* (a blindspot means not knowing what's going on as it's going on) about sales and inventory levels until IT provided the reports. To eliminate the problems, the company invested in data warehouse technology. (Data warehousing is discussed in detail in Chapter 10. For now, we are examining the impact of having access to accurate data.) Dashboard reporting tools were implemented in the call centers. See Figure 1.6 for examples of dashboard displays. Call center operators monitor their performance by looking at the dashboards on their computer screens.

Operators' dashboards are updated every 15 minutes. At a glance, they know how they are doing on key metrics (measurements) and how their performance compares to other operators. Color-coded round gauges on the left display the operator's closing ratio, average sale, and calls-per-hour for the day. Operators were also measured in terms of customer satisfaction, which was considered to be critical to customer loyalty, and ultimately sales growth and profitability. At month's end, operators are ranked based on a mix of metrics that contributed to profit—the *bottom line*. Operators in the top 80 percent receive bonuses base.

By linking operators' pay to the metrics that they can monitor on real-time dashboard displays, 1-800 CONTACTS improved

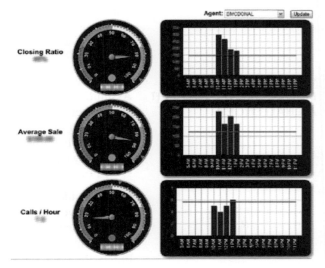

Figure 1.6 Examples of dashboards that report information in familiar graphical displays to keep operators informed of their sales performance.

sales by $50,000 per month and call quality remained high. As a result, every metric of strategic importance to the company also improved.

Sources: Comp led from *Microsoft SQL Server Case Study* (Hill, 2005), and Watson and Hill (2009). The Watson and Hill case study is available on the Teradata University Network (TUN). Visit *academicprograms.teradata.com/*. Registration (free) is required for access to TUN.

Discussion Questions: How did feedback at the operators' level lead to improved performance at the organizational level? Why have the dashboards created a beneficial competitive environment for the operators?

at 1-800-CONTACTS disrupted the status quo with a feedback system, thus motivating performance improvements and ultimately increasing sales revenues.

IT has evolved from narrowly focused data processing and routine reports in the mid-1970s to a function that increasingly supports business processes, manages relationships with customers and suppliers, and creates limitless possibilities in the 2010s, when out of touch means out of business.

Review Questions

1. Define an information system.
2. Describe the building blocks of an information system.
3. What business objectives are supported by ISs?

1.3 Business Performance Management and Measurement

Organizations and managers set goals and objectives; for example, to increase the number of new accounts by 4.0% within the next quarter or to decrease labor costs by 7.0% within six months. Performance is measured by how well those goals and objectives are met. Despite how simple this sounds, measuring business (or organizational) performance is extremely challenging. In this section, you will learn why performance measurement is so challenging in practice, how performance can be measured, and how ISs can help or hinder performance measurement.

WHAT IS PERFORMANCE MANAGEMENT? WHY IS IT A CHALLENGE?

What does *performance management* mean? How do you manage performance? Assume that a company's goals are increased sales and improved customer loyalty. Sales revenue is a rather easy-to-calculate quantitative metric. In contrast, customer loyalty is a qualitative metric and probably has a longer time dimension. You can immediately know how much customers have purchased on a particular day, but not how many customers you've lost that day.

In order to manage performance, two fundamental requirements are:

- **Being able to measure.** You cannot manage what you cannot measure. Stated in reverse, if you cannot measure a process, you cannot manage or control it. To be reliable, "measuring" needs to be fact-based and/or data-driven. Otherwise, managers are making decisions based on conditions of uncertainty. The more accurate and timely the data, the better the ability to measure.

- **Knowing that your indicator is measuring the right thing.** Not all performance metrics are clearly linked to the desired outcome. Consider the differences in measuring sales revenues (a quantitative metric) and customer loyalty (a qualitative metric). You often need to find surrogate quantitative measures for qualitative metrics that can reliably measure what you want measured. Even for quantitative metrics, measuring is challenging. If the goal is sales growth, then measuring sales revenues makes sense. But if the goal is to increase total profit (total profit = total sales revenues − total expenses), then multiple metrics are needed.

Measuring performance requires:

- Identifying the most meaningful measures of performance
- Being able to measure them correctly
- Selecting the set of measures that provides a holistic indicator of total business performance
- Identifying who should receive the reports and in what timeframe

Adding to the challenge is that rarely do managers agree on the answers about which sets of metrics are the right ones to track. As you can see, measuring performance requires a lot of managers' time and effort—and serves as a clear example of the critical role of people in IS success. We examine performance measurement processes next.

Performance Measurement Process. Measuring performance is a multistep cyclical process. The major steps in business performance management are:

Step 1. Decide on desired performance levels. Namely: *What does the company want to achieve*? Such targets are decided upon and expressed as goals and objectives, based on the organization's mission. Also, specific metrics should be set for desirable and measurable performance topics so that the company can evaluate its success.

Step 2. Determine how to attain the performance levels. The issue is: *How to get there*? This is determined by the corporate strategies and specific short-, medium-, and long-term plans.

Step 3. Periodically assess where the organization stands with respect to its goals, objectives, and measures. The issue here is to find: *How are we doing?* This is accomplished by monitoring performance and comparing it to the values set in Step 1.

Step 4. Adjust performance and/or goals. If performance is too low—that is, there is a negative gap between where we want to be and where we are—corrective actions need to be taken: *How do we close the gap?*

As with many topics introduced in this chapter, business performance management is discussed in later chapters.

In the remainder of this section, we examine in more detail two components—business environmental pressures and organizational responses.

Business Environmental Pressures. The business environment consists of a variety of factors—societal, legal, political, technological, and economic. Figure 1.7 shows major pressures and how that might affect each other. Also see Table 1.3.

Impact of Business Environment Factors. The business environment factors shown in Figure 1.7 can impact the performance of individuals, departments, and entire organizations. Some factors create constraints, while others cost a great deal of money or divert efforts away from the business. New laws and regulations almost always involve the implementation of new ISs for compliance, especially during the first years after they go into effect. Examples of such laws and regulations are the Sarbanes-Oxley Act (SOX), Foreign Corrupt Practices Act (FCPA), Basel III, Gramm-Leach-Bliley (GLB) Act, Environmental Protection Agency (EPA) requirements, and Heath Insurance Portability and Accountability Act (HIPAA).

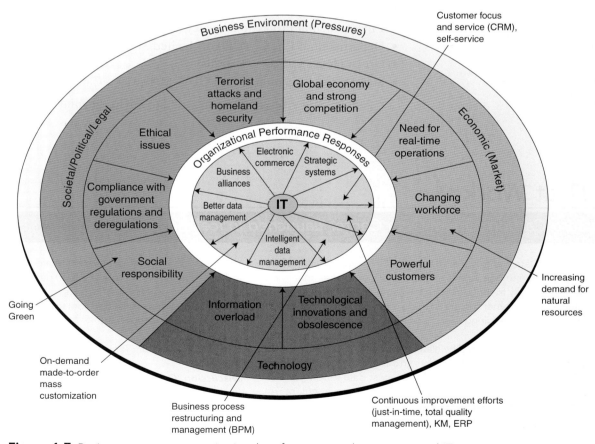

Figure 1.7 Business pressures, organizational performance and responses, and IT support.

Note that pressures may come from business partners. For example, Walmart mandated that its top suppliers adopt the RFID (radio frequency identification) technology. Similar requirements are imposed by other large buyers, including federal and state governments.

Green IT to Reduce Carbon and Energy Footprints. Concern about environmental damage and reducing a company's carbon and energy footprints on the planet has triggered efforts for **green IT.** Those footprints are a measure of the impact a business' activities have on the environment—in particular, climate change. It relates to the amount of greenhouse gases produced through burning fossil fuels for electricity and power production. For example, energy use in data centers (a data center is a facility used to house computer hardware and telecommunication systems) is a major concern to managers. IT purchase decisions regarding data center power, cooling, and space consumption affect a company's green status, as discussed in *IT at Work 1.4.*

Data center servers are known to be both power-hungry and heat-generating. PC monitors consume about 80 to 100 billion kilowatt-hours of electricity every year in the United States. Both Intel and AMD are producing new chips that reduce energy usage. Discarded PCs and other computer equipment are waste disposal problems. Green software refers to software products that help companies save energy or comply with EPA requirements.

Agencies worldwide are striving to reduce carbon footprints, including the following:

• Department for Environment, Food and Rural Affairs (DEFRA)—United Kingdom
• World Resource Institute (WRI) Greenhouse Gas (GHG) Protocol
• Vehicle Certification Agency (VCA)—United Kingdom
• Environmental Protection Agency (EPA)—United States
• Department of Energy (DOE)—United States
• Green House Office—Australia
• Standards Association (CSA) GHG Registries—Canada

Political and economic activities add to environmental complexity and chaos.

IT at Work 1.4

Zero-Carbon, Green Data Center Launched in Iceland

The Thor Data Center (THORDC) near Reykjavik, Iceland, offers several data storage hosting options for companies that want environmentally friendly, data center facilities. The data center is suitable for customer servers, storage, data backup and networking equipment requiring Tier 3 mechanical and electrical (M&E) infrastructure.

THORDC is powered by clean, renewable hydroelectric and geothermal energy sources. It offers an attractive value-proposition for companies that want a reliable, low-cost data hosting service in a 100 percent green, zero carbon footprint environment. All energy supplies in Iceland are sustainable.

Iceland's low-cost geothermal energy is an important factor in Thor's economics. It costs about 30 percent less than electricity in the UK. The center uses much less power because the low outside air temperature is used to cool the servers all year round such that chillers are unnecessary.

Sources: Compiled from *ThorDC.com* (2011) and Judge (2010).

Discussion Questions: What are the incentives to be eco-friendly? How can investments in energy-efficient data centers be justified?

TABLE 1.3	Organizational Responses to Pressures and Opportunities
Response/Action	**Description**
Develop strategic systems	Implement systems that provide strategic advantage; e.g., new features, low prices, super service, superb quality.
Introduce customer-focused systems, and customer loyalty programs	Meet customers' needs or priorities.
Improve decision making and forecasting	Use analytical methods to optimize operations, reduce cost, expedite decision making, support collaboration, automate routine decisions.
Restructure business processes and organization structure	Restructure business processes to make them more efficient or effective. Eliminate waste.
Use self-service approach	Have your customers, employees, or business partners use self-service whenever possible; e.g., track status, change an address, or manage your inventory.
Employ on-demand manufacturing/service and superb supply chain management	Meet the demands of your customers for standard or customized products/services efficiently and effectively.
Promote business alliances and partner relationship management	Create business alliances, even with your competitors, to reduce risks and costs. Collaborate effectively; provide benefits to your partners.
Use e-commerce	Automate business processes, procedures, and routine operations. Use new business models and electronic markets.
Share information and manage knowledge	Encourage information and knowledge creation, storage, and reuse.
Use enterprise and integrated systems	Integrate systems of internal information applications with partners' systems in order to facilitate collaboration, reduce costs and errors, and provide competitive advantage.
Go green	Save energy and the environment.
Reduce cycle time	Increase speed via automation, collaboration, and innovation.

ETHICS

Ethical Issues. IT creates challenging ethical issues ranging from monitoring employee e-mail to invading the privacy of customers whose data are stored in private and public databases. Ethical issues create pressures or constraints on business operations. **Ethics** relates to standards of right and wrong, and *information ethics* relates to standards of right and wrong in information management practices. Ethical issues are challenging, in part, because what is considered ethical by one person may seem unethical to another. Likewise, what is considered ethical in one country may be considered unethical in others.

Review Questions

1. Define business performance management and show its cycle.
2. Describe the impact of the business environment and list some of its components.
3. What is green IT and why has it become important?
4. List some environmental issues of data centers.
5. Describe organizational responses.
6. Define *ethics*.

1.4 Strategic Planning and Competitive Models

Strategic planning is critical for all organizations, including government healthcare, education, military, and other nonprofit and for-profit agencies. We start by discussing strategic analysis and then explain the activities or component parts of strategic planning.

WHAT IS STRATEGIC (SWOT) ANALYSIS?

There are many views on strategic analysis. In general, strategic analysis is the scanning and review of the political, social, economic, and technical environment of the organization. For example, any company looking to expand its business operations into a developing country has to investigate that country's political and economic stability and critical infrastructure. That strategic analysis would include reviewing the U.S. Central Intelligence Agency's (CIA) World Factbook (*cia.gov/library/publications/the-world-factbook/*). The World Factbook provides information on the history, people, government, economy, geography, communications, transportation, military, and transnational issues for 266 world entities. Then the company would need to investigate competitors and their potential reactions to a new entrant into their market. Equally important, the company would need to assess its ability to compete profitably in the market and impacts of the expansion on other parts of the company. For example, having excess production capacity would require less capital than building a new factory.

The purpose of this analysis of the environment, competition, and capacity is to learn about the strengths, weaknesses, opportunities, and threats (SWOT) of the expansion plan being considered. **SWOT analysis,** as it is called, involves the evaluation of strengths and weaknesses, which are internal factors, and opportunities and threats, which are external factors. Examples are:

- Strengths: reliable processes; agility; motivated workforce
- Weaknesses: lack of expertise; competitors with better IT infrastructure
- Opportunities: a developing market; ability to create a new market or product
- Threats: price wars or other fierce reaction by competitors; obsolescence

SWOT is only a guide and should be used together with other tools such as Porter's five-forces analysis model. Porter's models are described in an upcoming section. The value of SWOT analysis depends on how the analysis is performed. Here are several rules to follow:

- Be realistic about the strengths and weaknesses of your organization.
- Be realistic about the size of the opportunities and threats.
- Be specific and keep the analysis simple, or as simple as possible.
- Evaluate your company's strengths and weaknesses in relation to those of competitors (better than or worse than competitors).
- Expect conflicting views because SWOT is subjective, forward-looking, and based on assumptions.

SWOT analysis is often done at the outset of the strategic planning process. Now you can proceed to answer the question, "What is strategic planning?"

WHAT IS STRATEGIC PLANNING?

Strategic planning is a series of processes in which an organization selects and arranges its businesses or services to keep the organization viable (healthy or functional) even when unexpected events disrupt one or more of its businesses, markets, products, or services. Strategic planning involves environmental scanning and prediction, or SWOT analysis, for each business relative to competitors in that business's market or product line. The next step in the strategic planning process is strategy.

WHAT IS STRATEGY?

Strategy defines the plan for how a business will achieve its mission, goals, and objectives. It specifies the necessary financial requirements, budgets, and resources. Strategy addresses fundamental issues such as the company's position in its industry, its available resources and options, and future directions. A strategy addresses questions such as:

- What is the long-term direction of our business?
- What is the overall plan for deploying our resources?
- What trade-offs are necessary? What resources will it need to share?
- What is our position vis-à-vis competitors?
- How do we achieve competitive advantage over rivals in order to achieve or maximize profitability?

Two of the most well-known methodologies were developed by Porter. Their essentials are presented next.

PORTER'S COMPETITIVE FORCES MODEL AND STRATEGIES

Michael Porter's **competitive forces model,** also called the **five-forces model,** has been used to develop strategies for companies to identify their competitive edge. The model also demonstrates how IT can enhance competitiveness. Professor Porter discusses this model in detail in a 13-minute YouTube video from the Harvard Business School, which you can view at *youtube.com/watch?v=mYF2_FBCvXw* or by searching YouTube for the video.

The model recognizes five major forces (think of them as *pressures* or *drivers*) that could influence a company's position *within a given industry* and the strategy that management chooses to pursue. Other forces, such as those cited in this chapter, including new regulations, affect all companies in the industry and therefore may have a rather uniform impact on each company in an industry. Although the details of the model differ from one industry to another, its general structure is universal.

Basis of the Competitive Forces Model. Before examining the model, it's helpful to understand that it is based on the fundamental concept of profitability and profit margin.

- **PROFIT** = TOTAL REVENUES minus TOTAL COSTS. Profit is increased by increasing total revenues and/or decreasing total costs. Profit is decreased when total revenues decrease and/or total costs increase.
- **PROFIT MARGIN** = SELLING PRICE minus COST OF THE ITEM. Profit margin measures the amount of *profit per unit of sales* and does not take into account all costs of doing business.

Five Industry Forces. According to Porter's competitive forces model, there are five major forces in an industry that affect the degree of competition and thus impact profit margins and, ultimately, profitability. These forces interact, so although you will read about them individually, it is their interaction that determines the industry's profit potential. For example, while profit margins for pizzerias may be small, the ease of entering that industry draws new entrants into it. Conversely, profit margins for delivery services may be large, but the cost of the IT to support the service is a huge barrier to entry into the market.

Here is an explanation of the five industry (market) forces.

1. Threat of entry of new competitors. Industries with large profit margins attract more competitors (called *entrants*) into the market than do industries with small profit margins. It's the same principle that applies to jobs—people are attracted to higher-paying jobs, provided that they can meet or acquire the criteria for that job. In order to gain market share, entrants typically sell at lower prices or offer some incentive. Those companies already in the industry may be forced to defend their market share by lowering prices, which reduces their profit margin. Thus, this threat puts downward pressure on profit margins by driving prices down.

This force also refers to the strength of the **barriers to entry** into an industry, which is how easy it is to enter an industry. The threat of entry is lower (less power-ful) when existing companies have ISs that are difficult to duplicate or very expen-sive. Those ISs create barriers to entry that reduce the threat of entry.

2. Bargaining power of suppliers. Bargaining power is high where the supplier or brand is powerful; for example, Apple, Microsoft, and auto manufacturers. Power is determined by how much a company purchases from a supplier. The more powerful company has the leverage to demand better prices or terms, which increase its profit margin. Conversely, suppliers with very little bargaining power tend to have small profit margins.

3. Bargaining power of customers or buyers. This force is the reverse of the bargain-ing power of suppliers. Examples are Dell Computers, Walmart, and governments. This force is high where there a few large customers or buyers in a market.

4. Threat of substitute products or services. Where there is product-for-product sub-stitution, such as Kindle for Nook or e-mail for fax, there is downward pressure on prices. As the threat of substitutes increases, profit margin decreases because sellers need to keep prices competitively low.

5. Competitive rivalry among existing firms in the industry. Fierce competition involves expensive advertising and promotions, intense investments in research and development (R&D), or other efforts that cut into profit margins. This force is most likely to be high when entry barriers are low, threat of substitute products is high, and suppliers and buyers in the market attempt to control. That's why this force is placed in the center of the model.

The strength of each force is determined by the industry's structure. Existing companies in an industry need to protect themselves against the forces. Alternatively, they can take advantage of the forces to improve their position or to challenge indus-try leaders. The relationships are shown in Figure 1.8.

Companies can identify the forces that influence competitive advantage in their marketplace and then develop a strategy. Porter proposed three types of strategies—cost leadership, differentiation, and niche strategies.

In Table 1.4, Porter's three classical strategies are listed first, followed by a list of nine other general strategies for dealing with competitive advantage. Each of these

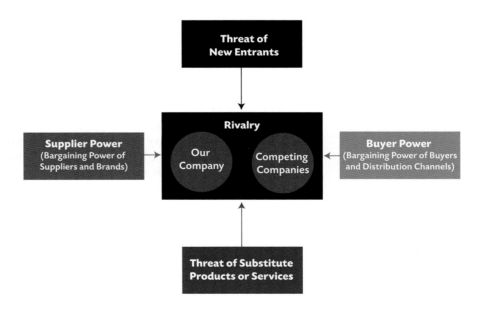

Figure 1.8 Porter's competitive forces model.

TABLE 1.4	Strategies for Competitive Advantage
Strategy	**Description**
Cost leadership	Produce product/service at the lowest cost in the industry.
Differentiation	Offer different products, services, or product features.
Niche	Select a narrow-scope segment (*market niche*) and be the best in quality, speed, or cost in that segment.
Growth	Increase market share, acquire more customers, or sell more types of products.
Alliance	Work with business partners in partnerships, alliances, joint ventures, or virtual companies.
Innovation	Introduce new products/services; put new features in existing products/services; develop new ways to produce products/services.
Operational effectiveness	Improve the manner in which internal business processes are executed so that the firm performs similar activities better than rivals.
Customer orientation	Concentrate on customer satisfaction.
Time	Treat time as a resource, then manage it and use it to the firm's advantage.
Entry barriers	Create barriers to entry. By introducing innovative products or using IT to provide exceptional service, companies can create entry barriers to discourage new entrants.
Customer or supplier lock-in	Encourage customers or suppliers to stay with you rather than going to competitors. Reduce customers' bargaining power by locking them in.
Increase switching costs	Discourage customers or suppliers from going to competitors for economic reasons.

strategies can be enhanced by IT, as will be shown throughout the book. Other chapters will show (1) how different ITs impact the five forces and (2) how IT facilitates the 12 strategies.

PORTER'S VALUE CHAIN MODEL

According to Porter's **value chain model,** the activities conducted in any manufacturing organization can be divided into two parts: *primary activities* and *support activities.*

Primary activities are those business activities through which a company produces goods, thus creating value for which customers are willing to pay. Primary activities involve the purchase of materials, the processing of materials into products, and delivery of products to customers. Typically, there are five primary activities:

1. Inbound logistics (incoming raw materials and other inputs)
2. Operations (manufacturing and testing)
3. Outbound logistics (packaging, storage, and distribution)
4. Marketing and sales (to buyers)
5. Services

The primary activities usually take place in a sequence from 1 to 5. As work progresses, value is added to the product in each activity. To be more specific, the incoming materials (1) are processed (in receiving, storage, etc.) in activities called **inbound logistics.** Next, the materials are used in *operations* (2), where significant value is added by the process of turning raw materials into products. Products need to be prepared for delivery (packaging, storing, and shipping) in the **outbound logistics** activities (3). Then *marketing and sales* (4) attempt to sell the products to customers, increasing product value by creating demand for the company's products. The value of a sold item is much larger than that of an unsold one. Finally, *after-sales service* (5), such as warranty service or upgrade notification, is performed for the customer, further adding value. The goal of these value-adding activities is to make a profit for the company.

Primary activities are supported by the following support activities:

1. The firm's infrastructure (accounting, finance, management)
2. Human resources management

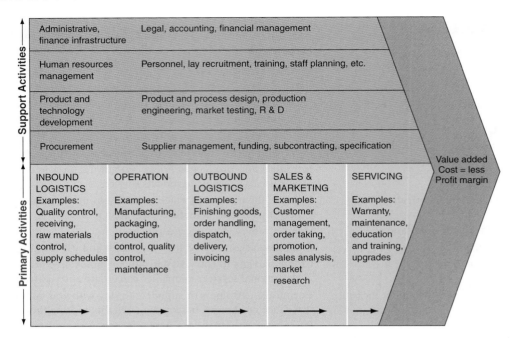

Figure 1.9 The firm's value chain. The arrows illustrate the flow of goods and services.

3. Technology development (R&D)
4. Procurement (purchasing)

Each support activity can be applied to any or all of the primary activities. Support activities may also support each other, as shown in Figure 1.9.

Innovation and adaptability are **critical success factors,** or CSFs, related to Porter's models. CSFs are those things that must go right for a company to achieve its mission. CSFs must be quantitative or measurable, such as the increase in the number of customers within a time period. An example of innovative strategy is provided in *IT at Work 1.5.*

Adaptive and Innovative Organizations. Charles Darwin, the renowned scientist, said, "It's not the strongest of species that survives, nor the most intelligent; but the one most responsive to change." What is true in nature is true today for organizations that operate in a rapidly changing environment, as you have read earlier. The digital revolution and rapid environmental changes bring opportunities and risks. Bill Gates is aware of this. Microsoft is continually developing new Internet and IT products and services to defend itself against Google. Google is defending itself against Facebook.

Competition exists not only among products or services but also among business models, customer service operations, and supply chains. The concept of value chain has been supplemented by the concepts of *value system* and *value network*.

A firm's value chain is part of a larger stream of activities, which Porter calls a value system. A **value system** includes the suppliers that provide the inputs necessary to the firm and their value chains. Once the firm creates products, they pass through the value chain of distributors, all the way to the buyers (customers). All parts of these chains are included in the value system. Gaining and sustaining a competitive advantage, and supporting that advantage by means of IT, this requires an understanding of the entire value system.

A *value network* is a complex set of social and technical resources. Value networks work together via relationships to create social goods (public goods) or economic value. This value takes the form of knowledge and other intangibles and/or financial value.

IT at Work 1.5

Daimler AG Relies on Data Analytics to Improve Performance

German automaker Daimler AG, located in Stuttgart, has several divisions including Mercedes-Benz Cars and Vans and Daimler Trucks and Buses. In 2009, Daimler sold 1.6 million vehicles, had revenues of 78.9 billion euros, and employed more than 250,000 people.

To better manage after-sales services and warranties on its numerous models, Daimler consolidated warranty, diagnostic, defect, and other quality-related data on sold vehicles on a system named *Advanced Quality Analysis*, or AQUA. In 2011, the automaker added data analysis tools to gain insights from the huge volume of data amassed in AQUA. The investment in data analysis supported Daimler's strategic goal to continuously improve vehicle quality and, ultimately, customer satisfaction. For example, engineers could analyze data so precisely that they were able to identify those vehicles that were at high risk of defects, thereby significantly decreasing the chances of a vehicle recall.

According to the head of IT, "The faster we can eliminate a problem in production, the easier it is to avoid future warranty and goodwill costs." With AQUA, Daimler has improved both the quality of its high-performance vehicles and its profitability.

Sources: Compiled from Dullaghan (2011) and *Teradata.com*.

Real-Time, On-Demand IT Support. Eliminating blindspots requires *real-time systems*. A **real-time system** is an IS that provides fast enough access to information or data that an appropriate decision can be made, usually before the data or situation changes (operational deadlines from event to system response). Fast enough may mean less than a second if you are buying a stock, or it may mean before a business opens in the morning if you are determining a price. It can be a day or two in other situations. When a patient is admitted to the hospital, the patient's medical records must be readily accessible. The longer the wait, the greater the risk to the patient. The real-time enterprise is a necessity since the basis of competition is often time or speed. Web-based systems (such as tracking stocks online) provide us with these capabilities. Some examples are the following:

- Salespeople can check to see whether a product is in inventory by looking directly into the inventory system.
- Suppliers can ensure adequate supplies by looking directly into the forecasting and inventory systems.
- An online order payment by credit card is checked for the balance, and the amount of the purchase is debited all in one second. This way, authorization is given "fast enough" for both a seller and a buyer.

Example of Real-Time IT Support. HyperActive Technologies (*hyperactive technologies.com*) has developed a system by which cameras mounted on the roof of a fast-food restaurant track vehicles pulling into the parking lot or drive-through. Other cameras track the progress of customers moving through the ordering queue. Using *predictive analysis*, the system predicts what customers might order. In addition, a database includes historical car-ordering data, such as 20 percent of cars entering the lot will usually order at least one cheeseburger at lunchtime. Based on the camera's input and the database, the system predicts what customers will order 1.5 to 5 minutes before they actually order. Cooks are better informed, minimizing customers' waiting time and the cost of overheated food without flavor. The real-time enterprise is also referred to as an on-demand enterprise. Such an enterprise must be able to fulfill orders as soon as they are needed.

Innovation and Creativity. Organizational responses usually occur in reaction to change in the business environment or to competitors' actions. Sometimes such response may be too late. Therefore, organizations can play a proactive role and make significant changes in their industry before anyone else. A first-mover strategy is risky but can be very rewarding if successful.

Information Systems Failures. So far, you have read several success stories. Unfortunately, IT projects are not always successful, and reasons for failure are often due to poor project management, which is a topic you will learn in Chapter 14. Some IT projects are doomed from the start because of inadequate budgeting or other resources.

We will show you some of these (marked with a "lessons from failures" icon) in this book or on our Web site. We can learn from failures as much as we can learn from successes.

Examples of three IT failures in different nations are the following:

• On February 24, 2008, about two-thirds of the world was unable to see YouTube for several hours. This happened when the Pakistan Telecommunication Authority decided to block offensive content in its own country. Its ISP, together with Hong Kong PCCW telecommunication, incorrectly programmed a block video on YouTube, causing the block to reach around the world instead (Claburn, 2008).

• The United Kingdom National Offender Management Information System project (NOMIS) failed due to mismanagement and vast budget overruns. The project to provide an IT system to support a new way of working with offenders was to be completed by January 2008. By July 2007, £155 million had been spent on the project, it was two years behind schedule, and estimated lifetime project costs had risen to £690 million. In January 2008, the NOMIS began work on a re-scoped program with an estimated lifetime cost of £513 million and a delivery date of March 2011 (Krigsman, 2009; NAO, 2009). The project offers an excellent case study relating failure directly to inadequate governance and oversight; it is discussed in the *public sector case* at the end of this chapter.

• The U.S. Census Bureau faced a loss of up to $2 billion on an IT project to replace paper-based data collection methods with handheld devices for the 2010 census. The Census Bureau had not implemented longstanding Government Accountability Office (GAO) recommendations, however, and had to scrap the program.

Review Questions

1. Describe strategic planning.
2. Describe SWOT analysis.
3. Explain Porter's five-forces model and give an example of each force.
4. Describe adaptive organization.
5. Describe real-time business and information systems.

1.5 Why IT Is Important to Your Career, and IT Careers

In this part of the chapter, we describe the importance of IT to your performance and its value to your organization.

In this chapter, you read that business is IT-dependent. For most organizations, if their computer network goes down, so does the business. Imagine not having Internet access for 24 hours—no texting, e-mail, Facebook, Twitter, data access, status reports, and so on. Looking at what you could still accomplish without IT gives a clear perspective of its importance and ubiquity.

IT DEFINES AND CREATES BUSINESSES AND MARKETS

IT creates markets, businesses, products, and careers. As you will continue to read throughout this book, exciting IT developments are changing how organizations and individuals do things. New technologies, such as 4G networks, 2D tags, mobile scanners, and e-readers point to groundbreaking changes. CNN.com, one of the most respected news media, has created a new market whose impacts are yet to be realized. Visit iReport at *ireport.com/*, where a pop-up reads "iReport is the way people like you report the news. The stories in this section are not edited, fact-checked or screened before they post." CNN.com invites everyone to become a reporter and to "take part in the news with CNN. Your voice, together with other iReporters, can help shape what CNN covers and how. At CNN we believe that looking at the news from different angles gives us a deeper understanding of what's going on. We also know that the world is an amazing place filled with interesting people doing fascinating things that don't always make the news" (*ireport.com/about.jspa, 2010*).

OCCUPATIONAL OUTLOOK FOR IS MANAGERS

According to the 2010–11 edition of the *Occupational Outlook Handbook*, published by the U.S. Bureau of Labor Statistics, the outlook for computer and information systems managers is as follows:

- Employment is expected to grow faster than the average for all occupations.
- A bachelor's degree in a computer-related field usually is required for management positions, although employers often prefer a graduate degree, especially an MBA with technology as a core component.
- Many managers possess advanced technical knowledge gained from working in a computer occupation.
- Job prospects should be excellent (*bls.gov/oco/ocos258.htm*).

IT as a Career: The Nature of IS and IT Work. In today's workplace, it is imperative that ISs work effectively and reliably. IS managers play a vital role in the implementation and administration of technology in their organizations. They plan, coordinate, and direct research on the computer-related activities of firms. In consultation with other managers, they help determine the goals of an organization and then implement technology to meet those goals. They oversee all technical aspects of an organization, such as software development, network security, and Internet operations.

IS managers can have additional duties, depending on their role in an organization. The **chief technology officers (CTO)** evaluates the newest and most innovative technologies and determines how they can be applied for competitive advantage. CTOs develop technical standards, deploy technology, and supervise workers who deal with the daily IT issues of the firm. When innovative and useful new ITs are launched, the CTO determines implementation strategies, performs cost-benefit or SWOT analysis, and reports those strategies to top management, including the chief information officer (CIO).

IT project managers develop requirements, budgets, and schedules for their firm's information technology projects. They coordinate such projects from development through implementation, working with their organization's IT workers, as well as clients, vendors, and consultants. These managers are increasingly involved in projects that upgrade the information security of an organization.

Earnings in the IT Field. According to the 2010–2011 analysis of the Bureau of Labor Statistics, wages of computer and information systems managers vary by specialty and level of responsibility. The median annual wage of these managers in May 2008 was $112,210. The middle 50 percent earned between $88,240 and $141,890. Median annual wages in the industries employing the largest numbers of computer and information systems managers in May 2008 were as follows:

- Software publishers, $126,840
- Computer systems design and related services, $118,120

- Management of companies and enterprises, $115,150
- Depository credit intermediation, $113,380
- Insurance carriers, $109,810

In addition to salaries, computer and information systems managers, especially those at higher levels, often receive employment-related benefits, such as expense accounts, stock option plans, and bonuses.

IT Job Prospects. As of 2010–2011, prospects for qualified IS managers should be excellent. Workers with specialized technical knowledge and strong communications and business skills, as well as those with an MBA with a concentration in ISs, will have the best prospects. Job openings will be the result of employment growth and the need to replace workers who transfer to other occupations or leave the labor force (Bureau of Labor Statistics, 2010–2011).

Management Issues

1. Recognizing opportunities for using IT and Web-based systems for strategic advantage and threats associated with not using them. These opportunities and threats are highlighted and discussed throughout the book.

2. Who will build, operate, and maintain the information systems? This is a critical issue because management wants to minimize the cost of IT while maximizing its benefits. Some alternatives are to use cloud computing, to use software-as-a-service (SaaS) models, to outsource IT activities, and to divide the remaining work between the IS department and the end users.

3. How much IT? This is a critical issue related to IT planning. IT does not come free, but *not* having it may be much costlier.

4. What social networking activities should be pursued? This is an explosive topic and covered extensively in Chapter 8.

5. How important is IT? In some cases, IT is the only approach that can help organizations. As time passes, the *comparative advantage* of IT increases.

GLOBAL

6. Globalization Global competition impacts most companies. At the same time, globalization creates opportunities, ranging from selling and buying products and services online in foreign markets to conducting joint ventures or investing in them. IT supports communications, collaboration, and discovery of information regarding all of the above.

ETHICS

7. Ethics and social issues The implementation of IT involves ethical and social issues that are constantly changing due to new developments in technologies and environments. These topics should be examined any time an IT project is undertaken.

Review Questions

1. Why is IT a major enabler of business performance and success?
2. Why is it beneficial to study IT today?
3. Why are IT job prospects so strong?

Key Terms

2D tag *3*	critical success factor *20*	primary activities *19*
agile enterprise *5*	ethics *15*	real-time system *21*
barriers to entry *18*	green IT *14*	strategic planning *16*
business model *7*	inbound logistics *19*	strategy *17*
chief technology officer (CTO) *23*	information system (IS) *8*	SWOT analysis *16*
commodities *7*	information technology (IT) *8*	value chain model *19*
competitive forces model *17*	interactivity application *2*	value proposition *8*
corporate strategy *2*	outbound logistics *19*	value system *20*

Chapter Highlights and Insights

❶ The importance of being an agile enterprise, which is one that has the ability to adapt rapidly, has never been greater because of struggling economic recoveries and advances in mobile technology.

❶ IT adds to profitability by enabling ways to connect with and push content to social networks and mobile devices.

❷ An information system collects, processes, stores, and disseminates information for a specific purpose.

❷ The business value of IT is determined by the people who use it, the business processes it supports, and the culture of the organization. That is, IS value is determined by the relationships among ISs, people, business processes, and organizational culture.

❸ Business performance management (BPM) is a cyclical process that begins with mission statement, goals, and targets, and then the strategy and plans of how to attain the targets. After measuring actual performance, one needs to compare it to the target. Finally, if a negative gap exists, corrective actions should be taken.

❸ Many market, technology, and societal pressures surround the modern organization, which is responding with critical response activities supported by information technology.

❸ Concern about environmental damage and reducing a company's carbon and energy footprints on the planet has triggered efforts for green IT.

❹ Strategic analysis is the scanning and review of the political, social, economic, and technical environment of the organization.

❹ IT is a major enabler of strategic systems. It can support organizational strategy or act as a direct strategic weapon.

❺ Learning about IT is essential because the role of IT is rapidly increasing in the support of organizations. We are getting more dependent on IT as time passes. Also, more IT-related jobs with high salaries are available.

Questions for Discussion

1. What is the business value of on-demand or interactivity applications?
2. Why do IT developments matter to managers?
3. How might mobile technologies disrupt the usual way business is done?
4. How has mobile technology influenced opportunities for entrepreneurs?
5. Explain how innovation can lead to profitable growth for businesses.
6. Explain the importance of culture and people in IS success.
7. How does green IT impact the bottom line?
8. Discuss why information systems might fail.
9. Explain why *measuring business performance in order to be able to manage it* is so challenging.

Exercises and Projects

1. Review three examples of IT applications in Chapter 1, and identify the business pressures in each example.
2. The market for optical copiers is shrinking rapidly. It is expected that by 2012 as much as 90 percent of all duplicated documents will be done on computer printers.
   a. How can a company such as Xerox Corporation survive? Visit Xerox's Web site for information to answer this question.
   b. Identify business pressures on Xerox.
   c. Find some of Xerox's response strategies (see *xerox.com, yahoo.com*, and *google.com*).
   d. What emerging risks might Xerox face due to changes in IT?
3. Identify a personal or professional use for a 2D tag. Then create or generate that 2D Tag at Microsoft's Web site, *microsoft.com/tag/*. Check the Chapter 1 Link List for additional helpful Web sites.

Group Assignments and Projects

1. Visit Teradata University Network (TUN) at *academicprograms.teradata.com/tun/* (ask your instructor for the password). Find and watch the *Partners 2009— Enterprise Rent-A-Car* video. You might also visit The Data Warehousing Institute at *tdwi.org* and find the case called "Enterprise Rent-A-Car's Data Warehouse Goes the Extra Mile with Decision-Making Horsepower." Link is: *http://tdwi.org/articles/1999/05/01/enterprise-rentacars-data-warehouse-goes-the-extra-mile-with-decisionmaking-horsepower.aspx?sc_lang=en*. Prepare a report identifying how IT improved business performance at Enterprise Rent-A-Car.
2. Visit Teradata University Network (TUN) at *academicprograms.teradata.com/tun/* (ask your instructor for the password). Find the Webinar "Turning Active Enterprise Intelligence into Competitive Advantage," by Imhoff, Hawkings, and Lee (2006). Identify the business environment pressures and real-time responses. Prepare a report.
3. Identify new business models related to or triggered by the power and performance capabilities of mobile devices. Identify older business models that are deteriorating because of these new models. Prepare a report.
4. Visit Facebook. Find five different types of organizations that are using Facebook. Identify two performance activities conducted by each organization (e.g., advertise, sell, recruit, collaborate).

Internet Exercises

1. Visit the Web site of UPS (*ups.com*), Federal Express (*fedex.com*), or a comparable logistics and delivery company. Select your country.
   a. Find out what information is available to customers before they send a package.
   b. Find out about the "package tracking" system; be specific.
   c. Compute the cost of delivering a 10″ × 20″ × 15″ box, weighing 20 pounds, from your location to another location. Compare the fastest delivery against the least cost.

   d. Prepare a spreadsheet for two different types of calculations available on the site. Enter data and solve for two different calculators. Use Excel.

4. Visit *YouTube.com* and search for two videos on Porter's strategic models. Report what you learned from each of these videos.

5. Visit *Dell.com* and *Apple.com* to simulate buying a laptop computer. Compare and contrast the selection process, degree of customization, and other buying features. What are the barriers to entry into this market, based on what you learned from this exercise?

BUSINESS CASE

IT and Reporting Infrastructure Critical to BP's Operations and Strategy

British Petroleum (BP) Global is one of the largest integrated global petrochemical (energy) companies. The global energy market is complex and competitive. BP relies on its data and reporting infrastructure to strengthen customer relationships and to support the diverse information requirements of its Chemical, Exploration, and Downstream businesses across the world. By 2008, BP also was relying on IT, communications, and reporting capabilities for its survival.

Restoring BP's Strategic and Competitive Edge

At a March 2008 meeting, BP chief executive officer (CEO) Tony Hayward warned managers that: "Despite having annual revenue of about $300 billion, BP had become a *serial underperformer.*" An oil and gas analyst at Morgan Stanley was predicting "BP will not exist in four to five years' time in its current form." Why? Because the company and its management had become bloated, passive, unfocused, and unconcerned with performance. They felt too big to fail. Management recognized that if they did not transform the way they did business, they would be wiped out by competitors.

The strategic goals were to restore revenue growth across all business, refocus attention on high performance and accountability, and reduce the complexity that was driving up costs.

The chief information officer (CIO) and the IT teams were charged with supporting the new strategic goals. Major changes had to be made in business processes to simplify and automate them as much as possible. For example, the CIO sought to simplify the global supply chain and reduce IT spending by £20 million. He did so by reducing their 540 hardware and software suppliers in Europe and the United States to just two resellers. This consolidation not only significantly reduced costs, but also eliminated most of the complexity from operations. Specifically, BP signed a five-year $150 million contract with the Computacenter and CompuCom as global reseller

partners to procure software licenses, servers, PC commodities and maintenance across Europe and the U.S. The five-year deal began on February 1, 2010.

Investments in enterprise-wide data analysis and reporting systems were needed in order to deliver operational (day-to-day) and strategic information throughout the business in 35 countries. Being able to better track operations and performance enables managers and workers to take immediate corrective action if necessary. For example, service stations are meant to take deliveries from the BP supply chain but in a few countries there are occasionally unauthorised deliveries of unbranded fuel. Being able to track sales patterns enables BP management to detect unusual or fraudulent activity and investigate promptly. In addition to operational support, BP is increasing its focus on Customer Relationship Management (CRM) to improve partner and customer relationships.

Sources: Compiled from *BP.com, UK.BusinessObjects.com,* Evans (2010), Kenart (2010), and *MicroScope.co.uk* (2010).

Questions

1. Why do you think giant organizations like BP Global, with enormous revenues, become "serial underperformers"?
2. How does complexity in business processes, such as procurement (purchasing), cause an increase in costs?
3. How can accurate reporting systems improve operational and strategic performance?
4. Visit *BP.com.* Read the BP strategy update and watch the strategy Webcast. What were the key issues discussed in the strategy update?
5. How has BP's management explained the causes of the explosion that in turn caused the massive Gulf of Mexico oil spill in 2010? What response to the oil spill did BP post on its Web site or social media? In your opinion, did these responses help restore its reputation?

PUBLIC SECTOR CASE

UK Prisoner Information Tracking Project Fails

National Offender Management Service (NOMS) is an agency of the UK Ministry of Justice, consisting of the Probation Service and Prison Service to more effective delivery of services. NOMS initiated the National Offender Management Information System, NOMIS, in 2004.

The NOMIS project was undertaken to develop single, integrated offender database and management systems for UK prisons and the probation services. ISA across 140 prisons and 42 administrative areas of the National Probation Service were to be integrated.

Clear Objectives, Bad Planning

From a technical perspective, NOMIS was to improve the continuity, consistency, and effectiveness of offender case management. Strategically, NOMIS was expected to help provide quality correctional services and interventions in order to reduce the risk of re-offending through "end-to-end" offender case management. This would involve making offender information available to the appropriate individuals within both the prison and probation services.

By July 2007, NOMS had spent £155 million and the project was two years behind schedule. Total expected costs had risen to £690 million. In summer 2008 the decision was made to put a hold on the project. The project was reduced in scope at a cost of £41 million, and was restarted in January 2008, the original due date. Lifetime costs were later expected to be £513 million, but it would no longer support "end-to-end" offender management as originally planned.

Mismanaged Organizational Project

The NOMIS project failed. NOMIS was treated as an independent IT project, rather than as a part of an IT-enabled organizational program. Other reasons for the project's failure were rather common. Three common reasons why projects fail so badly are:

1. **Poor-quality data.** The data used to assess the project is inadequate or just plain wrong. A project team may pick up an idea and run with it before critically evaluating the desired outcomes and alternatives.

2. **Optimism bias.** People are too optimistic about what can be achieved with the resources and deadlines available. The focus is on the benefits the project will achieve rather than what it will take to deliver the project.

3. **Strategic misrepresentation (deception).** There may be incentives to make the project look good on paper in order to get the project approved or to win the contract. So people may deliberately provide unrealistic cost estimates and delivery timetables.

In effect, the project had been abandoned and replaced by a much more limited system. Edward Leigh, chair of the National Audit Office, said the project was a spectacular failure and "a master class in sloppy project management."

Sources: Compiled from NAO (2009), Ministry of Justice (*noms. justice.gov.uk/*), Krigsman (2009), and Oates (2009).

Questions

1. Why did the NOMIS project fail?
2. Given what you have read, when was the project doomed to fail?
3. Dr. Cliff Mitchell, senior fellow and deputy director of the BP Managing Projects Programme at the Manchester Business School at the University of Manchester, stated: "We naturally believe we can achieve more, in less time, than historical data demonstrate. There is also a Western bias towards unrealistic macho management: we can get it done—we just need to drive harder." To what extent, if any, did the human dynamics mentioned by Dr. Mitchell play a role in the NOMIS project failure? Explain your answer.
4. Of the three reasons why projects go so wrong, which reason do you think is the most difficult to prevent? Explain your answer.

ANALYSIS USING SPREADSHEETS

Estimating Expected Improvement in Customer Retention

Notes: For this analysis, go to the Student Web Site to download the file. An image of that file, shown in Figure 1.10, is used to explain the scenario and required analysis.

Customer attrition rate is the rate at which a company loses customers. **Customer retention rate** is the opposite. It's the percent of customers that stay with the company. Mathematically, customer attrition rate = 100 percent − customer retention rate.

Scenario

InterMobile-2020 Company has asked you to prepare a spreadsheet that analyzes an expected improvement in customer retention. The company is considering implementing four new IT-based marketing campaigns to reduce customer attrition.

InterMobile-2020 estimates that they could control 6 percent of customer attrition with the right marketing strategies.

InterMobile-2020 Company

Number of customers, January 2011	**1,500,000**
Controllable Customer attrition rate (average rate per quarter) [CCAR]	**6%**

IT-based Strategies to reduce the Controllable Customer Attrition Rate (CCAR)	**Percent reduction in CCAR**
#1 - Launch campaign using 2D tags	1.25%
#2 - Create campaign on Facebook	0.50%
#3 - Launch viral marketing campaign	0.75%
#4 - Develop an iPhone app	1.50%
Total reduction in CCAR	**4.00%**

	2011				**Total loss of customers**
	Q1	**Q2**	**Q3**	**Q4**	
Expected loss of customers, no strategy (6% CCAR)	90,000	84,600	79,524	74,753	328,877
Number of customers remaining at end of Quarter	1,410,000	1,325,400	1,245,876	1,171,123	
Expected loss of customers, using all 4 marketing campaigns					
Number of customers remaining at end of Quarter					
Improvement (number of customers retained) due to IT-based campaigns					

Figure 1.10 Chapter 1 spreadsheet for analysis.

That is, with effective marketing campaigns they could prevent the entire 6 percent loss. They also have uncontrollable customer attrition, but that is irrelevant to this analysis.

As shown in the spreadsheet, the company estimates that the four new campaigns would reduce their quarterly controllable customer attrition rate (CCAR) by 4 percent. As of January 1, 2011, the company has 1.5 million customers. By the end of the fourth quarter (Q4) of 2011, the company will have lost an estimated 328,877 customers if no action is taken.

Analysis

See the example spreadsheet. Download or develop this spreadsheet to calculate the performance improvement that InterMobile-2020 can expect. You need to perform the calculations for the green-highlighted cells. Some of the analysis has already been completed. The results of this analysis will be combined with the costs of the campaigns (when those costs become known) to determine the value of these IT strategies. Keep a copy of your analysis for use in following chapters.

References

Apple iPad, *apple.com/ipad/*

BP.com

Bremmen, N. "Why MXit is Africa's largest social network," *Memeburn.com*, October 21, 2010. *memeburn.com/2010/10/why-mxit-is-south-africas-largest-social-network/*

Bureau of Labor Statistics (2010–2011), U.S. Department of Labor. *Occupational Outlook Handbook*, 2010–11 edition, "Computer and Information Systems Managers," *bls.gov/oco/ocos258.htm*

Business Objects, *.uk.businessobjects.com*

Central Intelligence Agency (CIA). World Factbook, *cia.gov/library/publications/the-world-factbook/*

China Post, "Paypal sets sights on Asia's appetite for wireless mobile purchasing," June 17, 2010. *chinapost.com.tw/business/company-focus/2010/06/17/261139/Paypal-sets.htm*

Conway, M., and G. Vasseur. "New Imperative for Business Schools," *The Business Intelligence Journal*, Third Quarter 2009. *findarticles.com/p/articles/mi_qa5525/is_200907/ai_n45878602/?tag=content;col1*

Digital Daya.com

Dresner, H. *The Performance Management Revolution: Business Results through Insight and Action*, John Wiley & Sons. 2007.

Dullaghan, A. "Daimler Drives High Performance," *Teradata Magazine*, Q1 2011, *Teradata.com/*

Duvall, M. "Boston Red Sox: Backstop Your Business," *Baseline*, May 14, 2004.

Duvall, M. "Monsanto Grows Green," *Baseline*, November 29, 2007a.

Duvall, M. "Playing By the Numbers: Baseball and BI," *Baseline*, October 29, 2007b.

Evans, B. "Global CIO: BP's Extraordinary Transformation Led By CIO Dana Deasy," *InformationWeek*, March 6, 2010.

Experian Hitwise, *weblogs.hitwise.com*

Feuilherade, P. "Social Networking Surges in Middle East," Suite101.com, May 26, 2010. *suite101.com/content/social-networking-surges-in-middle-east-a241274*

Hill, J. "Contact Lens Provider Has Clearer Vision of Business with New Data Warehouse," *Microsoft SQL Server Case Study*, 2005.

HyperActive Technologies, *hyperactivetechnologies.com*

Infocomm Development Authority of Singapore, 2011. *ida.gov.sg/*

iReport, *ireport.com/*

Judge, P. "Container-Based Data Centre Launches In Iceland," *eWeek Europe.* December 8, 2010. *eweekeurope.co.uk/news/container-based-data-centre-launches-in-iceland-15219*

Kinert, P. "BP to Streamline IT Supply Chain," *ComputerWeekly.com,* January 19, 2010.

Krigsman, M. "UK Prison IT: Massive and 'Spectacular' Failure," ZDNet Blog, March 14, 2009. *blogs.zdnet.com/projectfailures/?p=2353*

Leadership in Energy and Environmental Design (LEED), *usgbc.org/leed*

McKay, J., and P. Marshall, *Strategic Management of E-Business.* Milton Old, Australia, John Wiley & Sons, 2004.

Metropolitan Museum of Art (MoMA) *moma.org/interactives/exhibitions/2008/elasticmind/#/154/*

MicroScope.co.uk, "BP Signs Up Computacenter After Axing 540 Vendors," January 18, 2010.

Microsoft 2D Tags, *microsoft.com/tag/*

Microsoft Custom 2D Tags, *mediadl.microsoft.com/mediadl/www/t/tag/CreatingCustomTags.wmv*

Ministry of Justice, United Kingdom, *noms.justice.gov.uk/*

NAO (National Audit Office). "The National Offender Management Information System," Report by the Comptroller and Auditor General, March 12, 2009. *nao.org.uk/whats_new/0708-1/0809292.aspx*

Oates, J. "Failed probation system 'masterclass in sloppy management'." *The Register.* March 12, 2009. *theregister.co.uk/2009/03/12/nao_probation_report/*

PayPal.com

Pew Research, 2010. *stateofthemedia.org/2010/*

Plastic Logic, Que Reader, *quereader.com*

PR Newswire. "Digital Daya's Social Media Command Centre Buzzes in the UAE," January 27, 2011.

ThorDC.com

United Kingdom National Offender Management Information System project (NOMIS). *nao.org.uk/whats_new/0708-1/0809292.aspx*

Watson, H. J., and J. Hill. "What Gets Watched Gets Done: How Metrics Can Motivate," *Business Intelligence Journal,* 3rd Quarter 2009. Accessible from *academicprograms.teradata.com/*

Watson, B. "Cool Cash," *Baseline,* October 29, 2007.

Yankee Group, 2009. *yankeegroup.com/home.do*

Chapter 2

IT Infrastructure and Support Systems

Learning Objectives

❶ Understand the types of information systems and how they process data.

❷ Understand the types of information systems used to support business operations and decision makers.

❸ Describe how IT supports supply chains and business processes.

❹ Understand the attributes, benefits, and risks of service-based and cloud computing infrastructures.

Integrating *IT*

ACC   FIN   MKT   OM   HRM   IS

Blog on cloud computing *infoworld.com/blogs/david-linthicum*
Planners Lab, for building a DSS *plannerslab.com*
Supply Chain and Logistics Institute *SCL.gatech.edu/*
Salesforce.com cloud demos *salesforce.com*
U.S. Defense Information Systems Agency *disa.mil*
Supply Chain, Europe's strategic supply chain management resource *supplychainstandard.com*

QUICK LOOK at Chapter 2, IT Infrastructure and Support Systems

This section introduces you to the business issues, challenges, and IT solutions in Chapter 2. Topics and issues mentioned in the Quick Look are explained in the chapter.

Organizations have various types of information systems that collect and process data, distribute reports, and support decision making and business processes. Starting with transactions that take place at an interface (e.g., withdrawing money from an automatic teller machine, or ATM), a **transaction processing system (TPS)** processes the data (e.g., verifies available funds, subtracts withdrawal amount) and then stores or updates the data in a database. Data are extracted from the database and organized into reports using **management information systems (MIS)**. MIS refers to basic reporting systems that convert raw data into more meaningful information used by managers and employees. Information is an organization's most important asset, second only to people.

Decision making and problem solving require data and models for analysis; they are supported by **decision support systems (DSS)**. Corporations, government agencies, the military, healthcare, medical research, major league sports, and nonprofits depend on their DSSs at all levels of the organization. Innovative DSSs create and help sustain competitive advantages. DSSs reduce waste in production operations, improve inventory management, support investment decisions, and predict demand. The **model** of a DSS consists of a set of formulas and functions, such as statistical, financial, optimization, and/or simulation models.

Figure 2.1 shows how types of ISs relate to one another and how data flows among them. In this example, data from online purchases is captured and processed by the TPS, then stored in the transactional database. Data needed for reporting purposes is extracted from the database and used by the MIS to create periodic, ad hoc, or other types of reports. Data is output to a DSS, where it is analyzed using models. In effect, data collected by the TPS is converted into information by the MIS and DSS.

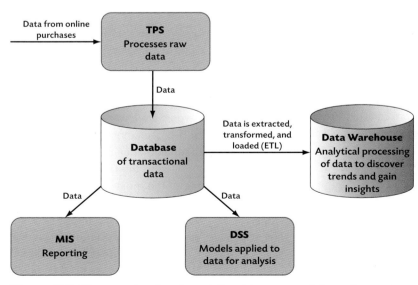

Figure 2.1 Diagram showing the relationships among information systems.

Customer, sales, and other critical data are selected for additional analysis, such as trend analysis or forecasting demand. That data is extracted from the database, transformed into a standard format, and then loaded into a data warehouse. Complex decision-making and problem-solving tasks cannot be done in a database because of its volatility. Those tasks need sophisticated systems, IT platforms, and data repositories, such as data warehouses.

In Chapter 2, you will learn how various types of systems and applications support managers, workers, work flows, business processes, and transactions with supply chain partners. The role of the IT department (or IT function, as it's sometimes called) is to ensure the reliability of the enterprise's IT infrastructure. **IT infrastructure** is the collection of hardware, software, processes, networks, and users. The design of the IT infrastructure determines the ability to efficiently store, protect, and manage data so that it can be made accessible, searchable, shareable, and, ultimately, actionable. In this chapter, you will learn why cost, complexity, and risk need to be considered when configuring an IT infrastructure. You will read about the growing use of software-as-a-service (SaaS) and cloud computing.

In the past, IT managers only had two options—to build or buy the technology. Now they also have the option of **cloud computing**, in which the technology is rented or leased on a regular or as-needed basis. Cloud computing gets its name from the Internet, which you usually see represented as a cloud. Examples are data storage and computing hardware that are accessed via the Internet instead of being company-owned and on-site in a data center. Cloud computing delivers IT capabilities as *services* over the Internet, allowing them to be managed and accessed via the Internet. A 2009 report from the University of California at Berkeley estimated that cloud computing services are five to seven times more cost effective than traditional data centers (Hasson, 2009). However, security risks had a dampening effect on the adoption of cloud strategies. According to a 2010 IDC survey, 88 percent of respondents said security was their biggest concern or challenge when considering cloud adoption.

FIN   OM   SVR

M&A at CIMB Group of Malaysia Depends on IT Integration

Basics of M&A

Mergers and acquisitions (M&A) are a common corporate growth strategy, and a way to form a stronger competitive organization. A **merger** is a combination of two companies to form a new company, while an **acquisition** is the purchase of one company by another with no new company being formed. In some cases, M&A may be necessary to the survival of the organizations. In other cases, M&A are a strategic action to create a leaner, more profitable company that is better positioned for growth.

In the banking sector, M&A occur in a majority of countries in the world, popular because of the global trend toward larger financial services institutions. In 2011, management consulting company Accenture (*Accenture.com*) predicted that the number of mergers and acquisitions worldwide would rise through 2015.

CIMB Group's M&A

CIMB Group (*cimb.com/*) of Malaysia is the fifth largest financial services organization in Southeast Asia. Headquartered in Kuala Lumpur, CIMB Group's main markets are Malaysia, Indonesia, Singapore, Thailand and Cambodia. In 2008, CIMB Group acquired two banks in Indonesia: the Bank Niaga and Lippobank. Bank Niaga had been the sixth largest Indonesian bank in term of assets and Lippobank had been the tenth largest. To comply with Indonesia Central Bank's single presence policy, CIMB merged the two banks it had acquired into the CIMB Niaga Bank (*cimbniaga.com/*). The objectives were to create a more solid and progressive banking institution, and to be the preferred bank of customers.

Merger Synergies Strongly Related to IT Integration and Consolidation

According to a study by McKinsey & Company (*mckinsey.com*), a global consulting company, more than half of the synergies (benefits) available in a merger of financial service institutions are strongly related to IT. Synergy takes the form of revenue improvements and cost savings. Synergies that can result from mergers are lower IT infrastructure costs or volume discounts for IT procurement (purchases). On the other hand, IT systems integration often presents a major hurdle.

Due to the IT-intensive nature of the banking business, one of the most important aspects of a bank merger is the integration of IT. Information systems, databases, and networks need to be integrated and consolidated for the merged bank to operate efficiently and gain synergies.

The speed of completing the CIMB Niaga Bank merger depended on the speed with which the banks' IT and operations could be integrated. That is, CIMB Niaga Bank could not operate as "one-bank" until the banks' IT infrastructures and support systems were consolidated.

Consolidating ISs is not simply changing over one company's TPS and MIS to match the other company's systems. And it's not achieved by moving one company's data into the databases of the other. Why? Because modifying legacy servers, databases, software applications, and reporting systems to make them compatible may not be feasible. Legacy systems are less flexible, and more expensive to maintain and operate.

Streamlining IT Systems for the Merged Bank

In any integration, IT streamlining is key to providing a seamless banking experience to customers and achieving operational efficiency. At CIMB Niaga, a majority of the IT effort was focused on consolidating hardware, merging of network communications, transforming and standardizing data, and leveraging of IT services.

For Class Discussion and Debate

1. **Scenario for Brainstorming and Discussion:** To compete on a global scale, organizations have increased their market share through M&A, both locally and internationally. Integrating the merged companies' data, information systems, and IT infrastructures may be much more complex, time-consuming, and expensive than senior management had expected. Studies were done in the mid-1990s to learn the impacts of the numerous mergers that occurred in the late 1980s. The evidence suggests that one of the main reasons for poor post-acquisition performance in the merger wave of the late 1980s was the failure of organizations to consider fully the complications of merging information systems and technologies (McKiernan and Merali, 1995). In 2008, researchers from Helsinki University of Technology and Copenhagen Business School reported that IS integration was among the most challenging tasks in corporate M&As (Alaranta and Henningsson, 2008).

   Imagine that two large banks in your region merged and that they were unable to integrate their customer information systems. How might the lack of IS integration negatively impact the newly merged bank's performance? Think in terms of "waste." Waste is effort, time, or investment that has no positive effect or worse—a negative ROI. Would the merged bank know how many customers it had

and which accounts each customer had? Explain your answer. How might not knowing which customers were the most profitable and which were the least profitable make it difficult for managers to improve performance?

2. **Debate:** Data that is inaccurate or incomplete is referred to as dirty data. The degree to which data is inaccurate or incomplete can be represented on a continuum, from "dirty and cannot be trusted" to "clean and can be reasonably trusted." Of course, keeping data accurate and complete so managers can trust it is expensive. All departments want and need trusted data at all times. For example, marketing knows that their campaign costs are lower with more accurate data. However, the IT department is limited by its budget and explains that such a degree of accuracy would consume too much of their budget. Take the position of the marketing manager, the IT manager, or the chief financial officer (CFO) who decides the budgets for each department. For those students who assume the role of the marketing or IT managers, present valid and convincing arguments to the CFO for an increased budget to improve data quality. For those students assuming the role of the CFO, challenge any unsupported arguments, ask questions, and then decide what to do about the IT budget.

Sources: Compiled from Sarrazin and West (2011), Alaranta and Henningsson (2008), *CIMB.com*, and Bank CIMB Niaga Report (2009).

2.1 Data and Software Application Concepts

Business software applications (apps) are computer programs that support a specific task or business process. Apps can support a single worker, a department or division, a functional area, or an entire enterprise. As you read in Chapter 1, there are apps specifically for the iPhone and BlackBerry. As you read throughout other chapters, you will see that apps can support relationships with customers, suppliers, and other business partners.

BUSINESS INFORMATION SYSTEMS

Multiple business apps form a system that supports a functional area—marketing, finance, human resources (HR), production, operations, accounting, and IT. Functional systems for planning and control are discussed in Chapter 9. A worker using a financial app is shown in the nearby photo.

© Steve Cole/iStockphoto

For instance, to support the HR function of the organization, a human resources information system (HRIS) typically consists of a suite or bundle of applications for screening job applicants, monitoring employee performance and turnover, processing payroll, documenting compliance with regulations, and tracking employee benefits. An HRIS collects data, from which reports containing information are generated. Even though the terms *data* and *information* seem to represent the same concept, their differences are important, as you will read about next.

DATA, INFORMATION, AND KNOWLEDGE

Information systems are built to achieve several goals. One key goal is to economically process data into information and knowledge.

Data, or raw data, refers to a basic description of products, customers, events, activities, and transactions that are recorded, classified, and stored. Data is the raw material from which information is produced; the quality, reliability, and integrity of the data must be maintained for the information to be useful. Examples are the number of hours an employee worked in a certain week or the number of new Toyota vehicles sold in the first quarter of 2010. A **database** consists of stored data organized for access, search, retrieval, and update.

Information is data that has been processed, organized, or put into context so that it has meaning and value to the person receiving it. For example, the quarterly sales of new Toyota vehicles from 2008 through 2010 is information because it would give some insight into how the vehicle recalls during 2009 and 2010 impacted sales.

Knowledge consists of data and/or information that has been processed, organized, and put into context to be meaningful and to convey understanding, experience, accumulated learning, and expertise as they apply to a current problem or activity. Knowing how to manage a vehicle recall to minimize negative impacts on new vehicle sales is an example of knowledge. Figure 2.2 illustrates the differences in data, information, and knowledge. Organizational knowledge—the expertise of its workers—is valuable to all employees and the bottom line.

Review Questions

1. Define *information system*.
2. What is an application program?
3. Define *data*, *information*, and knowledge.

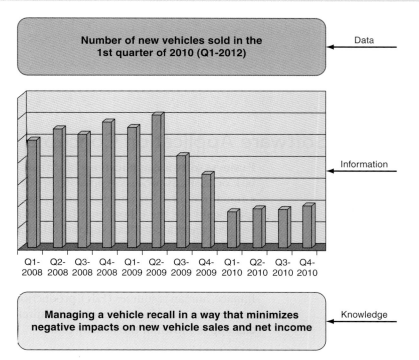

Figure 2.2 Example of data, information, and knowledge.

2.2 Types of Information Systems and Support

Information systems can be classified into two categories based on the general type of support they provide: managerial or operational support. Figure 2.3 represents this classification as management support systems and operations support systems, and it shows two examples of each.

TRANSACTION PROCESSING SYSTEMS (TPS)

Transaction processing systems are designed to process specific types of data input from ongoing transactions. TPSs can be manual, as when data is typed into a form on a screen, or automated by using scanners or sensors to capture data. Figure 2.4 illustrates input of barcode data via a handheld scanner.

Organizational data is processed by a TPS—sales orders, payroll, accounting, financial, marketing, purchasing, inventory control, and so on. Transactions are either:

• **Internal transactions:** Transactions that originate from within the organization or that occur within the organization. Examples are payroll, purchases, budget transfers, and payments (in accounting terms, they're referred to as *accounts payable*).

• **External transactions:** Transactions that originate from outside the organization, for example, from customers, suppliers, regulators, distributors, and financing institutions.

TPSs are critical systems. Transactions that do not get captured can result in lost sales, dissatisfied customers, and many other types of data errors. For example, if accounting issues a check as payment for an invoice (bill), and that transaction is not captured, the amount of cash on the financial statements is overstated and the invoice may be paid a second time. Or if services are provided but not recorded, the company loses that service revenue.

Batch vs. Online Real-Time Processing. Data captured by a TPS is processed and stored in a database; it is then available for use by other systems. Processing of transactions is done in one of two modes:

• **Batch processing:** A TPS in batch processing mode collects all transactions for a day, shift, or other time period and then processes and stores the data later. Payroll processing, which is typically done weekly or biweekly, is done in batch mode.
• **Online transaction processing (OLTP) or real-time processing:** The TPS processes each transaction as it occurs, which is what is meant by the term *real-time processing*. In order for online transaction processing (OLTP) to occur, the input device or Web site must be directly linked via a network to the TPS. Airlines need to process flight reservations in real time to verify that seats are available. E-commerce transactions also need to be processed in real time.

Batch processing costs less than real-time processing, with the obvious disadvantage that data is inaccurate because it is not updated immediately (in real time).

Data Quality. Processing improves data quality, which is important because reports and decisions are only as good as the data they are based upon. As data is collected

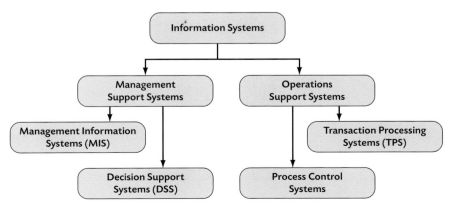

Figure 2.3 Information systems classified according to type of support.

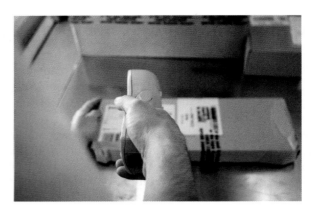

Figure 2.4 Scanners automate the input of data into a transaction processing system (TPS). (© Jan_Neville/iStockphoto)

or captured, it is validated to detect and correct obvious errors and omissions. For example, if a customer sets up an account with a company, such as Amazon.com, to purchase from its Web site, the TPS will validate that the address, city, and postal code are consistent and also that those data items match the address, city, and postal code of the credit card. If required fields of the online form are not completed or have obvious errors, the customer is required to make the corrections before the data is processed any further.

Data errors detected later may be difficult to correct, may expose the company to legal action, or may never be detected and corrected. You can better understand the difficulty of detecting and correcting errors by considering identity theft. Victims of identity theft face enormous challenges and frustration trying to correct data about them stored in databases.

Routine Business Transactions. Financial, accounting, and other repetitive business activities create routine business transactions. For example, employees are paid at regular intervals, customers place purchase orders and are billed, and expenses are monitored and compared to the budget. Table 2.1 presents a list of representative routine, repetitive business transactions in a manufacturing company.

TABLE 2.1	Routine Business Transactions in a Manufacturing Company
Payroll and personnel	Employee time cards
	Employee pay and deductions
	Payroll checks
	Fringe benefits
Purchasing	Purchase orders
	Deliveries
	Payments (accounts payable)
Finance and accounting	Financial statements
	Tax records
	Expense accounts
	Accounts receivable
	Accounts payable
Sales	Sales records
	Invoices and billings
	Sales returns
	Shipping
Production	Production reports
	Quality control reports
Inventory management	Material usage
	Inventory levels

MANAGEMENT INFORMATION SYSTEMS

The functional areas or departments—accounting, finance, production/operations, marketing and sales, human resource, and engineering and design—are supported by ISs designed for their particular reporting needs. General-purpose reporting systems are referred to as management information systems (MIS). Their objective is to provide reports to managers for tracking operations, monitoring, and control. The information systems department serves these departments, as shown in Figure 2.5.

Typically, a functional system provides reports about such topics as operational efficiency, effectiveness, and productivity by extracting information from databases and processing it according to the needs of the user. Types of reports are the following:

- **Periodic:** These reports are created or run according to a preset schedule, such as daily, weekly, or quarterly. Reports are easily distributed via e-mail, blogs, internal Web sites (called *intranets*), or other electronic media. Periodic reports are also easily ignored if workers don't find them worth the time to review.
- **Exception:** Exception reports are generated only when something is outside the norm, either higher or lower than expected. Sales in hardware stores prior to a hurricane may be much higher than the norm. Or sales of fresh produce may drop during a food contamination crisis. Exception reports are more likely to be read because workers know that some unusual event or deviation has occurred.
- **Ad hoc:** Ad hoc reports are unplanned reports. They are generated to a screen or in print on an *as-needed* basis. They are generated on request to provide more information about a situation, problem, or opportunity.

Reports can include tables of data and data charts, as shown in Figure 2.6. With easy-to-use multimedia technology, reports can also include video, audio, and links to other reports.

Functional information systems that support business analysts and other departmental employees can be fairly complex, depending on the type of employees supported. The following examples show the support IT provides to major functional areas.

1. Computerized analysis helps Texas collect $400 million additional taxes.
Tax gaps exist between taxes owed and the amount collected in many public entities.

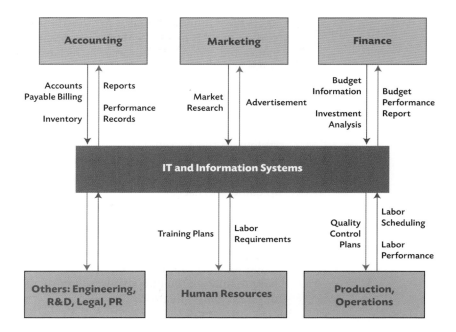

Figure 2.5 Functional information systems.

Figure 2.6 Sample report produced by an MIS. (© Damir Karan/iStockphoto)

The state of Texas is no exception. To overcome the problems, tax collectors perform audits, which are time-consuming and expensive to conduct manually. Also, many audits are unproductive, resulting in little or no tax recovery. In order to make better decisions on whom to audit to increase the percentage of productive audits, the state of Texas uses predictive analytics.

Millions of records are stored in the state data warehouse. Using data mining software from SPSS.com, the agency can cross-match millions of records identifying promising leads. Specifically, the system helps identify thousands of businesses that were operating in the state without complying with the tax obligations. Also, it helps field auditors in adopting better audit target selections. Once the employees gained confidence in the program, they started to use it extensively, saving over $150 million a year.

2. The Dallas Mavericks: Using IT for successful play and business. The Dallas Mavericks of the National Basketball Association (NBA) expect to fill every seat at every game in their stadium and to maximize sales from concessions and souvenir items.

To track attendance, the Mavs were the first NBA team to put barcodes on tickets and then scan them. The information encoded in the barcode enabled them to find out whether group sales and community organization giveaways were filling seats or whether those marketing efforts were just wasting tickets. The team's business managers have found other uses for the attendance information as well. By using forecasting models in a DSS, they more accurately predicted attendance for particular games and demand for beverages, which reduced beverage inventories by 50 percent—reducing inventory costs.

Each of the 144 luxury suites is equipped with a PC that handles orders for merchandise, food, and beverages. Wireless access from all seats in the arena is available so that fans can place orders directly from their seats. All 840 cash registers at concessions stands, restaurants, stores, and bars use a sophisticated point-of-sale (POS) system. In the big retail store on the ground floor, salespeople using handheld computing devices ring up credit card purchases when lines get too long. During a game, managers can see which concession stands are busy and which can be closed early to cut labor costs.

IT also supports the Mavs on the court. The team has 10 assistant coaches, and each has a laptop computer and a handheld computing device. Game films can be streamed over the Web for coaches to view on the road or at home. Another system developed in-house matches game footage with precise, to-the-minute statistics provided for every play of every game by the NBA. Coaches use data from the database to analyze the effectiveness of particular plays and combinations of players in different game situations.

Since 2002, the Mavs have used handheld computers to track the performance of each referee in every one of their games. The coaches look at patterns and trends—for example, to see which referee favors a given team or which one calls more three-second violations—and alert their players. Another system logs different offensive and defensive schemes used against the Mavs. It's used by coaches to make real-time adjustments based on statistics from previous games.

3. Army trains soldiers with virtual worlds. The U.S. Army uses video games and virtual worlds to teach soldiers interpersonal skills and cultural awareness for combat environments such as Iraq and Afghanistan. The IT supports computerized exercises that can sharpen physical reflexes and shooting skills. It prepares soldiers for a war and engenders the desire to win. The new systems train for difficult communication situations abroad (Gonsalves, 2008). For example, negotiation skills are heavily dependent on culture. Soldiers learn how to think and communicate under pressure and stress. The system is a multiplayer simulation game (up to 64 players on the networked computer system over an intranet). Players direct their avatars through the realistic war zone cyberspace. Participants serve as either role players or evaluators with tasks and experiences that vary according to role. Instructors can create or modify scenarios, monitor training, and jump in to change the direction of the game at any time. The interactions practiced in the game help soldiers deal with local customs, build trust with natives in foreign war zones, and equip and train locals to aid U.S. military efforts.

An integrated trade management system with DSS components used by Western Petroleum (Western Petro) to control costs is discussed in *IT at Work 2.1*.

IT at Work 2.1

Integrated Trade Management System for the Energy Sector

Western Petroleum Company (*WesternPetro.com/*) supplies over 2,000 customers in the United States and Canada with approximately 100,000 barrels per day of refined fuels, lubricants and propane. Western Petro buys petroleum products in bulk (e.g., 50,000 barrels) and resells them in smaller amounts (e.g., 5,000 barrels). As with all companies in the energy sector, uninterrupted operations are critical to their business performance. "When our oilfield customers need fuel, they need it immediately," says Perry P. Taylor, Western Petro president. "They don't want to hear excuses about delayed deliveries. If the drilling rigs run out of fuel, they have to shut down, and that can be very expensive."

Controlling Costs and Hedging Contracts. The company operates on a razor-thin profit margin, so controlling purchasing costs determines profitability. Costs are controlled by using an industry-specific software platform that facilitates trading and helps schedule employees.

The IT strategy has been to automate core business processes and to outsource all noncritical functions. A key piece of the automation strategy is PetroMan, from Sisu Group (*sisugrp.com*). PetroMan is a comprehensive trading system that triggers buying and selling activities and integrates contract management, risk management, accounting, and pipeline scheduler.

Using the PetroMan, the company can place bids and automatically capture a contract for refined products as well as schedule and confirm deliveries in pipelines. PetroMan also handles the resale of fuels, including electronic invoicing and a credit module that checks and tracks a customer's credit risk. This tracking is done by hedging large purchasing contracts by selling futures on the New York Mercantile (Commodities) Exchange. By hedging, the company protects itself against the risk of a large drop in oil prices. The software is plugged directly into the primary commodity exchanges, automating the process.

Accounting/financial data flows automatically from PetroMan to the company's financial application, a package called Global Financials (from Global Software). As a result, the entire process of buying and selling fuels and moving the accounting/financial information is fully automated.

Sources: Compiled from Duvall (2005), *westernpetro.com*, and *sisugrp.com/petroman.htm*

Discussion Questions: Which processes are being automated and why? Why is controlling risk important? Does PetroMan provide Western Petro with a competitive advantage? Explain. Visit *sisugrp.com/petroman.htm*. Why is PetroMan referred to as an enterprise information system?

DECISION SUPPORT
SYSTEMS

Decision support systems (DSS) are interactive applications that support decision making. Configurations of a DSS range from relatively simple applications that support a single user to complex enterprise-wide systems, as at Western Petro (described in *IT at Work 2.1*). A DSS can support the analysis and solution of a specific problem, evaluate a strategic opportunity, or support ongoing operations. These systems support unstructured and semistructured decisions, such as whether to make or buy products and what new products to develop and introduce into existing markets.

Degree of Structure of Decisions. Decisions range from structured to unstructured. Structured decisions are those that have a well-defined method for solving and the data needed to reach a decision. An example of a structured decision is determining whether an applicant qualifies for an auto loan or whether to extend credit to a new customer—and the terms of those financing options. **Structured decisions** are relatively straightforward and are made on a regular basis; an IS can insure that they are done consistently.

At the other end of the continuum are **unstructured decisions** that depend on human intelligence, knowledge, and/or experience—as well as data and models to solve. Examples include deciding which new products to develop or which new markets to enter. Semistructured decisions are in the middle of the continuum. DSSs are best suited to support these types of decisions, but they are also used to support unstructured ones. To provide such support, DSSs have certain characteristics to support the decision maker and the decision-making process.

Three Defining DSS Characteristics. Three defining characteristics of DSSs are:

• An easy-to-use interactive interface
• Models that enable sensitivity analysis, *what-if* analysis, goal seeking, and risk analysis
• Data from both internal databases and external sources, added to by the decision maker, who may have insights relevant to the decision situation.

Having models is what distinguishes DSS from MIS. Some models are developed by end users through an interactive and iterative process. Decision makers can manipulate models to conduct experiments and sensitivity, w*hat-if,* and *goal-seeking* analyses. What-if analysis refers to changing assumptions or data in the model to see the impacts of the changes on the outcome. For example, if sales forecasts are based on a 5 percent increase in customer demand, a what-if analysis would replace the 5 percent with higher and/or lower demand estimates to determine *what* would happen to sales *if* the demands were different. With goal seeking, the decision maker has a specific outcome in mind and needs to figure out how that outcome could be achieved and whether it's feasible to achieve that desired outcome. A DSS can also estimate the risk of alternative strategies or actions.

California Pizza Kitchen (CPK) uses a DSS to support inventory decisions. CPK has 77 restaurants located in various states in the United States. Maintaining the inventory of all restaurants at optimal levels was challenging. A DSS has made it easy for the managers to keep records updated and make decisions. Many CPK restaurants increased sales by 5 percent after implementing a DSS.

Building DSS Applications. Planners Lab is an example of software for building a DSS. The software is free to academic institutions and can be downloaded from *plannerslab.com*. Planners Lab includes:

• An easy-to-use model-building language
• An easy-to-use option for visualizing model output, such as answers to what-if and goal-seeking questions to analyze the impacts of different assumptions

These tools enable managers and analysts to build, review, and challenge the assumptions on which their decision scenarios are based. With Planners Lab, decision makers can experiment and play with assumptions to assess multiple views of the future.

Some DSS applications may be very similar to business intelligence (BI) applications, which are discussed in Chapter 11. *IT at Work 2.2* provides an overview of BI and shows the similarity between these applications and DSS. You will read about BI and DSS is greater detail in Chapter 11.

IT at Work 2.2

Architecture of BI Apps, Dashboards, and Data Mining

FIN   MKT

Business intelligence (BI) combines software architectures, databases, analytical tools, applications, graphical displays, and decision-making methodologies. BI's main objective is to enable timely and even interactive access to data and to give business managers and analysts the ability to conduct appropriate analysis. By analyzing historical and current data, situations, and performances, decision makers obtain valuable insights that enable them to make more informed and better decisions.

The Architecture of BI. A BI system has four major components:

1. A data warehouse or large database with its *source data*

2. Business analytics, a collection of tools for manipulating, mining, and analyzing the data in the data warehouse

3. Business performance management (BPM) tools for monitoring and analyzing performance

4. A user interface and display, such as a dashboard

A major component in BI and in BPM is the dashboard. A dashboard is a visual presentation of critical data (e.g., results of a report or analysis) for users, including executives. It allows users to see *hot spots* at a glance, such as deviations from targets, exceptional performance, or Web analytics summaries. An example is provided in Figure 2.7, which displays a number of key performance indicators (KPI) and critical data for a software company. From the dashboard, it is easy to see, for instance, that the KPIs are all good (i.e., they are all in the green), that for all stages of the pipeline the revenues are trending upward (i.e., they are all

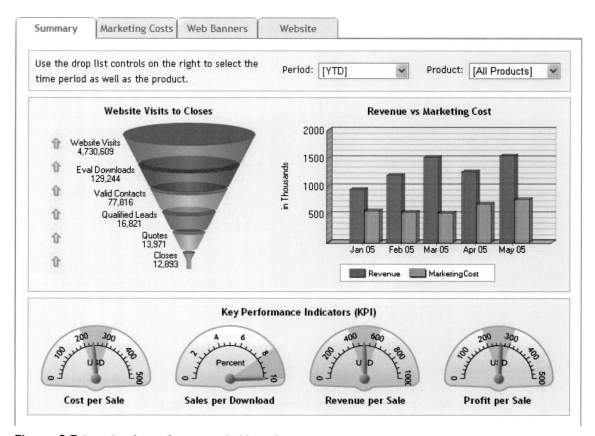

Figure 2.7 Sample of a performance dashboard.

green arrows pointing upward), and that the growth in revenues is outpacing the increase in marketing costs. This particular dashboard enables end users to see whether there are any differences by time period or product (the drop-downs on the upper right) and to further analyze marketing costs.

Data Mining. One major analytical tool in BI is data mining. **Data mining** is a computerized process for conducting searches in large amounts of data and information in an attempt to discover unknown valuable relationships in the data (e.g., among variables). Data mining helps in making predictions and decision making.

Examples of how data mining works: Two examples of useful applications that show how data mining can support organizations follow:

BI Example 1. The National Australia Bank uses data mining to aid its predictive marketing. The tools are used to extract and analyze data stored in the bank's Oracle database. Specific applications focus on assessing how competitors' initiatives are affecting the bank's bottom line. Data mining tools are used to generate market analysis models from historical data. The bank considers BI crucial to maintaining an edge in the increasingly competitive financial services marketplace.

BI Example 2. The FAI Insurance Group uses data mining to reassess the relationship between historical risk from insurance policies and the pricing structure used by its underwriters. The data analysis capabilities allow FAI to better serve its customers by more accurately assessing the insurance risk associated with a customer request.

MAIN TYPES OF SUPPORT SYSTEMS

The main types of support systems are listed in Table 2.2, together with the types of employees they support. Several of these support systems are discussed in later chapters.

TABLE 2.2	Main Types of Information Support Systems	
Information Systems	**Workers Supported**	**Description**
Management information system (MIS)	Middle managers	Provides routine information for planning, organizing, and controlling operations in functional areas
Decision support system (DSS)	Decision makers, managers	Combines models and data to solve semistructured problems with extensive user involvement
Business intelligence (BI)	Decision makers, managers, knowledge workers	Gathers and uses large amounts of data for analysis by business analytics and intelligent systems
CAD/CAM	Engineers, draftspeople	Allows engineers to design and test prototypes; transfers specifications to manufacturing facilities
Electronic records management system	Office workers	Automates management, archiving, and flow of electronic documents
Knowledge management system (KM)	Managers, knowledge workers	Supports the gathering, organizing, and use of an organization's knowledge
Data mining and text mining	Knowledge workers, professionals	Enables learning from historical cases, even with vague or incomplete information
Automated decision support (ADS)	Frontline employees, middle managers	Supports customer care employees and salespeople who need to make quick, real-time decisions involving small dollar amounts

Review Questions

1. Define *TPS* and provide an example.
2. What is a functional information system?
3. Explain why TPS needs to process incoming data before storing it in a database.
4. Define *MIS* and provide an example.
5. Define *DSS* and provide an example.

2.3 Supply Chain and Logistics Support

A company's supply chain can be viewed as two segments, the backstream and upstream, which are shown in Figure 2.8. Each segment can consist of multiple links, perhaps hundreds, to individual suppliers/sellers and to multiple customers. Every link an organization has to direct sources and/or direct customers needs to be managed. But not all links need to be managed to the same extent. For example, Walmart focuses its efforts on the backstream supply chain, as you will read in the next section. For a retailer, wholesalers and manufacturers are backstream; their customers are upstream. For manufacturers, their supply chain extends from raw materials through the recycling of the product.

Along with the physical flows of products and materials are the information flows and the financial flows that link companies in the supply chain. **Logistics** is the science concerned with managing material and information flows to optimize supply chain operations. Logistics has been described as having the right thing, at the right place, at the right time.

A company's competitive advantage—for example, low cost, reliability, quality, speed to market, and/or quick response—depends on how well the supply chain is aligned and managed. The importance of **supply chain management (SCM)** is understood by examining Walmart's global sourcing strategy. **Global sourcing** occurs when companies purchase goods or services from sellers located anywhere in the world.

Walmart's Global Sourcing Strategy for its Backstream Supply Chain. In March 2010, retail giant Walmart announced its new backstream SCM strategy. Because Walmart has thousands of suppliers and is constantly looking for new ones worldwide, it decided to invest in a new *global sourcing strategy*. **Sourcing** involves identifying sources (sellers) that could provide Walmart with products or services to sell in its stores and online. Its **sourcing strategy** is designed to reduce costs of goods, increase speed to market, and improve the quality of products.

Walmart's global sourcing strategy involves three things: (1) the creation of global merchandising centers (GMCs), (2) a change in leadership and structure, and (3) a strategic alliance with Li & Fung, a global sourcing organization. Li & Fung is building capacity that would enable it to act as a *buying agent* for goods valued around US$2 billion within the first year. Walmart vice-chairman Eduardo Castro-Wright said: "These centres will create alignment between sourcing and merchandising and drive efficiencies across various merchandise categories. Our new strategy and structure should drive significant savings across the supply chain" ("Wal-Mart Unveils," 2010).

Walmart has been a leader in global SCM best practices for many years. Its new global sourcing strategy shows that continuing efforts and investments to drive inefficiencies out of the supply chain are vital to competitiveness. Walmart's executives recognize that maintaining their low cost and huge product variety advantages depends on how well they manage their numerous supply chains. Supply chain management is a strategic concern of almost every organization. For many, particularly those in manufacturing, distribution, and retail, SCM is critical to survival. *IT at Work 2.3* gives an example of a company managing its internal operations— also referred to as the **internal supply chain**—and upstream supply chain.

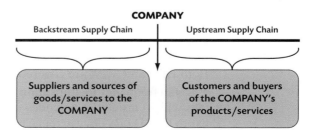

Figure 2.8 Backstream and upstream components of a supply chain.

IT at Work 2.3

Warehouse Control Systems in UK Distribution Center

OM

A warehouse control system (WCS) collects real-time information from various sources, such as automated material handling equipment, warehouse management systems, or enterprise resource planning (ERP) systems. Think of a WCS like a Universal Remote Control for a home-entertainment system—only much smarter. Based on information inputs, the WCS monitors and controls inventory and synchronizes order fulfillment and processing in the warehouse or distribution center. By doing so, the WCS maximizes throughput at the lowest operational cost.

Automated Distribution Center Supports Argos' Operations.
Argos (*argos.co.uk/*) is the largest non-food retailer in the United Kingdom (U.K.). Argos sells general merchandise and products for the home from over 700 stores in the U.K. and Ireland, online, and over the telephone. They serve over 130 million customers a year in their stores. In 2009, their sales were £4.3 billion and they employed 33,000 people. Approximately 26 percent of sales are online sales. The Argos Web site was the most visited high street retail site in the U.K. in 2008.

Argos partnered with VanDerLande Industries (*vanderlande. com*) on an automated distribution center, which lowered operational costs and improved efficiency, productivity and picking accuracy.

Faced with significant growth, Argos wanted to increase product availability, improve picking efficiency, and reduce costs. To do so, Argos centralized its distribution of small items. See an example of automation in Figure 2.9. Argos also wanted better control over the supply of direct imports, which make up a growing proportion of their products.

The automated distribution center includes a central warehouse for imported goods. Pallet handling is a vital part of their production and distribution processes. Pallet handling extends throughout the business process, from goods receiving to shipping of finished products or sorted deliveries. Therefore, fast, smooth, and efficient pallet handling is a critical success factor.

Figure 2.9 Automated handling of small products improves the efficiency of Argos' internal supply chain.

Integrated Operations. All automated processes are managed by VanDerLande Industries VISION WCS, which is integrated into Argos' warehouse management system. The automated distribution center significantly reduced Argos' operational costs by freeing up resources at the busy regional distribution centers. Managing direct imports in bulk yields greater savings and ensures continuity of supply.

Sources: Compiled from *argos.co.uk/* (2011), *vanderlande.com* (2011), and *supplychainstandard.com* (2008).

Discussion Questions: How has WCS benefited Argos? Why did Argos partner with a vendor for its warehouse management systems? Watch the video *A Major Advance in Logistics* about the Argos project at *yourlogisticstv.com*. Explain why Argos' project was a major advance in logistics.

Supply Chains Create Extended Enterprises. The supply chain—by linking a company with its suppliers, vendors, and customers—creates an extended enterprise. That extended enterprise depends on IT and information systems to share data and collaborate, similar to the way various departments within the company do. Supply chains can be grossly inefficient unless the companies in the supply chain can share data, collaborate, and respond to changes in demand efficiently and quickly.

ITs used for planning, organizing, coordinating, and controlling supply chain activities include the following:

• Enterprise resource planning (ERP) software: ERP helps manage both the internal and the external relationships with the business partners.

• Supply chain management software: SCM software helps in decision making related both to internal segments and to their relationships with external segments. Both ERP and SCM are covered in detail in Chapter 11.

• **Radio frequency identification** (RFID): RFID is a technology that uses electronic tags (chips) instead of barcodes to identify objects or items. This technology is similar to the 2D tags discussed in Chapter 1. RFID tags can be attached to or embedded in packages, physical objects, animals, or humans. RFID readers scan and input identifying information from the tags via radio waves.

Radio Frequency Identification (RFID) Systems. RFID systems are essential to any supply chain, but their ability to track and monitor also provides additional benefits. For example, in 2010 Gerry Weber International, a Germany-based manufacturer of women's fashions, began applying RFID tags to the 25 million garments it produces annually. The company rolled out RFID technology at 150 of its company-owned retail stores in Germany and abroad. The RFID system is designed to improve the efficiency of its incoming goods and inventory processes and also to function as an electronic article surveillance (EAS) system to deter theft. The RFID tags are embedded into the garment-care labels. The company is the first in Germany to sew RFID-enabled care labels into apparel, as well as the first to rely solely on RFID for EAS (*gerryweber-ag.de*, 2010; Wessel, 2009).

At a presentation at *RFID Journal LIVE! Europe 2009*, Ralph Tröger, an IT project manager at Gerry Weber, said his company learned from the logistics processes testing that it can gain "real value" from RFID, particularly by using the technology for picking and outbound shipping processes. It also learned that some RFID hardware was too large for retail distribution centers and that handheld readers required improved battery life and needed to be lighter.

Gerry Weber had significant time savings in the incoming goods receiving process because employees no longer had to manually count items or scan their barcodes to find out if an order was complete. Clerks simply scanned the barcode on the delivery note and scanned the RFID tags in garments to match up delivery receipts with actual items shipped. In addition, employees saved significant time by no longer having to attach and detach EAS security tags and take inventory. When a tagged item is purchased, a clerk reads the barcode on the price tag. The RFID system then reads the EPC number encoded to the garment's RFID tag and removes it from the database.

Sewing RFID tags into all garments it produces provides opportunities for suppliers and partners. The firm is encouraging all companies with which it does business to take advantage of its tagging in order to improve their processes and services, by implementing RFID read points in the supply chain or at other points. Gerry Weber's performance improvements represent major benefits of RFID—efficient tracking of the items in real time, automated inventory tracking, and aligning companies in the supply chain.

RFID implementation has been slow due to costs, privacy, and security concerns, especially when it involves consumers. On the other hand, an increasing number of companies use the technology internally, frequently in combination with other IT systems, as is done by Nokia. Security guards at Nokia carry a mobile phone handset with an attached RFID tag. RFID tags are also installed at various points around the facility. At the start of a shift, guards use the phone to read their RFID-enabled name badges. Then security guards do their rounds, operating the handsets to read the various tags as they pass by them. Details of the phone number and RFID tag just read are transmitted over the cell phone network. Supervisors are thus given accurate information as to when a particular guard started and finished a shift, whether the guard patrolled all of the required locations, and where the guard was at a particular point in time. In addition, supervisors can use the text and phone function to ask guards to recheck an area, vary their route, and the like.

For RFID implementation at Airbus Industries, see the Business Case at the end of this chapter.

Review Questions

1. Describe how IT can support the supply chain of a retailer.
2. What is meant by an extended enterprise?
3. What is an internal supply chain?
4. What is RFID? What are its major benefits?

2.4 IT Infrastructures, Cloud Computing, and Services

When employees log into the company network or e-mail accounts, or access data or documents to perform their jobs, the speed of the response and the reliability of the hardware are critical factors. Delays due to heavy network traffic or system crashes waste time and are frustrating. Of course, everyone wants fast response, quick processing, and rapid access to information or files from various ISs and databases. It is the company's IT infrastructure that determines the workload that ISs, apps, and mobile computing devices can handle and their speed. IT infrastructure is the collection of hardware, software, processes, networks, and users.

The design of the IT infrastructure allows (or limits) the ability to store, protect, and manage data so that it can be made accessible, searchable, shareable, and actionable. To improve performance or lower upfront costs, companies are turning to cloud computing options. The cloud—which is the term used to refer to the Internet—has greatly expanded the options for enterprise IT infrastructures. The general name for Internet-based infrastructures is *cloud computing*. The evolution to cloud computing is represented in Figure 2.10. Organizations may use any or all three types of infrastructures, depending on their needs. As you will read in *IT at Work 2.4,* the U.S. Department of Defense (DoD) has implemented a private cloud to service many military agencies at reduced cost but has not adopted cloud computing because of the sensitive nature of its data.

First we discuss IT infrastructures and then virtualization and cloud computing.

IT INFRASTRUCTURE

What an organization's IT infrastructure can support is determined by five major components: (1) hardware, (2) software, (3) networks and communication facilities, including the Internet and intranets, (4) databases and data workers, and (5) information management personnel. When making decisions about how to acquire hardware, software, or any of these five components, the following four characteristics of an IT infrastructure need to be considered.

- **Dependable.** Dependability means that the infrastructure meets availability, reliability, and scalability requirements of the company's information systems (TPS, MIS, DSS, etc) and applications. Applications inherit their dependability from the IT infrastructure. That is, the dependability of applications is limited by (is only as good as) the dependability of the IT architecture.
- **Manageable.** IT infrastructure determines the complexity of managing hardware and software required to deliver dependable applications. A wireless infrastructure is necessary for interactivity and mobile computing applications.
- **Adaptable.** When additional application capacity is needed, organizations are able to scale up the infrastructure as needed.
- **Affordable.** In today's IT reality, dependability, manageability, and adaptability are not as significant as affordability. For example, older infrastructures may need expensive redundancy, or backup systems, to ensure these characteristics.

With this understanding of IT infrastructure, we can intelligently examine the reasons enterprises are investing in new IT architectures, particularly those that are cloud-based.

Figure 2.10 Evolution to cloud computing.

VIRTUALIZATION

Cloud computing evolved from virtualization—an approach that enabled more flexible IT infrastructures and lower IT costs. **Virtualization** is a concept that has several meanings in IT and therefore several definitions. The major type of virtualization is hardware virtualization, which remains popular and widely used. Virtualization is often a key part of an enterprise's disaster recovery plan. In general, virtualization separates business applications and data from hardware resources. This separation allows companies to pool hardware resources—rather than to dedicate servers to applications—and assign those resources to applications as needed. The following are the major types of virtualization:

- *Storage virtualization* is the pooling of physical storage from multiple network storage devices into what appears to be a single storage device that is managed from a central console.
- *Network virtualization* combines the available resources in a network by splitting the network load into manageable parts, each of which can be assigned (or reassigned) to a particular server on the network.
- *Hardware virtualization* is the use of software to emulate hardware or a total computer environment other than the one the software is actually running in. It allows a piece of hardware to run multiple operating system images at once. This kind of software is sometimes known as a virtual machine.

Virtualization increases the flexibility of IT assets, allowing companies to consolidate IT infrastructure, reduce maintenance and administration costs, and prepare for strategic IT initiatives. Virtualization is not primarily about cost cutting, which is a tactical reason. More importantly, for strategic reasons, virtualization is used because it enables flexible sourcing and cloud computing.

THE MOVE TO ENTERPRISE CLOUDS

A majority of large organizations have hundreds or thousands of licenses for software, such as Microsoft Office or Oracle database management software, that are critical for building and running their databases and apps that support business processes. Managing software programs and their licenses—including deploying, provisioning, and updating them—is time-consuming and expensive. Productivity suffers when IT professionals cannot quickly access the tools they need at the right time. Putting software on a server with no management or usage tracking capabilities around them can cost even more. The latest trend, cloud computing, can overcome several problems and issues. The reduced complexity, lower costs, and improved scalability afforded by enterprise clouds are growing in appeal to many organizations. By offering computer power over the Internet, vendors can free their customers from having to pay for their own hardware, facilities, maintenance, and management.

The cloud idea is to store applications and information in the vendors' data centers rather than on local company-owned servers. This cloud concept refers to sources of stored data *outside a customer's internal network*. However, large companies or government agencies with multiple locations can set up their own clouds, called **private clouds**, on servers that they own if data confidentiality is a key requirement, as with military and defense agencies.

The move toward cloud computing, particularly cloud hosting by a vendor, is increasing with the introduction of new apps. For example, the vendor Rackspace (*rackspace.com/*) launched Cloud Pro in April 2010. Cloud Pro leverages the iPad's touch-screen interface to enable its customers to manage their servers. Using the iPad, network administrators (admins) can turn on backups for a server; create new servers from backups; manage backup scheduling; and reboot, rename, resize, and delete servers. The app was made available at no additional charge through iPad-maker Apple's iTunes store. This arrangement is of enormous benefit to start-up companies. The iPad tablet and Rackspace Cloud servers lower the entry barriers for Web start-ups because they no longer have to make large investments in hardware to get their businesses going.

CLOUD COMPUTING

One definition for cloud computing is that it is Internet-based computing, in which shared resources (such as hard drives for storage) and software apps are provided to computers and other devices on-demand, like a public utility (see Figure 2.11 for a model of cloud computing). That is, it's similar to electricity—a utility that companies have available to them on-demand and pay for based on usage. Companies don't generate their own electricity but obtain it from a "vendor," which in this case is an electric company. Major cloud vendors or providers are Google, Amazon, Microsoft, and Cisco. For example, Google Apps provides common business applications online that are accessed from a Web browser, while the software and data are stored on the servers.

Why Use the Cloud? Optimizing IT infrastructure became especially important during tough economic times when cost cutting became a priority. During challenging times, making the most of IT assets becomes imperative for competitive advantage and, ultimately, survival. The cloud typically offers a steep drop in IT costs because applications are hosted by vendors and provided on demand, rather than via physical installations or seat licenses. This rental arrangement with vendors is a key characteristic of cloud computing.

Cloud computing is often used to describe services such as Google's online word-processing application and Salesforce.com's customer service software, which are accessed online through a Web browser instead of stored on a computer. Another option is to pay to use Amazon.com's computing infrastructure—in effect, renting it—rather than buy more servers. *IT at Work 2.4* describes the potential of cloud computing in China.

The concept is catching on in the business world. *The New York Times* uses Amazon.com's cloud service to upload images of archived newspapers and convert them into a more readable format. Nasdaq OMX Group Inc. uses Amazon.com's service to provide historical trading information. Both companies pay only for the computing resources or services they use.

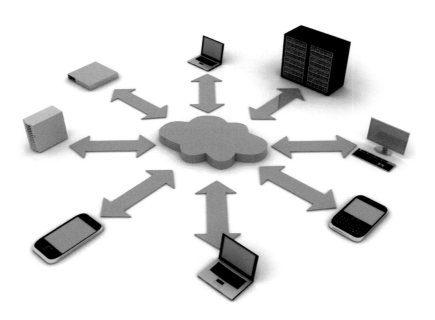

Figure 2.11 Cloud computing.
(*Alex Slobodkin/iStockphoto*)

IT at Work 2.4

Cloud Computing City is Being Built in China

IS   SVR

The world market for cloud computing will grow from $16 billion in 2009 to $55.5 billion in 2014, according to the research firm International Data Corp. (IDC). Cloud computing is a term used to describe the Internet as a method of delivering information, software apps, and other services.

In 2011, China-based Range Technology, an Internet data center services provider, and IBM formed a strategic partnership on cloud computing and software services. The partners are building a city-sized, cloud-computing data center in Langfang, near Beijing, which will be Asia's largest based on floor space. The 620,000 square meter facility, which will be owned by Range Technology and built to IBM specifications and international green building standards, will be completed in 2016. IDC forecasted data center services in China to reach $2.6 billion by the time the facility opens. The data centre will mainly serve government departments from China's capital and across the country, but will also be open to banks and private businesses.

Range Technology said in a statement that "This initiative plays a critical role in the economic development of China in light of the pressing demand for managed hosting in the areas of cloud computing and mobile devices."

"The data center offers the world-class infrastructure capabilities and advanced network-based services to support the business growth of our clients," said Madam Zhou Chaonan, Range Technology chairman.

Cloud computing operations and management will offer much higher efficiency and convenience than conventional computing and processing operations after they become more popular in China's market and win government support.

Sources: Compiled from Kass (2011), Kan (2011), and *IBM.com/cloud*

Discussion Questions: Search for recent information on the trend toward cloud computing. Include in your search content from *IBM.com/cloud*. Based on your research, discuss the importance of the Langfang cloud-computing data center to government departments, banks, and private businesses in China and to China's economy.

What Services Are Available in the Cloud? Cloud computing makes it more affordable for companies to use *services* that in the past would have been packaged as software and required buying, installing, and maintaining on any number of individual machines. A major type of service available via the cloud is called software-as-a-service.

Software-as-a-service (SaaS) is an increasingly popular IT model in which software is available to users as needed. Other terms for SaaS are *on-demand computing*, *utility computing*, and *hosted services*. The idea is basically the same: Instead of buying and installing expensive packaged enterprise applications, users can access software apps over a network, with an Internet browser being the only absolute necessity. Usually there is no hardware or software to buy since the apps are used over the Internet and paid for through a fixed subscription fee or per an actual usage fee. The SaaS model was developed to overcome the common challenge to an enterprise of efficiently meeting fluctuating demands on IT resources.

Cloud services are expanding. For instance, the use of cloud computing to lower accounting costs is becoming widespread, particularly with smaller companies, because there is practically limitless room for growth of the service. For example, a popular leading cloud software and services provider is *salesforce.com*. To emphasize its approach, its telephone number is 1-800-No-Software. Two clouds offered by Salesforce.com are:

• **Sales Cloud.** Sales Cloud is used by almost 80,000 companies. Sales representatives (reps) have almost everything they need to do their jobs in one place. They spend less time on administrative work and have more time to spend with customers and closing deals. For sales managers, the Sales Cloud gives real-time visibility into their team's activities.

• **Service Cloud.** Service Cloud is a platform supporting customer service activities that range from call (contact) centers to social Web sites. Tools provided by the Service Cloud include knowledge-as-a-service, giving agents and customers the ability to find answers online, 24/7; Twitter integration for real-time service conversations; and analytics that provide dashboards and real-time reports to monitor performance.

Issues in Moving Workloads from the Enterprise to the Cloud. With Amazon's EC2, Google's AppEngine, and Microsoft's Azure, cloud computing looks a lot less like a futuristic concept and more like a real IT architecture. But there are still plenty of critics and doubters of the cloud. Variable (on-demand as needed) computing capacity like Amazon's EC2 has its niche, but legacy (older) enterprise apps aren't leaving the data center, and you can't send critical business data to the cloud. However, the services offered by Amazon, Google, and Microsoft offer economies of scale.

But putting part of the IT workload into the cloud requires different management approaches and different IT skills. These include strategy questions, such as deciding which workloads should be exported to the cloud, which set of standards to follow for cloud computing, and how to resolve issues of privacy and security as things move out to the cloud. Two big questions are: How will departments or business units get new IT resources? Should they help themselves, or should IT remain a gatekeeper?

There are different vendor management skills. Staffs experienced in managing outsourcing projects will find parallels to managing work in the cloud, like defining and policing **service-level agreements (SLAs)** with vendors. There's a big difference, however, because cloud computing runs on a shared infrastructure, so the arrangement is less customized to a specific company's requirements. A comparison to help understand the challenges is that outsourcing is like renting an apartment while the cloud is like getting a room at a hotel.

With cloud computing, it may be more difficult to get to the root of performance problems, like the unplanned outages that occurred with Google's Gmail and Workday's human resources apps. The trade-off is cost versus control.

Demand for faster and more powerful computers is increasing, and increases in the number and variety of applications is driving the need for more capable IT architectures.

Review Questions

1. Define *information infrastructure*.
2. Describe virtualization.
3. Describe cloud computing.
4. What are the benefits of cloud computing?
5. Describe software-as-a-service and its benefits. Why is it referred to as utility computing?

Key Terms

ad hoc report *37*	data *34*	exception report *37*
batch processing *35*	data mining *42*	global sourcing *43*
business intelligence (*BI*) *41*	database *34*	information *34*
business software application *33*	decision support system	IT infrastructure *32*
cloud computing *32*	(DSS) *31*	knowledge *34*

Chapter Highlights and Insights

(Numbers refer to Learning Objectives)

❶ Organizations have various types of information systems that collect and process data, distribute reports, and support decision making and other business processes.

❶ Multiple business apps form an information system that supports a functional area—marketing, finance, human resources (HR), production, operations, accounting, and IT.

❷ Information systems can be classified into two categories based on the type of support they provide: managerial and operational support.

❷ Transaction processing systems (TPS) cover the core repetitive organizational transactions such as purchasing, billing, and payroll.

❷ The data collected in a TPS is used to build other support systems, especially MIS and DSS.

❷ Processing improves data quality, which is important because reports and decisions are only as good as the data they are based upon.

❷ The functional areas or departments—accounting, finance, production/operations, marketing and sales, human resource, and engineering and design—are supported by ISs designed for their particular information and reporting needs.

❷ Decision support systems (DSS) support unstructured and semistructured decisions, such as whether to make or buy products and what new products to develop and introduce into existing markets.

❸ A company's competitive advantage—for example, low cost, reliability, quality, speed to market, and/or quick response—depends on how well the supply chain is aligned and managed.

❸ The supply chain—by linking a company with its suppliers, vendors, and customers—creates an extended enterprise.

❸ Three of the major IT-supported managerial activities are (1) improving supply chain operations, (2) integrating departmental systems with ERP, and (3) introducing a variety of customer relationship management (CRM) activities. IT is a major enabler of all of these.

❹ IT infrastructure refers to the shared information resources (such as corporate networks and databases) and their linkages, operation, maintenance, and management.

❹ IT supports individual business processes in all functional areas (with MIS applications). It also supports activities along the supply chain such as procurement, relationship with suppliers, supply chain management, customer relationship management, and order fulfillment.

❹ The design of the IT infrastructure allows and limits the ability to store, protect, and manage data so that it can be made accessible, searchable, shareable, and, actionable.

❹ Virtualization increases the flexibility of IT assets, allowing companies to consolidate IT infrastructure, reduce maintenance and administration costs, and prepare for strategic IT initiatives.

❹ Cloud computing is Internet-based computing in which shared resources (such as hard drives for storage) and software apps are provided to computers and other devices on-demand, like a public utility.

❹ The major emerging technologies include cloud computing and software-as-a-service (SaaS).

Questions for Discussion

1. Explain the relationship between information systems and data stores.
2. Describe how raw data transform into information and information transforms into knowledge.
3. What critical functions do TPSs perform?
4. Explain how MIS supports the needs of middle-level managers.
5. Why are periodic reports often ignored? What types of reports are more valuable to managers?
6. Discuss the differences between structured and unstructured decisions. List an example of each type of decision that you've made within the past week.

7. Explain why a company's competitive advantage—such as low cost, reliability, quality, speed to market, and/or quick response—depends on how well the supply chain is aligned and managed.

8. How do the information systems that support supply chains create an extended enterprise?

9. RFID is considered superior to barcodes. Explain why.

10. Discuss the benefits of cloud computing.

Exercises and Projects

1. Classify each of the following systems as one (or more) of the IT support systems and design a business performance management for each:
   a. A student registration system in a university
   b. A system that advises farmers about which fertilizers to use
   c. A hospital patient-admission system
   d. A system that provides a marketing manager with demand reports regarding the sales volume of specific products
   e. A robotic system that paints cars in a factory

2. Visit *teradatastudentnetwork.com* (ask your instructor for the password) and find the Webcase on "BI Approaches in Healthcare, Financial Services, Retail, and Government" (2006). Explain the IT support. What challenges are common across the industries?

3. Visit *plannerslab.com*. Click onto YouTube in the Community. Watch the most recent Planners Lab video on YouTube. Explain how Planners Lab supports semi-structured and unstructured decisions. How does it support what-if analysis?

Group Assignments and Projects

1. Observe a checkout counter in a supermarket that uses a scanner. Find some material that describes how the scanned code is translated into the price that the customers pay.
   a. Identify the following components of the system: inputs, processes, and outputs.
   b. What kind of a system is the scanner (TPS, DSS, BI, ES, etc.)? Why did you classify it as you did?
   c. Having the information electronically in the system may provide opportunities for additional managerial uses of that information. Identify such uses.
   d. Checkout systems are now being replaced by self-service checkout kiosks and scanners. Compare the two.

2. Visit Planners Lab. Register to create an account, then download free trial software. Click on Models and Materials.
   a. Read the Tutorial Westlake *Lawn and Garden, University of Nebraska, Omaha.*
   b. Under "Example Models," select *Westlake Lawn and Garden, University of Nebraska, Omaha.* Load the Westlake model into Planners Lab.
   c. What are the most valuable decision support features of Planners Lab?
   d. How does Planners Lab support Westlake decision making?

Internet Exercises

1. Visit Rackspace at *rackspace.com/* and review the company's CloudPro products. Describe what CloudPro does. Explain how Rackspace CloudPro leverages the iPad's interface. What are the benefits of the iPad Cloud app?

2. Visit the Supply Chain and Logistics Institute at *SCL.gatech.edu/*. Describe two recent trends or issues of current interest.

3. Visit Teradata University Network (TUN). Search for and read an article or white paper on decision support systems (DSS). List four valuable *take-aways* (those are specific lessons learned) from the article.

4. Visit *oracle.com*. Describe the types of virtualization services offered by Oracle.

5. Visit *infoworld.com/blogs/david-linthicum*. Describe the key issues discussed in this blog.

BUSINESS CASE

High-Memory RFID Tags Improve Airbus' Logistics and Supply Chain

OM   IS

Airbus (*airbus.com/*) is a leading aircraft manufacturer head-quartered in Toulouse, France. Its parent company EADS (*eads.com/*) is a global leader in aerospace, defense, and related services and has a presence on every continent. Airbus itself is a global enterprise consisting of 52,500 employees; fully-owned subsidiaries in the United States, China, Japan and the Middle East; spare parts centers in Hamburg, Frankfurt, Washington, Beijing and Singapore; training centers in Toulouse, Miami, Hamburg and Beijing; and more than 150 field service offices around the world. Airbus also relies on industrial cooperation and partnerships with major companies all over the world, and a network of some 1,500 suppliers in 30 countries.

Airbus to Use High-Memory EPC Gen 2 RFID Tags by 2013

In 2010, Airbus signed a seven-year contract with a supplier of high-memory EPC (Electronic Product Code) Gen 2 radio frequency identification (RFID) tags. This deal is part of Airbus' plan to use RFID to track thousands of pressurized and non-pressurized parts and components on Airbus' new A350 extra-wide body (XWB) fleet, expected to be put into service in 2013.

Airbus will use the eight-kilobyte tags to track flyable aircraft parts and components and store detailed data about each part's initial construction and maintenance. Airbus plans to tag 3,000 parts per plane. Roughly 1,500 parts will require high-memory tags to store their huge volume of data; e.g., the complete birth record and maintenance history of the

aircraft part. By placing high-memory RFID tags on repairable parts, Airbus, aircraft owners, and aircraft repair companies will be able to improve their maintenance and warehouse logistics processes.

Value Chain Visibility

The A350 XWB will be the first aircraft in the Airbus fleet to use high-memory RFID tags on flyable parts. The RFID tags will enable Airbus to achieve its goal of value chain visibility. Value chain visibility enables better aircraft configuration management and line maintenance, repair-shop optimization, warehouse logistics, payload tracking, and life-limited parts monitoring.

Sources: Compiled from Wessel (2010), *RFID News* (2010), and *RFID Journal* (2011).

Questions

1. Why are high-memory tags needed on Airbus' aircraft parts?
2. What processes will be improved by the use of these RFID tags?
3. Explain the importance of value chain visibility.
4. How will these RFID tags reduce waste and other costs?
5. What other benefits will be gained by storing parts data on the high-memory RFID tags?
6. What are the performance management implications? (Relate to the book's model).

NONPROFIT CASE

Leveraging Data to Strengthen Patron Loyalty

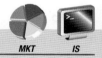

MKT   IS

The United Kingdom's nearly 100-year-old Royal Shakespeare Company (RSC) has grown to become one of the most respected theatrical companies in the world. The company is dedicated to keeping the spirit of William Shakespeare alive, and also stages classics and modern works. Over the past decade, the RSC staged 171 new productions, delivered 19,000 performances, sold 11 million tickets, and traveled from its home in Stratford-upon-Avon (Shakespeare's birthplace) to 150 towns and cities around the world. In fiscal year 2006, RSC had 700 employees and total income of approximately US$60 million (£32 million).

Audience Analytics Helps Save the Theatre

Theater companies, like other businesses, rely on customer loyalty for long-term success. RSC teamed with Accenture Ltd.

to conduct research into the characteristics of high-performance businesses. Accenture (*accenture.com*) is a global management consulting, technology services, and outsourcing company.

Despite its excellent reputation, securing its financial future in the 21st century depended on reaching a broader and more diverse audience as well as increasing repeat visits by current loyal patrons (customers). RSC relied on *audience analytics* to develop superior marketing capabilities to acquire new customers, retain existing customers, and cross-sell (sell more) to all customers.

Knowing How and When to Target Customers

RSC filtered through seven years of sales data for a marketing campaign that increased regular visitors by 70 percent.

Performing statistical analysis to forecast and discover correlations in sales and customer data had a huge pay-off. By examining more than 2 million transaction records, RSC learned about its best customers—income, occupation, and family status—which improved its ability to target marketing more precisely. This intelligence enabled RSC to substantially increase membership and fundraising revenues.

According to Mary Butlin, RSC's Head of Market Planning: "Our direct mail strategy for the last London season only took about 45 minutes to plan. The audiences to target were so clear cut, and we could even tell from Accenture's analysis exactly when to communicate with different groups to maximize response. As well as the campaign planning being much faster and more fact based, it is easier to predict likely response even in London, which is notoriously difficult."

Nonprofit Payoffs

By analyzing its transaction data with advanced analytics, RSC achieved the following improvements:

- The number of RSC's Stratford ticket buyers increased by more than 50 percent.

- The number of audience members in the Stratford segment defined as "regulars," who make the greatest overall contribution to RSC, increased by more than 70 percent, from 40,000 to 68,000.
- The number of audience members in the Stratford family show segment increased by more than 20 percent.

Sources: Compiled from Accenture (2008), rsc.org.uk/, and en.wikipedia. org/wiki/Royal_Shakespeare_Company

Questions

1. Why is customer loyalty critical to nonprofit organizations?
2. Explain the importance of data quality to the success of the RSC's marketing campaigns.
3. Discuss the benefits of more accurate forecasting to theater and other artistic companies.
4. What is audience analytics?
5. What can be learned from audience analytics to improve earnings?

ANALYSIS USING SPREADSHEETS

Managing Gasoline Costs

Notes: For this analysis, go to the Student Web Site to download the Excel file to help with this analysis.

The price of gasoline remains high, and demand for energy is increasing. Individuals, corporations, and government are involved in solving this issue. It is very likely that you are, too. What can you do? This assignment may help you learn how to reduce your carbon footprint on the environment.

To Do

1. Using the spreadsheet that you downloaded, calculate and compare the costs of driving a hybrid automobile and non-hybrid SUV from your location to a location 600 miles away.

2. How can you find the cheapest gas prices in your starting and destination locations? *Automotive.com* provides a free application (a widget), a real-time, continually updated tool that monitors gas prices.

3. You have just been promoted to fleet manager in a food company that uses 250 cars of different sizes. Prepare a report to top management on how to save on gas if the price is at $4, $5, $6, and $7 per gallon. A spreadsheet will help support your report (use the *what-if* option in Excel).

References

Accenture. "Helping the Royal Shakespeare Company Achieve High Performance through Audience Analytics, Segmentation and Targeted Marketing." April 2008.

Alaranta, M., and S. Henningsson. "An Approach to Analyzing and Planning Post-Merger IS Integration: Insights from Two Field Studies," *Information Systems Frontiers*, Vol. 10, Issue 3, July 2008.

Bank CIMB Niaga Merger Process and Achievement Report, January 2009. cimb.com/pdf/IR/Merger%20Report%20(6-7-09).pdf

"Gerry Weber International AG Is Awarded Coveted IT-Price for RFID Solution," press release, March 2010. gerryweber-ag.de/

Gonsalves, C. "Halo 3 Meets Second Life," *Baseline*, February 2008.

Hasson, J. "Will the Cloud Kill the Data Center?" *FierceCIO*, August 9, 2009. fiercecio.com/story/will-cloud-kill-data-center/2009-08-09

Kan, M. "IBM to build huge cloud computing data centre in China." *CIO.co.uk*, January 26, 2011. cio.co.uk/news/3258203/ibm-to-build-huge-cloud-computing-data-centre-in-china/

Kass, D.H. "IBM, Range Technology to Build Massive Cloud Computing Data Center in China." *IT Channel Planet. itchannelplanet.com/ enterprisenews/article.php/3922871/IBM-Range-Technology-to-Build-Massive-Cloud-Computing-Data-Center-in-China.htm*

Rackspace, *rackspace.com/*

RFID News, "MAINtag and Tego make RFIDs fly with Airbus." January 19, 2010. *rfidnews.org/*

Royal Shakespeare Company, *en.wikipedia.org/wiki/Royal_Shakespeare_Company*

Royal Shakespeare Company, *rsc.org.uk*

Sarrazin, H. and A. West. "Understanding the strategic value of IT in M&A." *McKinsey Quarterly.* January 2011, *mckinseyquarterly.com/ Understanding_the_strategic_value_of_IT_in_MA_2709*

Wal-Mart Unveils Global Sourcing Strategy. *"SupplyChainStandard.com,* March 29, 2010. *supplychainstandard.com/liChannelID/14/Articles/2840/ Walmart+unveils+global+sourcing+strategy.html*

Wessel, R. "Airbus Signs Contract for High-Memory RFID Tags," RFID Journal, January 19, 2010. *rfidjournal.com/article/view/7323*

Wessel, R. "Gerry Weber Sews in RFID's Benefits," *RFID Journal,* December 2009, *rfidjournal.com/article/view/7252/*

Chapter

3

Data, Text, and Document Management

Learning Objectives

❶ Describe data, text, and document management as well as their impacts on performance.

❷ Understand file management systems.

❸ Understand the functions of databases and database management systems.

❹ Describe the tactical and strategic benefits of data warehouses, data marts, and data centers.

❺ Explain how enterprise content management and electronic records management reduce cost, support business operations, and help companies meet their regulatory and legal requirements.

Integrating *IT*

ACC

FIN

MKT

OM

HRM

IS

Advizor Solutions, data analytics and visualization   *advizorsolutions.com/*
Clarabridge: How Text Mining Works   *clarabridge.com/*
SAS Text Miner   *sas.com/*
Tableau data visualization software   *tableausoftware.com/data-visualization-software/*
EMC Corp., enterprise content management   *emc.com/*
Oracle DBMS   *oracle.com/*

QUICK LOOK at Chapter 3, Data, Text, and Document Management

This section introduces you to the business issues, challenges, and IT solutions in Chapter 3. Topics and issues mentioned in the Quick Look are explained in the chapter.

Results of the *Information, Unplugged* research study published in mid-2010 by Informatica Corporation revealed that enterprises are drowning in their own data (Silva, 2010). The IT department faces enormous challenges because of the surge in data flowing through today's enterprise applications and databases. Some enterprise applications and databases increase in size by as much as 50 percent per year. More than 87 percent of respondents blamed database and network performance issues on data growth. Having more data makes it harder to find the information you need, or the cost of managing that data may exceed the value of the information.

The data explosion is in part the result of the many more channels bringing in data, more types of data, and more complete data. In this chapter, we focus on data and text management, business records, and data infrastructure. Data infrastructure refers to the fundamental structure of an information system (IS), which determines how it functions and how flexible it is in meeting future data requirements. This chapter covers how effective data management improves the performance and productivity of enterprises, managers, and data workers. You will learn the importance of master data management, which improves data sharing, and the regulatory and legal requirements for managing electronic records that all types of organizations currently face.

Performance of every type of organization, including police departments (as you will read in the public sector case at the end of this chapter), depends on timely access to data that can be quickly analyzed and used to anticipate needs of customers, suppliers, or business partners.

Daimler's AQUA Early Warning System

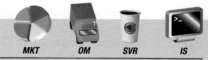
MKT   OM   SVR   IS

Global automaker Daimler AG (*daimler.com/*) distributes its products and services in almost every country. The company has production locations on five continents and more than 7,000 sales outlets worldwide. Daimler brand is comprised of diverse divisions: Mercedes-Benz smart, Mercedes-AMG, Maybach, Freightliner, Mitsubishi Fuso, Western Star, Detroit Diesel, Setra, Orion, and Thomas Built Buses.

Financial Crisis Hits Automobile Industry Worldwide

The worldwide economic and financial crisis that began in 2008 caused a drop in both production and sales across the entire automobile industry. By October 2008, all of the major auto companies had announced drastic slumps in sales and,

as a result, large cutbacks in production and workers. In 2009, Daimler scaled back output by 45,000 vehicles. Its sales fell from 2.1 million vehicles in 2008 to 1.55 million in 2009; it partially recovered with 1.89 million vehicles in 2010.

Data-Driven Quality Assurance, Customer Satisfaction, and Profitability

At the heart of Daimler's business are complete customer satisfaction and quality assurance, which is assured during design and production (see Figure 3.1). One way to maximize quality and customer satisfaction is to better analyze and use Daimler's immense volumes of data.

In 2011, Daimler implemented strategic and operational plans aimed at continuously improving vehicle quality and,

Figure 3.1 Production of the Mercedes Benz W class in the plant Sindelfingen of the Daimler AG assembly line. (© *vario images GmbH & Co.KG/Alamy*)

ultimately, customer satisfaction while holding costs down. Achieving these goals depended upon their ability to analyze huge volumes of warranty and diagnostic data on every vehicle sold, and to better manage all vehicle configurations and models. Daimler also sought to improve **failure management** of production machines and after-sales services by gaining insights from warranty and diagnostic data. Failure management refers to the corrective measures and preventive maintenance that are taken to avoid failures in mechanical equipment and keep production machines in working condition. Maintenance and failure costs of production machines increase the overall operating cost of a manufacturer and reduce the profit margin. The basic principle is that the faster problems in equipment or in the production process are detected and eliminated, the easier it is to avoid future warranty costs and loss of goodwill.

Advanced Quality Analysis—AQUA

To manage production and vehicle quality, Daimler consolidated diagnostic and quality data on an enterprise data warehouse (EDW) from Teradata with a powerful user interface from MicroStrategy. The new system is called Advanced Quality Analysis, or AQUA. With AQUA, managers and engineers can analyze both product and diagnostic effectiveness, and ensure the quality of repair and maintenance. AQUA enabled engineers, for instance, to identify vehicles at risk of defect so precisely that the costs of a vehicle recall decreased significantly. It also serves as an early warning system and supports Daimler's strategic goals of quality leadership, customer satisfaction, and profitability. Problems that arise in new vehicles, even those on the road for a month or so, can be identified with AQUA and used to correct production processes. This early warning capability has reduced long-term warranty costs.

Designing Future Vehicle Models

Better data management will be applied to the design of future vehicles and target marketing. A future goal is to integrate new warranty, diagnostic, early-warning, quality, and other data resources to target Daimler's vehicles more accurately to customers' needs and wants. Analyzing revolutions per minute (RPM), vibration behavior, and temperature data are expected to help uncover causes of defects based on actual driving experiences and influence the design and engineering of future vehicles—thereby strengthening Daimler's competitive advantages.

Sources: Compiled from Dullaghan (2011), *Daimler.com* (2011), Daimler Fact Sheet (2011), and Henning (2008).

For Class Discussion and Debate

1. Scenario for Brainstorming and Discussion: In making critical decisions for your company or agency, there is a cost ("a price to pay") to errors and/or ignorance. In every industry, managing customer satisfaction or service is essential to sustaining profit and growth. Select an industry, company, or public sector and identify some of the costs that result from ignorance about product quality. Explain how your selection can benefit from an early warning system such as AQUA. Compare and assess your answers with others in your class.

2. Debate: In the 1990 *Harvard Business Review* (HBR) article "No Excuses Management" (one of the most widely reprinted HBR articles), the author argued that companies seldom fail for lack of insight or vision. Rather, they fail because of poor execution. Execution refers to action taken based on those insights or visions. Now consider that if managers do not take action based on what they learn from data analysis, the IT investment might be a waste.

For this debate, consider the following. Engineering, production, customer service, and marketing departments are likely to be in favor of investments in near real-time data management and analysis systems such as AQUA, to spot problems as soon as possible. In contrast, finance and accounting departments might take the position that even if problems were spotted, the cost of fixing them may not be worthwhile, or that delays in fixing them would be unavoidable, so why bother.

To Do: Select one side of the argument, as just described. Debate whether the investment should be made even if no clear positive ROI (return on investment) from better execution can be determined in advance. Provide convincing arguments either for or against the investment.

3.1 Data, Text, and Document Management

Organizations' most strategic assets are their data, text, and documents. **Assets** are resources with recognized value that are under the control of an individual or organization.

Vast quantities of data, text, and documents are created or collected and then stockpiled through some type of storage method. Often data and documents get stored in multiple locations, perhaps five or more of them. Data, text, and document management helps companies improve productivity by ensuring that people can find what they need without having to conduct a long and difficult search. We use the term *data management* to refer to data, text, and document management, for simplicity, unless otherwise stated.

THE IMPORTANCE OF DATA MANAGEMENT

Why does data management matter? And how much does it matter? These are crucial questions because no enterprise can be effective without high-quality data that is accessible when needed. The goal of data management is to provide the infrastructure and tools to transform raw data into usable corporate information of the highest quality. Data is an organization's informational asset. Just as you study how to manage financial assets (i.e., identify, control, protect, analyze, and invest capital) to maximize their value in accounting and finance courses, here you learn how to manage informational assets. You will notice that the underlying concepts for managing financial and nonfinancial assets are similar. The basic rule is that to maximize earnings, companies invest in data management technologies that increase both of the following:

- opportunity to earn revenues (e.g., customer relationship management, or CRM)
- ability to cut expenses (e.g., inventory management)

When organizations analyze data, they need to consider all relevant expenses, including the expected costs of lost customers and earnings, penalties for noncompliance with regulations, and legal fines and losses stemming from the failure to protect confidential data from identity thieves. They calculate these costs by multiplying the probability of an event by the cost of the loss.

Managers and other decision makers need rapid access to correct, comprehensive, and consistent data across the enterprise if they are to improve their business processes and performance. They make decisions and service customers based on the data available to them. They rely on data retrieved from a data repository, such as a **database** or **data warehouse.** *Databases* store enterprise data that a company's business applications create or generate, such as sales, accounting, and employee data. Data entering the databases from POS terminals, online sales, and other sources is stored in an organized format so it can be managed and retrieved. A *data warehouse* is a specialized type of database that aggregates data from transaction databases so it can be analyzed. For example, management might scrutinize this data to identify and examine business trends in order to support planning and decision making, as you will read in Section 3.3.

Uncertainty: A Constraint on Managers. The viability of business decisions depends on access to high-quality data, and the quality of the data depends on effective approaches to data management. Too often managers and information workers are actually constrained by data that cannot be trusted because it is incomplete, out of context, outdated, inaccurate, inaccessible, or so overwhelming that it requires weeks to analyze. In those situations, the decision maker is facing too much uncertainty to make intelligent business decisions.

Data errors and inconsistencies lead to mistakes and lost opportunities, such as failed deliveries, invoicing blunders, and problems synchronizing data from multiple locations. In addition, data analysis errors that have resulted from the use of inaccurate formulas or untested models have harmed earnings and careers. Here are three examples of damages due to data analysis failures:

- TransAlta is a Canadian power generator company. A spreadsheet mistake led to TransAlta's buying more U.S. power transmission hedging contracts at higher prices than it would have if the decision had been based on accurate information. The data error cost the firm US$24 million (Wailgum, 2007).
- In the retail sector, the cost of errors due to unreliable and incorrect data alone is estimated to be as high as $40 billion annually (Snow, 2008).
- In the healthcare industry, one of the largest industries in the United States, data errors not only increase healthcare costs by billions of dollars but also cost thousands of lives.

Well-designed data infrastructures provide employees with complete, timely, accurate, accessible, understandable, and relevant data; this is what data management is about. Data management decisions require tough trade-offs among many complex factors, especially in recessionary times when cost cutting is a powerful force. Cost-cutting efforts should not make it more difficult to generate revenues, but that is what happens in the business, healthcare, and government sectors. In recessionary times, the payoff from having effective IT strategy and planning becomes more evident. We focus now on data management and infrastructure.

Data Management. Data management is a structured approach for capturing, storing, processing, integrating, distributing, securing, and archiving data effectively throughout its life cycle, as shown in Figure 3.2. The life cycle identifies the way data travels through an organization, from its capture or creation to its use in supporting data-driven solutions, such as supply chain management (SCM), CRM, and electronic commerce (EC). SCM, CRM, and EC are enterprise applications that require current and readily accessible data to function properly. One of the foundational structures of a business solution is the data warehouse. We

IT at Work 3.1

Cold Supply Chain Management in the Healthcare Industry

In 2011, the World Health Organization, or WHO (*who.int/*), reported that the world has invested enormous resources into the development of new, lifesaving vaccines over the past decade. Current vaccination or immunization programs are saving more than three million lives per year; new vaccines that focused on diseases affecting people in the poorest countries could save millions more. Because the medicine is perishable, the safety and effectiveness of vaccines depends on getting them to the right place, at the right time, and in the right condition.

According to the WHO, 25 percent of all vaccine products reach their destination in a degenerated state. This shows the need for system-enabled, cold chain data management, monitoring and transportation services to ensure correct order fulfillment. The *American Pharmaceutical Review* reported that more than half of the total pharmaceuticals sold in the world have temperature-sensitive transportation and handling needs.

Need for Cold Supply Chain Management. Vaccines and other temperature-sensitive medications need to be stored within the temperature range recommended by manufacturers, typically from +2°C to +8°C. Incorrect storage is not only wasteful; the

failure to store vaccines and medicines at the proper temperatures can degrade effectiveness and put people's health and lives at risk. Temperatures that are too cold can crack containers and contaminate the contents within. As such, distribution or supply chain systems need to be as advanced and innovative as the vaccines they support.

Immunization Systems and Technologies for Tomorrow is a collaboration between the WHO and PATH. PATH (*path.org/*) is an international nonprofit organization that creates sustainable, culturally relevant solutions, enabling communities in more than 70 countries to break longstanding cycles of poor health. WHO/PATH are putting technological and scientific advances to work to create supply chains that are flexible and robust enough to handle the demands of vaccines and medications.

Sources: Compiled from WHO (2011), PATH (2011), National Patient Safety Agency (2009), and Varghese (2010).

Discussion Questions: How does the nature of the healthcare industry make supply chain inefficiencies a matter of life and death? What are some of the challenges with cold supply chain management?

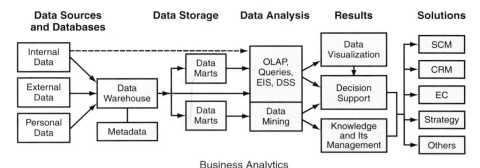

Figure 3.2 Data life cycle.

discuss managing data and applying it to solving business problems throughout this chapter.

Three general data principles illustrate the importance of the data life cycle perspective and guide IT investment decisions.

1. Principle of diminishing data value. Viewing data in terms of a life cycle focuses attention on how the value of data diminishes as the data ages. The more recent the data, the more valuable it is. This is a simple, yet powerful, principle. Most organizations cannot operate at peak performance with blindspots (lack of data availability) of 30 days or longer.

2. Principle of 90/90 data use. Being able to act on real-time or near-real-time operational data can have significant advantages. According to the 90/90 data-use principle, a majority of stored data, as high as 90 percent, is seldom accessed after 90 days (except for auditing purposes). Put another way, data loses much of its value after three months.

3. Principle of data in context. The ability to capture, process, format, and distribute data in near real time or faster requires a huge investment in data management infrastructure to link remote POS systems to data storage, data analysis systems, and reporting applications. The investment can be justified on the principle that data must be integrated, processed, analyzed, and formatted into "actionable information." End users need to see data in a meaningful format and context if the data is to guide their decisions and plans.

Data Visualization. To format data into meaningful contexts for users, businesses employ **data visualization** and decision support tools. Data or information visualization, as the name suggests, refers to presenting data in ways that are faster and easier for users to understand. To better understand this process, examine the two data displays in Figure 3.3. The tabular and graphical displays both depict one-day changes in the Dow Jones Industrial Average (DJIA). The table provides more precise data, whereas the graph takes much less time and effort to understand. Data presentation and visualization tools offer both display options.

Data visualization tools and technology are becoming more popular and widely used as they become less expensive and easier to manipulate. As one example, Dartmouth University's Development Department, which is responsible for fundraising, realized that its efforts to target alumni for contributions to its capital campaign were not as effective as they could be. To reduce missed opportunities, they invested in data visualization tools that they were able to use themselves. As described in *IT at Work 3.2*, these tools enabled the Development Department to overcome data limitations. That is, they knew where and when to invest their time to maximize return on that time. The value of the data visualization tools can be measured by Dartmouth's hugely successful capital campaign.

Last:	**11,893.690** Net Change:	−146.700% Change: −1.22%	
Open	12,039.090	52-Week High	14,198.100
High	12,094.210	52-Week Low	11,634.820
Low	11,819.690	Volume	07,579.268

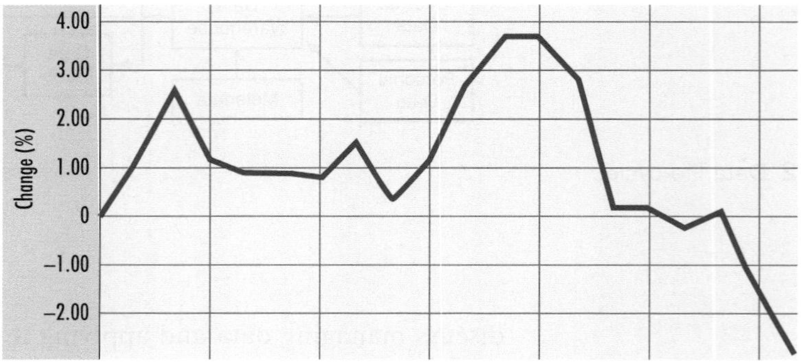

Figure 3.3 Dow Jones industrial average (DJIA) for a single day in tabular display and graphical display.

Data Management: Problems and Challenges. In *IT at Work 3.1*, you read about the problems and costs associated with nonstandardized, unsynchronized data among organizations in the healthcare supply chain. One widespread problem is that people do not get data in the format they need to do their jobs. Therefore, even if the data is accurate, timely, and clean, it still might not be usable. According to the market intelligence firm IDC (*idc.com*), organizations with at least 1,000 knowledge workers (workers who rely on data to perform their jobs) lose $5.7 million annually in time wasted by employees reformatting data as they move among applications. Just as workers waste time tracking down and correcting invoicing and ordering

IT at Work 3.2

Maximizing Return on Time

All organizations depend on their data—being able to capture, store, access, analyze, and make use of data when needed. Dartmouth University's Development Department faced the same data problems as small companies and major corporations. They had a huge volume of alumnae data, but no easy way to access them. They relied on the IT department for reports. Worse, these reports did not meet their needs. For example, reports could not answer basic questions that were critical to the success of a $1.3 billion capital campaign:

- Which alumni have the greatest donation potential?
- Which alumni segments are most likely to donate, and in what ways?
- Which prospects are not donating to their potential?

In order for the managers to navigate on their own and collect data that mattered to their current campaign, the university invested in visual discovery software tools from Advizor Solutions

(*advizorsolutions.com*). The Development Department used these tools to create a set of dashboards, which they made available over the Web. **Dashboards** are visual displays similar to the dashboard on an automobile (Figure 2.7 in Chapter 2 is an example). With the dashboards, managers now get answers within three minutes that used to take three weeks because of bottlenecks in the IT department. Most importantly, managers are targeting the most highly responsive prospective donors to maximize the return on their time and efforts.

Sources: Compiled from Advizor Solutions (*advizorsolutions.com*) and Teradata (2007).

Discussion Questions: Why were managers missing opportunities to obtain donations from prospective donors? How did end-user data visualization tools improve the managers' ability to perform their jobs?

errors among healthcare suppliers, they also spend significant amounts of time getting data into usable formats. In Chapter 4 you will read about how businesses resolve some of their data deficiencies using information or enterprise portals. **Enterprise portals** are a set of software applications that consolidate, manage, analyze, and transmit data to users through Web-based interface.

Managing, searching for, and retrieving data located throughout the enterprise is a major challenge, for various reasons:

- The volume of data increases exponentially with time. New data is added constantly and rapidly. Business records must be kept for a long time for auditing or legal reasons, even though the organization itself may no longer access them. Only a small percentage of an organization's data is relevant for any specific application or time.
- External data that needs to be considered in making organizational decisions is constantly increasing in volume.
- Data is scattered throughout organizations and is collected and created by many individuals using different methods, devices, and channels. Data is frequently stored in multiple servers and locations and also in different computing systems, databases, formats, and human and computer languages.
- Data security, quality, and integrity are critical yet easily jeopardized. In addition, legal requirements relating to data differ among countries, and they change frequently.
- Data is being created and used offline without going through quality control checks; hence, the validity of the data is questionable.
- Data throughout an organization may be redundant and out-of-date, creating a huge maintenance problem for data managers.

To deal with these difficulties, organizations invest in data management solutions. Historically, data management has been geared to support transaction processing by organizing the data in one location. This approach supports more secure and efficient high-volume processing. Because the amount of data being created and stored on end-user computers is increasing so dramatically, however, it is inefficient or even impossible for queries and other ad hoc applications to use traditional data management methods. Therefore, organizations have implemented relational databases, in which data is organized into rows and columns, to support end-user computing and decision making. Data organization is covered in Section 3.3.

With the prevalence of **client/server networks** (also called *client/server computing*) and Web technologies, numerous distinct databases are created and spread throughout the organization, creating problems in managing this data so that it's consistent in each location. Client/server networks consist of user PCs, called clients, linked to high-performance computers, called servers, which provide software, data, or computing services over a network. As businesses become more complex and their volumes of enterprise data explode, they increasingly are turning to master data management as a way to intelligently consolidate and manage these data.

MASTER DATA MANAGEMENT

Master Data Management. **Master data management (MDM)** is a process whereby companies integrate data from various sources or enterprise applications to provide a more unified view of the data. Although vendors may claim that their MDM solution creates "a single version of the truth," this claim is probably not true. In reality, MDM cannot create a single unified version of the data because constructing a completely unified view of all master data is simply not possible. Realistically, MDM consolidates data from various data sources into a **master reference file,** which then feeds data back to the applications, thereby creating accurate and consistent data across the enterprise. In *IT at Work 3.1*, participants in the healthcare supply chain were essentially developing a master reference file to obtain a more unified version of the data. A master data reference file is based on data entities. A **data entity** is anything real or abstract about which a company wants to collect and store data. Common data entities are a customer, a vendor, a product, and an employee.

Master Data Entities. **Master data entities** are the main entities of a company, such as customers, products, suppliers, employees, and assets. Each organizational department has distinct master data needs. Marketing, for example, is concerned with product pricing, brand, and product packaging, whereas production is concerned with product costs and schedules. A customer master reference file can feed data to all enterprise systems that have a customer relationship component, thereby providing a unified picture of the customers. Similarly, a product master reference file can feed data to all of the production systems within the enterprise. Three benefits of a unified view of customers are the following:

- Better, more accurate customer data to support marketing, sales, support, and service initiatives
- Better responsiveness to ensure that all employees who deal with customers have up-to-date, reliable information on the customers
- Better revenue management and more responsive business decisions

An MDM includes tools for cleaning and auditing the master data elements as well as tools for integrating and synchronizing data to make the data more accessible. MDM offers a solution for managers who are frustrated with how fragmented and dispersed their data sources are. According to Ventana Research (*ventanaresearch.com*), 4 percent of the 515 respondents to their survey said their organizations had implemented MDM, and 31 percent reported that their organizations had projects currently under way.

Transforming Data into Knowledge. Our discussion thus far has focused primarily on ways in which businesses accumulate and integrate data. Businesses do not run on raw data, however. They run on data that has been processed into information and knowledge, which managers apply to business problems and opportunities. As real-world examples throughout this chapter illustrate, knowledge learned from data fuels business solutions. Everything from innovative product designs to brilliant competitive moves relies on timely knowledge. However, because of the difficulties inherent in managing data, deriving knowledge from collected data is a complicated process.

Organizations transform data into knowledge in several ways. In general, this transformation process resembles the one shown in Figure 3.4. The desired data is

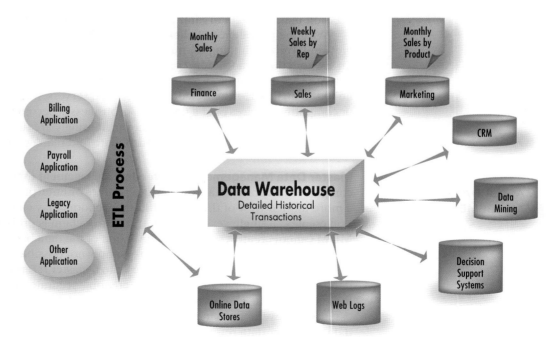

Figure 3.4 Model of an enterprise data warehouse. *(Source: From Syncsort, syncsort.com. Used with permission.)*

extracted from databases and preprocessed to fit the format of a data warehouse or a **data mart,** into which it is loaded. A data mart is a small data warehouse designed for a strategic business unit (SBU) or a single department. This series of processes is referred to as **ETL,** which stands for **extract, transform, and load.** Figure 3.4 shows the data transformation model of Syncsort Inc., which develops, markets, and services high-performance software for data management and data protection. ETL processes move data from multiple sources, reformat and cleanse them, and load them into another data warehouse or data mart for analysis or onto another operational system to support a business process.

Users then access the data warehouse or data mart and take a copy of the data needed for analysis. They scrutinize this material using data analysis and data mining tools. Data mining tools are specialized software used to analyze data to find patterns, correlations, trends, or other meaningful relationships. Data mining, which may also be called data discovery, is the process of analyzing data from different perspectives and summarizing it into information that can be used to increase revenue, decrease costs, or both. Data mining software allows users to analyze data from various dimensions or angles, categorize it, and find correlations or patterns among fields in the data warehouse. These activities ultimately generate valuable information and knowledge. Both the data (at various times during the process) and the knowledge (derived at the end of the process) may need to be sent and presented to users via visualization tools.

Data Quality and Integrity. Data collection is a highly complex process that can create problems concerning the quality of the data that is being collected. Therefore, regardless of how the data is collected, it needs to be validated so users know they can trust it. Classic expressions that sum up the situation are "garbage in, garbage out" (GIGO) and the potentially riskier "garbage in, gospel out." In the latter case, poor-quality data is trusted and used as the basis for planning. You have encountered data safeguards, such as integrity checks, to help improve data quality when you fill in an online form. For example, the form will not accept an e-mail address that is not formatted correctly.

Data quality is a measure of the data's usefulness as well as the quality of the decisions based on the data. It has the following five dimensions: accuracy, accessibility, relevance, timeliness, and completeness. As we have discussed, data frequently is inaccurate, incomplete, or ambiguous, particularly when it is stored in large, centralized databases. Examples of common data problems and possible solutions are listed in Table 3.1.

Although having high-quality data is essential for business success, numerous organizational and technical issues make it difficult to reach this objective. One problematic issue is data ownership. That is, who owns or is responsible for the data? Data ownership issues arise from the lack of policies defining responsibility and accountability in managing data. Inconsistent data quality requirements of various stand-alone applications create an additional set of problems as organizations try to combine individual applications into integrated enterprise systems. Interorganizational information systems add a new level of complexity to managing data quality. Companies must resolve the issues of administrative authority to ensure

TABLE 3.1	Data Problems and Solutions
Problems	**Solutions**
Data errors	Use automated data entry, Web forms for individuals entering data with data integrity checks and drop-down menus and radio buttons.
Duplicated data	Redesign the data model; normalize the relational database.
Compromised data	Implement a defense-in-depth approach to data security.
Missing data	Make fields mandatory on data entry forms.

IT at Work 3.3

Data Mining Used by Intelligence Agencies

National security requires the ability *to identify*—e.g., identify terrorist activities, such as money transfers and communications; identify and track individual terrorists through means such as travel and immigration records. National security also requires the ability to identify patterns and relationships and detect suspicious activities as early as possible. One of the tools used for intelligence efforts is data mining. Data mining involves the use of sophisticated data analysis tools to discover previously unknown, valid patterns and relationships in large data sets. These tools can include statistical models, mathematical algorithms, and machine-learning methods (algorithms that improve their performance automatically through experience, such as neural networks or decision trees). Consequently, data mining consists of more than collecting and managing data. It also includes analysis and prediction.

Data Mining as an Intelligence Tool. Data mining for intelligence purposes combines statistical models, powerful processors, and artificial intelligence (AI) to find and retrieve valuable information. There are two types of data mining systems: subject-based systems that retrieve data to follow a lead, and pattern-based systems that look for suspicious behaviors. An example of a subject-based technique is link analysis, which uses data to make connections among seemingly unconnected people or events. Link analysis software identifies suspicious activities, such as a spike in the number of e-mail exchanges between two parties (one of whom is a suspect), checks written by different people to the same third party, or airline tickets bought to the same destination on the same departing date. Intelligence personnel then follow these "links" to uncover other people with whom a suspect is interacting.

Intelligence Agencies. The MI6 (*intelligence.gov.uk/agencies/mi6.asp*) and Defense Intelligence Staff (DIS) (*intelligence.gov.uk/agencies/dis.asp*) in the United Kingdom, the Central Intelligence Agency (CIA, *cia.gov*) in the United States, and other intelligence agencies mine (search through) enormous amounts of data to monitor potential threats to national security. Some data collection methods might infringe on citizens' privacy rights. The DIS, for example, conducts intelligence analysis from both overt and covert sources.

Intelligence agencies track terrorists through their use of various tactics and technologies to carry out their destructive plans—hacking, spamming, phishing, identity theft, and Web site propaganda and recruitment. Computers seized in Afghanistan reportedly revealed that al-Qaeda was collecting intelligence on targets and sending encrypted messages via the Internet.

Experts consider intelligence efforts such as these to be crucial to global security. Some military experts believe that war between major nations is becoming obsolete and that our future defense will rely far more on intelligence officers with databases than on tanks and artillery.

Discussion Questions: Why is data mining important to national security? What are the two types of data-mining systems, and how do they provide value to defense organizations?

---

that each partner complies with the data quality standards. The tendency to delegate data quality responsibilities to the technical teams, who have no control over data quality, as opposed to business users, who do have such control, is another common barrier that stands in the way of accumulating high-quality data (Loshin, 2004).

Data Privacy and Ethics. Businesses that collect data about employees, customers, or anyone else have the duty to protect this data. Data should be accessible only to authorized people. Securing data from unauthorized access and from abuse by authorized parties is expensive and difficult. To motivate companies to invest in data security, the government has imposed enormous fines and penalties for data breaches, as you will read in Chapter 5.

Furthermore, providing information required by the government or regulators adds to the expense of data management. An example is the situation of homeland security described in *IT at Work 3.3.*

GAINING INSIGHT FROM TEXT AND DOCUMENTS

Managers who are committed to fact-based, data-driven decision making are recognizing the power hidden in text to yield insight into marketing, new product development, customer service, public relations, and competition. Techniques for analyzing text, documents, and other unstructured content are available from several vendors.

It's estimated that up to 75 percent of an organization's data is freeform or unstructured, consisting of word-processing documents, content of Web documents, tweets and other social media, e-mail and text messages, audio, video, images and diagrams, fax and memos, call center or claims notes, and so on. Increasingly, text analytics software is being used to gain insights from freeform content. Gaining business insight is the value of business analytics in general, regardless of the source of the data—textual, numerical, or categorical. Text mining and analytics help organizations manage the information overload.

Two innovative applications of text analytics by organizations are described here:

• Agata, an Italian company, uses social networking tools to implement an online lending system that matches borrowers and investors without intervention from traditional institutions. Its new credit scoring process not only includes quantitative variables from past history and well-defined risk categories; it also integrates qualitative evaluations collected from written descriptions of the projects and business plans to facilitate better decisions on credit risk.

• A Hong Kong government office was faced with the challenge of processing large volumes of structured and unstructured text in traditional Chinese, simplified Chinese, and English. It implemented SAS software to decode and analyze messages in any of these languages, including information from call centers. The result is better public service and increased public satisfaction with the government.

Text Mining and Analytics. Text mining is a broad category that in general involves interpreting words and concepts in context. Then the text is organized, explored, and analyzed to provide actionable insights for managers. With text analytics, information is extracted out of large quantities of various types of textual information. It can be combined with structured data in an automated process.

Text analytics addresses two major business challenges. The first is information organization and the *findability* of the content in documents. The second is discovery of trends and patterns to allow foresight from textual information.

The process of performing analysis on text to discover insights is similar to analyzing traditional data types.

1. Exploration. First, documents are explored. This might mean doing simple word counts in a document collection or manually creating topic areas to categorize documents by reading a sample of them. For example, what are the major types of issues (brake or engine failure) that have been identified in recent automobile warranty claims? A challenge of the exploration effort is misspelled or abbreviated words, acronyms, or slang.

2. Preprocessing. Before analysis or the automated categorization of the content, the text may need to be preprocessed to standardize it to the extent possible. As in traditional analysis, up to 80 percent of the time can be spent preparing and standardizing the data. Misspelled words, abbreviations, and slang may need to be transformed into consistent terms. For instance, "BTW" would be standardized to "by the way" and "left voice message" could be tagged as "lvm."

3. Categorizing and Modeling. Content is then ready to be categorized. Categorizing messages or documents from information contained in them can be achieved using statistical models and business rules. As with traditional model development, sample documents are examined to train the models. Additional documents are then processed to validate the accuracy and precision of the model, and finally new documents are evaluated using the final model (scored). Models can then be put into production for automated processing of new documents as they arrive.

There is considerable overlap between text and document management, but document management has unique issues, which are discussed next.

Document Management. All companies create **business records,** which are documents that record business dealings such as contracts, research and development, accounting source documents, memos, customer/client communications, and meeting minutes. **Document management** is the automated control of imaged and electronic documents, page images, spreadsheets, voice and e-mail messages, word-processing documents, and other documents through their life cycle in an organization, from initial creation to final archiving or destruction.

Document management systems (DMS) consist of hardware and software that manage and archive electronic documents and also convert paper documents into e-documents and then index and store them according to company policy. For example, companies may be required by law to retain financial documents for at least seven years, whereas e-mail messages about marketing promotions would be retained for a year and then discarded. DMS's have query and search capabilities so they can be identified and accessed like data in a database. These systems range from those designed to support a small work group to full-featured, Web-enabled enterprise-wide systems. DMS may be part of a newer integrated system called enterprise content management (ECM), which is discussed in Section 3.5.

Departments or companies whose employees spend most of the day filing or retrieving documents or warehouse paper records can reduce costs significantly with DMS. These systems minimize the inefficiencies and frustration associated with managing paper documents and paper workflows. Significantly, however, they do not create a paperless office, as had been predicted. Offices still use a lot of paper.

A DMS can help a business to become more efficient and productive by the following:

- Enabling the company to access and use the content contained in the documents
- Cutting labor costs by automating business processes
- Reducing the time and effort required to locate information the business needs to support decision making
- Improving the security of the content, thereby reducing the risk of intellectual property theft
- Minimizing the costs associated with printing, storage, and searching for content

The major document management tools are workflow software, authoring tools, scanners, and databases. When workflows are digital, productivity increases, costs decrease, compliance obligations are easier to verify, and **green computing** becomes possible. Green computing is an initiative to conserve our valuable natural resources by reducing the effects of our computer usage on the environment. Businesses also use a DMS for disaster recovery and business continuity, security, knowledge sharing and collaboration, and remote and controlled access to documents. Because DMS's have multilayered access capabilities, employees can access and change only the documents they are authorized to handle. Visit *altimate.ca/flash/viewer.html* to see how files can be opened directly within the Web browser without the file's native application being installed locally on the user's computer. When companies select a DMS, they ask the following questions:

1. Is the software available in the form needed by your organization? Two forms are (1) to purchase the DMS software to be installed on its network or (2) purchase the service.

2. Is the software easy to use and accessible from Web browsers, office applications and e-mail applications, and Windows Explorer? (If not, people won't use it.)

3. Does the software have lightweight, modern Web and graphical user interfaces that effectively support remote users via an intranet, a virtual private network (VPN, discussed in Chapter 4), or the Internet? A VPN allows a worker to connect to a company's network remotely through the Internet. A VPN is less expensive than having workers connect using a modem or dedicated line.

IT at Work 3.4 describes how several companies currently use DMS.

IT at Work 3.4

Portals and Electronic Document Management

Examples of how organizations are using portals and document management systems (DMS).

- A leading global corporate and investment bank (CIB) had an inefficient manual **loan processing system.** The system involved delivering documents via courier, fax or email and storing digitized copies on a network shared drive. The CIB implemented an electronic document management system to resolve business problems by providing controlled multiple user access, version control, and instantaneous distribution of documents, as well as reliable electronic backups.

- The European Court of Human Rights has implemented a Web-based knowledge portal and document and case management systems that support more than 700 internal users and millions of external users worldwide. The DMS has streamlined case processing, which in turn has made internal operations more efficient and has significantly improved the court's services to the public. The Human Rights Documents project has had a significant return on investment.

- In Toronto, Canada, the Department of Works and Emergency Services uses a Web-based document-retrieval solution. This DMS gives the department's employees immediate access to drawings and documents related to roads, buildings, utility lines, and other structures. The department has installed laptop computers loaded with maps, drawings, and historical repair data in each vehicle. Quick access to these documents enables emergency crews to solve problems and, more importantly, to save lives.

- The Surgery Center of Baltimore stores all medical records electronically, providing instant patient information to doctors and nurses anywhere and at any time. The system also routes charts to the billing department, which can then scan and e-mail any relevant information to insurance providers and patients. The DMS helps maintain the required audit trail, including providing records when they are needed for legal purposes. How valuable has the DMS been to the center? Since it was implemented, business processes have been expedited by more than 50 percent, the costs of these processes have been significantly reduced, and the morale of office employees in the center has improved noticeably.

Discussion Questions: What types of waste can DMS reduce? How? What is the value of providing access to documents via the Internet or a corporate intranet?

Review Questions

1. What is the goal of data management?
2. What constraints do managers face when they cannot trust data?
3. Why is it difficult to manage, search, and retrieve data located throughout the enterprise?
4. How can data visualization tools and technology improve decision making?
5. What is master data management?
6. What is text and document management?
7. What are three benefits of document management systems?

3.2 File Management Systems

The previous section discussed how businesses use computer systems, particularly DMS, to manipulate data much more efficiently and productively. In this section we explain how these systems actually work.

A computer system essentially organizes data into a hierarchy that begins with bits and proceeds to bytes, fields, records, files, and databases (see Figure 3.5). A **bit** represents the smallest unit of data a computer can process, which is either a 0 or a 1. A group of eight bits, called a **byte,** represents a single character, which can be a letter, a number, or a symbol. Characters that are combined to form a word, a group of words, or a complete number constitute a **field.** A key characteristic of a field is that all of the entries are related in some way. For example, a field titled "Cust_Name" might include the names of a company's customers. It would not, however, contain addresses or telephone numbers.

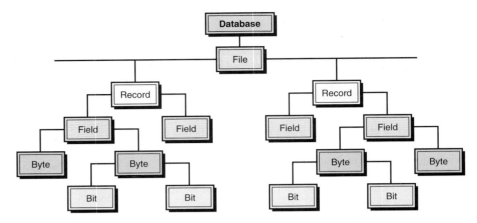

Figure 3.5 Hierarchy of data for a computer-based file.

Just as related characters can be combined into a field, related fields—such as vendor name, address, and account data—can constitute a **record.** Moving up the hierarchy, a collection of related records is called a **file** or data file. For example, the records of all noncommercial customers who have a mortgage loan at a financial institution would constitute a data file. Finally, as we saw in our discussion of data management, a logical group of related files would constitute a database. All customer loan files, such as mortgages and auto, personal and home equity loans, could be grouped to create a noncommercial loan database.

Another way of thinking about database components is that a record describes an *entity*. Each characteristic describing an entity is called an **attribute.** An attribute corresponds to a field on a record. Examples of attributes are customer name, invoice number, and order date.

Each record in a database needs an attribute (field) to uniquely identify it so that the record can be retrieved, updated, and sorted. This unique identifier field is called the **primary key.** Primary keys are typically numeric because they are easier to create. For example, the primary key of a product record would be the product ID. To find a group of records based on some common value (locating all products manufactured in Mexico) requires the use of secondary keys. **Secondary keys** are nonunique fields that have some identifying information (e.g., country of manufacture). **Foreign keys** are keys whose purpose is to link two or more tables together. Figure 3.6 illustrates primary and foreign keys.

Level 3 Customer Data Tables

Product Preferences Table

Field Name	Type	Length
Product SKU *	Number	12
Product name	Text	20
Product type	Text	12
Product characteristics	Number	30
Customer ID **	Number	8

Shop Locations Table

Field Name	Type	Length
Store number *	Number	8
Store neighborhood	Text	20
Store sales	Currency	8
Store customers	Number	5
Product SKU **	Number	12

Customer Contact Table

Field Name	Type	Length
Customer ID *	Number	8
Customer name	Text	20
Customer address	Text	30
Customer phone	Number	12

Product Sales Table

Field Name	Type	Length
Product SKU *	Number	12
Product name	Text	20
Product price	Currency	8
Product cost	Currency	8
Customer ID **	Number	8

Figure 3.6 Example of primary and foreign keys.

* Primary Key ** Foreign Key

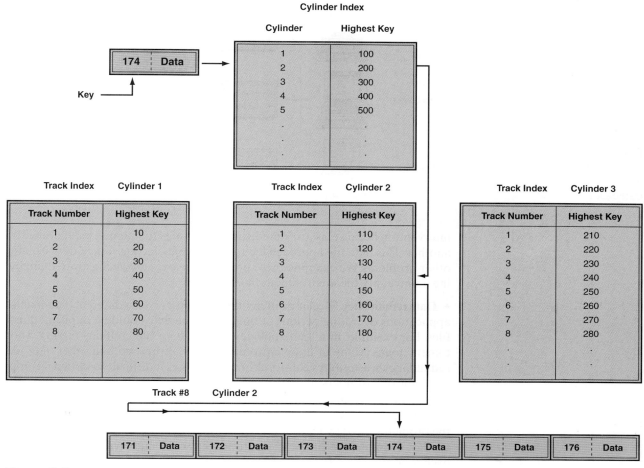

Figure 3.7 Indexed sequential access method.

Accessing Records from Computer Files. Records can be arranged in several ways on a storage medium. The arrangement determines how individual records can be accessed and how long it takes to access them. In **sequential file organization,** which is the way files are organized on tape, data records must be retrieved in the same physical sequence in which they are stored. The operation is like a tape recorder. In **direct file organization** or **random file organization,** records can be accessed directly regardless of their location on the storage medium. The operation is like a DVD drive. Magnetic tape uses sequential file organization, whereas magnetic disks use direct file organization.

The **indexed sequential access method (ISAM)** uses an index of key fields to locate individual records (see Figure 3.7). An *index* to a file lists the key field of each record and where that record is physically located on the storage media. Records are stored on disks in their key sequence. To locate a specific record, the system looks at the index (called track index) to locate the general location (identified by the cylinder and track numbers) containing the record. It then points to the beginning of that track and reads the records sequentially until it finds the correct record.

Limitations of the File Environment. When organizations began using computers to automate processes, they started with one application at a time, usually accounting, billing, or payroll. Each application was designed to be a stand-alone system that worked independently of other applications. For example, for each pay period, the payroll application would use its own employee and wage data to calculate and process the payroll. No other application would use this data without some manual

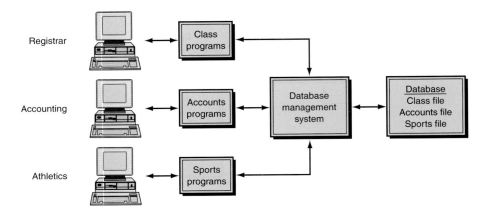

Figure 3.8 Database management system provides access to all data in the database.

intervention because, as just stated, the applications functioned independently of one another. This data file approach led to redundancy, inconsistency, data isolation, and other problems. We examine these problems below, and we illustrate them by showing a university file environment in Figure 3.8.

- **Data redundancy.** Because different programmers create different data-manipulating applications over long periods of time, the same data could be duplicated in several files. For example, in a loan application, each data file contains records about customers' loans. Many of these customers will be represented in other data files. This redundancy wastes physical storage media, makes it difficult to obtain a comprehensive view of customers, and increases the costs of entering and maintaining the data.

- **Data inconsistency.** Data inconsistency means that the actual data values are not synchronized across various copies of the data. Recall that unsynched data caused the problems faced by Dartmouth's development office, discussed earlier in this chapter. For example, if a financial institution has customers with several loans, and for each loan there is a file containing customer fields (e.g., name, address, e-mail, and telephone number), then a change to a customer's address in only one file creates inconsistencies with the address field in other files.

- **Data isolation.** File organization creates silos of data that make it extremely difficult to access data from different applications. For example, a manager who wants to know which customers owe more than $1,000 would probably not be able to obtain the answer from a data file system. To get the results, he would have to filter and integrate the data manually from multiple files.

- **Data security.** Securing data is difficult in the file environment because new applications are added to the system on an ad hoc basis. As the number of applications increases, so does the number of people who can access the data.

Data management problems arising from the file environment approach led to the development of better data management systems.

Review Questions

1. What are three limitations of the file management approach?
2. Why does each record in a database need a unique identifier (primary key)?
3. How do the data access methods of sequential file organization and direct file access methods differ?

3.3 Databases and Database Management Systems

Data flows into companies continuously and from many sources: clickstream data from Web and e-commerce applications, detailed data from POS terminals, and filtered data from CRM, supply chain, and enterprise resource planning applications. Databases are the optimal way to store and access organizational data.

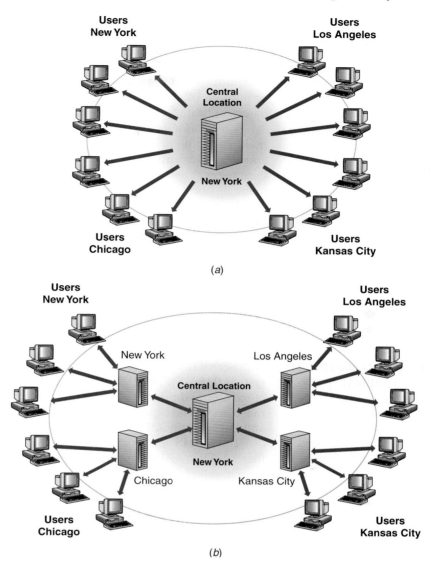

Figure 3.9 (a) Centralized database. (b) Distributed database with complete or partial copies of the central database in more than one location.

DATABASES

Database management programs can provide access to all of the data, alleviating many of the problems associated with data file environments. Therefore, data redundancy, data isolation, and data inconsistency are minimized, and data can be shared among data users. In addition, security and data integrity are easier to control, and applications are independent of the data they process. There are two basic types of databases: centralized and distributed.

Centralized Databases. A centralized database stores all related files in one physical location (see Figure 3.9). For decades the main database platform consisted of centralized database files on large, mainframe computers, primarily because of the enormous capital and operating costs associated with the alternative systems. Centralized databases offer many benefits to organizations. Files can generally be made more consistent with one another when they are physically kept in one location because file changes can be made in a supervised and orderly fashion. Also, files are not accessible except via the centralized host computer, where they can be protected more easily from unauthorized access or modification.

At the same time, however, centralized databases, like all centralized systems, are vulnerable to a single point of failure. That is, when the centralized database computer fails to function properly, all users are affected. Additionally, when users are widely dispersed and must perform data manipulations from great distances, they often experience transmission delays.

Distributed Databases. A *distributed database* has complete copies of a database or portions of a database (see Figure 3.9). There are two types of distributed databases: replicated and partitioned.

A *replicated database* stores complete copies (replicas) of the entire database in multiple locations. This arrangement provides a backup in case of a failure or problems with the centralized database. It also improves the response time because it is local (closer) to users. On the negative side, it is much more expensive to set up and maintain because each replica must be updated as records are added to, modified in, and deleted from any of the databases. The updates may be done at the end of a day or some other schedule as determined by business needs. Otherwise, the various databases will contain conflicting data.

In contrast, a *partitioned database* is divided up so that each location has a portion of the entire database—usually the portion that meets users' local needs. Partitioned databases provide the response speed of localized files without the need to replicate all changes in multiple locations. One significant advantage of a partitioned database is that data in the files can be entered more quickly and kept more accurate by the users immediately responsible for the data.

DATABASE MANAGEMENT SYSTEMS (DBMS)

A program that provides access to databases is known as a **database management system (DBMS).** The DBMS permits an organization to centralize data, manage it efficiently, and provide access to the stored data by application programs. DBMSs range in size and capabilities from the simple Microsoft Access to full-featured Oracle and DB2 solutions. Table 3.2 lists the major capabilities and advantages of DBMSs.

The DBMS acts as an interface between application programs and physical data files (see Figure 3.10). It provides users with tools to add, delete, maintain, display, print, search, select, sort, and update data. These tools range from easy-to-use natural

TABLE 3.2	Advantages and Capabilities of a DBMS

- **Permanence.** Data is permanently stored on a hard drive or other fast, reliable medium until explicitly removed or changed.
- **Querying.** Querying is the process of requesting data from various perspectives. Example: "How many trucks in Texas are green?"
- **Concurrency.** Many people may attempt to change or read the same data at the same time. Without rules for sharing changes, the data may become inconsistent or misleading. For example, if you change the color attribute of car 7 to be "blue" at the very same time somebody is changing it to "red," results are unpredictable.
- **Backup and replication.** Backup copies need to be made in case of equipment failure.
- **Rule enforcement.** Rules are applied to keep data clean and trustworthy. For example, a rule can state that each car can have only one engine associated with it (identified by engine number). If somebody tries to associate a second engine, the DBMS stops it and displays an error message. However, with new hybrid gas-electric cars, such rules may need to be relaxed. Rules can be added and removed as needed without significant redesign.
- **Security.** Limits on who can see or change attributes are necessary.
- **Computation.** Rather than have each computer application perform calculations, the DBMS performs them.
- **Change and access logging.** The DBMS creates a record and audit trail of who accessed what attributes, what was changed, and when it was changed.
- **Automated optimization.** If there are frequent usage patterns or requests, many DBMSs can adjust to improve the response time.

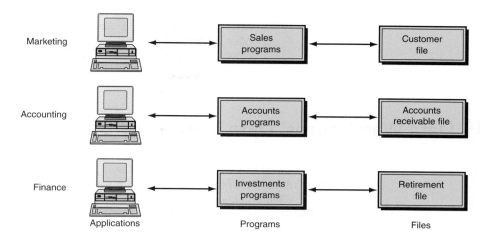

Figure 3.10 Computer-based files of this type cause problems such as redundancy, inconsistency, and data isolation.

language interfaces to complex programming languages used for developing sophisticated database applications. The major data functions performed by a DBMS are listed below.

- **Data filtering and profiling:** Inspecting the data for errors, inconsistencies, redundancies, and incomplete information.
- **Data quality:** Correcting, standardizing, and verifying the integrity of the data.
- **Data synchronization:** Integrating, matching, or linking data from disparate sources.
- **Data enrichment:** Enhancing data using information from internal and external data sources.
- **Data maintenance:** Checking and controlling data integrity over time.

Companies use DBMSs in a broad range of information systems. Some DBMSs, such as Microsoft Access, can be loaded onto a single user's computer and accessed in an ad hoc manner to support individual decision making. Others, such as IBM's DB2, are located on interconnected computers to support large-scale transaction processing systems, such as order entry and inventory control systems. DBMSs such as Oracle 11g, are interconnected throughout an organization's local area networks (LANs), giving departments access to corporate data. LANs are private networks owned and managed by the organization; they are discussed in detail in Chapter 4.

A DBMS enables many different users to share data and process resources. How can a single, unified database meet the differing requirements of so many users? For example, how can a single database be structured so that sales personnel can view customer, inventory, and production maintenance data while the human resources department maintains restricted access to private personnel data?

The answer is that a DBMS provides two views of the data: a physical view and a logical view. The physical view deals with the actual, physical arrangement and location of data in the direct access storage devices (DASDs). Database specialists use the physical view to configure storage and processing resources.

Users, however, need to see data differently from how they are stored, and they do not want to know all of the technical details of physical storage. After all, a business user is primarily interested in using the information, not in how it is stored. The logical view, or user's view, of data is meaningful to the user. What is important is that a DBMS provides endless logical views of the data. This feature allows users to see data from a business-related perspective rather than from a technical viewpoint. Clearly, users must adapt to the technical requirements of database information systems to some degree, but the logical views allow the system to adapt to the business needs of the users. The way in which you see data (the *logical view* or user's view) can vary; but the physical storage of data (*physical view*) is fixed.

Review Questions

1. What is a database? A database management system (DBMS)?
2. What are three data functions of a DBMS?
3. What is the difference between the physical view of and the logical view of data?

3.4 Data Warehouses, Data Marts, and Data Centers

It's not necessarily the biggest companies that are the most successful, but the smartest ones. Being a smart company means having on-demand access to relevant data, understanding it (usually with the help of data visualization tools), and using what you learn from it to increase productivity and/or profitability. Having complete information is critical to this process. Data warehouses enable managers and knowledge workers to leverage data for advantage from across the enterprise, thereby helping them make the smartest decisions.

Recall from our discussion of data management that a data warehouse is a repository in which data is organized so that it can be readily analyzed using methods such as data mining, decision support, querying, and other applications. Examples of uses of a data warehouse are revenue management, customer-relationship management, fraud detection, and payroll-management applications. To better understand data warehouses, it helps to compare them to databases.

COMPARING DATABASES TO DATA WAREHOUSES

Data warehouses and regular databases both consist of data tables (files), primary and other keys, and query capabilities. The main difference is that databases are designed and optimized to store data, whereas data warehouses are designed and optimized to respond to analysis questions that are critical for a business.

Databases are **online transaction processing (OLTP) systems** in which every transaction has to be recorded quickly. Consider, for example, financial transactions, such as withdrawals from a bank ATM or a debit account. These transactions must be recorded and processed as they occur, that is, in real time. Consequently, database systems for banking and debit cards are designed to ensure that every transaction gets recorded immediately.

Databases are volatile because data is constantly being added, edited, or updated. Consider a database of a bank. Every deposit, withdrawal, loan payment, or other transaction adds or changes data. The volatility caused by the transaction processing makes data analysis too difficult. To overcome this problem, data are extracted from designated databases, transformed, and loaded into a data warehouse. Significantly, these data are read-only data; that is, it cannot be updated. Rather, it remains the same until the next scheduled data extraction, transformation, and load (ETL). Unlike databases, then, warehouse data are not volatile. Thus, data warehouses are designed as **online analytical processing (OLAP) systems,** meaning that the data can be queried and analyzed much more efficiently than OLTP application databases.

REAL-TIME SUPPORT FROM A DATA WAREHOUSE

The modern business world is experiencing a growing trend toward real-time data warehousing and analytics. In the past, data warehouses primarily supported strategic applications, which did not require instant response time, direct customer interaction, or integration with operational systems. Today, businesses increasingly use information in the moment to support real-time customer interaction. Companies with an active data warehouse will be able to interact appropriately with a customer to provide superior customer service, which in turn improves revenues.

Companies, such as the credit card company Capital One, track each customer's profitability and use that score to determine the level of customer service. For example, when a customer calls Capital One, that customer is asked to enter the credit card number, which is linked to a profitability score. Low-profit customers get a voice response unit only; high-profit customers get a live person—a customer service representative (CSR).

Consider, for example, the case of Charles, who is calling the customer service center because of frequent dropped cell calls. Through the call center application (attached to the active data warehouse), the CSR accesses not only the complete history of Charles's calls to the company but also a full view of all the services to which he subscribes—DSL, Internet, and cellular—along with his customer profitability score, which lets the CSR know how profitable (valuable) he is to the company. Intelligent and selective customer service is possible because all service lines and calls to customer service are stored in the active data warehouse. The CSR uses the data and company information to determine the best action or offer to resolve this issue to Charles's satisfaction. Additionally, the CSR will have the insight to cross-sell or up-sell additional services based on the details in Charles' profile and company interaction information. In this example, the active data warehouse provided a view of the customer that indicated what intervention to take based on the customer's profitability to the company. Because Charles subscribes to the company's high-profit-margin services, the company wants to minimize the risk of losing him as a customer.

THE NEED FOR DATA WAREHOUSING

Many organizations built data warehouses because they were frustrated with inconsistent decision support data or they needed to improve reporting applications or better understand the business. Viewed from this perspective, data warehouses are infrastructure investments that companies make to support current and future decision making.

The most successful companies are those that can respond quickly and flexibly to market changes and opportunities, and the key to this response is to use data and information effectively and efficiently. Companies perform this task not only via transaction processing but also through analytical processing, in which company employees—frequently end users—analyze the accumulated data. Analytical processing, also referred to as business intelligence (BI), includes data mining, decision support systems (DSSs), enterprise systems, Web applications, querying, and other end-user activities.

BENEFITS OF DATA WAREHOUSING

According to Teradata Corp., the benefits of a data warehouse (DW) are both business- and IT-related. From the business perspective, companies can make better decisions because they have access to better information. From an IT perspective, DWs deliver information more effectively and efficiently. Several areas of an organization that benefit from a DW are the following:

- **Marketing and sales.** Use a DW for product introductions, product information access, marketing program effectiveness, and product line profitability. Use the data to maximize per-customer profitability.
- **Pricing and contracts.** Use the data to calculate costs accurately to optimize pricing of a contract. Without accurate cost data, prices may be below or too near to cost or prices may be uncompetitive because they are too high.
- **Forecasting.** The DW assists in the timely visibility of end-customer demand.
- **Sales performance.** Use the data to determine sales profitability and productivity for all territories and regions; can obtain and analyze results by geography, product, sales group, or individual.
- **Financial.** Use daily, weekly, or monthly results for improved financial management.

Figure 3.11 diagrams the process of building and using a data warehouse. The organization's data are stored in operational systems (left side of the figure). Not all data are necessarily transferred to the data warehouse. Frequently, only a summary of the data is transferred. The data that is transferred is organized within the warehouse in

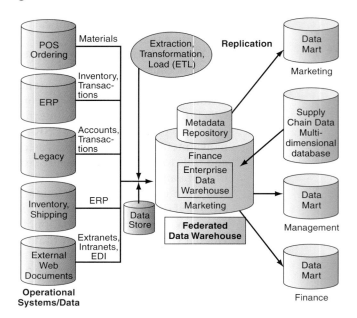

Figure 3.11 Data warehouse framework and views.

a form that is easy for end users to access and locate. The data is also standardized. Then the data is organized by subject, such as by functional area, vendor, or product.

CHARACTERISTICS OF A DATA WAREHOUSE

All types of data warehousing share nine major characteristics:

1. Organization. Data is organized by subject (e.g., by customer, vendor, product, price level, and region) and contains information relevant for decision support only.

2. Consistency. Data in different databases may be encoded differently. For example, gender data may be encoded 0 and 1 in one operational system, and "m" and "f" in another. In the warehouse it will be coded in a consistent manner.

3. Time variant. The data is kept for many years so it can be used for identifying trends, forecasting, and making comparisons over time.

4. Nonvolatile. Once the data are entered into the warehouse, they are not updated.

5. Relational. Typically the data warehouse uses a relational structure.

6. Client/server. The data warehouse uses the client/server architecture mainly to provide the end user an easy access to its data.

7. Web-based. Today's data warehouses are designed to provide an efficient computing environment for Web-based applications.

8. Integration. Data from various sources is integrated. Web Services are used to support integration.

9. Real time. Although most applications of data warehousing are not in real time, it is possible to arrange for real-time capabilities.

BUILDING A DATA WAREHOUSE

Building and implementing a data warehouse can present problems. Because a warehouse is very large and expensive to build, it's important to understand the key success factors in implementing one. Specifically, a company that is considering building a data warehouse first needs to address a series of basic questions:

- Does top management support the data warehouse?
- Do users support the data warehouse?
- Do users want access to a broad range of data? If they do, which is preferable: a single repository or a set of stand-alone data marts?
- Do users want data access and analysis tools?

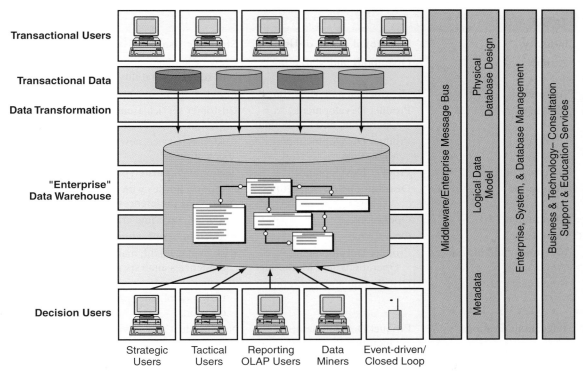

Figure 3.12 Teradata Corp.'s enterprise data warehouse. *(Source: Teradata Corporation [teradata.com], with permission.)*

- Do users understand how to use the data warehouse to solve business problems?
- Does the unit have one or more power users who can understand data warehouse technologies?

Architecture and Tools. There are several basic architectures for data warehousing. Two common ones are two-tier and three-tier architectures. In three-tier architecture, data from the warehouse is processed twice and deposited in an additional multidimensional database, in which it can be organized for easy multidimensional analysis and presentation or replicated in data marts.

There are two main reasons for creating a data warehouse as a separate data store. First, the performance of a separate data store is better because it is not competing (or waiting) for processing time. Second, modeling a database that can be used for both operational and analytical purposes can be difficult. Figure 3.12 represents an EDW developed by Teradata Corp. This centralized approach reduces the amount of data the technical team has to transfer, thereby simplifying data management and administration. Users are also provided with access to all of the data in the data warehouse instead of being limited to individual data marts.

Putting the Warehouse on the Intranet. Data warehouse content can be delivered to decision makers throughout the enterprise via an intranet. Users can view, query, and analyze the data and produce reports using Web browsers. This is an extremely economical and effective method of delivering data.

Suitability. Data warehousing is most appropriate for organizations that have some of the following characteristics:

- End users need to access large amounts of data.
- The operational data is stored in different systems.
- The organization employs an information-based approach to management.

TABLE 3.3	Strategic Uses of Data Warehousing	
Industry	**Functional Areas of Use**	**Strategic Use**
Airline	Operations and Marketing	Crew assignment, aircraft deployment, mix of fares, analysis of route profitability, frequent-flyer program promotions
Apparel	Distribution and Marketing	Merchandising, inventory replenishment
Banking	Product Development, Operations, and Marketing	Customer service, trend analysis, product and service promotions, reduction of IS expenses
Credit card	Product Development and Marketing	Customer service, new information service for a fee, fraud detection
Defense contracts	Product Development	Technology transfer, production of military applications
E-Business	Distribution and Marketing	Data warehouses with personalization capabilities, marketing/shopping preferences allowing for up-selling and cross-selling
Government	Operations	Reporting on crime areas, homeland security
Healthcare	Operations	Reduction of operational expenses
Investment and insurance	Product Development, Operations, and Marketing	Risk management, market movements analysis, customer tendencies analysis, portfolio management
Retail chain	Distribution and Marketing	Trend analysis, buying pattern analysis, pricing policy, inventory control, sales promotions, optimal distribution channel decisions
Telecommunications	Product Development, Operations, and Marketing	New product and service promotions, reduction of IS budget, profitability analysis

- The organization serves a large, diverse customer base (such as in a utility company or a bank; for example, AT&T's 26-terabyte data warehouse is used for marketing analysis by 3,000 employees).
- The same data is represented differently in different systems.
- Data is stored in highly technical formats that are difficult to decipher.
- Extensive end-user computing is performed (many end users performing many activities).

Table 3.3 summarizes some of the successful applications of data warehouses. Hundreds of other successful applications have been reported (e.g., see client success stories and case studies at Web sites of vendors such as Hyperion Inc., Business Objects, Cognos Corp., Information Builders, NCR Corp., Oracle, Computer Associates, and Software A&G). For further discussion of this topic, visit the Data Warehouse Institute (*tdwi.org/*).

Many organizations, buoyed by the success of their data warehouse efforts, are taking data warehousing public. One example is Wells Fargo. Its development effort uses the resources of a Teradata warehouse to provide an online tool that collects and summarizes transactions for consumers—credit card, debit card, online bill payments, checking account—and generates an analysis of online banking sessions. Consumers are better able to understand their spending patterns, and they have reported a higher level of customer satisfaction.

Another company that continues to grow its enterprise using a public data warehouse is Travelocity. Part of the company's success lies in its innovative use of its EDW for marketing and CRM.

DATA MARTS, OPERATIONAL DATA STORES, AND MULTIDIMENSIONAL DATABASES

Organizations frequently implement data marts, operational data stores, and multidimensional databases either as supplements or substitutes for data warehouses. In this section we take a closer look at these systems, beginning with data marts.

Data Marts. The high costs of data warehouses can make them too expensive for a company to implement. As an alternative, many firms create a lower-cost,

TABLE 3.4	Reasons Data Warehouses Fail

Data warehousing design:
- Unrealistic expectations
- Inappropriate architecture
- Vendors overselling capabilities
- Lack of development expertise
- Lack of effective project sponsorship

Data warehousing implementation:
- Poor user training
- Failure to align data warehouses and data marts
- Lack of attention to cultural issues
- Corporate policies not updated

Data warehousing operation:
- Poor upkeep of technology
- Failure to upgrade modules
- Lack of integration
- Poor data quality

scaled-down version of a data warehouse called a data mart. Data marts are designed for a strategic business unit (SBU) or a single department.

In addition to lower costs (less than $100,000 versus $1 million or more for data warehouses), data marts require significantly shorter lead times for implementation, often less than 90 days. In addition, because they allow for local rather than central control, they confer power on the using group. They also contain less information than the data warehouse. Thus, they respond more quickly, and they are easier to understand and navigate. Finally, they allow a business unit to build its own decision support systems without relying on a centralized IS department.

Operational Data Stores. An **operational data store** is a database for transaction processing systems that use data warehouse concepts to provide clean data. It brings the concepts and benefits of the data warehouse to the operational portions of the business at a lower cost. Thus, it can be viewed as being situated between the operational data (in legacy systems) and the data warehouse. An operational data store is used for short-term decisions involving mission-critical applications rather than for the medium- and long-term decisions associated with the regular data warehouse. These decisions require access to much more current information. For example, a bank needs to know about all the accounts for a customer who is calling on the phone.

System Failures. Unfortunately, despite their potential benefits, implementations of large information systems often fail. Examples and reasons for failures are summarized in Table 3.4. Suggestions on how to avoid data warehouse failure are provided at *datawarehouse.com*, at *bitpipe.com*, and at *teradatauniversitynetwork.com*.

DATA CENTERS

Data center is the name given to facilities containing mission-critical ISs and components that deliver data and IT services to the enterprise. Data centers store and integrate networks, computer systems, and storage devices. Data centers need to ensure the availability of power and provide physical and data security. The newest data centers are huge and include temperature and fire controls, physical and digital security, redundant power supplies such as uninterruptible power sources (UPS), and redundant data communications connections. For example, in 2008, Christus Health Medical Center in Texas built a $23 million data center to house its patient insurance records, CT scans, and other data and documents. The size of the data center is 48,000 square feet, which is over 10 times the size of the hospital's former 4,000-square-foot data center. Demands for imaging data are growing quickly as more types of health reports and records get digitized, stored, and archived for decades.

Many companies are building or reconfiguring their data centers to save money. Some cannot afford the electricity and cooling costs. Others need more computing, storage, or network capacity to handle new applications or to cope with acquisitions. Still others need to improve their disaster recovery capabilities. Creating—or reducing the cost of—a disaster recovery site is often part of a data center upgrade plan.

Next-generation data centers will be more efficient in lowering operating expenses and energy consumption. They will have greater availability (uptime) to meet business needs and will be easier to manage. A networking company, Cisco (*cisco.com*), offers several podcasts and video demos of data centers.

Review Questions

1. What is the main difference in the designs of databases and data warehouses?
2. Compare databases and data warehouses in terms of data volatility and decision support.
3. What is an advantage of an active data warehouse?
4. What are the data functions performed by a data warehouse?
5. How can a data warehouse support a company's compliance requirements and green initiatives?
6. Why are data centers important to performance?

3.5 Enterprise Content Management

Enterprise content management (ECM) has become an important data management technology, particularly for large and medium-sized organizations. ECM includes electronic document management, Web content management, digital asset management, and **electronic records management (ERM)**. ERM infrastructures help reduce costs, easily share content across the enterprise, minimize risk, automate expensive time-intensive and manual processes, and consolidate multiple Web sites onto a single platform.

Four key forces are driving organizations to adopt a strategic, enterprise-level approach to planning and deploying content systems:

- Compounding growth of content generated by organizations
- The need to integrate that content within business processes
- The need to support increasing sophistication for business-user content access and interaction
- The need to maintain governance and control over content to ensure regulatory compliance and preparedness for legal discovery

Modern businesses generate volumes of documents, messages, and memos that, by their nature, contain unstructured content (data or information). Therefore, the contents of e-mail and instant messages, spreadsheets, faxes, reports, case notes, Web pages, voice mails, contracts, and presentations cannot be put into a database. However, many of these materials are business records (as discussed in Section 3.1) that need to be retained. As materials are not needed for current operations or decisions, they are archived—moved into longer-term storage. Because these materials constitute business records, they must be retained and made available when requested by auditors, investigators, the SEC, the IRS, or other authorities. To be retrievable, the records must be organized and indexed like structured data in a database.

Records are different from documents in that they cannot be modified or deleted except in controlled circumstances. In contrast, documents generally are subject to revision. Figure 3.13 shows the differences between documents and records as well as the relationship between document management and records management.

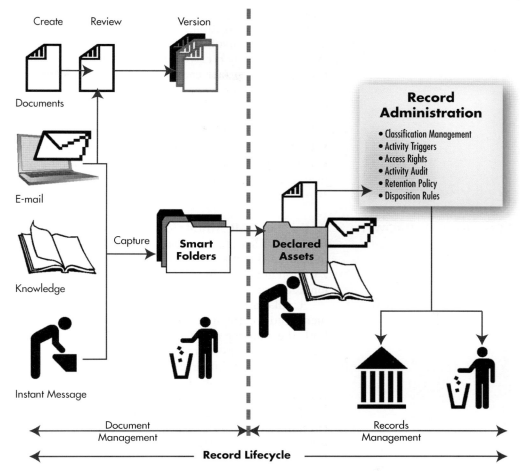

Create Review Version

Documents

E-mail

Knowledge

Instant Message

Capture

Smart Folders

Declared Assets

Record Administration

- Classification Management
- Activity Triggers
- Access Rights
- Activity Audit
- Retention Policy
- Disposition Rules

Document Management

Records Management

Record Lifecycle

Figure 3.13 Electronic records management from creation to retention or destruction.

Electronic Records and Document Management. In Section 3.1, you read that document management systems organize and store e-mail, instant messages, and other types of unstructured content. In this section, we examine the related topic of ERM.

Simply creating backups of records is not a form of ERM, because the content is not organized so that it can be accurately and easily retrieved. ERM requires the involvement of not only key players in recordkeeping, such as records managers or record librarians, but also IT personnel and administrators under a shared responsibility to establish ERM policies. Those policies include schedules for retaining and destroying records, which must comply with state and federal regulations.

The requirement to manage records—regardless of whether they are paper or electronic—is not new. What is new is the volume of electronic records that must be reviewed to determine whether they should be retained or destroyed. Properly managed, electronic records are strategic assets. Improperly managed or destroyed, they are liabilities.

THE BUSINESS VALUE OF E-RECORDS MANAGEMENT

Companies need to be prepared to respond to an audit, federal investigation, lawsuit, or any other legal action against it. Types of lawsuits against companies include patent violations, product safety negligence, theft of intellectual property, breach of contract, wrongful termination, harassment, discrimination, and many more.

Nearly 90 percent of U.S. corporations become engaged in lawsuits; at any one time, the average $1 billion company in the United States faces 147 lawsuits (Kish, 2006). Each lawsuit will involve discovery, or the request for information (which almost always involves the request for e-mail and other electronic communications).

Discovery is the process of gathering information in preparation for trial, legal or regulatory investigation, or administrative action as required by law. When electronic information is involved, the process is called electronic discovery, or e-discovery. When a company receives an e-discovery request, the company must produce what is requested—or face charges of obstructing justice or being in contempt of court.

Several cases where a company incurred huge costs for not responding to e-discovery are the following:

- Failure to save e-mails resulted in a $2.75 million fine for Phillip Morris.
- Failure to respond to e-discovery requests cost Bank of America $10 million in fines.
- Failure to produce backup tapes and deleted e-mails resulted in a $29.3 million jury verdict against USB Warburg in what became a landmark case, *Zubulake v. UBS Warburg.*

ECM AND ERM GROWTH

At the 2008 EMC World Conference in Las Vegas, 9,000 attendees heard about the future of EMC for content management, virtualization, and Web 2.0 storage—indicating the importance of these technologies. Stored data is expected to reach 2 trillion gigabytes by 2011. Keeping corporate data safe will be an incredible challenge, as you will read in Chapter 5.

Unlike any other aspect of business, planning and managing electronic documents and records are elements of every business process. This situation has increased both the number of ECM and ERM vendors and the capabilities they provide. Vendors sell suites of products, including document management, collaboration, portals, and business intelligence.

Numerous major IT companies have become ECM and ERM vendors. ECM vendors include IBM (*ibm.com*), Oracle (*oracle.com*), and EMC (*emc.com*).

Major ERM vendors include Hummingbird (*hummingbird.com*), Iron Mountain (*ironmountain.com*), Oracle (*oracle.com*), and AccuTrac (*accutrac.com*). Visit *ironmountain.com/services/tours/records.asp* or *ironmountain.com/services/tours/dms.asp* to view videos of electronic records management and a records management center.

Review Questions

1. Define *ECM.*
2. What is the difference between a document and a record?
3. Why is ERM important to an organization?
4. Define discovery and e-discovery.
5. How does creating backups of electronic records differ from ERM?

Key Terms

Chapter Highlights and Insights

❶ Data is the foundation of any information system and needs to be managed throughout its useful life cycle, which converts data to useful information, knowledge, and a basis for decision support. Viewed from the basic profitability or net income model (profit = revenues − expenses), profit increases when employees learn from and use the data to increase revenues, reduce expenses, or both.

❷ Managers and information workers may be constrained by data that cannot be trusted because it is incomplete, out of context, outdated, inaccurate, inaccessible, or so overwhelming that it requires too much time to analyze.

❷ Data errors and inconsistencies lead to mistakes and lost opportunities, such as failed deliveries, invoicing blunders, and problems in synchronizing data from multiple locations.

❷ Many factors that impact the quality of data must be recognized and controlled.

❸ Programs that manage data and provide access to the database are called database management systems (DBMSs).

❸ Data and documents are managed electronically. They are digitized, stored, and used in electronic management systems.

❸ The benefits of using a DBMS include improved strategic use of corporate data, reduced complexity of the data environment, reduced data redundancy and enhanced data integrity, improved security, reduced data maintenance costs, and better access to data.

❹ The logical view, or users' view, of data is meaningful to the user. Restricting access to data based on the users' job responsibilities increases data security.

❹ The logical model is a detailed view of the data in which high-level entities are broken down into manageable data entities (e.g., customer data into product preferences, customer contact, shop locations, and product sales).

❺ Data warehouses and data marts support the demanding data needs of decision makers. Relevant data is indexed and organized for easy access by end users.

❺ Electronic document management, the automated control of documents, is a key to greater efficiency in handling documents in order to gain an edge on the competition.

❺ How an organization manages its electronic records can directly affect its ability to compete intelligently, to comply with laws and regulations, to respond to litigation, and to recover from disaster. Regulatory requirements such as Sarbanes-Oxley, privacy requirements, and anti-fraud legislation have made managing information both a business priority and a legal obligation.

Questions for Discussion

1. What is the purpose of text mining?
2. Explain how having detailed real-time or near real-time data can improve productivity and decision quality.
3. Why does data and text management matter?
4. List three types of waste or damages that data errors can cause.
5. Explain the *principle of 90/90 data use.*
6. How does data visualization improve decision making?
7. Discuss the major drivers and benefits of data warehousing.
8. Why is master data management (MDM) important in companies with multiple data sources?
9. A data mart can substitute for a data warehouse or supplement it. Compare and discuss these options.
10. What ethical duties does the collection of data about customers impose on companies?
11. How are organizations using their data warehouses to improve consumer satisfaction and the company's profitability?
12. Relate document management to imaging systems.
13. Discuss the factors that make document management so valuable. What capabilities are particularly valuable?
14. Distinguish among operational databases, data warehouses, and data marts.

Exercises and Projects

1. Read *IT at Work 3.1,* "Daimler's Aqua Early Warning System." Answer the questions at the end. Then visit the SAS Web site at *sas.com* and search for their data synchronization or data integration solution. List the key benefits of the SAS solution.
2. Interview a manager or other knowledge worker in a company you work for or to which you have access. Find the data problems the person has encountered and the measures he or she has taken to solve them.
3. Read *IT at Work 3.2,* "Maximizing Return On Time." Answer the questions at the end. Then visit the Business Objects Web site at *businessobjects.com* and search for "Xcelsius 2008 Demos and Sample Downloads." Click on one of the images of a dashboard or model to launch an interactive demo. Use the simulated controls in the demo to see *Xcelsius 2008 in action* (or visit *businessobjects.com/product/catalog/xcelsius/demos.asp*). Identify the model or dashboard whose interactive demo you viewed. Explain the benefits to decision makers of that dashboard or model.
4. Visit Analysis Factory at *analysisfactory.com.* Click to view the Interactive Business Solution Dashboards. Select one type of dashboard and explain its value or features.

5. Read *IT at Work 3.3*, "Data Mining Used by Intelligence Agencies" Answer the questions at the end. Visit Oracle at *oracle.com* and do a search for Oracle Data Mining (ODM). Identify three functionalities of ODM.

6. At *teradatastudentnetwork.com*, read and answer the questions to the case "Harrah's High Payoff from Customer Information." Relate results from Harrah's to how other casinos use their customer data.

7. Go to *Teradata Magazine*, Volume 6, Number 2, and read "The Big Payoff." Then go to *teradatastudentnetwork.com* and read the case study "Harrah's High Payoff from Customer Information." What kind of payoff are they having from this investment in data warehousing?

8. At *teradatastudentnetwork.com*, read and answer the questions of the assignment entitled "Data Warehouse Failures." Choose one case and discuss the failure and the potential remedy.

Group Assignments and Projects

1. Prepare a report on the topic of data management and the intranet. Specifically, pay attention to the role of the data warehouse, the use of browsers for query, and data mining. Each group will visit one or two vendors' sites, read the white papers, and examine products (Oracle, Red Bricks, Brio, Siemens Mixdorf IS, NCR, SAS, and Information Advantage). Also, visit the Web site of the Data Warehouse Institute (*tdwi.org*).

2. Using data mining, it is possible not only to capture information that has been buried in distant courthouses but also to manipulate and cross-index it. This ability can benefit law enforcement but invade privacy. In 1996, Lexis-Nexis, the online information service, was accused of permitting access to sensitive information on individuals. The company argued that the firm was targeted unfairly because it provided only basic residential data for lawyers and law enforcement personnel. Should Lexis-Nexis be prohibited from allowing access to such information? Debate the issue.

3. Ocean Spray Cranberries, Inc. is a large cooperative of fruit growers and processors. Ocean Spray needed data to determine the effectiveness of its promotions and its advertising and to respond strategically to its competitors' promotions. The company also wanted to identify trends in consumer preferences for new products and to pinpoint marketing factors that might be causing changes in the selling levels of certain brands and markets.

Ocean Spray buys marketing data from InfoScan (*us.infores.com*), a company that collects data using barcode scanners in a sample of 2,500 stores nationwide and from A.C. Nielsen. The data for each product includes sales volume, market share, distribution, price information, and information about promotions (sales, advertisements).

The amount of data provided to Ocean Spray on a daily basis is overwhelming (about 100 to 1,000 times more data items than Ocean Spray used to collect on its own). All of the data is deposited in the corporate marketing data mart. To analyze this vast amount of data, the company developed a decision support system (DSS). To give end users easy access to the data, the company uses a data mining process called CoverStory, which summarizes information in accordance with user preferences. CoverStory interprets data processed by the DSS, identifies trends, discovers cause-and-effect relationships, presents hundreds of displays, and provides any information required by the decision makers. This system alerts managers to key problems and opportunities.

a. Find information about Ocean Spray by entering Ocean Spray's Web site (*oceanspray.com*).

b. Ocean Spray has said that it cannot run the business without the system. Why?

c. What data from the data mart is used by the DSS?

d. Enter *scanmar.nl* and click the Marketing Dashboard. How does the dashboard provide marketing and sales intelligence?

Internet Exercises

1. Conduct a survey on document management tools and applications.

2. Access the Web sites of one or two of the major data management vendors, such as Oracle, IBM, and Sybase, and trace the capabilities of their latest BI products.

3. Access the Web sites of one or two of the major data warehouse vendors, such as NCR or SAS; find how their products are related to the Web.

4. Access the Web site of the GartnerGroup (*gartnergroup.com*). Examine some of their research notes pertaining to marketing databases, data warehousing, and data management. Prepare a report regarding the state of the art.

5. Explore a Web site for multimedia database applications. Review some of the demonstrations, and prepare a concluding report.

6. Enter *microsoft.com/solutions/BI/customer/biwithinreach_demo.asp* and see how BI is supported by Microsoft's tools. Write a report.

7. Visit *www-306.ibm.com/*. Find services related to dynamic warehouse and explain what it does.

BUSINESS CASE

Generating Value from Data

Implementing ISs and networks to manage, process and distribute data and reports by themselves do not generate value, as measured by an increase in *profitability*. Viewed from the basic profitability or net income model (profit = revenues − expenses), profit increases when employees learn from and use the data to increase revenues, reduce expenses, or both. In this learn and earn model, managers learn—that is, gain insights—from their data to predict what actions will lead to the greatest increase in net earnings. *Net earnings* are also referred to as *net income* or the *bottom line*. Reducing uncertainty can improve the bottom line, as the examples in Table 3.5 show.

Applebee's Faces Competition in 21 Countries

Applebee's International, Inc. (*applebees.com*) had faced these and other common business uncertainties and questions, but the company lacked the data infrastructure to answer them. Applebee's International develops, franchises, and operates restaurants under the Applebee's Neighborhood Grill & Bar brand, the largest casual dining enterprise in the world. As of 2011, there were nearly 2,000 Applebee's restaurants operating in 21 countries.

Applebee's faced fierce competition in the casual dining restaurant sector. To differentiate from other restaurant chains and to build customer loyalty (defined as return visits), Applebee's management wanted guests to experience a good time while having a great meal at attractive prices. To achieve their strategic objectives, management had to be able to forecast demand accurately and to become familiar with customers' experiences and regional food preferences. For example, knowing which new items to add to the menu based on past food preferences helps motivate return visits. However, identifying regional preferences, such as a strong demand for steaks in Texas but not in New England, by analyzing the relevant data was too time-consuming when done with the company's spreadsheet software.

The problem many companies such as Applebee's face is the difficulty in bringing together huge quantities of data located in different databases in a way that creates value. Without efficient processes for managing vast amounts of customer data and turning this data into usable knowledge, companies can miss critical opportunities to find insights hidden in the data.

Point of Sale and Data Warehouse Solution

Applebee's International implemented an **enterprise data warehouse (EDW)** from Teradata with data analysis capabilities that helped management acquire an accurate understanding of sales, demand, and costs. An EDW is a data repository where data is analyzed and used throughout the organization to improve responsiveness and, ultimately, net earnings. Each day, Applebee's collects data concerning the previous day's sales from hundreds of point-of-sale (POS) systems located at every company-owned restaurant. The company then organizes this data to report every ticket item sold in 15-minute intervals. By reducing the amount of time required to collect POS data from two weeks to one day, the EDW has enabled management to respond quickly to guests' needs and changes in guests' preferences. With greater knowledge about their customers, the company is better equipped to market and provide services that attract customers and build loyalty.

Figure 3.14 illustrates Applebee's EDW and feedback loop. First, data are collected, processed, and stored in a data warehouse. They are then processed by analytical tools such as data mining and decision modeling. Knowledge acquired from this data analysis directs promotional and other decisions. Finally, by continuously collecting and analyzing fresh data, management can receive feedback regarding the success of management strategies.

Improved Earnings

Applebee's management gained clearer business insight by collecting and analyzing detailed data in near real time using an enterprise data warehouse. Regional managers can now select the best menu offerings and operate more efficiently. The company uses detailed sales data and data from customer satisfaction surveys to identify regional preferences, predict product demand, and build financial models that indicate which products are strong performers on the menu and which are not. By linking customer satisfaction ratings to specific menu items, Applebee's can determine which items are

TABLE 3.5	How Data Can Reduce Uncertainty and Improve Accuracy and Performance
Business Uncertainty	**Business Impact and Value**
What will be monthly demand for Product X over each of the next three months?	Knowing demand for Product X means knowing how much to order. Sales quantity and sales revenues are maximized because there are no inventory shortages or lost sales. Expenses are minimized because there is no unsold inventory.
Which marketing promotions for Product Y are customers most likely to respond to?	Knowing which marketing promotion will get the highest response rate maximizes sales revenues while avoiding the huge expense of a useless promotion.

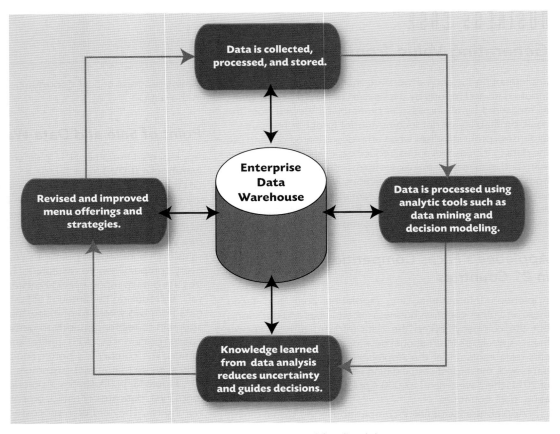

Figure 3.14 Applebee's enterprise data warehouse and feedback loop.

doing well, which ones taste good, and which food presentation is most appetizing.

With detailed, near real-time data, Applebee's International improved its customers' experience, satisfaction, and loyalty—and increased the company's earnings.

Sources: Compiled from *Applebees.com* (2011), Hoover's Company Records (2011), and Teradata (2007).

Questions

1. Why is learning important to managers?
2. How does learning influence net earnings?
3. What is the value of the feedback loop at Applebee's?
4. How necessary is near real-time data?
5. Is it easier for IT to support planning or execution? Why?

PUBLIC SECTOR CASE

Mobile IT and Biometrics Support UK Police

National Policing Improvement Agency (NPIA) is responsible for bringing high-tech equipment to the police service in England and Wales. NPIA published its *Science and Innovation in the Police Service 2010–2013*, a strategy for police service for years 2010–2013. Its three-year strategy includes a number of new ITs for police, including mobile fingerprinting and checking, wearable video devices, and digital forensics.

Mobile ID Devices

NPIA signed a contract with Cogent Systems, a biometrics firm, for mobile devices to check prints against those on the National Fingerprint Database at a cost of £9 million over three years. Deputy chief constable Peter Goodman, who leads mobile identification for the Association of Chief Police Officers (ACPO), said the MobileID devices would provide cost savings equivalent to releasing some 360 officers back to front-line policing each year. He stated: "At a time when funding is likely to be constrained or reduced, technical innovation has promise in saving the police service time and money as well as in aiding bringing criminals to justice more quickly."

MobileID is a device about the size of a BlackBerry that lets police officers take suspects' fingerprints on the street and check the prints against the National Fingerprint Database without having to return to the police station. The process takes about two minutes. MobileID is part of a larger project called Mobile Identification at Scene (Midas). The devices work by scanning both of the suspect's index fingers and communicating over an encrypted wireless link with the database.

The NPIA will also deliver the first elements of the *Police National Database* and make images of suspects available on officers' mobile devices. In 2012, the agency plans to deploy noncooperative facial recognition systems.

Applying IT on the Front Line

NPIA chief executive Peter Neyroud said in a statement: "By applying modern science on the front line, police officers are detecting criminals faster, staying on the beat for longer and making decisions based on better evidence about what works." He also explained that "Identification is crucial to police investigations, and giving officers the ability to do this on-the-spot within minutes is giving them more time to spend working in their communities, helping to fight crime,

bringing more offenders to justice and better protecting the public."

An overall goal is to help ensure that the police service in England and Wales continues to harness science effectively and remains one of the most innovative of its kind in the world. The NPIA recognizes the need to do more than improve the toolkit available to police officers. The success of its strategy requires putting public confidence first, for example, by meeting the public's concerns about personal privacy.

Sources: Compiled from NPIA (2010), Kable (2010), and Thurston (2010).

Questions

1. What are some of the ways the NPIA has cost-justified significant investments in innovative IT for police service?
2. How will the new ITs improve policing services in England and Wales?
3. In your opinion, why might the success of NPIA's strategy require putting public confidence first—for example, by meeting the public's concerns about personal privacy—rather than putting public safety first?
4. What are some potentials risks to privacy that MobileID might cause? Does encryption eliminate those risks?
5. Download the NPIA's publication at the textbook's Web site or from *npia.police.uk/en/docs/science_and_innovation.pdf.* What are the primary objectives of its three-year strategy? What ITs are needed to meet those objectives?

ANALYSIS USING SPREADSHEETS

Calculating the Cost of Poor Document Management

Spring Street Company (SSC, a fictitious company) faced rising costs not only from sky-high energy prices, but also from what it considered "hidden costs" associated with its paper-intensive processes. The employees jokingly predicted that if the windows in the offices blew open on a very windy day, there would be total chaos as the papers started flying. The financial implications were that, if such a disaster occurred, the business would grind to a halt.

The company's accountant, Sam Spring, decided to calculate the costs of the paper-driven processes to identify their impact on the bottom line. He recognized that several employees spent most of their day filing or retrieving documents. In addition, there were the monthly costs to warehouse old paper records. Sam observed and measured the activities related to the handling of printed reports and paper files. His average estimates are as follows:

• It takes an employee five minutes to walk to the records room, locate a file, act on it, refile it, and return to his or her desk.
• Employees need to locate a file, act on it, and so on five times per day.
• There are 12 full-time employees who perform these functions.
• Once per day a document gets "lost" (destroyed, misplaced, or covered with massive coffee stains) and must be re-created. The total cost of replacing each lost document is $220.

• Warehousing costs as of the present time for the current volume of stored documents are $75 per month.

Sam would prefer a system that lets employees find and work with business documents without leaving their desks. He's most concerned about the human resources and accounting departments. These personnel are traditionally heavy users of paper files and would greatly benefit from a modern document management system. At the same time, however, Sam is also risk averse. He would rather invest in solutions that would reduce the risk of higher costs in the future. He recognizes that the U.S. Patriot Act's requirements that organizations provide immediate government access to records apply to SSC. He has read that manufacturing and government organizations rely on efficient document management to meet these broader regulatory imperatives. Finally, Sam wants to implement a disaster recovery system.

Your Mission

Prepare a report that provides Sam with the data and information he needs to select and implement a cost-effective alternative to the company's costly paper-intensive approach to managing documents. You will need to conduct research to provide data to prepare this report. Your report should include the following information:

1. Explain the similarities and differences between document imaging systems and document management systems (DMS). List the benefits and the basic hardware and software requirements for each system. Put this information into a table to help Sam readily understand the comparison.

2. Discuss why a DMS transforms the way a business operates. How should SSC prepare for a DMS if it decides to implement one?

3. Collect estimates for the costs of buying or implementing a DMS at SSC.

4. Using the data collected by Sam, create a spreadsheet that calculates the costs of handling paper at SSC based on hourly rates per employee of $16, $22, and $28. Add the cost of lost documents to this. Then, add the costs of warehousing the paper, which increases by 10% every month due to increases in volume. Present the results, showing both monthly totals and a yearly total. Prepare graphs as visualization tools so that Sam can easily perceive the projected growth in warehousing costs over the next three years. Download the spreadsheet to help you get started from the textbook's Web site.

5. Identify at least one additional cost factor (other than better security) that might be reduced or eliminated with the DMS.

6. How can DMS also serve as a disaster recovery system in case of fire, flood, or break-in?

7. Submit your recommendation for a DMS solution. Identify two vendors in your recommendation.

References

Clarabridge, "Serving up Results through Text Analytics." White paper, 2010. *clarabridge.com/*

"Daimler Fact Sheet for Q4 and Full Year 2010," March 2, 2011. *daimler.com/Projects/c2c/channel/documents/1979737_Daimler_Q4___FY_2010_Fact_Sheet.pdf*

Dullaghan, A. "Daimler Drives High Performance," *Teradata Magazine*, Q1, 2011. *teradatamagazine.com/v11n01/Features/Daimler-Drives-High-Performance/*

Henning, D. "World financial crisis leads to auto industry layoffs across Europe," *World Socialist Web Site*, October 10, 2008. *wsws.org/articles/2008/oct2008/auto-o10.shtml*

Hoover's Company Records (2011).

Kable, B., "Police to Be Issued with Mobile Fingerprinting Devices," *ZDNet UK*, March 5, 2010. *zdnet.co.uk/news/security-management/2010/03/05/police-to-be-issued-with-mobile-fingerprinting-devices-40072975/*

Kish, L., "Most U.S. Companies Engaged in Lawsuits," *E-Discovery Advisor*, May 2006.

Loshin, D., "Issues and Opportunities in Data Quality Management Coordination," *DM Review*, April 2004.

National Patient Safety Agency (NPSA), 2009. *nrls.npsa.nhs.uk/alerts/?entryid45=66111*

NPIA (National Improvement Policing Agency), "Science and Innovation in the Police Service, 2010-2013." 2010. *npia.police.uk/en/docs/science_and_innovation.pdf.*

Silva, V., "Focus on Application Deployments Urgent: Informatica," *NetworkWorld*, April 8, 2010. *networkworld.com/news/2010/040810-focus-on-application-deployments-urgent.html*

Snow, C., "Embrace the Role and Value of Master Data Management," *Manufacturing Business Technology*, 26(2), February 2008.

Teradata, "Applebee's International," Video, 2007. *Teradata.com*

Thurston, T., "Police to Get Mobile Fingerprint-Checking Tech," *ZDNet UK*, March 25, 2010. *zdnet.co.uk/news/mobile-working/2010/03/25/police-to-get-mobile-fingerprint-checking-tech-40088449/*

Varghese, D.M. "Healthcare, Technology, and the Supply Chain," July 2010. *EnterpriseResilienceblog.typepad.com/*

Wailgum, T., "Eight of the Worst Spreadsheet Blunders," *CIO.com*, August 17, 2007. *cio.com/article/131500/Eight_of_the_Worst_Spreadsheet_Blunders.*

Chapter

4

Network Management and Mobility

Integrating *IT*

 ACC
 FIN
 MKT
 OM
 HRM
 IS

Google Wave   *wave.google.com/*   video: *wave.google.com/about.html#video*

Twitter network status   *status.twitter.com/*

Azulstar   *azulstar.com/*

Clear 4G WiMAX   *clear.com/*

International CTIA Wireless Tradeshows   *ctiawireless.com/*

Cisco   *cisco.com*

Microsoft SharePoint 2010   *sharepoint.microsoft.com/Pages/Default.aspx*

Cellular Telecommunications Industry Association   *ctia.org/*

WiMAX Forum   *wimaxforum.org/*

Packet switching flash demo   *pbs.org/opb/nerds2.0.1/geek_glossary/packet_switching_flash.html*

Cell phone radiation levels (SAR)   *reviews.cnet.com/2719-6602_7-291-2.html?tag=*

Kaiser Permanente *HealthConnect* video   *youtube.com/kaiserpermanenteorg*

QUICK LOOK at Chapter 4, Network Management and Mobility

This section introduces you to the business issues, challenges, and IT solutions in Chapter 4. Topics and issues mentioned in the Quick Look are explained in the chapter.

Every aspect of the enterprise depends on connectivity, and almost everyone wants mobility. Connectivity and mobility are network issues discussed in this chapter.

At work and in our personal lives, we need or expect immediate network connectivity to texts, tweets, social media, databases, news, apps, and everything else. We expect the Internet to be like water. Just turn it on and it's there . . . without any extra effort. The same view applies to all networks. For the most part, networks are transparent or invisible to us until service is degraded (slow) or the unthinkable happens—a crash or *unplanned downtime*. The social media meltdown in mid-2009 caused by hack attacks against Twitter, Facebook, blogging service LiveJournal, and gossip site Gawker was a pain point for hundreds of millions of users worldwide.

Recently, 4G networks—*purely digital networks*—have been deployed. Advances in 4G mobile broadband, primarily *WiMAX* and *LTE*, are making access to everything from anywhere a reality, as you will read in the opening case. The world's first dual network, *4G WiMAX and Wi-Fi*, on trains delivers wireless broadband Internet free to all passengers on the train and at the stations, and it also supports the operations of the train system. This innovative network uses WiMAX (802.16) technology for the connection to the train and Wi-Fi (802.11) technology

for passenger access on the trains and at the stations. The network provides speeds up to 6 Mbps download and 4 Mbps upload on trains moving at speeds up to 90 mph and can accommodate over 1,000 simultaneous users. This level of performance provides a true 4G network experience sufficient for data-intensive rail applications such as emergency phones, video displays in the trains and stations, and video surveillance equipment. As with all IT, what is now an amazing and blazing mobile network will soon become an expected level of service as 4G networks roll out worldwide. The combination of a 4G network with the killer features—device management, multitasking, social media aggregator, and/or unified e-mail inbox—of Apple's iPhone OS 4.0 (mobile operating system) or Sprint's HTC EVO 4G, released in summer 2010, allows commuters in New Mexico to be at work from the time they arrive at the train station.

Exciting developments and disruptions are occurring in networks and collaboration. New 4G networks, multitasking mobile operating systems, and collaboration platforms are revolutionizing work, business processes, and other things that we have not yet imagined. We look at networks, collaboration, and mobility in this chapter. All of this power carries an environmental price tag and health risk. We examine environmental and ethical issues associated with the huge energy consumption needed to support those networks as well as impacts on our lives and privacy.

Foodstuffs Mobilizes its Supply Chain in New Zealand

Foodstuffs (*foodstuffs.co.nz/*) is a wholesaler, distributor, and retailer of groceries with over 650 retail outlets across New Zealand and more than 6,000 employees. The company, which operates as a food cooperative, owns and manages extensive warehouse and transportation facilities, so its supply chain is a critical part of operations.

Foodstuffs' Supply Chain Processes

Foodstuffs' supply chain processes were complex, making them difficult and expensive to manage. There were two manual and paper-based systems that slowed and complicated Foodstuff's product distribution to outlets:

- Warehouse staff used a manual, paper-based system to pick and pack products for distribution to Foodstuffs' outlets. After deliveries were made at outlets, products were manually searched, counted, and marked—all time-intensive activities that were subject to errors.

- Store staff or sales representatives visited stores with print-outs of specific products and sales figures to do a manual stocktake, and then manually created orders. This ordering process took up to 30 minutes per order and occurred thousands of times each week.

Foodstuffs' management searched for and invested in ways to improve service to its customers, business partners, suppliers, and employees, and which also reduce costs. Simplifying its supply chain processes in order to keep partners informed of inventory and shipping status, increasing accuracy, and reducing costs became a top priority.

Enterprise Mobility for Simplicity and Better Visibility

Foodstuffs invested in **enterprise mobility,** which became one of the cooperative's most successful investments. Enterprise mobility refers to an organization's ability to connect to people and partners, and to control operations from any location at any time. Availability and affordability of app-driven portable devices with all-day batteries, high-speed wireless networks, and security and management software have made enterprise mobility feasible.

Enterprise mobility enables greater visibility and insight into operations with less complexity. By implementing enterprise mobility, Foodstuff's had fewer blind spots created by people and products on the move, which improved the ability to control operations.

Mobilizing the Supply Chain

Foodstuffs made the decision to deploy Symbol's Enterprise Mobility solution and Portable Shopping System (PSS) from

Figure 4.1 Foodstuffs progress through real-time ordering and delivery technology at Sainsbury's 700,000 square foot distribution depot. (© *RichardBakerWork/Alamy*)

Motorola (*motorola.com/Business/XA-EN/Enterprise+Mobility*). Murray Gray, Support Manager, explained:

> In the warehouse Symbol devices have reduced the amount of steps involved in picking, packing and delivering orders. Now, as soon as products are scanned they're automatically put into the database; there's no more double handling of data as it's entered into the system. Our forklifts have mounted units that tell drivers where to go, what to pick and allow drivers to scan products without leaving the vehicle. As products are packed, the system updates itself so that we can accurately track inventory, and this is linked to the ordering system so that buyers know if anything can't be supplied and can re-order quicker as well.

Core functions and benefits of enterprise mobility at Foodstuffs are:

- **Delivery processing:** Mobile devices track goods as they arrive at outlets. Upon delivery, products are scanned and matched to the original order. This real-time process automatically creates a list of overcharges or shortages and issues a credit note—speeding up the delivery process, detecting errors, and increasing accuracy.

- **Order processing:** Instead of doing manual stocktakes, staff use handhelds to scan products on the shelf and then place orders directly, using real-time ordering technology. This technology (see Figure 4.1) has cut the time it takes reps to place orders by 50 percent, drastically speeding up the supply chain.

- **Customer retention and greater share of budget:** Customer retention increased significantly and customers spend a greater proportion of their overall grocery budget with Foodstuffs.

Sources: Foodstuffs.com.nz (2011), Motorola Solutions (2011), and Foodstuffs Case Study (2008).

For Class Discussion and Debate

1. *Scenario for Brainstorming and Discussion:* Enterprise mobility within an organization and across its supply chain can create numerous opportunities for business improvement. For example, once business processes are automated and mobilized, managers can focus on higher value tasks such as customer acquisition and retention. The downside is that enterprise mobility also increases exposure to risks or threats.

a. What constraints and inefficiencies have been eliminated from Foodstuffs' supply chain? (Keep in mind that Foodstuffs is a wholesaler, distributor, and retailer of groceries—owner of many parts of the supply chain.)

b. Identify several risks or threats from enterprise mobility at Foodstuffs. Discuss how they might be minimized.

2. *Debate:* Consider the types of constraints or limitations on the deployment of enterprise mobility. Types of constraints or limitations are technology-related, people issues, inter-organization cooperation and trust issues, security and policy concerns, and organizational budgets. Select one type of constraint/limitation and debate why it might be the most difficult to overcome.

4.1 Business Networks

Business networks support four basic functions or needs: mobility, collaboration, relationships, and search. Brief descriptions of these functions are:

- **Mobility:** Secure, reliable access from anywhere at acceptable speeds.
- **Collaboration:** Working as a team or with others, with members having access to and sharing documents or other types of files.
- **Relationships:** Maintaining contact or interaction with customers, supply chain partners, shareholders, employees, regulators, and so on.
- **Search:** Looking for and finding data, documents, spreadsheets, e-mail messages, and so on easily and efficiently.

Common to all network functions is traffic (signals) and the circuits that transmit the traffic. The fundamentals of networks and network communalizations are discussed next.

NETWORK BASICS

Networks transmit signals between a sender (source) and a receiver (destination), as shown in Figure 4.2. Signals carry the voice or data being transmitted.

Switching Signals Along the Path from Sender to Receiver. Networks need to be connected to other networks, including the Internet. Transmission of a signal over a series of networks is made possible by *switches* and *routers*, which are hardware devices, and *nodes* on the network. Switches and routers make decisions about how to handle packets or frames. Signals lose energy as they travel along a network and need to be strengthened. Repeaters amplify or regenerate signals to keep them moving along their paths.

The transmission of the signal by the switches and routers is called *switching*. The two types of switching are:

- **Circuit switching:** Once a connection is made between the source and the destination, the path of the signal along the nodes is dedicated and exclusive. Circuit switching is older technology that was used for telephone calls. Plain old telephone service (POTS) and most wireline (wired) telephone calls are transmitted, at least

Figure 4.2 Overview of the transmission of a signal from a sender/source to a receiver/destination.

in part, over a dedicated circuit that is used only for that call. The distinguishing characteristic is that the circuit cannot be used by any other call until the session (connection) is ended.

- **Packet switching:** The path of the signal is digital and is neither dedicated nor exclusive. That is, the networks are shared. For example, a file or e-mail message is broken into smaller blocks, called **packets**. The network breaks a file or e-mail message into blocks (packets) of a specific size. Each packet carries part of the file or e-mail message as well as network information such as the sender's IP address, receiver's IP address, and instructions telling the network how many packets the file or e-mail message has been broken into. When packets are transmitted over a shared network, such as the Internet, they follow different paths to the destination, where they are reassembled into the original message once all of them have arrived. For a flash demo of packet switching, visit *pbs.org/opb/nerds2.0.1/geek_glossary/packet_switching_flash.html*

Wireless networks use packet switching and wireless routers. Routers are devices that forward packets from one network to another network. Routers connect networks that use different network technologies. Wireless routers are actually wired routers with **wireless access points (WAP)** built in, providing both wired and wireless at the same time. Figure 4.3 shows wireless routers, which use antennae to transmit and receive signals.

Network Terminology. To understand networks and the factors that determine their functionality, you need to be familiar with the following basic network terminology.

- **Bandwidth:** The throughput capacity of a network, which is a measure of the speed at which data is transmitted. Bandwidth depends on what protocol is used (802.11b, 802.11g, 802.11n, 802.16, etc.) and how much of the signal is available for processing. The weaker the signal, the lower the bandwidth, and the slower the transmission speed. As an analogy, consider a pipe used to transport water. The larger the diameter of the pipe, the greater the throughput (volume) of water that flows through it.
- **Protocol:** The standards or set of rules that govern how devices on a network exchange information (communicate) and how they need to function in order to "talk to each other." An analogy is a country's driving rules. In Australia, Bermuda, and the United Kingdom, the protocol is to drive on the left-hand side of the road. In China, Russia, and North American countries, the protocol is to drive on the right.
- **TCP/IP:** TCP/IP (Transmission Control Protocol/Internet Protocol) are the Internet protocols or the suite of Internet protocols. TCP/IP suite was created by the

Figure 4.3 Wireless routers use antennae to transmit signals.
(© *Joachim Wendler/iStockphoto*)

U.S. Department of Defense (DoD) to ensure and preserve data integrity as well as maintain communications in the event of catastrophic war. TCP/IP is used by most networks to ensure that all devices on the Internet can communicate.

- **Broadband:** This term is short for *broad bandwidth*. It's a general term that means fast transmission speed. In contrast, *narrowband* refers to slow speeds.
- **Download (speed):** How quickly data can be received from the Internet or other network, or how fast a connection can deliver data to a computer or mobile device.
- **Upload (speed):** How quickly data can be sent to a network or how fast a connection can transfer data from the source computer or mobile device. Typically, networks are configured so that downloading is faster than uploading.
- **Fixed-line broadband:** Describes either cable or DSL Internet connections. Fixed-line broadband differs from mobile broadband, which is wireless and uses a mobile broadband signal network.
- **Mobile broadband:** Describes various types of wireless high-speed Internet access through a portable modem, telephone, or other device. Various network standards may be used, such as GPRS, 3G, WiMAX, LTE UMTS/HSPA, EV-DO, and some portable satellite-based systems. These standards are discussed in the chapter.
- **3G:** Short for *third generation* of cellular telecommunications technology. 3G networks support multimedia and broadband services, do so over a wider range (distance), and at faster speeds than the prior generations—1G and 2G. 3G networks have far greater ranges because they use large satellite connections that connect to telecommunication towers.
- **4G:** Short for *fourth generation*. 4G mobile network standards enable faster data transfer rates.

3G AND 4G

4G technologies represent the latest stage in the evolution of wireless data technologies. 4G delivers average download rates of 3 Mbps or higher. In contrast, today's 3G networks typically deliver average download speeds about one-tenth of that rate. Even though individual networks, ranging from 2G to 3G, started separately with their own purposes, soon they will be converted to the 4G network. What is significant about 4G networks is that they do not have a circuit-switched subsystem, as do current 2G and 3G networks. Instead, 4G is based purely on the packet-based Internet Protocol (IP).

In general, users can get 4G wireless connectivity through one of two standards: WiMAX or LTE (long-term evolution).

- WiMAX is based on the IEEE 802.16 standard and is being deployed by Clearwire for wholesale use by Sprint, Comcast, and Time-Warner Cable to deliver wireless broadband.
- LTE is a GSM-based technology that will be deployed by Verizon, AT&T, and T-Mobile.

By the end of 2010, Clearwire had built out its 4G WiMAX network to all major markets in the United States and Verizon was offering its 4G LTE services commercially in 25 to 30 major U.S. markets.

IP NETWORKS

IP networks form the backbone of worldwide digital networking. They have encouraged the merger of voice, data, video, and radio waves, which can be digitized into packets and sent via any digital network. This convergence is happening on a global scale and is changing the way in which people, devices, and applications communicate. As shown in Table 4.1, improved network performance, which is measured by its *data transfer capacity*, provides fantastic opportunities for mobility, mobile commerce, collaboration, supply chain management, remote work, and other productivity gains.

TABLE 4.1	Growth of High-Capacity Networks			
Network Standard	Generation	Data Transfer Rates (Capacity)	Used by	Upgrades
GSM (Global System for Mobile Communications)	2G	9.6 Kbps	Cingular, T-Mobile, most European carriers	Upgrades include GPRS, EDGE, UMTS, HSDPA.
CDMA (Code Division Multiple Access)	2.5G	307 Kbps	Verizon, Sprint	Upgrades include 1xRTT, EV-DO, EV-DV.
EDGE (Enhanced Data for Global Evolution)	3G	474 Kbps	Cingular, T-Mobile	
EV-DO (Evolution, Data Only)	3G	2.4 Mbps	Verizon, Sprint	Third upgrade to CDMA.
EV-DV (Evolution, Data and Voice)	3G	3.1 Mbps	Not in the U.S.	Most advanced CDMA upgrade.
HSDPA (High-Speed Data Packet Access)	3.5G	10 Mbps (6–7 Mbps is more realistic)	Cingular	Most advanced GSM upgrade.
			Features and Advantages	
WiBro (Wireless broadband)	4G	50 Mbps	Provides *handover functionality* and, therefore, ubiquitous connection. 4G networks will integrate wired and wireless networks to enable seamless service anytime, anywhere. Developed and launched in South Korea.	
WiMAX (IEEE 802.16e) (Worldwide Interoperability for Microwave Access)	4G	70 Mbps	Enables delivery of the *last mile* (from network to user) wireless broadband access, as an alternative to cable and DSL. The technology has a technical lead over the competition.	
LTE (Long-Term Evolution)	4G	277 Mbps	This standard is developed by the Third Generation Partnership Project (3GPP), the same standards body already responsible for the GSM, GPRS, UMTS, and HSDPA standards.	

NETWORKED DEVICES

Devices must be able to communicate with a network; they do so based on protocols. Network devices and technologies—including laptops, PDAs, cell and smartphones, wikis, intranets, extranets, GPSs, POS (point of sale) terminals, and RFID (radio frequency identification)—communicate with networks to send/receive data. This data must be rapidly collected, processed, shared, and acted upon. New feature-rich wireless devices make collaboration easier and faster. Consider these developments in networked devices and developments that point toward a more integrated, always-connected business environment and lifestyle:

• In 2007, approximately 5,000 tweets were sent per day. By mid-2010, there were more than 50 million tweets per day or 600 tweets per second.

• By 2011, over 85 percent of handsets shipped globally included some form of browser. In mature markets, such as Western Europe and Japan, approximately 60 percent of handsets shipped were smartphones with sophisticated browsing capability.

• Sprint's first 4G phone, the HTC EVO 4G, was released in summer 2010 with speeds 10 times greater than 3G phones. The handset runs a combo of EV-DO Rev. A and WiMAX, with calls still being made over CDMA and the EV-DO/WiMAX options for data.

• On its first day of sale in April 2010, approximately 300,000 iPads were sold and iPad users downloaded more than 1 million apps and over 250,000 e-books from Apple's iBooks store.

- Within 30 hours of its release in June 2007, Apple sold 270,000 iPhones. iPhones combine a mobile phone, iPod media player, and Web accessibility running on AT&T's wireless network. By October 2008, sales of iPhones had reached 10 million units.

- Mobile handsets equipped with high-speed data transfer technology (e.g., HSDPA) were introduced in 2006. **HSDPA** (high-speed downlink (or data) packet access) allows for data speeds up to 10 Mbps, as shown in Table 4.1. In January 2007, Cingular launched Motorola's V3xx, the first 3G phone for Cingular capable of running on 3.6 Mbps HSDPA. The V3xx is tri-band GSM/EDGE/HSDPA, meaning that it can run on any of those three networks, as listed in Table 4.1.

- Advances in GPS positioning and short-range wireless technologies, such as Bluetooth and Wi-Fi, can provide unprecedented intelligence. They could, for example, revolutionize traffic and road safety. Intelligent transport systems being developed by car manufacturers allow cars to communicate with each other and send alerts about sudden braking. In the event of a collision, the car's system could automatically call emergency services. The technology could also apply the brakes automatically if it was determined that two cars were getting too close to each other.

Advancements in networks, devices, and RFID sensor networks are changing enterprise information infrastructures and business environments dramatically. The preceding examples and network standards illustrate the declining need for a physical computer, as other devices provide access to data, people, or services at anytime, anywhere in the world, on high-capacity networks using IP technology. Slow wireless speeds, compared to wireline speeds, had been a constraint. 4G networks and advanced handsets operating on multiple network standards offer universal connectivity/mobility.

Mobile Network Evaluation Factors. Pressures to deliver secure service to customers and business partners at reduced costs, to be environmentally responsible, and to support the 24/7 data needs of mobile and remote workers have increased demands on corporate networks. When evaluating mobile network solutions, the factors to consider are:

1. **Simple:** Easy to deploy, manage, and use
2. **Connected:** Always makes the best connection possible
3. **Intelligent:** Works behind the scenes, easily integrating with other systems
4. **Trusted:** Enables secure and reliable communications

Review Questions

1. What is the difference between circuit switching and packet switching?
2. What is the difference between 3G and 4G?
3. What is broadband?
4. What are the mobile network standards?
5. What factors should be considered when selecting a mobile network?

4.2 Wireless Broadband Networks

Enterprises are moving away from unsystematic adoption of mobile devices and infrastructure to a strategic build-out of mobile capabilities. As the technologies that make up the mobile infrastructure evolve, identifying strategic technologies and avoiding wasted investments are difficult. But the cost and competitive pressures to do so continue to intensify. Factors contributing to mobility include the following:

- New wireless technologies and standards
- High-speed wireless networks
- Multitasking mobile devices
- More robust mobile OSs and applications

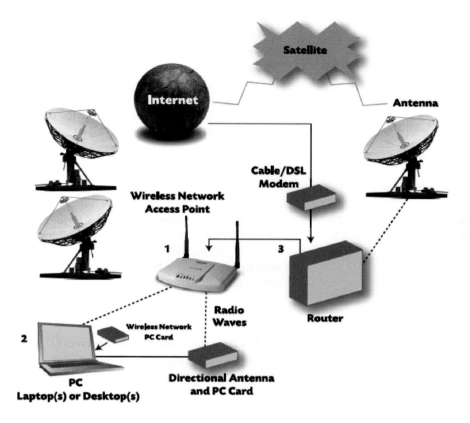

1   Radio-equipped access point connected to the internet
    (or via a router). It generates and receives radio waves
    (up to 400 feet).
2   Several client devices, equipped with PC cards, generate
    and receive radio waves.
3   Router is connected to the internet via a cable or
    DSL modem, or is connected via a satellite.

Figure 4.4 How Wi-Fi-works.

- Increased competitive pressure as others start adopting mobile technology
- Overall increased speed of business

Mobile Infrastructure. Mobile infrastructure consists of the integration of technology, software, support, security measures, and devices for the management and delivery of wireless communications.

**WI-FI NETWORKING
STANDARDS**

Wi-Fi is a technology that allows computers to share a network or Internet connection wirelessly without the need to connect to a commercial network. Wi-Fi networks beam large chunks of data over short distances using part of the radio spectrum, or they can extend over larger areas, such as municipal Wi-Fi networks. Municipal networks are not common because of huge expenses. The city of Philadelphia debated whether to go forward with its plans to install a wireless network, which would cost the 135-square-mile city $10 million to install, or about $75 per square mile. The cost for running the network the first two years would be $5 million.

Wi-Fi networks usually consist of a router, which transmits the signal, and one or more adapters, which receive the signal and are usually attached to computers. See Figure 4.4 for an overview of how Wi-Fi works. More powerful transmitters, which cover a wider area, are known as base stations. Wi-Fi networking standards are:

- **802.11b.** This standard shares spectrum with 2.4-GHz cordless phones, microwave ovens, and many Bluetooth products. Data is transferred at distances up to 300 feet.

- **802.11a.** This standard runs on 12 channels in the 5-GHz spectrum in North America, which reduces interference issues. Data is transferred about five times faster than with 802.11b, improving the quality of streaming media. It has extra bandwidth for large files. Since the 802.11a and b standards are not interoperable, data sent from an 802.11b network cannot be accessed by 802.11a networks.

- **802.11g.** This standard runs on three channels in 2.4-GHz spectrum, but at the speed of 802.11a. It is compatible with the 802.11b standard.

- **802.11n.** This standard improves on the previous 802.11 standards by adding multiple-input-multiple-output (MIMO) and many other newer features. Frequency ranges from 2.4 GHz to 5 GHz with a data rate of about 22 Mbps, but perhaps as high as 100 Mbps.

WIRELESS WIDE AREA NETWORKS (WWANS)

There are three general types of mobile networks: wide area networks (WANs), WiMAX (Worldwide Interoperability for Microwave Access), and local area networks (LANs). WANs for mobile computing are known as **WWANs (wireless wide area networks).** The breadth of coverage of a WWAN depends on the transmission media and the wireless generation, which directly affect the availability of services. Two components of mobile and wireless infrastructures are wireless local area networks and WiMAX.

WLAN (Wireless Local Area Network). WLAN is a type of local area network that uses high-frequency radio waves rather than wires to communicate between computers or devices such as printers, which are referred to as nodes on the network. A WLAN typically extends an existing wired LAN. WLANs are built by attaching a wireless access point (AP) to the edge of the wired network.

WiMAX. The WiMAX Forum (*wimaxforum.org*) describes WiMAX as "a standards-based technology enabling the delivery of last mile wireless broadband access as an alternative to cable and DSL." WiMAX is an 802.16-based broadband wireless metropolitan area network (MAN) access standard that can deliver voice and data services at distances of up to 30 miles, without the expense of cable or the distance limitations of DSL. WiMAX does not require a clear line of sight to function. Figure 4.5 shows the components of a WiMAX/Wi-Fi network.

Thirty-two percent of enterprise respondents to Forrester's *Enterprise Network and Telecommunications Survey of North America and Europe* in 2007 cited "mobile

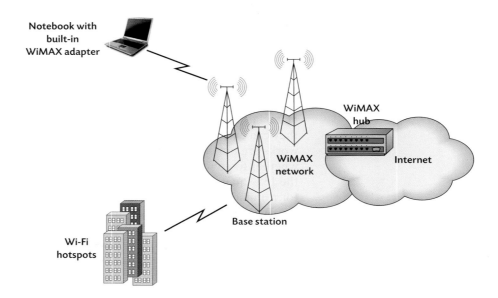

Figure 4.5 WiMAX/Wi-Fi network.

and wireless strategy and policies" as a priority (Forrester, 2007). An additional 15 percent stated that enterprise mobility is a critical priority for their business.

Review Questions

1. What factors are contributing to mobility?
2. How does Wi-Fi work?
3. What is a WLAN?
4. Why is WiMAX important?
5. What major vendors are helping drive the mobile enterprise?

4.3 Network Management and Portals

Effective communication is key to success in everything from business partnerships to personal and professional relationships. With few exceptions, when the network goes down or access is blocked, so does the ability to operate or function. Imagine a network meltdown in which you could not access the Internet, e-mail, voice-mail, software, and data files. At most companies, employees would have nothing to do without network connectivity. Obvious damages when a company cannot operate or fulfill orders include lost sales and productivity, financial consequences from not being able to send and receive payments, and inability to process payroll and inventory.

MODEL OF THE NETWORK, COLLABORATION, AND PERFORMANCE RELATIONSHIP

In the 21st century, performance depends on the capabilities and qualities of networks and collaboration technologies. Figure 4.6 presents a model of key network and collaboration factors that influence profitability, sales growth, and ability to innovate.

As the model in Figure 4.6 illustrates, an enterprise's network capability depends on proper planning, maintenance, management, upgrades, and bandwidth of the

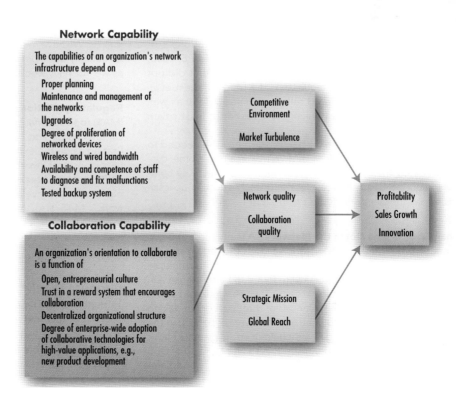

Figure 4.6 Model of network, collaboration, and performance relationship.

network to ensure that it has sufficient capacity and connectivity to link people, locations, and data. It also requires that those who need to access the network be equipped with the devices making it possible to do so. As a comparison, a highway system needs to be planned carefully to support peak traffic demands, monitored for compliance with driving rules, cleaned and maintained regularly, and expanded (upgraded) when it no longer meets the needs of those who rely on it.

When problems inevitably occur (e.g., a network crash or car crash), trained staff are needed to restore the network promptly or to switch to a backup system to minimize disruption during the restoration. *IT at Work 4.1* illustrates the importance of these factors and the consequences of bad planning and testing.

The network architecture is certainly critical because it provides the infrastructure for collaborative work within the company and with external partners and customers, regardless of their location. Often overlooked is the fact that the capability and willingness to collaborate depend on a corporate culture that people trust and that gives them the information, tools, and authority to plan and make decisions. When knowledge workers have such authority, the organization has a decentralized (also called *flatter*) organizational structure. A decentralized organization is more responsive to opportunities and problems than a centralized organization where top-level managers, who are typically less involved in day-to-day operations, make decisions.

The purpose of this model is to illustrate that network infrastructure alone does not improve business performance. Rather, what matters is how network capabilities combine with collaboration technologies to support employees and cross-functional work, connect remote locations, service customers, and coordinate with supply chain partners.

IT at Work 4.1

Monetary Authority of Singapore (MAS) Takes Action Against DBS Bank for Network Crash

DBS Bank, one of Singapore's largest financial institutions, suffered from a massive computer network crash on July 5, 2010, resulting in millions of dollars lost to transactions that did not push through. The network failure was the bank's largest ever, crippling over 1,000 automated teller machines (ATMs) as well as its Internet- and mobile-banking services for at least seven hours.

The outage frustrated many bank customers who needed to access online-banking services and ATMs urgently. Some customers vented their frustration on social media sites. Key complaints included being left cashless and unable to top up cash cards to pay for Electronic Road Pricing (ERP).

Human Error Brings Down the Network. A faulty cable and two engineers (from their IT vendor) who ignored the required steps to change the cable—and used the wrong procedure multiple times at DBS Bank's data center—were found to be the cause. On the fifth attempt, the data-storage system, which was linked to the mainframe computer by the faulty cable, shut itself down, taking the entire network with it. DBS had several layers of backup in the event of a failure, but the engineers' chain of errors over a 30-hour time period defeated those defenses. Piyush Gupta, CEO of DBS Group Holdings, reported: "Actually we have very good safe-

guards. We have multiple redundancies built into our systems and it's actually quite perplexing that the redundancies did not kick in as we normally would expect it to."

Regulatory Actions. The Monetary Authority of Singapore (MAS) took supervisory action and imposed an extra $230 million capital charge and censure against DBS for the network failure. Setting aside the extra capital reduces the bank's ability to make new loans and investments. In a stern statement, MAS said that DBS's systems breakdown "arose in part from the failure of the bank to put in place a robust technology risk management framework." MAS also instructed DBS to adopt additional security measures so that it would no longer "overly rely on a single service provider or a single vendor's products and services."

Sources: Compiled from Tan (2010), Ng (2010), and MAS (2010).

Discussion Questions:

1. Identify all the types of costs and losses that DBS suffered as a result of their network crash.

2. DBS relied on its IT vendor to fix a faulty cable, but MAS held DBS accountable for the crash. Do you agree that DBS should have been held accountable? Explain.

CONVERGENCE AND INTEROPERABILITY OF INFORMATION SERVICES

Various information services—data, documents, voice, and video—have functioned independently of each other. Traditionally, they were transmitted using different protocols (standards) and carried on either packet-switched or circuit-switched networks, as shown in Table 4.2. Multiple networks were needed because of the lack of **interoperability** or connectivity between devices. Interoperability refers to the ability to provide services to and accept services from other systems or devices. Lack of interoperability limited access to information and computing and communications resources—and increased costs. Technical details on interoperability and networking protocols are in Technology Guide 4 (TG4) on the book's Web site.

TCP/IP Architecture. The Internet protocol suite is the standard used with almost any network service. The Internet protocol suite consists of the IP (Internet Protocol) and TCP (Transmission Control Protocol), or TCP/IP. TCP/IP refers to the whole protocol family.

IP is the single most popular network protocol in the world, and it provides the architecture that made convergence possible. In preparation for transmission, data and documents are digitized into packets based on the Internet protocol and sent via packet-switched computer networks or **local area networks,** called **LANs.** LANs connect network devices over a relatively short distance. LANs are capable of transmitting data at very fast rates but operate in a limited area, such as an office building, campus, or home. They provide shared access to printers and file servers and connect to larger networks, such as **wide area networks (WANs)** or the Internet. WANs cover a much larger geographic area, such as a state, province, or country.

A comparison of the basic network protocols is presented in Table 4.2. Packets of data are transmitted using TCP. TCP does error checking to provide reliable delivery. If any packets are dropped along the way and never arrive at the destination,

TABLE 4.2	Networks, Protocols, and Transfer Methods of Information Services			
Information Service	Network	Format	Protocol	Transfer Method
Data and documents	Packet	Converted to packets based on Internet Protocol (IP).	TCP (Transmission Control Protocol)	Each packet can take a different route to the destination, where the packets are recompiled. If a packet does not arrive (gets dropped), the entire transmission is re-sent. For non-real-time data, documents, or e-mail, TCP provides for error correction, packet sequencing, and retransmission.
Voice	Circuit	Sent as analog signals between the telephone and telco's central office (*local loop*). Traffic between central offices is digital.		Whether analog or digital, each call creates a circuit that reserves a channel between two parties for the entire session. The entire message follows the same path in order.
Video streams	Packet	Compressed and converted to IP packets.	UDP (User Datagram Protocol)	Real-time data transfer with no checking for missing packets. Bad packets are dropped.
Voice over IP, or IP telephony	Packet	Voice communication is digitized into data packets.	Typically UDP, though sometimes TCP	Real-time. TCP/IP error checking is inappropriate for voice. Requesting retransmission because of dropped packets would delay and ruin the conversation.

TCP will request that the packets be re-sent. For data and document delivery, error checking is necessary to ensure that all content has been delivered. Since the error-checking process can cause delivery delays, TCP is not well suited for digital voice or video transmissions. For those transmissions, a dropped packet would be insignificant.

Voice that is sent as analog signals, or audio sound waves, is sent over circuits on circuit-switched telephone networks. Video streams are compressed and sent as IP packets using the **User Datagram Protocol (UDP).** This suite of protocols is referred to as the UDP/IP model. UDP does not check for errors; as a result, it has less overhead and is faster than connection-oriented protocols such as TCP. With UDP, the quality of the transmission (lack of errors) is sacrificed for speed. Compared to TCP, UDP sends packets much faster, but less reliably.

Voice over IP (VoIP), or **IP telephony,** involves an analog-to-digital conversion. With VoIP, voice and data transmissions travel over telephone wires, but the content is sent as data packets. VoIP has grown to become one of the most used and cost effective ways to communicate. IP telephony solutions make use of packet-switched connections from the Internet for the exchange of voice, fax, and other data formats instead of using the traditional dedicated circuit-switched connections. Benefits including cost savings, improved productivity, flexibility, and advanced features, make IP telephony an appealing technology.

IP telephony is evolving beyond basic telephony upgrades as enterprises look for increased flexibility and mobile solutions for their workers and business processes. It is more expensive to operate and manage two separate networks. A converged network that combines voice and data traffic on the same IP infrastructure could reduce administrative costs, while providing an easier path for growth and new applications. *IT at Work 4.2* explains the value of convergence and IP telephony at Thrifty Car Rental.

IT at Work 4.2

IS MKT OM

Thrifty Caters to Cost-Conscious Travelers

Thrifty Car Rental (*thrifty.com*) is one of the world's largest car rental companies that operates through corporate-owned and franchised stores. Thrifty operates at more than 1,200 locations in 70 countries and is one of the most widely recognized brands in the travel industry, catering to cost conscious business and leisure travelers.

Catering to Rate Shoppers. More than 30 percent of Thrifty's callers were rate shoppers. Agents spent too much of their time answering questions about car rates, which customers could have done for themselves using an automated self-help system or Web site. The company wanted to cut back on the use of agents, but still provide excellent customer service.

Rate checking and reservations at thrifty.com were growing rapidly. But the Web site did not offer the same level of high-quality customer service available by telephone. The company wanted to improve its Web-based customer service and differentiate from other car rental providers in its price-sensitive market.

Integrated Customer Service Solution. Its new customer-contact solution integrated human help with automated, self-help

services across all channels of interaction—phone, Web, chat, and e-mail. To integrate these channels and provide intelligent contact management, Thrifty invested in Cisco's **unified messaging (UM)** technology. UM brings together all messaging media such as e-mail, voice, mobile text, SMS, and fax into a combined communications medium. For example, UM can give users the ability to retrieve and send voice, fax, and e-mail messages from a single interface, such as handhelds or PCs.

Thrifty installed Web Collaboration Option, which enables customers to interact with agents over the Web, while conducting a voice conversation or text chat. Thrifty receives four million calls per year that require 150 agents in its two customer contact locations during regular seasons and 180 during the peak summer season. With the UM solution, between 35 and 40 fewer agents are required. Employee turnover has dropped to 20 percent from a high of 40 percent since installing the Cisco solution.

Sources: Compiled from Thrifty (*thrifty.com*) and Cisco Systems (*Cisco.com*).

Discussion Questions: Why did Thrifty Car Rental need UM? What costs were reduced or eliminated by the new IT solution?

**BARRIERS TO FULL
INTEGRATION OF
INFORMATION SERVICES**

Users will increasingly have the option to take broadband connections with them via *full-service broadband*—anytime, anywhere access from the screen or device of choice. While worldwide growth in wireline (wired) and wireless telecommunications (telecom) is forecasted to remain steady, the growth rate of wireless is eight times greater than the growth rate of wireline. Wireline usage will still be widely used because VoIP will lessen the migration to wireless.

Developing software for wireless devices had been challenging because there was no widely accepted standard for wireless devices. Therefore, software applications had to be customized for each type of device with which the application communicated. To keep down the cost of wireless services, software engineers have had to develop code that optimizes resource usage. Supporting different displays can force painstaking changes to multiple software modules and applications. Different CPUs, operating systems, storage media, and mobile platform environments create time-consuming porting and testing issues.

The Internet and WWW. Many people believe that the Web is synonymous with the Internet, but that is not the case. The Internet functions as the *transport mechanism*, and the Web (WWW) is an *application* that runs on the Internet, as do e-mail, IM, and VoIP. The Web is a system with universally accepted protocols for storing, retrieving, formatting, and displaying information via client/server architecture. The usual protocol is HTTP, which stands for hyper-text transport protocol.

Internet Application Categories. The Internet supports applications in the following categories:

• **Discovery or search.** Discovery involves browsing, finding, and retrieving information. It can involve querying, downloading, and processing information from databases. Software agents to contend with the vast information on the Internet and intranets can automate discovery.
• **Communication.** Developments in Internet-based and wireless communication such as podcasting, RSS, and micro-blogging are transforming business communications, marketing channels, and supply chain management—to name a few.
• **Collaboration.** Online collaboration between individuals, groups, and organizations is common. Numerous tools and technologies are available, ranging from online meetings with screen sharing to videoconferencing and group support systems. Collaboration software products, called groupware or workflow, can be used on the Internet and other networks.

**NETWORK COMPUTING
INFRASTRUCTURES**

In addition to the Internet and Web, intranets, extranets, information portals, and enterprise search engines are major infrastructures of network computing.

Intranets. An intranet is a network serving the internal informational needs of a company, using Internet tools. Intranets are portals (gateways) that provide easy and inexpensive browsing and search capabilities. Enterprise search engines are discussed later in this section. Using screen sharing and other groupware tools, intranets can be used to facilitate collaboration. Companies deliver policies and pay stub information for direct deposits, benefits, training materials, and news to their employers via their intranets.

IT at Work 4.3 describes Labatt Brewing Company's use of an intranet portal, named The Pub, for enterprise collaboration and search. The Pub was built using Microsoft Office SharePoint Server (MOSS) and Microsoft SharePoint Services (MSS). **SharePoint** is an integrated suite of capabilities that provides content (unstructured information) management and **enterprise search** to support collaboration.

IT at Work 4.3

The Pub, a Beer Information Portal

Labatt Breweries of Canada is part of Belgium-based Interbrew S.A., one of the largest brewing groups in the world, with more than 180 types of beer available in over 110 countries worldwide. And Labatt Blue is the best-selling Canadian beer in the world.

Traditionally, Labatt used employee meetings and postings on bulletin boards to keep employees informed. But with employees spread across Canada, delivering information to employees in a consistent and timely manner was challenging and expensive. Corporate information had been tough to find and share because it was stored in data silos belonging to various business units. The solution was to leverage the power of the SharePoint platform to build a world-class intranet portal.

Single Point of Data Access. After determining Labatt's business and IT requirements, the IT team decided that an intranet would provide the most efficient way for employees to access data. The intranet, which was named "The Pub," was built using Microsoft Content Management Server, Microsoft Office SharePoint Portal Server, and SharePoint Team Services.

Using The Pub, Labatt rolled out new programs to its employees, such as the *Innovation Database*. Labatt wanted innovative ways to improve every aspect of the business, and the Innovation Database provides a forum for employees to submit ideas and receive recognition and rewards for ideas that are implemented. About 70 percent of Labatt's employees use the portal, which has significantly improved productivity and collaboration across the board. With the robust search function within The Pub, employees are able to quickly locate the documents they need and obtain the information they require to make better business decisions.

Sources: Compiled from *Labatt.com*, Microsoft case study *Labatt Breweries of Canada*, and Imason (2010).

Discussion Questions: How do information silos block productivity? Why was a single point of access an important feature? How has sharing information via The Pub improved collaboration at Labatt?

An enterprise search system provides extensive capabilities for searching structured and unstructured data sources easily. The enterprise search system provides fast query response times and consolidated, ranked results (like the results of a Google search) that help users easily locate the information they need. Other elements of SharePoint are:

• Browser-based collaboration and document management platform.

• Content management system that allows groups to set up a centralized, password-protected space for document sharing. Documents can be stored, downloaded and edited, then uploaded for continued sharing.

• Web-based intranet that can improve management of and access to data.

• Enterprise information portal that can be configured to run intranet, extranet, and Internet sites.

Extranets. An extranet is a private, company-owned network that uses IP technology to securely share part of a business's information or operations with suppliers, vendors, partners, customers, or other businesses. Extranets can use virtual private networks (VPNs). VPNs are created using specialized software and hardware to encrypt/send/decrypt transmissions over the Internet. By encrypting transmissions, a VPN creates a private tunnel within the Internet or other public network, as shown in Figure 4.7. A VPN connects remote sites or users together privately. Instead of using a dedicated, physical connection such as a leased line, a VPN uses virtual connections routed through the Internet from the company's private network to the remote site or employee.

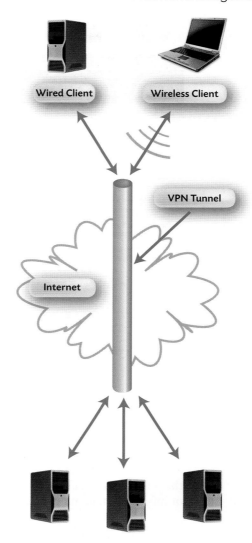

Figure 4.7 Virtual private network (VPN) created by encryption.

Basically, an extranet is a network that connects two or more companies so they can securely share information. In some cases, an extranet is an extension of the company's intranet that is designed to connect to a customer or trading partner for B2B commerce. In other cases, an extranet is a restricted portal that, for example, gives account customers instant access to their account details. In this way, customers can manage their own accounts quickly and easily. United Rentals' extranet portal at *URdata.UR.com* makes it convenient for account customers worldwide to request equipment, manage rental equipment by project, view invoices, calculate job costs, and so on—and at lower cost. Figure 4.8 illustrates the interface of an extranet, the use of usernames and passwords for access control and authentication, and self-help features.

Extranets usually have a central server that stores data, documents, and applications. Authorized users can remotely access them from any Internet-enabled device, which can drastically reduce storage space on individual hard drives. To protect the privacy of the information being transmitted, extranets need secure communication lines, encryption technologies, and access and authentication control.

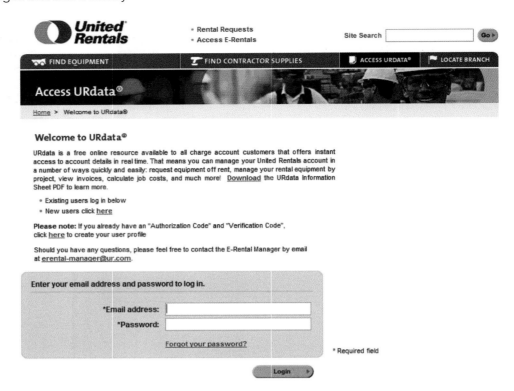

Figure 4.8 United Rentals' extranet portal.

ENTERPRISE SEARCH

As companies produce, store, and consume more and more business information, volume grows and the cost of managing it increases. Most content is difficult to manage and access. Fulcrum Research claims that 80 percent of enterprise content is unstructured—stored in Word documents, spreadsheets, and pdfs. Forrester Research estimates that content volume is growing at a rate of 200 percent a year. At this rate, the volume of data stored in many organizations reaches the point where the levels of information actually interfere with productivity rather than contribute to it.

What's Involved in Enterprise Search. Enterprise search (see Figure 4.9) starts with **content indexing,** which is created by software that crawls through directories

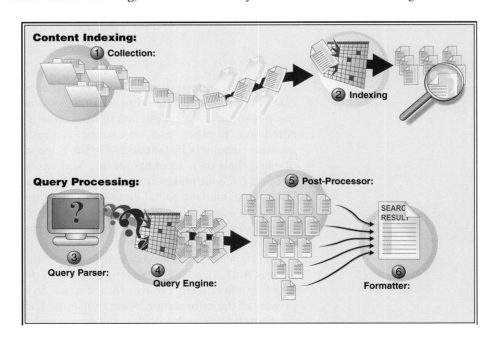

Figure 4.9 Overview of enterprise search.

and Web sites to extract content from databases and other repositories. Content indexing is done on a regular basis, so if one of those repositories is updated, the search engine will have some sort of procedure that enables it to go in and source and index that updated content.

Content that's been collected is *indexed*. That is, a searchable index of all the content is created. Additional processing, such as metadata extraction and autosummarization, might be done, depending on the search engine that is used.

Once the index is created, it can be queried—just as users do Google searches of the Internet. For example, to query an enterprise, a user enters search terms into a search box on the intranet screen. Of course, what matters is not how searchable the enterprise's content is, but finding the content that is needed.

INFORMATION PORTALS

Challenges facing workers are information overload and information scatter—huge amounts of information scattered across numerous documents, e-mail messages, and databases at different locations and in different systems. Accessing relevant, accurate, and complete information is time-consuming and requires access to multiple systems. To minimize wasting employee time, companies use portals. A **portal** (or information portal) is a Web-based gateway to content on a network, as you read in *IT at Work 4.3* about Labatt's intranet portal. Portals can include discussion boards, document sharing, and workspaces. Users can upload presentations or documents to share with peers.

It is estimated that Internet searchers are successful at finding what they seek only 50 percent of the time or less. Not surprisingly, the same problem applies to intranets. Consequently, companies incur the costs of time wasted searching for information that could not be found and then re-creating it—and costs arising from not being able to use existing information at the time it was needed.

Review Questions

1. How might a company's business performance be affected by its network's capabilities?
2. What are the benefits of an IP-based network?
3. What is a virtual private network (VPN)?
4. What is the difference between an extranet and an intranet?
5. What is enterprise search?
6. What is an information portal?

4.4 Collaboration

Collaboration is a key driver of overall performance in companies worldwide, according to the study "Meetings Around the World: The Impact of Collaboration on Business Performance." The survey was conducted by Frost & Sullivan and sponsored by Verizon Business and Microsoft Corp (Frost and Sullivan, 2006). The impact of collaboration on performance was twice as significant as a company's aggressiveness in pursuing new market opportunities (its strategic orientation) and five times as significant as the external market environment. The study also showed that while there is a global culture of collaboration, there are regional differences in how people in various countries prefer to communicate. Of all of the collaboration technologies that were studied, Web conferencing (also known as Web-based meetings) was used more extensively in high-performing companies than in low-performing ones. These results make sense when combined with estimates from *NetworkWorld* (*networkworld.com*) that 90 percent of employees work away from their company's headquarters and 40 percent work at a remote location, away from their supervisors.

Several factors are driving the need for messaging and collaboration. People need to work together and share documents. Groups make most of the complex decisions in organizations. And organizational decision making is difficult when team members are geographically spread out and working in different time zones. Nearly 87 percent of employees around the world work in remote offices.

Messaging and collaboration tools include older communications media such as e-mail, videoconferencing, fax, and IM—and newer media such as blogs, podcasts, RSS, wikis, VoIP, Web meetings, and torrents (for sharing very large files). As media move to IP, there will not be much left that is not converged onto data networks. One of the biggest components of many Web 2.0 sites and technologies is collaboration. Much of Web 2.0 is about harnessing the knowledge and work of many people.

VIRTUAL COLLABORATION

Leading businesses are quickly realizing the benefits of e-collaboration. For example, the real estate franchiser RE/MAX uses an e-collaboration platform to improve communications and collaboration among its nationwide network of independently owned real estate franchises, sales associates, and suppliers. Similarly, Marriott International, the world's largest hospitality company, started with an online brochure and then developed a collaborative e-commerce system that links corporations, franchisees, partners, suppliers, and customers around the world. There are many examples of collaboration.

Information Sharing Between Retailers and Their Suppliers: P&G and Walmart. One of the most publicized examples of information sharing is between Procter & Gamble (P&G) and Walmart. Walmart provides P&G access to sales information on every item Walmart buys from P&G. The information is collected by P&G on a daily basis from every Walmart store, and P&G uses the information to manage the inventory replenishment for Walmart.

Retailer–Supplier Collaboration: Asda Corporation. Supermarket chain Asda (*asda.com*) has begun rolling out Web-based electronic data interchange (EDI) technology to 650 suppliers. Web-EDI technology is based on the AS2 standard, an internationally accepted HTTP-based protocol used to send real-time data in multiple formats securely over the Internet. It promises to improve the efficiency and speed of traditional EDI communications, which route data over third-party value-added networks (VANs).

Lower Transportation and Inventory Costs and Reduced Stockouts: Unilever. Unilever's 30 contract carriers deliver 250,000 truckloads of shipments annually. Unilever's Web-based database, the Transportation Business Center (TBC), provides these carriers with site specification requirements when they pick up a shipment at a manufacturing or distribution center or when they deliver goods to retailers. TBC gives carriers all of the vital information they need: contact names and phone numbers, operating hours, the number of dock doors at a location, the height of the dock doors, how to make an appointment to deliver or pick up shipments, pallet configuration, and other special requirements. All mission-critical information that Unilever's carriers need to make pickups, shipments, and deliveries is now available electronically 24/7.

Reduction of Product Development Time: Caterpillar, Inc. Caterpillar, Inc. (*caterpillar.com*) is a multinational heavy-machinery manufacturer. In the traditional mode of operation, cycle time along the supply chain was long because the process involved paper-document transfers among managers, salespeople, and technical staff. To solve the problem, Caterpillar connected its engineering and manufacturing divisions with its active suppliers, distributors, overseas factories, and customers, through an extranet-based global collaboration system. By means of the collaboration system, a request for a customized tractor component, for example, can be transmitted from a customer to a Caterpillar dealer and on to designers and suppliers, all in a very short time. Customers can also use the extranet to retrieve and modify detailed order information while the vehicle is still on the assembly line.

GROUP WORK AND DECISION PROCESSES

Managers and staff continuously make decisions. They design and manufacture products, plan marketing strategies, develop policies, prepare financial statements, determine how to meet compliance mandates, design software, and so on. By design or default, group processes emerge, and those processes can be productive or they can be dysfunctional.

Group Decision Processes. Group work involves processes that can be quite complex depending on the task, human factors, and available decision support. Some characteristics of group work are:

- Group members may be located in different places or work at different times.
- Group members may work for the same or for different organizations.
- A group can be at a single managerial level or span several levels.
- There can be synergy (process and task gains) or conflict in group work.
- There can be gains and/or losses in productivity from group work.
- Some of the needed data, information, or knowledge may be located in many sources, several of which are external to the organization.
- The expertise of non-team members may be needed.
- Groups perform many tasks; however, groups of managers and analysts concentrate frequently on decision making.

Despite the long history and benefits of collaborative work, groups are not always successful. Process gains and losses from group work are listed in Tables 4.3 and 4.4.

TABLE 4.3	Benefits of Working in Groups, or Process Gains

- It provides learning. Groups are better than individuals at understanding problems.
- People readily take ownership and responsibility of problems and their solutions.
- Group members have their egos embedded in the decision, so they will be committed to the solution.
- Groups are better than individuals at catching errors.
- A group has more information (knowledge) than any one member. Groups can leverage this knowledge to create new knowledge. More creative alternatives for problem solving can be generated, and better solutions can be derived (e.g., through stimulation).
- A group may produce synergy during problem solving. The effectiveness or quality of group work can be greater than the sum of what is produced by independent individuals.
- Working in a group may stimulate the creativity of the participants and process.
- A group may have better and more precise communication working together.

TABLE 4.4	Dysfunctions of the Group Process, or Process Losses

- Social pressures to conform may result in groupthink. Groupthink refers to team members thinking alike, being intolerant of new or different ideas, or otherwise yielding to pressure to conform.
- Group work is a time-consuming serial process since only one member can speak at a time.
- Meetings can lack coordination and be poorly planned.
- Group members can display inappropriate behaviors, e.g., dominating a topic or the meeting time or fear of contributing because of groupthink.
- Group members can have a tendency to either dominate the agenda or free-ride by relying on others to do most of the work.
- Some members may be afraid to speak up.
- Groups have a tendency to produce compromised solutions of poor quality.
- These can be nonproductive times due to socializing, waiting for latecomers, or air-time fragmentation.
- Group members can have a tendency to repeat what was already said.
- Meetings can be costly because of travel, participation, and so on.

Improving Meeting Processes and Small-Group Dynamics. Meetings are a universal—and universally disliked—part of business operations. More and more companies are team-based (e.g., project management teams), with most work being done in meetings. Meetings can be more effective if one understands what can go wrong and intelligently manages decision processes and group dynamics to avoid problems. For example, newly formed groups whose members do not know each other have very different dynamics than groups with an established history and routine, and they need more socialization time before they become productive. Researchers have developed methods for improving the processes of group work, namely, increasing the benefits of meetings and minimizing the detriments. Some of these methods are known as group dynamics. The challenges of group work processes are more intense for virtual teams, as described in *IT at Work 4.4*. Virtual teams are groups of people who work interdependently with shared purpose across space, time, and organization boundaries, using technology to communicate and collaborate.

COLLABORATION SUPPORT TECHNOLOGIES

Enterprise collaboration tools have been popular for over a decade. Portals, intranets, extranets, and shared workspaces are examples. Lotus Notes, for example, has been around for over 10 years. More recent technologies—Web 2.0 or Enterprise 2.0 technologies such as wikis, blogs, and microblogs—provide more options to promote and support enterprise collaboration. These newer tools have a number of benefits—like a community-oriented paradigm and no software to install. However, Web 2.0 tools have not significantly displaced e-mail or texting, which remain the primary enterprise collaboration tools for information workers. Studies show e-mail and texts are used on an hourly basis.

Google Wave. **Google Wave** is a new type of platform consisting of e-mail, instant messaging, and documents. Google is positioning Wave as "what e-mail would look like if it were invented today." Google Wave attempts to be a complete collaboration solution, to solve this paradox, but its answer is currently incomplete. See *wave. google.com/* for the latest on Google Wave features.

What is a wave? According to Google, a wave is equal parts conversation and document. People can communicate and work together with richly formatted text, photos, videos, maps, and more. A wave is shared in that any participant can reply anywhere in the message, edit the content, and add participants at any point in the process. Playback is a feature that lets anyone rewind the wave to see who said what and when. Lastly, a wave is live. Participants can see what others are typing as they type, making conversations faster.

IT at Work 4.4

Subaru Uses WebEx for Online Training and Meetings

SVR   GLOBAL

When Subaru entered the luxury car market, the auto manufacturer needed to improve its level of customer service. Subaru launched the Owner Loyalty Program (OLP) to meet the needs of a high-end market that expects premium customer service. OLP focuses on predicting and fostering customer loyalty, which requires providing training to 600 dealerships. In order to have one person providing such extensive training, Subaru implemented the WebEx Training Center (*webex.com*). Using WebEx, the OLP trainer was able to reach 2,400 dealers within six months at a low cost of $0.75 per person.

WebEx Enterprise Edition was integrated throughout the organization for a variety of purposes. For instance, the IT department uses WebEx for internal application training, while regional vice presidents and training managers use Meeting Center to conduct meetings with dealers and salespeople located throughout large geographical territories. Subaru Service Technical Trainers also use WebEx to deliver diagnoses and just-in-time trainings to dealership technicians.

WebEx has improved efficiency, helped the company strengthen its dealer relationships, and positively impacted its customer loyalty program.

Information Content and Context. Storing content is not enough. Content needs to remain related to its context. Content management tools are emerging to manage content in context for regulatory reasons, such as to enable an audit trail of work done and to support enterprise search and organizational learning.

Review Questions

1. What is virtual collaboration?
2. Why is group work challenging?
3. What are the benefits of working in groups?
4. What are the dysfunctions of group processes?
5. What is Google Wave?
6. How are information content and context related?

4.5 Legal and Ethical Issues

Management needs to consider ethical and social issues, such as quality of working life. Workers will experience both positive and negative impacts from being linked to a 24/7 workplace environment, working in computer-contrived virtual teams, and being connected to handhelds whose impact on health can be damaging. A 2008 study by Solutions Research Group found that always being connected is a borderline obsession for many people. According to the study, 68 percent of Americans may suffer from disconnect anxiety—feelings of disorientation and nervousness when deprived of Internet or wireless access for a period of time. The study also found that 63 percent of BlackBerry users admitted to having sent a message from the bathroom. Technology addiction has gone so far that U.S. psychiatrists are considering adding this "compulsive-impulsive" disorder to the next release of the DSM (*Diagnostic and Statistical Manual of Mental Disorders*) in 2011. Approximately 25 percent of people stayed connected with work while on vacation in summer 2008, which was about double what it had been in 2006, according to a CareerBuilder.com survey (Perelman, 2008).

Consider these developments and their implications:

- **Debate over DWD** (Driving While Distracted). Several studies show cell phones are a leading cause of car crashes. Yet driving while talking, or DWD, is not illegal. It is estimated that cell phone–distracted drivers are four times more likely to be in a car wreck. Laws have been passed to discourage drivers from cell phone use when they should be paying attention to safety. The hands-free July 2008 California law is not expected to solve the problem of car accidents due to cell phone distractions based on New York City's lack of improvement after having had a hands-free law for several years. At any given moment, more than 10 million U.S. drivers are talking on handheld cell phones, according to the National Highway Traffic Safety Administration (*NHTSA.dot.gov*). Why is this a problem? Cell phones are a known distraction, and the NHTSA has determined that driver inattention is a primary or contributing factor in as many as 25 percent of all police-reported traffic accidents. This doesn't include the thousands of accidents that *are not* reported to the authorities.

- **Health risks.** The U.S. Food and Drug Administration (FDA) recommends minimizing potential risk by using hands-free devices and keeping cell phone talk to a minimum. A few studies have indicated that using a cell phone for an hour each day over a 10-year period can increase the risk of developing a rare brain tumor and that those tumors are more likely to be on the side of the head used to talk on the phone. More research is needed in this area.

- **RF emissions and SAR.** According to the Cellular Telecommunications Industry Association (*ctia.org/*), **specific absorption rate,** or **SAR,** is "a way of measuring the quantity of radio frequency (RF) energy that is absorbed by the body." For a phone to pass Federal Communications Commission (FCC) certification and be sold in the United States, its maximum SAR level must be less than 1.6 watts per kilogram (1.6 W/kg). Canada has the same (1.6 W/kg) cap as the United States. In Europe, the maximum level is 2 watts per kilogram. The SAR level that is reported shows the highest SAR level measured with the phone next to the ear as tested by the FCC. Keep in mind that SAR levels can vary between different transmission bands (the same phone can use multiple bands during a call) and that different testing bodies can obtain different results. Also, it's possible for results to vary between different models of the same phone, such as a handset that's offered by multiple carriers. In March 2010, Apple had banned an iPhone app that measures cell phone radiation (*news.cnet.com/8301-17852_3-10464388-71.html*), but other online sources of SAR are available.

The importance of understanding ethical issues has been recognized by the Association to Advance Collegiate Schools of Business (AACSB International, *aacsb.edu*). For business majors, the AACSB International has defined Assurance of Learning Requirements for ethics at both the undergraduate and graduate levels. In *Standard 15: Management of Curricula* (AACSB Accreditation Standards, 2006), AACSB identifies general knowledge and skill learning experiences that include "ethical understanding and reasoning abilities" at the undergraduate level. At the graduate level, *Standard 15* requires learning experiences in management—specific knowledge and skill areas are to include "ethical and legal responsibilities in organizations and society" (AACSB International Ethics Education Resource Center, 2006).

Life Out of Control. The technologies covered in this chapter blur work, social, and personal time. IT keeps people connected with no real off-switch. Tools that are meant to improve the productivity and quality of life in general can also intrude on personal time. Managers need to be aware of the huge potential for abuse by expecting 24/7 response from workers. See *IT at Work 4.5* for a look at life in a connected world.

IT at Work 4.5

Power of the Individual in the Connected Age

Communication technologies—writing, printing, cable, telephone, radio, and TV—have always played a central role in human history. Changes brought about by the Internet are as profound as previous historic milestones such as the Renaissance or Industrial Revolution. Every person can be a creative artist and freely distribute work to millions—characteristics of both the Renaissance and Industrial Revolution. Google's existence shows the power of the individual in the connected age—a better research tool than major corporations had in the 1990s. VoIP, wikis, and WiMAX enable anyone to call or share files for free.

Major companies face small but powerful challenges and competitors that are undermining traditional business models. Consumers and employees can counteract marketing strategies by posting harsh criticisms in blogs or social media. eBay shops can underprice. Intranets, extranets, and social networks are diminishing perimeters between companies and individuals' lives—and making them more transparent. People check Internet resources for ratings and prices before they buy books, vacations, cars, and so on. Amazingly, in places such as Tanzania, political activists worked on a new constitution using a wiki. Communication and collaboration tools can collectively create a compelling force whose impacts are not yet known.

Businesses have to learn to cope with a world that is far more competitive, dynamic, and connected.

Discussion Questions: How has the use of communication tools impacted your ability to get your work done? How has it impacted your personal life? How has IT been liberating or overwhelming? What ethical issue does this raise for managers?

Key Terms

3G *96*
4G *96*
bandwidth *95*
broadband *96*
circuit switching *94*
content indexing *108*
converged network *104*
download speed *96*
EDGE *97*
enterprise search *105*
EV-DO *97*
EV-DV *97*
extranet *106*
fixed-line broadband *96*
Google Wave *112*

GSM (Global System for
  Mobile Communications) *97*
HSDPA high-speed downlink *98*
interoperability *103*
intranet *105*
IP network *96*
IP telephony *104*
LTE *97*
mobile broadband *96*
packet *95*
packet switching *95*
portal *109*
protocol *95*
SAR (specific absorption rate) *114*
SharePoint *105*

TCP/IP *95*
Transmission Control
  Protocol (TCP) *95*
upload speed *96*
unified messaging (UM) *104*
User Datagram Protocol (UDP) *104*
voice over IP (VoIP) *104*
WAN (wide area network) *103*
Wi-Fi *99*
WiMAX *100*
wireless access point (WAP) *95*
WLAN (wireless local area
  network) *100*
WWWANs (wireless wide area
  networks) *100*

Chapter Highlights and Insights

(Numbers refer to Learning Objectives)

❶ In preparation for transmission, data and documents are converted into digital packets based on the Internet Protocol (IP) and sent via computer (i.e., packet-switched) networks or LANs.

❶ Data, voice, and video networks are converging into a single network based on packet technology, such as IP and VoIP.

❷ Real-time awareness, provided by Web-based collaboration solutions, can significantly improve the outcome of complex operations involving numerous remote or mobile workers.

❷ Convergence eliminates the need for separate networks. When all information services are handled the same way by one high-speed packet network, the technical barriers to collaborative work are eliminated. Multimedia applications become possible because the network does not restrict the kinds of computing devices that could be used.

❷ Broadband wireless computing allows users to collaborate via the Internet at any time, share files, or perform other group work functions that previously required a PC and wireline infrastructure.

❸ The major drivers of mobile computing are large numbers of users of mobile devices, especially cell phones; widespread use of cell phones throughout the world; new vendor products; declining prices; increasing bandwidth; and the explosion of collaboration tools.

❸ Intranets distribute frequently needed employee handbooks, government forms, policies, and other materials to employees over the company network.

❸ An extranet connects the company with its customers or trading partners for B2B commerce and real-time supply chain

management. Extranets give account customers instant access to their account details.

❸ Wireless technology can give a company a competitive advantage through increased productivity, better customer care, and more timely communication and information exchange.

❸ VoIP can be customized as a strategic tool because of its virtualization, customization, and intelligence capabilities. Location-based advertising and advertising via SMSs on a very large scale is expected.

❸ Mobile portals provide multimedia broadcasts and other content (e.g., news and sports) to billions.

❹ Messaging and collaboration tools include older media such as e-mail, videoconferencing, fax, and IM—and new media such as podcasts, RSS newsfeeds, wikis, VoIP, Web meetings, and torrents (for sharing very large files). As media move to IP, there will not be much left that is not converged onto data networks.

❺ Managers and staff continuously make decisions: They design and manufacture products, develop policies and strategies, prepare financial statements, determine how to meet compliance mandates, design software, and so on.

❺ Collaboration and communication technologies covered in this chapter blur work, social, and personal time. IT keeps people connected with no real off-switch. Tools that are meant to improve the productivity and quality of life in general can also intrude on personal time. Managers need to be aware of the huge potential for abuse by expecting 24/7 response from workers.

Questions for Discussion

1. Why will 4G wireless networks bring about significant changes in connectivity?
2. There is a growing demand for video to handheld devices. Explain at least three factors enabling or driving this demand.
3. Why attend class if you can view or listen to the podcast?
4. Discuss some of the potential applications of wireless technologies in the financial sector.
5. Discuss the components of a mobile communication network.
6. Explain the role of protocols in mobile computing and their limitations.
7. Discuss the impact of wireless computing on emergency response services.
8. Describe the ways in which WiMAX is affecting the use of cellular phones for m-commerce.
9. Which of the current mobile computing limitations do you think will be minimized within two years? Which ones will not?
10. Discuss the ethical issues of social networks and anytime, anywhere accessibility.
11. What health and quality-of-life issues are associated with social networks and a 24/7 connected lifestyle?

Exercises and Projects

1. CALEA is the Communications Assistance for Law Enforcement Act, a federal requirement to allow law enforcement agencies to conduct electronic surveillance of phone calls or other communications. What dilemmas are caused by the convergence of voice, video, and data and the requirements of CALEA?
2. Compare the various features of broadband wireless networks (e.g., 3G, Wi-Fi, and WiMAX). Visit at least three broadband wireless network vendors.
   a. Prepare a list of capabilities of each network.
   b. Prepare a list of actual applications that each network can support.
   c. Comment on the value of such applications to users. How can the benefits be assessed?
3. Compare the advanced features of three search engines.
   a. Prepare a table listing five advanced features of each search engine.
   b. Perform a search for "VoIP vendors" on each of those search engines.
   c. Compare the results.
   d. In your opinion, which search engine provided the best results. Why?
4. Read *IT at Work 4.2,* "Thrifty Caters to Cost-Conscious Travelers" and answer the discussion questions.

Group Assignments and Projects

1. Each team should examine a major vendor of mobile devices (Nokia, Kyocera, Motorola, Palm, BlackBerry, etc.). Each team will research the capabilities and prices of the devices offered by each company and then make a class presentation, the objective of which is to convince the rest of the class why one should buy that company's products.
2. Each team should explore the commercial applications of mobile communication in one of the following areas: financial services, including banking, stocks, and insur-ance; marketing and advertising; manufacturing; travel and transportation; human resources management; public services; or healthcare. Each team will present a report to the class based on its findings.
3. Each team will investigate an online (Web) meeting software suite, such as GoToMeeting or Lotus Sametime. Download the free trial version and/or video demonstra-tion. The teams will investigate the features and business purposes of the software and then present a report to the class based on their findings.

Internet Exercises

1. Visit *Sprint.com.* What are the features of its 4G phone that make it suitable for managers or business purposes?
2. Visit the Google Apps Web site. What types of collabora-tion support are available?

BUSINESS CASE

Greener Mobile Networks Cutting Carbon Footprint

Four incentives are driving mobile network operators (carriers) to develop greener mobile networks. The four incentives are:

- **To reduce costs.** Energy consumption is one of the biggest operating costs for both fixed and mobile networks.

- **To overcome limited availability of reliable electricity.** Many developing countries are high-growth markets for telecommunications, but they have limited reliable access to electricity.

- **To be more socially responsible.** Many organizations have adopted corporate social responsibility initiatives with the goal of reducing their networks' carbon footprints.

- **To gain competitive advantage.** Network infrastructure vendors are striving to gain competitive advantage by reducing the power requirements of their equipment.

All of these factors will continue to converge over the next several years, creating significant market potential for greener telecom networks.

Mobile network operators worldwide have embarked on bold initiatives to improve the energy efficiency of their wireless networks and reduce the carbon footprint and greenhouse gas (GHG) emissions associated with network operations. According to a Pike Research report (*pikeresearch. com/*), these green network initiatives will reduce network carbon emissions by 42 percent by 2013. Mobile operations in Asia Pacific, the leading region for the reduction of carbon

emissions by mobile operators, will be Asia and Pacific Islands, followed by Europe and North America.

In 2010, Clearwire, the largest 4G service provider in the United States, announced that it has begun trials in Chicago of its first high-efficiency "green" base station cabinets. This new generation of base station cabinets is capable of achieving up to 90 percent reduction in electrical operating expenses and would not require the use of HVAC equipment in the majority of the company's nationwide deployment. Following completion of the trials, the new base station designs are expected to be introduced throughout the Clearwire network.

Questions

1. Rank the four incentives according to how you believe they motivate a company to invest in greener IT.
2. Explain the reasons for your ranking.
3. Review predictions of global warming and related issues. Consider the expected surge in the use of 4G networks, which will increase electricity consumption to power the networks and cool the equipment. Based on your research, estimate the impact on the environment if mobile network operators did not invest in greener networks.
4. Bottom line: Is it profitable for operators to go green? Explain.

NONPROFIT CASE

Electronic Medical Records (EMR): A Strategic Healthcare Investment

Founded in 1945, Kaiser is a leading healthcare provider of nonprofit health plans in the United States. Their mission is to provide high-quality, affordable healthcare services and to improve the health of 8.6 million members. Medical teams are supported by industry-leading technology advances and tools for health promotion, disease prevention, state-of-the-art care delivery, and chronic disease management.

In mid-2010, every medical facility in its health system was connected to *Kaiser Permanente (KP) HealthConnect,* the largest private sector electronic medical records (EMR) system in the world. The development and implementation of KP HealthConnect took 10 years to build and represented a $4 billion strategic investment for Kaiser.

Connecting Healthcare Services

KP HealthConnect is a comprehensive health information system that securely connects more than 8.6 million people to their physicians, nurses, and pharmacists; their personal information; and the latest medical knowledge. KP HealthConnect:

- Includes bedside documentation, clinical decision support, and barcoding for medication administration

- Helps facilitate collaboration among both primary and specialty care teams

- Provides the healthcare teams with access to patient information and the latest, best practices all in one place to further improve patient safety and quality of care while increasing convenience and coordination.

The system has been in all 431 outpatient facilities since 2008. In 2009, more than 3 million people logged in a total of 27 million times to check their own records.

Healthy and Satisfied Customers

With easy-to-use, Web-based tools, all members have access to medical records and tools to communicate with their providers. *My Health Manager* on the Web site kp.org/myhealthmanager gives registered members the ability to manage their health online, such as:

- Scheduling appointments
- Ordering prescription refills
- Sending and receiving secure messages to/from their doctor over the Internet

- 24/7 online access to lab test results, eligibility, and benefits information—even their children's immunization records

In addition, all Kaiser physicians routinely use the EMR when caring for their patients in medical offices and hospitals.

In 2010, four regions rated Kaiser's health plans highest in customer satisfaction in the *J.D. Power and Associates 2010 U.S. Member Health Insurance Plan Study*. The study measures member satisfaction by examining seven key factors that reflect the relationship between the health plan and members: coverage and benefits, provider choice, information and communication, claims processing, statements, customer service, and approval processes.

According to Kaiser, the KP HealthConnect has improved the quality of care and service to its members, and communication between members and Kaiser professionals to help make getting well and staying healthy even more convenient. KP HealthConnect also coordinates patient care between the physician's office, the hospital, radiology, the laboratory, and the pharmacy, which helps to eliminate the pitfalls of incomplete, missing, or unreadable charts.

Sources: Compiled from Kaiser Permanente News Center (2010), Versel (2010a, 2010b).

Questions

1. To see Kaiser Permanente members, physicians, and employees talk about KP HealthConnect, view a video at *www.youtube.com/kaiserpermanenteorg*. What did you learn?
2. What benefits does KP HealthConnect offer healthcare providers? Members? Patients?
3. Research the annual rate of medical errors in one or two countries. What are several reasons for these errors? How does KP HealthConnect help to reduce medical errors?
4. Why is KP HealthConnect a strategic investment for Kaiser?

ANALYSIS USING SPREADSHEETS

Cost Comparison of Web Collaboration

DUMBO Company (a fictitious company) needed to cut travel costs and productivity losses (wasted time) but still maintain the benefits of person-to-person collaboration. One option was Web conferencing, which could be used internally for collaboration and externally for sales demonstrations to customers in geographically dispersed areas. The company's CFO, Eileen Griffin, decided to invest in one of the large vendors' Web meeting software, either on a pay-per-use basis or a per user licensing plan based on the number of seats or participants. Griffin estimated that Web conferencing cost estimates should be based on the following:

- Approximately 1,000 meetings per year (based on approximately three meetings per week)
- An average of eight participants per meeting
- Each meeting lasting about one hour (15 minutes of setup time and 45 minutes for the actual meeting)
- 300 unique participants, consisting of 100 employees and 200 0customers

Griffin wants you to research and develop a spreadsheet comparing the pay-per-use basis vs. buying seats (licenses) for Microsoft's LiveMeeting and Cisco's WebEx. Precise cost comparisons are difficult because there are so many variables, but a basic cost analysis between LiveMeeting and WebEx is feasible. Using a spreadsheet, perform the following calculations. Visit the book's Web site to download the spreadsheet to help with your analysis.

1. Calculate the total minutes per year for Web conferencing at DUMBO.
2. Research LiveMeeting and WebEx to find the costs for a pay-per-use basis or the cost to buy the software.
3. Prepare cost comparisons of the vendors' licensing options and pay-per-usage.
4. Identify other criteria that should be taken into account when making such a decision (for example, vendor support or the ability to integrate with Outlook).
5. Make a recommendation to CFO Griffin.

References

AACSB Accreditation Standards, Management of Curricula, 2006. *aacsb.edu/eerc/std-15.asp.*

AACSB International, Ethics Education Resource Center, Accreditation Standards, 2006. *aacsb.edu/resource_centers/EthicsEdu/standards.asp.*

Careless, J., Convergence Communications E-SPONDER, *Law and Order*, March 2006.

Cisco.com/

Foodstuffs Case Study, "Foodstuffs embraces enterprise mobility from the warehouse to the customer." 2008. *motorola.com/web/Business/Solutions/*

Forrester, *Business Data Services, Enterprise Network and Telecommunications Survey*, Q1 2007.

Frommer, D., "Smartphone Sales Soar, iPhone Grabs 27% of Market," Silicon Alley Insider, November 20, 2007. *alleyinsider.com/2007/11/smart-phone-sales-soar-iphone-grabs-27-percent-of-market.html*

Frost and Sullivan, "Meetings Around the World: The Impact of Collaboration on Business Performance," 2006. *newscenter.verizon.com/kit/collaboration/MAW_WP.pdf*

Imason, Inc. How Imason Helped Labatt Build a World-Class Intranet with SharePoint," 2010. *imason.com*

Kaiser Permanente News Center, 2010. *xnet.kp.org/newscenter/aboutkp/healthconnect/index.html.*

Labatt.com

MAS, "MAS Takes Supervisory Action Against DBS Bank Ltd For Breakdown of the Bank's Mainframe-Storage Area Network." Straits Times, 4 August 2010. *straitstimes.com/STI/STIMEDIA/pdf/20100804/MAS.pdf*

Motorola Solutions, *motorola.com/Business/XA-EN/Enterprise+Mobility. 2011*

Ng, V. "Singapore Bank's network crashes, millions possibly lost." Enterprise Innovation, July 7, 2010. *enterpriseinnovation.net/*

Perelman, D., "Has the Disconnected Vacation Become Extinct?" *eWeek.com*, May 5, 2008. *eweek.com/c/a/Careers/Has-the-Disconnected-Vacation-Become-Extinct/?kc=EWKNLCSM060308FEA*

Tan, C. "MAS hits DBS with $230m capital charge." Marshall Cavendish Business Information, August 5, 2010. *asiahoreca.com/*

Versel, N. "Kaiser Completes Systemwide EMR Rollout," *FierceEMR,* March 11, 2010a. *fierceemr.com/story/kaiser-completes-systemwide-emr-rollout/2010-03-11*

Versel, N. "Spotlight: Kaiser Completes Largest Private-Sector EMR Rollout," *FierceEMR,* March 12, 2010b. *fiercehealthcare.com/story/spotlight-va-preparing-re-start-health-data-exchange-dod/2010-03-12*

Chapter 5

IT Security, Crime, Compliance, and Continuity

Learning Objectives

❶ Understand the objectives, functions, and financial value of IT security.

❷ Recognize IS vulnerabilities, threats, attack methods, and cybercrime symptoms.

❸ Understand crimes committed against computers and crimes committed with computers.

❹ Explain key methods of defending information systems, networks, and wireless devices.

❺ Understand network security risks and defenses.

❻ Describe internal control and fraud and the related legislation.

❼ Understand business continuity and disaster recovery planning methods.

Integrating *IT*

 ACC
 FIN
 MKT
 OM
 HRM
 IS

Information Security Magazine *searchsecurity.techtarget.com/*
CIO Magazine, IT Security *cio.com/topic/3089/Security*
Computer and Internet Security *cnet.com/internet-security*
IT Governance Institute *itgi.org*
U.S. Computer Emergency Readiness Team (US-CERT) *us-cert.gov/cas/tips/*
SANS Information Security Reading Room *sans.org/reading_room/*
Privacy news from around the world *pogowasright.org/*
Government Computer News (GCN) *gcn.com/*
CompTIA *comptia.org/*
F-Secure *f-secure.com/en_US/security/security-center/*
Social engineering *symantec.com/connect/articles/social-engineering*

QUICK LOOK at Chapter 5, IT Security, Crime, Compliance, and Continuity

This section introduces you to the business issues, challenges, and IT solutions in Chapter 5. Topics and issues mentioned in the Quick Look are explained in the chapter.

Information security (*infosec*, for short) is about risk to data, information systems, and networks. These incidents create business and legal risks, such as when operations are disrupted or privacy laws are violated.

IT risk management includes securing corporate systems while ensuring their availability; planning for disaster recovery and business continuity; complying with government regulations and license agreements; maintaining internal controls; and protecting the organization against an increasing array of threats such as viruses, worms, spyware, and other forms of malware. In general, risk management is both expensive and inconvenient. Many users, for instance, complain about being forced to use strong passwords (i.e., at least 10 characters and must contain a digit and special character) that aren't easy to remember.

Managers have a **fiduciary responsibility** (legal and ethical obligation) to protect the confidential data of the people and partners that they collect, store, and share. To comply with international, federal, state, and foreign laws, companies must invest in IT security to protect their data, other assets, the ability to operate, and net income. Losses and disruptions due to IT security breaches can seriously harm or destroy a company both financially and operationally. As the effectiveness of the technology and tactics used by **cybercriminals**—people who commit crimes using the Internet—increases, so do the costs (and inconveniences) of staying ahead of deliberate attacks, viruses and other malware infections, and unintentional errors.

In this chapter we begin with an overview of enterprise-wide security issues. We discuss technologies, such as firewalls and malware, internal controls, information assurance, and the enterprise risk management (ERM) and COBIT framework. We base infosec on a risk exposure model for identifying what to protect and how much to invest in that protection.

FIN   IS   ETHICS   GLOBAL   Failure

HSBC Suisse Data Theft

In February 2011, Swiss financial regulator FINMA (Financial Market Supervisory Authority) reprimanded Swiss subsidiary HSBC Private Bank (Suisse) SA following its year-long investigation into massive security breach and theft of client account data. The accounts were held in Switzerland but the client base was international. FINMA concluded that there were deficiencies in the bank's IT infrastructure and oversight of its IT activities. Former HSBC IT employee Herve Falciani had stolen data from about 24,000 private accounts between late 2006 and early 2007. Ironically, Falciani allegedly stole the files during a project to transfer information to a more secure system.

Account information had been stored securely in encrypted files, but those files were carried out of the bank on a laptop by Falciani. HSBC was unaware that data had been stolen until after Falciani tried to sell it to the French authorities, who arrested him.

French, Italian, and German Authorities Gain Access to Private Bank Data

In January 2009, French police obtained the evidence—the encrypted files—after raiding Falciani's home in France. The French government has used the data to search for tax dodgers and has shared the data with Italy's prosecutors; data that included the identities of 5,728 Italian citizens and companies holding Swiss accounts valued at a total of $6.9 billion. While the information may not have been sold to identity thieves or other criminals, the clients whose data had been stolen may be facing legal problems in their own countries.

- **France:** Authorities in France are seeking to track down clients who hide assets in HSBC's private bank and to investigate suspected tax evasion by wealthy French taxpayers.
- **Italy:** Italian authorities are interested in the data for similar investigations into tax evasion and money laundering.

- **Germany:** According to German newspaper *Der Spiegel*, Falciani had also tried to sell details of 3,000 accounts and 1,300 names of German taxpayers to the German authorities for 2.5 million euros. The estimated tax recovery would be between 100 and 200 million euros. German Finance Minister Wolfgang Schaeuble said he would buy the data, which led to a public outcry: *How dare Germany seek to profit from an illegal act.*

HSBC Suisse Reacts with Tighter IT Security Procedures

HSBC Suisse invested an additional $93 million to upgrade its computer systems and data security procedures after the breach. However, that may be the least of their costs. The privacy invasion and legal exposure for tax evasion that clients faced when the authorities obtained the data may be devastating to the bank's reputation. As part of damage control, Alexandre Zeller, CEO of HSBC Suisse apologized to clients saying, "We deeply regret the situation and unreservedly apologize to our clients for this threat to their privacy." To help reassure clients, HSBC said it would refuse to help authorities use the stolen data for tax evasion investigations.

HSBC also faced very expensive legal problems. Swiss regulators were investigating whether HSBC broke the country's strict bank privacy laws, which carries severe penalties.

Sources: Compiled from Barrett (2010), HSBC-RI (2010), Leyden (2010), and PBI Editorial (2011).

For Class Discussion and Debate

1. *Scenario for Brainstorming and Discussion:* Complete (100%) security is impossible. Therefore, companies must decide how much to invest in infosec policies, procedures, and training, as well as the enforcement of those policies and procedures. Discuss why senior management's commitment and support are important to infosec. Brainstorm ways to determine how much to invest in infosec. Assume that a company's budget is fixed. Therefore, investment in infosec reduces funds available for other functions, such as marketing, new product development, etc.

2. *Debate on information privacy vs. public interests:* This incident has raised difficult questions about privacy and the ethics of how far authorities or law enforcement should be allowed to go to identify suspected tax dodgers, money launderers, or other types of criminals. Money laundering is known to be widely used to fund or support terrorism. Therefore, any

investigation into money laundering may be in the public's best interests but also an invasion of someone's privacy. Another perspective is best represented by the outcry *how dare Germany seek to profit from an illegal act.*

Is it ethical for authorities to use the private data that Falciani had stolen as evidence to investigate tax evasion and money laundering?

- If *yes*, then should there be any restrictions on the use of that data?
- If *no*, then if the public's safety or security were at potential risk, should the privacy of the clients' stolen data be allowed as evidence?

To Do: Select one side of the argument—either *in favor of privacy* or *in favor of public security*, as just described. Debate the ethical issues associated with your side of the argument.

5.1 Protecting Data and Business Operations

What is information and network security? Most people would mention hardware and software in their answers; for example, firewalls, encryption, antivirus, antispam, anti-spyware, anti-phishing, and so on. Firewalls and intrusion detection systems are placed throughout networks to monitor and control traffic into and out of a network, as shown in Figure 5.1.

Certainly, technology defenses are necessary, but they're insufficient because protecting data and business operations involves all of the following:

- Making data and documents available and accessible 24/7 while simultaneously restricting access
- Implementing and enforcing procedures and acceptable use policies for company-owned data, hardware, software, and networks
- Promoting secure and legal sharing of information among authorized persons and partners
- Ensuring compliance with government regulations and laws
- Preventing attacks by having network intrusion defenses in place
- Detecting, diagnosing, and reacting to incidents and attacks in real time
- Maintaining internal controls to prevent manipulation of data and records
- Recovering from business disasters and disruptions quickly

As the prior list shows, business policies, procedures, training, and disaster recovery plans as well as technology all play a critical role in IT security. **IT security** covers the protection of information, communication networks, and traditional and e-commerce operations to assure their confidentiality, integrity, availability, and authorized use.

Until 2002, infosec was mostly a technology issue assigned to the IT department. Incidents were handled on a case-by-case "cleanup" basis rather than by taking a pre-emptive approach to protect ahead of the threats. Infosec was viewed as a *cost* rather than as a *resource* for preventing business disruptions and satisfying governance responsibilities. The cost-based view turned out to be dangerously inadequate at securing the enterprise against dishonest insiders and the global reach of cybercrimes, malware, spyware, and fraud.

During 2010, hi-tech criminals were launching more than 100 attacks per second on computers worldwide, according to a report from IT security vendor Symantec. While most of these attacks didn't cause trouble, one attack every 4.5 seconds did affect a PC. Symantec identified almost 2.9 million items of malicious code during a 12-month period. The steep rise in malware was driven largely by the availability of free, easy-to-use, and/or powerful toolkits that novice cybercriminals were using to develop their own malware. For example, one malware toolkit named Zeus cost $700 (£458), and many had become so successful that their creators offered telephone

Figure 5.1 Firewalls protect networks by controlling incoming and outgoing traffic. (© *GodfriedEdelman/iStockphoto*)

support for those who could not get their worms or viruses to work. Cleanup costs after a single incident are already into the hundreds of millions of dollars.

KNOW YOUR ENEMY AND YOUR RISKS

Every enterprise has information that profit-motivated criminals (who may be across the globe or may be trusted employees) want to, and may actually attempt to, steal and/or sell. The opening case about HSBC Private Bank demonstrates why IT security risks are business risks. Those risks can stem from insiders, outsiders, cybercriminal organizations, or malware. **Malware** is short for *malicious software,* referring to viruses, worms, Trojan horses, spyware, and all other types of disruptive, destructive, or unwanted programs. Threats range from high-tech exploits to gain access to a company's networks and databases to nontech tactics to steal laptops and whatever else is available. Because infosec terms, such as *threats* and *exploits,* have precise meanings, the key terms and their meanings are listed in Table 5.1.

In general, IT security measures have focused on protecting against outsiders and malware. While controlling physical and remote access to databases and networks is still challenging, a majority of data breaches involve some sort of insider error or action—either intentional or unintentional. That is, the greatest infosec risks are employees and managers. Companies suffer tremendous loss from fraud committed by employees. It's a widespread problem that affects every company, regardless of size, location, or industry. You will read more about fraud in Section 5.3.

IT security is so integral to business objectives that it cannot be treated as a stand-alone function. Failures have a direct impact on business performance, customers, business partners, and stakeholders—and can lead to fines, legal action, and steep declines in stock prices as investors react to the crisis.

Internal Threats: Employees Threats from employees, referred to as **internal threats,** are a major challenge largely due to the many ways an employee can carry out malicious activity. Insiders may be able to bypass physical security (e.g., locked doors) and technical security (e.g., passwords) measures that organizations have in place to prevent unauthorized access. Why? Because defenses such as firewalls, intrusion detection systems (IDS), and locked doors mostly protect against external threats. As you have read, incidents that cause the greatest damages or losses are those carried out by insiders. Despite the challenges, insider incidents can be minimized with a layered defense strategy consisting of security procedures, acceptable use policies, and technology controls.

The following incidents, all of which were caused by insiders, could have been prevented if strict infosec policies and defenses had been enforced.

- In April 2010, Thomas A. Drake, a former high-ranking National Security Agency (NSA) official, was indicted for having used a secret, nongovernment e-mail account to transmit classified information that he was not authorized to access or disclose. The indictment alleged that in early 2006, Drake signed up for an account with Hushmail, which provides encrypted e-mail. He had contacted a reporter for a national newspaper, who also signed up for Hushmail, enabling them to exchange secret government documents. The reporter published reports about the NSA that contained classified Signals Intelligence information, which involves collection and analysis of foreign communications (Aftergood, 2010).
- Three HSBC business units were fined more than £3.2 million by the Financial Services Authority (FSA) for security failings that led to the loss of customers' sensitive personal details, exposing them to risk of identity theft and fraud. The FSA said that HSBC customer data had been lost twice in the mail. In 2007, HSBC actuaries lost an unencrypted disk in the mail with the personal details of 2,000 pension members, including birth dates, addresses, and insurance details. Despite apologies and a warning to staff from the bank about the need for effective security procedures, another unencrypted disk was lost in the mail in 2009 by HSBC Life, containing the personal details of 180,000 policyholders.

TABLE 5.1	IT Security Terms
Term	**Definition**
Threat	Something or someone that may result in harm to an asset
Risk	Probability of a threat exploiting a vulnerability
Vulnerability	A weakness that threatens the confidentiality, integrity, or availability (CIA) of an asset
CIA triad (confidentiality, integrity, availability)	The three main principles of IT security
Exploit	Using a tool or technique to take advantage of a vulnerability
Risk management	Process of identifying, assessing, and reducing risk to an acceptable level
Exposure	The estimated cost, loss, or damage that can result if a threat exploits a vulnerability
Access control	Security feature designed to restrict who has access to a network, IS, or data
Countermeasure	Safeguard implemented to mitigate (lessen) risk
Audit	The process of generating, recording, and reviewing a chronological record of system events to determine their accuracy
Encryption	Transformation of data into scrambled code to protect it from being understood by unauthorized users
Plaintext or clear-text	Readable text
Ciphertext	Encrypted text
Authentication	Method (usually based on username and password) by which an IS validates or verifies that a user is really who he or she claims to be
Malware (short for *malicious software)*	A generic term that refers to a virus, worm, Trojan horse, spyware, or adware
Scareware, also known as *rogueware* or *fake antivirus software*	Programs that pretend to scan a computer for viruses and then tell the user the computer is infected in order to convince the victim to voluntarily provide credit card information to pay $50 to $80 to "clean" the PC. When the victims pays the fee, the virus appears to vanish, but the machine is then infected by other malicious programs. It is one of the fastest-growing and most prevalent types of Internet fraud.
Biometrics	Methods to identify a person based on a biological feature, such as a fingerprint or retina
Perimeter security	Security measures to ensure that only authorized users gain access to the network
Endpoint security	Security measures to protect *endpoints*, e.g., desktops, laptops, and mobile devices
Firewall	Software or hardware device that controls access to a private network from a public network (Internet) by analyzing data packets entering or exiting it
Packet	A unit of data for transmission over a network with a *header* containing the source and destination of the packet
IP address (Internet Protocol address)	An address that uniquely identifies a specific computer or other device on a network
Public key infrastructure (PKI)	A system based on encryption to identify and authenticate the sender or receiver of an Internet message or transaction
Intrusion detection system (IDS)	A defense tool used to monitor network traffic (packets) and provide alerts when there is suspicious traffic or to quarantine suspicious traffic
Router	Device that transfers (routes) packets between two or more networks
Fault tolerance	The ability of an IS to continue to operate when a failure occurs, but usually for a limited time or at a reduced level
Backup	A duplicate copy of data or programs kept in a secured location
Spoofing	An attack carried out using a trick, disguise, deceit, or by falsifying data
Denial of service (DoS) or Distributed denial of service (DDoS)	An attack in which a system is bombarded with so many requests (for service or access) that it crashes or cannot respond
Zombie	An infected computer that is controlled remotely via the Internet by an unauthorized user, such as a spammer, fraudster, or hacker
Spyware	Stealth software that gathers information about a user or a user's online activity
Botnet (short for *Bot network*)	A network of hijacked computers that are controlled remotely—typically to launch spam or spyware. Also called software robots. Botnets are linked to a range of malicious activity, including identity theft and spam.

- In May 2006, the theft of a laptop during a home burglary of a Veterans Affairs employee cost taxpayers $100 million to remedy.
- In 2007, TJX Companies disclosed that data from 100 million credit and debit cards had been stolen by hackers starting in 2005. TJX's data heist was the largest breach ever to date, based on the number of records involved. Following the disclosure, banks said that tens of millions of dollars of fraudulent charges were made on the cards. The Massachusetts Bankers Association sued TJX for negligence. The FTC filed a complaint, alleging TJX did not have the proper security measures in place to prevent unauthorized access to the sensitive, personal customer information. The total cost of the data breach was an estimated $197 million.
- In November 2007, the United Kingdom's tax agency disclosed that it had lost unencrypted disks containing personal data, bank details, and national ID numbers on 25 million juvenile benefits claimants. Analyst firm Gartner Inc. estimated that closing compromised accounts and establishing new ones cost British banks about $500 million.

These incidents point out that victims of breaches are often third parties, such as customers, patients, social network users, credit card companies, and shareholders; costs to repair damage may be staggering.

Cloud Computing and Social Network Risks With the popularity of eReaders, netbooks, Google's Chrome OS, Facebook, YouTube, Twitter, LinkedIn, and other social networks, IT security dangers are getting worse. Social networks and cloud computing increase vulnerabilities by providing a single point of failure and attack for organized criminal networks. Critical, sensitive, and private information is at risk, and like previous IT trends, such as wireless networks, the goal is connectivity, often with little concern for security. As social networks increase their services, the gap between services and infosec also increases. E-mail viruses and malware have been declining for years as e-mail security has improved. This trend continues as communication shifts to social networks and newer smartphones. Unfortunately, malware finds its way to

IT at Work 5.1

Governments Worldwide Tighten Data Protection Laws   GOV   IS

Federal governments are passing new laws and reinforcing existing ones to pressure organizations into hardening their data-protection policies, procedures, technologies, and security-awareness training. These laws typically apply to any company doing business in, or transferring, data through the nation. Here are five examples.

- **China's Credit Card Protection Rules:** On January 13, 2011, the China Banking Regulatory Commission issued *Measures for the Supervision and Administration of the Credit Card Businesses of Commercial Banks* (Measures), which took effect that same day. The Measures are the first comprehensive regulations relating to credit card business in China, and regulate the protection of personal information by commercial banks.
- **India's Privacy Rules:** The Government of India's Ministry of Communications & Information Technology has published three draft rules: *Reasonable Security Practices and Procedures and Sensitive Personal Information; Due Diligence Observed by Intermediaries Guidelines,* and *Guidelines for Cyber Cafe.* The

first two of these rules affect international companies that provide digital services or process data in India.
- **Germany's Security Breach Notification Requirement:** On March 2, 2011, the German Federal government began revising data protection laws to comply with the data breach notification requirements in the European e-Privacy Directive.
- **Mexico's Private Sector Data Protection Regulations:** Mexico's Ministry of Economy and Federal Institute for Access to Information and Data Protection (IFAI) issued the first set of regulations implementing Mexico's new private sector data protection law in April 2011. These first regulations will cover the legal requirements to provide privacy notices to consumers and to appoint a designated privacy official.
- **South Korea's Protection of Personal Data Act:** South Korea's comprehensive privacy law requires nearly all businesses and government agencies to provide data breach protection, mandates the use of privacy assessments before establishing certain new databases, and establishes a right to file class actions in court over alleged violations of the law.

users through security vulnerabilities in these new services and devices. Web filtering, user education, and strict policies are key to preventing widespread outbreaks.

In Twitter and Facebook, users invite in others and build relationships with them. Cybercriminals hack into these trusted relationships using stolen log-ins. Fake antivirus and other attacks that take advantage of user trust are very difficult to detect.

An overriding reason why these networks and services increase exposure to risk is the **time-to-exploitation** of today's sophisticated spyware and mobile viruses. Time-to-exploitation is the elapsed time between when vulnerability is discovered and when it's exploited, or compromised by an attacker. That time has shrunk from months to minutes, so IT staff have ever-shorter timeframes to find and fix flaws before being compromised by an attack. Some attacks exist for as little as two hours, which means that enterprise IT security systems must have real-time protection. As of 2011, they will look to cloud services for enhanced security.

When new vulnerabilities are found in operating systems, applications, or wired and wireless networks, patches are released by the vendor or security organization. **Patches** are software programs that users download and install to fix the vulnerability. Microsoft, for example, releases patches that it calls **service packs** to update and fix vulnerabilities in its operating systems, including Vista, and applications, including Office 2007. Service packs are made available at Microsoft's Web site.

Left undetected or unprotected, vulnerabilities provide an open door for IT attacks, which lead to business disruptions and their financial damages. Despite even the best technology defenses, infosec incidents will occur mostly because of users who do not follow secure computing practices and procedures.

Phishing and Web-Based Threats Companies increasingly adopt external, Web-based applications and employees bring consumer applications into the enterprise. Criminal enterprises are following the money on the Internet, where they have a global market of potential victims.

(© Stuart Hickling/iStockphoto)

Since 2007, Web-based threats have been the primary way of stealing confidential data and infecting computers. In 2008, two-thirds of all known malware was created. Then in the first half of 2009, new malware exceeded all malware detected in 2008, phishing increased 585 percent, and more than 300 corporate brands were victimized. **Phishing** is a deceptive attempt to steal a person's confidential information by pretending to be a legitimate organization, such as PayPal, a bank, credit card company, or casino. Phishing messages include a link to a fraudulent phish Web site that looks like the real one. When the user clicks the link to the phish site, he or she is asked for a credit card number, Social Security number, account number, or password. In 2010 and 2011, phishing increased exponentially because unaware users still fall for the ruse.

Criminals use the Internet and private networks to hijack large numbers of PCs to spy on users, spam them, shake down businesses, and steal identities. But why are they so successful? The Information Security Forum (*securityforum.org*), a self-help organization that includes many Fortune 100 companies, compiled a list of the top information problems and discovered that nine of the top 10 incidents were the result of three factors:

• Mistakes or human error
• Malfunctioning systems
• Misunderstanding the effects of adding incompatible software to an existing system

Unfortunately, these factors can often overcome the IT security technologies that companies and individuals use to protect their information. A fourth factor identified by the Security Forum is motivation, as described in *IT at Work 5.2*.

Search Engine Manipulation Search engine manipulation is a method used by cybercriminals to exploit search engine algorithms to position hacked Web sites higher in the ranking results. Such manipulation drives users to malicious sites, such as bait pages that offer fake antivirus or *warez* (pirated software, games, music, etc.). Malware spread through search engines is also increasing because of the high degree of trust users place in search engines and the ease with which rankings can be manipulated.

IT at Work 5.2

Inter-Government FATF Fights Money Laundering and Terrorist Financing

The Financial Action Task Force (FATF) is an intergovernmental body whose purpose is the development and promotion of national and international policies related to anti-money laundering and counter-terrorist financing (AML/CFT). FATF (*fatf-gafi.org/*) is a policy-making body that works to generate AML/CFT laws and regulatory reforms. In order to protect the worldwide financial system, FATF identifies and works with jurisdictions that have AML/CFT deficiencies.

Why AML/CFT is Necessary. Transnational organized crime groups have long relied on money laundering to fund their operations. This practice poses national and international security threats. It undermines free enterprise by crowding out the private sector and threatens the financial stability of all countries.

Funds used to finance terrorist operations are very difficult to track. However, by adapting methods used to combat money laundering such as financial analysis and investigations, authorities can significantly disrupt the financial networks of terrorists, and build a paper trail and base of evidence to identify and locate leaders of terrorist organizations and cells.

Crime Syndicates. International organized crime syndicates, al-Qaeda groups, and other cybercriminals steal hundreds of billions of dollars every year. Cybercrime is safer and easier than selling drugs, dealing in black market diamonds, or robbing banks. Online gambling offers easy fronts for international money-laundering operations. Visit FATF Web site at *fatf-gafi.org/* to review the 40 + 9 recommended AML/CFT measures covering the criminal justice system and law enforcement, the financial system and its regulation, and international cooperation.

Fighting Corruption. The FATF attaches great importance to the fight against corruption because it has the potential to bring catastrophic harm to economic development, weaken the fight against organized crime, and diminish respect for the law and effective governance.

Sources: Compiled from the FATF (2011), U.S. Department of State (2008), and Altman (2006).

Discussion Questions: Why is it important for managers to stay up-to-date with FATF's most recent AML/CFT news, risks, and recommendations?

Multi-Link Attacks Attacks are getting more complex by being linked together. For example, search engine–manipulated links may connect to hacked blog pages that link to malware, which can download without the user's knowledge or consent. These linked attacks are designed to have a specific path; they do not work if the user does not follow that path. This *path-awareness* makes it very difficult for traditional Web crawlers to find and identify threats. Multi-link attacks will become part of more complex, blended threats as cybercriminals employ more layered approaches to avoid detection.

We now discuss government regulations and industry standards designed to force companies to invest in infosec defenses.

GOVERNMENT REGULATIONS

Data must be protected against existing and future attack schemes, and IT defenses must satisfy ever-stricter government and international regulations. Primary regulations are the Sarbanes-Oxley Act (SOX), Gramm-Leach-Bliley Act (GLB), Federal Information Security Management Act (FISMA), and USA Patriot Act in the United States; Japan's Personal Information Protection Act; Canada's Personal Information Protection and Electronic Document Act (PIPEDA); Australia's Federal Privacy Act; the United Kingdom's Data Protection Act; and Basel III (global financial services). All mandate the protection of personal data. The director of the Federal Trade Commission's (FTC) Bureau of Consumer Protection warned that the agency would bring enforcement action against small businesses lacking adequate policies and procedures to protect consumer data.

Two accepted models for IT governance are **enterprise risk management (ERM)** and **COBIT (Control Objectives for Information and Related Technology).** ERM is a risk-based approach to managing an enterprise that integrates internal control, the Sarbanes-Oxley Act mandates, and strategic planning. ERM is intended to be part of routine planning processes rather than a separate initiative. The ideal place to start is with buy-in and commitment from the board and senior leadership.

COBIT, which is described in *IT at Work 5.3*, is an internationally accepted IT governance and control framework for aligning IT with business objectives, delivering value, and managing associated risks. It provides a reference for management, users, and IS audit, control, and security practitioners.

IT at Work 5.3

IT Governance

ACC   FIN   HRM   IS   OM   ETHICS

Fundamental to information security is IT governance. **IT governance** is part of corporate governance that relates to the supervision, monitoring, protection, and control of the organization's IT assets. Everyone who uses IT resources has an ethical obligation to do so responsibly. IT governance is related to compliance with Basel III in Europe and Sarbanes Oxley in the U.S. Sarbanes-Oxley Act requires that companies provide proof that their financial applications and systems are controlled (secured) to verify that financial reports can be trusted. This requires that IT security managers work with business managers to do a risk assessment to identify which systems depend on technical controls rather than on business process controls.

The *IT Governance Institute* (*itgi.org*) publishes Control Objectives for Information and Related Technology (COBIT), which many companies use as their IT governance guide. COBIT can be downloaded from *isaca.org*. To meet COBIT, IT systems should be based on the following three principles:

- *Principle of economic use of resources:* This principle acknowledges that the cost of infosec needs to be balanced with its benefits. It's the basic cost-benefit principle that you're familiar with. For example, you wouldn't spend more to protect your auto, home, or other asset than they were worth. Because it's possible, for instance, for companies to set a very low value on the confidential data of customers and employers and therefore avoid basic infosec defenses, the next two principles try to make sure that doesn't happen.

- *Principle of legality:* This principle requires that companies invest in infosec to meet minimum legal requirements. This is a basic security principle, just like having hand railings on stairways, fire extinguishers, and alarm systems.

- *Accounting principles:* These principles require that the integrity, availability, and reliability of data and information systems be maintained.

INDUSTRY STANDARDS

Industry groups impose their own standards to protect their customers and their members' brand images and revenues. One example is the **Payment Card Industry Data Security Standard (PCI DSS),** created by Visa, MasterCard, American Express, and Discover.

PCI DSS is required for all members, merchants, or service providers that store, process, or transmit cardholder data. Section 6.6 of the PCI DSS went into full effect in June 2008. In short, this section of PCI DSS requires merchants and card payment providers to make certain their Web applications are secure. If done correctly, it could reduce the number of Web-related security breaches.

PCI DSS Section 6.6 mandates that retailers ensure that Web-facing applications are protected against known attacks by applying either of the following two methods:

1. Have all custom application codes reviewed for vulnerabilities by an application security firm.

2. Install an application layer firewall in front of Web-facing applications. Each application will have its own firewall to protect against intrusions and malware.

The purpose of the PCI DSS is to improve customers' trust in e-commerce, especially when it comes to online payments, and to increase the Web security of online merchants. To motivate following these standards, the penalties for noncompliance are severe. The card brands can fine the retailer and increase transaction fees for each credit or debit card transaction. A finding of noncompliance can be the basis for lawsuits.

CompTIA Infosec Survey In its 2008 information security survey, the Computing Technology Industry Association (CompTIA, *comptia.org*), a nonprofit trade group, reported how companies in the United States, United Kingdom, Canada, and China are attempting to improve their infosec standards. Key findings are the following:

- Nearly 66 percent of U.S. firms, 50 percent of U.K. and Chinese firms, and 40 percent of Canadian firms have implemented written IT security policies.

- The percentage of IT budget that companies dedicate to security is growing year after year. In the United States, companies spent 12 percent of their 2007 IT budget for security purposes, up from 7 percent in 2005. The bulk of the budget was used to buy security-related technologies.

- About 33 percent of U.S. firms require that IT staff be certified in network and data security; in China, 78 percent of firms require IT security certification.

Figure 5.2 Lower Manhattan, the most communications-intensive real estate in the world.

IT security remains a major concern of IT professionals around the world according to *CompTIA's 7th Annual Trends in Information Security: An Analysis of IT Security and the Workforce study.* As IT's role within an organization continues to expand, so does the potential for security breaches.

INFOSEC BREAKDOWNS BEYOND COMPANY CONTROL

Some types of incidents are beyond a company's control. The volcanic ash from Iceland in 2010 created prolonged disruptions and crises that had never been experienced by businesses. Uncertain events that can cause IS breakdowns, such as in the following incidents, require disaster recovery and business continuity plans, which are covered in Section 5.6.

Incident 1. Cybercriminals had launched an attack to extort money from StormPay, an online payment processing company. The attack shut down both of StormPay's data centers and its business for two days, causing financial loss and upsetting 3 million customers.

Incident 2. Lower Manhattan (see Figure 5.2) is the most communications-intensive real estate in the world. Many companies there lacked off-site-based business continuity plans and permanently lost critical data about their employees, customers, and operations in the aftermath of the September 11, 2001, attacks. Mission-critical systems and networks were brought down. They also lost network and phone connectivity when the World Trade Center (WTC) collapsed and Verizon's central office (CO)—which was located directly across from the WTC—suffered massive structural damage. In all, 300,000 telephone lines and 3.6 million high-capacity data circuits served by that CO were put out of service.

These incidents illustrate the diversity of infosec problems and the substantial damage that can be done to organizations anywhere in the world, as a result.

IT SECURITY DEFENSE-IN-DEPTH MODEL

Defense-in-depth is a multilayered approach to infosec. The basic principle is that when one defense layer fails, another layer provides protection. For example, if a wireless network's security was compromised, then having encrypted data would still protect the data provided that the thieves could not decrypt it.

The success of any type of IT project depends on the commitment and involvement of executive management, also referred to as the "tone at the top." The same is true of IT security. When senior management shows its commitment to IT security, it becomes important to others, too. This infosec *tone* makes users aware that insecure practices and mistakes will not be tolerated. Therefore, an IT security and internal control model begins with senior management commitment and support, as shown in Figure 5.3. The model views infosec as a combination of people, processes, and technology.

Step 1: Senior management commitment and support. Senior managers' influence is needed to implement and maintain security, ethical standards, privacy practices, and internal control. The Committee of Sponsoring Organizations of the Treadway

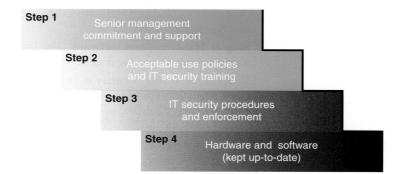

Figure 5.3 IT security defense-in-depth model.

Commission (COSO, *coso.org/key.htm*) defines **internal control** as a *process* designed to provide *reasonable* assurance of effective operations and reliable financial reporting. Internal control is discussed in Section 5.6.

Step 2: Acceptable use policies and IT security training. The next step in building an effective IT security program is to develop security policies and provide training to ensure that everyone is aware of and understands them. The greater the understanding of how security affects production levels, customer and supplier relationships, revenue streams, and management's liability, the more security will be incorporated into business projects and proposals.

Most critical is an **acceptable use policy (AUP)** that informs users of their responsibilities. An AUP is needed for two reasons: (1) to prevent misuse of information and computer resources and (2) to reduce exposure to fines, sanctions, and legal liability. To be effective, the AUP needs to define users' responsibilities, acceptable and unacceptable actions, and consequences of noncompliance. E-mail, Internet, and computer AUPs should be thought of as an extension of other corporate policies, such as those that address physical safety, equal opportunity, harassment, and discrimination.

Step 3: IT security procedures and enforcement. If users' activities are not monitored for compliance, the AUP is useless. Therefore, the next step is to implement monitoring procedures, training, and enforcement of the AUP. Businesses cannot afford the infinite cost of perfect security, so they calculate the proper level of protection. The calculation is based on the digital assets' risk exposure. The risk exposure model for digital assets is comprised of the five factors shown in Table 5.2.

FIN   HRM   MKT

Another risk assessment method is the **business impact analysis (BIA).** BIA is an exercise that determines the impact of losing the support or availability of a resource. For example, for most people, the loss of a smartphone would have greater impact than the loss of a digital camera. BIA helps identify the minimum resources needed to recover and prioritizes the recovery of processes and supporting systems. A BIA needs to be updated as new threats to IT emerge. After the risk exposure of

TABLE 5.2	Risk Exposure Model for Digital Assets
Factor	**Cost and Operational Considerations**
1. Asset's value to the company	What are the costs of replacement, recovery, or restoration? What is the recoverability time?
2. Attractiveness of the asset to a criminal	What is the asset's value (on a scale of low to high) to identity thieves, industrial spies, terrorists, or fraudsters?
3. Legal liability attached to the asset's loss or theft	What are the potential legal costs, fines, and restitution expenses?
4. Operational, marketing, and financial consequences	What are the costs of business disruption, delivery delays, lost customers, negative media attention, inability to process payments or payroll, or a drop in stock prices?
5. Likelihood of a successful attack against the asset	Given existing and emerging threats, what is the probability the asset will be stolen or compromised?

digital assets has been estimated, then informed decisions about investments in infosec can be made.

Step 4: Hardware and software. The last step in the model is implementation of software and hardware needed to support and enforce the AUP and secure practices.

Keep in mind that security is an ongoing and unending process, not a problem that can be solved with hardware or software. Hardware and software security defenses cannot protect against irresponsible business practices.

Review Questions

1. Why are cleanup costs after a single data breach or infosec incident in the tens of millions of dollars?
2. Who are the potential victims of an organization's data breach?
3. What is time-to-exploitation? What is the trend in the length of such a time?
4. What is a multi-link attack?
5. What is a service pack?
6. What are two causes of the top information problems at organizations?
7. What is an acceptable use policy (AUP)? Why do companies need an AUP?

5.2 IS Vulnerabilities and Threats

One of the biggest mistakes managers make is underestimating IT vulnerabilities and threats. Most workers use their laptops and mobiles for both work and leisure, and in an era of multitasking, they often do both at the same time. Yet off-time or off-site use of devices remains risky because, despite policies, employees continue to engage in dangerous online and communication habits. Those habits make them a weak link in an organization's otherwise solid security efforts. These threats can be classified as *unintentional or intentional.*

UNINTENTIONAL THREATS

Unintentional threats fall into three major categories: human errors, environmental hazards, and computer system failures.

- **Human errors** can occur in the design of the hardware or information system. They can also occur during programming, testing, or data entry. Not changing default passwords on a firewall or failing to manage patches create security holes. Human errors also include untrained or unaware users responding to phishing or ignoring security procedures. Human errors contribute to the majority of internal control and infosec problems.

- **Environmental hazards** include volcanoes, earthquakes, blizzards, floods, power failures or strong fluctuations, fires (the most common hazard), defective air conditioning, explosions, radioactive fallout, and water-cooling-system failures. In addition to the primary damage, computer resources can be damaged by side effects, such as smoke and water. Such hazards may disrupt normal computer operations and result in long waiting periods and exorbitant costs while computer programs and data files are re-created.

- **Computer systems failures** can occur as the result of poor manufacturing, defective materials, and outdated or poorly maintained networks (recall the network crash at LAX airport discussed in Chapter 4). Unintentional malfunctions can also happen for other reasons, ranging from lack of experience to inadequate testing.

INTENTIONAL THREATS

Examples of intentional threats include theft of data; inappropriate use of data (e.g., manipulating inputs); theft of mainframe computer time; theft of equipment and/or programs; deliberate manipulation in handling, entering, processing, transferring, or programming data; labor strikes, riots, or sabotage; malicious damage to computer resources; destruction from viruses and similar attacks; and miscellaneous computer abuses and Internet fraud. The scope (target) of intentional threats can be against an entire country or economy.

Hackers tend to involve unsuspecting insiders in their crimes, using tactics called **social engineering.** From an infosec perspective, social engineering has been used by criminals or corporate spies to trick insiders into revealing information or access codes that outsiders should not have. A common tactic used by hackers to get access to a network is to call employees, pretending to be the network administrator who wants to solve a serious problem. To solve the problem, they need the employee to give them their password. Of course, the tactic won't work on employees who have been trained not to give out passwords over the phone to anyone.

Malware creators have also used social engineering to maximize the range or impact of their viruses, worms, and so on. For example, the *ILoveYou* worm used social engineering to entice people to open malware-infected e-mail messages. The *ILoveYou* worm attacked tens of millions of Windows computers in May 2000 when it was sent as an e-mail attachment with the subject line: ILOVEYOU. Often out of curiosity, people opened the attachment named LOVE-LETTER-FOR-YOU.TXT.vbs—releasing the worm. Within nine days, the worm had spread worldwide, crippling networks, destroying files, and causing an estimated $5.5 billion in damages. Notorious hacker Kevin Mitnick, who served time in jail for hacking, used social engineering as his primary method to gain access to computer networks. In most cases, the criminal never comes face-to-face with the victim but communicates via the phone or e-mail.

Not all hackers are malicious, however. *White-hat hackers* perform ethical hacking, such as performing penetrating tests on their clients' systems or searching the Internet to find the weak points so they can be fixed. White-hat hacking by Finjan, an information security vendor, for example, led to the discovery of a **crime server** in Malaysia in April 2008, as described in *IT at Work 5.4.* A crime server is a server used to store stolen data for use in committing crimes. Finjan discovered the crime server while running its real-time code inspection technology to diagnose customers' Web traffic.

Social engineering is used for (noncriminal) business purposes, too. For example, commercials use social engineering (e.g., promises of wealth or happiness) to convince people to buy their products or services.

IT ATTACKS

There are many types of attack, and new ones appear regularly. Two basic types of deliberate attacks are data tampering and programming attack.

Data tampering is a common means of attack that is overshadowed by other types of attacks. It refers to an attack during which someone enters false or fraudulent data into a computer or changes or deletes existing data. Data tampering is extremely serious because it may not be detected. This is the method often used by insiders and fraudsters.

IT at Work 5.4

Malaysian Crime Server Found With Data Stolen from 10 Countries

In 2008, Finjan software researchers found compromised data from patients, bank customers, business e-mail messages, and Outlook accounts on a Malaysia-based server. Data included usernames, passwords, account numbers, Social Security and credit card numbers, patient data, business-related e-mail communications, and captured Outlook accounts containing e-mails. The stolen data, all less than one month old, consisted of 5,388 unique log files from around the world. The server had been running for three weeks before it was found. Data had been stolen from victims in the United States, Germany, France, India, England, Spain, Canada, Italy, the Netherlands, and Turkey. More than 5,000 customer records from 40 international financial institutions had been stolen.

A crime server held more than 1.4 gigabytes of business and personal data stolen from computers infected with Trojan horses. While gathering data, it also acted as a command-and-control server for the malware (also called crimeware) that ran on the infected PCs. The command-and-control applications enabled the hacker to manage the actions and performance of the crimeware, giving the hacker control over the uses of the crimeware and its victims. Since the crime server's stolen data was left without any access restrictions or encryption, the data was freely available to anyone on the Web. This was not an isolated situation. Two other crime servers holding similar information were found and turned over to law enforcement for investigation.

Sources: Compiled from Higgins (2008) and McGlasson (2008).

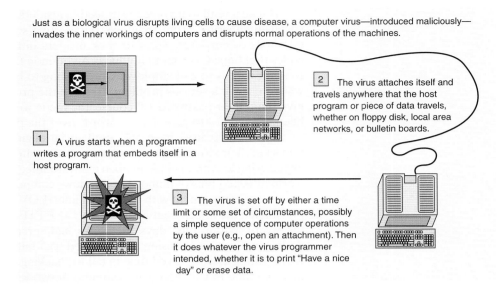

Just as a biological virus disrupts living cells to cause disease, a computer virus—introduced maliciously—invades the inner workings of computers and disrupts normal operations of the machines.

2 The virus attaches itself and travels anywhere that the host program or piece of data travels, whether on floppy disk, local area networks, or bulletin boards.

1 A virus starts when a programmer writes a program that embeds itself in a host program.

3 The virus is set off by either a time limit or some set of circumstances, possibly a simple sequence of computer operations by the user (e.g., open an attachment). Then it does whatever the virus programmer intended, whether it is to print "Have a nice day" or erase data.

Figure 5.4 How a computer virus can spread.

Programming attacks are popular with criminals who use programming techniques to modify other computer programs. For these types of crimes, programming skill and knowledge of the targeted systems are needed. Malware examples are viruses, worms, and Trojan horses. Several of the methods were designed for Web-based systems. Malware can be used to launch **denial of service (DoS) attacks.** A DoS attack occurs when a server or Web site receives a flood of traffic—much more traffic or requests for service than it can handle, causing it to crash.

A universal attack method is the **virus,** which is computer code (software program). It receives its name from the program's ability to attach itself to and infect other computer programs, without the owner of the program being aware of the infection, as shown in Figure 5.4. When the infected software is used, the virus spreads, causing damage to that program and possibly to others.

Unlike a virus, a **worm** spreads without any human intervention, such as checking e-mail or transmitting files. Worms use networks to propagate and infect anything attached to them—including computers, handheld devices, Web sites, and servers. Worms can spread via instant or text messages. Worms' ability to self-propagate through a network can clog and degrade a network's performance, including the Internet.

Trojan horses are referred to as backdoors because they give the attacker illegal access to a network or account through a network port. A network port is a physical interface for communication between a computer and other devices on a network. **Remote administration Trojans (RATs)** are a class of backdoors that enable remote control over the compromised (infected) machine. The crime server discussed in *IT at Work 5.4* involved RAT-infected computers for stealth data collection. RATs open a network port on a victim computer, giving the attacker control over it. Infected PCs are also called *zombies* or *bots*.

A Trojan attaches itself to a zombie's OS and always has two files, the client file and the server file. The server, as its name implies, is installed in the infected machine while the client is used by the intruder to control the compromised system. Trojan horse functions include managing files on the zombie PC, managing processes, remotely activating commands, intercepting keystrokes, watching screen images, and restarting and closing down infected hosts. Common Trojans are NetBus, Back Orifice (BO) 2000, SubSeven, and Hack'a'tack.

TARGETED ATTACKS ON ENTERPRISES

Corporate and government secrets are currently being stolen by a serious threat called **advanced persistent threat (APT).** Most APT attacks are launched through phishing. Typically, this type of attack begins with some reconnaissance on the part of attackers. This can include researching publicly available information about the company and its employees, often from social networking sites. This information is then used to create targeted phishing e-mail messages. A successful attack could give the attacker access to the enterprise's network.

APTs are designed for long-term espionage. Once installed on a network, APTs transmit copies of documents, such as Microsoft Office files and PDFs, in stealth mode. APTs collect and store files on the company's network, encrypt them, then send them in bursts to servers, typically in China.

A notorious APT is *Hydraq Trojan*, or *Aurora*. In January 2010, dozens of large companies were compromised by *Hydraq*. In the Hydraq attack, a previously unknown vulnerability in Microsoft Internet Explorer and a patched vulnerability in Adobe Reader and Flash Player were exploited to install the Trojan. Once installed, attackers had full remote access to do whatever they wanted. Typically, once they have established access within the enterprise, attackers use their access privileges to connect to other computers and servers and compromise them, too. They can do this by stealing credentials on the local computer or capturing data by installing a keystroke logger.

APT attacks are designed to remain undetected in order to gather information over prolonged periods. This type of attack has been observed in other large-scale data breaches that exposed large numbers of identities.

BOTNETS

A **botnet** is a collection of bots (computers infected by software robots). Those infected computers, called **zombies,** can be controlled and organized into a network of zombies on the command of a remote botmaster (also called *bot herder*). Storm worm, which is spread via spam, is a botnet agent embedded inside more than 25 million computers. Storm's combined power has been compared to the processing might of a supercomputer, and Storm-organized attacks are capable of crippling any Web site.

Botnets expose infected computers, as well as other network computers, to the following threats (Edwards, 2008):

- **Spyware:** Zombies can be commanded to monitor and steal personal or financial data.
- **Adware:** Zombies can be ordered to download and display advertisements. Some zombies even force an infected system's browser to visit a specific Web site.
- **Spam:** Most junk e-mail is sent by zombies. Owners of infected computers are usually blissfully unaware that their machines are being used to commit a crime.
- **Phishing:** Zombies can seek out weak servers that are suitable for hosting a phishing Web site, which looks like a legitimate Web site, to trick the users into inputting confidential data.
- **DoS Attacks:** In a *denial of service* attack, the network or Web site is bombarded with so many requests for service (that is, traffic) that it crashes.

Botnets are extremely dangerous because they scan for and compromise other computers, and can be used for every type of crime and attack against computers, servers, and networks.

MALWARE AND BOTNET DEFENSES

Since malware and botnets use many attack methods and strategies, multiple tools are needed to detect them and/or neutralize their effects. Three essential defenses are the following:

1. Antivirus software: Anti-malware tools are designed to detect malicious codes and prevent users from downloading them. They can also scan systems for the presence of worms, Trojan horses, and other types of threats. This technology does not provide complete protection because it cannot defend against *zero-day exploits. Zero-day* refers to the day the exploits hit the Internet. Anti-malware may not be able to detect a previously unknown exploit.

2. Intrusion detection systems (IDS): As the name implies, an IDS scans for unusual or suspicious traffic. An IDS can identify the start of a DoS attack by the traffic pattern, alert the network administrator to take defensive actions, such as switching to another IP address and diverting critical servers from the path of the attack.

3. Intrusion prevention systems (IPS): An IPS is designed to take immediate action—such as blocking specific IP addresses—whenever a traffic-flow anomaly is detected. ASIC (application-specific integrated circuit)-based IPSs have the power and analysis capabilities to detect and block DoS attacks, functioning somewhat like an automated circuit breaker.

Lavasoft (*lavasoft.com/*) offers free software, called Ad-Aware, to identify and remove Trojans and other infections at *lavasoft.com*. Its Web site also provides news about current malware threats.

In the next section, we discuss crime, one example of which is fraud, or white-collar crime. Companies suffer tremendous loss from occupational fraud. It is a widespread problem that affects every company, regardless of size, location, or industry. The FBI has labeled fraud one of the fastest-growing crimes.

Review Questions

1. Define and give three examples of an unintentional threat.
2. Define and give three examples of an intentional threat.
3. What is social engineering? Give an example.
4. What is a crime server?
5. What are the risks from data tampering?
6. List and define three types of malware.
7. Define *botnet* and explain its risk.
8. Explain the difference between an IDS and an IPS.

5.3 Fraud, Crimes, and Violations

Crime can be divided into two categories depending on the tactics used to carry it out: violent and nonviolent. Fraud is nonviolent crime because instead of a gun or knife, fraudsters use deception and trickery. Fraudsters carry out their crime by abusing the power of their position or by taking advantage of the trust, ignorance, or laziness of others.

FRAUD

Occupational fraud refers to the deliberate misuse of the assets of one's employer for personal gain. Internal audits and internal controls are essential to the prevention and detection of occupation frauds. Several examples are listed in Table 5.3.

High-profile cases of occupational fraud committed by senior executives, such as Bernard Madoff, have led to increased government regulation. However, increased legislation has not put an end to fraud. *IT at Work 5.5* gives some insight into Madoff's $50 billion fraud, which also led to the investigation of the agency responsible for fraud prevention—the SEC (Securities and Exchange Commission, *sec.gov/*).

TABLE 5.3	Types and Characteristics of Organizational Fraud	
Type of Fraud	**Does This Fraud Impact Financial Statements?**	**Typical Characteristics**
Operating management corruption	No	Occurs *off the books.* Median loss due to corruption: over six times greater than median loss due to misappropriation ($530,000 vs. $80,000)
Conflict of interest	No	A breach of confidentiality, such as revealing competitors' bids; often occurs with bribery
Bribery	No	Uses positional power or money to influence others
Embezzlement or "misappropriation"	No	Employee theft—employees' access to company property creates the opportunity for embezzlement
Senior management financial reporting fraud	Yes	Involves a massive breach of trust and leveraging of positional power
Accounting cycle fraud	Yes	This fraud is called "earnings management" or earning engineering, which are in violation of GAAP (generally accepted accounting principles) and all other accounting practices. See *aicpa.org*

IT at Work 5.5

Madoff's Ponzi Scheme: Biggest Fraud in Wall St. History

Bernard Madoff is in jail after pleading guilty in 2009 to the biggest fraud in Wall Street history.

For four decades, Madoff perpetrated a complex and sinister fraud. Prior to his arrest on December 11, 2008, Madoff was viewed as a charismatic man and stellar financier with favorable connections to power brokers on Wall Street and in Washington. Since his arrest, federal prosecutors have said that Bernard Madoff ran a scheme that bilked wealthy individuals and large nonprofits out of an estimated $64.8 billion.

Social Engineering. Fundamentally, Madoff relied on social engineering and the predictability of human nature to generate income for himself, not on financial expertise. Madoff would ask people to invest in his funds, which were by invitation only, to create the illusion of exclusivity. Madoff used this tactic to create the illusion that only the elite could invest because of consistent returns and his stellar Wall Street reputation. As he expected, wealthy investors mistook *exclusivity* to mean a secret formula for a *sure thing*.

Steady returns, an actual example of which is shown in Figure 5.5, were one of the many well-known red flags indicating fraud that investors and watchdogs chose to disregard. In fact, looking back, investors are saying they missed several glaring red flags.

Red Flags of Fraud. The classic red flags that made this fraud detectable much earlier (if those flags had not been ignored by many) include:

- Madoff was trusted because he was a Wall St. fixture, so his work was not given full scrutiny.
- The unbelievable returns defied the market. The returns were impossible, yet this fact was ignored.
- Madoff used a sense of exclusivity—a hook to play "hard to get." This false sense of exclusivity is a sign of a Ponzi scheme.

- There were steady returns. Reports of consistently good but never spectacular gains can lull all kinds of investors into a false sense of security over time.

Madoff and SEC Being Investigated. This scandal triggered investigations not only of Madoff but also of the watchdog agency, the Securities and Exchange Commission (SEC). The SEC was investigated by Congress and the agency's Inspector General for repeatedly ignoring whistleblowers' warnings about Madoff's operations. Created by Congress in 1934 during the Great Depression, the SEC is charged with ensuring that public companies accurately disclose their financial and business risks to investors and that brokers who trade securities for clients keep investors' interests first.

Madoff is not the only one at fault. He worked with dozens of feeder funds and other middlemen to lure money into his Ponzi scheme. Investigations have involved forensic accounting as well as computer forensics—the latter to discover a smoking-gun e-mail on other digital messages that reveal *who knew what* and *who did what*. Forensics experts are digging deep into the evidence to determine who else was complicit in the fraud.

Regulatory Reaction. In January 2009, the Senate Banking Committee introduced legislation to provide $110 million to hire 500 new FBI agents, 50 new assistant U.S. attorneys, and 100 new SEC enforcement officials to crack down on fraud.

Sources: Compiled from Antilla (2008), Appelbaum and Hilzenrath (2008), Chew (2009), Gold (2008), and Quinn (2009).

Discussion Questions: How important was trust to Madoff's scheme? What else did Madoff rely on to carry out his fraud? What is a *red flag*? In your opinion, how were so many red flags ignored given the risk that investors faced? Could a large investment fraud happen again—or are there internal fraud prevention and detection measures that would prevent it from happening? Explain your answer.

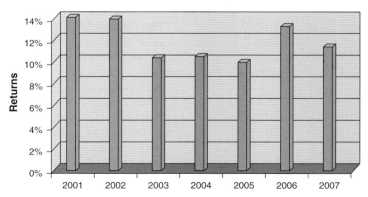

Figure 5.5 Annual Returns on a Madoff-Investor's Account from 2001–2007.

INTERNAL FRAUD PREVENTION AND DETECTION

ETHICS

IT has a key role to play in demonstrating effective corporate governance and fraud prevention. Regulators look favorably on companies that can demonstrate good corporate governance and best-practice operational risk management. Management and staff of such companies can then spend less time worrying about regulations and more time adding value to their brand and business.

Internal fraud prevention measures are based on the same controls used to prevent external intrusions—perimeter defense technologies, such as firewalls, e-mail scanners, and biometric access. They are also based on human resource (HR) procedures, such as recruitment screening and training.

Much of this detection activity can be handled by intelligent analysis engines using advanced data warehousing and analytics techniques. These systems take in audit trails from key systems and personnel records from the HR and finance departments. The data is stored in a data warehouse, where it is analyzed to detect anomalous patterns, such as excessive hours worked, deviations in patterns of behavior, copying of huge amounts of data, attempts to override controls, unusual transactions, and inadequate documentation about a transaction. Information from investigations is fed back into the detection system so that it learns. Since insiders might work in collusion with organized criminals, insider profiling is important to find wider patterns of criminal networks.

An enterprisewide approach that combines risk, security, compliance, and IT specialists greatly increases the prevention and detection of fraud. Prevention is the most cost-effective approach, since detection and prosecution costs are enormous, above and beyond the direct cost of the loss. Prevention starts with corporate governance culture and ethics at the top levels of the organization.

Identity Theft One of the worst and most prevalent crimes is identity theft. Such thefts, where individuals' Social Security and credit card numbers are stolen and used by thieves, are not new. Criminals have always obtained information about other people—by stealing wallets or digging in dumpsters. But widespread electronic sharing and databases have made the crime worse. Because financial institutions, data processing firms, and retail businesses are reluctant to reveal incidents in which their customers' personal financial information may have been stolen, lost, or compromised, laws continue to be passed to force those notifications. Examples in Table 5.4 illustrate different ways in which identity theft crimes have occurred.

TABLE 5.4	Examples of Identity Crimes Requiring Notification	
How It Happened	**Number of Individuals Notified**	**Description**
Stolen desktop	3,623	Desktop computer was stolen from regional sales office containing data that was password-protected but not encrypted. Thieves stole SSNs and other information from TransUnion LLC, which maintains personal credit histories.
Online, by an ex-employee	465,000	Former employee downloaded information about participants in Georgia State Health Benefits Plan.
Computer tapes lost in transit	3.9 million	CitiFinancial, the consumer finance division of Citigroup Inc., lost tapes containing information about both active and closed accounts while they were being shipped to a credit bureau.
Online "malicious user" used legitimate user's log-in information	33,000	The U.S. Air Force suffered a security breach in the online system containing information on officers and enlisted personnel, including personal information.
Missing backup	200,000	A timeshare unit of Marriott International lost a backup tape containing SSNs and other confidential data of employees and timeshare owners and customers.

1. What are the two types of crimes?
2. Define *fraud* and *occupational fraud*. Identify two examples of each.
3. How can internal fraud be prevented? How can it be detected?
4. Explain why data on laptops and computers should be encrypted.
5. Explain how identity theft can occur.

5.4 Information Assurance and Risk Management

The objective of IT security management practices is to defend all of the components of an information system, specifically data, software applications, hardware, and networks. Before they make any decisions concerning defenses, people responsible for security must understand the requirements and operations of the business, which form the basis for a customized defense strategy. In the next section, we describe the major defense strategies.

DEFENSE STRATEGY

The defense strategy and controls that should be used depend on what needs to be protected and the cost-benefit analysis. That is, companies should neither underinvest nor overinvest. The SEC and FTC impose huge fines for data breaches to deter companies from underinvesting in data protection. The following are the major objectives of defense strategies:

1. Prevention and deterrence. Properly designed controls may prevent errors from occurring, deter criminals from attacking the system, and, better yet, deny access to unauthorized people. These are the most desirable controls.

2. Detection. As with a fire, the earlier an attack is detected, the easier it is to combat and the less damage is done. Detection can be performed in many cases by using special diagnostic software, at a minimal cost.

3. Containment (contain the damage). Containment minimizes or limits losses once a malfunction has occurred. It is also called damage control. This can be accomplished, for example, by including a *fault-tolerant system* that permits operation in a degraded mode until full recovery is made. If a fault-tolerant system does not exist, a quick and possibly expensive recovery must take place. Users want their systems back in operation as fast as possible.

4. Recovery. A recovery plan explains how to fix a damaged information system as quickly as possible. Replacing rather than repairing components is one route to fast recovery.

5. Correction. Correcting the causes of damaged systems can prevent the problem from occurring again.

6. Awareness and compliance. All organization members must be educated about the hazards and must comply with the security rules and regulations.

A defense strategy also requires several controls, as shown in Figure 5.6. **General controls** are established to protect the system regardless of the specific application. For example, protecting hardware and controlling access to the data center are independent of the specific application. **Application controls** are safeguards that are intended to protect specific applications. In the next two sections, we discuss the major types of these two groups of information systems controls.

GENERAL CONTROLS

The major categories of general controls are physical controls, access controls, biometric controls, administrative controls, application controls, and endpoint controls.

Physical Controls Physical security refers to the protection of computer facilities and resources. This includes protecting physical property such as computers, data centers, software, manuals, and networks. It provides protection against most natural hazards

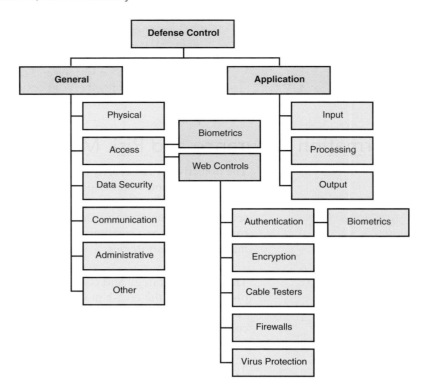

Figure 5.6 Major defense controls.

as well as against some human hazards. Appropriate physical security may include several controls, such as the following:

• Appropriate design of the data center; for example, ensuring that the data center is noncombustible and waterproof
• Shielding against electromagnetic fields
• Good fire prevention, detection, and extinguishing systems, including sprinkler system, water pumps, and adequate drainage facilities
• Emergency power shutoff and backup batteries, which must be maintained in operational condition
• Properly designed, maintained, and operated air-conditioning systems
• Motion detector alarms that detect physical intrusion

Access Controls Access control is the management of who is and is not authorized to use a company's hardware and software. Access control methods, such as firewalls and access control lists, restrict access to a network, database, file, or data. It is the major defense line against unauthorized insiders as well as outsiders. Access control involves authorization (having the right to access) and authentication, which is also called user identification (proving that the user is who he or she claims to be).

Authentication methods include:

• Something only the user knows, such as a password
• Something only the user has, such as a smart card or a token
• Something that is characteristic only of the user, such as a signature, voice, fingerprint, or retinal (eye) scan; implemented via biometric controls, which can be physical or behavioral

Biometric Controls A **biometric control** is an automated method of verifying the identity of a person, based on physical or behavioral characteristics. Most biometric systems match some personal characteristic against a stored profile. The most common biometrics are the following:

- **Thumbprint or fingerprint.** Each time a user wants access, a thumb- or fingerprint (finger scan) is matched against a template containing the authorized person's fingerprint to identify him or her.
- **Retinal scan.** A match is attempted between the pattern of the blood vessels in the retina that is being scanned and a prestored picture of the retina.
- **Voice scan.** A match is attempted between the user's voice and the voice pattern stored on templates.
- **Signature.** Signatures are matched against the prestored authentic signature. This method can supplement a photo card–ID system.

Biometric controls are now integrated into many e-business hardware and software products. Biometric controls do have some limitations: They are not accurate in certain cases, and some people see them as an invasion of privacy.

Administrative Controls While the previously discussed general controls are technical in nature, administrative controls deal with issuing guidelines and monitoring compliance with the guidelines. Examples of such controls are shown in Table 5.5.

Application Controls Sophisticated attacks are aimed at the application level, and many applications were not designed to withstand such attacks. For better survivability, information-processing methodologies are being replaced with agent technology. **Intelligent agents,** also called softbots or knowbots, are highly adaptive applications. The term generally means applications that have some degree of reactivity, autonomy, and adaptability—as is needed in unpredictable attack situations. An agent is able to adapt itself based on changes occurring in its environment, as shown in Figure 5.7.

In the next section, the focus is on the company's digital endpoints and the perimeter—the network. We discuss the security of wireline and wireless networks and their inherent vulnerabilities.

Endpoint Security and Control Many managers underestimate the business risk posed by unencrypted portable storage devices, which are examples of *endpoints*. Business data is often carried on thumb drives, smartphones, and removable memory cards without IT's permission, oversight, or sufficient protection against loss or theft. Handhelds and portable storage devices put sensitive data at risk. According to market research firm Applied Research-West, three of four workers save corporate data on thumb drives. According to their study, 25 percent save customer records, 17 percent store financial data, and 15 percent store business plans on thumb drives, but less than 50 percent of businesses routinely encrypt those drives and even less consistently secure data copied onto smartphones.

TABLE 5.5	Representative Administrative Controls

- Appropriately selecting, training, and supervising employees, especially in accounting and information systems
- Fostering company loyalty
- Immediately revoking access privileges of dismissed, resigned, or transferred employees
- Requiring periodic modification of access controls (such as passwords)
- Developing programming and documentation standards (to make auditing easier and to use the standards as guides for employees)
- Insisting on security bonds or malfeasance insurance for key employees
- Instituting separation of duties, namely, dividing sensitive computer duties among as many employees as economically feasible in order to decrease the chance of intentional or unintentional damage
- Holding periodic random audits of the system

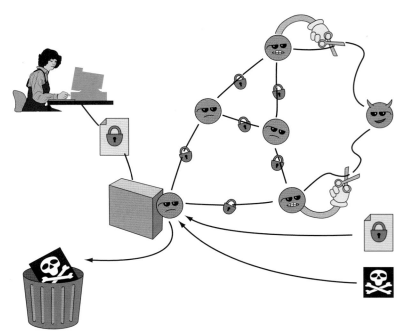

Figure 5.7 Intelligent agents. Agents in the collective communicate over secured links on the Internet or an intranet. Malicious agents (with horns) are detected and cut off from the collective. Properly authenticated data is allowed into the collective, but bad information is rejected. *Source: Courtesy of Sandia National Laboratories.*

Portable devices that store confidential customer or financial data must be protected no matter who owns it—employees or the company. If there are no security measures to protect handhelds or other mobile/portable storage, data must not be stored on them because it exposes the company to liability, lawsuits, and fines. For smaller companies, a single data breach could bankrupt the company.

Strong protection now requires more than native encryption. For example, locking a BlackBerry does not provide strong protection. Security company IronKey reported that Mantech Crowbar (*cybersolutions.mantech.com/*) can copy the contents of a BlackBerry's SD card quickly and crack a four-digit PIN in 30 seconds. Crowbar, which costs about $2,300, is designed to be simple and fast at doing its one job—cracking passwords on MMC/SD cards. The Crowbar can crack security on a handheld device without alerting the owner that the device's security has been compromised. The Crowbar also stores log-in information for the cracked handheld, allowing a hacker to access the hacked device again unless the user changes the password.

Review Questions

1. What are the major objectives of a defense strategy?
2. What are general controls? What are application controls?
3. Define *access control.*
4. What are biometric controls? Give two examples.
5. What is the general meaning of *intelligent agents*?
6. What is endpoint security?
7. How does Mantech Crowbar increase endpoint risk?

5.5 Network Security

As a defense, companies need to implement network access control (NAC) products. NAC tools are different from traditional security technologies and practices that focus on file access. While file-level security is useful for protecting data, it does not keep unauthorized users out of the network in the first place. NAC technology, on the other hand, helps businesses lock down their networks against criminals.

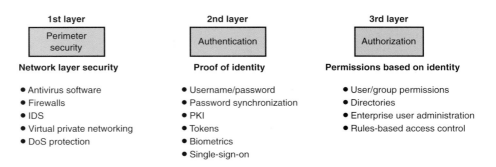

Figure 5.8 Three layers of network security measures.

Network security measures involve three types of defenses, which are referred to as *layers:*

- **First layer: Perimeter security** to control access to the network. Examples are antivirus software and firewalls.
- **Second layer: Authentication** to verify the identity of the person requesting access to the network. Examples are usernames and passwords.
- **Third layer: Authorization** to control what authenticated users can do once they are given access to the network. Examples are permissions and directories.

Details of these three defense layers are shown in Figure 5.8.

PERIMETER SECURITY AND FIREWALLS

The major objective of perimeter security is access control. The technologies used to protect against malware (e.g., firewalls, IDS, and IDP) also protect the perimeter. A firewall is a system, or group of systems, that enforces an access-control policy between two networks. It is commonly used as a barrier between a secure corporate intranet or other internal networks and the Internet, which is unsecured. Firewalls function by deciding what traffic to permit (allow) into and out of the network and what traffic to block. Firewalls need to be configured to enforce the company's security procedures and policies. A network has several firewalls, but they still cannot stop all malware (see Figure 5.9). For example, each virus has a signature that identifies it. Firewalls and antivirus software that have been updated—and know of that virus's signature—can block it. But viruses pass through a firewall if the firewall cannot identify it as a virus. For example, a newly released virus whose signature has not yet been identified or that is hidden in an e-mail attachment can be allowed into the network. That's the reason why firewalls and antivirus software require continuous updating.

All Internet traffic, which travels as packets, should have to pass through a firewall, but that is rarely the case for instant messages and wireless traffic, which, as a result, "carry" malware into the network and applications on host computers. Firewalls do not control anything that happens after a legitimate user (who may be a disgruntled employee or an employee whose username and password have been compromised) has been authenticated and granted authority to access applications on the network. For these reasons, firewalls are a necessary but insufficient defense.

NETWORK AUTHENTICATION AND AUTHORIZATION

As applied to the Internet, an authentication system guards against unauthorized access attempts. The major objective of authentication is the proof of identity. The attempt here is to identify the legitimate user and determine the action he or she is allowed to perform.

Because phishing and identity theft prey on weak authentication, and usernames and passwords do not offer strong authentication, other methods are needed. There are **two-factor authentication** (also called multifactor authentication) and two-tier authentication. With two-factor authentication, other information is used to verify the user's identity, such as biometrics.

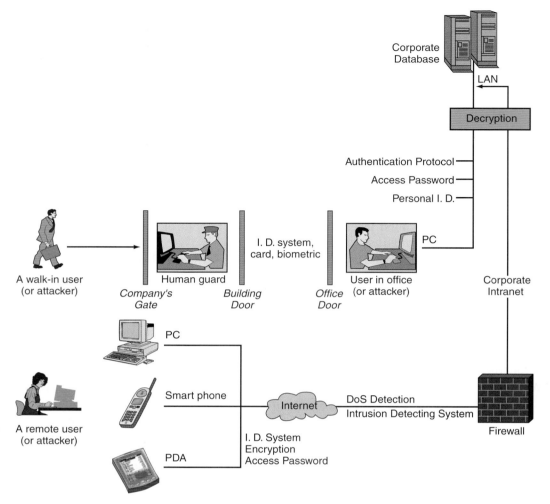

Figure 5.9 Where IT security mechanisms are located.

There are three key questions to ask when setting up an authentication system:

1. Who are you? Is this person an employee, a partner, or a customer? Different levels of authentication would be set up for different types of people.

2. Where are you? For example, an employee who has already used a badge to access the building is less of a risk than an employee or partner logging on remotely. Someone logging on from a known IP address is less of a risk than someone logging on from Nigeria or Kazakhstan.

3. What do you want? Is this person accessing sensitive or proprietary information or simply gaining access to benign data?

When dealing with consumer-facing applications, such as online banking and e-commerce, strong authentication must be balanced with convenience. If authentication makes it too difficult to bank or shop online, users will go back to the brick-and-mortars. There is a trade-off between increased protection and turning customers away from your online channel. In addition, authentication of a Web site to the customer is equally critical. E-commerce customers need to be able to identify whether it is a fraudulent site set up by phishers.

Authorization refers to permission issued to individuals or groups to do certain activities with a computer, usually based on verified identity. The security system, once it authenticates the user, must make sure that the user operates within his or her authorized activities.

SECURING WIRELESS NETWORKS

Wireless networks are more difficult to protect than wireline ones. All of the vulnerabilities that exist in a conventional wireline network apply to wireless technologies. Wireless access points (wireless APs or WAPs) behind a firewall and other security protections can be a backdoor into a network. Sensitive data that is not encrypted or is encrypted with a weak cryptographic technique used for wireless, such as **wired equivalent privacy (WEP),** and that is transmitted between two wireless devices, may be intercepted and disclosed. Wireless devices are susceptible to DoS attacks because intruders can gain access to network management controls and then disable or disrupt operations. Wireless packet analyzers, such as AirSnort and WEPcrack, are readily available tools that can be used to gain unauthorized access to networks, putting them at great risk. Unauthorized wireless APs could be deployed by malicious users—tricking legitimate users into connecting to those rogue access points. Malicious users then gain access to sensitive information stored on client machines, including log-ins, passwords, customer information, and intellectual property.

Although WEP is well known and has been widely used, it has inherent flaws in that WEP encryption is fairly easy to crack. As a result, more reliable encryption schemes have been developed, for example, the Wi-Fi Protected Access (WPA). WPA is a security technology for wireless networks that improves on the authentication and encryption features of WEP. In fact, WPA was developed by the networking industry in response to the shortcomings of WEP.

Review Questions

1. What are network access control (NAC) products?
2. Define *authentication*, and give an example of an authentication method.
3. Define *authorization*.
4. What is a firewall? What can it not protect against?
5. Explain the advantage of WPA over WEP.

5.6 Internal Control and Compliance

The **internal control environment** is the work atmosphere that a company sets for its employees. *Internal control (IC)* is a process designed to achieve the following:

- Reliable financial reporting
- Operational efficiency
- Compliance with laws, regulations, and policies
- Safeguarded assets.

INTERNAL CONTROLS NEEDED FOR COMPLIANCE

The Sarbanes-Oxley Act (SOX) is an anti-fraud law. It forces more accurate business reporting and disclosure of GAAP (generally accepted accounting principles) violations, thus making it necessary to find and root out fraud.

Section 302 deters corporate and executive fraud by requiring that the CEO and CFO verify that they have reviewed the financial report, and, to the best of their knowledge, the report does not contain an untrue statement or omit any material fact. To motivate honesty, executive management faces criminal penalties, including long jail terms for false reports. Table 5.6 lists the symptoms, or red flags, of fraud that internal controls can be designed to detect.

Section 805 mandates a review of the Sentencing Guidelines to ensure that "the guidelines that apply to organizations . . . are sufficient to deter and punish organizational criminal conduct." The Guidelines also focus on the establishment of "effective compliance and ethics" programs. As indicated in the Guidelines, a precondition to an effective compliance and ethics program is promotion of "an organizational culture that encourages ethical conduct and a commitment to compliance with the law."

TABLE 5.6	Symptoms of Fraud That Can Be Detected by Internal Controls

- Missing documents
- Delayed bank deposits
- Holes in accounting records
- Numerous outstanding checks or bills
- Disparity between accounts payable and receivable
- Employees who do not take vacations or who go out of their way to work overtime
- A large drop in profits
- A major increase in business with one particular customer
- Customer complaints about double billing
- Repeated duplicate payments
- Employees with the same address or telephone number as a vendor

Among other measures, SOX requires companies to set up comprehensive internal controls. There is no question that SOX, and the complex and costly provisions it requires public companies to follow, has had a major impact on corporate financial accounting. For starters, companies have had to set up comprehensive internal controls over financial reporting to prevent fraud and catch it when it occurs. Since the collapse of Arthur Andersen, following the accounting firm's conviction on criminal charges related to the Enron case, outside accounting firms have gotten tougher with clients they are auditing, particularly regarding their internal controls.

SOX and the SEC are making it clear that if controls can be ignored, there is no control. Therefore, fraud prevention and detection require an effective monitoring system. If the company shows its employees that it can find out everything that every employee does and use that evidence to prosecute that person to the fullest extent of the law, then the feeling that "I can get away with it" drops drastically.

Approximately 85 percent of occupational fraud could have been prevented if proper IT-based internal controls had been designed, implemented, and followed.

SOX requires an enterprise-wide approach to compliance, internal control, and risk management because they cannot be dealt with from a departmental or business-unit perspective. However, protecting against fraud also requires a worldwide approach, as many incidents have indicated, such as the crime server in Malaysia.

WORLDWIDE ANTI-FRAUD REGULATION

Well-executed internal fraud or money-laundering operations can damage the financial sector, capital (money) markets, and, as a result, a nation's economy. A capital market is any market where a government or a company can raise money to finance operations and long-term investment. Examples are the stock and bond markets.

Preventing internal fraud is high on the political agenda, with the Financial Services Authority (FSA) in the United Kingdom and the SEC in the United States both requiring companies to deal with the issue. In May 2007, the FSA fined French investment bank BNP Paribas €350,000 for systems and control failures at its London-based private banking unit that allowed a senior manager to steal €1.4 million from client accounts (Reuters UK, 2007). It was the first time a private bank was fined for weaknesses in anti-fraud systems by the FSA, which warned that it was "raising its game" against firms with lax controls.

Managing risk has become the single most important issue for regulators and financial institutions. Over the years, these institutions have suffered high costs for ignoring their exposure to risk. However, growing research and improvements in IT have improved the measurement and management of risk.

1. Define *internal control*.
2. How does SOX Section 302 deter fraud?
3. List three symptoms or red flags of fraud that can be detected by internal controls.

5.7 Business Continuity and Auditing

Fires, earthquakes, floods, power outages, and other types of disasters hit data centers. Yet business continuity planning and disaster recovery capabilities can be a tough sell because they do not contribute to the bottom line. Compare them to an insurance policy: If and only if a disaster occurs, the money has been well spent. And spending on business continuity preparedness can be an open-ended proposition—there is always more that could be done to better prepare the organization.

Disasters may occur without warning, so the best defense is to be prepared, as described in *IT at Work 5.6*. An important element in any security system is the **business continuity plan,** also known as the disaster recovery plan. Such a plan outlines the process by which businesses should recover from a major disaster. Destruction of all (or most) of the computing facilities can cause significant damage. It is difficult for many organizations to obtain insurance for their computers and information systems without showing a satisfactory disaster prevention and recovery plan.

IT managers need to estimate how much spending is appropriate for the level of risk an organization is willing to accept.

BUSINESS CONTINUITY PLANNING

Disaster recovery is the chain of events linking the business continuity plan to protection and to recovery. The following are some key thoughts about the process:

- The purpose of a business continuity plan is to keep the business running after a disaster occurs. Each function in the business should have a valid recovery capability plan.
- Recovery planning is part of *asset protection*. Every organization should assign responsibility to management to identify and protect assets within their spheres of functional control.
- Planning should focus first on recovery from a total loss of all capabilities.

IT at Work 5.6

Business Continuity and Disaster Recovery

Ninety-three percent of companies that suffer a significant data loss go out of business within five years. Even though business continuity/disaster recovery (BC/DR) is a business survival issue, many managers have dangerously viewed BC/DR as an IT security issue.

Disasters teach the best lessons for both IT managers and corporate executives who have not implemented BC/DR processes. The success or failure of those processes depends on IT, as the following case indicates.

The city of Houston, Texas, and Harris County swung into action by turning Reliant Park and the Houston Astrodome into a "temporary city" with a medical facility, pharmacy, post office, and town square to house more than 250,000 Hurricane Katrina evacuees. Coast Guard Lt. Commander Joseph J. Leonard headed up the operation, drawing on his knowledge of the National Incident Command System. As Leonard explained, ineffective communication between the command staff and those in New Orleans, who could have informed Houston authorities about the number

and special needs of the evacuees, caused a serious problem. In addition, agencies and organizations with poor on-scene decision-making authority hampered and slowed efforts to get things done.

Now businesses in hurricane alleys, earthquake corridors, and major cities are deploying BC/DR plans supported with software tools that allow them to replicate, or back up, their mission-critical applications to sites away from their primary data centers. In case of a disaster, companies can transmit vital accounting, project management, or transactional systems and records to their disaster recovery facilities, limiting downtime and data loss despite an outage at the primary location.

Sources: Compiled from Fagg (2006), *Fiber Optics Weekly* (2006), and the Infragard (*infragardconferences.com*).

Discussion Questions: Why might a company that had a significant data loss not be able to recover? Why are regulators requiring that companies implement BC/DR plans?

- Proof of capability usually involves some kind of what-if analysis that shows that the recovery plan is current.
- All critical applications must be identified and their recovery procedures addressed in the plan.
- The plan should be written so that it will be effective in case of disaster, not just in order to satisfy the auditors.
- The plan should be kept in a safe place; copies should be given to all key managers, or it should be available on the intranet. The plan should be audited periodically.

Disaster recovery planning can be very complex, and it may take several months to complete. Using special software, the planning job can be expedited.

Disaster avoidance is an approach oriented toward prevention. The idea is to minimize the chance of avoidable disasters (such as fire or other human-caused threats). For example, many companies use a device called uninterrupted power supply (UPS), which provides power in case of a power outage.

AUDITING INFORMATION SYSTEMS

An **audit** is an important part of any control system. Auditing can be viewed as an additional layer of controls or safeguards. It is considered to be a deterrent to criminal actions, especially for insiders. Auditors attempt to answer questions such as these:

- Are there sufficient controls in the system? Which areas are not covered by controls?
- Which controls are not necessary?
- Are the controls implemented properly?
- Are the controls effective? That is, do they check the output of the system?
- Is there a clear separation of duties of employees?
- Are there procedures to ensure compliance with the controls?
- Are there procedures to ensure reporting and corrective actions in case of violations of controls?

Auditing a Web site is a good preventive measure to manage the legal risk. Legal risk is important in any IT system, but in Web systems it is even more important due to the content of the site, which may offend people or be in violation of copyright laws or other regulations (e.g., privacy protection). Auditing e-commerce is also more complex since, in addition to the Web site, one needs to audit order taking, order fulfillment, and all support systems.

COST-BENEFIT ANALYSIS

It is usually not economical to prepare and protect against every possible threat. Therefore, an IT security program must provide a process for assessing threats and deciding which ones to prepare for and which ones to ignore or provide reduced protection against.

Risk-Management Analysis Risk-management analysis can be enhanced by the use of DSS software packages. A simplified computation is shown here:

$$\text{expected loss} = P_1 \times P_2 \times L$$

where:
P_1 = probability of attack (estimate, based on judgment)
P_2 = probability of attack being successful (estimate, based on judgment)
L = loss occurring if attack is successful
Example:

$$P_1 = .02, P_2 = .10, L = \$1,000,000$$

Then, expected loss from this particular attack is

$$P_1 \times P_2 \times L = 0.02 \times 0.1 \times \$1,000,000 = \$2,000$$

The amount of loss may depend on the duration of a system being out of operation. Therefore, some add duration to the analysis.

Ethical Issues Implementing security programs raises many ethical issues. First, some people are against any monitoring of individual activities. Imposing certain controls is seen by some as a violation of freedom of speech or other civil liberties. A Gartner Group study showed that even after the terrorist attacks of September 11, 2001, only 26 percent of Americans approved of a national ID database. Using biometrics is considered by many to be a violation of privacy.

Handling the privacy versus security dilemma is tough. There are other ethical and legal obligations that may require companies to "invade the privacy" of employees and monitor their actions. In particular, IT security measures are needed to protect against loss, liability, and litigation. Losses are not just financial, but also include the loss of information, customers, trading partners, brand image, and ability to conduct business, due to the actions of hackers, malware, or employees. Liability stems from two legal doctrines: *respondeat superior* and duty of care. *Respondeat superior* holds employers liable for the misconduct of their employees that occurs within the scope of their employment. With wireless technologies and a mobile workforce, the scope of employment has expanded beyond the perimeters of the company.

Under the doctrine of duty of care, senior managers and directors have a fiduciary obligation to use reasonable care to protect the company's business operations. Litigation (lawsuits) stems from failure to meet the company's legal and regulatory duties. According to a *Workplace E-Mail and Instant Messaging Survey* of 840 U.S. companies from the American Management Association and the ePolicy Institute (*epolicyinstitute.com*), more than one in five employers (21 percent) have had employee e-mail and IM subpoenaed in the course of a lawsuit or regulatory investigation.

Review Questions

1. Why do organizations need a business continuity plan?
2. List three issues a business continuity plan should cover.
3. Identify two factors that influence a company's ability to recover from a disaster.
4. What types of devices are needed for disaster avoidance?
5. Explain why business continuity/disaster recovery (BC/DR) is not simply an IT security issue.
6. Why should Web sites be audited?
7. How is expected loss calculated?
8. What is the doctrine of due care?

Key Terms

acceptable use policy (AUP) *131*
adware *135*
application controls *139*
audit *148*
biometric control *140*
business continuity plan *147*
business impact analysis (BIA) *131*
computer systems failures *132*
crime server *133*
data tampering *133*
denial of service (DoS) attack *134*
enterprise risk management (ERM) *128*
environmental hazard *132*

general controls *139*
human errors *132*
intelligent agents *141*
internal control *131*
internal threats *124*
IT security *123*
malware *124*
occupational fraud *136*
Payment Card Industry Data Security Standard (PCI DSS) *129*
phishing *127*
programming attacks *134*
remote administration Trojan (RAT) *134*

retinal scan *141*
service pack *127*
signature *141*
social engineering *133*
spam *135*
spyware *135*
thumbprint or fingerprint *141*
time-to-exploitation *127*
two-factor authentication *143*
virus *134*
wired equivalent privacy (WEP) *145*
worm *134*

Chapter Highlights and Insights

❶ Businesses that neglect to consider and implement privacy requirements are subject to enforcement actions, huge lawsuits, penalties, and fines that significantly increase expenses.

❶ A company's top line (revenue) suffers when customers discover that their private information has been compromised.

❶ Criminals invest considerable effort planning and preparing tactics to bypass company security measures.

❷ Responsibility for internal control and compliance rests directly on the shoulders of senior management and the board of directors. SOX and other anti-fraud regulations force better business reporting and disclosure of GAAP violations, thus making it necessary and easier to find and root out fraud.

❷ The chief privacy officer (CPO) and chief security officer (CSO) are corporate-level positions demonstrating the importance and changing role of IT security in organizations.

❸ Data, software, hardware, and networks can be threatened by internal and external hazards.

❸ One of the biggest mistakes managers make is underestimating vulnerabilities and threats.

❸ Computer criminals are increasingly profit-driven.

❹ The risk exposure model for digital assets has five factors: the asset's value to the company, attractiveness to criminals, legal liability attached to its loss or theft, impact on business performance, and likelihood of a successful attack.

❹ The consequences of wireless attacks include data theft, legal and recovery expenses, tarnished image, lost customers, and disrupted operations due to loss of network service.

❺ With two-factor authentication, two types of information are used to verify the user's identity, such as passwords and biometrics.

❺ Biometric controls are used to identify users by checking physical characteristics such as a fingerprint or voice-print.

❺ Encryption is extremely important for confidential data that is sent or stored.

❻ The Committee of Sponsoring Organizations of the Treadway Commission (COSO) defines internal control as a process designed to provide reasonable assurance of effective operations and reliable financial reporting.

❻ There is no such thing as small fraud, only large fraud that was detected and stopped early.

❼ Disaster recovery planning is an integral part of effective internal control and security management.

❼ Business continuity planning includes data backup and a plan for what to do when disaster strikes.

❼ Protecting critical infrastructures, including energy, IT, telecommunications, and transportation sectors, is a key part of national security.

❼ A large range of IT security tools, including intelligent agents and anti-fraud measures, help defend against counterterrorist activities.

Questions for Discussion

1. Many firms concentrate on the wrong questions and end up throwing a great deal of money and time at minimal security risks while ignoring major vulnerabilities. Why?

2. How can the risk of occupational fraud be decreased?

3. Why should information control and security be of prime concern to management?

4. Compare the computer security situation with that of insuring a house.

5. Explain what firewalls protect and what they do not protect. Why?

6. Why is cybercrime expanding rapidly? Discuss some possible solutions.

7. Why are authentication and authorization important in e-commerce?

8. Some insurance companies will not insure a business unless the firm has a computer disaster recovery plan. Explain why.

9. Explain why risk management should involve the following elements: threats, exposure associated with each threat, risk of each threat occurring, cost of controls, and assessment of their effectiveness.

10. Discuss why the Sarbanes-Oxley Act focuses on internal control. How does that focus influence infosec?

11. Discuss the shift in motivation of criminals.

Exercises and Projects

1. A critical problem is assessing how far a company is legally obligated to go. Since there is no such thing as perfect security (i.e., there is always more that you can do), resolving these questions can significantly affect cost.
   a. When are a company's security measures sufficient to comply with its obligations? For example, does installing a firewall and using virus detection software satisfy a company's legal obligations?
   b. Is it necessary for an organization to encrypt all of its electronic records?

2. The SANS Institute publishes the Top 20 Internet Security Vulnerabilities (*sans.org/top20*).
   a. Which of those vulnerabilities are most dangerous to financial institutions?
   b. Which of those vulnerabilities are most dangerous to marketing firms?
   c. Explain any differences.

3. Access the Anti-Phishing Working Group Web site (*antiphishing.org*) and download the most recent Phishing Activity Trends Report.
   a. Describe the recent trends in phishing attacks.
   b. Explain the reasons for these trends.

4. Assume that the daily probability of a major earthquake in Los Angeles is .07 percent. The chance of your computer center being damaged during such a quake is 5 percent. If the center is damaged, the average estimated damage will be $1.6 million.
   a. Calculate the expected loss (in dollars).
   b. An insurance agent is willing to insure your facility for an annual fee of $15,000. Analyze the offer, and discuss whether to accept it.

5. The theft of laptop computers at conventions, hotels, and airports is becoming a major problem. These categories of protection exist: physical devices (e.g., *targus.com*), encryption (e.g., *networkassociates.com*), and security policies (e.g., at *ebay.com*). Find more information on the problem and on the solutions. Summarize the advantages and limitations of each method.

6. Should an employer notify employees that their usage of computers is being monitored? Why or why not?

7. Twenty-five thousand messages arrive at an organization each year. Currently there are no firewalls. On average, there are 1.2 successful hackings each year. Each successful hack attack results in loss to the company of about $130,000. A major firewall is proposed at a cost of $66,000 and a maintenance cost of $5,000. The estimated useful life is three years. The chance that an intruder will break through the firewall is .0002. In such a case, the damage will be $100,000 (30%), or $200,000 (50%), or no damage. There is an annual maintenance cost of $20,000 for the firewall.
   a. Should management buy the firewall?
   b. An improved firewall that is 99.9988 percent effective and that costs $84,000, with a life of three years and annual maintenance cost of $16,000, is available. Should this one be purchased instead of the first one?

Group Assignments and Projects

1. Each group is to be divided into two parts. One part will interview students and businesspeople and record the experiences they have had with computer security problems. The other part of each group will visit a computer store (and/or read the literature or use the Internet) to find out what software is available to fight different computer security problems. Then each group will prepare a presentation in which they describe the problems and identify which of the problems could have been prevented with the use of commercially available software.

2. Create groups to investigate the latest development in IT and e-commerce security. Check journals such as *cio.com* (available free online), vendors, and search engines such as *techdata.com* and *google.com*.

3. Research a botnet attack. Explain how the botnet works and what damage it causes. What preventive methods are offered by security vendors?

Internet Exercises

1. Visit *cert.org* (a center of Internet security expertise). Read one of the recent Security Alerts or CERT Spotlights and write a report.

2. Visit *cert.org/csirts/services.html*. Discover the security services a CSIRT can provide in handling vulnerability. Write a summary of those services.

3. Visit *dhs.gov/dhspublic* (Department of Homeland Security). Search for an article on E-Verify. Write a report on the benefits of this verification program and who can benefit from it.

4. Visit *first.org* (a global leader in incident response). Find a current article under "Global Security News" and write a summary.

5. Visit *issa.org* (Information Systems Security Association) and choose a Webcast to listen to—one concerned with systems security. Write a short opinion essay.

6. Visit *wi-fi.org* (Wi-Fi Alliance) and discover what its mission is. Report on what you think about its relevance in the overall wireless security industry.

7. Visit *securitytracker.com* and select one of the vulnerabilities. Describe the vulnerability, its impacts, its cause, and the affected operating system.

8. Visit *cio.com* and search for a recent article on security, privacy, or compliance. Write a brief summary of the article.

9. Enter *scambusters.org*. Find out what the organization does. Learn about e-mail and Web site scams. Report your findings.

10. Enter *epic.org/privacy/tools.html* and examine one of the following groups of tools: snoop proof e-mail, encryption, or firewalls. Discuss the security benefits.

11. Access the Web sites of any three major antivirus vendors (e.g., *symantec.com*, *mcafee.com*, and *antivirus.com*). Find out what the vendors' research centers are doing. Also download VirusScan from McAfee and scan your hard drive with it.

12. Research vendors of biometrics. Select one vendor and discuss three of its biometric devices or technologies. Prepare a list of major capabilities. What are the advantages and disadvantages of its biometrics?

BUSINESS CASE

Facebook Used by Scammers for Profit

Facebook, with its 500 million users, has become one of spammers' favorite and biggest targets. The social media company says it is constantly evolving to try to outsmart the endless exploits that are targeted at its users. Fighting spam is a top priority, so the company employs a large team of investigators to defend against it. Facebook has successfully sued spammers, winning $2 billion in judgments. It has also added new security features, along with advice for users on how to protect against spam.

Attractive Target

But users are still at risk. Why? Because spammers make money by driving people to Web sites that pay them per click. If a scam works on just one percent of users, that's five million people. Spammers also depend on Facebook relationships to enhance their reach. If a spammer can get you, then he or she may get all your friends, and then get all their friends, and so on.

Another common exploit is phishing—using fake messages to direct users to sites for knockoff products, or to sites that can infect a computer, turning it into a zombie that floods friends with spam. One Internet worm hijacked Facebook accounts, sent messages to friends and then harvested their accounts and passwords.

April 2011 Spam Scam

In April 2011, spammers were exploiting millions of Facebook users by tricking them to click onto fake events and online survey scams. The scammers embedded instructions into the "More info" section of the event's summary, which led unsuspecting Facebook users into visiting Web pages for online surveys or competitions that earned commissions for those

behind the fraud. In some instances, users were asked for a mobile phone number, which then signed them up to an expensive, premium-rate phone service.

One of the frauds called *Who blocked you from his friend list?* gave directions to users curious to find out which Facebook members had them blocked. More than 165,000 people were tricked into signing up, while another 10.3 million users debated whether or not to respond. Once a Facebook invitee joined the event, they were presented with a 'security check' that had them 'verify' their account by selecting a prize, such as a gift card or *Coco Pops*. The user was then directed to Web pages off Facebook that were designed to trick visitors into participating in activities (e.g., surveys or competitions) that earned money for the scammers. Not surprisingly, many features and apps that scammers target are ones that members most frequently use.

Sources: Compiled from The Internet Safety Newswire (2011) and Sophos (2011).

Questions

1. *The best anti-spam tool is user awareness.* Do you agree with this statement? Explain.
2. Facebook users are reminded never to accept unsolicited invitations from suspicious events, and to always think twice before clicking on links received via Facebook. Why aren't these warnings effective? That is, why do users ignore these warnings?
3. Search for two recent scams and security breaches carried out via social networks. Describe the incidents. How are those incidents similar to the April 2011 Facebook scam? Are the incidents more or less sophisticated?

PUBLIC SECTOR CASE

Australia, Germany, and other Governments Investigate Google to Protect Citizens' Privacy

Australian Privacy Commissioner Karen Curtis led an investigation into Google's collection of unsecured Wi-Fi payload data in Australia using Street View vehicles. Street View is part of Google Maps and Google Earth, and provides panoramic pictures of streets and their surroundings across the globe. Google admitted in May 2010 that it had collected certain Wi-Fi content information, known as payload data, in 33 countries with special equipment mounted on its Street View photographic image–collection vehicles. Curtis found that such data collection violated Australian law. According to

Curtis: "Collecting personal information in these circumstances is a very serious matter. Australians should reasonably expect that private communications remain private."

Street View Data Collection

Google said the collection of personal information by its Street View cars, including e-mail addresses and other data, resulted from an error in the way its cars tracked the existence of wireless networks. They did wireless tracking (sniffing) in order to verify the location of the photos they were taking. Google said it was a coding error that led it to sniff as much as 600 gigabytes of data across dozens of countries as it was snapping photos for its Street View project. The data included Web pages that users visited and pieces of e-mail, video, and document files.

The privacy breach was discovered when German authorities asked to see the data that the company had been collecting. The privacy breach had Google tied up in regulatory investigations in dozens of countries, including the European Union, Australia, the U.S., and Canada.

Initial Settlement Conditions

As part of a settlement with the Australian Privacy Commissioner, Google has apologized publicly on its official blog at *google-au.blogspot.com/2010/07/were-sorry.html* for inadvertently collecting personal data from unprotected wireless networks via its Street View cars.

Google will also conduct a Privacy Impact Assessment (PIA) on any new Street View data-collection activities in Australia that include personal information, and regularly consult with the Australian Privacy Commissioner about personal data–collection activities arising from significant product launches in Australia.

Still Facing Regulatory and Lawsuit Threats

Google still faces legal and government sanctions in multiple countries over the Street View data collection. The company faces a possible investigation by Australia's federal police force. German authorities have undertaken an investigation that could lead to criminal penalties; in the U.S., there is a class-action lawsuit against Google. In some other countries, including Britain, Germany, France, and Italy, authorities have demanded that Google hand over the payload data so that it can be used in possible legal cases against the company.

Google Denies, then Admits Violations

Initially, Google denied that it had captured any personally identifiable information (PII), but later admitted that it had. In addition to breaching rules governing PII privacy in various countries, legal experts believe that Google may have also broken federal laws designed to prevent wiretapping.

Sources: Compiled from Official Google Australia Blog (2010), Ingram (2010), and Kravets (2010).

Questions

1. Why did governments consider Google's action a breach of privacy?
2. Do you consider it a breach of privacy? Explain your answer.
3. Research this incident for updated information on Google's legal issues or penalties. Report what you learn.
4. Why would Google first deny that it captured PII?
5. What might have motivated Google to admit their privacy violations?
6. Describe the ethical violations Google committed.

ANALYSIS USING SPREADSHEETS

Estimating Investments in Antispam Protection

It is difficult for companies to assess the costs of not implementing infosec defenses. Most companies do not do a proper postmortem, or if they do, they have no idea what to include in the analysis. Cost estimates may include the soft costs (i.e., hard to quantify costs) of diverting the IT department from a strategic project, lost sales, and customer attrition, or take a minimalist approach that only includes recovery costs. Rather than a single point estimate, several estimates can be made using a DSS to support the decision regarding infosec investments.

Using the model for estimating the cost of spam shown in Figure 5.10, design a DSS using Excel or other spreadsheet software. Enter the formulas as shown in the figure. Then enter data to calculate three scenarios—optimistic, realistic, and pessimistic. This is your cost analysis using a range of estimates.

Write a report that includes your DSS model (spreadsheet), showing the results. Estimate how much the company should invest in antispamware. Explain your answer.

Model for Estimating the Cost of Spam (Optimistic, Pessimistic, and Realistic Estimates)			
Labor Costs	**Optimistic**	**Pessimistic**	**Realistic**
A Number of employees	5	10	8
B Average employee annual salary	$ 50,000	$ 70,000	$ 60,000
C Average number of working days/year	245	250	248
D Average number of emails per day per employee	25	50	38
E Percentage of emails that are spam	20%	40%	30%
F Average time to process each one (seconds)	5	10	8
Technical Costs			
G Cost of bandwidth per year per site			–
H Number of sites			–
I Annual cost of bandwidth (G*H)			–
J Percentage of bandwidth used by email			–
K Total annual cost of bandwidth used by spam (I*J)			–
L Cost of email storage per GB			
M Size of average spam, in KB			
N Total annual cost of storing spam (A*C*E*M*0.000008) (storage cost/KB)			–
O Support costs per user per year			
P Percentage attributable to spam			
Q Total support cost of spam (O*P*A)			–
R Number of email servers			–
S Hardware cost (R*$5,000 per server)			–
T % of email server capacity used by spam			–
U Spam cost in hardware (S*T)			–
V Average annual cost of time lost per employee ((E*F)/60*C)*(B/((C*8)*60))			–
W Total productivity cost of spam (A*V)			–
Anti-Spam Costs			
X Annual cost of anti-spam software & tuning			–
Y Percentage of spam stopped by filters			–
Z Total cost of spam (K+N+Q+U+W)			–
Totals			
AA Total cost after filtering (Z*(1-Y)+X)			–
BB Total savings (Z-AA)			–
CC Total percentage cost savings (BB/Z)			–

Figure 5.10 Model for estimating cost of spam.

References

Aftergood, S., "Former Official Indicted for Mishandling Classified Info," *FAS*, April 15, 2010. *fas.org/blog/secrecy/2010/04/drake_indict.html*

Altman, H., "Jihad Web Snares Online Shops, Buyers," *Tampa Tribune*, February 20, 2006.

Antilla, S., "Red Flags Were There All Along; Suspicious Activities Largely Unquestioned." *The Gazette* (Montreal), December 16, 2008.

Appelbaum, B., and D. S. Hilzenrath. "SEC Ignored Credible Tips About Madoff, Chief Says." *Washington Post*, December 17, 2008.

Barrett, L., "HSBC Confirms Massive Database Security Breach," *eSecurityPlanett.com*, March 11, 2010. *esecurityplanet.com/features/article.php/3870071/HSBC-Confirms-Massive-Database-Security-Breach.htm*

"Blue Cross Mistake Releases Personal Info of 12K Members," April 16, 2010. *databreaches.net/*

Chew, R., "A Madoff Whistle-Blower Tells His Story." *Time*. February 4, 2009. *time.com/time/business/article/0,8599,1877181,00.html*

Edwards, J., "The Rise of Botnet Infections," *Network Security Journal*, February 13, 2008. *networksecurityjournal.com/features/botnets-rising-021308*

Fagg, S., "Continuity for the People," *Risk Management Magazine*, March 2006.

Fiber Optics Weekly Update, "Telstra Uses NetEx Gear," January 13, 2006.

Financial Action Task Force (FATF), 2011. *fatf-gafi.org/*

Gold, L., "Forensic Accounting: Finding the Smoking E-Mail; E-Discovery Is Now a Critical Part of Forensics—and of Firm Policy," *Accounting Today*, 22(8), May 5, 2008.

Higgins, K. J., "Crime Server Discovered Containing 1.4 Gigabytes of Stolen Data," *Dark Reading*, May 6, 2008. *darkreading.com/document.asp?doc_id=153058*

HSBC-RI (Blue Shield Blue Cross of Rhode Island), "Important Notice for BlueCHiP for Medicare Members," April 16, 2010. *bcbsri.com/BCBSRIWeb/about/newsroom/news_releases/2010/MemberInfoBreach.jsp*

Ingram, M. "Google Escapes with Apology in Australia, May Not Be So Lucky Elsewhere." BusinessWeek.com. July 9, 2010. *businessweek.com/technology/content/jul2010/tc2010079_071459.htm*

Kaplan, D., "ChoicePoint Settles Lawsuit over 2005 Breach," *SC Magazine*, January 28, 2008. *scmagazineus.com/ChoicePoint-settles-lawsuit-over-2005-breach/article/104649/*

Kravets, D. "Lawyers Claim Google Wi-Fi Sniffing 'Is Not an Accident'" Wired. June 3, 2010. *wired.com/threatlevel/2010/06/google-wifi-sniffing/*

Leyden, J., "Swiss HSBC Data Breach Victim Count Trebles," *Enterprise Security*, April 15, 2010.

McGlasson, L., "'Crime Server' Found with Thousands of Bank Customer Records: FBI Investigating Breach Affecting 40 Global Institutions," *Bank Info Security,* May 7, 2008. *bankinfosecurity.com/articles.php?art_id=846*

Official Google Australia Blog, 2010. *google-au.blogspot.com/2010/07/were-sorry.html*

PBI Editorial, "FINMA reprimands HSBC Suisse for data theft." *Private Banker International.* 28 February 2011. *vrl-financial-news.com*

Quinn, J. "On the Trail of Madoff's Missing Billions." *Sunday Telegraph* (London), January 18, 2009.

Reuters UK, "BNP Paribas Fined for UK Anti-Fraud Failings," May 10, 2007. *uk.reuters.com/article/UK_SMALLCAPSRPT/idUKWLA850120070510*

Sophos. "Facebook scammers invite over 10 million people to bogus event." Global Security Mag. April 2011. *globalsecuritymag.com/*

The Internet Safety Newswire. "Facebook Invite Scam." April 5, 2011. *internetsafetyproject.org*

U.S. Department of State, *state.gov,* 2008.

Chapter 6

E-Business and E-Commerce

Learning Objectives

❶ Describe e-business strategies and e-commerce operations.

❷ Understand effective business-to-consumer e-commerce applications.

❸ Understand business-to-business applications, logistics, procurement, order fulfillment, and payment systems.

❹ Describe e-government activities and public sector e-commerce.

❺ Understand e-commerce support services.

❻ Identify and describe ethical and legal issues of e-business.

Integrating *IT*

 ACC   **FIN**   **MKT**   **OM**   **HRM**   **IS**

Amazon.com's First Web site, August 1995   *digitalenterprise.org/images/amazon.gif*
e-Business forum   *ebusinessforum.com*
Google Merchant Center   *google.com/merchants*
Google Product Search   *google.com/products*
Shopzilla   *shopzilla.com*
U.S. Federal Trade Commission, the nation's consumer protection agency   *ftc.gov*
PCI Security Standards Council   *pcisecuritystandards.org/index.shtml*
Internet statistics   *internetworldstats.com*
Many Eyes (beta) data sets and visualization tools   *manyeyes.alphaworks.ibm.com/manyeyes/*
Washington, D.C., Data Catalog   *data.octo.dc.gov/*

QUICK LOOK at Chapter 6, E-Business and E-Commerce

This section introduces you to the business issues, challenges, and IT solutions in Chapter 6. Topics and issues mentioned in the Quick Look are explained in the chapter.

Electronic business (*e-business*) is business that uses the Internet and online networks as the **channel** to consumers, supply chain partners, employees, and so on. During the early Web era, the online channel was stand-alone. Typically, retailers rushed to build business-to-consumer (B2C) Web sites and set up online business units that were independent and separated from their **traditional (offline) channels.** Those e-business units were managed and evaluated according to different performance metrics, incentives, and operating models. Why? Because e-commerce was treated as something so fundamentally different, strange, or high-tech that traditional financial metrics did not apply. When dot-coms started failing on a massive scale in 2000, managers learned that financial principles and marketing concepts applied to e-commerce. Since then, numerous other e-commerce models have emerged, been implemented, and then been replaced by newer ones as Web and wireless technologies and applications emerged.

Today, as you know from personal experience, companies are **multichanneling**—integrating online and offline channels for maximum reach and effectiveness. As shown in Figure 6.1, the once purely online eBay opened a traditional channel—a store named eBay@57th—in New York City in November 2009. The 2D tags you read about in Chapter 1 have made it easier to multichannel.

In the 2010s, organizations continue to radically rethink their Web presence, e-business models and strategies, and

Figure 6.1 eBay added a traditional offline channel when it opened a physical store called eBay@57th in New York on November 20, 2009. The store offers previews of select items and Internet kiosks for consumers who want to shop online. (© *Richard Levine/Alamy*)

risks. Here are several types of changes impacting companies directly or indirectly.

• Retailers are advertising and selling through social channels, such as Facebook, Twitter, RSS feeds, and blogs, and via **comparison shopping engines.** Consumers use the Google Product Search, Shopzilla, TheFind, and NexTag comparison shopping engines to compare prices and find great deals for certain brands and products.

• Consumers are using handhelds to research brands, products, and services from multiple sources. What's

157

important is the extent to which consumers are exploring and challenging the information they've found as well as creating and posting their own opinions and detailed experiences. *TripAdvisor.com* is an example.

• Often business-to-business (B2B) sites lacked the helpful features and capabilities of B2C sites. Now manufacturers and distributors are revising their online B2B capabilities to meet the time-critical requirements of their buyers. With the growth of lean manufacturing and just-in-time inventory management, industrial buyers need on-demand access to supply and want well-designed, fast, and full-featured sites.

• Governments and agencies are expanding and refining their government-to-citizen (G2C) Web sites to improve services and outreach at reduced cost, as shown in Figure 6.2.

Figure 6.2 Public services are provided via Directgov, the U.K. government's Web site. (© *Stuwdamdorp/Alamy*)

• Malvertisements are harming e-business and increasing costs. **Malvertisements** are ads that, when clicked, will redirect to and load a malicious Web site, which is a replica of the site the user was expecting. Malvertising scams surged in 2010 as hackers tried to get their hands on some of the $30-billion-per-year e-commerce industry.

The *New York Times*, MySpace, and other popular and trusted sites were caught displaying mal-ads.

• In mid-2010, companies that host e-business platforms battled mysterious **mass Web attacks** that had silently infected a huge number of their customers' Web sites and blogs with malicious code. Many infected sites included encoded JavaScript that secretly installed malware on visitors' computers. A company official whose e-business was impacted summed up the frustration, costs, and revenue losses caused by mass Web attacks in the following comment:

We have spent at least a hundred hours over the past few weeks trying to repair our site, changing passwords at least 15 or 20 times . . . only to have it halfway working again. . . . Who's going to compensate us for the near complete loss of traffic and ad revenue from this problem?

• Increasingly, search engines are answering questions directly instead of only pointing to Web sites of dictionaries and other references. Google, for example, reworked its site so that it can give direct answers to certain economic questions. Google "unemployment rate" and it shows a chart with the national jobless rate. Search engines are diverting traffic away from reference sites.

In this chapter, you will learn about B2C, B2B, and G2C e-business models and specific e-commerce applications. **E-commerce** is the process of buying, selling, transferring, or exchanging products, services, or information via the public Internet or private corporate networks. We cover key advances in e-commerce, including IT platforms, benefits, limitations, and security risks to a company's or a brand's reputation. You will read about the compliance standards required by credit card companies and regulators to protect against fraud and other types of crime directly related to e-business operations. You frequently hear the term *e-commerce* (electronic commerce), which refers to a subset of e-business—mainly using Web sites for buying and selling. While *e-business* involves many more processes and interactions than *e-commerce*, the terms are used interchangeably, unless noted otherwise.

Rail Europe's Turnaround E-Business Strategy

When technology, economic conditions, and customers' tastes and expectations change, existing ways of doing business need to change too in order to remain competitive. Business survival and success may come to depend on a turnaround strategy—an overhaul, or reengineering, of the business strategy. Newer technologies—for example, 2D tags, 4G networks, and social media—and changes in customers' buying behavior have made e-commerce and mobile commerce

both easier to reach consumers, but control of e-business is often in their hands.

For example, companies are multi-channeling to extend their reach and to stay in contact with customers and prospects. But, in order to combat information overload from aggressive marketing, people are filtering content and blocking messages that they find irrelevant. In response to those tactics, smart companies are responding by reengineering their business strategies and delivering content that's meaningful enough to survive filtering and blocking, to beat out their competition. That's the approach Rail Europe has taken. In 2009, the company transformed its *RailEurope.com* Web site from a booking site that only helped customers find seats on European trains to a full-service e-commerce operation.

Uncompetitive Strategy

Rail Europe's e-commerce sales revenues were dropping for several years and for several reasons. Their e-business model was non-competitive, their Web site was outdated, and the recession had caused a drop in European travel (see Figure 6.3). Competing European travel sites offered more information and better features. Travel planners did not only want to buy tickets; they wanted reliable information and the ability to learn from others' good and bad experiences, to know about the best deals, and to be able to make flexible travel plans. Aware of their deficiencies, in 2009 Rail Europe's Web site became a full-featured European train travel portal.

Figure 6.3 European train station. (© *ynamaku/iStockphoto*)

Adding Social Media to E-Commerce Strategy

As part of its efforts to turn around declining sales, Rail Europe overhauled its Web site. Blogs (*blog.raileurope.com/*) with peer reviews, photos, maps, best-rate hotel reservation guarantees, and customer service options were added to provide content that would hold visitors' attention for longer. These social networking features improved the company's strategic position because its Web site became an early step in travelers' planning process. That is, people were visiting Rail Europe at the start of their planning. Previously, Rail Europe was catching customers too late in the process. Rail Europe's vice president of e-business, Frederick Buhr, explained the challenge he had to overcome and his strategy: "Today you get bypassed by the customer because they Google everything.

Although we enjoy being positioned by all the search engines, we knew that we needed to catch customers much earlier in their planning cycle."

Since the overhaul, RailEurope.com's conversion rate of visitors to customers increased 30 percent during April and May, when many people are planning summer vacations. Online sales increased 7 percent during that same period. These results are even more striking when compared to sales at other travel Web sites, which had dropped by up to 25 percent due to the recession.

FatWire Web Management Software

Rail Europe launched its new Web site using the FatWire (*fatwire.com/*) Content Server, which delivers multilingual content to visitors. FatWire's Web Experience Management (WEM) portfolio automates the WEM process, which includes content authoring, site design, content publishing and delivery, targeted marketing, Web site analytics, and user participation.

Through the Content Server interface, Rail Europe can set up and manage targeted online campaigns, keep Web content relevant and current, and maintain brand integrity. According to Rail Europe's CIO, "Over 60 percent of our customers interact with us through the Web, so we needed a Web content management solution that gave us the ability to constantly refresh information to encourage repeat online visits and referrals." Lots of content, photos, videos, interactive planners, and more than 500 pages of content were added.

Web Site Analytics and Intelligence

Content Server enabled Rail Europe to set up campaigns but did not provide the Web intelligence to know what campaigns would be most effective. To develop Web intelligence capabilities, Rail Europe invested in Web site analytics from Technology Leaders (*technologyleaders.com/*), a consulting firm. By analyzing online behavior data, for instance, managers learn which offers and promotions have the best conversion rates. Rail Europe hired Technology Leaders to develop and maintain (i.e., service) a Web analytics framework. Building that framework involved the following types of work:

- Retagging the entire site with JavaScript code and Webtrends tags.
- Setting up dashboards and KPIs (key performance indicators) for monitoring performance of the Web site.

Key benefits of the Web analytic framework are:

- Providing more detailed information for online marketing campaigns and better campaign reporting. Management sees which keywords and online campaigns lead to the sale of specific travel packages and products.

- Providing new conversion metrics, such as tracking newsletter registrations, to gauge their effectiveness.

Rail Europe's management now makes data-driven decisions supported by Web analytics. The travel portal's Web site is kept updated with the best and latest offers to attract visitors searching out the best deals, which encourages loyalty and repeat visits.

Sources: Compiled from *Wireless News* (2009), McKay (2009a, 2009b), *Fatwire.com*, *TechnologyLeader.com*, and *RailEurope.com* (2011).

For Class Discussion and Debate

1. Scenario for Brainstorming and Discussion: If a company had the same Web site and e-business features today that it had five years ago, the company would have lost customers. The same would be true if, five years from now, companies were still using today's e-commerce sites instead of expanding their efforts to include the latest Web and mobile apps.

a. First, discuss how e-commerce Web sites have changed over the past five years.

b. Next, select four different types of companies— for example, an auto manufacturer, a major software company, an online retailer (e-tailer), and a service provider—that have been in existence since at least 2000.

c. Then visit Internet archives of the Wayback Machine at *http://www.archive.org/web/web.php*. For each of the four companies you selected and also Rail Europe, view its latest archived Web site and its Web site from five years earlier. What important changes do you see in the five companies' e-commerce sites?

d. In your opinion, which of your selected companies would have suffered the greatest customer loss if it had not updated its e-commerce Web site? Why?

2. Debate: Rail Europe's Web site was redesigned to achieve its new e-business strategy. The redesign involved outsourcing some of the e-business site's platform and Web analytics to FatWire and Technology Leaders. Outsourcing partnerships require **service-level agreements** (SLAs). An SLA is a written legal contract between a service provider (e.g., vendor or consulting company) and the client (company) wherein the service provider guarantees a minimal level of service. One challenge is specifying exactly what the minimum service levels are and finding ways to measure them accurately. If the minimal level of service is not met, the contract is violated and the service provider typically faces a financial penalty. For reference, you can view FatWire's outline of its SLA on its Web site at *http://www.fatwire.com/support#tab3*.

SLAs are legal contracts that include an incentive for the service provider to fix the problem quickly and a way for the client to be compensated for losses due to failure to comply with the terms of the SLA. The provider's incentive is usually in the form of a financial penalty for problems it doesn't resolve within the specified timeframe. An outsourcing expert suggested (with some humor) that penalties can be set somewhere between the electric chair and a slight tap on the wrist. Generally, the stricter the SLA, the greater the cost of the SLA upfront, the more exact the minimal level of acceptable service, and the more precise the measurement of those levels. The more lenient the SLA, the less time and effort spent upfront defining levels and measures and actually monitoring those levels, but the greater the risk and costs in the future if something goes wrong. Interestingly, companies may outsource the monitoring of the SLA to another company. The point is that determining the SLA with a vendor and monitoring it are expensive, time-consuming, and require trade-offs. Excessively strict and lenient SLAs can be risky and expensive, but the risk and expenses may occur at different times in the life cycle of the SLA.

To Do: Assume either the role of the service provider or the role of the client. Debate whether the terms of the SLA should be strict or lenient to minimize overall risk and costs to your company. Consider all costs, including but not limited to: losses from downtime if the SLA was too lenient, the costs of the SLA contract if the SLA was strict, and the legal fees if the SLA's terms were not met. Debate compromises (trade-offs) you'd be willing to take as you negotiate the SLA terms.

6.1 E-Business Challenges and Strategies

The online explosion has given today's consumers greater control over where and how they interact with a business or a brand through a mix of online channels and media. To successfully compete in this online environment, managers need to understand and respond to changing consumer behavior or the needs of business customers, and they often have to deal with IT software vendors and consulting firms.

The opening case describes Rail Europe's overhaul of its e-business model and the reengineering of its e-commerce site—changes that required the help of at least two vendors. Due to the complexity of designing and implementing online business channels, companies may decide to outsource the development or hosting of the system, often using software-as-a-service (SaaS) or cloud computing, as you read in Chapter 2. However, developing an effective e-business model and competitive strategy is done in-house by managers from various functional areas—marketing, IT, operations, logistics, accounting, and so on. If the business model and strategy are wrong, then implementation would not matter in the long run.

To better understand the importance of sound models and strategies, in the next section you will read about the dot-com era.

THE DOT-COM ERA, 1995–2002

Companies rushed into e-commerce in the 1990s. Many far-fetched predictions and management assumptions were made that led to poor decisions and e-business failures. There were numerous debates, with one side arguing that *business over the Internet* had its own set of rules that differed (mysteriously) from traditional business models that valued positive earnings and cash flow. The opposing side argued that adding the prefix *e* to *business* did not eliminate the need to earn a profit, but risk-taking investors generally ignored this logic for several years.

From the mid-1990s to 2002, the media and Internet stock analysts hyped the *new economy* and the growth of dot-com businesses. (A few of those stock analysts were later arrested and/or fined for fraud and misleading investors.) The concept of a new economy helped fuel the theory that Internet companies were different (had new rules). In terms of the stock market, old-economy companies like Proctor & Gamble were out. New-economy companies like Yahoo.com (and many that went bankrupt within a few years) were in.

The Dot-Com Bubble Inflates. The new economy was the economy of the **dot-com era** (or **dot-com bubble**), which extended from roughly 1995 to 2000. In 1995, the number of Internet users sharply increased. Pure-play companies, nicknamed dot-coms, existed only on the Internet without a physical brick-and-mortar presence. These Internet-channel companies were set up to capture the new marketspace. *Marketspace* was the term used instead of the old economy's *marketplace*. (The new economy had new vocabulary, furthering the divide between traditional and e-business.)

Unrestrained by business models that required making a profit and having huge sums of money from venture capitalists (private investors), many dot-coms engaged in daring and sometimes fraudulent business practices. Their practices were aimed at building market share, which was believed to be the path to profitability. According to the dot-com business model, the objective was for companies to build up their customer base (market share) even if it meant selling at a loss in the short term (which many did) because they'd become profitable in the long run. Investors bought into these magical business models, and stock prices of dot-coms skyrocketed, attracting more investors. In reality, the dot-com bubble was really a stock market bubble. That is, stock prices were significantly overpriced and continued to rise (see Figure 6.4), inflating the size of the bubble until March 2000.

The Dot-Com Bubble Bursts and Deflates. Most dot-coms were listed on the NASDAQ, or National Association of Securities Dealers Automated Quotation System (*nasdaq.com*). On March 10, 2000, the NASDAQ composite index reached its peak of 5,048.62 points. From March 11, 2000, to October 9, 2002, the NASDAQ lost 78 percent of its value by dropping from 5,046.86 to 1,114.11 points as dot-com stock prices fell or lost all value. Figure 6.4 shows changes in the NASDAQ from the start of the bubble to 2003. March 10, 2000, is called the day the bubble burst because it was the turning point. The steady decline ended most debate over whether or not positive earnings, cash flow, and other financial metrics of brick-and-mortar (physical) commerce applied to e-commerce.

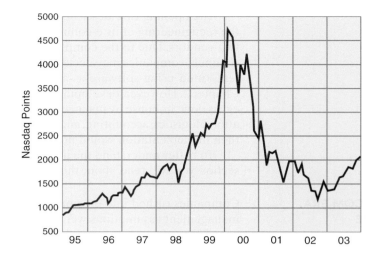

Figure 6.4 Changes in the NASDAQ during the dot-com era, which burst (started to decline) on March 10, 2000, and declined until October 2002.

Lessons are still being learned about B2C and B2B commerce as companies experiment with new features to gain even a slight or temporary competitive advantage. As you read in the chapter's introduction, new Web and wireless technologies and applications create new opportunities and capabilities.

Fundamental capabilities and challenges of e-commerce are briefly discussed next.

E-BUSINESS AND E-COMMERCE FUNDAMENTALS

Online channels and connectivity support or enable the following business activities, creating the following benefits for e-business:

- **Business processes.** Business processes are carried out and managed via networks for obvious reasons—namely, the fact that almost all business documents are digital and the availability of broadband wireless and wired networks, laptops, and mobiles/handhelds.

- **Service.** Self-service features reduce inefficiencies and costs of providing service to customers, clients, patients, citizens, and so on. For example, the Federal Express Web site lets customers track their shipments, calculate shipping costs, schedule pickups, and print their own labels. Airlines encourage travelers to print boarding passes before arriving at the airport.

- **Collaboration and training.** Telepresence minimizes the limitations of having to be physically present in a single location to collaborate or to give and receive live online training or education.

- **Community.** Social networks such as Facebook and Twitter are community centers on a scale possible only via online channels. You will read about social commerce in the next chapter.

Types of E-Business Transactions. There are several basic types of e-business transactions, which have been referred to in prior sections. Here are their definitions.

- **Business-to-business (B2B).** In B2B transactions, both the sellers and the buyers are business organizations. Over 85 percent of e-commerce volume is B2B—far exceeding B2C commerce.

- **Business-to-consumers (B2C).** In B2C, the sellers are organizations, and the buyers are individuals. B2C is also called *e-tailing* (electronic retailing).

- **Consumers-to-business (C2B).** In C2B, consumers make known a particular need for a product or service, and then suppliers compete to provide that product or service at the requested price. An example is Priceline.com, where the customer names a product or service and the desired price, and Priceline tries to find a supplier to fulfill the stated need.

- **Government-to-citizens (G2C) and to others.** In this case, a government agency provides services to its citizens via e-commerce technologies. Government units can engage in e-commerce with other government units—**government-to-government (G2G)** or with businesses—**government-to-business (G2B).**
- **Mobile commerce.** Transactions and activities are conducted using wireless networks.

E-BUSINESS WEB SITE REQUIREMENTS AND CHALLENGES

As a consumer, you've experienced first-hand e-commerce Web sites. You're likely to know most of the site characteristics and/or requirements. However, the number of integrated systems, networks, and maintenance tools needed to support e-business operations, including order fulfillment (getting the correct items to the customer in a reasonable amount of time), are less widely known. The following sections discuss the requirements and challenges of e-business.

Availability. Availability relates to the server side of e-business. An "always on" facility is needed to maintain the business-critical apps. Web sites need to be hosted on servers (specialized large-capacity hard drives) that are capable of supporting the volume of requests for access, or traffic, to the site. Figure 6.5 shows an example of Web hosting servers. Servers need to be connected to the Internet via huge capacity transmission (telecommunication) lines. Servers need to be taken offline for service or replacement, at which time hosting is switched to other servers or, if the business can tolerate it, the Web site is taken offline during the maintenance.

Recall that Rail Europe hosted its Web site on FatWire's Content Server and relied on its Web Experience Management (WEM) tools. Hosting on a third party's server is done if the company lacks infrastructure to host it themselves or the IT expertise to manage it. Another reason or benefit of third-party hosting is **scalability**—being able to add additional capacity incrementally, quickly, and as needed.

Accuracy and Quick Response. Not only must Web servers be available, the e-commerce software and databases need to respond quickly. Web software must be capable of searching; sorting; comparing product features; checking availability, balances, and/or delivery times; processing promotions and payments; verifying that a credit card number belongs to the person trying to use it; and confirming the purchase in real time. Particularly in time-sensitive B2B commerce, errors that delay delivery are intolerable.

Figure 6.5 Web hosting servers. (© Konstantnos Kokkinis/ Alamy)

TABLE 6.1	PCI DSS Principles and Requirements

The core of the PCI DSS is a group of principles and accompanying requirements, around which the specific elements of the DSS are organized:

Build and Maintain a Secure Network

Requirement 1: Install and maintain a firewall configuration to protect cardholder data

Requirement 2: Do not use vendor-supplied defaults for system passwords and other security parameters

Protect Cardholder Data

Requirement 3: Protect stored cardholder data

Requirement 4: Encrypt transmission of cardholder data across open, public networks

Maintain a Vulnerability Management Program

Requirement 5: Use and regularly update antivirus software

Requirement 6: Develop and maintain secure systems and applications

Implement Strong Access Control Measures

Requirement 7: Restrict access to cardholder data by business need-to-know

Requirement 8: Assign a unique ID to each person with computer access

Requirement 9: Restrict physical access to cardholder data

Regularly Monitor and Test Networks

Requirement 10: Track and monitor all access to network resources and cardholder data

Requirement 11: Regularly test security systems and processes

Maintain an Information Security Policy

Requirement 12: Maintain a policy that addresses information security

Security and PCI DSS Compliance. All of the servers, transmission lines, application software, databases, and connections must be secured; confidential data often must be protected with another layer of defense, typically encryption.

For Web sites accepting credit cards, an additional security standard is imposed by the payment card industry (PCI).

All e-commerce and brick-and-mortar merchants, regardless of size and sales volume, need to be PCI DSS compliant and certified to accept, hold, process, or exchange credit cardholder information of the major credit cards. The **PCI DSS (Payment Card Industry Data Security Standard)** is a set of information security requirements to help prevent credit card fraud. The PCI DSS was developed by the **Payment Card Industry Security Standards Council (PCI SSC)**, an organization founded by American Express, Discover Financial Services, JCB International, MasterCard Worldwide, and Visa, Inc.

Table 6.1 lists the PCI DSS principles and 12 accompanying requirements, around which the specific elements of the DSS are organized. The PCI Council publishes a list of Validated Payment Applications on its *pcisecuritystandards.org* Web site. Web sites built for e-commerce need to be hosted on software platforms that are PCI certified. Certification to verify that the credit card handling processes and Internet systems comply with PCI DSS must be done annually.

Building Competitive Advantage. No competitive innovation remains unique for long. Leading companies are always looking for next-generation capabilities to develop new competitive advantage. One approach is to integrate social networks. Companies can implement their own social networks and associated services or leverage Facebook or other existing ones. A strategic concern is how to control content, specifically because that content is not meant to be monitored and controlled.

Integration of E-Commerce Systems with Enterprise Systems. Another huge challenge is integrating e-commerce systems with legacy and other enterprise systems.

TABLE 6.2	Web Analytics and Intelligence Software Tools and Solutions	
Software	**Features and Functions**	**URL**
ClickTracks	Provides products, visualization tools, and hosted services for Web site traffic analysis, including visitor behavior	*clicktracks.com*
Coremetrics	A platform that captures and stores customer and visitor clickstream activity to build LIVE (Lifetime Individual Visitor Experience) profiles, which serve as the foundation for e-business initiatives	*coremetrics.com*
Google Analytics	Offers free Web analytics services with integrated analysis of Adwords and other keyword-based search advertising	*goggle.com/analytics/*
SAS Web Analytics	Automatically turns raw Web data into business information	*sas.com/solutions/webanalytics/*
Webtrends	Measures campaign performance, search engine marketing, Web site conversion, and customer retention	*webtrends.com*

There is growing interest in allowing better integration across all customer points of interactions. This challenge intensifies when companies are merged or acquired because then multiple Web sites that are built on a variety of technology platforms need to be integrated.

Web Analytics and Intelligence Software. Web site activities—such as what was clicked, how long a visitor viewed a page, the IP address of the visitor's computer, and items put into the shopping cart—are captured and stored in a log. Log data is analyzed to learn how visitors navigate the site, to assess advertising campaigns, and to determine other factors of interest. Many vendors offer Web analytics and intelligence software so managers can analyze Web traffic and other activities of visitors, as described in Table 6.2.

International E-Commerce. Too often international online shoppers have to work through several hurdles to buy from U.S. e-commerce companies. They face the challenge of finding out whether a site will ship to their country. Shipping costs tend to be higher than necessary, and delivery can be slow and unpredictable. In addition, prices are not converted into the shopper's native currency. The total cost of delivery for international customers is often too vague or incorrect. Customers may learn that they have to pay additional unexpected customs fees and taxes to receive their order, to return their order, or to correct errors.

E-BUSINESS MODELS

To better understand how e-business works, look at Figure 6.6. A company such as Dell (labeled "Our Company") provides products and/or services to customers, as shown on the right side. To do so, the company buys inputs such as raw materials, components, parts, or services from suppliers and other business partners in the procurement process. Processing the inputs is done in its production/operations department. Finance, marketing, IT, and other departments support the conversion of inputs to outputs and the sale to customers.

An objective of e-business is to *streamline* and *automate* as many processes as possible. A few examples of processes are credit card verification, production, purchasing,

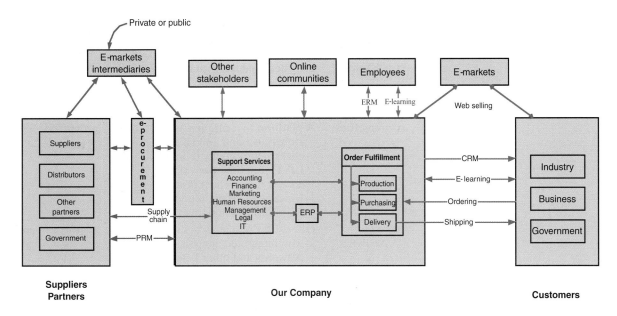

Figure 6.6 E-commerce model.

delivery, inventory management, or providing CRM (customer relationship management). This is done by e-commerce mechanisms such as e-markets, e-procurement, and e-CRM, as shown in Figure 6.6. Note that processes in the figure involve several types of transactions.

Recall that business models are the methods by which a company generates revenue. For example, in B2B one can sell from catalogs or in auctions. The major e-business models are summarized in Table 6.3. Forward and reverse auctions are explained in *IT at Work 6.1*.

TABLE 6.3	E-Business Models
E-Business Model	**Description**
Comparison shopping engines	TheFind, NexTag, and Google Product Search engines find products, compare prices, and find great deals—and are paid a commission.
Affiliate marketing	Vendors ask partners to place logos or banner ads on their sites. If customers click the logo, go to vendor's site, and buy, then the vendor pays a commission to partners.
Electronic marketplaces and exchanges	Transactions are conducted efficiently (more information to buyers and sellers, less transaction cost) in virtual marketplaces (private or public).
Information brokers and matching services	Brokers provide services related to e-commerce information, such as content, matching buyers and sellers, evaluating vendors and products.
Membership	Only members can use the services provided, including access to certain information, conducting trades, and so on.
Forward auctions	Sellers put items up for bid to many potential buyers and the highest bid wins, as on eBay.
Reverse auctions	Buyers put notices of items or services they want to buy on an auction site. Those notices are called **requests for quotes (RFQ)**. The lowest qualified bid wins.
Name-your-own-price	Customers decide how much they are willing to pay. An intermediary (e.g., *Priceline.com*) tries to match a provider.
Online auctions	Companies or individuals run auctions of various types on the Internet. This is a fast and inexpensive way to sell or liquidate items.
Online direct marketing	Manufacturers or retailers sell directly online to customers. This is very efficient for digital products and services.
Viral marketing	This involves relying on individuals to spread the marketing message.

IT at Work 6.1

E-Commerce Auctions

An **auction** is a competitive process in which either a seller solicits bids from buyers or a buyer solicits bids from sellers. The primary characteristic of auctions, whether offline or online, is that prices are determined dynamically by competitive bidding. Auctions have been an established method of commerce for generations, and they are well suited to deal with products and services for which conventional marketing channels are ineffective or inefficient. Electronic auctions generally increase revenues for sellers by broadening the customer base and shortening the cycle time of the auction. Buyers generally benefit from online auctions by the opportunity to bargain for lower prices and the convenience of not having to travel to an auction site to participate in the auction.

Auctions are used in B2C, B2B, C2B, e-government, and C2C commerce, and they are becoming popular in many countries. Auctions can be conducted from the seller's site, the buyer's site, or from a third party's site. Auctions are divided here into two major types: forward auctions and reverse auctions.

Forward Auctions. Forward auctions are auctions that sellers use as a selling channel to many potential buyers. The most popular forward auction site is eBay, which has an iPhone app, as shown in Figure 6.7. Usually, items are placed at an auction site and buyers can bid on items or services until the deadline. The highest bidder wins the items. Sellers and buyers can be individuals or businesses. The popular auction site eBay.com conducts mostly forward auctions, but there are many B2C and B2B online auctions. Forward online auctions are used to liquidate excess inventory or to increase the scope of customers, particularly for unique products or services. For example, Sears liquidates excess or discontinued inventory via auction and fixed price at *searsliquidations.com/*.

Reverse Auctions. In reverse auctions, a company or government agency that wants to buy items places a *request for quote* (RFQ) on its Web site or third-party bidding marketplace. Once RFQs are posted, sellers or preapproved suppliers submit bids

Figure 6.7 eBay store application for the iPhone. *(© ICP/Alamy)*

electronically. Reverse auctions can attract large pools of willing sellers, who may be manufacturers, distributors, or retailers. The bids are routed via the buyer's intranet to the engineering and finance departments for evaluation. Clarifications are made via e-mail, and the winner is notified electronically.

The reverse auction is the most common auction model for large-quantity purchases or high-priced items. Everything else being equal, the lowest-price bidder wins the auction. Governments and large corporations frequently mandate this RFQ approach for procurements because competition among sellers leads to considerable savings.

Discussion Questions: Why are auctions an efficient online sales channel? Search for two manufacturing and retail companies that are using auctions as an additional sales channel. What types of items are they selling via an auction site?

Review Questions

1. What was the dot-com bubble? What lessons were learned from it?
2. List benefits of e-business.
3. What are the major types of e-business transactions?
4. What are the requirements and challenges of e-business?
5. What is the importance of PCI DSS compliance?
6. Define a business model and list five e-business models.

6.2 Business-to-Consumer (B2C) E-Commerce

Retail sales via online channels, financial services, and travel services are widely popular forms of B2C commerce. The most well-known B2C site is Amazon.com, whose IT developments received U.S. patents that keep it ahead of competition; it is described in *IT at Work.6.2*.

IT at Work 6.2

IT Patents Are Amazon.com's Edge

Entrepreneur and e-tailing pioneer Jeff Bezos envisioned the huge potential for retail sales over the Internet and selected books for his e-tailing venture. In July 1995, Bezos started Amazon.com, offering books via an electronic catalog from its Web site. Key features offered by the Amazon.com mega e-tailer were broad selection, low prices, easy searching and ordering, useful product information and personalization, secure payment systems, and efficient order fulfillment. Early on, recognizing the importance of order fulfillment, Amazon.com invested hundreds of millions of dollars in building physical warehouses designed for shipping small packages to hundreds of thousands of customers.

Amazon has continually revised its business model by improving the customer's experience. For example, customers can personalize their Amazon accounts and manage orders online with the patented "One-Click" order feature. This personalized service includes an electronic wallet, which enables shoppers to place an order in a secure manner without the need to enter their address, credit card number, and so forth each time they shop. One-Click also allows customers to view their order status and make changes on orders that have not yet entered the shipping process. Amazon's other registered trademarks are EARTH'S BIGGEST SELECTION and IF IT'S IN PRINT, IT'S IN STOCK.

In addition, Amazon added services and alliances to attract more customers and increase sales. In January 2002, Amazon.com declared its first-ever profit for the 2001 fourth quarter; 2003 was the first year it cleared a profit in each quarter.

Amazon has invested heavily in its IT infrastructure, many of whose components it patented. The selected list of patents below gives a glimpse into the legal side of the e-tailer and explains why numerous major retailers, such as Sears and Sony, have used Amazon.com as its sales portal.

- 6,525,747—Method and system for conducting a discussion relating to an item

- 6,029,141—Internet-based customer referral system, also known as the Affiliate program
- 5,999,924—Method for producing sequenced queries
- 5,963,949—Method for data gathering around forms and search barriers
- 5,960,411—Method and system for placing a purchase order via a communications network (One-Click purchase)
- 5,826,258—Method and apparatus for structuring the querying and interpretation of semistructured information
- 5,727,163—Secure method for communicating credit card data when placing an order on a nonsecure network
- 5,715,399—Secure method and system for communicating a list of credit card numbers over a nonsecure network.

Amazon launched the e-reader Kindle in 2007. Its success proved the viability of the e-book market and led to the entry of numerous competitors, such as Barnes & Noble's Nook and the Apple iPad. Some analysts estimate that the Kindle accounted for about 60 percent of the e-reader market in 2010.

In mid-2010, Amazon started rolling out a software upgrade for Kindle, adding the ability for users to share e-book passages with others on Facebook and Twitter. The new social networking feature in version 2.5 adds another Web link to the standard Kindle and the larger Kindle DX, as Amazon finds itself in an increasingly competitive market because of the iPad's features. The iPad is designed for reading digital books, watching online videos, listening to music, and Web browsing.

Sources: Compiled from Gonsalves (2010), Rappa (2010), and *amazon.com.*

Discussion Questions: Why is order fulfillment critical to Amazon's success? Why did Amazon patent One-Click and other IT infrastructure developments? How has Amazon adapted the Kindle to new technologies? Why would other retailers form an alliance with Amazon.com?

Several of the leading online service industries are banking, trading of securities (stocks, bonds), and employment, travel, and real estate services.

Online Banking. Online banking includes various banking activities conducted via the Internet instead of at a physical bank location. Online banking, also called direct banking, offers capabilities ranging from paying bills to applying for a loan. Customers can check balances and transfer funds at any time of day. For banks, it offers an inexpensive alternative to branch banking. Transaction costs are about 2 cents per transaction versus $1.07 at a physical branch.

Most brick-and-mortar conventional banks provide online banking services and use e-commerce as a major competitive strategy. Customers are aware that if they are banking exclusively with a brick-and-mortar institution, they may be missing out on high-paying investment options or competitive loan rates that easily undercut many traditional banking entities. One of the high-interest, online-only banks is ING Direct. With prominent and sophisticated marketing, ING Direct has become one of the most successful direct banks, as described in *IT at Work 6.3.*

IT at Work 6.3

ING Direct Has Soaring Profits

ING Direct, a division of the Dutch financial services giant ING Group, has surpassed E*Trade Bank to become the largest online bank. ING Direct first opened for business in Canada in 1997. By 2007, ING Direct had become the most successful direct bank in the world, with more than 17 million customers in nine countries. Within five years of opening in the United States, ING had acquired 2.2 million U.S. customers and $29 billion in deposits.

Successful Marketing Tactics Have High-Payoff. ING has paid the highest rates on savings accounts, 2.6 percent compared to the .56 percent average rate being paid for money market accounts at traditional banks. The bank has invested heavily in online and offline marketing efforts to steal customers away from other banks. ING Direct's strategy of simple products, aggressive rates and marketing campaigns (see Figure 6.8), and direct distribution has created clear differentiation from its competitors. One of its successful marketing tactics was issuing a $25 check to customers for signing up.

Despite its high rates and huge marketing expenditures, ING Direct profits have soared. For example, the U.S. division earned a pretax profit of $250 million in 2004, more than double its pretax profit of $110 million in 2003.

The high-volume, low-margin business depends on using online efficiencies to offer a bare-bones service to low-maintenance customers. Originally, the bank did not offer checking accounts because that cost too much, but it added checking a few years later. ING Direct has almost no bricks and mortar other than four cafés to promote the bank in New York, Philadelphia, Los Angeles, and Wilmington (Delaware). Its headquarters is a converted Wilmington warehouse rather than an expensive office building.

Figure 6.8 Woman inside bank at Paris, France, exhibit of ING Direct Internet bank. (© *Directphoto.org/Alamy*)

ING Direct's competitive strategy was quickly copied by competitors. MetLife and New York's Emigrant Savings Bank have launched Internet banks offering high rates.

Sources: Compiled from *INGDirect.com* (2010), Stone (2005), and Ensor (2007).

Discussion Questions: How did ING Direct become the world's largest online bank? Why did ING Direct use both online and offline marketing campaigns? What attracted customers to online banking at ING Direct? What attracted brick-and-mortar banks into the online banking segment?

International and Multiple-Currency Banking. International banking and the ability to handle trading in multiple currencies are critical for international trade. Electronic fund transfer (EFT) and electronic letters of credit are important services in international banking. An example of support for e-commerce global trade is provided by TradeCard (*tradecard.com*). TradeCard offers a software-as-a-service (SaaS) model that provides supply chain collaboration and a trade finance compliance platform.

Although some international retail purchasing can be done by giving a credit card number, other transactions may require cross-border banking support. For example, Hong Kong and Shanghai Bank (*hsbc.com.hk*) has developed a special system, HSBC*net*, to provide online banking in 60 countries. Using this system, the bank has leveraged its reputation and infrastructure in the developing economies of Asia to rapidly become a major international bank without developing an extensive new branch network.

Online Job Market. Most companies and government agencies advertise job openings, accept résumés, and take applications via the Internet. The online job market is especially effective and active for technology-oriented jobs, for example, *dice.com and monster.com*. In many countries, governments must advertise job openings on the Internet. In addition, hundreds of job-placement brokers and related services are active on the Web. You can get help from *jobweb.com* to write your résumé.

ISSUES IN E-TAILING

Despite e-tailing's ongoing growth, many e-tailers continue to face several challenges that can interfere with the growth of its e-tailing efforts. Major issues are described next.

1. Resolving channel conflict. Sellers that are click-and-mortar companies, such as Levi's or GM, face a conflict with their regular distributors when they circumvent those distributors by selling online directly to customers. This situation is called **channel conflict** because it is a conflict between an online selling channel and physical selling channels. Channel conflict has forced some companies to limit their B2C efforts or not to sell direct online. An alternative approach is to try to collaborate in some way with the existing distributors, whose services may be restructured. For example, an auto company could allow customers to configure a car online but require that the car be picked up from a dealer, where customers could also arrange financing, warranties, and service.

2. Resolving conflicts within click-and-mortar organizations. When an established company sells online directly to customers, it creates conflict in its own offline operations. Conflicts may arise in areas such as pricing of products and services, allocation of resources (e.g., advertising budget), and logistics services provided by the offline activities to the online activities (e.g., handling of returns of items bought online). To minimize this type of conflict, companies may separate the online division from the traditional division. The downside is that separation can increase expenses and reduce the synergy between the two organizational parts.

3. Managing order fulfillment and logistics. E-tailers face tough order fulfillment and logistics problems when selling online because of the need to design systems to accept and process a huge volume of small orders, physically pick items from warehouse shelves and put them into boxes, be sure that the correct labels are applied, and accept returns. The return process is referred to as **reverse logistics.** Logistics is discussed in more detail in Section 6.4.

4. Determining viability and risk of online e-tailers. Many purely online e-tailers went bankrupt in the dot-com era, the result of problems with cash flow, customer acquisition, order fulfillment, and demand forecasting. Online competition, especially in commodity-type products such as CDs, toys, books, or groceries, became very fierce due to the ease of entry into the marketplace. As Porter's five-forces model explains, low entry barriers intensify competition in an industry. So a problem most new and established e-tailers face is determining how long to operate while they are still losing money and how to finance the losses.

5. Identifying appropriate revenue (business) models. One early dot-com model was to generate enough revenue from advertising to keep the business afloat until the customer base reached critical mass. This model did not work. Too many dot-coms were competing for too few advertising dollars, which went mainly to a small number of well-known sites such as AOL, MSN, Google, and Yahoo. In addition, there was a "chicken-and-egg" problem: Sites could not get advertisers to come if they did not have enough visitors. To succeed in e-commerce, it is necessary to identify appropriate revenue models and modify those models as the market changes.

ONLINE BUSINESS AND MARKETING PLANNING

Online marketing planning is very similar to creating any other marketing plan. It's strange to have separate plans for online and offline because that is not how customers perceive a business. Here are online business and planning recommendations:

- Build the marketing plan around the customer, rather than on products.
- Monitor progress toward the one-year vision for the business in order to be able to identify when adjustments are needed, and then be agile enough to respond.

- Identify all key assumptions in the marketing plan. When there is evidence that those assumptions are wrong, identify the new assumptions and adjust the plan.
- Make data-driven, fact-based plans.

Review Questions

1. Describe how digital content and services can lead to significantly lower costs.
2. What general features make the delivery of online services successful for both sellers and buyers?
3. How has Amazon maintained its competitive edge?
4. How did ING Direct attract customers to become the world's largest online bank?
5. List the major issues relating to e-tailing.
6. List three online marketing planning recommendations.

6.3 Business-to-Business (B2B) E-Commerce and E-Procurement

In *business-to-business (B2B) applications,* the buyers, sellers, and transactions involve only organizations. B2B comprises about 85 percent of e-commerce dollar volume. It covers applications that enable an enterprise to form electronic relationships with its distributors, resellers, suppliers, customers, and other partners. By using B2B, organizations can restructure their supply chains and partner relationships.

There are several business models for B2B applications. The major ones are sell-side marketplaces and e-sourcing (the buy-side marketplace).

SELL-SIDE MARKETPLACES

In the **sell-side marketplace** model, organizations sell their products or services to other organizations from their own private e-marketplace or from a third-party site. This model is similar to the B2C model in which the buyer is expected to come to the seller's site, view catalogs, and place an order. In the B2B sell-side marketplace, however, the buyer is an organization. The two key mechanisms in the sell-side model are forward auctions and online catalogs, which can be customized for each buyer.

Sellers such as Dell Computer (*dellauction.com*) use auctions extensively. In addition to auctions from their own Web sites, organizations can use third-party auction sites, such as eBay, to liquidate items. Companies such as Overstock.com help organizations to auction obsolete and excess assets and inventories.

The sell-side model is used by hundreds of thousands of companies and is especially powerful for companies with superb reputations. The seller can be either a manufacturer (e.g., IBM), a distributor (e.g., *avnet.com* is an example of a large distributor in IT), or a retailer (e.g., *Walmart.com*). The seller uses e-commerce to increase sales, reduce selling and advertising expenditures, increase delivery speed, and reduce administrative costs. The sell-side model is especially suitable to customization. For example, organizational customers can configure their orders online at *cisco.com* and other sites. Self-configuration of orders results in fewer misunderstandings about what customers want and much faster order fulfillment.

E-SOURCING

E-sourcing refers to the many procurement methods. The primary methods are auctions, RFQ processing, and private exchanges. E-sourcing also applies to all other secondary activities, which have added to the cycle time and cost of procurement transactions. Secondary activities include trading partner collaboration, contract negotiation, and supplier selection.

E-Procurement. Corporate procurement, also called **corporate purchasing,** deals with the buying of products and services by an organization for its operational and functional needs. Organizations procure materials to produce finished goods, which is referred to as **direct procurement,** and products for daily operational needs, which is referred to as **indirect procurement.** **E-procurement** refers to the reengineered procurement processes using e-business technologies and strategies. Strategies and solutions linked to e-procurement have two basic goals.

- **Control costs:** The first goal is to control corporate spending. Organizations want to spend intelligently for procurement activities to maximize the value of their spending; that is, ensure that money spent to procure items results in procuring the right products at the best value. Corporate e-procurement constitutes a substantial portion of an organization's operational spending. For example, it is common for a large manufacturing organization to spend millions of U.S. dollars in procuring products and services. Organizations thus design e-procurement systems to facilitate and control overall procurement spending.

- **Simplify processes:** The second goal is to streamline the procurement process to make it efficient. Inefficiencies in the procurement process tend to introduce delays in ordering and receiving items as well as tax internal resources.

The two goals of cost control and streamlining can be met in three ways:

1. Streamline the e-procurement process within an organization's value chain. Doing so reduces the number of employees needed to process purchasing, reduces the procurement cycle time to order and receive items, and empowers the organization's staff with enough information about the products and services to enable them to make intelligent decisions when procuring items.

2. Align the organization's procurement process with those of other trading partners that belong to the organization's virtual supply chain. Alignment can be achieved by automating the process from end to end, including trading partners' systems, and simplifies the buying process. This enables suppliers to react efficiently to buyers' needs.

3. Use appropriate e-procurement strategies and solutions. Organizations analyze spending patterns in an effort to improve spending decisions and outcomes.

Public and Private Exchanges. Exchanges are sites where many sellers and many buyers buy and sell. They may be public or private, depending on whether or not they are open to the public.

Vertical exchanges serve one industry (e.g., automotive, chemical) along the entire supply chain. *Horizontal exchanges* serve many industries that use the same products or services (e.g., office supplies, cleaning materials). There are four major types of exchanges:

1. Vertical exchanges for direct materials. These are B2B marketplaces where *direct materials*—materials that are inputs to manufacturing—are traded, usually in *large quantities* in an environment of long-term relationship known as **systematic sourcing.** An example is *PlasticsNet.com*, a vertical marketplace for industry professionals.

2. Vertical exchanges for indirect materials. Indirect materials in *one industry* are usually purchased on an as-needed basis, which is commonly called **spot sourcing.** Buyers and sellers may not even know each other. *ChemConnect.com* and *iSteelAsia.com* are examples. In vertical exchanges, prices change continuously (like a stock exchange), based on the matching of supply and demand. Auctions are typically used in this kind of B2B marketplace, sometimes done in private trading rooms, which are available in exchanges like *ChemConnect.com. IT at Work 6.4* describes this exchange.

3. Horizontal exchanges. These are e-marketplaces for indirect materials, such as office supplies, lightbulbs, and cleaning materials used by *any industry*. Because these products are used for maintenance, repair, and operations (and not sold to generate revenue), they are called **MRO.** Prices are fixed or negotiated in this systematic exchange. Examples are *EcEurope.com, Globalsources.com,* and *Alibaba.com.*

American Express applied its own experience with indirect purchasing to develop tools that improve compliance with established procurement rules on indirect purchases, or MRO supplies. Instead of a pile of catalogs or personal supplier preferences, the system relies on a master catalog that lists only approved products

IT at Work 6.4

Global Chemical Commodity Portal

MKT   GLOBAL

Buyers and sellers of chemicals and plastics meet electronically in the vertical commodity exchange ChemConnect (*chemconnect.com*), which formed in 1995. Using this exchange, global chemical industry leaders such as British Petroleum (BP), Dow Chemical, BASF, and Sumitomo reduce trading cycle time and costs while finding new markets and trading partners around the globe.

ChemConnect provides its customers on-demand solutions to improve their supply chain performance. Their *Negotiation Solutions* enable online dynamic bidding events, which are used to both buy materials at a lower cost and to sell finished goods at the highest price. The *Collaboration Hubs* are used by chemical companies around the world to share critical demand, inventory, and order data with their supply chain partners.

Supplier Hub. ChemConnect offers benefits to both suppliers and buyers who invest in the Supply Chain Connect's *Supply Hub,* including

• Up to 50 percent reductions in inventory and safety stocks

• 25 percent reduction in the total cost of processing and filling an order

• 20 percent less time spent on reconciling order, receipt, and invoice data

The cost of Supply Hub was justified by labor savings and lower inventories.

ChemConnect's private collaboration hubs provide supply chain partners with the ability to share critical real-time order, demand, and inventory information in real time. This capability uses both integrated and Web-based applications to reduce administration costs and lower inventory levels.

Sources: Compiled from *chemconnect.com*, and Case Study: ChemConnect (2008).

Discussion Questions: What are the advantages of the ChemConnect exchange? How can investments in the supplier portal or collaboration hub be justified? How long is the payback period? What are the benefits of Supply Hub?

---

from authorized vendors. One of the big gains is the elimination of **maverick buying.** Maverick buying is done outside the established system. If the procurement process is too complicated, people will go outside the system and buy from a local vendor. Maverick buying can prove costly not only because that vendor's prices may be high, but it can also keep the company from achieving volume levels that could trigger a new tier of discounts.

Since catalog purchases have high transaction costs, American Express put catalogs from multiple suppliers and from various categories of spending into its master catalog, *CatalogPro.* This catalog makes it easier for users to find the right items and purchase them at contract rates.

4. Functional exchanges. Needed services such as temporary help or extra space are traded on an as-needed basis. For example, *Employease.com* can find temporary labor using employers in its Employease Network. Prices are dynamic and vary depending on supply and demand.

Another important facet of managing procurement is **demand management**—knowing or predicting what to buy, when, and how much. The best procurement cost is zero, when people aren't buying what they don't need.

Review Questions

1. Briefly differentiate between the sell-side marketplace and e-sourcing.
2. What are the two basic goals of e-procurement? How can those goals be met?
3. What is the role of exchanges in B2B?
4. Explain why maverick buying might take place and its impact on procurement costs.

6.4 E-Government

E-commerce models apply to government and the public sector, as you have read in several case examples in prior chapters. Web technologies help the public sector to deal with economic, social, and environmental challenges and to manage their operations and growth the way that for-profits do. Here we examine the application of Web technologies to nonprofits.

E-government is the use of Internet technology to deliver information and public services to citizens, business partners and suppliers of government entities, and people who work in the public sector. Benefits of e-government are the following:

• Improves the efficiency and effectiveness of the functions of government, including the delivery of public services

• Enables governments to be more transparent to citizens and businesses by giving access to more of the information generated by government

• Offers greater opportunities for citizens to provide feedback to government agencies and to participate in democratic institutions and processes

As a result, e-government may facilitate fundamental changes in the relationships between citizens and governments.

E-government transactions can be divided into three major categories: G2C, G2B, and G2G. In the G2C category, government agencies increasingly are using the Internet to provide services to citizens. An example is *electronic benefits transfer* (EBT), in which governments transfer benefits, such as Social Security and pension payments, directly to recipients' bank accounts or to smart cards.

In G2B, governments use the Internet to sell to or buy from businesses. For example, *electronic tendering systems* using reverse auctions are often mandatory to ensure the best price and quality for government procurement of goods and services. G2G includes intragovernment e-commerce (transactions between different governments) as well as services among different governmental agencies.

E-GOVERNMENT IN THE CLOUD

Government officials, like corporate managers, did not easily embrace cloud computing. But their concerns about cloud computing are decreasing according to a survey of IT decision makers released in mid-2010. The survey conducted by the nonprofit Public Technology Institute (PTI) found that 45 percent of local governments are using some form of cloud computing for applications or services. The findings revealed that an additional 19 percent of local governments planned to implement some form of cloud computing within the year, while 35 percent had no intentions to do so.

Local governments have several options for cloud computing—a public cloud, a private cloud, a regional cloud, a government-operated cloud, or a cloud operated by a vendor on behalf of the government. Budget pressures are a leading factor moving governments into cloud computing solutions.

Two cases of e-government are the city of Carlsbad (*carlsbadca.gov/*), California, which selected a cloud solution, and the e-government use of smartphone apps to control drunken driving.

THE CITY OF CARLSBAD TURNS TO THE CLOUD

The city of Carlsbad employs 1,100 people and serves more than 100,000 local citizens. The city's workforce devotes a lot of time to team-based projects that depend on communication and collaboration. The city was faced with an outdated e-mail system and no collaboration system—and severe budget constraints. The city needed to replace the aging e-mail system that it managed in-house to provide its employees with improved collaboration.

The city first considered Microsoft Exchange Server 2007 and Microsoft Office Outlook. But the IT department was concerned with whether it would be cost-effective to spend its limited budget on the purchase of hardware and the hiring and training of staff to administer Exchange Server 2007. So the city sent out an RFP to various vendors to compare the costs of a hosted, managed, or on-premises solution. The IT staff explored how to acquire and use IT to get long-term savings. They worked with the consulting company Gartner to understand the value, security, and reliability ramifications of going with a hosted solution and learned that hosting was a viable option.

Therefore, given its limited budget and server expertise, the city decided on a cloud computing solution. This solution avoided on-premises investments with Microsoft's Business Productivity Online Standard Suite, a collaboration software hosted at Microsoft data centers. For a low per-user, per-month subscription fee, the suite offers hosted communication and collaboration services that include desktop and mobile e-mail, calendaring and contacts, instant messaging and presence, shared workspaces, and live audiovisual Web-conferencing applications.

In February 2009, the city began working with Microsoft Services to plan the migration of 880 GroupWise mailboxes to Exchange Online. On all of its desktops, the city installed Microsoft Office 2007 and the Microsoft Online Services client that provides a **single sign-on** to all online services in the suite. With single sign-on, users log in once and have access to all software and data sources that they are authorized to access. The city used a migration tool from Quest Software that facilitated the municipal government's migration from GroupWise directly to Exchange Online.

The city of Carlsbad is the first public sector entity to deploy the Microsoft Business Productivity Online Standard Suite. The city is benefiting from more flexibility in resource allocation, reduced costs, accelerated deployment, and improved employee productivity. Faced with tough economic times, the cloud solution provides the city with the ability to allocate its finite resources where they'll generate the greatest return on investment (ROI).

E-GOVERNMENT SERVES CITIZENS WITH APPS TO CURB DRUNKEN DRIVING

With widespread use of smartphone applications, several government agencies and app coders have found a promising way to curb drunken driving. In 2010, two iPhone apps were made available. One app called *R-U-Buzzed,* which was released by the Colorado Department of Transportation, estimates blood alcohol content. A mash-up program called *Stumble Safely* gives pedestrians in Washington, D.C., a safe route home after a night at the bar. The Stumble Safely app was submitted to the Apps for Democracy contest, which is described in *IT at Work 6.5.*

California's Office of Traffic Safety (OTS) partnered with the popular Taxi Magic app team to promote sober designated drivers, a cab driver in this case. California announced the partnership in May 2010. "It gives those who need to get someplace when they've had too much to drink an easy way to do it," said California OTS spokesman Chris Cochran. "It's one more tool in the anti-DUI [driving under the influence] tactics we have" (Wilkinson, 2010). The free Taxi Magic app, released in January 2009, has become one of the most downloaded apps in Apple's iTunes store. Users who are in a metropolitan area where the service is available can use the app's Magic Book feature to tap one button that phones the cab company and arranges pickup location details.

IT at Work 6.5

Using a Contest to Generate Open Source Apps for Citizens

In Fall 2008, the Office of the Chief Technology Officer asked iStrategyLabs how it could make Data Catalog (*data.octo.dc.gov/*) useful for citizens, visitors, businesses, and government agencies. The Data Catalog provides citizens with access to 431 data sets from multiple agencies, featuring real-time crime data feeds, school test scores, and poverty indicators, and is the most comprehensive public data source in the world. The solution was the creation of *Apps for Democracy* (*appsfordemocracy.org/*), a contest that had cost $50,000 and returned 47 iPhone, Facebook, and Web applications with an estimated value of $2,600,000 to the city.

The Apps for Democracy contest challenges citizens to make open-source applications that can access any of the data sets held by the government. The 2009 winning entry was an iPhone program in which users could submit 311 service requests to the district government. The application also interfaces with Facebook.

Sources: Compiled from Data Catalog (*data.octo.dc.gov/*) and Apps for Democracy (*appsfordemocracy.org*).

Discussion Questions: Visit the Data Catalog (*data.octo.dc.gov/*). What value does it provide citizens?

The state agency's partnership with Taxi Magic came at zero cost and fits its mission to encourage designated drivers and safe driving. The California OTS is the first state agency the company has partnered with, which Taxi Magic did in order to promote safety.

Review Questions

1. What are the benefits of e-government?
2. What is the advantage of using cloud computing as the platform for e-government?
3. What is the purpose of Apps for Democracy?
4. How do e-government apps help stop drunken driving?

6.5 E-Commerce Support Services: Payment and Order Fulfillment

Implementation of e-commerce requires support services. B2B and B2C applications require payments and order fulfillment; portals require content. Figure 6.9 shows the major e-commerce services, which include the following:

- **E-infrastructure:** technology consultants, system developers, integrators, hosting, security, wireless, and networks
- **E-process:** payments and logistics
- **E-markets:** marketing and advertising
- **E-communities:** citizens, audiences, and business partners
- **E-services:** CRM, PRM, and directory services
- **E-content:** Supplied by content providers

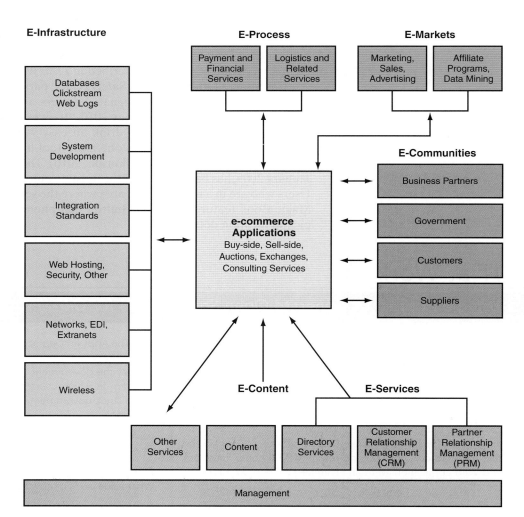

Figure 6.9 E-commerce support services.

All of these services support the e-commerce applications in the center of the figure, and all of the services need to be managed.

MARKET RESEARCH FOR E-COMMERCE

The goal of market research is to find information and knowledge that describe the relationships among consumers, products, marketing methods, and marketers. This information is used to discover marketing opportunities, establish marketing plans, better understand the purchasing process, and evaluate marketing performance. On the Web, the objective is to turn browsers into buyers. Market research includes gathering information about topics such as the economy, industry, firms, products, pricing, distribution, competition, promotion, and consumer purchasing behavior.

WEB ADVERTISING

One of the problems with direct-mail advertising is that advertisers knew very little about the recipients. Market segmentation by various characteristics (e.g., age, income, gender) helped, but did not solve the problem. The Internet introduced the concept of **interactive marketing,** which has enabled marketers and advertisers to interact directly with customers. In interactive marketing, a consumer can click an ad to obtain more information or send an e-mail to ask a question. Besides the two-way communication and e-mail capabilities provided by the Internet, vendors also can target specific groups and individuals on which they want to spend their advertising dollars.

Companies use Internet advertising as one of their advertising channels. At the same time, they also may use TV, newspapers, or other traditional channels. In this respect, the Web competes on a budget with the other channels. The two major business models for advertising online are (1) using the Web as a channel to advertise a firm's own products and services, and (2) making a firm's site a public portal site and using captive audiences to advertise products offered by other firms. For example, the audience might come to a P&G Web site to learn about Tide, but they might also receive additional ads for products made by companies other than P&G.

REPRESENTATIVE ADVERTISING STRATEGIES ONLINE

Several advertising strategies can be used over the Internet. In this section, we will present the major strategies used.

Affiliate Marketing and Advertising. Affiliate marketing is the revenue model by which an organization refers consumers to the selling company's Web site. Affiliate marketing is used mainly as a revenue source for the referring organization and as a marketing tool for sellers. However, the fact that the selling company's logo is placed on many other Web sites is free advertising as well. Consider Amazon.com, whose logo can be seen on about one million affiliate sites.

Viral Marketing. **Viral marketing** refers to word-of-mouth marketing in which customers promote a product or service by telling others about it. Promotion can be done by tweets, texts, and so on. Having people forward messages to friends, asking them, for example, to "check out this product," is an example of viral marketing. This marketing approach has been used for generations, but now its speed and reach are multiplied by the Internet. This ad model can be used to build brand awareness at a minimal cost because the people who pass on the messages are paid very little or nothing for their efforts.

Customizing Ads. The Internet has too much information for customers to view. Filtering irrelevant information by providing consumers with customized ads can reduce this information overload. The heart of e-marketing is a customer database, which includes registration data and information gleaned from site visits. The companies that advertise via one-to-one advertising use the database to send customized ads to consumers. Using this feature, a marketing manager can customize display ads based on users' profiles. The product also provides market segmentation.

ELECTRONIC PAYMENTS

Payments are an integral part of doing business, whether in the traditional way or online. Unfortunately, in several cases traditional payment systems are not effective for e-commerce, especially for B2B. Contrary to what many people believe, it may be less secure for the buyer to use the telephone or mail to arrange or send payment, especially from another country, than to complete a secured transaction on a computer. For all of these reasons, a better way is needed to pay for goods and services in cyberspace. This better way is *electronic payment systems*, such as PayPal.

There exist several alternatives for paying for goods and services on the Internet. The major ones are summarized in Table 6.4.

The most common methods, paying with credit cards and electronic bill payments, are discussed briefly here.

Electronic Credit Cards. Electronic credit cards make it possible to charge online payments to one's credit card account. For security, only encrypted credit cards should be used. Credit card details can be encrypted by using the SSL protocol in the buyer's computer (available in standard browsers).

Here is how electronic credit cards work: When you buy a book from Amazon, your credit card information and purchase amount are encrypted in your browser, so the information is safe during transmission on the Internet. Furthermore, when this information arrives at Amazon, it is not opened, but transferred automatically in encrypted form to a clearing house, where the information is decrypted for verification and authorization. The complete process of how e-credit cards work is shown in Figure 6.10. Electronic credit cards are used mainly in B2C and in shopping by SMEs (small-to-medium enterprises).

TABLE 6.4	Electronic Payments Methods
Method	**Description**
Electronic funds transfer	Popular for paying bills online. Money is transferred electronically from payer's account to the recipient's.
Electronic checks	Digitally signed e-check is encrypted and moved from the buying customer to the merchant.
Purchasing e-cards	Corporate credit cards, with limits, work like regular credit cards but must be paid more quickly (e.g., in one week).
E-cash—smart cards	Cards that contain considerable information can be manipulated as needed and used for several purposes, including transfer of money.
E-cash—person-to-person	Special online account from which funds can be sent to others is created. PayPal is the best-known company (an eBay company). You can pay businesses as well. Another example is Yahoo Pay Direct.
Electronic bill presentment and payments	Bills are presented for payer's approval. Payment is made online (e.g., funds transfer). Examples: *CheckFree.com*, Yahoo Bill Pay.
Pay at ATMs	ATMs allow you to pay monthly bills (e.g., to utility companies) by transferring money from your account to the biller.
Micropayments	Payments are too small to be paid with credit cards. Can be paid with stored-value money cards or with special payment methods, including payments from cell phones.
B2B special methods	Enterprise invoice presentment and payment, wire transfer, and electronic letter of credit are popular methods.

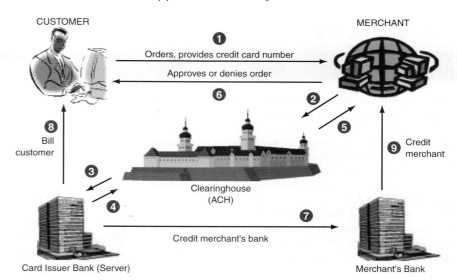

Figure 6.10 The sequence of activities involved in e-credit card processing.

Electronic Bill Payments. There are three major ways to pay bills over the Internet:

1. Online banking. The consumer signs up for a bank's online bill-paying service and makes all payments from a single Web site. Some banks offer the service for free with a checking account or if the account holder maintains a minimum balance.

2. Biller direct. The customer makes payments at each biller's Web site either with a credit card or by giving the biller enough information to complete an electronic withdrawal directly from the customer's bank account. The biller makes the billing information available to the customer (presentment) on its Web site or the site of a billing hosting service. Once the customer views the bill, he or she authorizes and initiates payment at the site. The payment can be made with a credit/debit card or by using the Automated Clearing House (ACH) transfer system. The biller then initiates a payment transaction that moves funds through the payment system, crediting the biller and debiting the customer. This method is known as electronic bill presentment and payments (EBPP).

3. Bill consolidator. The customer enrols to receive and pay bills for multiple billers with a third-party bill consolidator. The customer's enrolment information is forwarded to every biller that the customer wishes to activate (service initiation). For each billing cycle, the biller sends a bill summary or bill detail directly to the consolidator. The bill summary, which links to the bill detail stored with the biller or the consolidator, is made available to the customer (presentment). The customer views the bill and initiates payment instructions. The consolidator initiates a credit payment transaction that moves funds through the payment system to the biller.

SECURITY IN ELECTRONIC PAYMENTS

Two main issues need to be considered under the topic of payment security: (1) what is required in order to make e-commerce payments safe and (2) the methods that can be used to do so.

Security Requirements. Security requirements for conducting e-commerce are the following:

• **Authentication.** The buyer, the seller, and the paying institutions must be assured of the identity of the parties with whom they are dealing.

• **Integrity.** It is necessary to ensure that data and information transmitted in e-commerce, such as orders, replies to queries, and payment authorizations, are not accidentally or maliciously altered or destroyed during transmission.

IT at Work 6.6

E-Money Lifestyle

You walk through the crowded train station in central Tokyo, heading straight for the entry barriers, and you can ignore the people in line at the ticket machines. You take out your mobile phone and wave it at a card reader. A beep is heard and you can pass through, ready for your train.

The growing e-money lifestyle in Japan is making life more convenient for consumers by allowing a number of transactions to be conducted via mobile phone, instead of traditional paper bills and coins given at the cash register. The system, called Mobile Suica, debuted publicly in January 2006 as an offering by NTT DoCoMo, which is the leading Japanese mobile phone provider, and East Japan Railway. Mobile Suica is a cell phone–based smart card that can be used for buying rail tickets or for accessing buildings. It is based on RFID.

Europe is updating, too, in places such as France, where Societe Generale, in partnership with Visa Europe and Gemalto, introduced a Visa Premier "contactless" bank card in July 2007 for consumers to make small purchases with. In England, the *Evening Standard,* a popular newspaper, is sold at special kiosks where the only contact made is between card and scanner.

The Bank of Japan has not released any figures regarding e-money, but analysts say e-money represents about 20 percent of the ¥300 trillion (US$2.8 trillion) in Japanese consumer spending. Experts say the new technology will promote the growth of e-money. "With contactless Mobile Suica on your mobile phone, you can check your balance and upload more money into your account at anytime, from anywhere," said an expert (see Figure 6.11).

There are causes for concern, however, especially for security. "Losing my phone would be like losing my money," said a consumer. To address these, some mobile phone providers have already introduced biometric security measures that include fingerprint, facial, and voice recognition needed to activate phones.

Sources: Compiled from *International Herald Tribune* (2008), *nttdocomo.com,* and *slashphone.com.*

Figure 6.11 Contactless Mobile Suica on your mobile phone. (© *Kyodo/Landov LLc*)

- **Nonrepudiation.** Merchants need protection against the customer's unjustified denial of placing an order. On the other hand, customers need protection against merchants' unjustified denial of payments made. (Such denials, of both types, are called *repudiation*.)
- **Privacy.** Many customers want their identity to be secured. They want to make sure others do not know what they buy. Some prefer complete anonymity, as is possible with cash payments.
- **Safety.** Customers want to be sure that it is safe to provide a credit card number on the Internet. They also want protection against fraud by sellers or by criminals posing as sellers.

ORDER FULFILLMENT

Any time a company directly sells customers a product that is delivered physically, it is involved in various **order fulfillment** activities. It must perform the following activities: quickly find the products to be shipped; pack them; arrange for the packages to be delivered speedily to the customer's door; collect the money from every customer, either in advance, by COD, or by individual bill; and handle the return of unwanted or defective products.

It is very difficult to accomplish these activities both effectively and efficiently in B2C, since a company may need to ship small packages to many customers quickly. For this reason, both online companies and click-and-mortar companies often have difficulties in their B2C supply chain, and they outsource deliveries and sometimes packaging. Here, we provide a brief overview of order fulfillment.

Order fulfillment includes not only providing customers with what they ordered and doing it on time, but also providing all related customer service. For example, the customer must receive assembly and operation instructions to a new appliance. In addition, if the customer is not happy with a product, an exchange or return must be arranged. Order fulfillment is basically a part of what is called a company's *back-office operations*. *Back-office* activities are inventory control, shipment, and billing.

Order Fulfillment Process. A typical e-commerce fulfillment process is shown in Figure 6.12. The process starts on the left, when an order is received and after verification that it is a real order. Several activities take place, some of which can be done simultaneously; others must be done in sequence. Demand forecasts and accounting are conducted at various points throughout the process.

• **Activity 1:** Assurance of customer payment. Depending on the payment method and prior arrangements, the validity of each payment must be determined. In B2B, the company's finance department or financial institution (i.e., a bank or a credit card issuer) may do this. Any holdup may cause a shipment to be delayed, resulting in a loss of goodwill or a customer.

• **Activity 2:** Check of in-stock availability. Regardless of whether the seller is a manufacturer or a retailer, as soon as an order is received, an inquiry needs to be made regarding stock availability. Several scenarios are possible here that may involve the material management and production departments, as well as outside suppliers and warehouse facilities. In this step, the order information needs to be connected to the information about in-stock inventory availability.

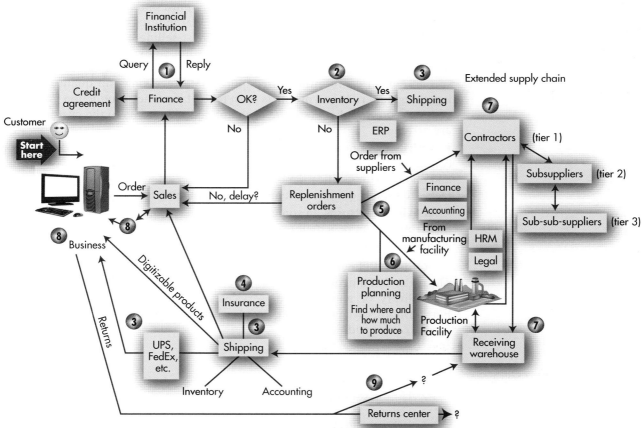

Note: Demand forecasts and accounting are conducted various points throughout the process.

Figure 6.12 Order fulfillment and logistics system.

- **Activity 3:** Shipment arrangement. If the product is available, it can be shipped to the customer right away (otherwise, go to step 5). Products can be digital or physical. If the item is physical and it is readily available, packaging and shipment arrangements need to be made. It may involve the packaging or shipping departments and internal shippers or outside transporters.

- **Activity 4:** Insurance. Sometimes the contents of a shipment need to be insured. This could involve both the finance department and an insurance company, and, again, information needs to flow not only inside the company but also to and from the customer and insurance agent.

- **Activity 5:** Replenishment. Customized orders will always trigger a need for some manufacturing or assembly operation. Similarly, if standard items are out of stock, they need to be produced or procured. Production can be done in-house or by contractors. The suppliers involved may have their own suppliers (subsuppliers or tier-2 suppliers).

- **Activity 6:** In-house production. In-house production needs to be planned. Production planning involves people, materials, components, machines, financial resources, and possibly suppliers and subcontractors. In the case of assembly, manufacturing, or both, several plant services may be needed, including possible collaboration with business partners. Services may include scheduling of people and equipment, shifting other products' plans, working with engineering on modifications, getting equipment, and preparing content. The actual production facilities may be in a different country than the company's headquarters or retailers. This may further complicate the flow of information and communication.

- **Activity 7:** Contractor use. A manufacturer may opt to buy products or sub-assemblies from contractors. Similarly, if the seller is a retailer, such as in the case of Amazon.com or walmart.com, the retailer must purchase products from its manufacturers. Several scenarios are possible. Warehouses can stock purchased items, which is what Amazon.com does with its best-selling books, toys, and other commodity items. However, Amazon.com does not stock books for which it receives only a few orders. In such cases, the publishers or intermediaries must make the special deliveries. In either case, appropriate receiving and quality assurance of incoming materials and products must take place. Once production (step 6) or purchasing from suppliers (step 7) is completed, shipments to the customers (step 3) are arranged.

- **Activity 8:** Contacts with customers. Sales representatives need to keep in constant contact with customers, especially in B2B, starting with notification of orders received and ending with notification of a shipment or a change in delivery date. These contacts are usually done via e-mail and are frequently generated automatically.

- **Activity 9:** Returns. In some cases, customers want to exchange or return items. Such returns can be a major problem, as more than $100 billion in North American goods are returned each year.

Order fulfillment processes may vary, depending on the product and the vendor. The order fulfillment process also differs between B2B and B2C activities, between the delivery of goods and of services, and between small and large products. Furthermore, certain circumstances, such as in the case of perishable materials or foods, require additional steps.

Review Questions

1. What are the major e-commerce support services?
2. List the security requirements for e-commerce.
3. Describe the issues in e-commerce order fulfillment.
4. List the nine steps of the order fulfillment process.
5. What is the meaning of Internet market research?
6. What are some online advertisement strategies?

6.6 E-Business Ethics and Legal Issues

Ethical standards and laws frequently lag behind technological innovation. E-commerce is taking new forms and enabling new business practices that may bring numerous risks—particularly for individual consumers—along with their advantages. We begin by considering ethical issues relating to e-business. We then examine the legal environment in which e-commerce operates.

ETHICAL AND IMPLEMENTATION ISSUES

Many of the ethical and implementation issues related to IT in general also apply to e-business.

Privacy. Most electronic payment systems know who the buyers are; therefore, it may be necessary to protect the buyers' identities. A privacy issue related to employees also involves tracking: Many companies monitor employees' e-mail and have installed software that performs in-house monitoring of Web activities to discover employees who extensively use company time for non-business-related activities, including harassing other employees. Many employees don't like being watched, but companies may be obligated to monitor.

Web Tracking. Log files are the principal resources from which e-businesses draw information about how visitors use a site. Applying analytics to log files means either turning log data over to an application service provider (ASP) or installing software that can pluck relevant information from files in-house. By using tracking software, companies can track individuals' movements on the Internet. Programs such as cookies raise privacy concerns. The tracking history is stored on your PC's hard drive, and any time you revisit a certain Web site, the computer knows it. In response, some users install programs such as Cookie Cutter, CookieCrusher, and Spam Butcher, which are designed to allow users to have some control over cookies. Or they delete their cookie files.

However, the battle between computer end users and Web trackers has just begun. There are more and more "pesticides" for killing these "parasites." For example, Privacy Guardian, MyPrivacy, and Tracks Eraser Pro are examples of software that can protect users' online privacy by erasing a browser's cache, surfing histories, and cookies. Programs such as Ad-Aware are specially designed to detect and remove spyware.

Loss of Jobs. The use of e-commerce may result in the elimination of some company employees as well as brokers and agents. The manner in which these unneeded workers are treated may raise ethical issues, such as how to handle the displacement and whether to offer retraining programs.

Disintermediation and Reintermediation. One of the most interesting e-commerce issues relating to loss of jobs is that of intermediation. Intermediaries provide two types of services: (1) matching and providing information and (2) value-added services such as consulting. The first type of services (matching and providing information) can be fully automated, and therefore these services are likely to be assumed by e-marketplaces and portals that provide free services. The second type of services (value-added services) requires expertise, and these can be only partially automated. Intermediaries who provide only (or mainly) the first type of service may be eliminated, a phenomenon called **disintermediation** (elimination of the intermediaries).

For example, airlines sell tickets directly to customers, eliminating some travel agents. Direct sales from manufacturers to customers may eliminate retailers. On the other hand, brokers who provide the second type of service or who manage electronic intermediation are not only surviving, but may actually prosper. This phenomenon is called reintermediation. In **reintermediation** of travel agents, for example, new activities may include organizing groups that go to exotic places. Intermediaries may therefore fight manufacturers because of fear that the traditional sales channel will be negatively affected by online channels. For instance, Walmart and Home Depot warned Black & Decker that they would take its products off their shelves if Black & Decker began to sell its products directly through the Internet. Also, confronted with dealer complaints, Ford executives recently agreed to discontinue plans for future direct online car sales.

LEGAL ISSUES SPECIFIC TO E-COMMERCE

Many legal issues are related to e-commerce. When buyers and sellers do not know each other and cannot even see each other (they may even be in different countries), there is a chance of fraud and other crimes over the Internet. During the first few years of e-commerce, the public witnessed many such instances, ranging from the creation of a virtual bank that disappeared along with the investors' deposits to manipulation of stock prices on the Internet. Unfortunately, fraud on the Internet is increasing.

Review Questions

1. List some ethical issues in e-commerce.
2. List the major legal issues of e-commerce.
3. Define *disintermediation*. Give an example.
4. Define *reintermediation*. Give an example.

Key Terms

auction *167*
business-to-business (B2B) *162*
business-to-consumers (B2C) *162*
channel *157*
channel conflict *170*
comparison shopping engine *157*
consumers-to-business *162*
corporate purchasing *171*
demand management *173*
direct procurement *171*
disintermediation *183*
dot-com era (bubble) *161*
e-business model *158*
e-commerce *158*
e-government *174*

e-procurement *171*
e-sourcing *171*
government-to-business *163*
government-to-citizens (G2C) *163*
government-to-government *163*
indirect procurement *171*
interactive marketing *177*
malvertisement *158*
maverick buying *173*
mass Web attack *158*
mobile commerce *163*
MRO *172*
multichanneling *157*
Payment Card Industry Data Security Standard (PCI DSS) *164*

Payment Card Industry Security Standards Council (PCI SSC) *164*
requests for quotes *166*
reintermediation *183*
reverse logistics *170*
scalability *163*
sell-side marketplace *171*
service-level agreement (SLA) *160*
single sign-on *175*
spot sourcing *172*
systematic sourcing *172*
viral marketing *177*

Chapter Highlights and Insights

(Numbers refer to Learning Objectives)

❶ E-commerce offers many benefits to organizations, consumers, and society, but it also has limitations (technological and nontechnological). The current technological limitations are expected to lessen with time.

❷ The major mechanism of e-commerce is the use of electronic markets, which frequently include online catalogs.

❷ Another mechanism of e-commerce is auctions. The Internet provides an infrastructure for executing auctions at lower cost, and with many more involved sellers and buyers, including both individual consumers and corporations. Two major types of auctions exist: forward auctions and reverse auctions. Forward auctions are used in the traditional process of *selling* to the highest bidder. Reverse auctions are used for *buying*, using a tendering system to buy at the lowest bid.

❸ B2C e-tailing can be pure (such as Amazon.com) or part of a click-and-mortar organization (such as Walmart). Direct marketing is done via solo storefronts or in malls. It can be done via electronic catalogs or by using electronic auctions. The leading online B2C service industries are banking, securities trading, job markets, travel, and real estate.

❸ The major issues faced by e-tailers are channel conflict, conflict within click-and-mortar organizations, order fulfillment, determining viability and risk, and identifying appropriate revenue models.

❸ The major B2B applications are selling from catalogs and by forward auctions (the sell-side marketplace), buying in reverse auctions and in group and desktop purchasing (the buy-side marketplace), and trading in electronic exchanges.

4 E-government commerce can take place between government and citizens, between businesses and governments, or among government units. It makes government operations more effective and efficient.

5 New electronic payment systems are needed to complete transactions on the Internet. Electronic payments can be made by e-checks, e-credit cards, purchasing cards, e-cash, stored-value money cards, smart cards, person-to-person payments via services such as PayPal, electronic bill presentment and payment, and e-wallets.

5 Order fulfillment is especially difficult and expensive in B2C because of the need to ship relatively small orders to many customers. Several activities take place, some of which can be done simultaneously; others must be done in sequence. Activities that take place in order fulfillment include (1) making sure the customer will pay, (2) checking for in-stock availability, (3) arranging shipments, (4) insurance, (5) replenishment, (6) in-house production, (7) use of contractors, (8) contacts with customers, and (9) returns (if applicable).

6 Ethical and legal issues are persistent and must constantly be addressed.

Questions for Discussion

1. Discuss the reasons for having multiple e-commerce business models in one company.
2. Distinguish between business-to-business forward auctions and buyers' bids for RFQs.
3. Discuss the benefits to sellers and buyers of a B2B exchange.
4. What are the major benefits of e-government? How are they changing?
5. Discuss the various ways to pay online in B2C.
6. Why is order fulfillment in B2C difficult?
7. Discuss the reasons for e-commerce failures.
8. Discuss the role of recommendation agents in e-commerce.
9. What are two of the most pressing ethical issues related to e-commerce?

Exercises and Projects

1. Assume you're interested in buying a car. You can find information about cars at *autos.msn.com*. Go to *autoweb.com* or *autobytel.com* for information about financing and insurance. Decide what car you want to buy. Configure your car by going to the car manufacturer's Web site. Finally, try to find the car from *autobytel.com*. What information is most supportive of your decision-making process? Was the experience pleasant or frustrating?

2. Visit *amazon.com* and identify at least three specific elements of its personalization and customization features. Browse specific books on one particular subject, leave the site, and then go back and revisit the site. What do you see? Are these features likely to encourage you to purchase more books in the future from Amazon.com? Check the One-Click feature and other shopping aids provided. List the features and discuss how they may lead to increased sales.

3. Compare the various electronic payment methods. Specifically, collect information from the vendors cited in the chapter and find more with *google.com*. Pay attention to security level, speed, cost, and convenience.

4. Go to *nacha.org*. What is the National Automated Clearing House Association (NACHA)? What is its role? What is the ACH? Who are the key participants in an ACH e-payment? Describe the "pilot" projects currently underway at ACH.

5. Visit *espn.com*. Identify at least five different ways it makes revenue.

6. Visit *manyeyes.alphaworks.ibm.com/manyeyes/*. Select visualizations from the left-side menu bar. Generate two visualizations. How does visualization improve understanding of the data sets?

Group Assignments and Projects

1. Have each team study a major bank with extensive e-commerce offerings. For example, Wells Fargo Bank is well on its way to being a cyberbank. Hundreds of brick-and-mortar branch offices are being closed. In Spring 2003, the bank served more than 1.2 million cyberaccounts (see *wellsfargo.com*). Other banks to look at are Citicorp, Netbank, and HSBC (Hong Kong). Each team should attempt to convince the class that its e-bank activities are the best.

2. Assign each team to one industry. Each team will find five real-world applications of the major business-to-business models listed in the chapter. (Try success stories of vendors and e-commerce-related magazines.) Examine the problems the applications solve or the opportunities they exploit.

3. Have teams investigate how B2B payments are made in global trade. Consider instruments such as electronic letters of credit and e-checks. Visit *tradecard.com* and

examine their services to SMEs. Also, investigate what Visa and MasterCard are offering. Finally, check Citicorp and some German and Japanese banks.

4. Conduct a study on selling diamonds and gems online. Each group member investigates one company such as *bluenile.com, diamond.com, thaigem.com, tiffany.com,* or *jewelryexchange.com*.

a. What features are used in these sites to educate buyers about gemstones?
b. How do the sites attract buyers?
c. How do the sites increase trust for online purchasing?
d. What customer service features are provided?
e. Would you buy a $5,000 diamond ring online? Why or why not?

Internet Exercises

1. Use the Internet to plan a trip to Paris. Visit *lonely-planet.com, yahoo.com,* and *expedia.com*.
a. Find the lowest airfare.
b. Examine a few hotels by class.
c. Get suggestions of what to see.
d. Find out about local currency, and convert $1,000 to that currency with an online currency converter.
e. Compile travel tips.
f. Prepare a report.

2. Access *realtor.com*. Prepare a list of services available on this site. Then prepare a list of advantages to users and advantages to realtors. Are there any disadvantages? To whom?

3. Visit *alibaba.com*. Identify the site's capabilities. Look at the site's private trading room. Write a report. How can such a site help a person who is making a purchase?

4. Visit *campusfood.com*. Explore the site. Why is the site so successful? Could you start a competing one? Why or why not?

5. Enter *housevalues.com* and find the various services it provides under several URLs. What is its revenue model?

BUSINESS CASE

Web 2.0 in South African Vineyards

Stormhoek Vineyards is a small winery in South Africa (*stormhoek.com*). Annual sales in 2005 were only $3 million, but with Web 2.0 technologies, sales grew to $10 million in 2007 and were projected to reach $30 million in 2010. The company devised a marketing campaign called "100 Geek Dinners in 100 Days." Each dinner was to be hosted by one person and used for wine tasting by several dozen guests in the United Kingdom and the United States. How can you get 100 people to host a wine tasting and how do you find 40 to 60 guests for each event? The answer: Web 2.0 technologies. The company's plan consisted of the following:

• *Blogging.* The CEO of Orbital Wines, Stormhoek's parent company, in collaboration with a well-known blogger, Hugh Macleod, wrote dozens of blog entries about the events, soliciting volunteer hosts, including bloggers (*stormhoek.com/blog)* and wine enthusiasts.
• *Wiki.* Each volunteer was provided with contact and location information on a wiki. The wiki technology was mainly used for customer relations management (CRM). The wiki included wine-related cartoons and other entertainment and advertising.
• *Podcasts.* Web-content feed enabled by an RSS was used to push information to participants' inboxes. Information included wine news, wine analyses, and descriptions of the 100 parties.
• *Video and photo links.* The corporate blog supported video links. Bloggers could cut and paste embedded links to YouTube videos directly into an entry. The company also posted videos on YouTube (*youtube.com/stormhoekwines*) and pictures at *flickr.comflickr.com/search/?w=all&q=stormhoek&m=text*.

• *Shopping.* The blog site acted as a portal to Stormhoek and included support for order placement and shopping carts for promotional "swag," such as posters and T-shirts.
• *Mashups.* An interactive map was integrated into the wiki using mashup software. This allowed dinner hosts to display a map of the location of the event. Also, guests could click an event on the map to make a reservation, get a reservation confirmation, send a query to the host, and receive photos of the house and the hosts. The company's wiki also had a link to host-blogger's home page.
• *Social networks.* The company has a page at Facebook with news, a discussion group, information, photos, videos, and a dedicated group.

The parties were attended by over 4,500 people, and the publicity enabled the vineyard to triple sales in two years, mainly in the United Kingdom. The only problem was of *blog spam*—random comments that were automatically posted by marketers for promotions. This required a daily cleaning of unwanted postings.

The blogging resulted in word-of-mouth publicity. The blogging was done by a professional blogger, Hugh Macleod, at *gapingvoid.com*. The blog offered a free bottle of wine. Macleod also organized the 100 dinners described earlier. RSS pioneer Dave Winer attended one of the dinners. A final word: Stormhoek wine is really good. Viral marketing cannot sell bad wine.

Sources: Compiled from Bennett (2007), McNichol (2007), *stormhoek.com,* and *New Communications Review* (2006).

Questions

1. What was the corporate blog used for?

2. What were the hosts' blogs used for?

3. What capabilities were introduced by the mashups?

4. How did the wiki help in communication and collaboration?

5. Why do you think the Web 2.0 technologies were successful in increasing sales?

6. What is blog spam and why is it a problem?

NONPROFIT CASE

IT Integration at Canadian Food for the Hungry International

Canadian Food for the Hungry International (CFHI, fhcanada.org/) is a nonprofit agency located in British Columbia, Canada. CFHI sends emergency relief supplies—food, water, bedding, medical supplies, and other essentials—to disaster-struck and impoverished areas around the world.

CFHI has been expanding its role. It is also a leader in *sustainable development* by working with communities and teaching them to build the skills and resources they need to thrive. Like any growing organization, CFHI found that as its workload increases, so does the need to operate efficiently and to enhance its ability to reach donors via its Web site. CFHI's IT platform could not support the growth and real-time capabilities that the organization needed to continue its mission, which is to make the world a little better.

CFHI implemented NetSuite (netsuite.com). According to CFHI IT manager Mark Petzold, the organization needed to integrate its disparate systems and improve its ability to update its Web site immediately to reflect a natural disaster that had just occurred anywhere in the world. NetSuite was selected because of its flexibility and features, for example, it can put up links on the Web site to take donations almost immediately after a natural disaster. After the 2008 earthquake in China and cyclone in Myanmar, CFHI was taking and getting donations the very next day. That lets the organization get help to those who need it faster.

Speed and Inventory Management are Crucial to Nonprofits

At a nonprofit, speed is of the essence, marketing and customer relationships are crucial, and so is having cutting-edge IT to make it all happen. At CFHI, all of those capabilities and tools are critical for the following reasons.

• Communities in distress need help fast—and that means donations need to stream in quickly via CFHI's Web site.

• Supply inventories need to be tracked and managed carefully.

• Donors must be treated like customers—able to see results, get answers, and occasionally be reminded that there are even more ways they can help.

CFHI has benefited tremendously from its new IT platform, which supports e-commerce, CRM, inventory management, reporting, marketing, and accounting.

Improved Donor Relationships and Loyalty

Donors want to see the disaster relief efforts in need of their financial support. Now, links on CFHI's Web site can be created almost instantaneously in NetSuite. With the organization's previous system, the same Web site redesign usually took a week and required outside help. With easily configurable e-commerce software, online donations come in faster following a disaster—and get to where they needed faster. The two key benefits are:

• Online donations have increased by almost 300 percent.

• Reports that used to take one week to compile now take one minute.

B2E—Business-to-Employee Enhancement

Another benefit with NetSuite's Web-based architecture is that CFHI staff can work from any location. Being able to access the CFHI system via the Web greatly enhances employees' productivity.

Dashboards give employees live data on their handhelds. Employees can click and see how many kids they are sponsoring, see how many new donors and donations have come in, and how these numbers compare to past numbers. They get instant insight into how they are doing and where to focus to best achieve their objectives and mission.

Employees in the call center can access a complete, up-to-date record when a donor calls in, letting them see the caller's history and enabling them to provide more personalized service. That creates a sense of professionalism that helps retain repeat donors.

Sources: Compiled from Canadian Food for the Hungry International (2009) and Netsuite (2010).

Questions

1. Explain the similarities between CFHI's "business" needs and those of a for-profit organization.

2. Compare donor loyalty to customer loyalty.

3. Why does real-time data matter to donors?

4. What are the benefits of NetSuite's architecture?

5. Why are dashboards important to performance?

6. What other enhancements might improve the mission of CFHI?

ANALYSIS USING VISUALIZATION

Creating Visualizations Using Public Online Data Sets

Visit ManyEyes and click onto data sets, *manyeyes.alphaworks.ibm.com/manyeyes/datasets*. Click on "create visualization" and read how to *create a visualization in three easy steps*.

1. Then select a recent data set that has been uploaded to Many Eyes. The link in the "data" column takes you to a view of the data set itself. The blue "Visualize" button lets you visualize the data.

2. Read the other sections of "Learn More."
3. Create four different visualizations and save each to a file or print your results. Many Eyes uses Java applet technology. In a few browsers, you may need to download Sun's Java Plugin to see the visualizations.
4. Review and compare your results.
5. What is the value of visualization?

References

Bennett, E., "Winery Blogs to Turn Browsers into Buyers," *Baseline*, June 2007.

Canadian *Food for the Hungry International*, 2009, cfhi.ca

Case Study: Chem Connect, 2008. *digitalenterprise.org/cases*

Ensor, B., "The Sources of ING Direct's Success," *Forrester*, April 25, 2007.

Flynn, L. J., "Like This? You'll Hate That. (Not All Web Recommendations Are Welcome)," *New York Times*, January 23, 2006.

Gonsalves, A. "Amazon Kindle 2.5 Adds Social Networking," *Information Week*, May 3, 2010.

International Herald Tribune, "Cellphones in Japan Make Wallets Obsolete," February 25, 2008.

McKay, L. "Analytics Are Just the Ticket," *CRM Magazine*. October 1, 2009a.

McKay, L. "Information Overload," *CRM Magazine*, December 2009b.

McNichol, T., "How a Small Winery Found Internet Fame," *Business 2.0*, August 8, 2007.

Netsuite, "Canadian Food for the Hungry International," 2010. *netsuite.com/portal/industries/nonprofit.shtml*

New Communications Review, "Award of Excellence–Business Category: Stormhoek Winery," October 31, 2006.

Rappa, M., Case Study: Amazon.com," DigitalEnterprise.com, 2010. *digitalenterprise.org/cases/amazon.html*

Stone, A., "ING Direct: Bare Bones, Plump Profits," *BusinessWeek*, March 14, 2005.

Wilkinson, K., "States Targeting Drunken Driving with Smartphone Apps," *Government Technology*, May 4, 2010. *govtech.com/gt/759850?topic=117673/*

Wireless News, "Rail Europe Launches Website Using FatWire Software," July 10, 2009.

Chapter

7

Mobile Computing and Commerce

Learning Objectives

❶ Understand mobile computing technologies.

❷ Describe the emergence of the mobile financial services industry.

❸ Understand the growing role of mobile computing in shopping, entertainment, gaming, hospitality and travel, and advertising.

❹ Describe the growth of location-based services and commerce.

❺ Identify the expansion of enterprise handhelds that make use of mobile computing technology.

Integrating *IT*

 ACC
 FIN
 MKT
 OM
 HRM
 IS

Ecommerce Times' M-Commerce   *ecommercetimes.com/perl/section/m-commerce/*
Mobile Commerce Daily   *mobilecommercedaily.com*
Storefront Backtalk   *storefrontbacktalk.com/*
Lo-So (Location-based social networking)   *Foursquare.com*
Augmented Reality on Smartphones   *youtube.com/watch?v=b64_16K2e08*
Mobile payments threaten retail banks and credit cards   *youtube.com/watch?v=vpw9KcqgVvE*
Wearable Computer by Motorola   *youtube.com/watch?v=zNYNZ03WH1E*
Innovative Mobile Payment System by Square   *youtube.com/watch?v=iBieYjxUj5Q*
Mobile Inventory Management   *youtube.com/watch?v=6ekR-CUDD9o*

QUICK LOOK at Chapter 7, Mobile Computing and Commerce

This section introduces you to the business issues, challenges, and IT solutions in Chapter 7. Topics and issues mentioned in the Quick Look are explained in the chapter.

Mobile computing has changed dramatically since 2008. Portable devices that connect wirelessly to the Internet are lighter, smaller, thinner, and much more powerful. Widely popular smartphones are now capable of performing functions like playing full-length movies that weren't even available on desktop computers a few years ago. Web-enabled computers for navigation and entertainment are available in most luxury vehicles and are becoming an option in mid-priced ones.

New categories of handhelds have emerged and been rapidly adopted, such as e-readers—Amazon's Kindle and Apple's iPad. Wireless hotspots to connect to the Internet are everywhere in urban areas and on transportation lines, and access to high-speed 3G and 4G networks has made interoperability a standard, as you also read in Chapter 1. Consumer and enterprise apps for mobile computing and commerce continue to expand the capabilities of this in-demand technology.

In this chapter, we review the technological foundations for mobile computing and commerce and identify the factors that impact the usability of these tools. You will read how companies are gaining customer loyalty and other competitive benefits from mobile commerce and wireless networks as well as how mobile operating systems (OS) and apps are accelerating the growth of and demand for mobile computing.

IS   ETHICS

Mobile Technology Used to Manage Epidemics, Disasters, and Healthcare

Epidemics, disasters, and healthcare are data-driven and information-intensive events and activities where outcomes are significantly improved with mobile technologies. Handhelds, mobile apps, and mobile networks play major roles in disease, disaster, and healthcare management worldwide, as shown in the following examples.

Kenya Polio Epidemic and Public Health Intervention

Mobile technology revolutionized the way contagious diseases are monitored in sub-Saharan Africa. Health officials in Kenya used the life-saving application, *EpiSurveyor*, after refugees fleeing violence in Somalia introduced the first case of polio into the country in more than 20 years. In 2008, Kenyan health workers downloaded the EpiSurveyor app onto PDAs to log patients' symptoms and the treatment they received. The data was used to track the emergency vaccination campaign and, ultimately, to stop a potential epidemic in its tracks. According to Dr Patrick Nguku from the Kenyan Health Ministry: "We used EpiSurveyor to basically control our supplies, monitor which areas needed to be vaccinated, and the quick flow of information helped us in achieving very good results."

In prior emergency situations, data had been collected and reported using paper. In many countries, a lack of timely and accurate data is one of the greatest obstacles to overcoming long-standing public health challenges. While using mobile apps and devices:

- Data quality improved because of the ability to enforce data validation—to help ensure that every data value was correct and accurate.
- Data collection to analysis time was reduced because field staff performed the data entry themselves. The time taken to record epidemiological information can be slow when healthcare workers have only paper and pen to record which children have been immunized, or where vital stocks of medication have been sent.
- Data collection was cheaper because the mobile system eliminated costs of printing, paper, and data-entry staff.

The EpiSurveyor app trial in Kenya has been so successful that the World Health Organization (WHO) expanded the project to another 20 countries in Africa, with funding provided by the United Nations Foundation, Vodafone Foundation, and the WHO.

Japan Earthquake, Tsunami, and Mobile Technology

When natural disasters hit, mobile technology takes on a crucial role transmitting information to and from devastation sites. Following the 8.9-magnitude earthquake and seven-meter tsunami that struck Japan in March 2011, mobile devices and networks provided the connectivity that helped save lives, locate people, and support relief efforts. Throughout the Pacific region, many lives were saved thanks to early tsunami warnings sent and received via mobiles, which directed people to higher, safer grounds.

Google launched a Japanese-language and English-language *Person Finder* tool, as shown in Figures 7.1 and 7.2, at *http://japan.person-finder.appspot.com* and, at a shorter URL *http://goo.gl/sagas* for mobiles, to help victims and families locate one another. With Person Finder, family and

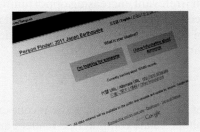

Figure 7.1 Google *Person Finder* initiated for the Japan earthquake, in English. (© *Richard Wareham Fotografie/Alamy*)

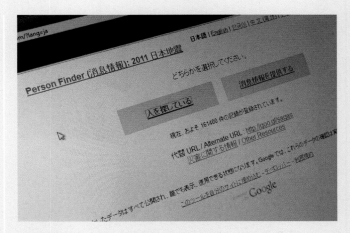

Figure 7.2 Google *Person Finder* initiated for the Japan earthquake, in Japanese. (© *Richard Wareham Fotografie/Alamy*)

friends can search for loved ones and input information about missing persons.

Healthcare via Handheld Mobile Computing and Electronic Records

Research studies of medication errors in the United Arab Emirates (UAE), Europe, and the U.S., show an alarmingly high rate of errors (six percent or more) that could lead to patient disability or even death. The financial cost of this problem is significant at a national level, and an agonizing problem for individuals and families on a personal level.

Using handheld, mobile-computing devices, medical personnel can reduce the chance of errors when prescribing medicines. Handhelds can scan barcodes on hospital patient bracelets to correctly identify patients and to retrieve electronic records with information about the patient's condition, drug allergies, and other medications they are taking. The physician can also call up information about the medicine they are considering for the patient, identifying any potential dangerous interactions that might occur. Once the doctor determines the proper medication, information can be transmitted directly to the pharmacy (see Figure 7.3), eliminating the chances of error due to unclear handwriting, loss, theft or fraudulent alteration of the script.

When nursing staff or other medical personnel arrive at the patient's bedside to administer the medicine, a handheld, mobile device is used to scan the patient's barcoded bracelet to confirm identity. Barcodes on the medicine are then scanned to confirm that the appropriate drug and dose is consistent with what the physician ordered. Alert systems warn medical personnel if there are any discrepancies between physician's orders and what has been delivered. Once the medication is administered, this information is recorded to

Figure 7.3 Handwriting errors can lead to potentially dangerous medical problems. (© *Sean Locke/iStockphoto*)

prevent additional medication being delivered until the appropriate time.

Faced with such a significant problem and a solution with very obvious benefits, one would think that electronic prescription systems would be readily embraced by the healthcare industry. Unfortunately, several obstacles are slowing the adoption of these mobile-computing solutions, including (1) insufficient knowledge of the concept, (2) required start-up financial investment, (3) lack of technology standardization, (4) provider resistance, and (5) regulatory restrictions or indecisiveness.

Sources: Compiled from Konovalov and Kumlander (2010), BBC (2008), Joia and Magalhães (2009), Papshev and Peterson (2009).

For Class Discussion and Debate

The Healthcare Industry is one of the largest industries in most countries and can benefit significantly from on-demand, location-independent, high-quality data. However, many healthcare professionals are unfamiliar with the business, information, and IT solutions or are reluctant to apply them to their field.

1. *Scenarios for Brainstorming and Discussion:*

Cost-Benefit Analysis: Start-up costs are a barrier to implementation of mobile technologies, particularly in poor economic regions. Explain why investments in mobile IT to better manage epidemics, disasters, and healthcare would be financially sound decisions—and a positive ROI. In your analysis, identify the benefits and attempt to quantify them.

2. *Debate:* Mobile networks have been *networks of convenience*. It may be argued that mobile networks, handhelds, and apps have become *critical infrastructures*. Select one of these two perspectives and support your position in a debate.

7.1 Mobile Computing Technology

The mobile computing landscape has evolved rapidly over the last two decades. Traditionally, computers were primarily used in fixed locations. They were connected via wires to peripheral devices, other computers, and networks. This lack of mobility significantly constrained the performance of people whose work took place outside of the office, such as salespeople, repair people, students, law enforcement agents, utility workers, and so on.

Wireless technology makes location irrelevant, increasing opportunities for businesses through mobile computing and commerce. In this section, you will read about the three technological foundations of mobile computing: mobile devices, mobile operating systems and software, and wireless networks.

MOBILE COMPUTING DEVICES

For consumers, the most exciting part of mobile computing is the recent explosion in new computing devices. Powerful smartphones, slate computers, e-readers, and computing devices that we can wear as clothing generate considerable media attention at electronics shows around the world. For some consumers, mobile devices have become fashion statements. For others, the mobile device a person carries can define how sophisticated or cool that person is. Companies with brands like *BlackBerry*, *iPad*, and *Android* have become experienced at launching sophisticated marketing campaigns designed to build consumer demand and excitement prior to the launch of new products.

Constant innovation in the mobile technology marketplace makes categorization of end-user devices difficult. As capabilities and functionality are added to devices, the differences between PC, e-reader, smartphone, and PDA get blurred. For the discussion below, we will rely on current trends in terminology and categorization but recognize that as mobile hardware evolves, new categories will emerge and traditional categories will become irrelevant.

Laptops, Notebooks, Netbooks, and Tablets. Mobility started when computers became portable. These early devices were only slightly smaller than desktop computers but had external cases that made it somewhat easier to transport them. They were still heavy and bulky. Portable computers evolved into laptop computers. There are currently several variations of this device:

- **Standard laptops** and **desktop replacements.** Perform most of the basic functions of a desktop computer; weigh over 3.6 kg/8 lb.
- **Notebooks.** Smaller, but less powerful than the standards and weigh from 2.7 to 3.6 kg/6 to 8 lb.
- **Netbooks** (*mini-notebook*, *ultra-portable*). Designed for Internet access and cloud computing. Much of their functionality is based on the presumption that users will be able to connect to a network. They have limited RAM, processing power, and storage capabilities and weigh less than 1.8 kg/4 lb.
- **Ultra-thin laptops.** Serve the needs of users who need very light and thin computers. As with notebooks, some processing power and functionality are sacrificed to achieve the size and weight requirements, typically 1.8 to 2.7 kg/4 to 6 lb.
- **Tablet PCs.** Have a tough screen that might also swivel so they can be used like a notebook. When needed, the screen can be folded down flat on the keyboard and used as an electronic tablet. Other tablet PCs are called *slates* because they lack a dedicated keyboard, relying primarily on stylus input. Tablet PCs are popular in healthcare, education, and the hospitality field and weigh 1 to 1.8 kg/2 to 4 lb.

Other variations are UMPC (ultra mobile personal computer), smartbook (combines features of a netbook and a smartphone), gaming laptops, and rugged computers designed for industrial settings or for use in challenging climatic conditions.

Smartphones. The mobile phone market consists of people who own feature phones and smartphones (see Figure 7.4). Smartphones are mobile phones capable of Internet connectivity and a variety of mobile computing capabilities. Feature phones are more basic devices that offer little if any Internet access or computing capability. As of 2010, there were over 4.6 billion cell phone users globally, or 60.6 percent of the world's population. Cell phone sales to end users totaled over 314 million worldwide in the first quarter of 2010. Smartphone sales totaled 54.3 million units during this same period, a 48.7 percent increase over 2009 figures (Gartner, 2010).

The Nielsen Company (*nielsen.com/*) estimates that smartphones now account for 23 percent of the U.S. cell phone market, up from 16 percent almost a year earlier (Kellogg, 2010). While the market trend is definitely toward increased use of smartphones, it should be noted that even feature phones can be used in limited ways for m-commerce.

Other Handheld Devices—PDAs, iPad, E-readers. A number of other handheld devices have emerged recently that make use of mobile networks, LCD screens, and compact processing and data storage technology. Many of these devices have received significant publicity and interest by consumers. **Personal data assistants (PDAs)** have been around for a number of years and have proven popular with the business community. These handheld devices initially focused on organization applications such as calendars, address books, to-do lists, and memo pads. Users frequently

Figure 7.4 Google's Android phone (shown here) along with Apple's iPhone represent popular innovations in the smartphone market. (© *Hugh Threlfall/Alamy*)

synchronize these applications with applications on their personal computers. While PDAs have proven extremely popular, it is likely that this device category will disappear because many PDA manufacturers are integrating cell phone technology in the devices. Likewise, most smartphones contain applications that effectively turn them into PDAs. The difference between a smartphone with PDA apps and a PDA with cell phone capability is practically zero.

E-readers are devices that look similar to slate tablet computers but are positioned primarily as a way for users to read electronic books. Some of the leading devices have been promoted by book sellers like Amazon (the Kindle) and Barnes and Noble (the Nook). The Apple iPad is expected to present both of these devices with significant competition. The iPad is similar in size and appearance to other e-readers but offers greater functionality. The iPad is yet another illustration of a device that blurs the lines between mobile device categories. It shares similarities with slate tablet PCs, e-readers, and PDAs. All three of the devices discussed above are capable of connecting to online stores through Wi-Fi technology or 3G connections (see below) so that users can purchase books, music, and software applications that will run on the machines.

Wearable Devices. People who work on buildings, electrical poles, or other difficult-to-climb places may be equipped with a special form of mobile wireless computing device called a wearable device. These devices come in a variety of forms, including wrist devices, small screens worn close to the eyes, voice-activated equipment, and keyboards built into gloves or clothing. For an expanded description of these devices and a history of their development, see *en.wikipedia.org/wiki/wearable_computing*. *Glaciercomputer.com*, *kopin.com*, and *Lxe.com* manufacture a variety of wearable computers. Examples can be viewed on their Web sites.

MOBILE COMPUTING SOFTWARE

There are three dominant PC operating systems (OSs): Microsoft Windows, Apple, and Linux. Most laptops and related devices are powered by these OSs. Programmers who write software apps target one or more of these platforms for their programs. Writing apps for handhelds is more difficult because there are more than twice as many systems to write for. Here is a brief summary of the most popular mobile OSs:

- **BlackBerry OS** (RIM). Made by Research in Motion, this is currently the dominant smartphone OS in the United States and number two globally. It powers a variety of BlackBerry-style smartphones manufactured by RIM.
- **iOS** (Apple, Inc.). Formerly called the iPhone OS, this innovative platform is often credited, in part, with spurring growth in the smartphone segment. The iOS is used in Apple's iPhone, iPod Touch, and iPad products. A distinctive feature of these devices is the touch screen. Apple has encouraged third-party development of apps for the iOS, generating further functionality and excitement about these devices.
- **Windows Mobile OS** (Microsoft). This OS by software giant Microsoft was preceded by an earlier version called Pocket PC, which pioneered the use of multiple computing apps in a small handheld. While the Windows Mobile OS holds a respectable market share in the United States, it continues to lose ground globally to other newer platforms.
- **Android OS** (Google/Open Handset Alliance). This OS is receiving very favorable reaction in the marketplace and is predicted by some to compete fiercely against Apple's popular iOS. Like the Apple product, its use is not limited to smartphones and it can be found in smaller tablet computers, notebooks, and e-readers.
- **Palm OS** (Palm, Inc.). Originally designed to power Palm's PDA devices, this mobile OS has been enhanced for use in smartphones as well as PDAs.
- **Linux OS** (Linux). The iOS, Android, and Palm operating systems described above are all based on modifications of the Linux Kernel (see *wikipedia.org/wiki/Linux_kernel*). Other manufacturers like Motorola and Samsung have used Linux to power their mobile phone devices.
- **Symbian OS** (Symbian Foundation). While this open-source software platform enjoys only a fractional market share in the United States, globally it is the

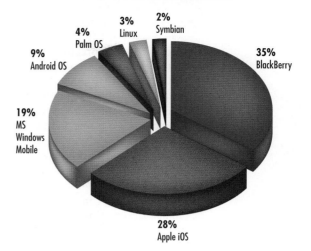

Smartphone Marketshare—Qtr 1, 2010

2% Symbian
3% Linux
4% Palm OS
9% Android OS
19% MS Windows Mobile
35% BlackBerry
28% Apple iOS

Figure 7.5 Smartphone operating system market share in the United States. (*Source: Adapted from The Nielsen Company.*)

dominant smartphone OS and runs mainly on phones manufactured by Nokia. The fourth generation of this OS became available in 2011.

Consumers expect to access Web sites from their smartphones and other devices and are frustrated by companies that do not have Web sites developed for this OS and purpose. This presents special challenges for business and Web site programmers because now they must design Web sites for access from the various mobile browsers. If a company is unable to develop mobile sites for all available devices, then knowing the relative market share of mobile OSs will help target the most dominant platforms. Figures 7.5 and 7.6 illustrate the relative share of these platforms in the United States and worldwide.

WIRELESS NETWORK GROWTH

As you read in Chapter 4, mobile devices must be able to connect with high-speed wireless networks. The mobile computing and commerce environment relies on two basic approaches to Internet connectivity: short-range wireless technologies such as Wi-Fi, and longer-range telecommunications technologies such as 3G and 4G networks (e.g., WiMAX). Most laptops today rely on Wi-Fi technology that requires being in range of a network access point. Cell phones communicate over a 3G network. However, it is possible for laptops and other mobile devices to connect with 3G networks using peripheral devices.

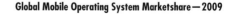

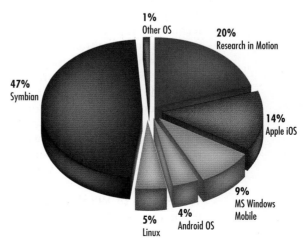

Global Mobile Operating System Marketshare—2009

1% Other OS
20% Research in Motion
14% Apple iOS
9% MS Windows Mobile
4% Android OS
5% Linux
47% Symbian

Figure 7.6 Global smartphone OS market shares. (*Source: Adapted from Gartner, 2010.*)

TABLE 7.1	Wi-Fi Locations and Applications

- iWire has a searchable registry of 317,585 free and for-purchase Wi-Fi locations in 144 countries at *v4.jiwire.com/search-hotspot-locations.htm*
- Most major airports today offer complimentary or fee-based wireless access to the Internet. Lufthansa offers in-flight Wi-Fi service on its long-haul fleet. The hotspots on the planes are connected to the Internet via satellites. American Airlines, Alaska Airlines, JetBlue, and Virgin America offer connection to the Web to fliers as of 2008.
- McDonald's offers free Wi-Fi hotspots in more than 11,500 restaurants, and the number is increasing daily. Local service providers provide high-quality wireless service.
- Using a wireless ticketing system, Universal Studios in Hollywood is shortening the waiting lines for tickets at its front gate. The ticket sellers, armed with Wi-Fi–enabled devices and belt mounted printers sell tickets and provide information to guests.
- Several mining companies in Europe installed hundreds of Wi-Fi hotspots in their coal mines. Information from drills and trucks, such as their positions and the weight of their loads, is transmitted wirelessly to the control center. It increases both productivity and safety.

Wireless Local Area Networks and Wi-Fi. Wireless local area networks have been making their way to the wireless forefront (see Table 7.1). A wireless LAN (WLAN) is like a wired LAN without cables. WLANs transmit and receive data over the airwaves from a short distance in what is known as Wi-Fi, which is short for Wireless Fidelity. Wi-Fi technology is described in Chapter 4.

The growth of Wi-Fi networks globally is one of the factors fueling the growth of mobile computing. As the number of access points or **hotspots** grows, use of mobile devices becomes easier, more convenient, and more reliable, increasing the attractiveness of the technology to end users. Across the world, businesses—especially restaurants and hotels—and municipalities are increasingly offering access to Wi-Fi as a free benefit. Business and residential users are rapidly expanding their Wi-Fi networks. Manufacturers of Wi-Fi equipment reported double-digit growth in 2010 from the previous year, a further indication that Wi-Fi network coverage will continue to expand.

Wi-Fi is used to support business and compliance requirements. By now we're aware of the terrible mining accidents that occur from time to time in various parts of the world. After the Sago mine disaster in West Virginia in January 2006, the U.S. Congress passed the Mine Improvement and New Emergency Response (MINER) Act, which requires underground coal-mining firms to upgrade procedures, equipment, and technology. These companies must provide two-way communications between underground and surface personnel and an electronic tracking system that allows surface personnel to determine the location of any persons trapped underground. The solution is to use Wi-Fi to monitor underground conditions.

3G and 4G Networks. 3G and 4G networks have evolved from telecommunications technology. Earlier forms of these networks were used primarily for voice communications, but now data transmission constitutes a major portion of the information flowing over these networks. These technologies allow greater ubiquity than Wi-Fi, and coverage is widespread, access is very good throughout most metropolitan areas and, depending on the carrier, may be strong across the country. The historical trade-off between the telecommunications networks and Wi-Fi has been coverage versus speed. Wi-Fi was faster but required users to be near an open network access point. With 3G networks, a user could be traveling down the road in an automobile and reasonably expect to access the network, but at speeds slower than Wi-Fi. With 4G technologies, the telecommunications networks are becoming faster, approaching speeds offered by Wi-Fi.

The Future of Wireless Networking. It remains to be seen how the global wireless network system will evolve. For the foreseeable future, telecommunications and

Wi-Fi technologies will coexist. With the growth of free or public Wi-Fi access points, many users are likely to view this technology as an adequate, low-cost approach to certain types of mobile computing. While access to a telecommunications network is only available through a paid subscription, other users may see the cost as well worth the benefit of constant connectivity. It is simply too early to tell whether one or the other of these technologies will eventually become dominant or whether market forces and user behavior will continue to support a dual approach. One thing is certain—because both technologies are expanding geographically, along with increases in speed and functionality, overall mobile computing is projected to grow dramatically in the near future.

Review Questions

1. What are the three technological foundations of mobile computing?
2. List some of the reasons why it can be difficult to categorize mobile computing devices.
3. What factors have led to the recent growth of the smartphone market?
4. From an end-user perspective, what are the basic trade-offs between Wi-Fi and telecommunications technology (e.g., 3G and 4G)?

7.2 Mobile Financial Services (MFS)

Mobile banking is generally defined as carrying out banking transactions and other related activities via mobile devices. The services offered include bill payments and money transfers, account administration and checkbook requests, balance inquiries and statements of account, interest and exchange rates, and so on.

Banks and other financial institutions let customers use mobile devices for a wide range of services. The most common of these mobile banking services are the following (Mobile Marketing Association, 2009):

- Account alerts, security alerts, and reminders
- Account balances, updates, and history
- Customer service via mobile
- Branch or ATM location information
- Bill paying (e.g., utility bills), delivery of online payments by secure agents and mobile phone client apps
- Fund transfers
- Transaction verification
- Mortgage alerts

People access these financial services using a combination of mobile media channels including Short Message Service (SMS), mobile Web browsers, and customized smartphone apps. Mobile banking is a natural extension of online-banking services, which have been growing in popularity over the last decade.

Short Codes. Many m-commerce transactions utilize SMS texts in conjunction with **short codes.** This is true of financial services as well. A short code works like a telephone number, except that it is only five or six characters long and easier to remember. For example, mobile banking customers of PNC Bank can send an SMS text message to short code 762265 to retrieve account information. In the body of the text, they might include messages such as BAL for account balance or LAST CHK1 to retrieve information about recent transactions.

Businesses lease short codes from the Common Short Code Association (CSCA) for $500 to $1,000 a month. The lower price is for randomly assigned codes, companies that want a specific short code pay a higher monthly rate. Once a company has leased its short code, it can begin using it in promotions and interactivity with customers.

One example of nonbanking short-code use is voting on the popular television show *American Idol*. Each contestant is assigned a specific short code, and viewers are encouraged to send text messages indicating which performer they like the best. The annual *MTV Movie Awards* also uses short-code voting, which allows viewers to pick the winning entry in certain prize categories. For a related example, see the Starbucks business case at the end of this chapter. On some telecommunications networks, ringtones are sold using short codes and SMS texts.

MOBILE BANKING AND STOCK TRADING

Throughout Europe, the United States, and Asia, an increasing percentage of banks offer mobile access to financial and account information. In 2009, ABI Research evaluated 29 U.S. banks on accessibility of their mobile banking services. Six of the banks received top marks: BB&T, Eastern Bank, Fifth Third Bank, Northeast Bank, USAA, and Wells Fargo. Bank of America and Chase also received positive evaluations (ABI Research, 2009).

In Sweden, Merita Bank has pioneered many services, and The Royal Bank of Scotland offers mobile payment services. Banamex, one of Mexico's largest banks, is a strong provider of wireless services to customers. Many banks in Japan allow for all banking transactions to be done via cell phone. Experts predict that growth in the mobile banking services sector could reach between 894 million and 1.5 billion customers globally by 2015. The Asia-Pacific region is expected to emerge as the predominant market for mobile banking services. (Berg Insight, 2010; Global Industry Analysts, 2010).

As the wireless transmission speeds improve, the rate of mobile banking services is increasing. The same holds true for other mobile insurance and stock market trades (see Figure 7.7).

Security Issues. At present, the benefits associated with mobile banking seem to outweigh potential security threats. However, as the number of people who engage in mobile banking increases, the likelihood that criminals will target mobile financial activity is sure to grow as well. What kinds of threats exist to mobile banking? Table 7.2 lists several mobile banking risks.

MOBILE ELECTRONIC PAYMENT SYSTEMS

According to the Mobile Marketing Association (2010), about one in five U.S. adults is now using **mobile commerce.** As interest in mobile commerce grows, there is a greater demand for innovative payment systems that make transactions from smartphones and other mobile devices convenient, safe, and secure. A number of businesses have attempted to meet this demand with a variety of approaches. There are two basic types of transactions of interest: the online purchase of goods and services

Figure 7.7 Mobile banking, stock trading, and payment services have increased in recent years. (© *Daniel Heighton/Alamy*)

TABLE 7.2	Mobile Banking Security Risks

Cloning. Duplicating the electronic serial number (ESM) of one phone and using it in a second phone—the clone. This allows the perpetrator to have calls and other transactions billed to the original phone.

Phishing. Using a fraudulent communication, such as an e-mail, to trick the receiver into divulging critical information such as account numbers, passwords, or other identifying information.

Smishing. Similar to phishing, but the fraudulent communication comes in the form of an SMS message.

Vishing. Again, similar to phishing, but the fraudulent communication comes in the form of a voice or voice-mail message encouraging the victim to divulge secure information.

Lost or stolen phone. Lost or stolen cell phones can be used to conduct financial transactions without the owner's permission.

Sources: Compiled from Howard (2009), Mobile Marketing Association (2009), and McGee (2008).

using a mobile device (e.g., ordering a book from *Amazon.com*) and using a hand-held to pay for goods and services in a traditional brick-and-mortar retail store. Here are examples of recent innovations approaches:

Charge to phone bills with SMS confirmation (see *Boku.com*). Using this approach, mobile users text a message to a short-code number specified by the payee. The amount of the charge is then added to the payer's phone bill, and the telecom carrier remits this amount to the payee. Telecom companies may deduct a service charge from the amount paid.

Near-field communications (see *Blingnation.com*). Another approach to mobile payment uses a small microchip containing account information that users attach to their mobile device. The mobile user simply passes or taps the phone on a merchant terminal and payment is transferred. Users receive an SMS text message confirmation. A variation on this approach involves the use of a smart card in the user's mobile phone.

Payment by credit card via phone number and SMS (see *Zong.com* and *Paypal.com*). Mobile buyers create an account at a company like *zong.com*. This account links a mobile phone number with a credit card. When shopping online, the buyer clicks a payment button and enters his or her telephone number, which is easier to remember than a credit card number. An SMS text is sent to the buyer asking for payment confirmation. When confirmed, a charge is made to the buyer's credit card.

Credit card + Web form. Using a mobile Web browser, buyers make online purchases by entering their credit card number and other identifying information just as they would if they were using a personal computer. This process can be cumbersome, given the smaller screen and keyboards on mobile devices, but it is an option.

Transfer funds from payment account using SMS (see *obopay.com* and *paypal.com*). Using this approach, the user creates an account at a company like *obopay.com* and transfers money into it from a bank or credit card account. Using a mobile phone and SMS, the user can then transfer money to anyone else with a mobile phone number. The receiver must create an account at the payment company in order to retrieve the funds.

Mobile phone card reader (see *square.com*). This novel approach requires mobile phone users to use a small card reader that plugs into the audio input jack of most mobile devices. The card reader, which resembles a small cube, allows those with accounts at *square.com* to make or receive credit card payments without a merchant account.

2D tags (see *Cimbal.com*). This payment system uses QR or 2D tags to identify the merchant or payee. The buyer scans the merchant's tag using a special smartphone app and then approves the fund transfer when it shows up on the device.

Person-to-person transfers are also possible, since the app can generate custom QR tags that individuals can scan from one another's mobile devices.

"Bumping" iPhones with payment applications (see *bumptechnologies.com*). Using an iPhone app called bump, two individuals can transfer money to each other simply by tapping their phones together.

Phone displays barcode that retailers scan (see *Facecash.com*). When it comes time for buyers to pay for goods and services, they present their mobile device, which displays their photograph for identification purposes and a barcode linked to a payment account that they've established with *facecash.com*. The merchant scans the barcode with a reader and completes the transaction.

Almost all of the payment systems described above are illustrated by videos on *YouTube.com*. Interested readers are encouraged to view these video resources for a more complete explanation of how they work.

Wireless payment systems transform mobile phones into secure, self-contained purchasing tools capable of instantly authorizing payments over the cellular network. Many of the above systems bypass traditional credit card companies or banks, decreasing transaction costs for merchants. In addition, the payment of small sums, called **micropayments,** is less problematic since many of the systems are specifically designed to accommodate smaller transactions. The ability to make micropayments allows individuals to use their mobile devices to do things like purchase a beverage from a vending machine or make a payment to a municipal parking meter. Many cities in Europe, and a growing number in the United States that have adopted mobile phone payment systems for parking, have reported dramatic increases in revenue because of the reduction in loss due to theft, broken meters, and the reduced expense associated with collecting cash from traditional meters.

Mobile (wireless) wallets are yet another payment system. An *e-wallet* is a piece of software that stores an online shopper's credit card numbers and other personal information so that the shopper does not have to reenter that information for every online purchase. While mobile e-wallets, called **m-wallets,** have been around for a few years, adoption of these apps has been limited because users perceive them to be of limited value. Companies that promote m-wallets are attempting to make them more attractive by expanding their functionality beyond simple payment systems. Their goal is to make the m-wallet an attractive replacement for a person's physical wallet. New m-wallets will be capable of storing not only credit card information but also driver's license, passport, and healthcare information (Swartz, 2010). Furthermore, many of the new m-wallet products are server-side apps. This means that crucial information in a user's wallet is not stored on the mobile device. Instead, the information is stored on secure servers and accessed, when needed, by mobile phones or other devices. This increases the safety and security of critical information by minimizing the risk associated with lost or stolen mobile devices. Makers of m-wallet apps hope that these changes will spur wide-scale adoption of m-wallets.

Review Questions

1. What are the two kinds of basic transactions requiring mobile payment systems?
2. What are short codes and how are they used to conduct transactions?
3. Why have e-wallets not been widely adopted and what are makers of m-wallets doing to make their apps more attractive?
4. What are the most common security risks associated with mobile banking?
5. Describe some of the mobile payment systems.

7.3 Mobile Shopping, Entertainment, and Advertising

Mobile commerce B2C apps are expanding in several areas—retail shopping for products and services, mobile entertainment, mobile gaming, travel and hospitality services, and sales of digitized content (e.g., music, news, videos, movies, or games).

SHOPPING FROM WIRELESS DEVICES

An increasing number of online vendors allow customers to shop from handheld devices. For example, customers use smartphones to shop at sites like *target.com*, *amazon.com*, and *buy.com*. Customers use handhelds to perform quick searches, compare prices, use a shopping cart, order, pay, and view the status of their order. Specialized devices like Amazon's e-reader Kindle allow users to purchase and download books from the store. Using Apple's iPod touch, users can purchase and download music from iTunes. Many national restaurant chains offer consumers the ability to search menus, order, and pay for food via their mobile devices.

Handheld users can also participate in online auctions. For example, eBay offers mobile apps for a variety of smartphones. They also use a voice-based service called Unwired Buyer that can contact bidders minutes before their auction is going to close to let them know the status of their bid. eBay subsidiary PayPal allows users to pay for their merchandise by phone. Consumers are increasingly using their phones to get product and price information while shopping in traditional stores. *Pricegrabber.com*, *slifter.com*, and *froogle.com* are just some of the price-comparison sites that allow people to search for product information from their mobile phones. Experts are now advising retailers to take these savvy shoppers into consideration when developing their mobile strategy. The ability to identify in-store mobile shoppers and to deliver meaningful information and value through price-matching offers or other incentives is vitally important.

Mobile commerce in Japan is growing exponentially and now represents the largest volume of m-commerce sales in the world. Over 60 million Japanese are making purchases with cell phones, for example, buying their train tickets while riding the train. Mobile shopping is popular with busy single parents, executives, and teenagers, who are doing over 80 percent of their EC shopping from cell phones.

In Japan, most food products are tagged with QR codes, allowing consumers to quickly find information about the goods they are shopping for (see Figure 7.8). According to the Daiwa Institute of Research, impulse shopping accounts for most of the purchases that are done on mobile phones, but only if the users are on flat-fee-based service.

Figure 7.8 QR codes linked to specific goods and services are used by mobile phone users to retrieve product information. (© *jeremy suttonhibbert/Alamy*)

MOBILE ENTERTAINMENT

Mobile entertainment is expanding on wireless devices. Most notable are music, movies, videos, games, adult entertainment, sports, and gambling apps.

Sports enthusiasts enjoy a large number of apps and services on their mobile devices. Apps exist to check game scores; track news updates about specific athletes, teams, or sports; participate in fantasy team contests like fantasy football; and participate in sports-oriented social networking services. Numerous sports-related games like mobile golf and sports trivia apps are widely available. There are even handhelds designed to provide tips and information for improving your own athletic performance. An app that analyzes a person's golf swing and provides advice for improving performance is available for the iPhone.

ESPN's Sport Center, in partnership with Sanyo, offers a cell phone that comes preloaded with several sports-related apps. You can get quick access to news of your favorite teams. Video clips of up to 30 seconds are available, and so is a built-in camera. To occupy the owner during waiting time, sports-trivia questions are installed on the phone. Sports-related alerts are sent to the phone via text message.

Industry analysts are predicting that recent improvements in mobile computing device hardware will lead to an even bigger increase in the number of people who watch video clips, movies, and television programs on their mobile devices. The screen size of devices like Apple's iPad makes watching videos more appealing than on a smartphone. However, the number of people viewing videos on smartphones seems to be increasing as well. Companies like *theChanner.com* and FLO TV, among others, offer television programs to mobile device users. Fox Mobile recently introduced a mobile app that will allow smartphone users to view television content from its Web site *hulu.com*.

IT at Work 7.1

Mobile Godiva

Belgian Godiva Chocolatier is recognized worldwide as the leader in fine chocolates. From its famous truffles and shell-molded chocolate pieces to its European-style biscuits, gourmet coffees, and hot cocoa, Godiva Chocolatier has been dedicated to excellence and innovation in the tradition for 80 years.

When it came time to continuing the tradition of innovation and excellence in the mobile channel, Godiva launched the Godiva Mobile initiative. Godiva Mobile was designed as a way to purchase goods and build intimate customer relationships. A device-resident app, Godiva Mobile includes Godiva's best-selling products and can integrate with other applications on a BlackBerry smartphone, including the address book and mapping applications. Consumers purchase products by simply scrolling and clicking.

Godiva Mobile includes:

- Quick access to Godiva Chocolatier's most popular products
- The ability to complete a shopping transaction in less than 30 seconds
- Rich product descriptions and full-color images
- Address book integration, allowing users to ship with just a few clicks
- A "One-Touch Store-Locator" that uses GPS or cell towers to automatically identify stores close to the user's location
- Secure transactions and password-protected buying

Discussion Questions: Why is Mobile Godiva a good application for Godiva? In your answer, consider the fact that Godiva chocolates and other products are usually bought as a gift rather than for oneself.

The iTunes Store continues to be a leader in making digital music, movies, and podcasts available to consumers for a fee. Mobile users can also access music from digital streaming sites like *pandora.com* and *grooveshark.com*. Both of these services offer free streaming music. Users can upgrade their accounts by paying a subscription fee, which then limits the amount of advertising that occurs during their listening.

While still relatively small, the mobile gambling industry is expected to grow substantially in the next few years. Some predict this type of mobile commerce could generate as much as $20 billion in the near future. Primary growth of this market is expected to take place in Japan and other Asian countries.

Many handhelds exist to enhance home-based entertainment activities. The Food Network has an app with tips and recipes for fine dining and entertaining. *Mobilewinelist.com* offers a way to inventory your wine collection, rate wines, and share information about wine with other enthusiasts through your mobile device. Mobatech is the maker of a mobile bartending app with numerous recipes for cocktails and party drinks. Mobile Godiva is discussed in *IT at Work 7.1*.

MOBILE GAMES

With smartphones, the potential audience for mobile games is substantially larger than the market for other platforms, PlayStation and X-box included. Nearly half (45 percent) of smartphone users play games and spend an average of $41 on gaming handhelds. Experts expect that this market will continue to grow as network speeds increase and mobile devices become more powerful, adding increased richness to the gaming experience. In Japan, where millions of commuters "kill time" during long train rides, cell phone games have become a cultural phenomenon. Now mobile games are very popular in many countries.

In July 2001, Ericsson, Motorola, Nokia, and Siemens established the Mobile Games Interoperability Forum (MGIF) (*openmobilealliance.org*) to define a range of technical standards that will make it possible to deploy mobile games across multigame servers and wireless networks, as well as across different mobile devices.

HOTEL SERVICES AND TRAVEL GO WIRELESS	A number of hotels now offer their guests in-room wireless or wireline (wired) high-speed Internet connections. Some of these same hotels offer Wi-Fi Internet access in public areas like the lobby and in meeting rooms. One of these is Marriott, which manages about 3,000 hotels worldwide. Most other large hotel chains (e.g., Best Western) as well as small hotels offer Internet connections.

Airports and other transit centers are increasingly offering Wi-Fi access to the Internet to accommodate travelers. Major airlines are exploring the ability to offer broadband Internet access during flights to users of laptops and other computing devices. Some rail services also provide in-transit Internet access to travelers.

In addition to providing guests with Internet access via Wi-Fi access points, a small number of hotels are exploring use of mobile Web sites for guests to check in, book spa or restaurant reservations, and order room service. Other technologies are being developed that would allow guests to open their hotel room door using SMS text messages or by passing their NFC (near field communications) enabled phone next to the door lock.

MOBILE SOCIAL NETWORKING	**Mobile social networking** is social networking in which two or more individuals converse and connect with one another using smartphones or other mobile devices. Much like Web-based social networking, mobile social networking occurs in virtual communities. All of the most popular social networking sites now offer apps that allow users to access their social network accounts from a smartphone or other mobile device. Some experts predict that mobile social media will be one of the most popular consumer applications and, along with gaming apps, will be a driving force in the growth of the mobile market.

OTHER MOBILE COMPUTING SERVICES FOR CONSUMERS	Many other mobile computing services exist for consumers in a variety of categories. Examples include information services for news, city events, weather, and sports reports; online language translations; information about tourist attractions (e.g., hours, prices); and emergency services. Many other services are available to cell phones with Internet access. For example, Skype offers its voice, text, and video service for free.

TARGETED ADVERTISING	The growth of mobile computing and m-commerce is attractive to advertisers. Smartphones enabled with GPS capabilities can convey information about a user's location to advertisers. This information can be used, along with user preferences or surfing habits, to send user-specific advertising messages to mobile devices. Advertising can also be location-sensitive, providing information about stores, malls, and restaurants close to a potential buyer. SMS messages and short paging messages can be used to deliver this type of advertising to cell phones and pagers, respectively. Many companies are capitalizing on targeted advertising. See *IT at Work 7.2* for an illustration.

As more wireless bandwidth becomes available, content-rich advertising involving audio, pictures, and video clips will be generated for individual users with specific needs. The obvious challenge for advertisers will be to use this information to communicate with users in ways they find helpful and not annoying.

MOBILE PORTAL	A mobile portal is a customer channel, optimized for mobility, that aggregates and provides content and services for mobile users. These portals offer services similar to those of desktop portals such as AOL, Yahoo!, and MSN. Many companies host mobile portals today, as shown in Table 7.3.

IT at Work 7.2

Wireless Marketing and Advertising in Action

MKT

Industry analysts expect advertising in the mobile channel to heat up. Increasing numbers of smartphones, better browsers, enhanced GPS capabilities, and better ways of measuring advertising effectiveness are all factors powering this growth. The following are a few examples of wireless advertising in action.

Foursquare.com is one of the latest entries in the growing field of mobile advertising. Structured as a kind of mobile social media game, users "check in" from their phones when they visit retail stores and restaurants. They can provide information and ratings based on their reaction to these outlets. This information is shared with advertisers and their friends who are also part of the Foursquare network. Over time, Foursquare develops a profile of users based on the kinds of businesses they frequent and can use this information to better target consumers with advertising messages. Foursquare reinforces member use of the service by awarding *badges* to members for various types and levels of usage. Members who are the most frequent shopper at a particular location are awarded the title of *Mayor* and may receive special attention and discounts from the retailer. Foursquare provides advertisers with information about target customers that they usually don't have: location. This helps advertisers deliver timely messages that can be more relevant and meaningful to consumers, increasing the chances that the ads will be acted on.

Augmented reality (AR) apps are a special technology that will become more commonplace in the future. Augmented reality involves computer-generated graphic images being superimposed on pictures of real things (e.g., people, rooms, buildings, roads, etc.). This technology is used by advertisers in several ways. For instance, a mobile phone user might point his or her phone camera at an office building and activate an AR app that generates the logos of all food service outlets (e.g. Starbucks, Subway, McDonald's) inside the building. Furniture retailer IKEA offers shoppers an AR app that allows them to project images of its products onto pictures of the rooms in their homes so they can "visualize" how the products will look there. Industry experts expect that AR advertising will grow as smartphone users become more familiar with the concept. You can watch a fascinating video of an iPhone handheld developed by Yellow Pages at *youtube.com/watch?v=tOw8X78VTwg/*.

Hoping to become the king of location-based Web domains, Go2Online (*go2.com*) helps mobile travelers find everything from lodging to Jiffy Lube stations. Partnering with Sprint, Nextel, Verizon, and Boost, Go2 makes its services available on every Web-enabled phone, Palm i705, and BlackBerry RIM pager in America. Entering "JiffyLube" or any of hundreds of other brand names into the Go2 system will bring up the nearest location where one can find that product or service.

Sources: Compiled from Moore (2010) and Whitfield (2010).

Discussion Questions:

1. What benefit do advertisers derive from knowing a customer's location?

2. What are some similarities between *foursquare.com* and other social networking services?

3. What privacy concerns do you think are important for users of location-based services like *foursquare.com* to consider?

4. How might augmented reality apps be more effective than traditional directory services?

The services provided by mobile portals include news, sports, e-mail, entertainment, and travel information; restaurants and event information; leisure-related services (e.g., games, TV and movie listings); community services; and stock trading. A sizable percentage of the portals also provide downloads and messaging; music-related services; and health, dating, and job information. Mobile portals frequently charge for their services. For example, you may be asked to pay 50 cents to get a weather report over your mobile phone. Alternatively, you may pay a monthly fee for the portal service and get the report free anytime you want it. In Japan, for example, i-mode generates revenue mainly from subscription fees.

TABLE 7.3	Mobile Portals
Name	**Address**
iGoogle	*google.com/m/ig*
Yahoo Mobile	*m.yahoo.com*
MSN	*mobile.msn.com*
Windows Live	*mobile.live.com*
AOL	*wap.aol.com/portal/*
Redcliff (India)	*mobile.rediff.com*
Nokia Here and Now	*nokia.mobi/hereandnow/*

VOICE PORTALS

A **voice portal** is a Web site that can be accessed by voice. Voice portals are not really Web sites in the normal sense because they are not accessed through a browser.

In addition to providing information, some sites provide true interaction. *iPing.com* is a reminder and notification service that allows users to enter information via the Web and receive reminder calls. In addition, *iPing.com* can call a group of people to notify them of a meeting or conference call. *Tellme.com* and *quack.com* also offer voice-based services.

Voice portals are used extensively by airlines, for example, enabling customers to make reservations, find flight status, and more. Many other organizations use voice portals to replace or supplement help desks. The advantage to the company is cost reduction. Users can save time, since they do not have to wait for help.

A benefit for Internet marketers is that voice portals can help businesses find new customers. Several of these sites are supported by ads; thus, the customer-profile data they have available helps them deliver targeted advertising. For instance, a department-store chain with an existing brand image can use short audio commercials on these sites to deliver a message related to the topic of the call.

Review Questions

1. Describe how shoppers use mobile devices to enhance their shopping experience.
2. How is targeted advertising done wirelessly?
3. Describe a mobile portal.
4. What is a voice portal?
5. List types of mobile entertainment available to consumers.
6. How are hotels using mobile computing technology to increase guest satisfaction?

7.4 Location-Based Services and Commerce

Location-based commerce (l-commerce) refers to the delivery of advertisements, products, or services to customers whose locations are known at a given time [also known as location-based services (LBSs)]. Location-based services are beneficial to consumers and businesses alike. From a consumer's viewpoint, l-commerce offers safety. For instance, you can connect to an emergency service with a mobile device and have the service pinpoint your exact location. The services offer convenience because you can locate what is near you without having to consult a directory, pay phone, or map. The services offer increased productivity because you can decrease your travel time by determining points of interest in close proximity. From a business supplier's point of view, l-commerce offers an opportunity to sell more. (See *IT at Work 7.3.*)

The basic l-commerce services revolve around five key concepts:

1. Location. Determining the basic position of a person or a thing (e.g., bus, car, or boat) at any given time

2. Navigation. Plotting a route from one location to another

3. Tracking. Monitoring the movement of a person or a thing (e.g., a vehicle or package) along the route

4. Mapping. Creating digital maps of specific geographic locations

5. Timing. Determining the precise time at a specific location

L-COMMERCE TECHNOLOGIES

Providing location-based services requires the following location-based and network technologies, shown in Figure 7.10:

• **Position-determining equipment (PDE).** This equipment identifies the location of the mobile device either through GPS or by locating the nearest base station. The position information is sent to the mobile positioning center.

• **Mobile positioning center (MPC).** The MPC is a server that manages the location information sent from the PDE.

IT at Work 7.3

New mobile innovations are creating an immersive, multichannel consumer experience that bridges the gap between online and in-store shopping experiences. One innovation of great interest to e-business managers is location-based commerce, or l-commerce. Retailers are integrating l-commerce into their mobile strategies.

Retailers often rely on third-party, location-based services such as Foursquare and Shopkick to roll out location-aware mobile coupons. Or retailers may develop location services into their own mobile shopping apps beyond the basic store-finder feature to create new ways to gain the attention of customers or interact with shoppers via their smartphones.

Retailers are using geo-fences defined within the vicinity of their brick-and-mortar stores to attract consumers who are nearby by sending them relevant, timely, and location-aware offers or incentives to smartphones (see Figure 7.9).

Discussion Questions: What types of businesses would benefit the most from l-commerce?

Figure 7.9 Location-aware offers are sent to nearby potential customers. (© *Brownstock/Alamy*)

- **Location-based technology.** This technology consists of groups of servers that combine the position information with geographic- and location-specific content to provide an l-commerce service. For instance, location-based technology could present a list of addresses of nearby restaurants based on the position of the caller, local street maps, and a directory of businesses. It is provided via the content center via the Internet.
- **Geographic content.** Geographic content consists of digitized streets, road maps, addresses, routes, landmarks, land usage, zip codes, and the like. This information must be delivered in compressed form for fast distribution over wireless networks.
- **Location-specific content.** Location-specific content is used in conjunction with the geographic content to provide the location of particular services. Yellow Pages directories showing the location of specific businesses and services are examples of this type of content.

Figure 7.10 also shows how these technologies are used in conjunction with one another to deliver location-based services that are managed via the service center. Underlying these technologies are global positioning and geographical information systems.

Global Positioning System (GPS). A **Global Positioning System (GPS)** is a wireless system that uses satellites to determine where the GPS device is located anywhere on earth. GPS equipment has been used extensively for navigation by commercial airlines and ships, and for locating trucks and buses.

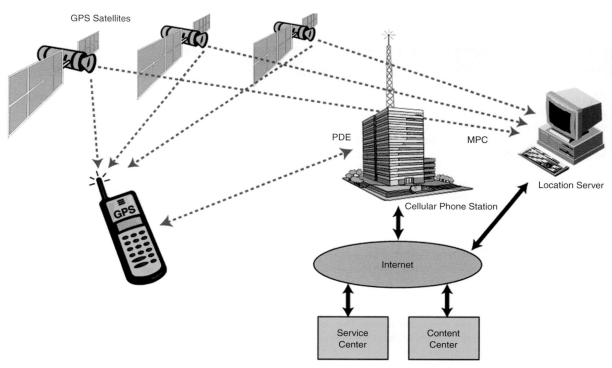

GPS Satellites

PDE

MPC

Location Server

Cellular Phone Station

Internet

Service Center

Content Center

Figure 7.10 Smartphone with GPS in location-based commerce.

GPS is supported by 24 U.S. government satellites, plus three backup satellites, that are shared worldwide. Each satellite orbits the earth once every 12 hours on a precise path, at an altitude of 10,900 miles. At any point in time, the exact position of each satellite is known, because the satellite broadcasts its position and a time signal from its onboard atomic clock, which is accurate to one-billionth of a second. Receivers also have accurate clocks that are synchronized with those of the satellites.

GPS handsets can be stand-alone units or can be plugged into or embedded in a mobile device. They calculate the position of the handsets or send the information to be calculated centrally. Knowing the speed of the satellite signals, 186,272 miles per second, engineers can find the location of any receiving station—its latitude and longitude—to within 50 feet by *triangulation*, using the distance from a GPS to *three* satellites to make the computation. GPS software then computes the latitude and longitude of the receiver. This process is called **geocoding.** (See *IT at Work 7.4.*)

Geographic Information System (GIS). The location provided by GPS is expressed in terms of latitude and longitude. To make that information useful to businesses and consumers, it is necessary in many cases to relate those measures to a certain place or address. This is done by inserting the latitude and longitude onto a digital map, which is known as a **geographic information system (GIS).** The GIS data visualization technology integrates GPS data onto digitized map displays. Companies such as *mapinfo.com* provide the GIS core spatial technology, maps, and other data content needed in order to power location-based GIS/GPS services.

IT at Work 7.4

Real-Time Public Transport System

Commuters in Finland, the U.S., and several other countries rely on their smartphones or other handhelds, and a real-time public-transport system to find out when a bus is likely to arrive at a stop. Knowing the location of a fleet of buses and factoring in traffic patterns and weather reports, NextBus (*nextbus.com*) calculates the estimated time of arrival of the bus to each stop on the route. Arrival times are also displayed on the Internet and on a public screen at each bus stop. Figure 7.11 shows how the NextBus system works. The core of the NextBus system is a GPS satellite that can tell the NextBus information center where a bus is at any given time.

Riders can set an alarm to warn them that it's time to head for the bus stop so they don't accidently miss the bus. They can choose to receive an e-mail, an SMS message, or an alert on the Web via a simple and unavoidable pop-up. The alerts can be one time only, set for weekdays or for everyday of the week. Different alerts can be set for multiple stops and routes. The automatic alerts can be a critical commuting component for busy students and employees who need to be on time.

Sources: Compiled from *en.wikipedia.org/wiki/NextBus* and *nextbus.com*.

Discussion Questions: How can NextBus generate revenues? Who might be good sponsors of the service?

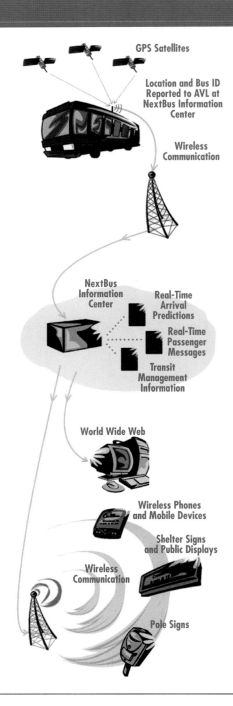

Figure 7.11 NextBus operational model. (*Source: nextbus.com/corporate/works/index.htm, 2008. Used with permission of NextBus Information Systems.*)

Review Questions

1. Define location-based services.
2. How does location-based EC work? Provide an example.
3. Describe GPS. What is it used for?
4. Describe GIS and its advantages.
5. Describe some location-based applications, particularly advertising.

7.5 Mobile Enterprise Applications

More organizations are looking to create a full range of mobile apps—from back-office to consumer-centric apps. Leading organizations are building a marketing and sales strategy that is built on connecting with customers via mobile devices. These connections extend beyond Facebook and Twitter to include the ability to be aware of mobile coupons, advertisements, or product offerings, and then engage with companies via their mobile devices.

The limitations that come from two-inch or four-inch smartphone screens are being eliminated by the iPad and other mobile tablets—and expanding the possibilities of mobile computing and mobile enterprise applications.

Whether the apps are for internal or external users, organizations need to develop plans to manage apps and keep them updated. Greater adoption of mobile apps will change the way that organizations deal with both internal and external customer service and support. However, few organizations have yet developed a plan for mobile customer service and support.

The next section looks at how mobile devices and technologies can be used *within*, *outside*, and *between* organizations.

MOBILE APPS

Many companies offer innovative mobile and wireless apps in the enterprise. In this section, you will read about examples of how organizations are deploying mobile solutions to conduct business. Mobile apps include the following:

- Supporting salespeople while they are waiting on customers
- Supporting field employees doing repairs or maintenance on corporate premises or for clients
- Supporting executives, managers, or other employees when they are traveling or otherwise not at the corporate site
- Supporting employees while they do work inside the enterprise at places where there is no easy access to desktop computers, for example, in a warehouse, at outdoor facilities, or in large retail stores
- Supporting employees driving trucks while they are on the road

Investments in mobile enterprise apps are made to provide employees with communication and collaboration tools as well as access to data, information, and people inside the organization.

Mobile POS (Point of Sale). Traditional POS technology involves a computerized cash register connected to a server via a wired local area network (LAN). These stations are fixed, requiring customers to bring their merchandise to a specific location in the store, where they wait in line for their turn to check out. Long lines frustrate customers. Some studies show that at least one in 10 customers will abandon a long line, leaving the store without completing a purchase.

Mobile POS stations can be set up as needed by using handhelds, scanners, and printers. During periods of high volume, employees can set up temporary mobile checkout stations capable of scanning merchandise barcodes, processing credit card payments, and printing receipts. Employees can even walk through a fixed-station line offering to expedite checkout for those customers paying with credit card.

Inventory Management. Inventory management and tracking represent a significant expense for retailers. Using barcodes and handhelds or wearable wrist devices, retailers can record when merchandise enters the store, where it is stored, and when it is moved to the floor. Delivery drivers use mobile devices to enter invoices and other shipping data into the store's database at the point of delivery, making billing and accounting easier. As merchandise is sold, inventory levels are updated, triggering replacement orders and reducing the chances of stock-out situations. The benefits are a reduction in lost sales due to missing or unavailable merchandise and theft.

If a customer asks an employee to help find a particular product, the employee can check its location from a handheld device or order it and arrange for drop-shipping directly to the customer's home. Immediate response reduces the probability that the customer will purchase the product from another business.

Finally, the cumbersome process of changing prices on in-store merchandise is made easier using mobile devices. Employees can walk the aisles of a store, scanning merchandise and checking the posted price against the price in the store's UPC (Universal Product Code) database. If the employee finds a discrepancy, he or she can use the device to print a new price tag.

Customer Service. Because wireless devices can be quickly set up or moved throughout a store, retailers can position mobile price-check devices in convenient locations for customers to verify prices or retrieve product information by simply scanning the UPC code on a product. These devices can be moved without incurring the costs of rewiring the units. Wireless self-help kiosks can be positioned in each department, allowing customers to identify the location of products and obtain other information to facilitate their purchase. Stores can program the devices to identify inventory levels of a product at nearby locations in the chain, if necessary. Some devices have a voice-activated feature allowing customers to request assistance from store employees carrying handheld devices capable of voice communications. This prevents customers from having to search for someone to help when they need assistance — or leaving because they can't get help.

Job Dispatch. Mobile devices are becoming an integral part of groupware and work-flow handhelds. For example, nonvoice mobile services can be used to assist in dispatch functions — to assign jobs to mobile employees, along with detailed information about the tasks.

A dispatching handheld for wireless devices allows improved response with reduced resources, real-time tracking of work orders, increased dispatcher efficiency, and a reduction in administrative work. For example, Michigan CAT (*michigancat.com*), a large vendor of used heavy machinery equipment, offers an interesting solution. Michigan CAT's system uses Cloudberry from Air-Trak (*airtraksoftware.com*), which supports both cellular and satellite networks. It entails a hybrid approach to the use of a GPS tracking and messaging system that enables information and forms generated by Caterpillar's database (DBS) and Service Technician Workbench (STW) software to be transmitted wirelessly between the field operations staff and service vehicles equipped with a laptop. Data gathered from the field can be easily integrated into a back-end system. A simple extraction program was created to move data, service reports, and time sheets from one program to the other, eliminating duplicate keying of the same information into separate systems. Other dispatchers can access the information to add comments or notes. The system's benefits include increased productivity; reduced staff time; timely parts ordering; faster invoicing; and secure, precise service information with seamless integration between the company's systems.

 Mobile App Failure. However, not all mobile apps are successful. An example is the U.S. Census Bureau's mobile snafu. For the 2010 Census, the government allocated $3 billion for handhelds to improve interviewers' performance in the field. Unfortunately, due to poor program management, a poor contract estimate, and hardware and software delays, the program had to be delayed until the 2020 Census. The cost of manual data taking and programming increased the cost of the project by $2.2–3 billion.

CUSTOMER SUPPORT AND MOBILE CRM

Mobile access extends the reach of customer relationship management (CRM) — both inside and outside the company — to both employees and business partners on a 24/7 basis, to any place where recipients are located.

In the large software suites, such as Siebel's CRM (an Oracle company), the two CRM functions that have attracted the most interest are *sales force automation* and *field service*. For instance, a salesperson might be on a sales call and need to know the recent billing history for a particular customer. Or a field service representative on a service call might need to know the current availability of various parts in order to fix a piece of machinery. It is in these sorts of situations that real-time mobile access to customer and partner data is invaluable. Two popular offerings are Salesforce.com's App Exchange Mobile (*salesforce.com/*) and Oracle's CRM On Demand (*oracle.com/crmondemand/index.html*).

MOBILE SUPPLY CHAIN MANAGEMENT (MSCM)

Mobile computing solutions are also being applied to B2B and supply chain relationships. Such solutions enable organizations to respond faster to supply chain disruptions by proactively adjusting plans or by shifting resources related to critical supply chain events as they occur. Furthermore, mobile computing may have strategic implications regarding supply chains by improving efficiency, reducing delays, and improving supplier and customer relationships.

With the increased interest in collaborative commerce comes the opportunity to use wireless communication to collaborate along the supply chain. There is no longer any need to call a partner company and ask someone to find certain employees who work with your company. Instead, you can contact these employees directly or access ordering systems using mobile devices. For this to take place, interorganizational information systems integration is needed.

By enabling sales force employees to type orders or queries directly into ERP (Enterprise Resource Planning) systems while at a client's site, companies can reduce clerical mistakes and improve supply chain operations. If salespeople can check production schedules and inventory levels and access product configuration and availability as well as capacity available for production, they can obtain quantities and real-time delivery dates. Thus, companies empower their sales force to make more competitive and realistic offers to customers. Today's ERP systems tie into broader supply chain management solutions that extend visibility across multiple tiers in the supply chain. Mobile supply chain management empowers the workforce to leverage these broader systems through inventory management and ATP/CTP functionality that extend across multiple supply chain partners and take into account logistics considerations.

For example, sales teams at Adidas America use BlackBerry's Enterprise Solution and PDAs to check inventory levels from anywhere in real time. This enables better customer service and increases sales productivity. For details, see *na.blackberry.com/eng/ataglance/get_the_facts/rapid_roi.pdf*.

Review Questions

1. Describe mobile apps used inside organizations.
2. Describe wireless sales force apps.
3. Describe mobile CRM.
4. Describe how mobile computing is used to improve supply chain management.

Key Terms

Chapter Highlights and Insights

1 Mobile commuting and commerce are based on a foundation of mobile devices, mobile software (operating systems and handhelds), and wireless networks.

1 Mobile computing devices include laptop computers, handheld devices like smartphones and PDAs, e-readers and slate computers, as well as wearable computers.

1 A wide variety of mobile operating systems exist to power smartphones and other mobile devices. This presents a challenge for mobile Web site and handheld programmers.

1 Wireless networks based on Wi-Fi and telecommunications technology (e.g., 3G and 4G) have expanded considerably in the last few years, offering wide-scale coverage for mobile users.

2 People are increasingly using mobile devices, specifically smartphones, to perform financial transactions, including banking, credit card transactions, and stock purchases.

2 Numerous mobile electronic payment systems have been developed. It remains to be seen which one(s) will be accepted by merchants and consumers.

2 People access financial services using a combination of mobile media channels including Short Message Service (SMS) text and short code, mobile Web browsers, and customized smartphone apps.

3 Mobile retail shopping has grown considerably in recent years. Japanese consumers have embraced mobile commerce more than any other group, but American interest in mobile retail is growing.

3 Shoppers are increasingly using their mobile devices to find product and price information while shopping in traditional stores.

3 Smartphones and other mobile devices are becoming a key channel for entertainment such as music, movies, and games.

3 Hotels and others in the hospitality and travel industry are expanding their use of mobile apps to provide greater service and convenience to travelers.

3 Mobile social networking is expected to grow dramatically over the next decade, and experts predict it will be a primary driver of mobile computing technology.

3 Advertising through the mobile channel is attractive to businesses because it allows them to send targeted messages to prospective customers. In some cases, these messages may be based on a user's location, which can be determined using GPS technology.

3 A mobile portal is a customer channel, optimized for mobility, that aggregates and provides content and services for mobile users.

4 Location-based commerce or services refers to the delivery of advertisements, products, information, or services to customers whose locations are known at a given time.

4 An increasing number of handhelds are evident in several industries, particularly in transportation. These handhelds relate mainly to customer service, advertising/marketing, and operations.

5 Many organizations are using mobile computing technology to improve their operations, automate their sales force, and improve employee communications and interactions. These uses are referred to as mobile enterprise apps.

5 Retailers are increasingly using mobile technology to improve operations in their stores and to provide enhanced customer service and inventory management.

5 Mobile supply chain management (MSCM) refers to the use of mobile computing technology to manage the flow of goods from the point of manufacture to the end user.

5 Mobile computing technologies allow different business organizations in a supply chain to communicate and share information in order to improve the efficiency of the whole distribution system.

5 CRM (customer relationship management) systems are increasingly being enhanced with mobile technology to improve the ability of businesses and their partners to provide greater service and value to end users.

Questions for Discussion

1. Explain how mobile computing technology is being used to enhance the safety and effectiveness of the healthcare industry.

2. Describe some of the latest advances in mobile computing devices. What trends do you see in the development of this equipment? Speculate on how future devices might look or function.

3. Based on how other industries have developed over time, what do you predict will occur in the area of mobile device operating systems? (Hint: How does this market compare to the operating system market for personal computers?)

4. Describe some of the key developments in wireless network technology that have taken place in the last few years.

5. How are people using mobile devices to conduct banking and other financial services?

6. Evaluate the various mobile electronic payment processes described in the chapter. Which ones do you think are likely to emerge as the dominant method for mobile payment? Explain your answer.

7. What are some of the risks for consumers related to mobile banking and other financial transactions that take place using mobile devices?

8. What are the key benefits of using a mobile wallet? Do you think new improvements to this handheld will make it more attractive to end users?

9. How has mobile computing changed the retail shopping behavior of consumers?

10. What can stores do to utilize mobile technology to make shopping in traditional stores more attractive?

11. Describe the mobile entertainment market and ways people can use their mobile devices to have fun.

12. Why is mobile social networking expected to grow dramatically in the next few years?

13. How is mobile computing creating an attractive opportunity for advertisers? Will consumers be receptive to this type of communication? Why or why not?

14. List some location-based services and explain their value to mobile device users.

15. How do businesses, governments, and other organizations use mobile computing to enhance their productivity, efficiency, and profitability?

Exercises and Projects

1. Conduct research on the relative advantages/disadvantages of Apple's iOS versus the Android OS, developed by Google and the Open Handset Alliance. Based on your research, predict which system will become more popular with mobile device users.

2. Take a poll of your classmates and friends to see how many are using feature phones versus smartphones. Briefly interview a handful of people in each group to identify their reasons for owning the kind of phone they do. Summarize your findings in a brief report.

3. Investigate how your college or university is using mobile computing technology. (Note: you may have to speak to several different people.) Specific areas you should examine include admissions, instructional uses, operations, and information services. Conduct research to see how other campuses employ mobile technology. Prepare a brief report comparing your campus with others.

4. Prepare a brief report comparing Apple's iPad with various copy-cat products that are on the market (e.g., the Apad, the LifePad, the iPed). How do these products compare with the iPad? Do they represent a competitive threat to Apple's new slate computer?

5. Conduct research on the way telecommunications companies are charging for mobile access to the Internet. Identify providers that offer fixed or flat rate pricing versus those that charge based on usage.

Group Assignments and Projects

1. When patient medical records are stored electronically, it is easier for patients, doctors, and other healthcare providers to access medical information during treatment. Unfortunately, it also increases the possibility that unauthorized individuals may be able to gain access to sensitive information. Each team brainstorms the potential benefits associated with electronic medical records (EMR). Then, create a list of the potential risks associated with this approach. Finally, discuss the potential trade-offs associated with moving to the kind of mobile computing handheld discussed in the opening case. Compare the teams' answers.

2. Along with other students, sign up for an account at *foursquare.com*. Make connections with your group members on the service. Use Foursquare for a week or two, checking into the retail locations you visit. At the conclusion of this experience, meet with your group and compare reactions. Was it fun? Did the group gain valuable information from one another? Was the experience compelling enough that you'll want to maintain your account?

3. *Yelp.com* is a social networking directory service. It helps people find local businesses based on location, ratings, and recommendations from friends. With other students from your class, sign up for an account on Yelp and download its mobile handheld. Connect with your classmates (and other friends) on the Yelp service. Use Yelp for two weeks and then prepare a presentation with your group on the advantages and disadvantages of this new service.

4. Have each member of your group contact their bank to identify what mobile banking services, if any, are offered. Create a table that lists the mobile banking services offered by each bank. Finally, discuss among yourselves how receptive you all are to the idea of banking on your mobile devices. Identify the reasons why people want to engage in mobile banking and reasons why they are reluctant.

Internet Exercises

1. Visit ME, a news site for the mobile entertainment industry (*mobile-ent.biz/*). Select an entertainment category and study recent developments in that area. Prepare a report summarizing the current status of and predicting future developments in the category.

2. Using *youtube.com* or any other video-sharing site, watch examples of augmented reality handhelds and promotional campaigns. Write a brief report describing your reaction to this new technology and predict whether it will become more commonplace in the future.

3. If you have a smartphone and an appropriate mobile network access plan, download apps for *pandora.com* and *grooveshark.com*. Use these two services for a few

days to listen to music. Prepare a presentation that compares the services, listing the strengths and weaknesses of each. (Caution: These services use a lot of bandwidth, so you should check with your cell phone carrier prior to using these handhelds to make sure you won't incur unexpected expenses on your phone bill.)

4. If you have a smartphone, download one or more comparison shopping apps (e.g., Citishopper, Shopsavvy, or Sidebar). Visit a local mall or retail store and practice using the handhelds. Prepare a report or presentation

about your experience, noting the strengths and weaknesses of each handheld. Explain whether or not you think you will continue using one of the apps.

5. If you have a Facebook account, download the Facebook mobile app and use it for approximately one week. Prepare a report describing how your mobile experience on the social networking site compares with your experience using a personal computer. Do you think you could use the mobile handheld as your primary interface with Facebook? Why or why not?

BUSINESS CASE

Starbuck Builds Customer Loyalty with Short Codes and Tags

Mobile commerce is a source of competitive advantage. Starbucks (*starbucks.com/*), the global coffee-beverage retailer, has engaged in several mobile commerce initiatives.

In Mexico, Text "Venti"

In Mexico, Starbucks used in-store signs to encourage on-site customers to text the word "Venti" to short code 80080 in order to receive offers for discounts and drink upgrades (see Fig. 7.12). This mobile commerce campaign also included the distribution of postcards in malls, universities, and other public areas that encouraged cell phone users to text "Starbucks" to the same short code. Consumers who responded via text received instructions for downloading a 2D barcode to their phones. (You read about 2D codes in Chapter 1.)

Figure 7.12 Starbucks Venti coffee. (© *Exotic eye/Alamy*)

When consumers visited a Starbucks store, the baristas would scan the code on their phones to determine which offer the customer was eligible to receive. To keep customers coming back and the campaign interesting, Starbucks continually modified the offer—for instance, offering a 2-for-1

drink special or a free upgrade on the size of a customer's drink order.

Redemption of these 2D barcode coupons was approximately 60 percent, more than double the effectiveness of other types of coupon promotions. This clearly demonstrated the effectiveness of the mobile campaign. Mobile commerce enabled Starbucks to differentiate between new and existing customers and alternate their offers accordingly.

Figure 7.13 A Starbuck's branch in the Polanco district of Mexico City. (© *Keith Dannemiller/Alamy*)

iPhone Loyalty Card

Starbucks also has an app that allows iPhone users to turn their device into a Starbucks loyalty card. Users register the card, track their balance, and pay for their orders at over 1,000 Target and Starbucks stores. A second iPhone app helps users locate nearby stores based on their location.

In another mobile initiative, Starbucks builds loyalty and traffic in its stores using the Foursquare social app. Foursquare customers who visit and check in to Starbucks locations frequently can earn a *Barista badge* on the social networking service. For a limited time, Foursquare members who earned the status of *Mayor* at particular store locations qualified for discounted beverages during the promotion.

Starbucks coordinated with MTV in a promotion for its Frappuccino drinks. During the *MTV Movie Awards*, viewers were encouraged to text a vote for their favorite movie to short code 66333. Viewers then received a *thank you* along with a promotional message from Starbucks. This cross-promotion with MTV demonstrates how mobile commerce can be used in interactive promotions in which consumers choose to participate in two-way communications with businesses.

Testing M-Commerce

While Starbucks initiatives in the mobile commerce have created lots of attention (which is a great marketing benefit), some critics think the effort falls short. Schuman (2009) notes that the apps allow users to select favorite store locations and beverage preferences, but there isn't anything the customer can do with that information. Schuman blames this shortcoming on Starbucks' fear of customers uploading information that might interfere with its POS (point of sale) system. Others have suggested that this is a common problem for companies

that are testing the waters with mobile commerce. They develop nice-looking apps that don't really do anything of value for end users. But in this case, they get discounts at Starbucks, which customers apparently appreciate.

Sources: Compiled from Butcher (2009), Roldan (2010), Tsirulnik (2010a, 2010b), Van Grove (2010) and Schuman (2009).

Questions

1. What advantages do mobile coupons have for businesses over traditional methods of coupon promotions?
2. What advantages do mobile coupons have for consumers compared to traditional coupons?
3. How does Starbucks use mobile promotions to engage its customers?
4. Why do you think Starbucks partnered with MTV for its Frappuccino promotion? What benefits were there to both companies?
5. How can Starbucks take mobile commerce to the next level? What more can it do to engage the mobile consumer?

NONPROFIT CASE

Micro-Donations Support Charities and Relief Efforts

Since 2008, many charities have employed a novel approach to raising money in response to natural disasters and other emergencies. mDonations involve the use of mobile devices, usually cell phones, to make contributions to charitable organizations and disaster relief efforts. Mobile donations have played an important role in raising money to address the growing needs of people affected by events like Hurricane Katrina, the 2010 earthquakes in Haiti and Chile, and the devastation caused by British Petroleum's (BP) Gulf Coast oil spill. Other charity and not-for-profit organizations have developed integrated fund-raising campaigns that make use of mDonations as an ongoing giving channel.

Micro-payments and Micro-donations

Most mobile donations are made using SMS text messaging. In one approach, the giver sends a simple pre-determined message to a short code specified in an advertisement or public announcement. A second text message is required to confirm the transaction. The donation, usually $5 or $10, is then added to the user's mobile phone bill. A variation on this approach involves users sending a SMS text message to a short-code number. In response, they are sent a link to a mobile Internet site that allows them to specify an amount they'd like to give. As with the previous method, the amount is then added to the giver's monthly phone bill. At the end of the month, the phone company sends a payment to the charity for all the donations it has received.

Some experts have speculated that the micro-donation format, combined with the use of familiar mobile technology, makes this kind of philanthropy particularly appealing to a new generation of givers. Young people are comfortable with cell

phones, and mobile technology makes it easy for them to respond to appeals by charities, particularly when the cause is compelling. The mobile donation process encourages spontaneous giving, since it is less cumbersome than donation methods that involve sending paper checks or submitting credit card numbers on a Web page.

In order for an organization to solicit charitable donations via mobile devices in the United States, there are guidelines it must follow. Organizations must be organized under Section 501(c)3 of the U.S. tax code and recognized by the Internal Revenue Service as a not-for-profit organization. The Mobile Giving Foundation (MGF) and *mGiving.com* provide verification services for the telecommunications companies that collect the donations, ensuring that only legitimate organizations collect money using this method.

Integrated Mobile Campaigns

Mobile donations to assist victims of Hurricane Katrina in 2005 amounted to only $250,000. Just a few years later, there was much greater interest in mobile giving. As of February 2010, the Red Cross had raised over $31 million for victims of the Haiti earthquake through mobile donations. The organization has used these funds along with donations received through traditional channels to provide food, water, shelter, and medical services to earthquake victims.

Successful campaigns typically integrate other media—print ads, television, radio, and social media (e.g. Twitter and Facebook). Capital Area United Way, located in Baton Rouge, Louisiana, used traditional media and distributed pamphlets prior to a LSU football game. During the first timeout of the game, a message was shown on the stadium Jumbotron asking the 90,000 fans to send a text message "LSU" to short code 864833 to donate $5 to Capital Area United Way, resulting in over $9,000 in donations (*mGive.com*, 2009). Other charities have partnered with celebrities who announce mobile-giving opportunities during concerts or shows.

While the dramatic nature of disasters caused by hurricanes, earthquakes, or environmental devastation are more likely to make the news headlines, many charities not involved with disaster relief are exploring ways to generate funding from mobile philanthropy. For example, the National Public Radio program *This American Life* has raised over $140,000 from listeners who donated using their mobile devices.

Many of the organizations that offer to partner with not-for-profit organizations by providing technological support for mobile giving say that 100 percent of the donations are passed on to the charity. However, this doesn't mean that the mobile donation process is free. While most, if not all, donations are conveyed to the charitable organization, the partner organizations charge charities a number of fees associated with running a mobile donation campaign. Many charge setup fees ranging from $350 to $500, monthly fees that can range

from several hundred dollars to thousands of dollars, and almost all charge some type of transaction fee. A typical transaction fee amounts to $0.35 per transaction plus 3 percent of the donation.

Sources: Compiled from Strom (2010), Green (2010), Heatwole (2010), mGive.com (2009), and Fisher-Thompson (2010).

Questions

1. What changes in the behavior of mobile device users has led to the increase in mobile donations from Hurricane Katrina in 2005 to the Haitian earthquake in 2010?

2. Why do some people find it easier to make mobile donations compared with traditional methods of giving?

3. Do you think it is reasonable for organizations that facilitate mobile giving to charge setup fees and transaction fees to charitable organizations? Are the fees discussed in the case reasonable? Explain your answer.

4. Why is it important for charitable organizations to integrate their mobile giving campaigns with traditional and social media communications?

ANALYSIS USING SPREADSHEETS

Estimating the Financial Benefits of Increased Customer Loyalty

Customer loyalty is a bond between a targeted customer and an organization whereby the customer consistently spends a significant amount of money on the supplier's goods or services. Loyal customers add value to a supplier's bottom line by one or more of the following:

- Generating new sales by referring other customers
- Paying a price premium
- Buying a broader mix of goods and services
- Reducing the company's selling and servicing costs

Enhancing loyalty in target customers can lead to sustainable and profitable sales growth. Starbucks' mobile commerce strategy, as you read in the Business Case, is aimed at increasing customer loyalty.

You are tasked with completing the analysis using spreadsheet software. Create a spreadsheet with the data shown in Figure 7.14. Then use formulas or functions to calculate the blue-shaded cells. The results represent the NPV and ROI of the mobile commerce campaigns.

Estimating Financial Benefits of Increased Customer Loyalty

		Year 1	Year 2	Year 3	Total	Present Value (PV)
(a)	Benefit	$ 803,300	$ 722,970	$ 650,673		
(b)	Cost	317,060	301,207	286,147		
(a) – (b)	Net Cash Flow					
	Net Present Value (NPV)					
	ROI					

Figure 7.14 Spreadsheet for estimating financial benefits of increased customer loyalty.

References

"29 US Banks Receive Mobile Banking 'Report Card' from ABI Research," Press Release, ABI Research, September 2009. *abiresearch.com/press/1488-29+US+Banks+Receive+Mobile+Banking+%93Report+Card%94+From++ABI+Research*

BBC, "Mobiles Combat Kenyan Polio Outbreak," September 18, 2008. *news.bbc.co.uk/2/mobile/technology/7619473.stm*

Berg Insight, "Berg Insight Predicts 894 Million Mobile Banking Users by 2015," *Berginsight.com*, April 2010. *berginsight.com/News.aspx?m_m=6&s_m=1*

Butcher, D., "Starbucks Runs Mobile Coupon Loyalty Program," *Mobile Marketer*, April 22, 2009. *mobilemarketer.com/cms/news/database-crm/3085.html*

Fisher-Thompson, J., "Mobile Phone Donations Break Records for Haiti Earthquake Relief," *America.gov*, 2010. *america.gov/st/develop-english/2010/February/201002041707471ejrehsiF0.8422663.html&distid=ucs*

Gartner, Inc., "Gartner Says Worldwide Mobile Phone Sales Grew 17 Per Cent in First Quarter 2010," May 19, 2010. *gartner.com/it/page.jsp?id=1372013*

Global Industry Analysts, "Global Mobile Banking Customer Base to Reach 1.1 Billion by 2015, According to New Report by Global Industry Analysts, Inc," February 2010. *prWeb.com/releases/2010/02/prWeb3553494.htm*

Green, C., "Inside Scoop on Mobile Donations—Part Two," *Beyondnines.com*, 2010. *beyondnines.com/blog/fundraising/mobile-donations-part-two/*

Heatwole, A., "Radio and Text Donations: *This American Life's* Experience with Mobile Giving," *MobileActive.org*, 2010. *mobileactive.org/american-life-joins-mobile-giving-revolution*

Howard, N., "Is It Safe to Bank by Cell Phone?" *MSN Money*, July 2009. *articles.moneycentral.msn.com/Banking/FinancialPrivacy/is-it-safe-to-bank-by-cell-phone.aspx?page=2*

Joia, L., and C. Magalhães, "Implementation of an Electronic Prescription System in a Brazilian General Hospital: Understanding Sources of Resistance," *The Electronic Journal of Information Systems in Developing Countries*, Vol. 39, 2009. *ejisdc.org/ojs2/index.php/ejisdc/article/view/607*

Kellogg, D., "iPhone vs. Android," *NeilsonWire.com*, June 4, 2010. *blog.nielsen.com/nielsenwire/online_mobile/iphone-vs-android/*

Konovalov, R., and D. Kumlander, "Using Clinical Decision Support Software in Health Insurance Company." *Advanced Techniques in Computing Sciences and Software Engineering*. Edited by Khaled Elleithy, Springer, 2010.

Krizner, K., "DEA Proposes Rule to Allow Electronic Prescriptions for Controlled Substances," *Drug Topics*, August 11, 2008. *drugtopics.modernmedicine.com/drugtopics/Business+and+Management/DEA-proposes-rule-to-allow-electronic-prescription/ArticleStandard/Article/detail/534506*

McGee, B., "Mobile Banking Security—Phishing for Answers?" *Netbanker.com*, January 2008. *netbanker.com/2008/01/mobile_banking_security_phishi_2.html*

mGive.com, "Using Mobile Donations at In-Stadium College Events Case Study: Capital Area United Way," 2009. *blog.mgive.com/wp-content/uploads/2009/11/Case-Study-Capital-Area-UWay-In-Stadium.pdf*

MobiAdNews.com, "IKEA Uses Mobile Augmented Reality to Engage Shoppers' Imagination," August 2009.

Mobile Marketing Association, "Mobile Banking Overview (NA)," January 2009. *mmaglobal.com/mbankingoverview.pdf*

Mobile Marketing Association., "One in Five U.S. Adult Consumers Now Using Mobile Commerce," May 2010. *mmaglobal.com/news/one-five-us-adult-consumers-now-using-mobile-commerce*

Moore, G., "Foursquare Leads New Mobile Advertising Model," *Masshightech.com*, April 2010. *masshightech.com/stories/2010/04/26/daily10-Foursquare-leads-new-mobile-advertising-model.html*

Papshev, D., and A. Peterson, "Extent of Electronic Prescribing Implementation as Perceived by MCO Pharmacy Managers," *Journal of Managed Care Pharmacy JMCP* Vol. 8, No. 1, January/February 2002.

Roldan, C., "Starbucks Unveils National Foursquare Promotion; Local Mayors Pounce on Perks," *The Palm Beach Post*. May 17, 2010. *blogs.palmbeachpost.com/techtonic/mobile/starbucks-unveils-national-foursquare-promotion-local-mayors-pounce-on-perks/*

Schuman, E., "Starbucks Rules Out M-Commerce That Can't Really Buy Anything." *Storefronttalkback.com* October 1, 2009. *storefrontbacktalk.com/e-commerce/starbucks-roll-out-an-m-commerce-app-that-cant-really-buy-anything/*

Strom, S., "A Deluge of Donations via Text Messages," *The New York Times*. January 19, 2010. *nytimes.com/2010/01/19/us/19charity.html*

Swartz, N., "Mandatory M-Wallets," *Connected Planet*, June 2010, *connectedplanetonline.com/wireless/mag/wireless_mandatory_mwallets/*

"The Regulatory Plan," *Federal Register*, Vol. 66, No. 232, December 2001.

Tsirulnik, G. "Starbucks Rolls Out Largest Mobile Payments Effort Nationwide." *Mobile Marketer*, March 31, 2010a. *mobilemarketer.com/cms/news/commerce/5818.html*

Tsirulnik, G., "Starbucks Pushes Frappuccino Drink in MTV On-Air SMS Call to Action," *Mobile Commerce Daily*, June 11, 2010b. *mobilecommercedaily.com/starbucks-pushes-frappuccino-drink-in-mtv-on-air-sms-call-to-action/*

Van Grove, J., "Mayors of Starbucks Now Get Discounts Nationwide with Foursquare," *Mashable.com*, May 17, 2010. *mashable.com/2010/05/17/starbucks-foursquare-mayor-specials/*

Whitfield, T., "Augmented Reality for Mobile Advertising," *Econsultancy.com* February 2010. *econsultancy.com/blog/5397-augmented-reality-for-mobile-advertising/*

Chapter

8

Web 2.0 and Social Media

Learning Objectives

❶ Understand the nature of Web 2.0 and its business applications.

❷ Understand online communities and how social networking services are evolving.

❸ Describe how businesses are using Web 2.0 applications to carry out a variety of business functions more effectively.

❹ Understand how businesses evaluate the effectiveness of their social media strategies and tactics.

❺ Describe how the Internet is evolving and the significant changes that will take place in the near future.

Integrating *IT*

ACC   FIN   MKT   OM   HRM   IS

Web 2.0 . . . The Machine Is Us/ing Us—Michael Wesch   *youtube.com/user/mwesch#p/u/9/*
NLlGopyXT_g
Social Media Revolution—Is It a Fad?   *youtube.com/watch?v=lFZ0z5Fm-Ng*
The Mashable Social Media Guide   *mashable.com/social-media/*
Cluetrain Manifesto   *cluetrain.com/*
O'Reilly Media   *oreilly.com/community/*
World Wide Web Consortium   *w3.org/Consortium/*
Read, Write, Web technology blog   *readwriteweb.com/*

QUICK LOOK at Chapter 8, Web 2.0 and Social Media

This section introduces you to the business issues, challenges, and IT solutions in Chapter 8. Topics and issues mentioned in the Quick Look are explained in the chapter.

In his popular 2007 video, *Web 2.0 . . . The Machine Is Us/ing Us*, cultural anthropologist Michael Wesch notes that enhancements to the Internet known as **Web 2.0** will cause us to rethink a lot of our assumptions about things as diverse as ethics, privacy, governance, family, and even love. We will rethink our assumptions because the interactive nature of the modern Internet allows for social connections between individuals, organizations, governments, and other entities that were not previously possible.

In this chapter, you learn about the technologies and capabilities known as Web 2.0. You will examine how **online communities** are evolving into **social networks** and how businesses are responding to this new development. And you read how organizations are benefiting from **enterprise social networks.** Naturally, the magnitude of change occurring online has created some unease on the part of traditional-minded businesses and individual users.

We explore the use of **social media metrics** that help businesses determine the effectiveness of their communication strategies in this new environment. Finally, we take a quick glance at our crystal ball and speculate on what the future holds for the next evolution of the Internet.

Viral Video Hit and Social Media Fail, *United Breaks Guitars*

IS   MKT   FAILURES

David Carroll is a Halifax musician and the lead singer of Canadian band *Sons of Maxwell*. In March 2008, Carroll and his band saw their guitars being thrown around by United Airlines (UAL) baggage handlers at Chicago's O'Hare Airport. Carroll tried but failed to get any UAL employee to rescue the instruments from baggage handlers. After reaching his final destination, Carroll discovered that his $3,500 Taylor guitar had been smashed.

Power of the Social Media Space

For one year Carroll tried to get compensation for the damages but, instead, was frustrated by what he believed was a corporate runaround. He then wrote and produced a series of music videos detailing his bad experiences. His first song

Figure 8.1 United Airlines did not know to respond to the damage from David Carroll's Internet campaign against its poor customer service. (© *Andrew Paterson/Alamy*)

United Breaks Guitars went viral shortly after it was uploaded to YouTube in July 2009. He sang:

> "United, you broke my Taylor Guitar/United, some big help you are. You broke it, you should fix it/ You're liable, just admit it/ I should've flown with someone else/Or gone by car/ 'Cause United breaks guitars."

Within days his video received over 2.5 million views. Then the story was picked up and covered by major news media in the U.S., Canada, and the U.K. Within a year of its original post, the *United Breaks Guitar* video had been viewed over 8.5 million times (YouTube, 2010). Carroll released two more songs about his trials and tribulations with UAL, and his story has been retold and shared via countless blogs, Facebook pages, Tweets (Twitter messages), and this textbook.

Carroll's ability to use social media to damage the reputation of a major corporation has both fascinated and terrified many in the business world. The 2010 business case "United Breaks Guitars" by Harvard Business School professor John Deighton and research associate Leora Kornfeld, details the damaging impact a viral campaign can have on a company's brand, reputation, and customer relationships. They discuss the complexities of dealing with viral videos, companies' limited options for countering negative publicity, and the difficulties that unprepared companies face when responding to viral campaigns.

Facing Viral Threats

The response in the social media space was tremendously supportive of Carroll and vicious toward UAL. Negative viral videos posted by customers are a potential threat that cannot be ignored. Companies and their executives can no longer afford to hide behind slick advertising campaigns and press releases to protect their public image; nor can they insu-late themselves from unhappy customers with call center employees who can't solve problems when they arise. Motivated consumers, using the tools of social media, have the power to spread viral messages that can severely damage a company's brand image and expose it to ridicule and significant financial consequences. New communication strategies that utilize social media involve listening to customers, responding to their concerns, engaging them in conversation, and mobilizing them toward mutually beneficial goals.

In an interesting post script to this story, the *New York Times* reported that Dave Carroll flew UAL several months after his video went viral. On that flight, UAL lost his luggage.

Capitalizing on Viral Opportunities

Several businesses capitalized on the situation. Bob Taylor used the popularity of Carroll's videos to promote his own company, Taylor Quality Guitars (*taylorguitars.com*) and their service center, which provides quality repairs of damaged guitars of any make. On July 10, 2009, Taylor released a video on YouTube to "lend his support to Dave Carroll and guitar players everywhere." In the two-minute video, Taylor directs viewers to the Taylor guitars Web site for advice on traveling with guitars. His video received almost 500,000 views.

United Makes Peace with the Band

UAL and the band have since made peace, according to a follow-up statement by Carroll, posted on YouTube. In his statement-via-video, *United Breaks Guitars—A statement from Dave Carroll*, Carroll mentions that UAL offered him generous *but late* compensation.

Sources: Compiled from Erickson (2009), Reynolds (2009), Negroni (2009) and *YouTube.com* (2010), Harvard Business School Working Knowledge (HBSWK, 2010).

For Class Discussion and Debate

1. Scenario for Brainstorming and Discussion: There's an old saying, "Nobody is perfect." Even when companies mean well and do everything reasonable to please the customer, something is going to go wrong some of the time.

To hear Dave Carroll's first-hand account of the story and to watch his videos, visit *davecarrollmusic.com* or *YouTube.com*. View the videos and then brainstorm answers to the following questions:

a. Discuss the notion of social media as *insurgent media*, that is, better at attack than at defense.

b. When you engage your customers in a conversation, they may tell you (and others) things you don't want to hear. They might criticize your product, service, management, and/or employees. Would it be smarter for companies to limit their online exposure to Web sites that project a well-thought-out message and do not encourage or allow responses from customers?

c. Once Carroll posted his videos on YouTube, what steps could UAL have taken to minimize the damage and possibly turn things around so that it could maintain a positive brand image in the marketplace? (Hint: The major themes in social media communication are "conversation" and "relationship." What do you do when you've hurt someone's feelings?)

d. Apart from this situation, what are some ways that UAL's management should consider using social media to build relationships with existing and prospective customers?

e. Did Bob Taylor expose his company, Taylor Guitars, to any risk? Explain.

2. *Debate:* Social media can be a source of risk to a company's brand or image. One example is that Dave Carroll's complaint, propagated by social media, received a lot of attention. However, many complaints via social media do not. If the issue is not new, not interesting, or not presented in an entertaining way, it is very unlikely to go viral.

a. Take the position either that companies need a damage control strategy for negative social media or that such a strategy is unnecessary and not worth the investment. Defend your position with persuasive evidence.

b. In your debate, consider the probability of the risk and how feasible it is for a company to prevent situations like this from happening.

c. Debate the ethical issues, including the use of damaging social media by competitors. Address this question: What's to stop anyone with an axe to grind from using social media to ruin the reputation of well-run, customer-oriented businesses?

8.1 Web 2.0 and Social Media

In your lifetime, there has been a dramatic change in the way people use the Internet. In the early 1990s, many people did not have regular access to the Internet, and those who did typically "dialed up" their network from a home or office telephone. Dial-up access meant long waits as content from Web pages "downloaded" onto the screen. Some users joked that the letters "www" in a Web address stood for "world wide wait." E-mail was the primary mechanism for social interaction. Online communities were often like public bulletin boards where all members of the community could read the messages that others posted. Web sites were static—essentially online billboards for the businesses that created them. Online purchasing (e-commerce) was rare and risky because there were few safeguards protecting credit card information. But all that has changed.

NEW MODELS DRIVEN BY WEB 2.0

Today, most of us access the Internet using wired or wireless broadband technology, chewing up bandwidth that was unheard of a few years ago. We expect to be able to stream audio and video files as well as watch feature-length films over wireless connections or on smartphones. We surf Web pages that constantly change their appearance in response to how we interact with them. While e-mail is still a standard form of communication in business, young people tend to view it with disdain in favor of tweets, texts, or social networking sites like Facebook. We keep track of our world, interests, and hobbies by reading blogs and online newspapers, sharing them with friends and family by postings on profile pages.

Some people write their own blogs, post videos on YouTube, or share pictures using sites like Flickr or Photobucket. E-commerce continues to grow as we buy books from Amazon, sell on eBay, download music and videos from iTunes, book travel arrangements on *Travelocity.com*, and buy concert tickets from Ticketmaster.

The transformation has happened so smoothly that we frequently don't recognize many of the implications to businesses, agencies, and individuals. As Michael Wesch notes, we may need to rethink a lot of things.

BROADCAST VS. CONVERSATION MODELS

Internet interactivity allows for robust social connections between individuals, organizations, governments, and other entities. Organizations previously communicated with their audiences using a broadcast model, where messages flowed from the sender to the receiver. Now, they must learn to use a conversation model, where communication flows back and forth between sender and receiver. This model is made possible by IT and a change in the expectations and behavior of Internet users (Li and Bernoff, 2008).

TABLE 8.1	Web 1.0 vs Web 2.0
Web 1.0	**Web 2.0—the Social Web**
Static pages, HTML	Dynamic pages, XML and Java
Author-controlled content	User-controlled content
Computers	Computers, cell phones, televisions, PDAs, game systems, car dashboards
Users view content	Users create content
Individual users	User communities
Marketing goal: influence	Marketing goal: relationships
Top down	Bottom up
Data: single source	Data: multiple sources, e.g., mashups

Source: Barefoot (2006), O'Reilly (2005)

In the next section, you will read about the technological aspects of Web 2.0. It's important to recall that while IT provides the platform for this phenomenon, the changing behavior of users represents the biggest challenge and opportunity for businesses today.

Because of Web 2.0, people have different attitudes about how they want businesses to interact with them. They have higher expectations for a company's character, ethical behavior, responsiveness, and ability to meet their individual needs. Customers expect businesses to use Web 2.0 capabilities to satisfy their needs. Those companies that don't respond face a growing weakness.

Web 2.0 also represents opportunities for those who understand and master the new way of doing things. Managers who invest the time to understand and become proficient in new approaches to identifying, communicating with, and building relationships with customers online will have a tremendous advantage over managers who limit themselves to traditional methods.

WHAT IS WEB 2.0?

Experts don't always agree on a definition for **Web 2.0.** Many writers have identified characteristics that differentiate the new Web from what is called Web 1.0 (see Table 8.1). Others maintain that the term Web 2.0 is simply an inevitable, incremental advance from earlier capabilities. In a 2006 interview, Tim Berners-Lee, originator of the World Wide Web, suggests the term Web 2.0 is simply "a piece of jargon, nobody even knows what it means." Berners-Lee maintains that the Internet has been about connecting people in an interactive space from the beginning.

While the applications that are labeled as Web 2.0 may simply be an extension of earlier advances, it is the change in user behavior that matters most to businesses around the world. The new technologies dramatically increase the ability of people to interact with businesses and each other, to share and find information, and to form relationships. This perspective explains why Web 2.0 is often called the Social Web (see Figure 8.2).

Figure 8.2 Web 2.0 is also referred to as the Social Web. (© *Kheng Ho Toh/Alamy*)

Figure 8.3 WordPress is one of the leading platforms for online blogs. (© *digitallife/Alamy*)

WEB 2.0 APPLICATIONS

The following technologies and tools are valuable capabilities commonly associated with Web 2.0:

Blogs. Blog is short for "Web log"; it is a Web site where users regularly post information for others to read. Blogs allow readers to comment on each posting. Blog authors, or bloggers, use this approach to share opinions, commentary, news, technical advice, personal stories, and so on. Blogs are relatively easy to create and are used by individuals and businesses as a way of communicating. Wordpress, Typepad, and Blogger offer easy-to-use software (see Figure 8.3). Because it is a common practice for bloggers to use a special kind of hyperlink called a **trackback** to reference other blogs in their writing, blogs are collectively referred to as the **blogosphere.** In a sense, bloggers and those who follow them form an online social network.

Blogs are a key tool for organizations that practice **content marketing,** where valuable information is shared with current or prospective customers. Bloggers can establish a lot of credibility for themselves and their organizations by providing helpful information to people who are part of their target market. Politicians practice a similar strategy when they use blogs to communicate with their constituency. Chief executives and other managers use blogs targeted to their employees to motivate, inspire, and provide information about company goals.

Wikis. A **wiki** is a Web site that allows many people to add or update information found on the site. Wikis are a collaborative work that benefits from the efforts of many participants. Wikipedia is an online encyclopedia that is the most popular general reference work on the Internet (*Alexa Topsites*, 2010). Businesses can create wikis for a particular product and allow employees and customers to contribute information that will form a knowledge base resource for those who need information about the product.

Social Networking Services. A **social networking service (SNS)** is a Web site where individuals, who are defined by a *profile*, can interact with others. This interaction can take the form of posting messages, sharing photographs or videos, sharing links to online material, instant messaging, and so on. Social networking sites are different from the broader category of *online communities* in that they usually allow individuals to control who can access information they post to the site. For instance, on Facebook, people "friend" one another to gain access to information. An individual's social network consists of all the friends they've acknowledged or *friended* on the site. LinkedIn uses a similar feature, allowing users to add *contacts* and to approve or deny requests to establish a connection with others.

Figure 8.4 YouTube, a video-sharing site, is the third most popular site on the Internet.
(© *David J. Green-lifestyle themes/Alamy*)

Sharing Sites. Some sites are dedicated to sharing various kinds of media, including video, audio, and pictures. YouTube is the best-known Web site for sharing video files (see Figure 8.4). However, YouTube is also a form of social networking site in that users interact with one another by leaving comments about videos, posting video responses, creating and sharing video playlists, and even creating *channels* for their video content.

Some sites allow users to load **podcasts,** or audio/video files that people download onto devices like computers and MP3 players. Picture-sharing sites like Flickr and Photobucket have expanded beyond simple photo sharing and now include video capabilities as well as organization and editing tools; they also let people sell photos or order products with their photo images (e.g., calendars, coffee mugs, and T-shirts). Like YouTube, they contain elements of social networking by allowing users to interact and comment on things that are posted to the site.

Widgets and Mashups. Widgets are stand-alone programs that can be embedded into Web pages, blogs, profiles on social networking sites, and even computer desktops. Common widgets include clocks, visitor counters, weather reporters, and chat boxes. Businesses frequently sponsor the development and distribution of widgets as a way of promoting themselves. For instance, *ESPN.com* offers users a number of widgets that can receive and display sports information such as scores and news and broadcast schedules. See *IT at Work 8.1* for more details.

RSS (Really Simple Syndication). RSS feeds allow users to aggregate regularly changing data—such as blog entries, news stories, audio, and video—into a single place called a news aggregator or **RSS reader** (see Figure 8.5). RSS pushes content

IT at Work 8.1

Mashups: Interactive Web Apps

The term **mashup** refers to an application or Web page that pulls information from multiple sources, creating a new functionality. For instance, assume that you find a Web page with a listing of popular restaurants in your community. By placing the cursor over a particular restaurant's name, a small window opens with a map showing the location of the restaurant as well as summary review information from people who have eaten there before. When you move the cursor away from the restaurant

name, the window disappears.

Discussion Questions: To better understand mashup applications, visit the Tall Eye Web site at *map.talleye.com/index.php*. At that site, use a mashup application to answer such questions as "If I dig a hole all the way through the earth, where will I come out?" and "If I walk a straight line all the way around the globe, what places will I pass through?"

Figure 8.5 Users can subscribe to online content using RSS technology. (©AKP Photos/Alamy)

to users so they can avoid the hassle of having to visit several different sites to get the information they are interested in. Popular RSS readers include FeedDemon, GoogleReader, and NewzCrawler. RSS enables content management, allowing users to filter and display information in ways they find most helpful. RSS readers are a special kind of mashup application.

Social Bookmarking and Tag Clouds. People have traditionally kept track of sites they wanted to remember by using the *bookmark* feature or *favorites list* on their browser. These methods allowed users to store and organize Web site addresses in folders they had created. However, as lists become long, this folder system becomes unwieldy and disorganized. Using self-defined **tags,** such as "business partners," "travel," and "IT vendors," users can classify sites, allowing them to be searched using those tags. Online content posted at sites like Flickr and YouTube can also be tagged, which helps other users find that content.

Tag clouds are graphic representations of all the tags that people have attached to a particular page. Figure 8.6 shows three examples of tag clouds. The varying font sizes of words in a tag cloud represent the frequency of keywords at the site. *Delicious.com* is perhaps the most popular social bookmarking site. It also allows users to see Web pages that others have tagged with certain labels and to perform searches for sites that have a combination of tags.

While *delicious.com* is positioned as a social bookmarking site, it also maintains a wiki, a blog, and uses RSS feeds. This shows that many popular Web sites can't be easily categorized by a single technology.

AJAX Technologies. AJAX, or **Asynchronous JavaScript** and **XML,** refers to a group of technologies that create Web pages that respond to users' actions without requiring the entire page to reload. AJAX languages are JavaScript, XML, HTML, and CSS, which are defined in Table 8.2. AJAX makes it possible for Web developers to create small apps that run on a page instead of on a server. This capability makes content run much faster and increases the functionality of Web sites. Why? Because without AJAX, every time you clicked a hyperlink, you would need to wait for a page to load. AJAX apps run faster because it doesn't involve waiting for an entire page to load in a browser.

Social Media. Collectively, these Web 2.0 applications are commonly referred to as **social media** because they have moved the locus of control for mass communications from large organizations to individual users. In other words, people as well as organizations control both the message and the medium. Organizations and individual users can easily share their thoughts, opinions, and experiences interactively with each

Figure 8.6 Examples of word tag clouds. **(a)** Tag clouds illustrate the content and frequency of specific words on a Web page. **(b)** Tag cloud illustrating financial terms. **(c)** Tag cloud illustrating terms for supply chain management. (© *Equinox Imagery/Alamy*)

other. Instead of a large organization broadcasting a single message to a mass audience, a massive number of conversations take place.

Nobody has complete control over the message or the medium, yet everyone can play a part if they choose to. The challenge for businesses today is to develop strategies that take advantage of social media. A new mindset is required. Businesses that

TABLE 8.2	AJAX Languages for Web 2.0

HTML: Hypertext Markup Language is the predominant language for Web pages. It provides a means to create structured documents by denoting structural semantics for text, such as headings, paragraphs, and lists as well as for links, quotes, and other items.

XML: Extendable Markup Language is a set of rules and guidelines for describing data that can be used by other programming languages. It is what makes it possible for data (information) to be shared across the Web.

CSS: Cascading Style Sheets is a style sheet language used to enhance the appearance of Web pages written in a markup language.

JavaScript: JavaScript is an object-oriented language used to create apps and functionality on Web sites. Some examples of JavaScript applications include popup windows, validation of Web form inputs, and images that change when a cursor passes over them.

(*Source: Wikipedia.com*, 2010)

TABLE 8.3	Excerpts from The Cluetrain Manifesto

- Markets are conversations.
- Markets consist of human beings, not demographic sectors.
- These networked conversations are enabling powerful new forms of social organization and knowledge exchange to emerge.
- As a result, markets are getting smarter, more informed, more organized. Participation in a networked market changes people fundamentally.
- People in networked markets have figured out that they get far better information and support from one another than from vendors. So much for corporate rhetoric about adding value to commoditized products.
- Corporations do not speak in the same voice as these new networked conversations. To their intended online audiences, companies sound hollow, flat, literally inhuman.
- Companies need to realize their markets are often laughing. At them.
- Most marketing programs are based on the fear that the market might see what's really going on inside the company.
- Networked markets can change suppliers overnight. Networked knowledge workers can change employers over lunch. Your own "downsizing initiatives" taught us to ask the question: "Loyalty? What's that?"

Source: Levine et.al, (2000).

used to spend most of their time developing sophisticated ways of getting their message heard must now develop sophisticated strategies for listening and responding to what their consumers are saying.

WEB 2.0 ATTITUDE

As you have read, the availability of Web 2.0 applications is changing not only how people behave but also the way they think about things. This new way of thinking is captured in a provocative list of 95 statements called the Cluetrain Manifesto (*cluetrain.com*). Perhaps the fundamental principle of the manifesto is described by its first thesis: *Markets are conversations.* Other excerpts from the Manifesto are listed in Table 8.3. Over time, successful companies will learn to engage customers in conversations as an alternative to the unidirectional or broadcast method of communication. While the Cluetrain Manifesto seemed idealistic, impractical, and revolutionary when it was first written in 2000, we are starting to see more examples of companies finding ways of turning those principles into action.

Most companies still struggle with the concept of *conversation.* Forrester researchers Charlene Li and Josh Bernoff (2008) describe a number of companies that recognize the power of what they call the **groundswell,** "a spontaneous movement of people using online tools to connect, take charge of their own experience and get what they need—information, support, ideas, products, and bargaining power—from each other."

Businesses are learning to participate in the groundswell by using Web 2.0 tools to implement **Integrated Social Media (ISM)** strategies. Organizations that fail to participate effectively in the groundswell risk becoming irrelevant.

Because of the relatively low cost and ease of use, social media is a powerful democratization force; the network structure enables communication and collaboration on a massive scale. Figure 8.7 shows the emergence and rise of mass social media. The figure compares traditional and social media and illustrates the new tools of social media, such as blogs and video blogs (vlogs), as being in the consumer's control. Content is produced and consumed by people in the social media, rather than pushed to or observed by people in the traditional media.

Notice that traditional media content goes from the technology to the people, whereas in social media, people create and control the content.

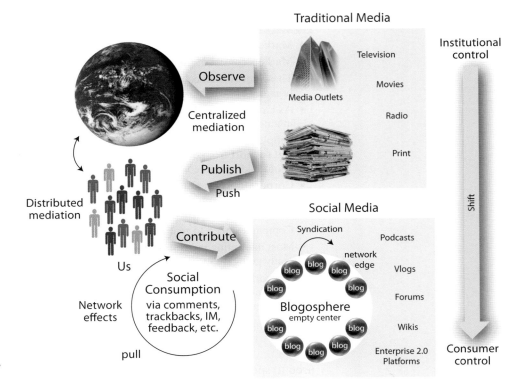

Figure 8.7 The emergence and rise of mass social media. (*Source*: Hinchcliffe, Web 2.0 Blog, *web2.wsj2.com.*)

Review Questions

1. How has Web 2.0 changed the behavior of Internet users?
2. What are the basic tools or applications that characterize Web 2.0?
3. Why is Web 2.0 referred to as the *Social Web*?
4. What are some of the benefits or advantages that Web developers gain from using AJAX technologies?
5. What are some of the most important messages for business organizations in the *Cluetrain Manifesto*?

8.2 Virtual Communities and Social Networking Services

Online or **virtual communities** parallel typical physical communities, such as neighborhoods, clubs, and associations, except that they are not bound by political or geographic boundaries. These communities offer several ways for members to interact, collaborate, and trade. Virtual or online communities have been around for a long time and predate the World Wide Web. The **Usenet** (*usenet.com*) provided the initial platform for online communities by making it possible for users to exchange messages on various topics in public **newsgroups,** which are similar in many ways to online bulletin board systems. While the Usenet is technically not part of the Internet, much of the content can be accessed from Internet sites like Goggle Groups.

Some of the first major online Internet communities include The Well (1985), GeoCities (1994), The Globe (1994), and Tripod (1995). Of these, only The Well continues to operate as an online community. The others have either changed their business model to Web hosting or have gone out of business entirely. Table 8.4 lists several types of online communities.

Online communities can take a number of forms. For instance, some people view the blogosphere as a community. YouTube is a community of people who post, view, and comment on videos. Epinions (*epinions.com*) is a community of people who share their experiences and opinions about products and companies. Flickr, Photobucket,

TABLE 8.4	Types of Online Communities

Associations. Many associations have a Web presence. These range from Parent-Teacher Associations (PTAs) to professional associations. An example of this type of community is the Australian Record Industry Association (*aria.com.au*).

Ethnic communities. Many communities are country or language specific. An example of such a site is *elsitio.com*, which provides content for Spanish- and Portuguese-speaking audiences, mainly in Latin America and the United States. A number of sites, including *china.com, mymailhk.com, sina.com, and sohu.com,* cater to the world's large Chinese-speaking community.

Gender communities. *ivillage.com* is a large community that focuses on women's interests, while *askmen.com* is an online community that caters to men.

Affinity portals. These are communities organized by interest, such as hobbies, vocations, political parties, unions [(e.g., *edmunds.com* (cars), *democraticunderground.org* (politics)], and so on. Many communities are organized around a technical topic (e.g., a database) or a product (e.g., BlackBerry smartphones). A major subcategory here is medical- and health-related sites like *webmd.com*. According to Johnson and Ambrose, almost 30 percent of the 90 million members who participated in communities in 2005 were in this category.

Young people—teens and people in their early twenties. Many companies see unusual opportunities here. Alloy Digital has created a number of Web sites in this space— including *alloy.com, gurl.com, teen.com, takkle.com,* and *channelone.com*—which it claims reach over 30 million young people every month.

B2B online communities. B2B exchanges support community programs such as technical discussion forums, blogs, interactive Webcasts, user-created product reviews, virtual conferences and meetings, experts' seminars, and user-managed profile pages. Classified ads can help members to find jobs or employers to find employees. Many also include industry news, directories, links to government and professional associations, and more.

Social networking sites. These are megacommunities, such as MySpace, Facebook, LinkedIn, and Bebo, in which millions of unrelated members can express themselves, find friends, find jobs, exchange photos, view videotapes, and more.

Webshots, and similar sites are photo-sharing communities. Wikipedia is a community of people who create, edit, and maintain an online knowledge base. Obviously, social networking sites like Facebook and MySpace are communities and have seen tremendous growth in recent years. The mass adoption of social networking Web sites points to an evolution in human social interaction (Weaver and Morrison, 2008).

Social network analysis (SNA) is the mapping and measuring of relationships and flows between people, groups, organizations, computers, or other information- or knowledge-processing entities. The nodes in the network are the people and the groups, whereas the links show relationships or flows between the nodes (see Figure 8.8). SNA provides both a visual and a mathematical analysis of relationships. In its corporate communications, Facebook has begun using the term **social graph** to refer to the global social network reflecting how we are all connected to one another through relationships. Facebook users can access a social graph application that visually represents the connections among all the people in its network. Berners-Lee (2007) extended this concept even further when he coined the term "**giant global graph.**" This concept is intended to illustrate the connections between people and/or documents and pages online. Connecting all points on the giant global graph is the ultimate objective goal for creators of the **Semantic Web,** which you will read about in Section 8.5.

Online communities have received increasing attention from the business community. Online communities can be used as a platform for the following:

- Selling goods and services
- Promoting products to prospective customers; that is, advertising
- Prospecting for customers

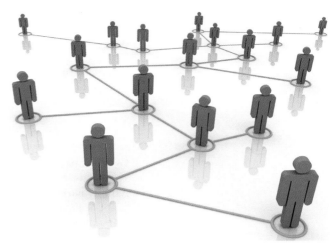

Figure 8.8 A social graph uses nodes and ties to illustrate relationships between individuals and groups of people.
(© Alex Slobodkin/iStockphoto)

- Building relationships with customers and prospective customers
- Identifying customer perceptions by "listening" to conversations
- Soliciting ideas for new products and services from customers
- Providing support services to customers by answering questions, providing information, and so on
- Encouraging customers to share their positive perceptions with others; that is, word of mouth
- Gathering information about competitors and marketplace perceptions of competitors
- Identifying and interacting with prospective suppliers, partners, and collaborators (see Enterprise 2.0 in the next section)

In recent years, several companies have created online communities for the purpose of identifying market opportunities through crowdsourcing. **Crowdsourcing** is a model of problem solving and idea generation that marshals the collective talents of a large group of people. Using Web 2.0 tools, companies solicit, refine, and evaluate ideas for new products and services based on input from their customers. Business organizations that have implemented this approach include Fiat, Sara Lee, BMW, Kraft, Proctor & Gamble, and Starbucks. *Openinnovators.net* lists other examples.

SOCIAL NETWORKING SERVICES (SNS)

Social networking sites represent a special type of virtual community and are now the dominant form of online community. With social networking, individual users maintain an identity through their profile and can be selective about which members of the larger community they choose to interact with. Over time, users build their network by adding contacts or friends. On some social network platforms, organizations create an identity by establishing discussion forums, group pages, or some other presence. Social networking has increased substantially in recent years. The Nielsen Company (2010) reported that users spent on average over six hours on social networking sites in March 2010, more than a 100 percent increase over the previous year. Figure 8.9 shows the growth rate of time spent on social networking sites.

The number of social networking services has grown tremendously in recent years. It is expected that it will segment and consolidate in the future just like other industries. Among the general purpose SNS platforms, MySpace, with 113 million users (*myspace.com*), used to be the leader but has been overtaken by Facebook, with over 500 million users. Facebook is the second most visited site on the Internet after Google according to *Alexa.com* (2010), and it has publicly said it wants to be number one (Harvey, 2010; Vogelstein, 2009). Many have observed that if Facebook were a country, it would be the third largest in the world. Other large, general social network services are listed in Table 8.5.

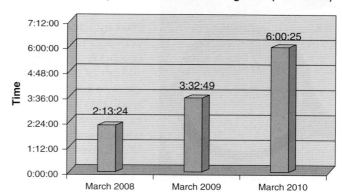

Figure 8.9 Time spent on social networking services increased dramatically in 2010. (*Source: The Nielsen Company, 2010.*)

TABLE 8.5	Large Social Network Services	
Qzone	Caters to users in mainland China	200 million users
Habbo	Caters to teens in 31 countries.	162 million users
Orkut	Popular in Brazil and India	100 million users
Friendster	Popular in Southeast Asia	90 million users
Hi5	Popular in India, Portugal, Mongolia, Thailand, Romania, Jamaica, Central Africa, and Latin America	80 million users

The leading SNSs in the United States from 2008 through 2010 are compared in Figure 8.10. The landscape of SNS services is changing rapidly. Fortunately, a constantly updated list of SNS sites is maintained by Wikipedia. See the "List of social networking Web sites" at *Wikipedia.com*.

While SNS sites share some common features, they are not all alike. As the category matures, sites are differentiating themselves in a variety of ways. For instance, the SNS services in Wikipedia's list differ in terms of the following:

- Target age group
- Geographic location of users
- Language
- Interest area; for example, music, photography, gaming, travel
- Social vs. professional networking
- Interface; for example, profile page, micro blog, virtual world

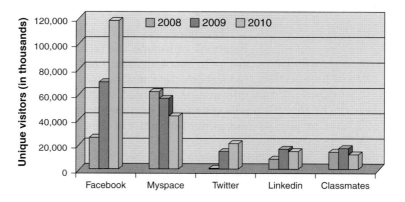

Figure 8.10 Unique visitors to U.S. social networks, 2008–2010. (*Source: The Nielsen Company, 2010*).

Figure 8.11 Facebook has a simple interface that people of all ages find easy to use. (© PSL Images/Alamy)

Facebook Becomes Leading SNS. Facebook is the largest social networking service in the world, with more than 500 million active users. Facebook was launched in 2004 by a former Harvard student, Mark Zuckerberg. Photos, groups, events, marketplace, posted items, and notes are the basic applications already installed in Facebook. Apart from these basic applications, users can develop their own apps or add any of the millions of Facebook-available apps that have been developed by other users. In addition, Facebook owns two special features called "news feed" and "mini-feed" that allow users to track the movement of friends in their social circles. For example, when a person changes his or her profile, updates are broadcast to others who subscribe to the feed. Facebook also launched an application called "People You May Know" that helps new users connect with their old friends (Vander Veer, 2008).

When Zuckerberg first created Facebook, he had very strong social ambitions aimed at helping people connect to others on the Web. Facebook was initially an online social space for college students. It started by connecting students to all others at the same school. In 2006, Facebook expanded to anyone 13 years or older with a valid e-mail address (see Figure 8.11). The lack of privacy controls (i.e., tools that restrict who sees your profile) has been the biggest reason why many businesspeople resisted joining Facebook.

In 2008, Facebook introduced new controls that allow users to set different levels of access to information about themselves for each of their groups, such as family, friends from school, and friends from work. For example, close friends might see your cell phone number, music favorites, e-mail address, and so forth, while other friends might see only the basics of your résumé (Abram and Pearlman, 2008). More recently, however, Facebook has made changes in its privacy policies, often igniting a wave of complaints from users. This highlights an ongoing tension between the corporate goals of Facebook, which depend on a high level of access to user data, and the desire of individual users to control access to their personal information.

Facebook has expanded to the rest of the world with the help of its foreign language members: Engineers first collected thousands of English words and phrases throughout the site and invited members to translate those bits of text into another language. Members then rate translations until a consensus is reached. The Spanish version was done by about 1,500 volunteers in less than a month. The German version was done by 2,000 volunteers in less than two weeks. In early March 2008, Facebook invited French members to help out. They did the translations in a few days. Today Facebook exists in over 70 different languages, and approximately 70 percent of its members are outside of the United States (Facebook, 2010).

A primary reason that Facebook wants to expand is the *network effect:* More users mean more value. In April 2010, Mark Zuckerberg announced that Facebook would begin a new initiative called the **open graph.** Facebook wants to connect all the different relationships that exist on the Internet. It proposes to do this by linking other Web sites to Facebook. Programmers at external Web sites are being encouraged to include a Facebook "like" button on their Web sites. That way, when Facebook members visit the Web site, they can click the "like" button and their relationship with that Web site will be reflected back on their Facebook page for friends to see.

Facebook will also encourage other Web sites to allow people to use their Facebook username and password to sign in or create accounts. For instance, if you are a Facebook member and you visit *pandora.com* (a music service) or *yelp.com* (a local directory service), you can just sign into the sites using your Facebook access information. Facebook will then share your profile information with those sites. This new initiative is exciting for its potential to enhance the social richness and ease of use of the Internet. On the other hand, there are very serious privacy and security concerns.

And Now, for Something Different: Second Life. Second Life is a social network service unlike most others. What makes it unique is that it uses a 3-D virtual world

Figure 8.12 Residents on Second Life use avatars to navigate the virtual world. While most avatars are humanoid in form, they can actually take on any shape. (© *Friedrich Stark/Alamy*)

interface in which users, called *residents,* are represented by **avatars,** or cyberbodies that they create (see Figure 8.12).

Residents on Second Life, developed by Linden Research in 2003, communicate with others in the virtual world through chat or voice communications. Residents can create and trade things they make in Second Life, including virtual clothes, art, vehicles, houses, and other architectural structures. They can also earn money by providing services such as instruction in a foreign language or serving as a DJ in a virtual club. This has led to the evolution of a Second Life economy with its own currency, the Linden dollar (L$). While most of the economic activity remains in the Second Life world, there are news reports of a few entrepreneurs who have made considerable sums of real money. Residents who make a lot of Linden dollars can exchange them at a rate of about 250 L$ for every U.S. dollar.

Real-world businesses use the virtual world, too. For example, IBM uses it as a location for meetings, training, and recruitment. American Apparel was the first major retailer to set up shop in Second Life. Starwood Hotels used Second Life as a relatively low-cost market research experiment in which avatars visit Starwood's virtual Aloft hotel. The endeavor created publicity for the company, and feedback on the design of the hotel was solicited from visiting avatars. This information was used in the creation of the first real-world Aloft hotel, which opened in 2008 (Carr, 2007). Starwood subsequently donated its Second Life property to a not-for-profit educational organization.

Will Second Life eventually replace Facebook and other 2-D SNS platforms? Probably not, in spite of its impressive interface. While Second Life is visually compelling, it requires users to master a much larger range of controls and technology to become fully functional. Its aesthetic similarity to video games may cause some to underestimate its potential for more serious applications. Also, avatars interact in real time, so users need to be online at the same time as their friends and acquaintances in order to interact. That said, there are some niche applications that show promise. Using speakers and microphones, groups of people can conduct meetings in Second Life. Teachers can interact with their students in Second Life. How would you like it if your professor held office hours on a virtual beach? Linden Labs has revamped the special browser that residents use to participate in the virtual world and is actively promoting its use for interesting business applications, but it is unlikely to achieve the same level of attention as Facebook in its present form. We believe, however, that Second Life will continue to provide benefit as a fascinating niche player in the overall SNS marketplace.

Figure 8.13 Twitter is a microblogging SNS that limits users to messages of 140 characters or less. (© *2020WEB/Alamy*)

Twitter: Microblogging. Twitter is a social networking site where users send short messages called tweets of 140 characters or less to their network of *followers* (see Figure 8.13). Started in 2006, Twitter is now among the top 15 Web sites in terms of traffic.

Like Facebook, it has experienced tremendous growth over the last few years as businesses and individual users discover ways of using the **microblogging** site to meet their needs. Twitter is used by athletes and other celebrities as a way of maintaining frequent contact with their fan base and by businesses and bloggers as a way of directing traffic to updates on Web sites.

Breaking news is distributed through Twitter networks by major news organizations and private citizens who witness events first-hand. Twitter has become an integral part of many social media campaigns directed to consumers. Even though sending and receiving tweets is like instant messaging, the site allows individuals to broadcast messages to very large groups of followers. In turn, followers can reply to tweets or interact with each other, which add a strong social element to the service.

Basic Twitter service is simple and efficient, but many third-party apps have been developed to enhance the service, and some are considered essential tools in the life of the power Twitter user:

- TweetDeck is an advanced, split-screen Twitter interface that allows users to view messages streaming from followers, people being followed, and people the user might wish to follow. It also makes it easy to quickly reply to incoming tweets, increasing the frequency of Twitter conversations.
- Twitpic allows users to add photos to their tweets.
- Twitterfeed automatically tweets posts published on a blog using RSS technology.
- Twitterholic is a service that ranks users by number of followers, friends, and updates.

Private SNS Services. Many business and professional organizations have found it desirable to create their own focused social networking services. Several companies offer platforms for just this purpose. One of the most popular is *ning.com*. Until recently, you could create a private social network service on Ning for free. However, in May 2010, Ning announced that it was phasing out its free service by converting its networks to premium (paid) service or eliminating them. There are, however, several other free, premium, and open-source alternatives to Ning.

There are many reasons why organizations create private social networks. Companies that wish to better understand their customers can create social networks that will attract individuals from their target market. This gives them the ability to monitor or listen to customers and identify important issues that their customers are discussing. Businesses can also develop social networks for internal use, limiting access to employees.

Not-for-profit organizations can build communities for donors or users interested in particular causes. Li and Bernoff warn, however, that building a private social networking service is not an easy undertaking and requires considerable resources, even when the SNS platform is "free." Organizations are cautioned not to enter into the project lightly and to carefully plan their strategy and resource allocations prior to launch. Building a community with all of its social and relationship implications, only to abruptly terminate it because of resource limitations, is likely to be a public relations disaster. For companies that execute this approach properly, however, the private social network can yield numerous benefits in terms of marketing information and fruitful customer relationships.

Social networking services are perhaps the most social applications of Web 2.0. It is expected that growth and innovation in this sector will continue as individual users and business organizations discover its power for building networks and relationships. We expect that Facebook will continue to dominate the field but that smaller SNSs will stake out strong positions in niche markets using traditional market segmentation strategies—focusing on the needs of specific geographic, cultural, age, or special-interest segments.

IT at Work 8.2

Social Privacy?

Privacy rights are too easily abused. Governments and industry associations are trying to control these abuses through legislation and professional standards, but they frequently fail to provide adequate protection. One of the most effective deterrents is fear of backlash from abuses that become public and cause outrage. So it is important to identify privacy issues that pertain to social media and specifically social networking services. Examples of privacy violations are:

- Posting pictures of people on social networking sites without their permission
- Tricking people into disclosing credit or bank account information or investing in "work at home" scams
- Sharing information about members with advertisers without the members' knowledge or consent
- Disclosing an employer's proprietary information or trade secrets on social networking sites
- Posting information on social networking sites that could compromise people's safety or make them targets for blackmail

Taking Control of Your Privacy. The most important thing that users can do to protect themselves is to understand that they're responsible for protecting their own information. The basic solution is common sense. Unfortunately, most social networking sites create the illusion of privacy and control. This can sometimes lull even the most vigilant users into making mistakes. Sites like Facebook, MySpace, and others make us feel like our information is only going to be seen by those we've allowed to become part of our network. Wrong. Listed below are commonsense guidelines:

- Don't post private data. Nothing, absolutely nothing, you put on a social networking site is private. You should avoid posting personal information, including full birth date, home address, phone number, and so on. This information is used for identity theft.
- Be smart about who you allow to become part of your network. It is not uncommon for teenagers to "friend" hundreds of individuals on their Facebook accounts. With this many contacts, there is no way to protect profile or other information.
- Don't rely on current privacy policies. Social networking sites change their privacy policies regularly. Many have accused Facebook of doing this specifically to wear down user vigilance with regard to maintaining desired privacy settings. Regularly review your social network service privacy policies. Set your privacy settings at the level offering maximum protection—operating as if you have no privacy whatsoever.
- Minimize your use of applications, games, and third-party programs on social networking sites until you have carefully investigated them. They can expose you to malicious programs or viruses. Do not automatically click on links that look like they were sent to you by members of your network.

Discussion Questions: Which of these guidelines is the easiest to follow? Which is the toughest? Explain why.

Review Questions

1. What are the major differences between social networking services and other online communities?
2. What is the basic difference between the social graph and Berners-Lee's concept of the giant global graph?
3. Explain Facebook's open graph initiative and how it plans to expand its influence across the World Wide Web.
4. What are some potential ways that business organizations can take advantage of Second Life's unique virtual world interface?
5. Why would a business want to create a private SNS? What are some of the challenges associated with doing this?

8.3 Enterprise 2.0 Tools

The term **Enterprise 2.0** is being used increasingly to refer to Web 2.0 technologies used for some business or organizational purpose. According to Harvard professor Andrew McAffee (2008), Enterprise 2.0 applications are valuable because they don't impose anything on users, give them free environments to work in, and let structure emerge over time. The goal is to promote increased collaboration and knowledge exchange among employees, consultants, and company partners. McAffee is among a growing number of IT experts who advocate using the Web 2.0 applications to either supplement or replace the closed intranet platforms that are widely used by business organizations today.

According to Cecil Dijoux (2009), Enterprise 2.0 is likely to lead to changes in organizational culture the same way that Web 2.0 is creating fundamental changes in the broader culture. Dijoux claims that organizations will need to communicate with their employees using a conversation rather than a broadcast model. Important ideas are more likely to come from the bottom up (the workforce) than from managers at the top. Managers won't be able to rely as much on their job title to maintain respect. They'll have to earn it on the enterprise social network. Other benefits include greater transparency in the organization, increased agility and simplicity, creation of a sharing culture, and the emergence of more efficient and effective organizational structures.

BUSINESS USE OF WEB 2.0 TECHNOLOGIES

How are businesses using these new technologies? According to a recent report (Network Solutions, 2010), social media use in the small business sector doubled from 12 to 24 percent in 2009. Another study shows that approximately 18 percent of Fortune 500 companies have public-facing blogs (Barnes and Mattson, 2009).

Recruiting and Professional Networking. According to Econsultancy, a company that compiles social media statistics, over 80 percent of companies used LinkedIn as their primary recruiting tool (Hird, 2009). Social networking among business professionals has exploded over the last few years. Begun in 2003, LinkedIn is the largest professional networking service, with over 65 million users across the globe as of 2010 (see Figure 8.14). Most users join LinkedIn for free, but many who wish to use all the benefits and tools of the site upgrade to a premium account by paying a subscription fee. LinkedIn allows users to create profiles that include their résumés, professional affiliations, educational history, and so on. Members can also update their status to let others in their network know what they are doing. LinkedIn allows people to post endorsements of others, which provides a way for sharing testimonials. Users expand their networks by either directly asking to connect with others or through referrals and introductions from people in their existing network. Savvy recruiters use the popular professional networking site in a number of ways, as described in *IT at Work 8.3*.

Just as recruiting strategies are changing, job-hunting strategies will change as well. Job hunters will need to master various social media tools in order to make contact with and establish relationships with potential employers. LinkedIn provides a way for candidates to gain visibility by expanding their network, joining LinkedIn groups, building their reputations by participating in Q&A discussions, generating testimonials (called *referrals* on LinkedIn), and integrating these activities with other

IT at Work 8.3

Social Networking Differs by Culture

Do people in China use social-networking sites the way you do? Do people in Japan use mobile phones more or less? How does technology use differ around the world?

Researcher Dr. Larissa Hjorth is a digital ethnographer—a person who charts cultures as *technocultures*—at RMIT University's School of Media and Communication. Dr. Hjorth has been studying the role of the user in mobile communication, gaming and virtual communities in the Asia-Pacific region since 2000. She reported:

"Each culture massages and transforms a technology. So devices such as the mobile phone are used in different ways according to the cultural context. An 18-year-old using a mobile phone in China will use it in a totally different way to 18-year-olds using their mobiles in Australia, Sweden or Japan."

For the first time in 2009, Internet penetration rates in China exceeded the global average level with more than 298 million users, of which 279 million were broadband users. In 2010, China Internet Network Information Center (CINNC) statistics noted a sharp increase in lower-income and less-educated people using the Internet.

Social-networking sites have also grown in popularity in China. For example, the site Xiaonei (like Facebook) is used predominantly by university students; Kaixin is used by female, white-collar workers; and sites QQ and Fetion can be accessed via mobiles and computers. QQ is popular among young adults leaving home to study in another city or country.

Sources: Compiled from RMIT (2010) and *NOMAD.net.au/index.php* (2010)

Figure 8.14 LinkedIn is used as the primary recruiting tool by 80 percent of companies. (© Alex Segre/Alamy)

social media tools. Other professional networking sites that can be used for recruiting include Plaxo, Ecademy, Jobfox, and Jobster.

Marketing, Promotion, and Sales. Many companies believe that social media has great potential to boost marketing and sales efforts. They see social media as the new way to communicate with current and potential customers. Throughout this chapter, we have cited several examples of how companies use social media technology to build and enhance customer relationships. Companies use blogs to disseminate information about their products, and they work hard to influence the attitudes and opinions of those who are writing blogs about them. Business organizations are finding ways to have a presence on popular SNS sites like Facebook and MySpace so that they can engage their customers.

YouTube has become a popular way for companies to promote themselves using viral videos. The BlendTec YouTube video is an excellent example, discussed in *IT at Work 8.4.* The company monitors blogs and discussion boards in order to listen to its customers and even participates in these discussions in order to build meaningful relationships. Companies find that promoting through social media is more effective and often less expensive than traditional advertising efforts. However, the field is so new that companies are learning how to apply ISM strategies through trial and effort, and they sometimes struggle to measure the effectiveness of their efforts.

Internal Collaboration and Communication. Most large and medium-sized companies utilize an intranet for internal collaboration and communication. An **intranet** is a network that utilizes Web-based technology, but its access is restricted to authorized users, typically employees. Company employees access the intranet with usernames and passwords. Businesses exercise a good deal of control over how and what happens on their intranets. According to Toby Ward (2010), most intranets are based on Web 1.0 technology and appear "flat" when compared to modern Web 2.0 capabilities. The other feature lacking in many intranets is a social element.

Russell Pearson (2010) and James Bennett (2009) believe that intranets will need to evolve with the behavior of "social" employees who join companies and expect to be able to communicate as professionals in the same ways they have communicated prior to joining the workforce. This means that intranets may need to evolve to allow file sharing, blogging, social tagging or bookmarking, wikis, and so on. In addition, management will need to balance their innate desire for control with the more important goal of enhancing communication with and among the workforce. Consequently, a new set of management skills will need to be developed.

As you read earlier, managers will need to learn how to use social technology to engage in conversations with employees, listen to their ideas, and motivate them toward mutually beneficial goals. Sending out a paper memo from headquarters or even a mass e-mail and expecting a desired response from company employees will be increasingly ineffective.

IT at Work 8.4

Will it Blend? Goes Viral

Let's say you have a great product that costs much more than any of your competitors, and your advertising budget is tight. Sound like a recipe for business failure? Not for BlendTec, a high-end brand of kitchen blenders. This company has leveraged a limited marketing budget using an Integrated Social Media (ISM) strategy and, in the process, established a huge fan base.

BlendTec had enormous success with YouTube videos featuring CEO Tom Dickson using his durable blenders to destroy everything from marbles and hockey pucks to an Apple iPhone. The videos are short and fun to watch but effectively illustrate the durability and strength of BlendTec's products. What started out as an inside joke at the company has become an Internet sensation. BlendTec hosts its own channel on YouTube, with over 50 different "Will it Blend?" segments.

Blendtec's Integrated Social Media (ISM) Strategy. The company had almost zero name recognition prior to its viral campaign, but now has one of the most-watched YouTube video collections. Most of the videos on the BlendTec channel have been viewed hundreds of thousands of times, and several have been seen by millions. The most popular video features the blended destruction of an iPhone, which had over 8 million views. A more recent entry features the demolition of an Apple iPad and was viewed over 6 million times in a single month (YouTube, 2010).

RSS, Blogs, and Videos. While the YouTube videos are the most visible part of BlendTec's social media efforts, the company utilizes an ISM strategy with a variety of tactics. The most popular videos are also featured on BlendTec's company Web page. Viewers at this site help BlendTec spread the word by sharing videos with their social network by clicking on buttons for Facebook or Twitter. They can even subscribe to the site

using RSS technology. The "Will It Blog" is used to provide information about products and upcoming videos. BlendTec regularly updates its followers with new videos and blog posts using Twitter. The company's Facebook page has over 34,000 fans who comment on the videos and request, sometimes plead, for certain objects to be blended in future videos. According to Dickenson, company sales have increased fivefold since the viral campaign was launched. That's a lot of enthusiasm for something as simple as a blender!

Sources: Compiled from Helm (2006), Dilworth (2007), and YouTube.com (2010).

Discussion Question:

1. BlendTec's videos are certainly fun to watch, but content isn't the only thing that has led to the viral nature of their campaign. What other elements of social media does the company use to optimize the success of their strategy?
2. How is BlendTec's video campaign any different from a television advertising campaign? What are the advantages for the company and the consumer?
3. Review the varying popularity of BlendTec's videos (YouTube shows the number of times a video has been viewed.) Can you identify any factors that might explain why some are more popular than others? What recommendations would you make to the company for future "Will it Blend" videos?
4. Read Dan Ackerman Greenberg's tips on how to make a video go viral (*techcrunch.com/2007/11/22/the-secret-strategies-behind-many-viral-videos/*), then visit the BlendTec Web site. How many of Greenberg's strategies are employed by the blender company?

Supply Chain Management 2.0. Supply chain management (SCM) refers to the set of activities that support the production and distribution of goods and services to end users. Activities that are typically associated with SCM include acquisition of raw materials, production processes and scheduling, inventory control, logistics, and coordination of channel members—wholesalers, distributors, and retailers. Supply chains are, by nature, social entities. They involve a number of people and organizations that must work together in order to create and deliver goods and services to consumers.

SCM 2.0 simply involves the use of social media tools to increase the effectiveness of this communication and enhance the acquisition of information necessary to make optimal decisions. Consider how enterprise social network systems could aid in the identification of new suppliers or buyers. Channel members can use blogs to share ideas about best practices and mashup apps to coordinate inventory levels throughout the channel and aid in transportation and shipping decisions. Any tool that increases the ability of channel partners to communicate, coordinate, and solidify relationships will make a business more competitive.

Just as social media is changing things about the social world we live in, it is also changing how businesses behave and operate.

Review Questions

1. How does a social networking service like LinkedIn fundamentally differ from Facebook or MySpace?
2. Identify some specific ways in which managers or leaders of organizations will need to change in response to the opportunities and challenges presented by social media.
3. Explain why social media tools are likely to make supply chains more efficient and productive in the future.
4. What are some specific ways in which workers will rely on social media tools to be more productive in their professions?

8.4 Social Media Objectives and Metrics

Management depends on data-driven measurements, or metrics. Businesses are constantly evaluating the efficiency and effectiveness of their activities. As part of the strategic planning process, companies identify goals, objectives, strategies, and tactics. In this way, they identify and focus on those activities that lead to revenue and profits and reduce their emphasis on activities that don't support company goals.

WHY MEASURE SOCIAL MEDIA?

While standard **metrics** exist for many traditional business activities, the field of social media and the related issue of **social media metrics** are so new that there are few standard ways of evaluating social media activities. We identify key methods of measuring the effectiveness of social media efforts but acknowledge that there are many variations on what we describe.

DASHBOARDS AND SCORE CARDS

As you have read since Chapter 1, managers keep informed by using performance **dashboards** or **balanced score cards** to summarize the effectiveness of activities and progress toward goals. These graphic representations show how well a company is performing on key metrics. In many cases, information technology is used to continuously feed data into dashboards or scorecards so that managers have access to real-time information. This has a significant advantage over using monthly or quarterly reports for assessing progress toward goals and helps to increase organizational responsiveness to a variety of situations. When automated, the scorecard or dashboard is an example of a mashup, a Web 2.0 application that pulls data from multiple sources and displays it in one location.

But what should a management team track in terms of social media in its dashboard or score card? In the next section, we discuss metrics that organizations find meaningful and effective.

TYPES OF SOCIAL MEDIA OBJECTIVES

Literally hundreds of metrics exist to track how people respond to social media. The list in Table 8.6 is just a sample of the many factors that can be tracked. New companies are springing up every day to offer tools for tracking social media activity. Companies are attracted into this market (think in terms of Porter's five-forces model) because businesses need to know if their social media efforts are effective and worth the expense. There are many different kinds of metrics because social media can be used to do so many things. Therefore, the question of what kind of information a company tracks depends on what it is trying to accomplish with its social media efforts. For instance, if a company wants to increase traffic to its Web page, then it would start tracking the number of visitors who arrive at its Web site from a tweet, the company's Facebook fan page, and all other sources.

On the other hand, if a company wants to learn how customers feel about its products, it would track the number of positive vs. negative blog posts and videos about the company, its products, services, senior management, or business practices.

Traditionally, business organizations developed media objectives around various models called **response hierarchies.** A common response hierarchy includes the

TABLE 8.6	**Examples of Social Media Metrics**

Activity Metrics
- Pageviews
- Unique number of visitors
- Posts
- Comments and trackbacks
- Time spent on site
- Contributors
- Frequency: of visits, posts, comments

Survey Metrics
- Satisfaction
- Quality and speed of issue resolution
- Content relevance

ROI Measurements
- Sales and marketing
  - Cost per number of prospects
  - Number of leads per period
  - Cost of leads
  - Conversion of leads to customers
  - Customer lifetime value (CLV)
- Product development
  - Number of new product ideas
  - Idea to development initiation cycle time
- HR
  - Hiring and training costs
  - Employee attrition
  - Time to hire

Individual Metrics (for members) NEW
- Number of friends met online that users have met offline
- Number of friends met online that member has subsequently collaborated with

General Internet Tracking (outside of enterprise-sponsored communities)
- Net promoter score (*netpromoter.com*)
- Number of mentions (tracked via Web or blog search engines)

Source: Adapted from Happe (2008).

following stages: awareness, knowledge, liking, preference, and purchase. Using this model, advertisers set measurable objectives for each stage. For instance, a company might set an objective, such as:

- Achieve 45 percent brand awareness in our primary market within the first quarter.
- Increase the conversion rate from preference to purchase by 2 percent over the next six months.

Once these objectives are set, advertisers use marketing research to track their progress toward reaching the objectives and can evaluate the success of their promotional activities.

Businesses could apply response hierarchy models to the area of social media. However, response hierarchy models are based on an advertising or broadcast approach to communication and fail to capture the full potential of the social media environment. The real potential of social media goes far beyond sending messages that influence people. Interactive social media can be used to collect information as well as send it. It can be used to reduce costs associated with customer service. It can be used to gather intelligence on competitors and much more. Because there are so many applications, companies need to be very clear about what they want to accomplish with their social media efforts; this in turn will drive what information they track to assess the effectiveness of their actions.

At this point, it seems that there are primarily four basic approaches to social media metrics: *tool-based metrics, tactical metrics, strategic metrics,* and *ROI metrics.* The four approaches are not mutually exclusive. It is common for some specific metrics to be used in each of the four approaches. The difference between each approach is how a business defines its objectives, or what it is trying to accomplish, as explained next.

Tool-Based Metrics. Metrics are driven by objectives. The metrics a company uses are determined by what the company is trying to achieve. In some cases, a company will define its objectives based on a specific Web 2.0 tool. **Tool-based metrics** are designed to identify information about a specific applications. For instance, a company might want to determine if it should advertise on a popular blog or sponsor the creation and distribution of a useful widget application. Companies that use Twitter might track the number of followers; number of times other people mention the company in tweets; number of times people forward messages, called retweets. A 2009 report by the Interactive Advertising Bureau (IAB) specified definitions for three widely used Web 2.0 tools: blog metrics, social network metrics, and widget metrics. Advertisers view these tools as channels for reaching consumers and are therefore interested in both the volume of traffic related to a particular tool, as well as the nature of the interaction or "conversations" occurring because of the tool. Examples of specific metrics identified by the IAB for these tools are listed in Table 8.7.

Tactical Metrics. Another way for organizations to define their objectives for social media is by tactical objectives. For instance, a company may express its tactical objectives as follows:

- Increase traffic to our Web site by 10 percent
- Increase requests for product information via our Web site by 15 percent
- Increase the number of people who create a user account on our Web site by 12 percent
- Increase the number of people who download our informational brochure by 25 percent

TABLE 8.7	Tool-Specific Metrics	
Blog Metrics	**Social Network Service Metrics**	**Widget Metrics**

• Number of conversation-relevant posts on the site
• Number of links to conversation-relevant posts on the site
• Earliest post date for conversation-relevant posts
• Latest post date for conversation-relevant posts
• Duration between earliest and last post date for conversation-relevant posts
• Mean-time between conversation-relevant posts
	• Unique visitors
	• Cost per unique visitor
	• Page views
	• Return visits
	• Proportion of visitors who interact with an ad or application
	• Time spent on site
	• Activity metrics related to:
	  • Contest/sweeps entries
	  • Coupons downloaded/redeemed
	  • Uploads (e.g., images, videos)
	  • Messages sent (e.g., bulletins, updates, e-mails, alerts)
	  • Invites sent
	  • Newsfeed items posted
	  • Comments posted
		• Number of application installations
		• Number of active users
		• Audience profile—user demographics from self-reported profile information
		• Unique user reach
		• Percentage of users who have installed application among the total social media audience
		• Growth of users within a specific time frame
		• Influence—average number of friends among users who have installed application.

Source: Adapted from Social Media Ad Metrics Definitions, Interactive Advertising Bureau (2009).

Based on these tactical objectives, companies can develop specific actions that support the objectives and then monitor progress. For instance, in order to increase traffic to the Web site, a company might start its own blog, identify and communicate with people who blog about the company or industry, or begin a Twitter campaign. It

IT at Work 8.5

Search Engine Optimization and Social Media

Haley Marketing Group is a New York marketing services company started in 1996 whose mission is to help companies in the staffing services industry develop long-term, profitable relationships with their customers. According to Haley's president David Searns, "In the early days, direct mail was our main communication vehicle for nurturing relationships. That evolved into e-mail marketing. Now, social media allows us and our clients to create, maintain and enhance relationships in ways that were never possible before."

Haley Marketing Group makes strategic use of social media. Everything they do online is part of an integrated plan to accomplish specific business objectives. Chief operating officer (COO) Victoria Kenward notes, "While we are a marketing company, we don't have an unlimited marketing budget. Like our clients, we need to maximize the impact of every dollar we spend to promote the company. That's why we don't do anything unless we have a very clear objective, and we track everything to make sure that we're getting the return we need on our efforts."

Getting Higher Ranks. Like other businesses, Haley Marketing want their company to rank near the top when prospective clients use Google or other search engines to identify companies in their industry. **Search engine optimization (SEO)** involves a number of strategies to influence how search engines categorize and rank Web pages. Search engine rankings are strongly influenced by the amount of traffic that flows to a Web site. More traffic means a higher ranking on search results.

Sales Leads. Haley Marketing Group relies on inbound marketing techniques for sales leads. Historically, direct mail and e-mail marketing had provided a sufficient quantity of well-qualified sales leads, but in recent years, the response from these lists declined. The volume of sales leads being produced was insufficient to meet corporate goals.

Integrated Social Media. The heart of Haley Marketing's strategy is the creation and distribution of content. The company Web site was reengineered in 2008 to be a platform for educational resources and information on Haley Marketing's services. In 2009, the site was augmented with landing pages offering free webinars, free e-book downloads, and other complimentary resources. In addition, the company produces a monthly e-mail newsletter, called *The Idea Club*, and Searns and all other employees are required to contribute a minimum of two blog posts a month to the *Ask Haley Blog*, which offers marketing tips and advice for staffing industry professionals.

According to Searns, "the greatest challenge we face is getting our target audience to become aware of, and engage with, the content we offer." To drive Web traffic, the company employs a variety of channels, including five monthly e-mail communications

to an opt-in list of staffing professionals, consistent promotion via social networks, search engine optimization, and online PR.

In terms of integrated social media, Searns, Kenward, and most of the company employees maintain an active presence on LinkedIn, a professional social networking service that has become the primary recruiting tool for many companies. When new content is created or events are scheduled, company employees use their LinkedIn status, LinkedIn events calendar, and LinkedIn groups to notify associates.

The company also maintains a Facebook page. Whenever new content is added to the *Ask Haley Blog*, the corporate Facebook page is automatically updated, and those individuals who have "liked" Haley Marketing are notified about the new content.

Haley Marketing also uses multiple Twitter accounts as another means of driving traffic to its site. Updates from the *Ask Haley* blog are automatically fed to the Twitter accounts of several employees, and the Twitter feeds are then fed to LinkedIn.

Members of Haley Marketing's network that want to subscribe to the blog can do so using an RSS feed button positioned next to each post. Readers also help promote the *Ask Haley Blog* by sharing links with their Facebook, LinkedIn, or Twitter networks simply by clicking on a small button next to the post.

344 Percent Increase in Traffic. Traffic to the Haley Marketing Group Web site has increased by 344 percent in the 18-month period that the company has employed its ISM strategy. Unique visitors to the site have increased 504 percent, and page views have increased by 105 percent. Most importantly, the volume of traffic from search engines has steadily increased from about 300 per month to over 1,500.

Source: Gregory R. Wood's personal interviews with David Searns and Victoria Kenward, 2010.

Review Questions

1. How did Haley Marketing Group define their objectives? What type of metric—for example tool, tactical, strategy or ROI—did they use to evaluate the success of their ISM strategy?

2. Did Haley Marketing Group use appropriate metrics for evaluating their efforts? What additional metric should they consider?

3. Compare Haley Marketing's traditional approach to communication with its social media tactics. What advantages does the company gain by using social media?

4. While the case discusses Haley Marketing Group's attempt to optimize Search Engine Optimization (SEO), what other social media objectives might they pursue with the tools they are using?

5. Research the issue of SEO online. What additional steps can a company like Haley Marketing Group take to increase rankings on popular search engines?

can then track traffic to the Web site, noting changes in total volume as well as identifying where the traffic is coming from. Using **tactical metrics** of this nature, the company can determine the relative impact that each of these specific social media activities is having on its objective.

Strategic Metrics. Various authors have attempted to identify higher-level objectives that more fully capture the potential of social media than what is described by focusing on a specific Web 2.0 tool or tactical objectives. In their influential book on social media strategies, Li and Bernoff (2008) identify five strategic objectives that companies can pursue using social media.

- **Listening:** Learn about your customers by paying attention to what they are saying online to one another or directly to you.
- **Talking:** Communicate with your customers by engaging in conversations.
- **Energizing:** Encourage current customers and fans to spread the word through ratings, reviews, and other positive "buzz."
- **Support:** Help customers solve problems by providing information and online resources like user forums, knowledge bases, and other tools.
- **Embracing:** Invite customers to generate ideas for new products and services.

Organizations that seek to optimize their performance in each of these areas will identify and implement social media tactics as well as track related metrics to evaluate progress toward goals. For instance, companies that use crowdsourcing to generate new product ideas might count the number of ideas submitted, the number of people who vote on the ideas, the number of positive vs. negative comments made about each idea, and so on. Companies that want to strategically "listen" to their markets might measure the number of "conversations," identify who is "talking," identify what people are saying, and so on.

A number of **social media monitoring services** have sprung up in recent years to provide this kind of data to business organizations, including Radian 6, Visible Technologies, Buzzlogic, and Cymfony. Most of these services use IT to track online content and then feed summary statistics into dashboards that can be used by their clients. However, smaller companies can use a variety of cost-free approaches to monitoring. *Moreover.com* and Yahoo track aggregated news about companies and industries. Technorati specifically tracks social media sites. Services such as Google Blog Search, Comments, and Blogpulse all offer ways to follow activity in the blogosphere. Once companies decide on the strategies they want to follow, they must identify information related to those strategies and then use a monitoring service to track the metrics.

ROI Metrics. Finally, many experts in the field of social media metrics emphasize the importance of what they call **social media ROI** (return on investment). This approach attempts to monetize the return on the cost of implementing social media strategies. This concept has inherent appeal because it addresses the need of the business organization to engage in activities that will contribute to its revenue goals. The ROI concept inspires considerable debate, however. Some maintain that the qualitative contributions of social media (e.g., relationships, conversations, trust, etc.) cannot be meaningfully expressed in monetary or quantitative terms. However, despite the potential difficulty associated with capturing all contributions of social media to a company's bottom line, the attempt must be made. Unless a reasonable link can be established between the costs associated with social media and a company's financial performance, some executives are unlikely to support social media initiatives, particularly in a depressed economy.

Sometimes the calculation of ROI for social media is easy. For instance, if an online retailer can increase traffic to its Web site by publishing a blog, then the company can track how many of these customers ultimately make a purchase after reading the blog. That data can be used to determine the blog's contribution to sales revenue. If a company notices an 18 percent drop in calls to its customer service line after implementing an online support forum, the reduction in call center expense can be readily calculated. Companies that see their sales leads increase because of their presence on a social network can estimate the resulting sales volume by applying their *yield rate* to this new set of inquiries (e.g., 1,000 new leads times a 7 percent yield rate equals 70 new customers). If a company knows how much each new customer is worth, then it can estimate the total revenue produced by its presence on the social network. Each of these is an example of a quantitative or **hard ROI metric.**

Other times, the link between important social media activity and a firm's financial performance is less direct. For instance, what is the relationship between an increase in the number of positive blog postings about a company's product and sales of the product? What is the relationship between the number of users who download a widget application sponsored by the company and company sales performance? To answer questions like these, it is necessary to make assumptions about consumer behavior or to make assumptions about the conversion rate of customers as they pass through stages—similar to the response hierarchy models discussed at the beginning of this section. For instance, a company that wishes to increase awareness for its brand or product may sponsor the distribution of a popular desktop widget or create a viral video for YouTube. While the company can track the number of people who use the widget or view the video, it would need to make some assumptions about the conversion rate, or the number of people who ultimately purchase something from the company as a result of these initiatives.

Considerable work remains to be done in the area of ROI metrics. However, we believe that companies will be most likely to adopt social media strategies when there is a clear link to their financial performance. As managers become comfortable with their capabilities and experience success in this area, they become less risk averse to engaging in social media activities to support strategic goals even when the link to revenues or costs is difficult to measure.

Review Questions

1. Why should companies use metrics to track social media activity?
2. List examples of tool-based metrics. What questions can an organization answer with this kind of information?
3. List social media strategies that businesses might pursue. What kind of information could they collect to see if they are being effective with social media?
4. Why do businesses find ROI metrics to be so compelling?
5. Why are ROI metrics for social media sometimes difficult to use or identify?

8.5 The Future of Social Media

If there's one thing that history has taught us, it's that the future is hard to predict. It might seem silly to try to predict what the future Internet will look like when it's clear that so many people are having trouble trying to understand all the implications of the Internet we have now. However, forward-thinking businesses and individuals are beginning to plan for the next evolution, which is being called **Web 3.0.** In an attempt to predict what the future Web will look like, Sramana Mitra (2007) has approached the question differently from others, who focus on specific apps or technologies that may emerge as part of the future Internet. Instead, she proposes a model that describes the characteristics of Web 3.0 from the user's perspective. According to Mitra (2007), the future Web will be defined as:

$$\text{Web } 3.0 = (4C + P + VS)$$

where
   3C = Content, Commerce, Community
4th C = Context
    P = Personalization
  VS = Vertical Search

The current Web is disjointed, requiring us to visit different Web sites to get content, engage in commerce, and interact with our network of relationships (community). The future Web will use context, personalization, and vertical search to make the 3Cs—content, commerce, and community—more relevant.

- **Context** defines the intent of the user; for example, trying to purchase music, find a job, or share memories with friends and family.
- **Personalization** refers to the user's personal characteristics that impact how relevant the 3C's are to the individual.
- **Vertical search** refers to a search strategy that focuses on finding information in a particular content area, such as travel, finance, legal, and medical.

Future Web sites, therefore, will maximize user experience by increasing performance on the factors outlined in this model.

SEMANTIC WEB

Tim Berners-Lee, creator of the technology that made the World Wide Web possible, is the director of the **World Wide Web Consortium (W3C).** This group is working on programming standards designed to make it possible for data, information, and knowledge to be shared even more widely across the Internet. In effect, it hopes to turn the Internet into one large database (or rather, a collection of databases) that we can access for wide-ranging purposes. The W3C is developing standards for a **metadata** language, or ways of describing data so that it can be used by a wide variety of applications. Much of the world's data is stored in files structured so that they can only be read by the programs that created them. With metadata, the information in these files can be tagged with information describing the nature of the data, where it came from, or how it's arranged. That way it can be read and used by a wide variety of applications.

It is helpful to think about the **Semantic Web** against the background of earlier Internet function. According to Jim Hendler and Tim Berners-Lee (2010), leading developers of the Semantic Web:

The Internet allowed programmers to create programs that could communicate without having to concern themselves with the network of cables that the communication had to flow over. The web allows programmers and users to work with a set of interconnected documents without concerning themselves with details of the computers that store and exchange those documents. The Semantic Web raises this to the next level, allowing programmers and users to make reference to real-world objects—whether people, chemicals, agreements, stars or whatever else—without concerning themselves with the underlying documents in which these things, abstract and concrete, are described.

THE LANGUAGE(S) OF WEB 3.0

The early Web was built using **Hypertext Markup Language (HTML).** As noted earlier, Web 2.0 was made possible, in part, by the development of languages like XML and JavaScript. The Semantic Web utilizes additional languages that have been developed by the W3C. These include **RDF (Resource Description Framework), OWL, and SPARQL.** RDF is a language used to represent information about resources on the Internet. It will describe these resources using metadata **URIs (uniform resource identifiers)** like "title," "author," "copyright and license information." It is one of the features that allow data to be used by multiple applications.

SPARQL is a Protocol and RDF Query Language. As the name implies, it is used to write programs that can retrieve and manipulate data stored in RDF format. OWL is the W3C Web Ontology Language used to categorize and accurately identify the nature of things found on the Internet. These three languages, used together, will enhance the context element of the Web, producing more fruitful and accurate information searches. Work continues by the W3C with input by programmers and the broader Internet community to improve the power and functionality of these languages.

In addition to these new programming languages, we expect to see a rise in the use of **Application Programming Interfaces (APIs).** An API is essentially a tool that allows programs to talk to or interact with one another. This makes it possible for one program to get information from another program. For instance, a popular API in current use is the Google Maps API (*code.google.com/apis/maps/*), which allows programmers to embed Google Maps into their own Web site applications. While many Web sites make use of APIs currently, this trend is expected to accelerate as more and more data becomes structured through the use of RDF and other Semantic Web programming tools (Iskold, 2007).

ARTIFICIAL INTELLIGENCE

Some people believe that the future Internet will be an intelligent Web. The application of **artificial intelligence (AI)** to our Internet experience could make things even more efficient and effective. Over time, our computers could learn about us, our interests, our information needs, our friends, and so on. This would create searches that produced more relevant information and tools for improving decision making and problem solving. To put it simply, the Semantic Web will vastly increase the amount of information that is available—so much so that human users are likely to be overwhelmed and unable to find relevant information that meets their specific needs. AI provides a potential solution, using rule-based systems to specify the context of an information search. The development of AI technologies will be a significant element in the potential success of the Semantic Web (Hendler and Berners-Lee, 2010).

AI may even change the way we interface with the Internet. Imagine a Web browser that can engage in conversation and ask questions to clarify the tasks we ask it to perform. The stage is being set for exactly this kind of experience. Visit *alicebot.org/logo-info.html* and click the "Chat with A.L.I.C.E." link for an example.

MOBILITY

We have already seen tremendous expansion in the kinds of equipment used to access the Internet. It is expected that this phenomenon will continue as Web browsers are built into smart phones, PDAs, e-readers, and other wireless devices. Many expect that the demand to stay connected to social networking services through wireless devices will increase. As smartphones, e-readers, and electronic pads and tablets move into the mainstream, Web programmers will increasingly be compelled to create sites that display nicely on small screens (see Figure 8.15). A number of mobile social networking services are emerging such as *foursquare.com* and *gowalla.com*. You read about several of these trends in Chapter 7.

Figure 8.15 Experts predict that demand for access to social networking services will drive the development of new technology for smartphones and other wireless devices.
(© *TheProductGuy/Alamy*)

BARRIERS TO BE
OVERCOME

Closed Data Sources. Obviously, the key to an information-rich Web is information. However, not everyone is particularly interested in having their data made available to anyone who wants it. You can probably think of many of situations in which data should be protected to prevent intrusions on privacy, to maintain public safety, and to protect national security. For many businesses, information is a key to their competitive position in the marketplace. The last thing they want to do is give away something of value and get nothing in return.

So what information should be made public? What should be kept private? The truth is that technology will be used to determine who has access to different kinds of information. W3C is working to develop such standards. Once companies are convinced that they can reliably restrict access of their data to an audience that they determine, they will be more likely to tag the data so that it can be accessed using Web 3.0 technologies by authorized users.

Incompatible Data Structures and Format. While the W3C is working to develop standards for tagging information with metadata labels, we must remember that across the Web, data exists in many different forms and structures. It is a formidable undertaking to layer all data files with information that makes it possible to be read by everyone. It remains to be seen how long it will be until most commonly used information is appropriately tagged to be used by Web 3.0 applications. While we sometimes talk about Web 3.0 as a future evolution, in fact, the new Web is already here—it just hasn't gotten very far yet.

Web developers are already hard at work applying Web 3.0 technologies. Companies like Evri, Kngine, and Lexxe have already created search engines based on Web 3.0 technologies. However, it won't be until much more data has been tagged and categorized that we'll begin to experience the power of these new search engine capabilities.

Interoperability Across Mobile Equipment, Web Sites, and Software. As the number of devices used to access online content proliferates, it makes it very difficult for Web programmers to keep up multiple versions of their site that work well in each format. This creates what some call a *fractured Web*, where each device can only access a portion of the available online content because of incompatibility.

Lack of Net Neutrality. Currently, most Internet content flows freely through networks maintained by large telecom companies. While these companies charge us for access to the Internet, they are not allowed to control the content that flows through the networks. This maintains a level playing field, guaranteeing that all Web content is equally accessible. If big telecom companies get their way, however, in the future they will be able to charge organizations for access to a "fast lane" on the Internet. This means that larger companies like Facebook, Microsoft, and Google will be able to pay to have their information delivered more quickly to your browser, while smaller companies and individuals with blogs and Web sites would be relegated to a relatively slow data pipe.

This might reduce the power of individuals and smaller, innovative companies, changing the democratic and social nature of the Internet. Opponents of net neutrality argue that they have spent billions on creating the infrastructure for high-speed Internet and should be able to manage it without interference from the government. They call concerns that smaller players will be pushed aside unrealistic and alarmist. Some even suggest that heavy-handed government regulation will slow the innovation of new and exciting online services. For an online debate of this topic, see the Opposing Views Web site: *opposingviews.com/questions/should-the-government-regulate-net-neutrality*.

Review Questions

1. Independent of any specific technology, what three capabilities does Sramana Mitra predict will become enhanced in Web 3.0?
2. What is the purpose of metadata labels used to tag data files?
3. What is the Semantic Web? How is it different from Web 2.0?
4. How might artificial intelligence play a role in the evolution of the future Web?
5. What are some of the barriers or challenges to be overcome in creating Web 3.0?

Key Terms

AJAX (Asynchronous JavaScript and XML) *225*
Application Programming Interface (API) *246*
artificial intelligence (AI) *246*
avatar *233*
balanced score card *239*
blog *223*
blogosphere *223*
content marketing *223*
context *245*
crowdsourcing *230*
CSS (Cascading Style Sheets) *226*
dashboard *239*
Enterprise 2.0 *235*
enterprise social network *219*
giant global graph *229*
groundswell *227*
hard ROI metrics *244*
HTML (Hypertext Markup Language) *226*
Integrated Social Media (ISM) *227*
intranet *237*
JavaScript *226*

mashup *224*
metadata *245*
metrics *239*
microblogging *234*
net neutrality *247*
newsgroups *228*
online communities *219*
open graph *232*
OWL (Web Ontology Language) *245*
personalization *245*
podcast *224*
Really Simple Syndication (RSS) *224*
Resource Description Framework (RDF) *245*
response hierarchies *240*
RSS reader *224*
SCM 2.0 *238*
Semantic Web *229*
sharing site *224*
Search engine optimization (SEO) *242*
social bookmarking *225*
social graph *229*
social media *225*
social media metrics *219*

social media monitoring services *243*
social media ROI metrics *243*
social network *219*
social network analysis (SNA) *229*
social networking service (SNS) *223*
SPARQL (Protocol and RDF Query Language) *245*
tactical metrics *243*
tag *225*
tag cloud *225*
tool-based metrics *241*
trackback *223*
URI (uniform resource identifier) *245*
Usenet *228*
vertical search *245*
virtual community *228*
Web 2.0 *219*
widget *224*
wiki *223*
World Wide Web Consortium (W3C) *245*
XML (Extendable Markup Language) *225*

Chapter Highlights and Insights

(Numbers refer to Learning Objectives)

❶ Web 2.0 consists of several tools that allow for enhanced social interaction on the Web.

❶ The new social Web is changing the way people communicate, their behavior, and their expectations for how business organizations will interact with them.

❶ Typical Web 2.0 applications include blogs, wikis, social networking services, sharing sites, RSS, widgets, mashups, and social bookmarking.

❷ Online communities predate the World Wide Web and can take a variety of forms.

❷ The social graph describes how we are all connected to one another through relationships. The giant global graph describes connections between people and/or documents and pages online.

❷ Social networking services are the dominant form of online community today and include companies like Facebook, Qzone, Orkut, and Habbo.

❸ Enterprise 2.0 refers to the use of Web 2.0 technologies for business use.

❸ The use of social media tools by businesses is likely to change the behaviors of employees and the way that managers lead their organizations.

❸ Businesses are using social media tools in human resources, marketing and sales, supply chain management, internal collaboration and communication, and other areas.

❹ Businesses use metrics to evaluate the efficiency and effectiveness of their social media efforts.

❹ Social media metrics fall into four categories: tool metrics, tactical metrics, strategic metrics, and ROI metrics.

❺ Technology is being created to make information search on the Web more effective. The future Internet is frequently referred to as the Semantic Web.

❺ The Semantic Web will make use of new languages such as RDF, OWL, and SPARQL. In addition, the use of Application Programming Interfaces (APIs) are expected to increase.

❺ A number of obstacles to Web evolution exist, including closed data sources, incompatible data structures, interoperability across equipment and software, and so on.

Questions for Discussion

1. Explain some of the fundamental differences between Web 1.0 and Web 2.0.

2. Compare the methods that companies used to communicate with their customers using the broadcast model vs. ways that companies can have conversations with their customers using Web 2.0 tools.

3. Describe why it is increasingly difficult to neatly categorize Web sites as purely blogs, social network services, sharing sites, wikis, and so on.

4. Is there really any meaningful difference between Web 2.0 and Enterprise 2.0?

5. How will the Social Web and individual user expectations for communication shape the workplace of the future? What are some specific ways in which managers or business leaders will have to adjust to this new environment?

6. Describe the fundamental changes that need to take place before the Semantic Web concept becomes widespread.

7. What role might artificial intelligence play in the Semantic Web? How will AI tools be helpful in the future?

8. How will concern for individual privacy affect the growth and expansion of social networking services and other Social Web applications?

Exercises and Projects

1. Using online sources, research Facebook's open graph initiative. Make a list of pros and cons regarding these changes from the viewpoint of a Facebook user.

2. Visit *youtube.com/user/SearchStories* and watch some Google Search Stories made by others. Then, using the tools on the site, make one of your own. Have fun and be creative. Share with your class.

3. If you are a member of Facebook and have over 100 "friends," use the social graph application to map out your Facebook network. See if you can identify any patterns or groupings that occur.

4. Using Google's blog search tool, identify some active blogs on a topic of interest to you. Leave comments in the response section (if available). See if the blog author or other readers reply.

5. Set up an account on two different RSS readers and use them to subscribe to some blogs that are of interest to you. Prepare a report or presentation comparing the strengths and weaknesses of each application.

6. Prepare a report on the economic activity that takes place on Second Life. Describe how people make money in the virtual world and identify the opportunities and challenges associated with making a living in Second Life.

Group Assignments and Projects

1. It seems like everyone is on Facebook, but there are other popular social networking services. Divide the class into teams of four or five students. Have each team create accounts on a lesser known SNS. For a period of one week, team members should interact on the new SNS and prepare a brief presentation on their experience. Be sure to discuss ways in which the alternative SNS is better or worse than Facebook.

2. Form a team of four or five people willing to set up accounts on Second Life, the virtual world SNS. Spend a week learning to control your avatar and interacting with your team members in the virtual world. Prepare a report or presentation on your experiences.

3. Have each team identify a topic on Wikipedia that it feels could be updated or enhanced with additional

information. Conduct research using credible sources and carefully make editorial changes to the Wikipedia page. Report back to the class on your experience.

4. Using online sources, have two teams research each side of the net neutrality debate. In class, each team should make a 5- to 10-minute presentation to support its position. At the end of the presentations, allow the rest of the class to ask questions. Conduct a vote to see which team made the most convincing argument.

5. Have each member of your team identify a social media monitoring service and explore the kind of information that companies like these can collect. Working together, prepare a report outlining the kind of data that is available to companies that want to know if their social media activities are effective.

Internet Exercises

1. Set up an account on *Twitter.com*. Also, download Tweetdeck, a useful interface for Twitter. Identify and "follow" people who seem to be sending messages that are of interest to you. Prepare a report on your experiences. Evaluate Twitter as a tool for social networking.

2. Visit the LinkedIn page for college graduates: *grads.linkedin.com/*. Using the information on this page, create a LinkedIn account and begin building your

professional network. Search the Internet for additional tips on using LinkedIn to find jobs and prepare a brief report on your findings.

3. Using a search engine, find four examples of mashup applications. Prepare a report describing each one. If possible, identify the Web site(s) the data is pulled from to create the application.

4. Create an account on *delicious.com*, the social bookmarking site. Actively use it to tag and categorize Web pages that you want to remember for future viewing. Use the search engine on delicious to find pages that other users have tagged. Compare the effectiveness of your searches to similar searches using Google and Yahoo.

5. Using a search engine, identify a list of Web 3.0 companies. Prepare a brief report that describes three or four of these firms and specifically identify the characteristics or capabilities that associate them with the new Semantic Web described in the chapter.

BUSINESS CASE

International Powerhouse Gets Ideas from Crowdsourcing

MKT   ETHICS

Since opening in 1971, Starbucks has grown into an international powerhouse with 15,000 stores in 50 countries. The typical Starbucks store serves drip-brew coffee, espresso, and other hot and cold drinks. They carry a variety of sandwiches, salads, and pastries. The company creates store environments that encourage people to come together to meet, socializing, work or relax (see Figure 8.16).

Figure 8.16 Starbucks is popular for its gourmet coffee drinks and the social environment it creates in its stores. (© Niall McDiarmid/Alamy)

In 2008, the company started *mystarbucksidea.com*, a social media site designed to solicit ideas and feedback from its customers. The site was built around four key themes:

• **Sharing:** Community members can post their ideas for Starbucks products, services, community contributions, or changes in operations.

• **Voting:** Anyone can create an electronic suggestion box. One of the things that makes *mystarbucksidea.com* special is that members can vote on the ideas. This helps the company prioritize ideas that are most likely to be attractive to its customers.

• **Discussing:** In addition to voting, members can provide feedback by commenting on the ideas of others. Designated "idea partners" (company employees) participate in these discussions, answer questions, and provide insights.

• **Seeing:** Community members can track an idea's progress toward implementation. A running tally of the votes (thumbs up or thumbs down) is displayed next to each entry. Next, ideas are tagged by the company with one of four status icons: "under review," "reviewed," "in the works," and "launched." This feedback helps demonstrate responsiveness.

Over 85,000 ideas have been submitted to the company through its crowdsourcing site since the launch. The company's social media initiative was rewarded in 2008 by Forrester Research with a Groundswell Award, recognizing it as an excellent example of using social media to embrace customers.

Credibility Gap?

However, the company's approach to tapping into customer wants and desires hasn't impressed everyone. John Moore (2010) questions how many of the ideas the company says its customers generated really came from the community, suggesting that most of the implemented ideas were already under consideration by the company. The biggest concern seems to be about credibility. Some critics say the overwhelmingly positive tone of the message postings and the relative lack of negativity suggests the possibility of censorship. That runs against the cultural norms of the social Web. Others suggest that if Starbucks was really interested in engaging people, it would be taken more seriously by participating in conversations at existing Web sites where people talk about the company (see *starbucksgossip.typepad.com/*).

Sources: Compiled from Board of Innovation (2009), Foley (2010), Suesz (2008), Moore (2010), Forrester Research (2008), Carroll (2008).

Questions

1. Visit *mystarbucksidea.com* and look around the site. What is your overall impression? Do you think the company is sincere in its approach to identifying new products and services?

2. What are the key elements of Starbucks' crowdsourcing site? How are they more than just an electronic suggestions box?

3. What are the chief concerns voiced by critics of *mystarbucksidea.com*? Do you think they are valid?

4. All things considered, do you think Starbucks took the right approach in using social media to engage its customers?

NONPROFIT CASE

NPOs and NGOs Use Social and Virtual Media

Charitable and not-for-profit organizations (NPOs) try to make a positive contribution to their local, national or global communities. The key word here is *community*. These organizations have a high probability of benefiting from the latest social media trends, but may lack the resources and staff to integrate the latest technology into their strategies. That's where NetSquared, and its parent organization, TechSoup Global come in.

Promoting Social Change

These organizations help NPOs and nongovernmental organizations (NGOs) use the social nature of the Web to increase their impact and promote positive social change. Their goals are to train and assist NPOs and NGOs to use social media to:

• Improve/increase advocacy efforts
• Find new supporters (around the globe)
• Reengage the supporters
• Have greater influence on national and global policy
• Get more and better press
• Increase value for NPO supporters (opportunities to be creative/engage/things to do)
• Reinvent the possibilities of collaboration on a global scale
• Build more and better partnerships
• Help millions of NPO and NGO constituents to become more active and accomplish more through their NPO and NGO Internet communities.

First and foremost, NetSquared and TechSoup Global demonstrate to other organizations how to use social media by actively using Web 2.0 tools themselves. Their Web sites are communities, offering opportunities for representatives of NPO/NGO organizations to communicate, collaborate, and interact around the topics of IT and social media use. They maintain active blogs and encourage dialogue and exchange. Both organizations maintain Facebook pages with a combined audience of over 3,000 fans. They use the social network service to promote new blog posts, events, and relevant third-party information. Twitter is also a key tool, used to promote webinars and new Web site content as well as engage in conversations with followers.

Virtual Worlds

Perhaps one of the most innovative things they've done is to create a virtual community on Second Life called "Nonprofit Commons." Nonprofit Commons is actually a collection of four virtual locations on the 3-D social network service. One goal is to help NPO community members learn how to use the virtual world to accomplish their objectives. Meetings, training sessions, networking, and informal discussion all take place in the Nonprofit Commons.

NetSquared is particularly focused on social media use and encourages broad-based collaboration among its 20,000 registered users. In 2004, NetSquared organized a Challenge Program designed to identify, define, and accelerate innovative projects. Using social media tools to implement a crowdsourcing strategy, the community proposes worthwhile projects, selects the ones with most potential, provides feedback to project teams, and provides ongoing support until the projects are completed. This collaborative, community-based approach is now being used by other organizations that recognize the value of collective response to community problems.

Extended Reach and Contributions

Implementing these social media practices has yielded impressive results for TechSoup Global and NetSquared. The organizations interact with over 400,000 individuals worldwide, who in turn are committed to improving their communities. Their community reaches people in over 190 countries, and they collaborate with over 35 major technology providers such as Microsoft, Adobe, Cisco Systems, and Intuit to provide product donations and support to charitable and community organizations around the world. They estimate that their combined contributions to the NPO/NGO sector saved these organizations as much as 1.5 billion dollars in 2010.

Sources: TechSoup Global Annual Report (2010), *Techsoupglobal.org* (2010), *NetSquared.org* (2010), Guthrie (2009) and *nonprofitcommons.org* (2010).

Questions

1. Why is social media a particularly attractive alternative to traditional communication methods for NPOs?
2. Describe the different "audiences" NPOs might try to reach using social media.
3. Many NPOs, NGOs, and government agencies serve the poor and disadvantaged, many of whom have limited access to the Internet. Identify some ways that social media might still be an important tool for these groups.
4. How has Netsquared leveraged the unique features of Second Life? What benefits does this approach offer to traditional ways of accomplishing the same thing?
5. How might these organizations utilize social media metrics to evaluate the effectiveness of their efforts?

ANALYSIS USING SPREADSHEETS
Estimating the ROI of Social Media

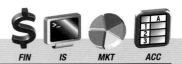

FIN   IS   MKT   ACC

Notes

For this analysis, go to the Student Web Site to download the file. An image of that file is used to explain the scenario and required analysis.

Refer to the *Analysis Using Spreadsheets* exercise in Chapter 1. The Chapter 1 analysis exercise stated that the results of the analysis will be combined with the costs of the campaigns (when those costs become known) to determine the value of these IT strategies now that those costs are known. In this analysis, you are asked to include the social media campaign costs to calculate the estimated ROI.

Recall that customer attrition rate is the rate at which a company loses customers. Customer retention rate is the percent of customers that stay with the company. Mathematically, customer attrition rate = 100% − customer retention rate.

Scenario

InterMobile-2020 Company has asked you to prepare an additional analysis on the spreadsheet to estimate the ROI of the four social media investments.

The cost of each campaign is shown in Figure 8.17. The estimated average profit per retained customer is $10. The total value of the campaigns is represented as:

IMPROVEMENT = increase in number of retained customers • $10

The investment cost is the sum of the four campaign costs.

INVESTMENT COST = $2,000,000 (see Figure 8.17)

InterMobile-2020 Company

ROI Calculation

Number of customers, January 2011	1,500,000
Controllable Customer Attrition Rate (average rate per quarter) [CCAR]	6%

Average Profit per Customer	$	10

IT-based Strategies to Reduce the *Controllable Customer Attrition Rate* (CCAR)	Percent Reduction in CCAR	Estimated Cost of the Campaign or App	
#1 - Launch campaign using 2D tags	1.25%	$	700,000
#2 - Create campaign on Facebook	0.50%	$	425,000
#3 - Launch viral marketing campaign	0.75%	$	525,000
#4 - Develop an iPhone app	1.50%	$	350,000
Total Reduction in CCAR	4.00%	Total Investment $	2,000,000

	2012			
	Q1	Q2	Q3	Q4
Expected Loss of Customers, no Strategy (6% CCAR)	90,000	84,600	79,524	74,753
Number of Customers Remaining at End of Quarter	1,410,000	1,325,400	1,245,876	1,171,123
Expected Loss of Customers, Using All 4 Marketing Campaigns (2% CCAR)	30,000			
Number of Customers Remaining at End of Quarter	1,470,000			

IMPROVEMENTS DUE TO IT-BASED CAMPAIGNS — INCREASED # OF RETAINED CUSTOMERS

Improvement in # of Customers Retained Due to Campaigns (Difference Between the Q4 Numbers)	
Average Profit per Customer	$ 10
TOTAL VALUE OF CAMPAIGNS [improvement • $10]	$ —
ROI = (Total Value of Campaigns − Total Investment)/Total Investment * 100%=	

Figure 8.17 ROI spreadsheet for Chapter 8.

The general formula for ROI is:

ROI = (IMPROVEMENT − INVESTMENT COST) / INVESTMENT COST • 100%

A positive ROI indicates that the investment in the campaigns makes a positive contribution to profits.

Analysis

You may want to refer to your completed spreadsheet from Chapter 1 or start the analysis using the spreadsheet on the textbook's Web site. Perform the calculations to estimate the ROI. Figure 8.17 illustrates that spreadsheet and the highlighted cells requiring formulas to calculate the ROI.

Based on the results of your ROI analysis, what do you recommend?

References

Abram, C., and L. Pearlman, *Facebook for Dummies.* Hoboken, NJ: John Wiley & Sons, 2008.

Alexa Topsites, May 2010. *alexa.com/topsites*

Barefoot, D., "Web 1.0 vs Web 2.0," DarrenBarefoot. May 2006. *darrenbarefoot.com/archives/2006/05/web-10-vs-web-20.html*

Barnes, N, and E. Mattson, "The Fortune 500 and Social Media: A Longitudinal Study of Blogging and Twitter Usage by America's Largest Companies," 2009. *umassd.edu/cmr/studiesresearch/2009f500.cfm*

Bennett, J., "Will Social Media Kill Off the Intranet in Years to Come?" *Internalcommshub.com,* 2009. *internalcommshub.com/open/channels/whatsworking/intranetend.shtml*

Berners-Lee, T. "Giant Global Graph", Timbl's blog, Decentralized Information Group, Nov. 2007. *Dig.csail.mit.edu/breadcrumbs/blog/4*

Board of Innovation, "My Starbucks Idea, Free Crowdsourcing of Product Ideas," July 2009. *boardofinnovation.com/2009/07/11/my-starbucks-idea-free-crowdsourcing-of-product-ideas/*

Carr, D. "Is Business Ready for Second Life?," *Baseline Magazine,* March, 2007. *Baselinemag.com*

Carroll, B., "Re-Experiencing Starbucks: Update 5—MyStarbucksIdea," Customers Rock, March 2008. *customersrock.wordpress.com/2008/03/28/re-experiencing-starbucks-update-5-mystarbucksidea/*

Dijoux, C. "Enterprise 2.0 Explained to Our Managers in 10 Principles," Hypertextual, November 2009. *ceciiii.wordpress.com/2009/11/08/enterprise-2-0-managers-in-10-principles/*

Dilworth, D. "Blendtec Mixes Online Video to Raise Brand Awareness." DMNews. June 06, 2007 *dmnews.com/blendtec-mixes-online-video-to-raise-brand-awareness/article/95826/*

Erickson, D. "Revenge of the Customer: United Breaks Guitars," eStrategy Internet Blog, July 2009. *e-strategyblog.com/2009/07/revenge-of-the-customer-united-airlines-breaks-guitars/*

Facebook Statistics, 2010. *facebook.com/press/info.php?statistics*

Foley, M., "MyStarbucksIdea.com—The Truth Behind the Hype," PluggedIn.com, March 2010. *pluggedinco.com/blog/bid/31075/MyStarbucksIdea-com-the-truth-behind-the-hype*

Forrester Research, 2008. "Forrester Groundswell Awards Winners." *forrester.com/Groundswell/embracing/mystarbucksidea.html*

Guthrie, J., "TechSoup Sees Upside for Nonprofits in Downturn," *San Francisco Chronicle,* March 22, 2009. *articles.sfgate.com/2009-03-22/business/17214653_1_increase-donations-charities-grant-makers*

Happe, R. "Social Media Metrics," *The Social Organization,* 2008. *http://www.thesocialorganization.com/social-media-metrics.html*

Harvard Business School Working Knowledge (HBSWK) First Look, May 4, 2010. *hbswk.hbs.edu/item/6418.html*

Harvey, M., "Facebook Sets Up Google-War with Vast Expansion Through Open Graph," *Times Online,* 2010. *technology.timesonline.co.uk/tol/news/tech_and_web/the_web/article7104354.ece*

Helm, B. "As Seen on YouTube. Order Now!" *Newsweek.* December, 2006. *nybw.businessweek.com/the_thread/brandnewday/archives/2006/12/as_seen_on_youtube_order_now-html*

Hendler, J., and T. Berners-Lee, "From the Semantic Web to Social Machines: A Research Challenge for AI on the World Wide Web," *Artificial Intelligence,* 174, 2010.

Hird, J., "20+More Mind Blowing Social Media Statistics," Digital Marketing Blog. August 2009. *econsultancy.com/blog/4402-20+-more-mind-blowing-social-media-statistics.*

Hof, R. D., "My Virtual Life," *BusinessWeek*, May 1, 2008.

Johnson, G. J., and P. J. Ambrose, "Neo-Tribes: The Power and Potential of Online Communities in Health Care," *Communications of the ACM,* January 2006.

Iskold, A., "The Structured Web—A Primer," Read Write Web, October 2007. *readwriteweb.com/archives/structured_web_primer.php*

Levine, R., C. Locke, D. Searls, and D. Weinberger, D., *The Cluetrain Manifesto: The End of Business as Usual,* Perseus Books, Cambridge, MA, 2000.

Li, C. and J. Bernoff, *"Groundswell: Winning in a World Transformed by Social Technologies,"* Boston: Harvard Business Press, 2008.

McAffee, A., "Interview: Andrew McAfee—What Is Web/Enterprise 2.0?" 2008. [Video File] *youtube.com/watch?v=6xKSJfQh89k*

Mitra, S., "Web 3.0=(4C + P + VS)," Sramanamitra.com, 2007. *sramanamitra.com/2007/02/14/web-30-4c-p-vs*

Moore, J.,"Tough Love for Starbucks," *BrandAutopsy.com,* 2010. *brandautopsy.typepad.com/brandautopsy/2010/01/tough-love-for-starbucks.html*

Negroni, C., "With Video, a Traveler Fights Back." *The New York Times,* October 2009. *nytimes.com/2009/10/29/business/29air.html*

Network Solutions and The Robert H. Smith School of Business, University of Maryland, "The State of Small Business Report: December 2009 Survey of Small Business Success," *Grow Smart Business,* 2010. *growsmartbusiness.com/sbsi-wave-iii/introduction/*

O'Reilly, T., "What Is Web 2.0: Design Patterns and Business Models for the Next Generation of Software," September 2005. *oreilly.com/web2/archive/what-is-web-20.html*

Pearson, R., "Imagineering a Windows (Social) Media Player," *The Parallax View.* 2010. *theparallaxview.com/2010/04/windows-social-media-player/*

Reynolds, C., "Smashed Guitar, YouTube Song—United Is Listening Now," *L.A. Times Daily Travel and Deal Blog,* July 2009. *travel.latimes.com/daily-deal-blog/index.php/smashed-guitar-youtu-4850/*

RMIT News, "Social networking around the world." February 19, 2010. *rmit.com.au*

Social Media Ad Metric Definitions, Interactive Advertising Bureau. 2009. *iab.net/ugc_metrics_definitions*

Suesz, E., "MyStarbucksIdea.com: A Half-Full Idea," Get Satisfaction Blog, March 2008. *blog.getsatisfaction.com/2008/03/30/mystarbucksideacom-a-half-full-idea/*

TechSoup Global Annual Report, "Our Currency Is Contribution: New Equations for Social Change," 2010. *techsoupglobal.org/*

The Nielsen Company "Facebook and Twitter Post Large Year over Year Gains in Unique Users", May, 2010. *blog.nielsen.com/nielsenwire/global/facebook-and-twitter-post-large-year-over-year-gains-in-unique-users/*

Vander Veer, E., *Facebook: The Missing Manual.* Cambridge, MA: Pogue Press, 2008.

Vogelstein, F., "Great Wall of Facebook: The Social Network's Plan to Dominate the Internet—And Keep Google Out," *Wired Magazine.* June 2009. *wired.com/techbiz/it/magazine/17-07/ff_facebookwall*

Ward, T., "The Social Intranet," *IntranetBlog.com,* 2010. *intranetblog.blogware.com/blog/_archives/2010/4/19/4509510.html*

Weaver, A., and B. Morrison, "Social Networking," *Computer,* February 2008.

Wesch, M., "Web 2.0 . . . The Machine Is Us/ing Us," [video file] March 2007. *youtube.com/watch?v=NLlGopyXT_g*

Wikipedia, "Ajax (Programming)," 2010. *en.wikipedia.org/wiki/Ajax_programming*

Chapter

9

Operational Planning and Control Systems

Learning Objectives

❶ Describe how functional systems support managers and workers at the operational level.

❷ Understand the support provided by manufacturing and production/operations systems.

❸ Understand the support provided by marketing and sales systems.

❹ Understand the support provided by accounting and finance systems.

❺ Understand the support provided by human resources systems.

Integrating *IT*

ACC   FIN   MKT   OM   HRM   IS

QUICK LOOK at Chapter 9, Operational Planning and Control Systems

This section introduces you to the business issues, challenges, and IT solutions in Chapter 9. Topics and issues mentioned in the Quick Look are explained in the chapter.

Operational-level information systems (or simply **operational ISs**) capture and record all of the company's data from operations and perform the routine transactions needed to conduct business on an ongoing day-to-day basis. They are planning and control systems. At their best, operational ISs put the right information in the right hands at the right time, giving those on the front-line the ability to respond to customers and suppliers, resolve production issues, and react to changing conditions as quickly as possible. The support provided by operational ISs can be broken into two components:

• **Operational awareness:** The ability to see at any given time what's happening in the department or functional area. The business functions are manufacturing and production, accounting, finance, sales and marketing, and human resources (HR).

• **Operational responsiveness:** The ability to respond to unexpected changes in conditions and customer demands as they occur, enabling business units to take advantage of opportunities, to protect against threats, and/or to improve efficiency.

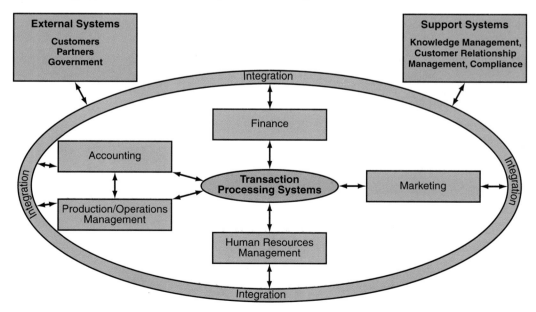

Figure 9.1 Functional areas, TPS, and integration connection. Note the flow of information from the TPS to the functional systems. Flow of information between and among functional systems is done via the integration component.

In this chapter, you learn more about functional information systems that support the operational level of the organization. Functional ISs get much of their data from transaction processing systems, TPSs, which you read about in Chapters 1 and 2. Most applications in business intelligence, e-commerce, and customer relationship management (CRM) use data from several functional ISs. As such, getting a complete view of what's going on requires integrating the functional systems with the TPS and with external business apps and support systems, as diagrammed in Figure 9.1.

The focus of this chapter is on information systems that support the operational level, or operations, and the benefits and issues of integrating functional ISs shown in Figure 9.1. These systems are critical to the organization's ability to conduct business and to its performance.

Delivery Chain Integration Benefits Scandinavian Food Group

OM   MKT   IS

In 1999, Axfood AB was formed by the merger of over 1,300 Scandinavian (Sweden and Finland) food retailers. The purposes of the merger were to build brand recognition, to be able to respond better to changing customer demands, and to improve efficiency. In 2006, the company consolidated sales of 28.8 billion SEK (Sweden Kronor; approximately 3 billion Euros) and over 7,000 employees.

Merger Results in Incompatible IT Solutions

Axfood invested approximately 200 million SEK (20.4 million euros) in a common IT platform for the Axfood Group's core businesses to fully integrate its wholesale and retail operations. Mats Munkhammar, Axfood's chief of IT architecture, explained: "As a direct consequence of this consolidation, we were left with a very diverse IT infrastructure with many different solutions. So we had to go and look for a central integration engine, a platform that would allow us to keep our existing solutions while adding on new components and removing old ones when the time came."

New Flex and Scalable Architecture

Axfood selected two Progress software (*progress.com*) products: Progress SonicMQ and Progress Sonic ESB (enterprise service bus). Progress Software Corporation is a global software company that helps enterprises respond quickly to changing conditions and customer interactions. (Visit *progress.com*, and click on the tab *What We Offer* to view their **tag cloud**, which you read in Chapter 8.) Sonic ESB combines messaging, Web services, XML transformation, and intelligent routing—all of which are used by managers and workers to connect to apps throughout the enterprise.

Figure 9.2 POS terminals collect operational data.
(© *Joshua Hodge Photography/iStockphoto*)

With integrated operational systems, Axfood can handle high-volume POS (point-of-sale) data as well as the following:

- Coordinate secure, reliable transmission of POS data from retail locations to a central data warehouse, enabling more efficient inventory management and business activity monitoring.
- Connect suppliers and logistics, which cut the *order-to-delivery* time by 33 percent—from three days to two days.
- Add new solutions for future business processes with minimal incremental investment.
- Keep shelves stocked with the products consumers want, which increased sales.

For Class Discussion and Debate

1. Scenario for Brainstorming and Discussion: Supermarkets, food retailers, and others in the grocery industry operate on thin (low) profit margins. To maintain profits, they attempt to make up for thin margins with volume. Visit *data360.org* to compare the profit margins (shown as Data Graphs) of selected industries. The data graph shows that the profit margin of *grocery sales* in 2005 Q4 was .90% (less than 1.00%). In contrast, the profit margins of *Internet companies* were 21.30% and those of security software were 17.90%. You can see the detailed data by clicking "Generate CSV," which generates a spreadsheet.

a. Discuss why it makes sense for Axfood to invest approximately 200 million SEK (20.4 million euros or US$25.6 million) to integrate operations despite its thin profit margin.

b. Was it necessary for the food retailers to merge prior to investing in the IT to integrate operations? Explain.

2. Debate: Refer to Porter's five competitive forces that shape strategy model, which you read about in Chapter 1. You can also view Porter discussing that model on YouTube (*youtube.com/*).

a. Debate how and to what extent the increased use of IT to manage operations in the grocery industry and to connect to suppliers, as Axfood has done, impact each of those five forces.

b. Two possible outcomes are that the degree of competition in the grocery industry increases because of required IT investments or it decreases the degree of competition. Select one of those two positions and explain it. You may need to make reasonable assumptions to support your position.

9.1 Management Levels, Functions, and Operational Systems

Three levels of management and decision making are modeled as a pyramid to show their hierarchy. Starting at the bottom of the pyramid shown in Figure 9.3, the levels are operational, managerial or administrative, and strategic. Each level of management has its own data needs, decision-making responsibilities, and time horizons.

• At the **strategic level,** senior or top-level management plan and make decisions that set or impact the long-term direction of the entire organization. These decisions are visionary and future-oriented, defining the mission, objectives, and strategy. External data about the economy, competitors, and business trends is essential to management's SWOT (strengths, weaknesses, opportunities, and threats) analysis, planning, and decisions.

• At the **managerial or administrative level,** middle-level managers make tactical decisions that focus on intermediate-term issues to fulfill the organization's mission, objectives, and strategy. Control is important at this level. Middle-level managers set goals for their departments or business units that are consistent with organizational goals set by senior management. External and internal data are important for decision making, which often has a one- to three-year time horizon.

Figure 9.3 Robert Anthony's model of organizational levels, decision making, planning, and control.

258

- At the **operational level,** lower-level managers, supervisors, and workers need detailed data, in real time or near real time, and the ability to respond to what they learn from functional ISs. Decision making is for the immediate or short-term because decisions are made to control the day-to-day activities or operations. The purpose of control is to identify deviations from objectives and plans as soon as possible in order to take corrective action. Tracking sales, inventory levels, orders, and customer support are examples of control activities. Internal data is most important at this level.

TRADITIONAL FUNCTIONAL IS DESIGNS

Traditionally, ISs were designed within each functional area to support and increase its effectiveness and efficiency. However, the traditional functional structure may not be the best structure for some organizations, because certain business processes involve activities that are performed in several functional areas. Suppose, for example, a customer wants to buy a particular product. When the customer's order arrives at the marketing department, the customer's credit needs to be approved by finance. Someone in production/operations (see Figure 9.4) determines whether the product is in the warehouse. If it is there, then picking and shipping departments pack the product, print the mailing label, and arrange for delivery. Accounting prepares a bill for the customer, and finance may arrange for shipping insurance. The flow of work and information between the different departments may not work well, and coordination may be difficult, creating delays or poor customer service.

One solution is to integrate the functional departments via ISs that facilitate communication, coordination, and control.

OPERATIONAL SYSTEMS AND DATA QUALITY

The various operational functions interact, passing data from one to the other. For example, when products are produced and shipped, then production and shipping departments inform the accounting department to process and charge the buyer's credit card or issue an accounts payable (A/P). In the process, files are generated to record the details of the activity. The data requirements of the operational-level units are extensive and routine, rarely changing because they depend on fixed sources of input and **standard operating procedures (SOP).** As the term implies, a standard operating procedure, or SOP, is a clearly defined and mandatory procedure to be followed without deviation to complete a process or function, such as a quality control process or function. SOPs document the step-by-step ways in which activities are to be performed.

Data in a TPS has a different significance to many other systems. If data is lost, it has financial implications. As such, it is critical that businesses have procedures to ensure that data is secure and accurate and that data integrity is maintained.

- **Data security:** Data needs to be protected from malicious or unintentional corruption, unauthorized modification, theft, or natural hazards such as fire. Infosec is covered in greater detail in Chapter 5.

Figure 9.4 Preparing factory orders for shipping. (© API/Alamy)

TABLE 9.1	Key Characteristics of a TPS

- Large volumes of data are processed.
- Data sources are mostly internal, and the output is intended mainly for internal users and trading partners.
- Data is processed on a regular basis: hourly, daily, weekly, biweekly, and so on.
- Processing is done at high speed due to the high volume.
- Current or past data is monitored and collected.
- Input and output data are structured. Processed data are fairly stable, so they are formatted in a standard fashion.
- There is a high level of detailed raw data.
- There is low computation complexity, such as basic math and statistical calculations.
- Accuracy, data integrity, and security are critical. Privacy of personal data is strongly related to TPSs.
- High reliability is required. The TPS is the lifeblood of the organization. Interruptions in the flow of TPS data can disrupt operations and damage the organization.
- Quick search and query processing capacities are a must, often in real time.

- **Data accuracy:** Every effort is needed to ensure that data is accurate and in standardized format. Data validation is used to detect and correct data entry errors as well as to standardize address data, names, and other data types.
- **Data integrity:** The overall reliability of the data must be ensured. Data integrity with real-time systems involves the ACID test, which is short for atomicity, consistency, isolation, and durability:
  - *Atomicity:* If all steps in a transaction are not completed, then the entire transaction is canceled.
  - *Consistency:* Only operations that meet data validity standards are allowed. For instance, systems that record checking accounts only allow unique check numbers for each transaction. Any operation that repeated a check number would fail to ensure that the data in the database is correct and accurate. Network failures can also cause data consistency problems.
  - *Isolation:* Transactions must be isolated from each other. For example, bank deposits must be isolated from a concurrent transaction involving a withdrawal from the same account. Only when the withdrawal transaction is successfully completed will the new account balance be reported.
  - *Durability:* Backups by themselves do not provide durability. A system crash or other failure must not cause any loss of data in the database. Durability is achieved through separate transaction logs that can be used to re-create all transactions from a known checkpoint. Other ways include database mirrors that replicate the database on another server.

Other key characteristics of TPSs are summarized in Table 9.1.

OPERATIONAL SUBSYSTEMS

Functional systems are composed of subsystems, or modules, that support specific activities performed in the functional area. Examples of subsystems of the key functional areas are:

- **Manufacturing and production:** purchasing, quality control, scheduling, shipping, receiving
- **Accounting:** accounts receivable, accounts payable, general ledger, budgeting
- **Finance:** cash management, asset management, credit management, reporting
- **Sales and marketing:** order tracking, pricing, sales commissions, market research
- **HR:** payroll, employee benefits, training, compensation, employee relations, staffing, performance appraisal

TRANSACTION PROCESSING SYSTEMS AND CORE OPERATIONS

Figure 9.5 Server at a café uses a mobile scanner to process customers' credit card payment. (© *Chris Cooper-Smith/Alamy*)

Core operations are supported by TPSs that monitor, collect, store, process, and disseminate information for all financial and nonfinancial (e.g., hiring) transactions. Transactions occur when a company produces a product or provides a service. For example, to produce cell phones, a manufacturer needs to order materials and parts, pay for labor and electricity, create a shipment order, and bill customers. The bank that maintains the cell phone company's checking account keeps the account balance up-to-date, disperses funds for the checks written, accepts deposits, and posts statements.

Every transaction generates additional transactions. Purchasing materials changes the inventory level; paying employees reduces cash-on-hand. Because the computations involved in most transactions are simple and the transaction volume is large and repetitive, such transactions are fairly easy to computerize.

Activities and Methods of TPS. Regardless of the specific data processed by a TPS, a fairly standard process occurs, whether in a manufacturer, in a service firm, or in a government organization. First, raw data is collected by people or sensors, and then the data is entered into the computer via input device, as shown in Figure 9.5.

Generally speaking, organizations try to automate the TPS data entry as much as possible to minimize errors and data entry time.

Next, the system processes data in one of two basic ways: *batch* or *online processing*. In **batch processing,** the firm collects data from transactions as they occur and stores it. The system then prepares and processes the collected data periodically, such as at the end of the workday. Batch processing is useful for operations that require processing for an extended period of time. Once a batch job begins, it continues until it is completed. Examples are payroll and billing.

In **online processing,** data is processed as soon as the transaction occurs, in *real time*.

Examples. When a component part is used, an order for a new one is placed. When you place an order online, your credit card authorization is done instantly.

To implement online transaction processing, master transaction files containing data about business entities are stored in an operational database (see Figure 9.6).

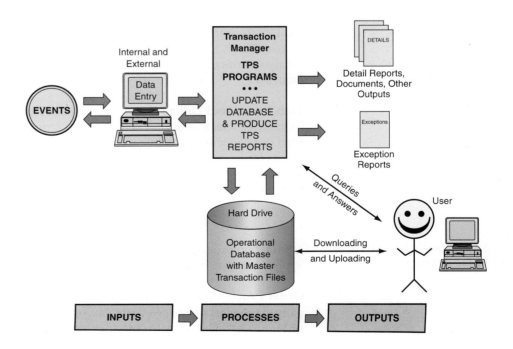

Figure 9.6 Flow of information in transaction processing.

IT at Work 9.1

Cut Costs and Delivery Time with TPS

Here are examples of how TPSs have saved time or money.

FedEx-Kinko's. Each time you make a copy at Kinko's, both a copying transaction and a payment transaction occur. In the past you received a device (a card the size of a credit card) and inserted it into a control device attached to the copy machine, which recorded the number of copies that you made. Then you stood in line to pay: The cashier placed the device in a reader to see how many copies were made. Your bill was computed, with tax added. Kinko's cost was high with this system, and some customers were unhappy about standing in line to pay for only a few copies. With Kinko's new system, you insert your credit card into a control device, make the copies, print a receipt, and you're done.

Carnival Line. Carnival Line, an operator of cruise ships, needs to rapidly process up to 2,500 people leaving the ship at the ports of call and later returning to the ship. The company used to use printed name lists for manual checkmarks. Today, passengers place a smart card into a reader so the company knows who left the ship, when they left, and who returned. Each smart card reader can process over 1,000 people in 30 minutes. In the past, 10 to 15 employees processed passengers leaving and returning to the ship, which took almost an hour. Now, one person supervises two card readers.

Sprint Nextel. Sprint Nextel has improved its order processing for new cell phones. In the past it took a few days for a customer to get a new telephone line. With its new system, Sprint can process an order in a few hours. The order application itself takes less than 10 minutes, experiences fewer errors, and can be executed on electronic forms on a salesperson's desktop or laptop computer.

Discussion Questions: Could FedEx-Kinko's operate completely without employees at its outlets? What effect does Carnival's smart-card reader have on security? Whose time is being saved at Sprint Nextel?

In **online transaction processing (OLTP),** transactions are processed as soon as they occur. Data can be accessed directly from the operational database. The transaction files containing data about business activities, such as items ordered, are also stored in online files until they are no longer needed. This series of processes ensures that transaction data is available to all applications and that all data is kept updated. Data from the TPS can be further processed and stored in a data warehouse.

The flow of data in a TPS is shown in Figure 9.6. An event, such as a customer purchase, is recorded by the TPS program via a barcode reader at a retail checkout. The processed data (output) can be in the form of a report. Users can query the TPS for information, such as "How many units of item A were sold each month of year 20XX?" The system will provide the appropriate answer by accessing a database containing transaction data, as shown with the bidirectional arrows in Figure 9.6.

Web-Based and Online Transaction Processing Systems. With OLTP and Web technologies such as portals and extranets, suppliers can look at the firm's inventory level or production schedule in *real time*. Suppliers are then able to assume responsibility for inventory management and ordering in what is known as **vendor-managed inventory (VMI).** Customers, too, can enter data into the TPS to track orders directly. Other Web-based applications are described in *IT at Work 9.1.*

TASKS IN TRANSACTION PROCESSING

Transaction processing exists in all functional areas. Here we describe in detail one application that crosses several functional areas—order processing.

Order Processing. Orders for goods or services may flow from customers to a company via a smart device, Web site, fax, or other electronic method. Fast and effective order processing is a key to customer satisfaction. Orders can also be internal—from

IT at Work 9.2

First Choice Ski Beats Its Competition with Yahoo! Web Analytics

First Choice Ski (*firstchoice-ski.co.uk/*) holds a 14 percent market share of the online U.K. ski market. TUI Travel, its parent company, is an international leisure travel group that operates in 180 countries and serves more than 30 million customers.

Increasing Margins by Tracking Customers. Margins are tight in the highly competitive tour operator industry. As a result, real-time reporting is key to maintaining a profitable business. By implementing Yahoo! Web Analytics (*web.analytics.yahoo.com/*), First Choice Ski could stay informed in near-real time of its customers' online behaviors. Customers spend a lot of time researching and selecting their vacation. Simon Rigglesworth, e-commerce manager, explained: "We see users return multiple times from multiple sources such as paid search, e-mail and even social networking as they try to find the vacation that suits them the best. Capturing as much information as possible allows us to identify the best way to complete the sale and optimize for it."

Yahoo! Web Analytics. After experimenting with fee-based analytics packages, First Choice Ski selected Yahoo! Web Analytics (YWA), which is free. Web analyst Penelope Bellegarde used the *Search Phrases Report* in YWA to leverage factors driving visitors to First Choice Ski. She said: "If we notice a specific destination is driving a lot of visits to the site, then it is very likely we will promote that destination on the homepage."

The *Internal Campaign Report* is valuable because of the numerous travel promotions on First Choice Ski. Bellegarde monitors the number of clicks and number of sales generated by the campaigns; when a low ratio of sales to clicks is noticed, she adjusts the campaign accordingly.

Using YWA tools, TUI redesigned the First Choice Ski homepage. There was an 18 percent decrease in bounce rate, a 13 percent decrease in exit rate, and a 266 percent increase in Web sales. Over two-thirds of these improvements are directly attributed to these changes.

"We are now generating quantifiable, actionable, data-driven processes for prioritizing and reviewing website developments," says Rigglesworth.

Sources: Compiled from *firstchoice-ski.co.uk/* and *Yahoo.com/*.

Discussion Questions: How is being able to respond quickly to visitors' clickstream behavior related to the company's profit margin? Recall the principle: If you can't measure it, you can't manage it. Explain how this case illustrates this principle. Does Web analytics impact barriers to entry and rivalry among incumbents in this industry?

---

one department to another. Once orders arrive, an order processing system needs to receive, document, route, summarize, and store the orders.

Some companies spend millions of dollars reengineering their order processing as part of their transformation to e-business. IBM, for example, restructured its procurement system so its purchasing orders (POs) are generated quickly and inexpensively in its e-procurement system.

Web Analytics. **Web analytics** is the analysis of data generated by visitors' behavior on a company's Web site. That data is referred to as **clickstream data.** Web analytics begins by identifying the data that can be used to assess the effectiveness of the site's goals and objectives. For example, frequent visits to the site map may indicate navigation problems. Abandoning shopping carts repeatedly when the shipping charges are added indicates another problem.

Next, analytics data is collected, such as where site visitors are coming from, what pages they look at and for how long, and how they interact with the site's information. For example, the data can reveal the impact of an online advertising campaign, the effectiveness of Web site design and navigation, and, most important, visitor buying behavior. Because the goal of e-commerce sites is to sell a product or service, the most valuable Web analytics are those related to step-by-step conversion of a visitor to a customer.

Other typical TPS activities performed by managers in various functional areas are summarized in Table 9.2.

TABLE 9.2	Descriptions of TPS Activities
Activities	**Description**
General ledger	An organization's financial accounts. Contains all of the assets, liabilities, and owners' equity accounts.
Accounts payable (A/P) and accounts receivable (A/R)	Records of all accounts to be paid and those owed by customers. Automated systems send reminder notes about overdue accounts.
Receiving and shipping records	Records of all items sent or received, including returns.
Inventory-on-hand records	Records of inventory levels as required for inventory control and taxation. Use of barcodes and 2-D improves ability to track inventory.
Fixed-assets management	Records of the value of an organization's fixed assets, which include buildings and machines. Tracks depreciation rates and major improvements made in assets, for taxation purposes.
Payroll	Detailed and summary payroll records.
Personnel files and skills inventory	Files of employees' history, evaluations, and records of training and performance.
Sales reports	Reports on sales and for commissions on sales.
Reports to government	Reports on compliance with government regulations, taxes, and so on.

WHAT IF A TPS FAILS? TPS failure can cause a disaster. The U.S. Social Security Administration had some major TPS failures, as did insurance companies, hospitals, and banks.

IT at Work 9.3

Microsoft Excel and OLAP Connector Tool

Microsoft Excel is one of the world's most popular data-analysis tools. Using Excel pivot tables and charts, you can slice, dice, drill, and explore data arranged into multi-dimensional (three-dimensional, 3D) cubes. Once you generate a 3D cube, for instance, you can review the data without any help from the IT department. You can swap dimensions from rows to columns, add and remove measures, and filter certain criteria. This interactive and real-time exploration is critical to finding answers to business questions. But to use pivot tables or charts, you need to extract the data from a data store, often a data mart or warehouse. This leads to the *spread-mart problem*, which involves users having inconsistent data because they extract the data at different times. Users then save results to their own computers, where they remain inaccessible to others.

OLAP Connector. A tool called *OLAP connector* allows for seamless connectivity from Excel to the data mart or warehouse. OLAP stands for *online analytic processing*. Advantages of OLAP connector include:

- Familiar user interface
- Real-time data access
- Lower total cost of ownership (TCO)
- Consistent results and numbers across the organization

Several vendors offer OLAP connector tools, including Teradata (*Teradata.com/*) and SAP (*SAP.com*).

1. Explain Robert Anthony's management hierarchy (see Figure 9.3).
2. List the major characteristics of TPSs.
3. Describe the importance of high-quality (error-free) data entry.
4. List five typical TPS activities.
5. Describe the importance of Web analytics and show some of its applications.

9.2 Manufacturing and Production Systems

OM

The production and operations management (POM) function in an organization is responsible for the processes that transform inputs into useful outputs, as shown in Figure 9.7. Compared to other functional areas, POM covers diverse activities. It also differs considerably among organizations. For example, manufacturers use completely different processes than service organizations, and a hospital operates much differently than a government agency.

Next, we present two IT-supported POM topics: in-house logistics and materials management and computer-integrated manufacturing (CIM).

IN-HOUSE LOGISTICS, AND INVENTORY CONTROL AND MANAGEMENT

Logistics management deals with ordering, purchasing, inbound logistics (receiving), and outbound logistics (shipping) activities. In-house logistics activities are processes that cross several functional departments. Both conventional purchasing and e-procurement result in incoming raw materials and parts, which constitute inventory or stock. Materials are tracked from the time they are received until they're distributed—or disposed of when they become obsolete or their quality becomes unacceptable.

Scanners, RFID, and voice technologies support inspection, and robots can perform distribution and materials handling. **Robots** are programmable machines. Large warehouses use robots to bring materials and parts from storage, when needed. Parts are stored in bins, and the bins are stacked one above the other similar to the way safe deposit boxes are organized in banks. Whenever a part is needed, the stockkeeper keys in the part number. The mobile robot travels to the part's location, takes the bin out of its location using magnetic force, and brings the bin to the stockkeeper. Once a part is taken out of the bin, the robot is instructed to return the bin to its permanent location.

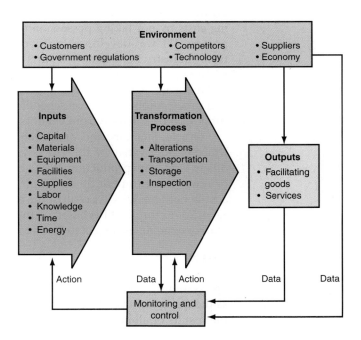

Figure 9.7 Production operations management (POM) functions transform inputs into useful outputs.

Figure 9.8 Industrial robot handles boxes of sugar. (© *David J. Green-industry/Alamy*)

Figure 9.8 is a photo of an industrial robot that's used to handle and transport inventory from storage. In intelligent buildings in Japan, robots bring files to employees and return them for storage. In some hospitals, robots dispense medications.

Inventory Control. The function of **inventory control** (also called stock control or inventory management) is to minimize the total cost of inventory. The objective is to maintain optimal inventory levels by reordering the correct quantity at the right time. POM departments may keep **safety stock** as a hedge against running out of inventory. Safety stock is extra inventory in case of unexpected events, such as spikes in demand or longer delivery times. It is often called **buffer stock.** The absence of inventory is called a **shortage.**

Managing inventory is important to profits because there are numerous costs associated with inventory. Inventory control systems minimize the following three categories of cost:

1. Cost of holding inventory: warehousing costs, security costs, insurance, losses due to theft or obsolescence, inventory financing costs based on the interest rate.

2. Cost of ordering and shipping: employees' time ordering and receiving, shipping fees.

3. Cost of inventory shortage: production delays and forgone revenues because of stockouts.

Because of these costs, the POM department has two decisions to make:

- When to order
- How much to order

One inventory model that is used to answer both questions is the **economic order quantity (EOQ)** model. The EOQ model takes all of those costs into consideration. A tutorial on EOQ, including its assumptions and equations, is available at *scm.ncsu.edu/public/inventory/6eoq.html.*

Dozens of other inventory control models exist because inventory scenarios can be diverse and complex. A large number of commercial inventory software packages to automate the application of these models are available at low cost. Minimizing inventory costs is a major objective of supply chain management.

Just-in-Time Inventory Management and Lean Manufacturing. Just-in-time (JIT) inventory management is an alternative method whose objective is to minimize holding costs by not taking possession of inventory until it is needed in the production process. JIT was developed by Toyota and is used extensively in the auto manufacturing industry. For example, if parts and subassemblies arrive at a workstation exactly when needed, there is no need to hold inventory. There are no delays in production, and there are no idle production facilities or underutilized workers, provided that parts and subassemblies arrive on schedule and in usable condition. Many JIT systems are supported by software from vendors such as HP, IBM, CA, and Cincom Systems.

Oracle, Siemens, and other vendors offer demand-driven **lean manufacturing,** which is a derivative of JIT. The objective of lean manufacturing is to remove waste of any kind from production. Waste can be unnecessary labor, material space, energy, or rework due to poor quality control. Like any IS, JIT needs to be justified with a cost-benefit analysis. Also, all of the assumptions that the JIT model is based on must exist. For example, JIT is based on the assumption that inventory will arrive on schedule. For companies subject to bad weather or labor strikes, that assumption is not valid.

Quality Control. Manufacturing quality control (QC) systems can be stand-alone systems or can be part of an enterprise-wide total quality management (TQM) effort. QC systems provide data about the quality of incoming materials and parts, as well as the quality of in-process semifinished and finished products. Such systems record the results of all inspections and compare actual results to expected results.

QC data may be collected by Web-based sensors and interpreted in real time, or it can be stored in a database for future analysis. Also, RFID systems collect data.

Periodic reports are generated, such as percentage of defects or percentage of rework needed, and management can compare performance among departments on a regular basis or as needed. For example, KIA Motors introduced an intelligent QC system to analyze customer complaints so it could more quickly investigate and make corrections. The analysis was done with data mining tools.

Project Management. A **project** is a collection of tasks to achieve a result, such as implementing a new JIT inventory management system. Projects have a defined beginning and end as well as a scope, resources, and a budget. Projects are approved before they are allocated resources. *Projects* differ from *operations*, or *business as usual*, because of their uniqueness.

Projects have these characteristics:

- Are unique undertakings
- Have a high degree of uncertainty with respect to costs and completion times due to the generally long length
- Involve participation of outsiders, which is difficult to control
- Require extensive interaction among participants
- May compete and conflict with other business activities, making changes in planning and scheduling difficult
- Involve high risk of delay, failure, and costly changes, but also have high profit potential or benefit

The management of projects is enhanced by computerized project management tools such as the *program evaluation and review technique* (PERT) and the *critical path method* (CPM). For example, developing a social media campaign can be a major project, and several IT tools are available to support and help manage the tasks.

Other POM Areas. Many other areas of POM are improved by IT. Web-based production planning optimization tools, product routing and tracking systems, order management, factory layout planning and design, and other tasks can be supported by POM subsystems. For example, a Web-based system at Office Depot matches employee scheduling with store traffic patterns to increase customer satisfaction and reduce costs. Schurman Fine Papers, a manufacturer/retailer of greeting cards and specialty products, uses special warehouse management software to improve demand forecasting and inventory processes. Its two warehouses efficiently distribute products to over 30,000 retail stores.

COMPUTER-INTEGRATED MANUFACTURING

Computer-integrated manufacturing (CIM) is a concept promoting the integration of various computerized factory systems. CIM has three basic goals: (1) the *simplification* of all manufacturing technologies and techniques, (2) *automation* of as many of the manufacturing processes as possible, and (3) *integration and coordination* of all aspects of design, manufacturing, and related functions via computer hardware and software.

The major advantages of CIM are its comprehensiveness and flexibility. These are especially important in business processes that are being completely reengineered or eliminated. Without CIM, it may be necessary to make large investments to change existing ISs to fit the new processes.

Review Questions

1. What is the function of POM in an organization? How can it be enhanced with IT?
2. What is a robot? How does it differ from a machine?
3. What are the three categories of inventory costs?
4. Explain the difference between EOQ and JIT inventory models.
5. Explain the difference between a project and operations.
6. What is CIM?

9.3 Sales and Marketing Systems

In Chapters 1, 7, and 8, you read about marketing channels, interoperability, e-commerce, and social media—all are types of sales and marketing ISs. In this section, we describe marketing systems for best-in-class performance.

In general, sales and marketing systems support market research, getting products and services to customers, and responding to customers' needs. Many of these systems and subsystems are shown in Figure 9.9. As you notice, marketing ISs have numerous components—sales, research, intelligence, reporting, procurement, logistics, and delivery. Interoperability enhances market power and presence.

Chapters 7, 8, and 10 cover sales and marketing systems and strategies, including e-commerce and customer relationship management (CRM). This section will focus on data-driven marketing and components of marketing ISs.

DATA-DRIVEN MARKETING

Marketing ISs are more than a system of data collection or a set of information technologies. They consist of people, equipment, and procedures to gather, sort, analyze, evaluate, and distribute relevant, timely, complete, and accurate data for use by marketing decision makers to improve their marketing planning, implementation, and control. The focus is on data-driven, fact-based marketing. Data mining, discussed in Chapter 10, is the primary method for data-driven marketing.

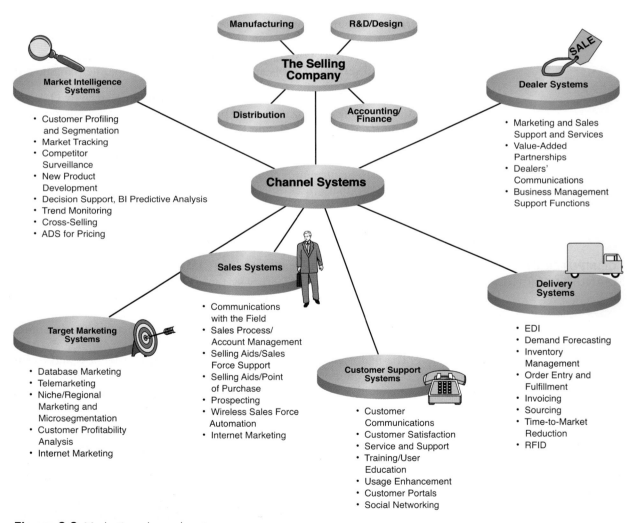

Figure 9.9 Marketing channel systems.

There is no shortage of customer and sales data, but there is a shortage of reliable, high-quality data and insight about how to use that data for better decisions that improve performance. In the August 2008 benchmark study, "Customer Analytics: Segmentation Beyond Demographics," all respondents identified that their top two data-related challenges were poor data quality (62 percent) and the inability to collect or access the data needed to calculate key performance metrics (31 percent) (Aberdeen Group, 2008).

DISTRIBUTION CHANNELS

Organizations distribute their products and services through a combination of electronic, mobile, and physical channels. Here are representative topics relating to distribution channels.

• Kiosks at 7-Eleven stores in some countries can be used to place orders on the Internet. In Macy's, you can check the current price on computerized screens with barcode readers.

• Some stores that have many customers who pay by check have installed check-writers. All you have to do is submit the blank check to the cashier, who runs it through a machine attached to the cash register. The machine prints the name of the store as the payee and the amount, you sign the check, and in seconds the check is validated, your bank account is debited, and you are out of the store with your merchandise.

• The Exxon Mobil Speedpass allows customers to fill their tanks by waving a token, embedded with an RFID device, at a gas-pump sensor. Then the RFID starts an authorization process, and the purchase is charged to your debit or credit card. Customers no longer need to carry their Mobil corporation credit cards.

• An increasing number of retailers are installing self-checkout machines. For example, Home Depot has self-checkouts in its stores. Not only does the retailer save the cost of employees' salaries, but customers are happier for saving time. And some enjoy "playing cashier" briefly. A major vendor is U-Scan, which is used in many supermarkets, shown in Figure 9.10. RFIDs are improving the process even further.

MARKETING MANAGEMENT

Here are some representative examples of how marketing management is being done.

Pricing of Products or Services. Sales volumes are largely determined by the prices of products or services. Price is also a major determinant of profit. Pricing is a difficult decision, and prices may need to be changed frequently, as is true for First Choice Ski, which is discussed in *IT at Work 9.2*. For example, in response to price changes made by competitors, a company may need to adjust its prices quickly or take other actions. Checking competitors' prices is commonly done by retailers, often using wireless price checkers, such as PriceMaster Plus, from SoftwarePlus. These devices make data collection easy.

Figure 9.10 U-Scan kiosk.
(© *Sonda Dawes/The Image Works*)

Salesperson Productivity. Salespeople differ from each other; some excel in selling certain products while others excel in selling to a certain type of customer or in a certain geographic zone. This information, which is usually collected in the sales and marketing TPS, can be analyzed using a comparative performance system in which sales data categorized by salesperson, product, region, and even time of day is evaluated. Actual current sales can be compared to historical data and to standards. Multidimensional spreadsheet software facilitates this type of analysis. Assignment of salespeople to regions and/or products and the calculation of bonuses can also be supported by this system. Wireless systems are used extensively by salespeople.

In addition, sales productivity can be boosted by Web-based call centers. When a customer calls a sales rep, the rep can look at the customer's history of purchases, demographics, services available where the customer lives, and more. This information enables reps to work faster while providing better customer service.

Sales automation software is especially helpful to small businesses, enabling them to rapidly increase sales and growth. A leading software is *salesforce.com,* which is a CRM application that is offered as a software-as-a-service (SaaS). You will read about Salesforce.com in the CRM section of Chapter 10.

Profitability Analysis. In deciding on advertising and other marketing efforts, managers need to know the profit contribution of certain products and services. Profitability metrics for products and services can be derived from the cost-accounting system. For example, profit performance analysis software available from IBM, Oracle, SAS, and Microstrategy is designed to help managers assess and improve the profit performance of their line of business, products, distribution channels, sales regions, and other dimensions critical to managing the enterprise. Several airlines, for example, use automated decision systems to set prices based on profitability.

New Products, Services, and Market Planning. The introduction of new or improved products and services can be expensive and risky. An important question to ask about a new product or service is, "Will it sell?" An appropriate answer calls for careful analysis, planning, and forecasting. These can best be executed with the aid of IT because of the large number of determining factors and the uncertainties that may be involved; for example, see the discussion of using predictive analysis in Chapter 10. Market research also can be conducted on the Internet.

Marketing activities conclude the primary activities of the value chain. Next we look at the functional systems that are *support activities* (also called *secondary activities*) in the value chain: accounting/finance and human resources management.

Review Questions

1. Define *data-driven marketing.*
2. Identify several distribution channels.
3. How does IT support marketing and sales?
4. What marketing strategies can be enhanced by the Web?

9.4 Accounting and Finance Systems

Accounting and finance control and manage cash flows, assets, liabilities, and net income or profit as well as issue financial statements to regulatory agencies. Another critical responsibility is the prevention, detection, and investigation of fraud.

In companies with lax accounting systems, it is too easy for employees to misdirect purchase orders and payments, bribe a supplier, or manipulate accounting data. If senior managers are involved in the fraud, preventing fraud is extremely tough. Consider Bernie Madoff, who committed record-setting fraud for many years even after the Sarbanes-Oxley Act was passed to prevent financial fraud.

IT at Work 9.4

ACC   FIN

Forensic Accountants Learn about Employee Fraud

Chris became a compulsive gambler. Her problem began at work when a casino Web site popped up on her computer as she surfed the Internet during lunch. She placed a few bets using the free credits offered by the site to entice first-time players, which she won—as did all first time gamblers. Winning gave her a thrilling feeling, she would later explain to fraud investigators. Two years later, as the payroll manager of a medium-sized manufacturing firm, Chris had defrauded her employer of over $750,000.

Stealing from Payroll to Pay Off Gambling Losses. Why did Chris (and many like Chris) commit fraud? To pay off her gambling losses, which averaged $7,000 a week. How was she able to do it? By taking advantage of the lack of proper controls in her company's payroll and accounting information systems. Chris had worked at the company for over 10 years. Her performance reviews described her as hardworking, reliable, and loyal but did not mention that she felt underpaid. Chris was bitter, thinking her employer didn't treat her fairly. When her gambling began to spiral out of control, she turned to fraud. "As far as I was concerned, they owed me," she told the forensic accountants.

No One Watching. The company's HR manager and comptroller were supposed to review Chris's work. But the HR manager focused on providing her with the correct data for employees'

wages and benefits. The comptroller appeared not to have exercised control over payroll processing, which Chris knew.

Chris set up two phony employees on the company's hourly payroll system. She altered the payroll records from an external payroll provider (EPP) because there was no oversight. She deposited the payroll check for the phony employees into her account. At year-end, Chris made adjustments to the payroll register to eliminate the amounts paid to the phony employees. When she went on vacation, she deactivated the two phony names from the payroll.

Expanding the Fraud. Still in need of cash, Chris started paying herself for unauthorized overtime. she paid herself for 1,500 hours of overtime over two years, but actually worked 50 hours overtime. Chris again falsified records until the HR manager finally noticed. When she was confronted with the evidence, she confessed that she had spent all the money on gambling and could not repay.

Discussion Questions: What role did trust play in Chris's ability to commit fraud for so long (that is, the employer's trust in Chris)? What role did weak accounting ISs play in her ability to commit fraud? In your opinion, if Chris knew that strong accounting ISs were in place, would that have deterred her from trying to steal from her company?

AUDITING INFORMATION SYSTEMS

Fraud is easy to commit and hard to detect. Just ask any auditor. There are countless ways to hide fiscal malfeasance. The problem may be exacerbated in government and nonprofit entities, which rarely have adequate accounting and internal control systems. The problem is so bad at the federal level that auditors are unable to express an opinion on the fairness of the consolidated financial statements of the United States. For example, NASA, the space agency, was unable to explain $565 billion in year-end adjustments to its books. It could have been the result of bad accounting, fraud, waste, or abuse. Without adequate records, no one really knows. This amount is astounding, especially when one considers that the combined cost of fraud in the Enron and WorldCom scandals was less than $100 billion in shareholder equity.

Because physical possession of stolen property is no longer required and it's just as easy to program a computer to misdirect $100,000 as it is $1,000, the size and number of frauds have increased tremendously. See *IT at Work 9.4*, which describes a real-life case.

FINANCIAL PLANNING AND BUDGETING

Management of financial assets is a major task in financial planning and budgeting. Managers must plan for both the acquisition of financial resources and their use. Financial planning, like any other functional planning, is tied to the overall organizational planning and to other functional areas. It is divided into short-, medium-, and long-term horizons, much like activities planning.

Financial and Economic Forecasting and Budgeting. Knowledge about the availability and cost of money is a key ingredient for successful financial planning.

Especially important is the projection of cash flows, which tells organizations what funds they need and when, as well as how, they will acquire them. In today's tough economic conditions with tight credit and limited availability of funds, this function has become critical to the company's survival.

Inaccurate cash flow projection is the number one reason why many small businesses go bankrupt. The inability to access credit led to the demise of the investment bank Lehman Brothers in September 2008.

The best-known part of financial planning is the annual budget, which allocates the financial resources of an organization among participants, activities, and projects. The budget is the financial expression of the organization's plans. It allows management to allocate resources in the way that best supports the organization's mission and goals. IT enables the introduction of financial logic and efficiency into the budgeting process.

Several software packages, many of which are Web-based, are available to support budget preparation and control. Examples are budgeting modules from Oracle (*oracle.com*) and *capterra.com*, which facilitate communication among participants in budget preparation. Software support for budgeting and forecasting is available from Prophix (*prophix.com*). The key benefits of the package are a familiar Windows Explorer interface, customizable flexibility that supports a variety of budgeting templates, a controlled database that secures data and allows for multiple user accessibility, and data manipulation tools for complex budgeting.

The major benefits of using budgeting software are that it can reduce the time and effort involved in the budget process, explore and analyze the implications of organizational and environmental changes, facilitate the integration of the corporate strategic objectives with operational plans, make planning an ongoing, continuous process, and automatically monitor exceptions for patterns and trends.

Capital Budgeting. Capital budgeting is the process of identifying the financing of assets, including software, that need to be acquired or developed. It includes comparing alternatives or evaluating buy-versus-lease options.

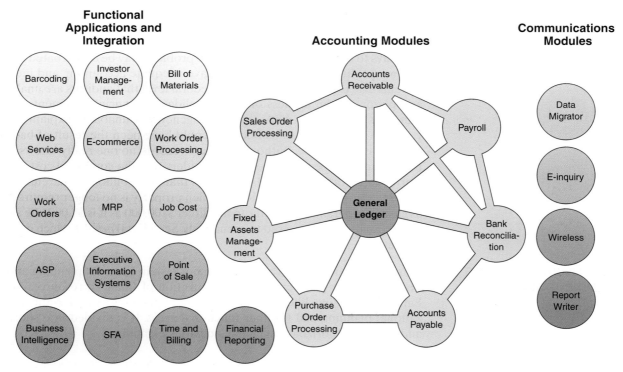

Figure 9.11 Integrated accounting/business software.

Capital budgeting analysis uses standard financial models, such as net present value (NPV), internal rate of return (IRR), and payback period to evaluate alternative investment decisions. Excel and other spreadsheet packages include built-in functions of these models.

Accounting/finance ISs are also responsible for gathering the raw data necessary for the accounting/finance TPS, transforming the data into information, and making the information available to users, whether it is aggregate information about payroll, the organization's internal reports, or external reports to stockholders or government agencies, which is illustrated in Figure 9.11.

The accounting/finance TPS also provides a complete, reliable audit trail of all routine transactions transmitted through the network. This feature is vital to accountants and auditors.

XBRL: eXtensible Business Reporting Language. As you read in Chapter 8, **XBRL** is a programming language and an international standard for electronic transmission of business and financial information. As of September 2005, it can be used to file financial reports electronically with the SEC and FDIC. With XBRL, all of the company's financial data is collected, consolidated, published, and consumed without the need to use Excel spreadsheets. Figure 9.12 illustrates how XBRL works. Such submissions allow government analysts to validate information

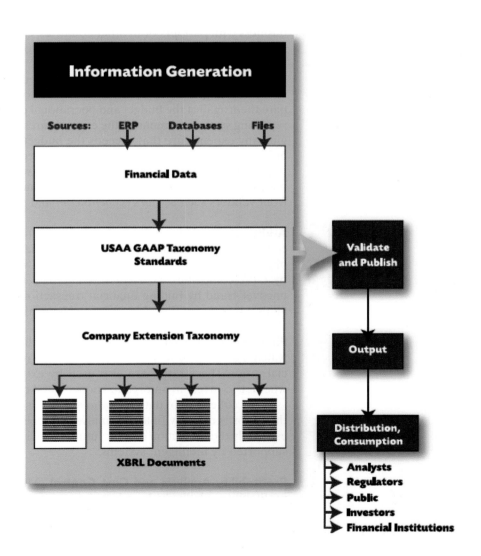

Figure 9.12 How XBRL works.

within a matter of hours instead of weeks. XBRL helps financial institutes do the following:

- Generate cleaner data, including written explanations and supporting notes
- Produce more accurate data with fewer errors that require follow-up by regulators
- Transmit data faster to regulators and meet deadlines
- Increase the number of cases and amount of information that staffers can handle
- Make information available faster to regulators and the public
- Address issues and concerns in their filings rather than after the fact
- Reduce report cycle time
- Lead to a more efficient capital market

CONTROL AND AUDITING

As you have read, a major reason organizations fail is their inability to forecast and/or secure sufficient *cash flow*. Underestimated expenses, overspending, financial mismanagement, and fraud, can lead to disaster. Good planning is necessary, but not sufficient, and must be supplemented by skillful control. Control activities in organizations take many forms, including control and auditing of the information systems themselves. Information systems play an extremely important role in supporting organizational control, as we show throughout the text. Specific forms of financial control are presented next.

Risk Analysis and Budget Control. Companies need to analyze the risk of doing business with partners or in other countries. Giving credit to customers can be risky, so one can use products such as FICO from *fairisaac.com* for calculating risk. Regulators mandate risk management.

Once the annual budget has been decided upon, it is divided into monthly allocations. Managers at various levels then monitor departmental expenditures and compare them against the budget and operational progress of the corporate plans. Simple reporting systems summarize the expenditures and provide *exception reports* by flagging any expenditure that exceeds the budget by a certain percent or that falls significantly below the budget. More sophisticated software attempts to tie expenditures to program accomplishment. Numerous software programs can be used to support budgetary control; most of them are combined with budget preparation packages from vendors such as *claritysystems.com* and *capterra.com*.

Auditing. The major purpose of **auditing** is to protect and defend the accuracy and condition of the financial health of an organization. Internal auditing is done by the organization's accounting/finance personnel, who also prepare for external auditing by CPA companies. IT facilitates auditing. For example, intelligent systems can uncover fraud by finding financial transactions that significantly deviate from previous payment profiles. Also, IT provides real-time data whenever needed.

Financial Ratio Analysis. A major task of the accounting/finance department is to watch the financial health of the company by monitoring and assessing a set of financial ratios. These ratios are also used by external parties when they are deciding whether to invest in an organization, extend credit, or buy it.

The collection of data for ratio analysis is done by the TPS, and computation of the ratios is done by financial analysis models. The interpretation of the ratios, and especially the prediction of their future behavior, requires expertise and is sometimes supported by intelligent systems.

Profitability Analysis and Cost Control. Many companies are concerned with the profitability of individual products or services as well as with the financial health of the entire organization. Profitability analysis DSS software allows accurate computation of profitability and allocation of overhead costs. One way to control cost is by properly

estimating it. This is done by using special software. Profitability Management from Hyperion, an Oracle Company, provides potent multidimensional and predictive analysis as well as proven query, reporting, and dashboard functionality with ease of use and deployment. The solution delivers powerful, insightful, activity-based cost analysis and what-if modeling capabilities to help create and test new business strategies. Sophisticated business rules are stored in one place, enabling analyses and strategies to be shared easily across an entire enterprise.

Review Questions

1. How are financial planning and budgeting facilitated by IT?
2. Explain how accounting ISs help deter fraud.
3. Define *capital budgeting*.
4. Why is XBRL important?
5. What is the purpose of auditing?

9.5 Human Resource Systems

Human Resources (HR) is a field that deals with policies, procedures, compliance requirements, and best practices. Developments in online systems increased the use of human resources information systems (HRISs) as of the late 1990s. HRISs have been moved to intranets and the cloud, where HR apps are leased in a software-as-a-service (SaaS) arrangement. This benefits companies by freeing HR staff from routine tasks by shifting them to employees (self-entry of an address change) so that they can focus on their legal and compliance responsibilities, employee development, hiring, and succession planning. In the following sections, we describe in more detail how IT facilitates HR management.

To better understand how IT facilitates the work of the HR department, review Figure 9.13. The figure summarizes the role HR plays in acquiring and keeping people in organizations. Note that the activities are cyclical in nature.

Recruitment. Recruitment is finding employees, testing them, and deciding which ones to hire. Some companies are flooded with viable applicants, while others have difficulty finding the right people. With millions of résumés online, it is not surprising that companies are trying to find appropriate candidates on the Web, usually with

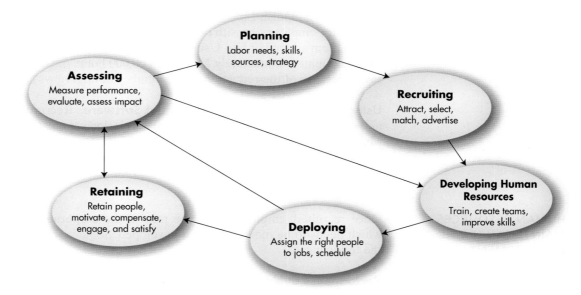

Figure 9.13 HR management activities.

IT at Work 9.5

IPG's HR Management Apps

Interpublic Group (IPG, *ipg.com*) is a global provider of advertising and marketing services. A Fortune 500 company, IPG is the parent company of Reprise Media (*reprisemedia.com/*), McCann-Erikson Worldgroup (*mccannworldgroup/*), and numerous other agencies that offer customized search and marketing solutions to the world's largest advertisers. IPG covers a range of specialties from public relations and consumer advertising to mobile and search engine marketing (SEM).

With 45,000 employees and hundreds of offices in more than 100 countries, IPG's role as the holding company is to provide human resources (HR) and IT support to their agencies, including recruitment. In 2008, IPG sought out an automated **applicant tracking system (ATS)** to find prospective job applicants for its agencies. As a global company, IPG was looking for a solution that could provide international functionality.

Applicant Tracking System (ATS) with International Support. IPG needed a highly scalable and configurable ATS solution. IPG selected iCIMS' implementation program (*icims.com*) because it could be tailored to each client's needs, processes, and recruitment goals. iCIMS offered multiple languages, workflows and talent initiatives, and 24/5 international support.

According to Christine McGay, HR director, "At IPG, we were looking for a partner that could give us outstanding customer service, a competitive price, flexibility to expand, and a company that had a good rating within the ATS market. . . . iCIMS delivered in all areas, and we felt confident they'd be able to successfully implement a solution that would meet our company's complex needs."

Key benefits of the ATS solution are:

- Training programs and a detailed implementation process to ensure high user adoption
- Highly configurable and flexible platform that has the ability to expand to agencies
- Global functionality and cost-effectiveness

Discussion Questions: Visit *icims.com/* and click *Demos*. View the free online demos of iCIMS' *Candidate Management Software* and *Employee Management Software* apps. Registration is required. Describe what you learned about candidate and employee management. Why would IPG and other global enterprises need to use ATS solutions?

---

the help of specialized search engines. Online recruiting is able to "cast a wide net" to reach more candidates, which may bring in more qualified applicants at lower cost.

Recruitment online is beneficial for candidates as well. They are exposed to a larger number of job offerings, are able to get details of the positions quickly, and can begin to evaluate the prospective employer. To check the competitiveness of salary offerings both locally and in several other countries, job candidates go to *monster.com*.

Example. The Finish Line Corp. had to process more than 330,000 candidates that applied for employment with the company in a 12-month period. More than 75 percent of them applied online. Using screening software by Unicru, 112,154 candidates were eliminated immediately. More than 60,000 hours of store managers' time were saved because of the reduction in the number of interviews conducted.

Using Social Networks and Intelligent Software. Recruitment at virtual worlds and social networking sites is very popular. It is done at most major sites—LinkedIn, MySpace, Facebook, Craigslist, and Second Life. Recruitment online is frequently supported by intelligent software agents. For an example of how this is done, see *IT at Work 9.5*.

HUMAN RESOURCES MAINTENANCE AND DEVELOPMENT

Once recruited, employees become part of the corporate human resources pool, which needs to be maintained and developed. Some activities supported by IT are the following.

Performance Evaluation. Most employees are evaluated periodically by their immediate supervisors. Peers or subordinates may also evaluate others. Evaluations are usually recorded on paper or electronic forms. Using such information manually is a tedious and error-prone job. Once digitized, evaluations can be used to support many decisions, ranging from rewards to transfers to layoffs. For example, Cisco Systems is known for developing an IT-based human capital strategy. Many universities evaluate professors online. The evaluation form appears on the screen, and the students fill it in. Results can be tabulated in minutes. Corporate managers can analyze employees' performances with the help of intelligent systems, which provide systematic interpretation of performance over time. Several companies provide software for performance evaluation; e.g., *people_trak.com* and *talco.com.*

Wage review is related to performance evaluation. For example, Hewlett-Packard's Atlanta-based U.S. Field Services Operations (USFO) Group has developed a paperless wage review (PWR) system. The Web-based system uses intelligent agents to deal with quarterly reviews of HP's 15,000 employees. (A similar system is used by most other groups, covering a total of 150,000 employees.) The agent software lets USFO managers and personnel access employee data from both the personnel and functional databases. The PWR system tracks employee review dates and automatically initiates the wage review process. It sends wage review forms to first-level managers by e-mail every quarter.

Training and Human Resources Development. Employee training and retraining is an important activity of the human resources department. Major issues are planning classes and tailoring specific training programs to meet the needs of the organization and employees. Sophisticated human resources departments build a career development plan for each employee. IT can support the planning, monitoring, and control of these activities by using workflow applications.

Some of the most innovative developments are in the areas of live online training (LOT) using WebEx (*webex.com*) or other online meeting software. YouTube, Teradata University Network (TUN), and *CNN.com* offer excellent educational videos. Flash animations and simulations are easily made available. Social media, such as Second Life, discussed in Chapter 8, offers the latest in training options. The aircraft industry has been using flight simulators for decades for training pilots. Second Life has a special forum on training and learning using virtual worlds. An example of how interactive simulation is utilized in training for the use of complex equipment is provided in *IT at Work 9.6*.

HR PLANNING, CONTROL, AND MANAGEMENT

In some industries, labor negotiation is an important aspect of HR planning, and it may be facilitated by IT. For most companies, administering employee benefits is also a significant part of the human resources function. Here are some examples of how IT can help.

Personnel Planning and HR Strategies. The HR department forecasts requirements for people and skills. In some geographic areas and for overseas assignments, it may be difficult to find particular types of employees. In such cases, the HR department plans how to find or develop from within sufficient human resources.

Benefits Administration. Employees' contributions to their organizations are rewarded by salary/wage, bonuses, and other benefits. Benefits include those for health and dental care as well as contributions for pensions. Managing the benefits system can be a complex task, due to its many components and the tendency of organizations to allow employees to choose and trade off benefits. In large companies, using computers for self-benefits selection can save a tremendous amount of labor and time for HR staff.

Providing flexibility in selecting benefits is viewed as a competitive advantage in large organizations. It can be successfully implemented when supported by computers. Some companies have automated benefits enrollments. Employees can self-register for specific benefits using the corporate portal or voice technology, and self-select desired benefits from a menu. Payroll pay cards are now in use in numerous

IT at Work 9.6

Using Interactive Simulation in Training

An effective technology for e-training and e-learning is visual inter-active simulation (VIS), which uses computer graphic displays to present the impact of decisions. It differs from regular graphics in that the user can adjust the decision-making process and see the results of the intervention. Some learners respond better to graph-ical displays, and this type of interaction can help students and managers learn about decision-making situations. For example, VIS was applied to examining the operations of a physician clinic environment within a physician network to provide high-quality, cost-effective healthcare in a family practice. The simulation sys-tem identified the most important input factors that significantly affected performance. These inputs, when properly managed, led to lower costs and higher service levels.

VIS can represent a static or a dynamic system. Static mod-els display a visual image of the result of one decision alternative at a time. Dynamic models display systems that evolve over time, and the evolution can be represented by animation.

The learner can interact with the simulated model, watch the results develop over time, and try different decision strategies online. Enhanced learning, both about the problem and about the impact of the alternatives tested, can and does occur.

The major potential benefits of such systems are the following:

- Shortening the trainee's learning time
- Easing the learning of operating complex equipment
- Enabling self-learning, any place, any time
- Achieving better memorization
- Lowering the overall cost of training
- Recording the learning progress of individuals and improving it

Several companies provide the necessary software and learning procedure. One product is SimMAGIC, from Hannastar Technology Co., Ltd., in Taiwan. Figure 9.14a shows application in a pharmaceu-tical company; Figure 9.14b shows trainee progress charts.

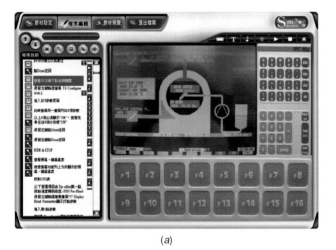

(a)

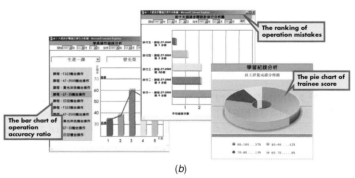

(b)

Figure 9.14 SimMagic training app and progress charts. **(a)** SimMagic training application in the pharmaceutical industry. **(b)** SimMagic data presentation of the training process. (*Courtesy of HamStar Technology Ltd.*)

companies, such as Payless Shoes, which has 30,000 employees in 5,000 stores. The system specifies the value of each benefit and the available benefits balance of each employee. Some companies use intelligent agents to assist the employees and mon-itor their actions.

Employee Relationship Management. In their effort to better manage employees, companies are developing human capital management, facilitated by the Web, to streamline the HR process. These Web applications are more commonly referred to as employee relationship management. For example, self-services such as tracking personal information and online training are very popular in ERM. Improved rela-tionships with employees result in better retention and higher productivity.

ETHICS

HRM applications are especially prone to ethical and legal considerations. For example, training activities that are part of HRM may involve ethical issues in recruiting and selecting employees, and in evaluating performance. Likewise, TPS data processing and storage deal with private information about people, their performance, and so forth. Care should be taken to protect this information and the privacy of employees and customers.

Review Questions

1. List IT-supported recruitment activities.
2. How can training be done online?
3. Explain HR information systems.
4. Describe IT support for employee selection, promotion, and development.

Key Terms

auditing *274*	lean manufacturing *266*	robot *265*
batch processing *261*	online processing *261*	safety stock *266*
buffer stock *266*	online transaction processing	shortage *266*
clickstream data *263*	(OLTP) *262*	standard operating procedures
computer-integrated manufacturing	operational awareness *256*	(SOP) *259*
(CIM) *267*	operational-level information	tag cloud *257*
economic order quantity (EOQ) *266*	systems *256*	vendor-managed inventory (VMI) *262*
inventory control *266*	operational responsiveness *256*	Web analytics *263*
just-in-time (JIT) *266*	project *267*	XBRL *273*

Chapter Highlights and Insights

(Numbers refer to Learning Objectives)

❶ Information systems applications support many functional activities. The major business functional areas are production/operations management, marketing, accounting/finance, and human resources management.

❶ The backbone of most information systems applications are TPSs, which keep track of the routine, mission-central operations of the organization.

❷ The major area of IT support to production/operations management is in logistics and inventory management: JIT, mass customization, and CIM.

❸ Marketing and sales information systems deal with all activities related to customer orders, sales, advertising and promotion, market research, customer service, and product and service pricing. Using IT can increase sales, customer satisfaction, and profitability.

❹ Financial information systems deal with topics such as investment management, financing operations, raising capital, risk analysis, and credit approval.

❹ Accounting information systems also cover many non-TPS applications in areas such as cost control, taxation, and auditing.

❺ Most tasks related to HR development can be supported by human resources information systems. These tasks include employee recruitment and selection, hiring, performance evaluation, salary and benefits administration, training and development, labor negotiations, and work planning.

❺ Online HR systems are extremely useful for recruiting and training.

Questions for Discussion

1. Explain Robert Anthony's management hierarchy.
2. Which functional areas are related to payroll, and how does the relevant information flow?
3. Describe how XBRL can help financial institutions.
4. Discuss how IT facilitates the capital budgeting process.
5. Discuss the role IT plays in auditing.
6. What is the value of lean manufacturing?
7. What is the objective of EOQ?
8. Describe waste and give three examples.
9. What are the risks of JIT?
10. Investigate the role of the Web in HR management.
11. Discuss the need for sharing data among functional areas.

Exercises and Projects

1. Visit Teradata Student Network and find the podcast titled "Best-Practice Enterprise Risk Management" (by R. M. Mark). View the presentation and write a report on how IT can help a company with its risk management.

2. Visit Teradata Student Network and find the assignment regarding Advent Technology. Use the MicroStrategy Sales Force Analysis Module and answer the questions about sales at Advent.

3. Visit *secondlife.com* and find an island that interests you. For accountants, we suggest looking at the "CPA Island." Make a list of 10 major activities conducted on the site.

Group Assignments and Projects

1. Each group should visit (or investigate) a large company in a different industry and identify its channel systems. Then find out how IT supports each of those components. Finally, suggest improvements in the existing channel system that can be supported by IT technologies and that are not in use by the company today. Each group presents its findings.

2. The class is divided into groups of four. Each group member represents a major functional area: production/operations management, sales/marketing, accounting/finance, or human resources. Find and describe several examples of processes that require the integration of functional information systems in a company of your choice. Each group will also show the interfaces to the other functional areas. For example, accounting students can visit *accountantsworld.com* just to be surprised at what is there, and *1040.com* can be useful to both the accounting and finance areas.

3. Each group investigates an HR software vendor (Oracle, SAP, Lawson Software). The group prepares a list of all HR functionalities supported by the software. Then each group makes a presentation to convince the class that its vendor is the best.

4. Analyze the financial crisis of 2008. In your opinion, what roles did IT play to accelerate the crisis? Also, how did IT help to rectify some of the problems? Be specific.

Internet Exercises

1. Find free accounting software online. Download the software and try it. Write a report on your findings.

2. Search for an explanation of EOQ. Explain the formula.

3. Finding a job on the Internet is challenging; there are almost too many places to look. Visit the following sites: *careerbuilder.com, craigslist.org, LinkedIn.com, careermag.com, hotjobs.yahoo.com, jobcentral.com,* and *monster.com*. What do these sites provide you as a job seeker?

4. Visit *sas.com* and access revenue optimization there. Explain how the software helps in optimizing prices.

5. Enter *sas.com/solutions/profitmgmt/brief.pdf* and download the brochure on profitability management. Prepare a summary.

6. Visit *techsmith.com/camtasia/features.asp* and take the product tour. Do you think it is a valuable tool?

7. Examine the capabilities of the following financial software packages: TekPortal (from *teknowledge.com*), Financial Analyzer (from *oracle.com*), and Financial Management (from *sas.com*). Prepare a report comparing the capabilities of the software packages.

8. Review *salesforce.com*. What functional support does the software provide?

BUSINESS CASE

Microsoft Dynamics NAV Supports SunWest Foods

SunWest Foods is California's second-largest rice and wild rice producer, milling up to 73 metric tons (80 tons) per hour at seasonal peaks. In 2010, SunWest employed 100 staff in three processing and warehouse locations and a marketing office. SunWest buys from 350 farms, then packages, distributes, and sells domestically and internationally.

An incompatible mix of ISs and data silos made it necessary for staff to enter and re-enter data manually for each order—up to 10 times—wasting time and creating errors. Staff spent weeks compiling business reports because of numerous data formats that needed to be converted into usable data. At times, financial and operations decisions had to be made in blind spots, that is, before data could be compiled and made available.

Jim Errecarte, SunWest President and CEO explained, "the impacts of our patchwork system were many extra steps and rushed business decisions based on incomplete reports we couldn't wait for—particularly in our commodity positions. We were overdue for one cohesive, end-to-end solution to encompass purchasing, sales, production, distribution, finances, and trend prediction." To improve decisions, financial control, and operations, SunWest implemented Microsoft Dynamics NAV software, which is a complete enterprise resource planning (ERP) solution. Software demos of Dynamics NAV are available from Microsoft's Web site or *microsoft.com/en-us/dynamics/products/nav-demos.aspx.*

Fast Financial, Accounting, and Pricing Data

SunWest has improved enterprise-wide financial controls, planning, and P&L (profit and loss) reporting. What used to take 10 to 15 staff-hours per month to prepare financial and accounting reports dropped to a few minutes. Errecarte creates most reports he needs in Microsoft Dynamics NAV without pulling others off-task. He gets the data four weeks faster and in formats he can easily use, which is critical to run a commodity food business.

SunWest previously had a generalized price list for each market sector. Now it has customer-specific prices, which gives the company a competitive advantage. A summary of key benefits are:

• Data re-entry time dropped 80 percent, making perfect orders the rule and freeing up 30 staff hours weekly.

• Commodity reports that took weeks are now instant and save 15 hours monthly.

• Marketing's wild rice reports, which had lagged by three months, are now real time.

• Panic calls on incomplete orders dropped from monthly to less than quarterly.

Sources: Compiled from Microsoft (2010) and SunWest (2010).

Questions

1. Why were multiple data entries of the same data necessary?
2. Prior to integration, why did SunWest have fragmented ISs?
3. Explain the waste at SunWest prior to integration. Why was there so much waste?
4. What functional areas have benefited from the integrated IS solution?
5. Why is real-time reporting and trusted data critical to SunWest?

NONPROFIT CASE

FIN   IS

Banco Compartamos: Micro-Finance Institution for Poor in Latin America

Established in 1990 as a nonprofit, Banco Compartamos became a financial institution in 2000. Banco Compartamos is a micro-finance (micro-loan) institution based in Mexico City. It contributes to Latin America's economic development by providing financial services to low-income entrepreneurs. Clients consist of small business owners—98 percent of which are women—who provide services and produce food and clothing for their communities, and who need capital to create a better future for their families.

Challenged by Fraud and Slow Customer Service

Banco Compartamos faced the high risk of fraud and poor customer service. A cause of these problems was poor data quality—multiple versions of information, data inconsistencies and delayed reporting. To address these business problems and create opportunities, Banco Compartamos invested in data-warehouse solutions. Data warehousing provided managers with up-to-date data for analysis, in order to make better and faster decisions on credit or loan applications. Managers also needed to be able to forecast demand while reducing business users' dependence on IT to develop reports. Reducing dependence on IT was important because it often took at least one week to get the right information for decision making.

Roadmap: A Visual Planning Model

Banco Compartamos began with an enterprise data warehousing (EDW) roadmap to create a visual planning model and a business plan. The roadmap enabled the company to understand strategic and operational objectives and to identify the type of data needed to accomplish those objectives. The roadmap was very important because it involved the key users in the project, which was crucial for acceptance of the project. Once goals were specified, the IT team developed the project plan to reach the end results.

Data Warehousing Project Rollout

The data warehouse was rolled out in phases based on priorities and the roadmap. Data regarding customers, employees, credit, insurance, and risk were consolidated so the organization could:

• Provide easier access to consistent, comprehensive information and feedback for better decision making

- Provide single-view reports and dashboards containing business results and goal achievements from different lines of business
- Understand customers and their financial behavior
- Cut costs by cutting time and people who consolidated, validated, and maintained data.

Banco Compartamos expanded its operations, services, and its client base. It has grown to serve more than 1.5 million entrepreneurs, becoming the largest micro-finance institution in Latin America.

Social and Economic Value

According to Federico Hernandez, COO of Banco Compartamos, "As a micro-finance institution, our business is to generate opportunities of development in communities by providing financial services to the low-economic segment, allowing our clients to invest in their most important assets— themselves." The bank helps Mexico and Latin America by generating social, economic, and human value through its humanitarian business model. The data-warehouse solution provided the data, analysis, and reporting capabilities needed to add the following:

- **Social value.** Provides micro-loans to the greatest number of people possible when they need it.
- **Humanitarian value.** Provides the only financial opportunity for many poor people to support themselves and improve their communities.

Sources: Compiled from Zack (2010) and Compartamos Banco (2011) *compartamos.com/wps/portal*

Questions

1. What were Banco Compartamos' problems?
2. What factors or practices contributed to those problems?
3. To what extent does accurate and quick decision making matter?
4. How have the obstacles to fulfilling its missions been solved?

ANALYSIS USING SPREADSHEETS

Calculation of Labor Savings at SunWest Foods

FIN   IS   ACC

Refer to the preceding Business Case *Microsoft Dynamics NAV Supports SunWest Foods.* Design a spreadsheet to calculate the savings in labor costs. Use the data from the case to estimate the reduction in wasted time. Assume that the hourly labor rate for staff workers is $15.00 and the rate for managers and senior executives is $100 per hour.

References

Aberdeen Group, "Customer Analytics: Segmentation Beyond Demographics," August 31, 2008. aberdeen.com.

Compartamos Banco (2011). *compartamos.com/wps/portal*

Salesforce.com, 2010.

Supply Chain Management and Logistics, "Health Care: Safety and Security in the Spotlight," June 1, 2004.

SunWest Foods, Microsoft Case Study, April 30, 2010.

Zack, J. "Small Loans, Huge Impact," *Teradata Magazine*, March 2010.

Learning Objectives

❶ Understand how enterprise systems support cross-functional and multinational operations.

❷ Understand why companies need enterprise resource planning (ERP) systems.

❸ Describe supply chain management (SCM) networks and solutions.

❹ Understand collaborative planning, forecasting, and replenishment (CPFR).

❺ Describe customer relationship management (CRM) systems.

❻ Discuss benefits of knowledge management systems.

Integrating *IT*

 ACC
 FIN
 MKT
 OM
 HRM
 IS

Comparison of top 10 ERP vendors *top10erp.org/*
ERP Vendor Shootout *erpshootout.com/*
Oracle *oracle.com*
SAP *sap.com*
SSA Global *ssaglobal.com/solutions/erp/ln.aspx*
Microsoft Dynamics *microsoft.com/dynamics/en/us/default.aspx*
Teradata *Teradata.com*

QUICK LOOK at Chapter 10, Enterprise Information Systems

This section introduces you to the business issues, challenges, and IT solutions in Chapter 10. Topics and issues mentioned in the Quick Look are explained in the chapter.

Companies have many of the database and software applications that they had invested in over the past several decades. These older information systems (IS), called **legacy systems,** have been built with various outdated technologies. As business strategies and technologies changed over the years, the legacy systems were modified repeatedly and patched to the point where they just cannot be modified anymore. Typically, legacy systems are inflexible and expensive to maintain for two reasons:

1. They either cannot be updated or cannot be updated without significant effort.
2. They either cannot interface (connect to) and exchange data with newer information technologies (IT) or cannot be interfaced without significant effort.

Regardless of their limitations and age, a company's legacy systems may be **mission-critical.** That means that if one of these systems crashes or stops working, one or more business operations may grind to a halt. Think about the chaos you'd be caught in if you were at an airport when your airline's reservation system crashed. Passengers would not be able to make connections and their luggage would not be checked in. You can imagine—or might have experienced—other aggravating consequences.

New IT may also be mission-critical. Our dependence on newer IT infrastructures was made obvious on August 6, 2009, when a hack attack took down the microblogging site Twitter. In some companies and in some countries, Twitter has turned into a critical infrastructure. Over 45 million Twitter users worldwide were left speechless—so to speak—by the attack, including companies that relied on Twitter for marketing and consumer outreach.

Given the situation that organizations of all types find themselves in with their legacy systems, when they need to upgrade mission-critical ISs or implement global systems, they turn to enterprise information system software. **Enterprise information systems,** or simply **enterprise systems,** are integrated ISs that support core business processes and functions. Business processes and functions include marketing, accounting, finance, information security, human resources (HR), compliance, production, purchasing, and logistics. Integration is achieved by linking databases and data warehouses so they can share data from:

• Internal functions: Functions that take place within the company, which are referred to collectively as the **internal supply chain.**
• External partners: Business or supply chain partners, such as customers or suppliers, which are referred to as the **external supply chain.**

As you read in greater detail in this chapter, key enterprise systems are:

• ERP: Enterprise resource planning
• SCM: Supply chain management
• CPFR: Collaborative planning, forecasting, and replenishment
• CRM: Customer relationship management
• KM: Knowledge management

The key benefit of enterprise systems is data integration. Integration enables the sharing or exchange of data. For example, ERP is integrated with SCM to improve supply chain performance, and KM is integrated with CRM to identify profitable and unprofitable customers. Improvements in business processes are highly dependent on data accuracy, completeness, context, and access to it—which all of the ISs discussed in this chapter help achieve.

Enterprise systems are a top issue in IT management and corporate strategy because of their potential to increase both the *top line* (growth in net revenues) and the *bottom line* (growth in net income). **Corporate strategy** is the collection of activities and actions a company chooses to invest in and perform as well as those it chooses not to invest in or perform.

The greatest challenges when implementing enterprise systems are not the technical ones. Rather, the biggest challenges are process and change management. Companies that have inconsistent or outdated business processes along their supply chains tend to have poor-quality data. To improve data quality, companies reengineer those processes and consolidate them into an integrated enterprise system.

Under Armour Competes on Global Playing Field

MKT OM ACC IS GLOBAL

In the mid-1990s, Nike, Adidas, and Reebok dominated the athletic footwear and sportswear industry—and operated in over 40 countries. (Reebok is no longer a separate company. In 2006, Adidas, the German athletic apparel and the world's second-biggest sports goods maker after Nike, acquired Reebok). Competing successfully with them on a global playing field would be tough, and near impossible for a new company just entering their industry. Yet in 1996 that's what former University of Maryland football player and entrepreneur Kevin Plank did with Under Armour Inc. (*underarmour.com/*).

Under Armour is the originator of performance apparel that's made of fabric to keep athletes cool, dry, and light throughout their games and workouts. The company develops, markets, and distributes Under Armour apparel, footwear, and accessories. The brand's synthetic fabrics are engineered in many different designs and styles for wear in any climate. Their products are sold worldwide and worn by athletes at all levels and ages, from youth to professional. Under Armour has headquarters in Maryland and Amsterdam, and offices in Denver, Toronto, Hong Kong, and Guangzhou, China.

Figure 10.1 Under Armour competes with Nike and Adidas. (© *Under Armour, Inc. 2010.*)

Global Distribution and Growth Constrained by Outdated IT

Success eventually caused problems. Under Armour's IT could no longer support its extensive product line, global distribution, and ambitious growth strategy. Specifically:

- ISs did not provide sufficient agility to outpace competitors and enable the company to reinvent itself every six months—a goal important to top management.
- ISs with multicurrency and multicompany processing capabilities were needed to support international expansion.
- Software applications could not support growth of the product lines or the company's expansion into several other countries.

Available-to-Promise (ATP) Capabilities

To improve its brand and channel management, the company needed to replace its time-consuming manual allocation processes with dependable **available-to-promise (ATP)** capabilities. ATP is a business function that provides data about resource availability and delivery dates to keep customers informed of their orders' status. ATP also supports order fulfillment in order to manage demand and match it to production plans. The software takes a lot of work out of the order fulfillment process—and less effort means lower cost and fewer errors.

SAP ERP Solution

Management reviewed various software vendors' products to identify the one that best met the company's needs. The company selected an ERP solution from SAP (*sap.com*). The ERP gave them the ability to accelerate time-to-market of new products, to improve customer service, and to take advantage of growth opportunities. Under Armour implemented the *SAP Apparel and Footwear Solution for Consumer Products* module to the ERP.

Within eight months, a 20-person project team from operations, IT, and ERP consulting company Metamor managed the implementation. Web-based SAP NetWeaver Business Intelligence software was also implemented to provide managers with reports accessible on demand or on schedule.

Benefits of Improved Operational Visibility

With the SAP ERP, products module, and exchange infrastructure, Under Armour increased both its top line—*growth in sales*—and bottom line—*growth in net income*. With automated ATP processes, the data is reliable and inventory management is efficient and lower cost. Multiple currencies and companies are supported. Managers have a clear view of timely data to drive better decisions and business performance. Under Armour can close its books faster than ever and bring new operations onboard quickly.

The Under Armour case illustrates the operational and strategic benefit of enterprise systems to insure quick response to market changes and customer needs. Doing so is not a simple task, as you will read in this chapter.

Sources: Compiled from Business Wire (2009), SAP (*sap.com*), and Under Armour (*underarmour.com*, 2010).

For Class Discussion and Debate

1. Scenario for Brainstorming and Discussion: Many factors contributed to Under Armour's success in the fiercely competitive sports apparel industry.

a. Identify all of the factors, reasons, and conditions that contributed to Under Armour's success.

b. Discuss the importance of each factor, reason, and condition. Decide which are the top three success factors and explain why.

2. Debate: Based on your answers to 1(a) and (b), debate how and to what extent a company wanting to enter that market today—given today's economic and market conditions—could succeed for the same reasons and factors.

10.1 Enterprise Systems

Enterprise information systems, or **enterprise systems** for short, are systems that help managers and companies improve their performance by enabling them to seamlessly share data among departments and with external business partners. Enterprise systems allow workers to access and analyze real-time information and transaction processes across the entire organization. These systems integrate the functional systems that you read about in Chapter 9, such as accounting, finance, marketing, and operations. Another advantage of enterprise systems is that processes become more automated or totally automated, which increases efficiency. For example, by automating finance processes, a company can do things such as accept online orders and do business-to-business (B2B) transactions electronically instead of via e-mail or offline methods such as telephone or fax.

Prior to selecting and implementing an ERP or other enterprise system, it's essential that a company identify the problems to be solved, the goals to be achieved, and the type of support the IS is to provide. For example, Under Armour's management wanted real-time or near-real-time data and sufficient agility to respond quickly to operational and market conditions. **Agility** is the ability to thrive and prosper in an environment of constant and unpredictable change. Agility is a result of streamlining processes on the shop floor to speed up order fulfillment, which in turn maximizes capacity for increased productivity.

TYPES OF ENTERPRISE SYSTEMS AND THEIR FUNCTIONS

Several examples of enterprise systems are listed and described in Table 10.1. Companies implement most or all of these systems, not just one.

TABLE 10.1	Descriptions of Enterprise Systems	
Name	**Abbreviation**	**Description**
Enterprise resource planning	ERP	ERP is the software infrastructure that links an enterprise's internal applications and supports its external business processes.
		ERP systems are commercial software packages that integrate business processes, including supply chains, manufacturing, finance, human resources, budgeting, sales, and customer service.
Supply chain management	SCM	SCM software refers to software that supports the steps in the supply chain—manufacturing, inventory control, scheduling, and transportation.
		SCM improves decision making, forecasting, optimization, and analysis.
Collaborative planning, forecasting, and replenishment	CPFR	CPFR is a set of data-driven business processes designed to improve the ability to predict and coordinate with supply chain partners.
		With CPFR, suppliers and retailers collaborate in planning and demand forecasting in order to ensure that members of the supply chain will have the right amount of raw materials and finished goods when they need them.
Customer relationship management	CRM	CRM creates a total view of customers to maximize share-of-wallet and profitability. Also, it is a business strategy to segment and manage customers to optimize their long-term value.
Knowledge management	KM	KM helps organizations identify, select, organize, disseminate, and share information and expertise.

REASONS COMPANIES MIGRATE TO ENTERPRISE SYSTEMS

The reasons companies migrate to enterprise systems stem from limitations with their existing legacy systems. Here are several reasons for the migration from legacy systems to enterprise systems:

- **High maintenance costs.** Maintaining and upgrading legacy systems are some of the most difficult challenges facing CIOs (chief information officers) and IT departments.
- **Business value deterioration.** Technological change weakens the business value of legacy systems that have been implemented over many years and at huge cost.
- **Inflexibility.** Monolithic legacy architectures are inflexible. That is, these huge systems cannot be easily redesigned to share data with newer systems, unlike modern architectures.
- **Integration obstacles.** Legacy systems execute business processes that are hardwired by rigid, predefined process flows. Their hardwiring makes integration with other systems such as CRM and Internet-based applications difficult and sometimes impossible.
- **Lack of staff.** IT departments find it increasingly difficult to hire staff who are qualified to work on applications written in languages no longer used in modern technologies.

IMPLEMENTATION CHALLENGES AND BEST PRACTICES

Implementing an enterprise system is challenging because it requires extensive changes in processes, people, and existing systems. Three required changes are:

1. **Redesign of business processes.** Processes need to be simplified and redesigned so that they can be automated, either totally or partially. Tasks that are no longer necessary are removed from the processes.

2. **Changes in how people perform their jobs.** Jobs and how they are performed will change to accommodate the new processes. Enterprise systems require retraining of end users, whose productivity will slow initially as they adjust to a new way of doing their jobs.

3. Integration of many types of information systems. Integrating information systems is necessary so that data can flow seamlessly among departments and business partners. Automated data flows are essential to productivity improvements.

A best practice is to examine the inefficiencies in existing processes to find ways to improve on or significantly simplify the process. For example, manual document-intensive processes (such as order entry and billing) create major headaches for workers. These processes require users to manually review documents for approval, enter data from those documents into a back-office system, and then make decisions. Automated order entry systems track customer orders from the time of initial order placement through the completion of those orders; they also perform backorder processing, analysis, invoicing, and billing.

Because of their complexity, enterprise systems are leased or licensed from vendors and customized with support from IT personnel who are familiar with their company's business processes. The trend toward *ERP as a service* continues to increase. In fact, the term ERP commonly refers to commercially available software systems. For examples of monthly costs and a comparison of 10 ERP vendors' products, visit *top10erp.org/*. To simplify and reduce the cost of the ERP software selection process (the selection process itself is complex and critical), an annual event called the ERP Vendor Shootout (*erpshootout.com/*) is held and geared toward ERP selection teams and decision makers for companies with manufacturing, distribution, or project-oriented requirements.

ENTERPRISE SYSTEMS INSIGHTS

Here are three other insights related to enterprise systems to better understand the current state of enterprise systems and their potential:

1. One of the IT department's most important roles is to provide and support applications that enable workers to access, use, and understand the data. These applications need to be tightly aligned with well-defined and well-designed business processes—a standard that few enterprises are able to achieve.

2. Customer loyalty helps drive profits, but only for customers who are profitable to the company. Many companies don't know how to recognize or encourage the kind of customer loyalty that's worth having. Using data about buying behaviors (e.g., amount spent per month, purchase of high-margin products, return activity, and demands for customer service) helps a company identify its loyal customers and which ones are profitable.

3. Companies all over the world are spending billions of dollars on the design and implementation of enterprise systems. Huge investments are made in ERP systems from vendors such as Oracle, Peoplesoft (acquired by Oracle), JD Edwards (also acquired by Oracle), SAP, Microsoft, and BAAN to create an integrated global supply chain. Interorganizational ISs play a major role in improving communication and integration among firms in a global supply chain.

Next you will read about ERP systems, which despite their name, are not limited to planning functions. Although most types of companies now have an ERP system, ERP evolved from the manufacturing industry.

Review Questions

1. Explain the purpose of an enterprise system.
2. Describe five types of enterprise systems.
3. What are two challenges of legacy systems?
4. Explain the three types of changes needed when an enterprise system is implemented.

10.2 Enterprise Resource Planning (ERP) Systems

What is an **ERP (enterprise resource planning) system?** From a technology perspective, ERP is the software infrastructure that links an enterprise's internal applications and supports its external business processes, as you read in the opening case on Under Armour. ERP applications are modular, and the modules are integrated with each other to expand capabilities.

TABLE 10.2	Characteristics of ERP Applications

- Bring silos of information together to enable managers to really understand what is going on
- Provide the information access, integrated business processes, and modern technology platform necessary to become and remain competitive
- Support all, or a great majority, of a company's business functions and processes
- Expand a company's reach beyond its internal networks to its suppliers, customers, and partners

An ERP helps managers run the business from front to back. Departments can easily stay informed of what's going on in other departments that impact their operations or performance. Being informed of potential problems and having the ability to work around them improves the company's business performance and customer relations. For example, an ERP enables a manufacturer to share a common database of parts, products, production capacities, schedules, backorders, and trouble spots. Responding quickly and correctly to materials shortages, a spike in customer demand, or other contingency is crucial because small initial problems are usually amplified down the line or over time. Table 10.2 lists the characteristics of ERP suites and applications.

ERP: A STRATEGIC WEAPON FOR FOOD MANUFACTURERS

Food manufacturing is a highly competitive and regulated environment. Major challenges facing food manufacturers are margin pressures, food safety and regulations, and constantly changing consumer tastes. An integrated business software system is essential for controlling costs, managing inventory, and meeting government regulations. Another challenge is knowing how to evaluate a new enterprise-wide software system.

Figure 10.2 shows the subsystems that need to share data and support the operations of most manufacturers.

Food Safety and Agri-Food Regulations. In a survey conducted by *Food Engineering* magazine, the top concern of the agri-food industry was food safety, in large part because worldwide distribution systems have increased the risk and range of contaminated food entering the food supply. In 2009, the *New York Times* reported that a single hamburger could contain beef products from several slaughterhouses on several continents (Moss, 2009). An estimated 76 million people in the United States get sick every year with foodborne illnesses and 5,000 die, according to the U.S. Centers for Disease Control and Prevention (CDC).

The threats and potential costs associated with food safety are high and rising. Contaminated spinach, peanut butter, beef, imported seafood, pet food, and many other food products, in addition to life-threatening and ethical issues, result in litigation, bad publicity, and recall costs that damage or destroy companies' reputations.

The European Food Safety Authority (*efsa.europa.eu/*) applies a "from the farm to the fork" integrated approach based on transparency, risk analysis and prevention,

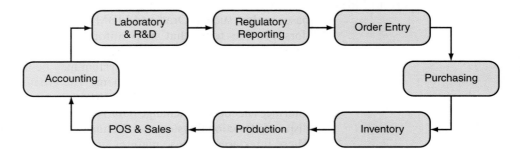

Figure 10.2 An ERP system integrates all function ISs of a food manufacturer around a single set of data.

and consumer protection. The U.S. Congress responded to terrorism by passing the Public Health Security and Bioterrorism Preparedness and Response Act (Bioterrorism Act) in 2002. In 2009, Congress passed a food safety law creating new traceability requirements for the food supply chain and giving greater facility inspection power to the Food and Drug Administration (FDA).

Using IT to Deal with Complexity. All of these challenges have one thing in common: They add complexity, and that adds costs. The challenge for today's food manufacturer is how to meet the regulatory requirements, ensure a safe food supply, constantly improve business processes, and make a profit. The answer has been investments in IT.

The first software purchased is an accounting package to handle the financial aspects of running a business. As the company grows, companies invest in IT to manage inventory, process sales and purchase orders, and control production. This progression of IT investments addresses the needs of individual departments or functions. As a result, companies have separate ISs for accounting, sales and purchasing, and inventory management—with the same data being held in multiple systems. This leads to duplicate data entry and differing versions of the truth.

Integrated ERP System. A well-designed ERP system can help integrate all aspects of an organization around a single set of data. Key benefits of an integrated ERP system to a food manufacturer are improved operational performance, a framework to meet regulatory mandates and reporting requirements, and cost control. Many food manufacturers are replacing multiple software applications with a single integrated ERP system to manage their complex businesses to maximize productivity and profitability. Specifically, the ERP gives manufacturers a single point of control for data, thereby:

- Eliminating the need to enter data in multiple systems
- Reducing common data entry errors and costs
- Allowing for the posting of transactional data in real time for instant access to up-to-date information
- Being able to respond quickly to food recalls
- Meeting requirements of the Bioterrorism Act or other regulations for accurate recordkeeping in order to support the discovery of and quick response to food chain supply threats

Like many other companies, food manufacturers are being squeezed at both ends. Increased pressure for food safety and regulation add costs to the food processing supply chain. Higher energy bills and distribution further reduce profit margins. These pressures are leading to investments in enterprise systems to integrate data silos.

FROM STAND-ALONE DATA SILOS TO AN INTEGRATED ENTERPRISE SYSTEM

When companies need to replace their disparate (stand-alone) or labor-intensive legacy systems, they often invest in enterprise systems. Doing so requires migrating databases and applications from legacy to enterprise systems. Not surprisingly, database vendors such as Oracle and IBM are also enterprise system vendors. These vendors provide tools that help automate both the database migration and the application migration, which occur separately.

Implementing an enterprise system may be a competitive necessity for companies with data management problems. The greater the number of applications and databases, the greater the complexity of data management because of the numerous interfaces needed to exchange data. As you see in the left-side diagram of Figure 10.3, disparate functional systems—HR, finance, operations—involve numerous interfaces. These interfaces increase maintenance efforts and costs as well as the risk of dirty

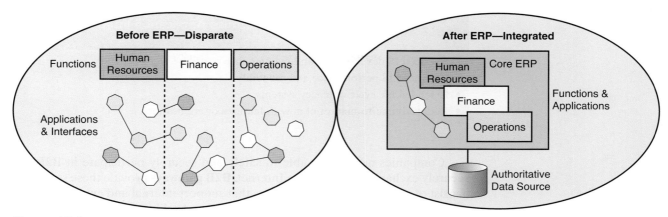

Figure 10.3 Comparison of disparate systems within an enterprise to an integrated ERP system.
(Courtesy of U.S. Army Business Transformation Knowledge Center (2009), *army.mil/armyBTKC/*.)

data. An ERP integrates functions, including a suite of IT modules that can be purchased as needed by the company.

Enterprise Application Integration Layer. In Figure 10.4, you see how an ERP fits into an enterprise's IT infrastructure. The core ERP functions are integrated with other systems or modules that are bolted-on, including SCM, PLM, CRM, and BI. In the example shown in Figure 10.4, the ERP interfaces with legacy applications through an **enterprise application integration (EAI)** layer and with external business partners through a B2B gateway (explained in the next section). EAI is middleware that connects and acts as a go-between for applications and their business processes. Benefits of EAI are listed in Table 10.3.

B2B Gateway Layer. Business-to-business integration (B2Bi) is vital to ensure the efficient, accurate, and timely flow of data across internal ISs and external business partners. (See left side of Figure 10.4.) Companies that implement B2Bi are realizing enormous competitive advantage through faster time to market, reduced cycle times, and increased customer service. Through integration of business and technical processes, companies are able to strengthen relationships with partners and customers, achieve seamless integration inside and outside the enterprise, gain real-time views of customer accounts, increase operational efficiencies, and reduce costs.

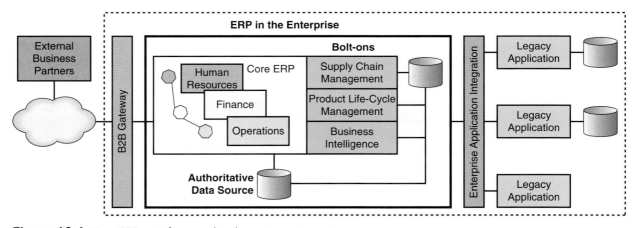

Figure 10.4 How ERP interfaces with other enterprise systems.
(Courtesy of U.S. Army Business Transformation Knowledge Center (2009), *army.mil/armyBTKC/*.)

TABLE 10.3	Benefits of the Enterprise Application Integration (EAI) Middleware Layer

- Reduced IS development and maintenance costs
- Enhanced IS performance and reliability
- Extended life cycle of legacy systems
- Reduced time-to-market of new IS features or applications

Companies need to be able to safely and securely participate in B2Bi and to securely exchange data over the Internet. **B2B gateways** provide these services. They consist of a suite of software products that support internal and external integration and business processes. B2B gateways provide a backbone for the secure exchange of data, files, and documents—intracompany and with external parties. As such, they increase real-time visibility into business activity and performance.

JUSTIFYING AN ERP

Why are ERP systems worth their cost? Because decisions are only as good as the timeliness and completeness of the data on which they're based. The more complete the data, the less the uncertainty and risk involved in the decision process. An ERP provides the integration and automation that makes timely and complete data possible. So it's not surprising that establishing a reliable pipeline of data from internal functions and external business partners is a priority for businesses in every industry and of all sizes.

ACQUIRING AN ERP

Typically, ERP systems are acquired by purchasing or leasing packaged software. The purchased or leased ERP software is customized to meet the company's need by adding modules. ERP systems include modules for manufacturing, order entry, accounts receivable and payable, general ledger, purchasing, warehousing, transportation, and HR. ERPs are not built in-house or built using proprietary software because the costs and time to do so would be staggering. You will read more about IS acquisition in Chapter 11.

The current major ERP vendors are the following. Note that acquisitions continue to consolidate the industry.

- Oracle, *oracle.com,* which acquired PeopleSoft and JD Edwards
- SAP, *sap.com*
- SSA Global, *ssaglobal.com/,* which acquired BAAN
- Microsoft Dynamics, *microsoft.com/dynamics/en/us/default.aspx*

Vendors charge license fees based on the number of users and annual revenues, as shown in Table 10.4. Table 10.4 lists the types of ERP vendors, whose systems range from Tier 1 to Tier 5. Tier 1 ERP systems are able to support the largest global corporations—those with annual revenues over $200 million, with 500 or more employees. Tier 5 systems support the smallest companies with less than $5 million in annual revenues and fewer than 10 employees. Tier 1 vendors are SAP, Microsoft, and Oracle. These revenues and license fees for the five tiers are only general figures, and vendors may use their own cut-off points. In addition to the license fees,

TABLE 10.4	Types of ERP Vendors Based on the Size of the Company They Can Support		
Tier	Annual Revenues	Number of Employees	License Fees
1	Over $200 million	500 and over	> $300,000
2	$50 million to $200 million	100–499	> $150,000
3	$10 million to $50 million	50–99	> $50,000
4	$5 million to $10 million	10–49	> $5,000
5	Less than $5 million	1–9	> $100

IT at Work 10.1

Achieving Efficient Flexible Manufacturing

Manufacturing companies have two goals: to be efficient and flexible. Production efficiency is achieved by removing waste. Unused, excessive inventory is considered waste. Flexibility means the company is able to respond quickly to changes in customer demand, which can increase waste; thus, efficiency and flexibility can be conflicting goals if they are treated separately. Achieving efficient and flexible manufacturing is complex (and beyond the scope of this text), but there are a few basic concepts and ITs for you to understand.

Linking production and sales forecasts can help. For example, by linking manufacturing schedules into sales demand forecasts within an ERP system, companies can:

- manufacture what customers demand, which improves customer responsiveness, and
- increase inventory turnover, which reduces capital tied up in inventory and obsolescence.

Inventory turnover (or inventory turn) is the number of times that inventory cycles or "turns over" in a year. A higher turnover indicates less waste. Inventory turnover is calculated using this formula: (Cost of Goods Sold in Past 12 Months)/(Average Inventory Cost in Past 12 Months).

Sample calculation: During 2013, a company's Cost of Goods Sold = $50 million and Average Inventory Costs = $10 million. In 2013, the company had five inventory turns ($50 million/$10 million).

ERP System for Visibility. As demand forecast accuracy improves, the ability to meet market needs (be responsive) also improves and inventory waste decreases. All of these capabilities depend on enterprise systems, typically ERP, which improve visibility throughout the production processes. Ultimately, you cannot improve what you cannot measure, so visibility into processes enterprise-wide is necessary for efficient, flexible manufacturing and supply-chain improvement.

Discussion Questions: What competitive advantages do efficiency and flexibility provide to a manufacturing company? Are those competitive advantages sustainable? Why or why not? Based on the inventory turn formula, what are the two ways a manufacturer can increase its inventory turn within a year?

---

there are implementation, training, and maintenance costs. The conventional wisdom is that you buy a software license, and then you buy maintenance and support separately, which usually costs 20 percent of the original license cost annually. For a $1,000 software license, maintenance and support cost an additional $200 per year.

Lesser known ERP vendors tend to be less expensive and provide more specialized (customized) features than traditional ERP options. For example, complex design-to-order, low-volume manufacturers are not going to want a package that supports high-volume, make-to-stock manufacturing. Rather, they need a solution that handles their customized type of business very well rather than one that tries to be everything to everyone.

As the Under Armour opening case and *IT at Work 10.1* illustrate, improved agility can create a competitive advantage. ERP provides the infrastructure needed for the agility for quick correction and response, which can be exploited to improve profitability, market share, or customer service.

UNDERSTANDING ERP SUCCESS AND FAILURE FACTORS

Managers and other decision makers tend to think that if an enterprise system works for the best companies, it will work for them too. But that's not true. In fact, as you read in Table 10.5, several of the best companies have suffered devastating consequences that led to multimillion-dollar losses, bankruptcy, or lawsuits. Most often, the ERP eventually is fixed and remains in use, which gives the false impression that the ERP was successful from the start.

The success of ERP depends on organizational and technological factors that occur prior to, during, and after the implementation. Knowing what to do and what not to do are important. Both the successes and failures teach valuable lessons, too, as you will read in this section.

Be aware that reading vendor white papers and viewing Webcasts or demos may give you a biased view of the benefits of their software. You need to conduct your own research to learn the full story of an enterprise system implementation. Problems may be skipped over or ignored. While blogs and YouTube posts may be good sources of objective data, many vendors have blogs and YouTube videos that are designed to appear to be neutral when, in fact, they're not.

TABLE 10.5	ERP Failures
Company and Industry	**Description of ERP Failure**
Hershey Foods, manufacturer of chocolates, confectionaries, and beverages	Hershey's spent three years implementing a $115 million ERP system with SAP, Siebel, inventory, and Manugistics. The ERP was to replace all legacy systems and to integrate inventory, production, order processing, payroll, accounting, and finance. Hershey's devastating mistake was trying to implement all systems in all departments at the same time and at its busiest time of the year. Hershey's suffered heavy losses in profits and sales, which led to an 8 percent drop in its stock price, and filed a lawsuit against the vendors.
Nike, athletic shoe and apparel manufacturer	Nike implemented i2's (*i2.com*) demand and supply planner software, which it wanted up and running before introducing an SAP ERP to handle all supply chain and sales order processes. The i2 system created duplicate orders, deleted customer orders, and deleted manufacturing requests to Asian factories. Adding to the problems, the ERP was not designed to handle Nike's large number of products. Many legacy systems had been left in use that lacked the ability to communicate with the supply chain software, causing huge delays and system crashes. The $400 million upgrade to Nike's supply chain and ERP systems caused $100 million in lost sales, a drop of 20 percent in stock price, and class-action lawsuits. Nike blamed the failure on underestimating the needed resources for the i2 system and rolling out the SAP prematurely.
FoxMeyer, bankrupted; formerly the fourth largest pharmaceuticals distributor	FoxMeyer's ERP could not process the transactions needed to supply its customers with their orders. FoxMeyer had been processing 425,000 invoice lines per day on its legacy software. Its ERP was limited to 10,000 invoice lines per day. This decreased order processing capability, quickly put the company into bankruptcy protection, and ultimately shut down the business.
Waste Management, garbage-disposal giant	As of mid-2009, Waste Management was embroiled in a $100 million legal battle with SAP over an 18-month installation of its ERP software. In the lawsuit filed in March 2008, Waste Management claimed that SAP executives participated in a fraudulent sales scheme and demo that resulted in the massive failure. SAP countersued, alleging that Waste Management violated its contract agreement.

Cases of ERP Failure. ERP implementations are complex, so it's not surprising to learn that there have been horror stories of ERP projects gone wrong. Dell canceled an ERP system after spending two years and $200 million on its implementation. Hershey Foods Corp. brought widely publicized lawsuits against ERP software vendors because of their failed implementations. Table 10.5 presents Hershey's and other cases of ERP failures. In cases of extreme failure, companies have sued their vendors or consulting firms because their ERP software failure made it impossible to ship products or, at the extreme, led to a shutdown of the entire business.

ERP Success Factors. What factors increase the likelihood of ERP success and minimize the risk of problems? Many managers assume that success or failure depends on the software and, furthermore, that a failure is the fault of the software that's purchased or licensed. In reality, 95 percent of a project's success or failure is in the hands of the company implementing the software, not the software vendor.

The results of a 2008 survey to identify what ERP experts had found to be most important to successful ERP projects are shown in Figure 10.5. These ERP experts were given a list of five factors and asked to select only one of them as *most important*. The sixth alternative was *all five factors*. The results (which sum to 100 percent) are:

1. Strong program management: 6 percent
2. Executive support and buy-in: 19 percent
3. Organizational change management and training: 13 percent
4. Realistic expectations: 8 percent
5. Focus on business processes: 5 percent
6. Interaction of all five factors: 49 percent

Survey responses to the question:
What is most important to successful ERP projects?

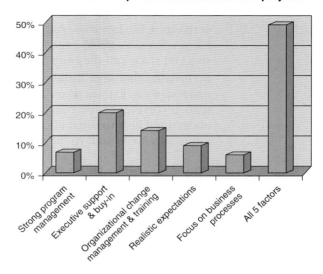

Figure 10.5 Experts identify what's most important to the success of an ERP.

That is, 49 percent of the ERP experts have found that success depended on all five factors. Stated another way, nearly half of the experts indicated that the failure of any one of these five factors would or could cause the ERP to fail.

The following recommendations explain why ERP success depends on several key factors being done right.

1. Focus on business processes and requirements. Too often, companies get caught up in technical capabilities or platforms on which the ERP runs. But compared to business processes, none of this really matters. What matters is how managers want business operations to run and what the key business requirements are. Once management and IT have defined them, they can more effectively choose the software that fits their unique business needs.

2. Focus on achieving a measurable ROI. Developing a business case to get approval from upper management or the board of directors is essential, but not sufficient. Establish key performance measures, set baselines and targets for those measures, and then track performance after going live.

3. Use a strong project management approach and secure commitment of resources. The success of an ERP project depends on how it is managed. Responsibility for the management of the ERP implementation project cannot be transferred to vendors or consulting firms. Because of the business disruption and cost involved, ERP projects require the full-time attention and support of high-profile champions from the key functions for a long period of time, from six to 12 months on average. It's also known that ERP projects cannot be managed by people who *can be spared*. They must be managed by people who are *indispensable* personnel. Without powerful champions and the necessary budget (discussed next), expect the ERP to fail.

4. Ensure strong and continuing commitment from senior executives. Any project without support from top management will fail. No matter how well run a project is, there will be problems, such as conflicting business needs or business disruptions, that can only be resolved by someone with the power and authority to cut through the politics and personal agendas.

5. Take sufficient time to plan and prepare up front. An ERP vendor's goal is to close the deal as fast as possible. The company needs to make sure it correctly defines its needs and what it can afford to achieve in order to intelligently evaluate and select the best vendor. Do not be rushed into a decision. Too often, companies jump right into a project without validating the vendor's understanding of business requirements or its project plan. The principle of "measure twice, cut once" applies to vendor selection. The more time the company spends ensuring that these things are done right at the start, the lower the risk of failure and the less time spent fixing problems later. Filing a lawsuit against a vendor (see Table 10.5) is not a fix. Lawsuits are both expensive and risky, and they add nothing to the company's performance.

6. Provide thorough training and change management. Another key principle to understand is that when you design an ERP, you redesign the organization. ERP systems involve dramatic change for workers. An ERP loses value if people do not understand how to use it effectively. Investing in training, change management, and job design are crucial to the outcome of any large-scale IT project.

Why Companies Don't Invest in ERP. One of the IT department's most important roles is to provide and support applications that ensure that workers can access, use, and understand the data they need to perform their jobs effectively. An ERP would seem to be the perfect solution. Despite their potential benefits, not all companies invest in ERP, typically because they are unable to meet or overcome the following requirements:

- Applications must be tightly aligned with well-defined and well-designed business processes, which is a standard that few enterprises are able to achieve.
- Selecting the appropriate ERP is time-consuming, complex, and expensive.
- Business processes must be modified to fit the software.
- Initial costs to purchase or lease and set up the ERP may be extremely high.
- The complexity of the applications might make it too difficult for employees to use the ERP correctly for maximum efficiency and ROI.

In addition, justifying an ERP becomes more difficult during an economic downturn.

Review Questions

1. Define ERP and describe its objectives.
2. Briefly describe the challenges of legacy systems that motivate the migration to ERP.
3. Describe how ERP enables agility.
4. List and briefly describe three ERP implementation success factors.
5. Describe two barriers to ERP implementation.

10.3 Supply Chain Management (SCM) Systems

The journey that a product travels, as shown in Figure 10.6, starting with raw material suppliers, then to manufacturers or assemblers, then forward to distributors and retail sales shelves, and ultimately to customers, is its **supply chain.** The supply chain is like a pipeline composed of multiple companies that perform any of the following functions:

- Procurement of materials
- Transformation of materials into intermediate or finished products
- Distribution of finished products to retailers or customers
- Recycling or disposal in a landfill

Supply chains vary significantly depending on the type, complexity, and perishability of the product. For example, in a simplified sense, the food supply chain begins with the livestock or farm, moves to the manufacturer (processor), then through the distribution centers and wholesalers to the retailer and final customer. In *IT at Work 10.2*, you read how track and trace technologies are being used to improve food safety and reduce costs.

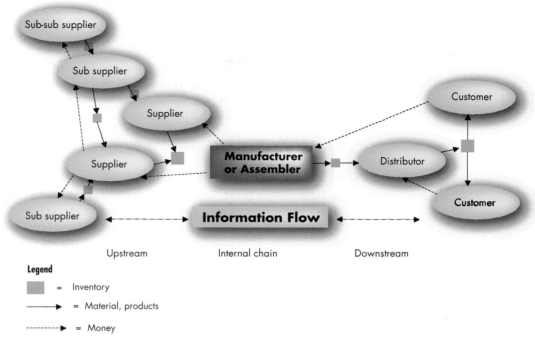

Upstream   Internal chain   Downstream

Legend

▉ = Inventory

——▶ = Material, products

------▶ = Money

Figure 10.6 Structure of a typical supply chain.

IT at Work 10.2

Improving Food Supply Chain Safety with Track and Trace IT

Beef patties, pet food, peanut butter, lettuce, and spinach are a few of the recent high-profile food recalls due to contamination. Consumers worldwide are worried about the safety and source of their food. One solution is to implement track and trace technologies that follow food products throughout their supply chain, primarily through the use of barcodes and radio frequency identification (RFID). Barcoding and RFID enable the tracking of food through the food supply chain from "farm to fork." Without the capability to identify the scope of the contamination and contain it, the food recall is much more extensive than necessary as a safety precaution. For example, when *E.coli*-tainted spinach was discovered in 2007, using the barcode on a bag of bad spinach, investigators traced its origin to California's Salinas Valley. But then they had to do an intense and expensive search for the specific grower in that valley. And during that search time, all spinach was being pulled from grocery stores, distribution plants, and processing plants and destroyed. A growers' organization estimates the recall cost the spinach industry $74 million. It would have been much faster to track the contaminated leaves to the grower if spinach bags and containers had carried RFID tags with complete histories of the contents' origins.

With detailed information, companies can streamline the distribution chain and lower spoilage and contamination rates. Reducing the rates of spoilage and contamination is important for reasons related to safety and costs.

Consumer product and retail industries lose about $40 billion annually, or 3.5 percent of their sales, due to supply chain inefficiencies.

In the Canadian Province of Manitoba, a full traceability network was developed, connecting more than 16 supply chain partners, including beef and pork producers, animal feed ingredient producers, feed manufacturers, farmers, processing plants, truckers, and a retail grocery chain. Using Global Traceability Network (GTNet) software from TraceTracker, an IBM partner, the Manitoba project shows it is possible to securely and accurately collect and process data about a piece of meat from a variety of sources and share that information at any step in the process.

Track and trace technologies are also being used at Germany's METRO Future Store (*future-store.org/*), where butchers not only cut meat but also apply RFID smart labels. Each package is identified with an RFID tag and recorded when it is placed into the refrigerated display case. All cases are equipped with RFID readers and antennas to scan the label of each product as it goes in, as it sits on the shelf, and as it goes back out with a consumer. Real-time data helps the store maintain fresh products, control the storage environment, and manage inventory levels.

Sources: Compiled from METRO Future Store (*future-store.org*, 2009), *CDC.gov*, IBM (*ibm.com*), and Weier (2007).

Discussion Questions: Where does the food supply chain start and end? What costs are reduced during a food recall if the food has RFID tags? How has barcoding and RFID improved the food supply chain?

MANAGING THE FLOW OF MATERIALS, DATA, AND MONEY

Supply chains involve the flow of materials, data, and money. Descriptions of these three main flows are:

1. **Material or product flow:** This is the movement of materials and goods from a supplier to its consumer. For example, chipmaker Intel supplies computer chips to its customer Dell. Dell supplies its computers to end users. Products that are returned make up what is called the **reverse supply chain** because goods are moving in the reverse direction. For any location on the supply chain, the immediate previous source is **one-back** and the immediate subsequent recipient is **one-up.** For example, in the food chain, each immediate previous supplier of food is a one-back and the immediate subsequent recipient (customer) of the food product is the one-up. For a manufacturer, raw material suppliers are one-back in the supply chain while retailers are one-up in that chain.

2. **Information flow:** This is the movement of detailed data among members of the supply chain, for example, order information, customer information, order fulfillment, delivery status, and proof-of-delivery confirmation. Most information flows are done electronically, although paper invoices or receipts are still common for noncommercial customers.

3. **Financial flow:** This is the transfer of payments and financial arrangements; for example, billing payment schedules, credit terms, and payment via **electronic funds transfer (EFT).** EFT provides for electronic payments and collections. It is safe, secure, efficient, and less expensive than paper check payments and collections.

Supply chain links are managed. Think of the chain in terms of its links because the entire chain is not managed as a single unit. A company can only manage the links it actually touches. That is, a company will manage only partners who are one-back and one-up because that's the extent of what a company can manage.

ORDER FULFILLMENT AND LOGISTICS

Order fulfillment is the set of complex processes involved in providing customers with what they have ordered on time and all related customer services. Order fulfillment depends on the type of product/service and purchase method (online, in-store, catalog, etc). For example, a customer who has ordered a new appliance via the *Sears.com* Web site needs to receive it as scheduled, with assembly and operating instructions as well as warranty and return information. The customer can receive a paper manual with the product or download the instructions from the Sears Web site. In addition, if the customer is not happy with a product, an exchange or return can be arranged via the Web site.

Order fulfillment is a part of **back-end** (or **back-office) operations,** which are activities that support the fulfillment of orders, such as accounting, inventory management, and shipping. It also is closely related to **front-office operations,** or *customer-facing activities,* which are activities, such as sales and advertising, that are visible to customers. The key aspects of order fulfillment are the delivery of materials or products at the right time, to the right place, and at the right cost.

Logistics is defined by the Council of Logistics Management as "the process of planning, implementing, and controlling the efficient and effective flow and storage of goods, services, and related information from point of origin to point of consumption for the purpose of conforming to customer requirements" (*Logisticsworld. com*). Note that this definition includes inbound, outbound, internal, and external movements and the return of materials and goods. It also includes *order fulfillment.* The distinction between logistics and order fulfillment is not always clear, and the terms are sometimes used interchangeably because logistics is a large part of order fulfillment.

STEPS IN THE ORDER FULFILLMENT PROCESS

The order fulfillment process consists of the flows of orders, payments, information, materials, and parts, all of which need to be coordinated with various departments and external partners. The order fulfillment process starts when an order is received and includes the following nine activities that are supported by software or may be automated:

Step 1. Make sure the customer will pay. Depending on the payment method and prior arrangements with the customer, verify that the customer can and will pay and the payment terms. This activity is done by the finance department for B2B sales or an external company, such as PayPal or a credit card issuer such as Visa for B2C sales. Any holdup in payment may cause a shipment to be delayed, resulting in a loss of goodwill or a customer. In B2C, the customers usually prepay by credit card, but the buyer may be using a stolen card, so verification is crucial.

Step 2. Check in-stock availability and reorder as necessary. As soon as an order is received, the stock (inventory) is checked to determine the availability of the product or materials. If there's not enough stock, the ordering system places an order, typically automatically using EDI (electronic data interchange). To perform these operations, the ordering system needs to be connected to the inventory system to verify availability and to suppliers' ordering systems. Several scenarios are possible that may involve the material management department and production department as well as outside suppliers and warehouse facilities. Most often buyers can check availability by themselves using the Web.

Step 3. Arrange shipments. When the product is available, shipment to the customer is arranged (otherwise, go to Step 5). Products can be digital or physical. If the item is physical and it's readily available, packaging and shipment arrangements are made. Both the packaging/shipping department and internal shippers or outside transporters may be involved. Digital items are usually available because their "inventory" is not depleted. However, a digital product, such as software, may be under revision and thus unavailable for delivery at certain times. In either case, information needs to flow among several partners.

Step 4. Insurance. Sometimes the contents of a shipment need to be insured. Both the finance department and an insurance company could be involved, and, again, information needs to flow not only inside the company but also to and from the customer and insurance agent.

Step 5. Replenishment. Customized (build-to-order) orders will always trigger a need for some manufacturing or assembly operation. Similarly, if standard items are out of stock, they need to be produced or procured. Production can be done in-house or by contractors.

Step 6. In-house production. In-house production needs to be planned, and actual production needs to be scheduled. Production planning involves people, materials, components, machines, financial resources, and possibly suppliers and subcontractors. In the case of assembly and/or manufacturing, several plant services may be needed, including collaboration with business partners. Production facilities may be in a different country than the company's headquarters or retailers. This may further complicate the flow of information.

Step 7. Use suppliers. A manufacturer may opt to buy products or subassemblies from suppliers. Similarly, if the seller is a retailer, such as in the case of *amazon.com* or *walmart.com,* the retailer must purchase products from its manufacturers. In this case, appropriate receiving and quality assurance of incoming materials and products must take place.

Once production (Step 6) or purchasing from suppliers (Step 7) is completed, shipments to the customers (Step 3) are arranged.

Step 8. Contacts with customers. Sales representatives need to keep in close contact with customers, especially in B2B, starting with notification of orders received and ending with notification of a shipment or a change in delivery date. These contacts are usually done via e-mail and are frequently generated automatically.

Step 9. Returns. In some cases, customers want to exchange or return items. The movement of returns from customers back to vendors is *reverse logistics.* Overall,

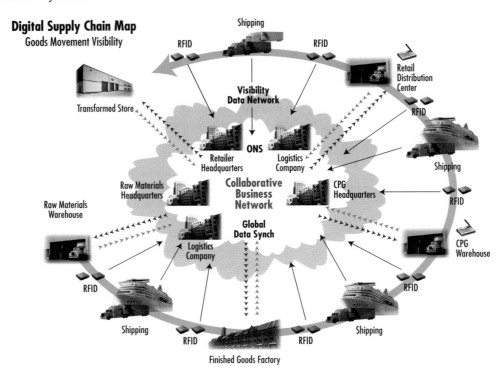

Digital Supply Chain Map
Goods Movement Visibility

Figure 10.7 Managing a supply chain with RFID.

between $50 and $100 billion in U. S. goods are returned each year. Such returns can be a major problem, especially when they occur in large volumes.

We now take a more in-depth look at supply chain management concepts.

SUPPLY CHAIN
MANAGEMENT
CONCEPTS

Supply chain management (SCM) is the efficient management of the flows of material, data, and money in the supply chain, as shown in Figure 10.7. **SCM software** refers to software that supports the steps in the supply chain—manufacturing, inventory control, scheduling, and transportation. SCM software concentrates on improving decision making, forecasting, optimization, and analysis. SCM software is configured to achieve the following business goals:

• To reduce uncertainty and variability in order to improve the accuracy of forecasting
• To increase control over the processes in order to achieve optimal inventory levels, cycle time, and customer service

The benefits of SCM have long been recognized in business, government, and the military. In today's competitive business environment, efficient, effective supply chains are critical to survival and fully dependent on SCM software, which depends on up-to-date and accurate data. If the network goes down or data is outdated, those managing the supply chain are mostly working blind.

The use of RFID in the supply chain provides a major opportunity to reduce costs and increase operating efficiencies. Figure 10.8 illustrates how RFID can improve the efficiency of a supply chain by improving data quality.

MANAGING ON-DEMAND
ACTIVITIES

The current business environment contains the elements of an *on-demand enterprise* with *real-time* operations. To review those concepts:

• **On-demand enterprise.** The concept of an on-demand enterprise is based on the premise that manufacturing or service fulfillment operations will start only after an order is received. We also refer to this approach as *build-to-order*. Enterprises have added this approach to their traditional **produce-to-stock** manufacturing. As the term indicates, *produce-to-stock* is the manufacture of products to stockpile inventory so the company is ready to respond to future demand. An obvious example of produce-to-stock is automobile dealerships, which have huge inventories of vehicles on their lot.

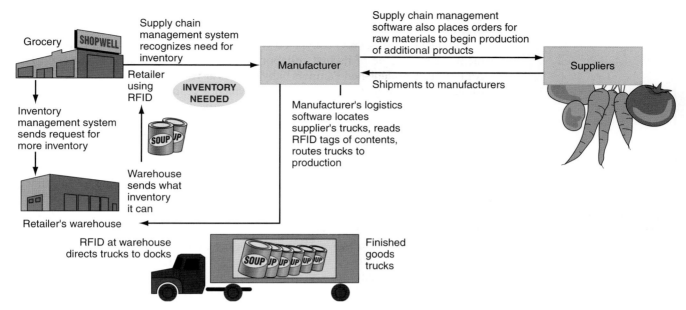

Figure 10.8 How RFID tags provide the data needed to manage the supply chain.

• **On-demand and real-time processes.** An on-demand process in the fulfillment cycle is one that is primed to respond to real-time conditions. There will be no back-orders, safety stock, lag time, or excess inventory. This principle is not fully achievable, but it is the direction that high-tech companies are headed in. Laptop and netbook manufacturers build-to-order as much as possible to reduce inventory, holding, and obsolescence costs. Inventory holding costs can greatly add to the cost of a product and narrow the profit margin.

These on-demand concepts have revolutionized the design and management of supply chains. To achieve on-demand and real-time processes, companies must reengineer their supply chain and add SCM to their ERP capabilities.

The market for SCM software applications and services reached $6.68 billion in 2008, a 4 percent increase over 2007, according to AMR Research (*amrresearch.com*). Leading SCM software vendors SAP and Oracle both posted significant percentage gains in 2008, with SAP up nearly 12 percent and Oracle growing by nearly 9 percent. In 2009, growth declined because of the bad economy. In a recession, companies do not make major investments in supply chain software unless it is mission-critical.

Review Questions

1. Define a *supply chain*.
2. List four functions performed in a supply chain.
3. List and describe the three main flows being managed in a supply chain.
4. Describe SCM.
5. What is order fulfillment?
6. Define *logistics*.

10.4 Collaborative Planning, Forecasting, and Replenishment (CPFR) Systems

There is a lot of uncertainty in product demand. The most common solution to supply chain uncertainties is to build inventories, or *safety stock,* as insurance. High levels of safety stock increase the costs of holding inventory. High inventories at multiple points in the supply chain can result in the bullwhip effect, described below. Low inventory levels increase the risk of stockouts (insufficient supply) and lost revenues when demand is high or delivery is slow. In either event, the total cost—including the cost of holding inventories, the cost of lost sales opportunities, and bad reputation—can be very high. Thus, companies strive to optimize and control inventories. A leader in inventory management for several decades has been Procter & Gamble (P&G).

In the late 1980s, P&G convinced Walmart to implement its continuous replenishment software. One of its first collaborations was with Walmart. For example, P&G continuously replenished Pampers baby diapers at Walmart stores. Continuous replenishment is a supply chain relationship in which a vendor continuously monitors the inventory of a retailer or distributor and automatically replenishes its inventory when levels hit the reorder point. In this vendor-managed inventory (VMI) situation, a vendor manages the inventory of its customers, eliminating the need for customers to send purchase orders. The advantage to the vendor is having more advanced notice of product demand. The advantage to the retailer or distributor is minimizing inventory costs. Having the correct item in stock when the end customer needs it benefits all partners.

BULLWHIP EFFECT IN THE SUPPLY CHAIN

P&G logistics executives examined the order patterns for one of their best-selling products, Pampers diapers. At retail stores, Pampers sales were fluctuating, but the variability was not excessive. However, as they examined orders of distributors, the executives were surprised by the higher degree of variability. When they looked at P&G's orders of materials—the manufacturing level—to its suppliers such as 3M, they discovered that the swings (variability) in the size of orders were even greater. Figure 10.9 shows how the swings, which look like bullwhips, intensify from retailers to distributors to manufacturers.

At first glance, the variability did not make sense. While the consumers, in this case *babies*, consumed diapers at a steady rate, the demand order variability in the supply chain gets amplified at the manufacturer. This phenomenon is called the **bullwhip effect,** which occurs when companies significantly cut or add inventories. Economists call it a *bullwhip* because even small increases in demand can cause a big increase in the need for parts and materials further down the supply chain.

The bullwhip has broad implications today, as companies rush to fill orders while also restocking warehouse shelves. It touches everyone from retailers to the industrial companies that supply the grease, bolts, and coal needed to churn out more products. The manner in which companies, large and small, respond to market shifts determines which ones emerge first from the slump and start growing again.

A big question as the economy starts to recover is how well suppliers are positioned to ramp up production. Bottlenecks may occur as spot shortages cause unexpected price hikes and hamper companies' ability to meet demand. That's why heavy-equipment manufacturer Caterpillar took the unusual step late in 2009 of visiting with key suppliers to ensure that they had the resources to quickly increase output. In extreme cases, Caterpillar is helping suppliers get financing.

Example. Caterpillar said that even if demand for its equipment was flat in 2010–2011, it would still need to boost production in its factories by 10 to 15 percent, just to restock dealer inventories and meet ongoing customer demand. Mechanical Devices Co. was already feeling the crack of the whip. The small factory in Bloomington, Illinois, supplies Caterpillar with metal parts. It struggled through 2009, shedding about 100 of its 275 workers and scrounging for other clients to keep its machines running.

Quantity Ordered

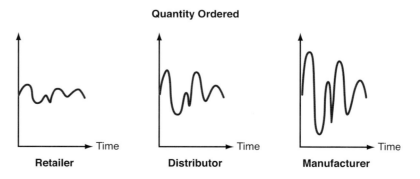

Figure 10.9 Bullwhip effect.

One reason Caterpillar is so attuned to the inventory cycle is its history. The company went through a massive growth spurt in the past decade, fueled by the twin forces of a commodity boom and a housing boom. Sales of the company's iconic yellow machines grew to $51 billion in 2008 from $20 billion in 2002.

How the Effect Works. SCM systems generate demand forecasts for a planning period, such as a quarter, month, or week. Participating sales representatives generate the sales forecasts. Based on these forecasts, the SCM systems stage, source, and schedule production and distribution facilities to meet your forecasted demand. Unfortunately, the sales force often changes the order quantities for a product before the close of the planning period. These deviations from the forecast are significant enough to cause a mismatch between what a company planned for production and what is actually needed to meet the amended orders. The deviations from the planned number of sales orders ripple through the supply chain, causing the bullwhip effect.

Amended sales orders exaggerate deviations as the information travels up the supply chain. If I am a component supplier one step up the chain, I will order raw material to build additional components and procure some material for safety stock. Next, my supplier will add its own safety stock to my amended order. These changes will continue up the supply chain, magnifying the original small deviation from planned orders. These oscillations cause all the firms in the supply chain to revamp their sourcing, manufacturing, and distribution plans. They now scramble to get additional raw material, add production lines, and restock distribution lines to meet the amended sales order quantities.

As a result of these oscillations from the bullwhip effect, firms across the supply chain are saddled with excess inventory, procurement cost overruns, additional warehousing and shipping costs, and, most importantly, quality problems. The upstream firms have the option of taking the loss resulting from amended orders or passing on the costs by reducing other product attributes. Component quality is the biggest casualty of rush orders. Distributors or retailers often return products manufactured to meet the amended demand signals, thus placing additional burden on the supply chain.

IMPROVING B2B EC

The most promising source of performance improvement in B2B e-commerce is collaboration in the supply chain. Supply chain collaboration can increase profit margins by as much as 3 percent for supply chain partners, which is a significant improvement. For the collaboration effort to succeed, business partners must *trust* each other and each other's information systems. Many supply chain problems have been solved through *sharing information* along the supply chain. Such information sharing is frequently referred to as the **collaborative supply chain.** It may take several different formats, as described next.

COLLABORATIVE PLANNING, FORECASTING, AND REPLENISHMENT

The concepts of continuous replenishment, VMI, and collaboration evolved into the more comprehensive model known as **collaborative planning, forecasting, and replenishment (CPFR).** CPFR is a set of data-driven business processes designed to improve the ability to predict and coordinate with supply chain partners. With CPFR, suppliers and retailers collaborate in planning and demand forecasting in order to ensure that members of the supply chain will have the right amount of raw materials and finished goods when they need them. CPFR streamlines product flow from manufacturing plants all the way to customers' homes.

The Voluntary Interindustry Commerce Solutions (VICS) Association (*vics.org*) describes the structure of CPFR activities and guidelines for implementing them. Since 1986, VICS Association has worked to improve the efficiency and effectiveness of supply chains. CPFR comprises four main collaboration activities:

- **Strategy and planning:** Setting the ground rules for the collaborative relationship and specifying the product mix.
- **Demand and supply management:** Forecasting consumer demand and order and shipment requirements over the planning horizon.
- **Execution:** Performing activities, such as placing orders, shipping and delivery, receiving, stocking, tracking sales transactions, and making payments.

• **Analysis:** Monitoring outcomes of planning and execution, assessing results and key performance metrics, sharing insights with partners, and adjusting plans to improve results.

Large manufacturers of consumer goods, such as Warner-Lambert (WL), have superb supply chains resulting from their use of CPFR. As part of a pilot project, WL shared strategic plans, performance data, and market insights with Walmart. The company realized that it could benefit from Walmart's market knowledge, just as Walmart could benefit from WL's product knowledge (see Figure 10.10). See *IT at Work 10.3* for details.

IT at Work 10.3

Demand Management and CPFR

In 2000, Warner-Lambert (WL) was acquired by Pfizer (*pfizer.com*), creating the world's fastest-growing pharmaceutical company. One of its major products is Listerine mouthwash. The materials for making Listerine come mainly from eucalyptus trees in Australia and are shipped to the WL manufacturing plant in New Jersey. Like all manufacturers, WL wanted answers to the one burning question that drives many decisions: "What are we going to sell this week or month?" Its key concern is accurately *forecasting overall demand* to determine how much Listerine to produce. Once demand is determined, WL calculates how much raw material is needed and when. A wrong forecast results in excess raw material or finished product inventories, or in shortages. Inventories are expensive to keep; shortages may result in loss of business to competitors.

WL forecasts demand using JDA Demand Management System (*jda.com/*). Used with other SCM software, the system analyzes manufacturing, distribution, and sales data against expected demand and business climate information. Its goal is to help WL decide when and how much Listerine and other products to produce. For example, the model can anticipate the

impact of seasonal promotion or a production line being down. WL's supply chain excellence stems from its collaborative planning, forecasting, and replenishment (CPFR) program.

Demand Management. WL's demand management system analyzes manufacturing, distribution, and sales data against expected demand and business climate information to help WL decide how much product to make and distribute. Because WL can smooth out the effects of seasonality in forecasts, it has dramatically cut manufacturing and raw materials inventory costs. Data transfer between companies is done using **electronic data interchange (EDI).** EDI is a communication standard that enables the electronic transfer of routine documents, such as purchase orders, between business partners. It formats these documents according to agreed-upon standards.

Sources: Compiled from *JDA.com* (2009) and *VICS.org*.

Discussion Questions: What other supply chain management solutions are offered by JDA? For what industries, besides retailing, would such collaboration be beneficial?

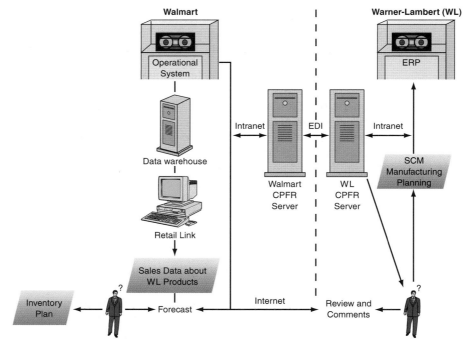

Figure 10.10 Model of CPFR.

Review Questions

> 1. How does demand uncertainty affect inventory? Give an example.
> 2. Describe a collaborative supply chain.
> 3. Define *CPFR* and describe how it works.
> 4. Describe how vendor-managed inventory works.

10.5 Customer Relationship Management (CRM) Systems

Every company depends on customers for revenues and growth. Marketing managers run campaigns, promotions, commercials, and advertisements to attract new customers, or to increase sales to existing customers, or both. Attracting new customers is expensive; for example, it costs banks roughly $100 to acquire a new customer. Newly acquired customers are unprofitable until they have purchased enough products or services to exceed the cost to acquire and service them. Therefore, retaining customers that generate revenues in excess of the costs (e.g., customer service, returns, promotional items, and the like) is critical—and the underlying reason for **customer relationship management** (CRM). **CRM** refers to the methodologies and software tools to leverage customer information in order to achieve the following:

- Build greater customer loyalty and therefore greater profitability per customer
- Deter customer attrition (loss of a customer)
- Acquire new customers who are most likely to become profitable
- Up-sell (sell more profitable products/services) or cross-sell (sell additional products/services) to unprofitable customers to move them to a profit position
- Reduce inefficiencies that waste advertising dollars

The purpose of frequent-purchase programs offered by airlines, supermarkets, credit card issuers, retailers, casinos, and other companies is to track customers for CRM purposes and build customer loyalty to improve financial performance.

According to management guru Peter Drucker, "Those companies who know their customers, understand their needs, and communicate intelligently with them will always have a competitive advantage over those that don't." For most types of companies, marketing effectiveness depends on how well they know their customers; specifically, knowing what their customers want, how best to contact them, and what types of offers they are likely to respond to positively. According to the *loyalty effect*, a 5 percent reduction in customer attrition can improve profits by as much as 20 percent. Customer-centric business strategies strive to provide products and services that customers want to buy. One of the best examples is the Apple iPhone and iPod—devices that customers were willing to camp out on sidewalks to buy to guarantee getting one on the day of their release. In contrast, companies with product-centric strategies need to create demand for their products, which is more expensive and may fail.

CRM EXAMPLE: TRAVELOCITY

CRM is best understood by looking at a familiar company's CRM strategy. Consider *travelocity.com,* the online travel agency. Travelocity implemented CRM software from Teradata (*teradata.com*) in 2001 to better understand, serve, and communicate with its 40 million customers. Its CRM software has enabled Travelocity to:

- Analyze clickstream data and discover how customers use the Web site. This information is leveraged to better personalize messages in realtime (that is, while customers are using the site).
- Test the value of specific messages and offers on various customer segments.
- Identify customers who have booked a flight, but not a hotel or car rental, and then make them a compelling offer. Adjusting offers or taking action based on customer behavior is referred to as *event-based marketing*.

Building CRM capabilities takes time and requires a data warehouse for the analytics. Travelocity started with the building blocks to learn about its customers and the best ways to deliver targeted market campaigns to them. In addition, Travelocity can respond quickly to offers from its suppliers. For example, at 8 A.M. a major airline offered travel agencies a special fare from Los Angeles to San Juan, Puerto Rico. Travelocity quickly scanned its customers' browsing behavior, pulled the e-mail addresses of 30,000 people in the Los Angeles area who had browsed but not bought tickets to the Caribbean, and then generated an e-mail message to them. The response rate was incredible: 25 percent of the recipients who had been e-mailed booked flights. This was an effective campaign measured by the response rate, or take rate, as well as a highly efficient one as measured by the ROI from the profit on sales of those extra tickets.

CRM IS MULTICHANNEL

CRM is implemented across multiple sales channels.

Dell Computer uses direct mail, e-mail, media advertising, and the Internet in combination with personal contacts by sales representatives and special intranet Web sites for large Dell accounts to stay connected with its customers.

Barnes & Noble's (*BN.com*) multichannel strategy allows customers to browse and buy products at any of its stores or online. The "Readers Advantage" loyalty program offers customers additional discounts and benefits.

1-800-FLOWERS.com uses e-mail, Web sites, telephone, retail stores, and catalogs to deploy its multichannel marketing strategies. The company's customer-centric focus has enabled it to achieve up to 35 percent growth for several years.

CRM IS AN ENTERPRISEWIDE INITIATIVE

CRM is an enterprise-wide effort to acquire and retain profitable customers. CRM focuses on building long-term and sustainable customer relationships for the purpose of increasing the company's profitability. A common misconception about CRM is that it's about providing services and perks to delight or keep customers happy. As the Travelocity example shows, CRM is a data-driven, fact-based business strategy to select and manage customers to optimize sales and profit.

Key components of CRM are shown in Figure 10.11 and described below:

- Customers
- Call center
- Marketing department
- Sales department
- Customer support

CRM is basically a simple idea: *Treat different customers differently* according to their current or potential value to the company. CRM involves much more than just sales and marketing because a firm must be able to change how its products are configured or its services are delivered based on the needs of individual customers or customer segments. Smart companies encourage the active participation of customers in the development of products, services, and solutions.

E-CRM

There's one key advancement created by Web 2.0 that organizations must force themselves to recognize: "Your customers have technology, too, and if you don't deliver a customer experience that's of value to them, they will let the community know."

CRM has been practiced manually by corporations for generations. However, since the mid-1990s, various types of information technologies have enhanced CRM. CRM technology is an evolutionary response to changes in the business environment, making use of new IT devices and tools. The term **e-CRM (electronic CRM)** was

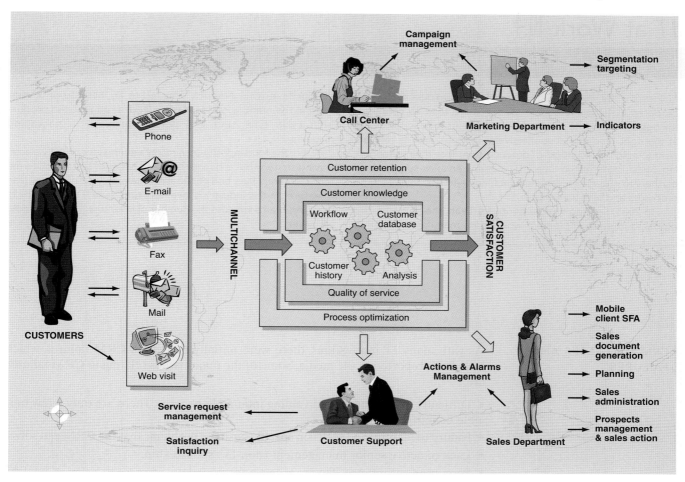

Figure 10.11 CRM.

coined in the mid-1990s, when businesses started using Web browsers, the Internet, and other electronic touchpoints (e-mail, POS terminals, call centers, and direct sales) to manage customer relationships. E-CRM covers a broad range of topics, tools, and methods, ranging from the proper design of digital products and services to pricing to loyalty programs.

Through Internet technologies, data generated about customers can be easily fed into marketing, sales, and customer service applications for analysis. Electronic CRM also includes online applications that lead to segmentation and personalization. The success of these efforts can be measured and modified in real time, further elevating customer expectations. In a world connected by the Internet, e-CRM has become a requirement for survival, not just a competitive advantage. In this section we will discuss several issues related to e-CRM and its implementation.

Loyalty programs are programs that recognize customers who repeatedly use the services (products) offered by a company. A well-known example is the airlines' *frequent-flyers* program. Casinos use their players' clubs to reward their frequent players. Many supermarkets use some kind of program to reward frequent shoppers, as do many other companies. These programs include some kind of database (or data warehouse) to manage the accounting of the points collected and the rewards. Analytical tools such as data mining are then used to explore the data and learn about customer behavior.

IT at Work 10.4

Kellogg's K-Lean Programs in Latin America

Kellogg's is the world's leading breakfast cereal manufacturer. It produces in 19 countries and sells in more than 16 countries. Kellogg's manages its supply chain to place its products in stores at the right time and cost-effectively. Kellogg's and its retailers want to hold limited stocks of products to reduce their warehousing costs. Using just-in-time (JIT) systems enables supply chain partners to engage in lean manufacturing—that is, to streamline processes and eliminate waste.

In 2008, Kellogg's implemented *K-Lean*, the name for the global journey to implement world-class manufacturing at all its plants in Latin America. This led to an increase of 50 percent in the number of boxes produced, a reduction in production cycle time, and a 4 percent increase in packaging capacity.

For the food industry, lean manufacturing is not simply a cost-saving strategy but is directly linked to issues of sustainability, the environment, ethics and public accountability. One of the key lean measures in this industry is inventory turns (see IT at Work 10.1). Lean programs increase the number of inventory turns a business achieves.

CRM SUCCESSES AND FAILURES

As with many IT innovations, there were initially numerous CRM failures, which have been reported in the media. Some of the major issues relating to CRM failures are:

- Difficulty in measuring and valuing intangible benefits. There are only a few tangible benefits to CRM.
- Failure to identify and focus on specific business problems that the CRM can solve.
- Lack of active senior management (non-IT) sponsorship.
- Poor user acceptance. This can occur for a variety of reasons, such as unclear benefits—that is, CRM is a tool for management, but it may not help a rep sell more effectively—and usability problems.
- An attempt to automate a poorly defined business process in the CRM implementation.

Example of a Failure. Citizen National Bank's experience is an example of a failure that became a success with the change of CRM vendors. The lessons learned, at a cost of $500,000, were

- Be absolutely clear about how the CRM application will add value to the sales process.
- Determine if and why sales people are avoiding CRM.
- Provide incentives for the sales team to adopt CRM.
- Find ways to simplify the use of the CRM application.
- Adjust the CRM system as business needs change.

Justifying e-CRM. One of the biggest problems in CRM implementation is the difficulty of defining and measuring success. Additionally, many companies say that when it comes to determining value, intangible benefits are more significant than tangible cost savings. Yet companies often fail to establish quantitative or even qualitative measures in order to judge these intangible benefits.

A formal business plan must be in place before the e-CRM project begins—one that quantifies the expected costs, tangible financial benefits, and intangible strategic benefits, as well as the risks. The plan should include an assessment of the following:

- **Tangible net benefits.** The plan must include a clear and precise cost-benefit analysis that lists all of the planned project costs and tangible benefits. This portion of the

IT at Work 10.5

CRM and e-CRM Apps

Most corporations have formal CRM and e-CRM systems. Here are a few examples of how companies have benefitted from t systems:

- Micrel Inc., a leading manufacturer of integrated circuit solutions for enterprise, consumer, industrial, mobile, telecommunications, automotive, and computer markets, has become known for being "fast on its feet" in responding to customer needs. To improve response time and relevancy of information delivered to customers online, the company uses a sophisticated self-service search and navigation engine that directs customers to the right information at the right time to help them reach buying decisions. As a result, Web site traffic grew by 300 percent, retention rate for new site visitors increased by 25 percent, the company saved $40,000 a year, and customer satisfaction increased significantly.

- The Kassel region in Germany uses a CRM-based social networking platform to attract businesses, tourists, and potential residents. The site won the Most Innovative CRM Deployment Award at the *CRM Expo*, Europe's largest CRM show.

- Boots the Chemists, a U.K. retailer of over 1,400 health and beauty stores, uses e-CRM analytics to learn about customers in its e-loyalty programs. The retailer uses data mining to acquire insights into customer behavior. Customer service agents can analyze, predict, and maximize the value of each customer relationship.

- FedEx's CRM system enables the company to provide superb service to millions of customers using 56 call centers. Each of its 4,000 call center employees has instant access to a customer's profile. The profile tells the employee how valuable the customer is and the details of the current transaction. The more an agent knows about the customer, the better the service provided. Customers use one phone number regardless of where the company is or the destination of the package. The CRM reduced calls for help, increased customer satisfaction, and enabled better advertising and marketing strategy.

Discussion Questions: What are the common elements of CRM in these examples? CRM systems provide managerial benefits. What are they? Why is data mining becoming so important in CRM?

---

plan should also contain a strategy for assessing key financial metrics, such as ROI, NPV, or other justification methods.

- **Intangible benefits.** The plan should detail the expected intangible benefits, and it should list the measured successes and shortfalls. Often, an improvement in customer satisfaction is the primary goal of the e-CRM solution, but in many cases this key value is not measured.

- **Risk assessment.** The risk assessment is a list of all of the potential pitfalls related to the people, processes, and technology that are involved in the e-CRM project.

Having such a list helps to lessen the probability that problems will occur. And, if they do occur, a company may find that, by having listed and considered the problems in advance, the problems are more manageable than they would have been otherwise.

While a special approach is recommended for all enterprise systems, the CRM approach is most challenging, as you will find in the *Analysis Using Spreadsheets* at the end of this chapter.

Tangible and Intangible Benefits. Benefits typically include increases in staff productivity (e.g., closing more deals, avoiding costs, increasing revenues, and increasing margins) as well as reductions in inventory costs (e.g., due to the elimination of errors). Other benefits include increased customer satisfaction, loyalty, and retention.

Potential Pitfalls and Risks of e-CRM

- Taking on more than can be delivered. The e-CRM solution should target specific sales or service business functions or specific groups of users. Additionally, it is essential to manage the project's scope, goals, and objectives throughout the project development phase and deployment.
- Getting over budget and behind schedule.
- Poor user adoption. Ease of use and adequate training are essential.
- Expensive maintenance and support.
- Isolation. The effectiveness of a project may suffer if the CRM data is not used throughout the company.
- Garbage in–garbage out (GIGO). Because e-CRM systems require so much data entry, users often put in placeholders, misguided estimates, or inaccurate information, which leads to poor analytical results and decision-making errors.
- Failure to measure success. Measurement of pre-project status and post-project achievements is essential for a company to show success.

On-Demand CRM. Like several other enterprise systems, CRM can be delivered in two ways: on-premises and on-demand. The traditional way to deliver such systems was on-premises—meaning users purchased the system and installed it on-site. This was very expensive, with a large upfront payment. Many SMEs (small and medium-sized enterprises) could not justify it, especially because most CRM benefits are intangible.

The solution to the situation is to lease the software. *Salesforce.com* pioneered the concept for its several CRM products, including supporting salespeople, under the name of *On-Demand CRM,* offering the software over the Internet. The concept of on-demand is known also as *utility computing* or *software-as-a-service* (SaaS). On-demand CRM is basically CRM hosted by a vendor on the vendor's premises, in contrast to the traditional practice of buying the software and using it on-site.

On-demand CRM must be weighed against the following implementation problems:

- Service providers can go out of business, leaving customers without service.
- It is difficult, or even impossible, to modify hosted software.
- Upgrading could become a problem.
- Relinquishing strategic data to a hosting vendor can be risky.
- Integration with existing software may be difficult.

The benefits are:

- Improved cash flow due to savings in upfront purchase
- No need for corporate software experts
- Ease of use with minimal training
- Fast time-to-market
- Vendors' expertise available

Review Questions

1. Define *CRM*.
2. List the major types of CRM.
3. What is e-CRM?
4. List some customer-facing, customer-touching, and customer-intelligent CRM tools.
5. What is on-demand CRM?

10.6 Knowledge Management (KM) Systems

Forrester Research and IBM estimated that up to 85 percent of a company's *knowledge* is not stored in databases. Knowledge is dispersed in social media, e-mail, texts, intranets, drops (*drop.io*), Word documents, spreadsheets, and presentations on individual computers and mobile devices. Knowledge typically is unstructured and has strong experiential and reflective elements that distinguish it from information in a given context.

KNOWLEDGE

Having knowledge implies that it can be used to solve a problem, whereas having information does not. The ability to act is an integral part of being knowledgeable. For example, two people in the same context with the same information may not have the same ability to use the information with the same degree of success. There is a difference in the human capability to add value. The differences in ability may be due to different experiences, different training, different perspectives, and other factors.

Whereas data, information, and knowledge may all be viewed as assets of an organization, knowledge provides a higher level of meaning about data and information. It conveys meaning and tends to be much more valuable, yet more ephemeral.

In the IT context, knowledge is very distinct from data and information. See Figure 10.12. Whereas data is a collection of facts, measurements, and statistics, information is organized or processed data that is timely and accurate. Knowledge is information that is contextual, relevant, and actionable.

KNOWLEDGE MANAGEMENT (KM)

Knowledge management (KM) is a process that helps organizations identify, select, organize, disseminate, and transfer important information and expertise that are part of the organization's memory. The goal of KM systems is to identify, capture, store, maintain, and deliver useful knowledge in a meaningful form to anyone who needs it, anyplace and anytime, within an organization. KM systems support sharing, decision making, and collaborating at the organization level regardless of location.

KM initiatives focus on identifying knowledge, explicating it in such a way that it can be shared in a formal or systematic manner, and leveraging its value through reuse.

Through a supportive organizational climate and IT, an organization can bring its entire organizational memory and knowledge to bear upon any problem anywhere in the world and at any time. For organizational success, *knowledge, as a form of capital, must be exchangeable among persons, and it must be able to grow.* Knowledge about how problems are solved can be captured, so that KM can promote organizational learning, leading to further knowledge creation.

For example, a map giving detailed driving directions from one location to another could be considered data. An up-to-the-minute traffic bulletin along the

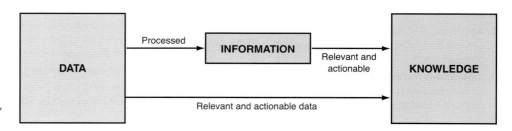

Figure 10.12 Data, information, and knowledge.

freeway that indicates a traffic slowdown due to construction could be considered information. Awareness of an alternative, back-roads route could be considered knowledge. In this case, the map is considered data because it does not contain current relevant information that affects the driving time and conditions from one location to the other. However, having the current conditions as information is useful only if the individual has knowledge that will enable him or her to avoid the construction zone. Having knowledge implies that it can be used to solve a problem, whereas having information does not carry the same connotation.

KM Systems. **Knowledge management systems (KMSs)** refer to the use of the Internet, intranets, extranets, LotusNotes, software filters, agents, and data warehouses to systematize, enhance, and expedite intra- and interfirm knowledge management. KMSs are intended to help an organization cope with turnover, rapid change, and downsizing by making the expertise of the organization's human capital widely accessible. They are being built in part from increased pressure to maintain a well-informed, productive workforce. They also help organizations retain the knowledge of departing employees. Many organizations have been building KM systems in order to capitalize on the knowledge and experience of employees worldwide. For an example, see the case of Petronas in *IT at Work 10.6*.

IT at Work 10.6

Knowledge Management in PETRONAS

GLOBAL　ETHICS　IS　ACCT　FIN

PETRONAS (*Petroliam Nasional Berhad*) is an oil and gas business fully owned by the Malaysian Government. The company, founded in 1974, has presence in more than 30 countries. PETRONAS ranked among the Top 100 FORTUNE Global companies, was the thirteenth most profitable company worldwide, and the most profitable company in Asia in 2009.

PETRONAS Starts Doing KM Strategically. PETRONAS started to do KM strategically across the entire organization in 2006. Before that, there were pockets of KM initiatives at the department level, and KM focus had been on content and information management. KM has since matured from managing content to a greater emphasis on managing connections, relationships, and extracting and transferring tacit knowledge of staff. Reasons for the new strategic KM initiative were:

1. **Aging workforce:** A good percentage of the PETRONAS workforce was retiring within the next five to 10 years. KM was needed to preserve their expertise such that it could be used to increase productivity and accelerate growth of young engineers.

2. **Attrition:** Skilled employees were being hired away by competitors. KM helped retain and grow skills to remain competitive.

3. **Operations increasingly international:** KM helped assimilate oil and gas plants to operate the *PETRONAS way* and transmit relevant knowledge assets across borders.

KM Requires Changing Behavior. When the strategic KM program first started, the focus was on technology because their disparate databases made sharing difficult. However, like other organizations they learned that changing technology is easy compared to the difficulty of changing people's behavior. Most efforts were focused on strengthening *Communities of Practice* (CoP) for connecting people to people.

SharePoint. PETRONAS developed their own KM platform using Microsoft SharePoint (*sharepoint.microsoft.com/*). Microsoft SharePoint makes it easier for people to work together. The KM systems have modest features including discussion forums, document library, yellow pages, CoP portal, and a search engine for groupwide knowledge sharing and collaboration.

Sources: Compiled from KMTalk (2009), PETRONAS Gas News (2011), IKMS.org (2008).

Discussion Questions:

1. KM can be done at any level within an organization—department, division, or enterprise-wide. Why did PETRONAS expand KM from department to enterprise-wide?

2. What were the challenges?

3. Review the latest version of Microsoft SharePoint at *sharepoint. microsoft.com./* List SharePoint's features.

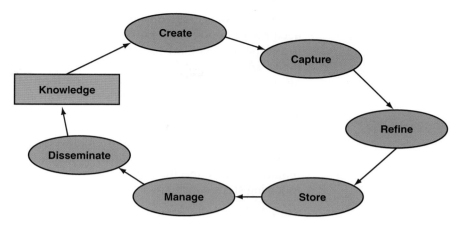

Figure 10.13 The knowledge management system cycle.

KM Systems Cycle. A functioning KMS follows six steps in a cycle, which is shown in Figure 10.13. The system is cyclical because knowledge is acquired and refined over time. The cycle works as follows:

1. Create knowledge. Knowledge is created as people determine new ways of doing things or develop know-how. Sometimes external knowledge is brought in.

2. Capture knowledge. New knowledge must be identified as valuable and be represented in a reasonable way.

3. Refine knowledge. New knowledge must be placed in context so that it is actionable. This is where human insights (tacit qualities) must be captured along with explicit facts.

4. Store knowledge. Useful knowledge must then be stored in a reasonable format in a knowledge repository so that others in the organization can access it.

5. Manage knowledge. Like a library, the knowledge must be kept current. It must be reviewed to verify that it is relevant and accurate.

6. Disseminate knowledge. Knowledge must be made available in a useful format to anyone in the organization who needs it, anywhere and anytime.

COMPONENTS OF KM SYSTEMS

KM systems are developed using the following sets of technologies: *communication* and *collaboration*, and *storage* and *retrieval*.

Communication and collaboration technologies allow users to access needed knowledge and to communicate with each other and with experts. Communication and collaboration also allow for knowledge solicitation from experts.

Storage and retrieval technologies originally meant using a database management system to store and manage knowledge. This worked reasonably well in the early days for storing and managing most explicit knowledge, and even explicit knowledge about tacit knowledge. However, capturing, storing, and managing tacit knowledge usually requires a different set of tools. Electronic document management systems and specialized storage systems that are part of collaborative computing systems fill this void. *Desktop search* is a major tool in knowledge retrieval.

KM SYSTEM IMPLEMENTATION

In the early 2000s, KMS technology evolved to integrate collaborative computing, databases, and network technology (previously independent of each other) into a single KMS package. Today, these include enterprise knowledge portals and knowledge management suites. These are sold with other enterprise systems packages, especially CRM, and are available on an on-demand basis, so even SMEs can use them. In addition, there were some innovative specific applications, such as expert locating systems.

Finding Experts Electronically and Using Expert Location Systems. People who need help can post their problem on the corporate intranet, blogs, or social media to ask for help. Similarly, companies may ask for advice on how to exploit an opportunity. IBM frequently uses this method. Sometimes it obtains hundreds of useful ideas within a few days. This method is a form of brainstorming. The problem with this approach is that it may take days to get an answer, if an answer is even provided, and the answer may not be from the top experts.

Therefore, companies use expert location systems. **Expert location systems (ELSs)** are interactive and help employees find and connect with colleagues—whether they are across the country or across the room—who possess the expertise required to solve specific, critical business problems quickly. The process includes the following steps, which are also listed in Figure 10.14:

Step 1. An employee submits a question into the ELS.

Step 2. The software searches its database to see if an answer to the question already exists. If it does, the information (research reports, spreadsheets, etc.) is returned to the employee. If not, the software searches documents and archived communications for an "expert."

Step 3. Once a qualified candidate is located, the system asks if he is able to answer a question from a colleague. If so, he submits a response. If the candidate is unable to respond (perhaps he is in a meeting or otherwise indisposed), he can elect to pass on the question. The question is then routed to the next appropriate candidate until one responds.

Step 4. After the response is sent, it is reviewed for accuracy and sent back to the querist. At the same time, it is added to the knowledge database. This way, if the question comes up again, it will not be necessary to seek real-time assistance.

IT at Work 10.7 demonstrates how an ELS works for the U.S. government.

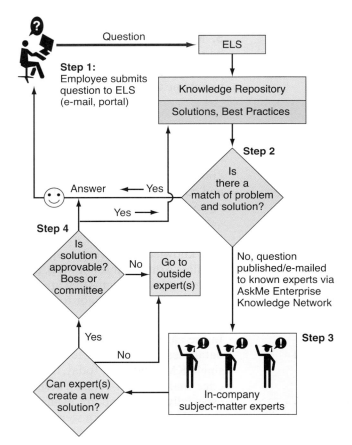

Figure 10.14 Expert location system of AskMe Corp.

IT at Work 10.7

AskMe Expert Location System (ELS)

The Commercial Service Division at the U.S. Department of Commerce (DOC) employs specialists who research or call on experts to answer questions asked by corporations. A software company contacted Brad Anderson, a DOC specialist, for advice about a tax issue with a customer in Poland. The Polish buyer wanted to charge a 20 percent withholding tax—a tax it attributed to Poland's recent admission into the European Union (EU). Was the tax legitimate?

DOC Insider. To find the answers, Anderson used *DOC Insider*, an ELS from AskMe. After typing in his question, Anderson found documents related to his query, but they did not fully explain the EU tax code. Anderson then asked the system to search the Commercial Service 1,700-expert list for a live expert, and within seconds he was given a list of 80 people in the DOC who might

be able to answer. Of those, he chose the six people he felt were most qualified and then forwarded his query.

Before the DOC Insider was in place, Anderson says it would have taken him about three days to get the answer to the question. He would have to make many phone calls and deal with time zones. With *DOC Insider*, he had three responses within minutes, a complete answer within an hour, and the sale went through the following morning. Anderson estimates that he now uses the system for roughly 40 percent of the work he does. In the first nine months, ELS saved more than 1,000 hours of work.

Sources: Compiled from D'Agostino (2004) and Fox (2004).

Discussion Questions: What are the benefits of an ELS? Will the system impact privacy? Can it be integrated with wireless devices? If so, for what purposes?

INTEGRATION OF KM SYSTEMS WITH OTHER ISS

Since a knowledge management system is an enterprise system, it is usually integrated with enterprise and other information systems in an organization. Obviously, when a KMS is designed and developed, it cannot be perceived as an add-on application. It must be truly integrated into other systems. Through the help of the organizational culture, a knowledge management system and its activities can be directly integrated into a firm's business processes. For example, a group involved in customer support can capture its knowledge to provide help on customers' difficult problems. In this case, help-desk software would be one type of package to integrate into a KMS, especially into the knowledge repository. A major challenge is to integrate data that resides in a variety of systems, locations, and formats.

Review Questions

1. Define *KM* and relate it to knowledge and intellectual capital. What are the major benefits of KM to a company?
2. Distinguish knowledge from data and information.
3. Draw the KM life cycle and explain the major steps.
4. Describe the major components of a KM system.
5. Describe an expert location system.
6. Relate KM to training.

Key Terms

agility *286*
available-to-promise (ATP) *285*
back-office operation *298*
B2B gateway *292*
bullwhip effect *302*
collaborative planning, forecasting, and replenishment (CPFR) *303*
customer relationship management (CRM) *305*

e-CRM (electronic CRM) *306*
electronic data interchange (EDI) *304*
electronic funds transfer (EFT) *298*
enterprise application integration (EAI) *291*
enterprise information systems *286*
enterprise resource planning (ERP) *288*
external supply chain *284*

financial flow *298*
front-office operations *298*
information flow *298*
internal supply chain *284*
knowledge management (KM) *311*
knowledge management system (KMS) *312*
legacy system *284*
logistics *298*

Chapter Highlights and Insights

(Numbers refer to Learning Objectives)

❶ Enterprise systems are information systems that support several departments and/or the entire enterprise. The most notable are ERP, which supports supply chains, and CRM.

❶ Supply chains connect suppliers to a manufacturing company, departments inside a company to one another, and a company to its customers. The supply chain must be completely managed, from the raw materials to the end customers. Typical supply chains involve three segments: upstream, internal, and downstream. Most supply chains are supported by a variety of IT application programs.

❷ It is difficult to manage the supply chain due to the uncertainties in demand and supply and the need to coordinate several (sometimes many) business partners' activities. One of the major problems is known as the bullwhip effect, in which lack of coordination and/or communication results in large, unnecessary inventories.

❷ A number of solutions to supply chain problems are supported by IT, such as appropriate inventory management, vertical integration, information sharing, VMI, supply chain collaboration, RFID, supply chain teams, virtual factories, and wireless solutions.

❸ The next step in SCM was to integrate routine transactions, including internal suppliers/customers and external suppliers/customers, in ERP and extended ERP software. The latest step in the evolution of integrated supply chain software is the addition of business intelligence and CRM applications.

❹ CRM is an enterprise-wide activity through which an organization takes care of its customers and their needs. It is based on the idea of one-to-one relationships with customers. CRM is done by providing many communication and collaboration services, most of which are IT-supported and many of which are delivered on the Web.

❺ Knowledge management is a process that helps organizations identify, select, organize, disseminate, and transfer important information and expertise that typically reside within the organization in an unstructured way. The knowledge management model involves following cyclical steps: create, capture, refine, store, manage, and disseminate knowledge.

❺ A variety of technologies can make up a knowledge management system: the Internet, intranets, data warehousing, decision-support tools, groupware, and so on. Intranets are the primary means of displaying and distributing knowledge within organizations.

❻ KM has many potential benefits resulting from reuse of expertise. The problem is how to collect, store, update, and properly reuse the knowledge. It is difficult to measure the success of a KMS. Traditional methods of financial measurement fall short, as they do not consider intellectual capital an asset. Nonfinancial metrics are typically used to measure the success of a KM, yet some firms have been able to determine financial payoffs.

Questions for Discussion

1. Distinguish between ERP and SCM software. In what ways do they complement each other? Why should they be integrated?

2. Discuss the benefits of e-procurement.

3. Find examples of how two of the following organizations improve their supply chains: manufacturing, hospitals, retailing, education, construction, agribusiness, and shipping. Discuss the benefits to the organizations.

4. It is said that supply chains are essentially "a series of linked suppliers and customers; every customer is in turn a supplier to the next downstream organization, until the ultimate end user." Explain. Use of a diagram is recommended.

5. Discuss why it is difficult to justify CRM.

6. A supply chain is much more powerful in the Internet marketplace. Discuss how Internet technologies can be used to manage the supply chain.

7. Explain how vendor-managed inventory can save costs in the supply chain.

8. State the business value of enterprise systems and how they can be used to make management of the supply chain more effective.

9. Discuss each of the steps in the ERP selection process.

10. What are the problems in implementing ERP systems? State solutions that make implementations more successful.

11. Describe and relate the different characteristics of knowledge.

12. Explain why it is important to capture and manage knowledge.

13. Compare and contrast tacit knowledge and explicit knowledge.

14. How can employees be motivated to contribute to and use KM systems?

15. Explain how the Internet and its related technologies (Web browsers, intranets, and so on) enable knowledge management.

16. Discuss the value for expert locating systems over simply using the Internet.

Exercises and Projects

1. Identify the supply chain(s) and the flow of information described in the opening case. Draw it. Also, answer the following.
   a. "The company's business is not to make the product, but to sell the product." Explain this statement.
   b. Why was it necessary to use IT to support the change?
   c. Identify all of the segments of the supply chain.
   d. Identify all supporting information systems in this case.

2. Visit Teradata Student Network and find the podcasts that deal with CRM and supply chains. Identify the benefits cited in the podcasts.

3. Enter Teradata Student Network and find the most recent Web seminar on data integration. Relate these tools to the integration issues discussed in this chapter.

4. Based on your own experience or on the vendor's information, list the major capabilities of a particular knowledge management product, and explain how it can be used in practice.

5. Visit *sap.com* and identify all modules that are related to financial management and all those related to HRM.

Group Assignments and Projects

1. Each group in the class will be assigned to a major ERP/SCM vendor such as SAP, Oracle, Microsoft, and so forth. Members of the groups will investigate topics such as (a) Web connections, (b) use of business intelligence tools, (c) relationship to CRM and to KM, (d) major capabilities, and (e) availability of ASP services by the specific vendor.

    Each group will prepare a presentation for the class, trying to convince the class why the group's software is best for a local company known to the students (e.g., a supermarket chain).

2. Create groups to investigate the major CRM software vendors, their products, and the capabilities of those products in the following categories. (Each group represents a topical area of several companies.)
   - Sales force automation (Oracle, Onyx, Salesforce, Saleslogix, Pivotal)
   - Call centers [Clarify, LivePerson, NetEffect, Inference, marketing automation (Annuncio, MarketFirst)]

   - Customer service [Brightware (from Oracle), Broadvision]
   - Sales configuration (Selectica, Cincom)

    Start with *searchcrm.com* and *crmguru.com* (to ask questions about CRM solutions). Each group must present arguments to the class to convince class members to use the product(s) the group investigated.

3. Search the Internet for knowledge management products and systems and create categories for them. Assign one vendor to each team. Describe the categories you created and justify them. Examine Tolisma Knowledge base (see *knowledgebase.net*) and Intactix Knowledge base (from JDA Software, *jda.com*). What did the vendors' knowledge bases accomplish?

4. Visit Teradata Student Network and find the First American Corporation Case (by Watson, Wixon, and Goodhue), regarding CRM implementation. Write an executive summary listing the key lessons that you learned.

Internet Exercises

1. Visit *ups.com*. Examine some of the IT-supported customer services and tools provided by the company. Write a report on how UPS contributes to supply chain improvements.

2. Visit *supply-chain.org, cio.com, findarticles.com*, and *google.com* and search for recent information on supply chain management integration.

3. Visit *sap.com*. Search for the Advanced Planner and Optimization (APO). What value does SAP APO offer?

4. Visit *i2.com* and review its SCM products that go beyond ERP. Examine the OCN Network and Rhythm. Write a report.

5. Visit *oracle.com*. Find the ERP modules offered by Oracle and identify their connection to CRM and customer services.

6. Visit *salesforce.com* and take the tour. What enterprise-wide system does the company support? How?

7. Enter *2020software.com*. Find information about the top 10 ERP solutions. View the demo; write a report on your findings.

8. How does knowledge management support decision making? Identify products or systems on the Web that help organizations accomplish knowledge management. Start with *brint.com, decisionsupport.net*, and *knowledge-management.ittoolbox.com*. Try one out and report your findings to the class.

9. Visit *internetdashboard.com*. View its products and relate them to the different enterprise systems described in this chapter.

BUSINESS CASE

Impact of Japan Quake on Apple iPad 2 Supply Chain

FIN   POM

Apple sold fewer than 4.7 million iPad 2s in the first quarter of 2011 (1Q2011), which was 1.6 million fewer devices than Wall Street expected. Demand was not the problem; in fact, demand for the iPad 2 was stronger than estimated. iPad buyers faced sold-out stock at Apple stores and long wait times ordering online. The problem was a bottleneck on the supply side. Apple's iPad production lines were blocked by various manufacturing problems, among them:

- quality concerns with liquid crystal display (LCD) panels
- production shortages of the new speaker
- lamination issues with one of the touch suppliers
- end-unit production shortages

Apple faced production slowdowns with iPads because its key components were made in Japan. Factories weren't damaged, but parts delivery and logistics were extremely delayed. As early adopters well know, Apple has dealt with supply constraints before. The iPhone 4 faced delays for months after its launch, and the original iPad was also difficult to come by.

Earthquake Disrupts Logistics and Supply Chain

The 2011 Japanese earthquake disrupted logistics that led to supply shortages of the iPad 2. Several iPad components were manufactured in the disaster-stricken area—including a hard-to-replace electronic compass, the battery, and possibly the advanced technology glass in the display. Market research firm iSuppli (isuppli.com/) identified five parts sourced from Japanese suppliers: NAND flash from Toshiba Corp., dynamic random access memory (DRAM) made by Elpida Memory Inc., an electronic compass from AKM Semiconductor, the touch-screen overlay glass that is likely from Asahi Glass Co., and the system battery from Apple Japan Inc.

While some of these suppliers' facilities were undamaged, delivery of components from all of them was impacted by logistical problems in the quake zone. Suppliers had difficulty shipping out products and getting raw materials supplied and distributed. They also faced difficulties with employee absences because of transport system problems. These challenges were made worse by interruptions in the electricity supply, which can have a major impact on delicate processes such as semiconductor lithography.

In 2Q2011, Apple announced that it was on track to increase its production volume. But it was still falling substantially short of its target production goal for April 2011.

Sharp Drop in Stock Price Linked to Supply Problems

In March 2011, Apple shares did something they rarely do: they fell nearly 7 percent in two days. Apple's stock price dropped sharply—more than twice as much as the decline in technology stocks overall. The large drop was due in part to worries over how Japan's supply-chain crisis would harm Apple's ability to produce iPad 2s and other high demand products. Some investors feared that Apple's inability to meet the demand for iPad 2s would worsen as critical components were delayed further. Analysts were concerned about the supply of BT resin, a product used to produce circuit boards for iPhone and iPad chips, manufactured primarily by a Mitsubishi facility in Japan that was temporarily shut down.

Apple's Power in the Supply Chain

Other analysts did not consider Apple to be at risk. They believed that Apple has enough pull in the supply chain, due to its size and supply agreements with upfront payments, to get more than its fair share of supplier output. In addition, after the quake, Apple employees and partners showed "outstanding teamwork and unprecedented resilience," working together to come up with contingency plans.

Sources: Compiled from DeWitt (2011), Helft (2011), and Ha (2011).

Questions

1. Describe the impact Japan's quake had on Apple.
2. Rank the impacts in terms of their severity on Apple.
3. Explain the connection between supply chain and market price.
4. What reduced the impact of the supply shortage of components on Apple?
5. Explain the competitive advantage of supply chain power.
6. Visit the Web site of market research firm iSuppli (isuppli.com/). Search for the latest information on Apple's supply chain. Describe what you learned.

PUBLIC SECTOR CASE

Member Relationship Management App Built with MS Dynamics

IS   MKT

Arbor Day Foundation (*arborday.org/*) is the world's largest tree-planting organization. The foundation has 1 million members and many conservation and education programs. As the foundation expanded, leaders recognized the need to replace its aging legacy system with a flexible solution. The challenge was to be better able to manage a huge volume of interactions with diverse supporting organizations.

The Arbor Day Foundation selected Microsoft Dynamics CRM to rapidly develop and deploy customized relationship management applications for its many environmental conservation programs.

Held Back by Legacy Systems

The foundation had a custom-built member relationship management (MRM) application which it relied on for nearly two decades. This legacy MRM app was designed around interactions with only a few existing outreach programs. The foundation's six-person app development team had extended the system whenever possible to handle changes in communicating with corporate partners and government entities and to support newly launched programs. Over time, however, this legacy model became unsustainable. Developing add-ons and applications to enhance existing functionality often required specialized skills sets, inevitably increasing project costs and delaying deployment. And with each new app, IT staff had to create and maintain huge amounts of custom code, which increased the risk of failure and decreased IT efficiency.

As the Arbor Day Foundation grew, adding dozens of new partners and programs in the last decade, a flexible and robust MRM system became necessary. According to Mike Ashley, IT Director for the Arbor Day Foundation: "Previously, 75 percent or more of our operations centered on working directly with members. As we've engaged more supporters, partners, and sponsors in connection with new conservation and education programs, our need to manage interactions with various groups has intensified."

Performance Improvements

With MS Dynamics CRM as the new platform for its MRM, the foundation was able to reduce new app development time by up to 300 percent and strengthen overall productivity. The top three benefits were:

- Increased employee productivity: Over the course of six months, the foundation continued to add programs and expand relationships with partners and supporters without the need to increase staffing levels.
- Provided greater scalability of operations: The ability to deploy new applications in substantially less time means that the Arbor Day Foundation can cost-effectively meet the unique needs of its emerging programs.
- Reduced application development time by 300 percent: Ashley estimates that his team completed development of the application to support the Tree Campus USA program three times faster than would have been possible with the organization's previous system. "We set a time frame of four weeks from start to finish for building and rolling out the application, and we comfortably hit that target," says Ashley. "We estimate that it would have taken three months or more to extend our old system in the same way."

Sources: Compiled from *Microsoft.com* and *ArborDay.org*.

Questions

1. Why are changes to legacy ISs needed? Why were changes needed at the Arbor Day Foundation?
2. Why do organizations finally decide to replace their legacy systems?
3. In your opinion, what problems would the foundation be facing today if it had not replaced its legacy systems with the CRM software?
4. Compare and contrast constituent relationship with customer relationship management.

ANALYSIS USING SPREADSHEETS

FIN   HRM   ACC

Assessing the Value of E-CRM

Design a spreadsheet to perform the analysis detailed below.

Managers of a large food processing company would like to find the cost/benefit of installing an e-CRM application. The managers created a list of both tangible and intangible costs and benefits of the project.

Your assignment is to develop a spreadsheet in which you:

1. Calculate the tangible costs and benefits for one year.
2. List the intangible costs (and risks) for the year.

3. List the intangible benefits for the year.

The data to use for the one-year analysis are:

- E-CRM software licensing: Cost per user $1,200; number of users 86 (including 50 direct sales employees)
- Technical support and maintenance: $20,000
- Training of 86 users for five days: Productivity loss $120/day

- Training of four supervisors: Productivity loss $200/day
- Fees to trainers: $8,000
- Additional hardware, networks, and so forth: $27,000
- Annual operating cost: two IT employees at $72,000 each; other costs $18,000

- Average *monthly* sales per direct sales employee: $50,000; gross profit from sales = 8 percent
- Productivity increase per CRM employee using the new system = 12 percent
- Overhead cost computed at 10 percent

References

Bartholomew, D., "A Banker's $500,000 Lesson in CRM," *Baseline*, February 2007.

Boucher–Ferguson, R., "10 Cool CRM Developments," *eWeek.com*, March 24, 2008. *eweek.com/c/a/CRM/10-Cool-CRM-Developments*

Business Wire, "Research and Markets: Recent Overview of the Performance Apparel Markets," April 17, 2009.

Center for Disease Control (CDC), *CDC.gov/*

Chan, I., and C. K. Chao, "Knowledge Management in Small and Medium-Sized Enterprises," *Communications of the ACM*, April 2008.

D'Agostino, D. "Expertise Management: Who Knows About This? *CIO Insight,* July 1, 2004.

DeWitt, P.E. "Why Apple couldn't build iPad 2s fast enough to meet demand." Fortune. April 22, 2011. *tech.fortune.cnn.com/2011/04/22/*

EFSA.europa.eu/

Feldman, S. "What Are People Searching For, and Where Are They Looking?" *KMWorld*, February 29, 2008.

Fox, P. "Using IT to Tap Experts' Know-How," *Computerworld,* March 15, 2004.

Garud, R., and A. Kumaraswamy, "Vicious and Virtuous Circles in the Management of Knowledge: The Case of Infosys Technologies," *MIS Quarterly,* (29)(1), March 2005.

Ha, A. "Apple says supply chain safe despite Japanese quake." VentureBeat. April 20, 2011. *venturebeat.com/2011/04/20/apple-supply-chain-japan-quake/*

Helft, M. "Supply Concerns Thwart Apple's Magic." *New York Times.* March 23, 2011.

House.gov/

IKMS.org

Intel, "Building the Digital Supply Chain: An Intel Perspective," *Intel Solutions White Paper*, January 2005.

KMTalk, "KM in PETRONAS, Malaysia." 2009. *kmtalk.net/blog/?p=125 #more-125*

Moss, M., "The Burger That Shattered Her Life," *New York Times,* October 2, 2009. *nytimes.com/2009/10/04/health/04meat.html?_r=1*

PETRONAS Gas News, 2011. *petronasgas.com/*

UnderArmour.com/

Weier, M. H., "Food Industry Looks to RFID to Avoid Next Catastrophe," *InformationWeek,* February 5, 2007.

Learning Objectives

❶ Understand organizations' need for business intelligence (BI), BI technologies, and how to make a business case for BI investments.

❷ Describe BI architecture, data mining, predictive analytics, dashboards, scorecards, and other reporting and visualization tools.

❸ Understand the value of data, text, and Web mining.

❹ Understand managerial decision-making processes.

❺ Describe decision support systems (DSSs), benefits, and structure.

❻ Take a forward look at the future of BI in the form of mobile intelligence (MI).

Integrating *IT*

| ACC | FIN | MKT | OM | HRM | IS |

Business Intelligence Journal *businessintel.org/*

The Data Warehousing Institute (TDWI) *tdwi.org/*

Cloud9 Analytics, on-demand (SaaS) *cloud9analytics.com/*

Information Builders *informationbuilders.com/*

WebFOCUS BI platform *informationbuilders.com/products/webfocus/*

IBM Cognos 8 BI *www-01.ibm.com/software/data/cognos/*

Oracle *Oracle.com*

SAS BI *sas.com/technologies/bi/*

SAP AG *Sap.com*

Microsoft BI *microsoft.com/bi/default.aspx*

Tableau Software *tableausoftware.com/*

QlikTech *qlikview.com*

iDashboards *idashboards.com*

Honoring Those Who Use IT to Benefit Society (ComputerWorld) *cwhonors.org/*

QUICK LOOK at Chapter 11, Business Intelligence and Decision Support

This section introduces you to the business issues, challenges, and IT solutions in Chapter 11. Topics and issues mentioned in the Quick Look are explained in the chapter.

American businessman John Wanamaker, who's regarded as the father of modern advertising, remarked about 100 years ago, "Half the money I spend on advertising is wasted; the trouble is I don't know which half." Business intelligence (BI), data mining, and the decision support systems (DSS) discussed in this chapter are used to minimize *uncertainty* (the reverse of *intelligence*) and/or to be able to make faster, smarter decisions—often in real time. For example, marketers use BI to track, day by day, the effect of marketing campaigns on sales. Customer service and call center representatives (reps) access BI reports for up-to-the-minute status for problem resolution or to schedule service calls.

Today, BI vendors offer products or software-as-a-service (SaaS) packages to support each management level—strategic, tactical, or operational. BI packages are affordable to organizations of all sizes including SMEs (small and medium enterprises). According to analyst firm Gartner, "BI is truly for everybody because there is no company or role without information needs that cannot be described as BI" (2010). When managers and workers have the intelligence they need to respond *correctly and quickly* to opportunities, threats, and mistakes, they and their companies significantly outperform those that don't.

You read in prior chapters that responsiveness maximizes revenues, efficiency minimizes costs, and not doing the wrong thing minimizes waste. In this chapter, we introduce another factor: proper resource allocation. **Proper resource allocation** is the optimal distribution of resources to a specific place at a specific time to achieve a specific purpose. Ineffective resource allocation—one symptom of which is long wait times—can prevent delivery of products or services when needed. This, in turn, frustrates customers and hurts revenues. BI, properly applied, can improve a company's allocation of resources and profitability—and show a clear return on investment (ROI).

We also introduce the latest topic in BI—mobile intelligence driven by the convergence of mobile computing and BI. We look at intriguing transformations such as changes in the functions of hardware. For example, smartphones are becoming PCs, PCs are becoming servers, servers are becoming the cloud, and the cloud is the new app source.

Why Would Companies Invest in Another Set of IT Apps?

Innovations in IT and real-time media, like Twitter and Foursquare, add to or leverage capabilities of smartphones, improving your ability to be well informed in real time. Many people are notified of live news via tweets or alerts to their mobiles (see Figure 11.1). This type of leveraging to get up-to-the-moment data also applies to BI and decision support apps. BI leverages existing

Figure 11.1 iPhone showing tweets on a mobile Twitter app. (© ICP-UK/Alamy)

reporting systems by delivering real-time information through dashboards, mashups, and reports to employees, managers, partners, and customers.

In this chapter, you learn about the tools for intelligence, prediction, operational responsiveness, and resource allocation. You read how BI and DSS collect data from various data sources that you are now familiar with—TPS, CRM, ERP, and POS databases—then compile and analyze the data using data mining and predictive models. Since the latest BI tools provide a high degree of self-sufficiency, reducing managers' dependence on analysts and tech staff, you can expect to be a hands-on user of these tools during your career.

Operational BI at DIRECTV

Figure 11.2 DirecTV provides television and sports entertainment via satellite dish. (© Frances Roberts/Alamy)

DIRECTV (*directv.com/*) is the world's largest pay-TV provider with net sales of $24.1 billion in 2010. DIRECTV and related Sky brands have subsidiaries in Argentina, Brazil, Colombia, Venezuela, Mexico, other Latin American countries, and the United States. DIRECTV provides TV service, including video-on-demand, via satellite dishes (see Figure 11.2) to over 28 million customers as of mid-2011.

Business Goals

DIRECTV operates in a highly competitive market that has high rates of **customer churn** (customers switching to a competitor). Its biggest challenges were minimizing churn and supporting needs of its customer service representatives (reps) who average 600,000 customer calls per day and handle of huge volumes of transaction data. Every day over 10 terabytes of transaction data are compiled and made available in real-time

reports to the reps. Consistent with the nature of its business, DIRECTV set the following goals:

- Maintain high-quality customer care for its millions of customers by optimizing field technician routes for new installations and service calls.
- Prevent fraud by proactively alerting field service teams to avoid new customers who are potentially fraudulent
- Attract new customers at lower cost through highly targeted marketing campaigns and quick feedback.

Information and Reporting Needs

As in most competitive industries, acquiring and retaining customers are top priorities. DIRECTV invests heavily in advertising and incentive campaigns. Managers want to know which types of campaigns are the most effective and which are a waste. Evaluating and managing marketing efforts requires accurate, real-time information, and the ability to take action. Managers also needed access to reports that detailed the purpose and outcome of customer calls and other call center activity metrics.

The IT that could meet all of its data and reporting requirements was an *operational BI system*. With operational BI systems, front-line workers and operational managers spend less time trying to locate and access information and more time on activities that benefit the business.

Outcomes of Operational BI

DIRECTV's operational BI was built on data mining and integration software from GoldenGate Software and a data warehouse from Teradata. GoldenGate software reads data logs and within seconds of a transaction, streams relevant data to the data warehouse over the wide area network (WAN). In essence, software grabs transactional data in real time as it is entered, and then delivers data to wherever it is needed within the IT infrastructure.

The BI system handles 45 million transactions per day, 1,500 customer service agents running 8,000 reports daily, and the logging of a million calls per day to its CRM application. Reps have access to detailed customer reports, which has reduced churn. For example, reps get fresh data listing customers who had moments earlier asked to be disconnected, and within hours contacts them with a new offer.

Data mining and real-time operational reports are also used for order management and fraud detection. With real-time order information on brand new customers, investigators are able to identify and cancel fraudulent orders saving the cost of a driver/installer and the truck.

The company significantly improved its call center performance, customer service, customer re-acquisition rate, which contributed to sales growth and net profit. In 2009, DIRECTV posted the highest customer service rating in the *American Customer Satisfaction Index*—beating all major cable companies for the ninth consecutive year. In Latin America, performance was even more impressive. DIRECTV set new records for most of its key metrics, including net customer additions, revenues, and operating profit before depreciation and amortization.

Sources: Compiled from DIRECTV 2009 annual report, *investor.directv.com/* (2010), and Briggs (2009).

For Class Discussion and Debate

1. Scenario for Brainstorming and Discussion: Highly accurate and trusted reports are often the strongest argument in the business case for investing in operational BI.

a. What does *information accuracy* mean?

b. Does information accuracy differ depending on the level in the organization—strategic, managerial, or operational—or the type of organization? For example, in order for data to be considered "accurate," must it be refreshed every day or be in real time or some other timeframe? In your discussion, compare credit card companies and supply chain operations.

2. Debate: Proactive vs. reactive approaches to resource allocation.

Perhaps you've been in one or more of the following situations:

- Waiting in a very long checkout line (queue) at the store and noticing there were five other registers not being used.

- Waiting to check in luggage at an airport counter being covered by only one attendant, while three other attendants talk on the phone or do other things unrelated to passengers trying to check in.

- Deciding to go to a restaurant because it has been promoting a specialty meal only to find the kitchen had run out of it.

These three situations were not due to lazy workers or incompetent supervisors. They were the result of poor resource allocation, which can be remedied with the implementation of an operational BI system. However, economic conditions have significantly impacted the budgets. Companies are being conservative about spending for fear of a deeper and extended recession. This has made it more difficult to gain funding for BI initiatives.

There are two approaches to the resource allocation problem:

1. Proactive approach: Companies can take a proactive approach and simply stock more products and/or hire more employees. In this approach, the company is prepared for the highest level of demand for service or products to prevent lost sales or poor customer service.

2. Reactive approach: Companies can take a reactive approach. After a resource runs short, employees are redistributed or more products are ordered. Additional resources are only deployed after they are needed. For example, when the line at the supermarket gets too long, workers are moved from other departments to the front registers. Or a restaurant may increase its food order for the next promotion—and be left with overstock if there's a poor turnout.

Select either the proactive or reactive approach to resource allocation. In the debate, present arguments explaining why your approach is better than the other approach. Make reasonable assumptions, as needed. In the debate, include a consideration of all relevant costs of labor and holding inventory, the state of the economy with tight credit and high interest rates on borrowing, and the benefits of customer satisfaction and loyalty.

Notice that each approach has high costs associated with it. The improper resource allocations that cause these costs can be minimized by implementing BI.

11.1 Business Intelligence (BI) for Profits and Nonprofits

Organizations are often overloaded with data, simultaneously having too much data but somehow not enough. Managers may not have the right data, may not have a way to interpret so much data, or may not be able to compile data to get reports out quickly enough. To combat these types of problems, many organizations use apps that fall under the BI umbrella. *Business intelligence* refers to a collection of ISs and technologies that support managerial decision making or operational control by providing information on internal and external operations. Due to the complexity of BI implementations, most BI vendors offer highly integrated collections of apps—including connections to ERP and CRM systems—that are Web enabled.

It's tough to fully understand BI because BI apps are not stand-alone systems, nor do they support a specific objective, as do supply chain management (SCM) or customer relationship management (CRM). To help you appreciate the value of BI, in the next section you will read about three cases representing diverse uses of BI by for-profit and nonprofit organizations—and then how to recognize the need for BI.

BI CASES

The performance of nonprofits and the profitability of for-profit enterprises depend on the quality and timeliness of information. Enterprises are getting more value from BI by extending information to all managerial levels and to employees, maximizing the use of existing data assets. Visualization tools, including dashboards and mashups, are the user interfaces that help people understand the numbers. Dashboards are apps that pull data from a data warehouse or other data store and then graphically depict the data in meaningful displays. The term *mashup* started in the music world but has been adopted by IT to mean an application that combines data from different sources into a new application. BI systems are very good at filtering and aggregating huge data volumes into information. By combining mapping mashup capabilities with aggregated data, the result is a **data mashup** that can improve the understandability of the information.

In the examples and cases throughout this chapter, you learn how industry-specific analytical tools support analysis and informed decision making from the top level to the user level. BI takes advantage of existing IT technologies to help companies leverage their IT investments and use their legacy and real-time data. In many instances, BI implementation is a competitive or operational necessity. Here are three such cases.

WildTrack (*wildtrack.org/*) Monitors and Verifies Endangered Rhinos in Africa. WildTrack is using a noninvasive footprint identification technique and BI data analysis solution from SAS (*sas.com/*) to track and monitor their constantly changing inventory—endangered African rhinos. Like for-profit businesses, the organization uses BI as a means to cut costs and to make better-informed decisions. Using SAS BI software, WildTrack has already helped save the black rhino population in Zimbabwe and has provided a census of white rhinos in Namibia (see Figure 11.3). In addition, the use of BI solutions has generated ROI in terms of providing local employment for the indigenous workers of Namibia's Waterberg Plateau.

"Increasingly, governments and authorities require hard evidence of the existence of endangered animals before they will listen to guidance about protecting its habitat. Moving forward, we hope to incorporate biometrics and other technology into our projects to help speed up the identification of animals," said Zoe Jewell, cofounder of WildTrack.

United Way (*unitedway.org/*) Monitors Fund Raising Campaigns and Generates Reliable Reports. The United Way is dedicated to improving lives by raising money for local groups that address community issues. Fundraising is an essential component. The United Way has a mandate to closely monitor and track fundraising campaign

Figure 11.3 Endangered black rhinoceroses are tracked using BI. (*© Photoshot Holdings Ltd/Alamy*)

Figure 11.4 Jamba Juice store managers rely on BI to perform marketing and accounting. (© David Zanzinger/Alamy)

profits and make that information available to the public. Problems with its previous data management platform included inflexible reporting practices and the inability to perform important analytics on campaign results. Staff would manipulate large spreadsheets and require several months to complete their reporting after the yearly campaign ended. Each office conducted its own reporting, but there was no standardized process and reports required significant effort to produce.

After the United Way implemented an integrated BI solution, it was able to ensure consistent measurement of fundraising results throughout the organization. Workers can easily track and monitor donor data and make better sense of data analysis. With a 360-degree view of internal processes, staff can better track trends and opportunities, allowing for better future fundraising planning and initiatives.

Jamba Juice (jambajuice.com/) Monitors Customers' Preferences and Captures Data for Fast, Reliable P&L and Financial Reporting. Jamba Juice (see Figure 11.4) is a provider of healthy, on-the-go food and beverages. When the economic downturn slowed its growth, managers decided to implement newer IT across Jamba Juice stores as a way to support increased productivity and, ultimately, profitability.

Store managers had trouble finding information they needed to effectively run their stores. The company maintained what it called an "originals" folder on the company-wide shared network drive, which contained more than 1,000 documents. Everything — equipment manual, store directories, tax forms, and marketing guides — was in the *originals* folder. Every week or two, Jamba Juice corporate employees would push out necessary information to those in the field (in this case, the store managers) by placing it into the originals folder. This process was cumbersome and unreliable because there was no version control on the documents. Store managers had no way of knowing if the document they found was the most accurate. They had to spend at least two hours each week gathering and typing in data that Jamba Juice corporate wanted for analysis purposes. Store managers also struggled to manually update their stores' profit-and-loss (P&L) and other accounting data that their district and regional managers needed.

Even when the information was in the Jamba Juice system, employees were uncertain about the integrity of the data gathered because of conflicting sets of metrics between store and corporate resources. Poor-quality data was damaging profits, so traditional BI was deployed at the corporate level and operational BI was deployed at the store level.

• By deploying BI tools at the corporate level, data about everything from the popularity of each smoothie flavor to regional sales trends are tracked and analyzed to identify trends and to determine how to make the most of customer behavior patterns.

• Deploying BI at the store level to inform marketing decisions, such as promoting certain menu items in certain markets and/or during a specific time period, enabled store managers to be more strategic in their marketing efforts.

These three organizations, as well as DIRECTV (opening case), the military, and disease research centers that are covered in this chapter, recognized the need for BI and could justify their BI investments. They were under pressure to be informed; to make frequent, quick, and/or complex decisions; and to compile trusted data in order to report quickly and frequently to internal or external entities.

TYPES OF BI

BI technology has progressed to the point where companies are implementing BI for various types of users, as shown in Table 11.1 and explained next.

Traditional BI and Operational BI. Strategic BI and tactical BI are referred to as **traditional BI.** Most companies use traditional BI for strategic and tactical decision making, where the decision-making cycle spans several weeks or months. Competitive pressures, however, were forcing companies to react on a daily or real-time basis to changing business conditions and customer demands — and to extend BI systems to their operational employees.

TABLE 11.1	Strategic, Tactical, and Operational BI: Business Focus and Users		
	Strategic BI	**Tactical BI**	**Operational BI**
Primary business focus	To achieve long-term enterprise goals and objectives	To analyze data; deliver alerts and reports regarding the achievement of enterprise goals	To manage day-to-day operations
Primary users	Executives, analysts	Executives, analysts, line-of-business managers	Line-of-business managers, operations
Measures	Measures are a feedback mechanism to track and understand how the strategy is progressing and what adjustments need to be made to the plan.	Measures are a feedback mechanism to track and understand how the strategy is progressing and what adjustments need to be made to the plan.	Measures are individualized so each line manager gets insight into performance of his or her business processes.
Timeframe	Monthly, quarterly, yearly	Daily, weekly, monthly	Immediately, intraday
Data types or uses	Historical, predictive	Historical, predictive modeling	Real time or near real time

Sources: Adapted from Oracle (2007) and Imhoff (2006).

Operational BI is relatively new and can be implemented in several ways. One way is by improving the responsiveness of traditional data warehouse and BI processing. Another way is to embed the BI directly into operational processes. These approaches are often used together.

HOW TO RECOGNIZE THE NEED FOR BI

You can better understand BI by learning how to recognize the need for it. The following list represents seven difficult situations—common in companies, government agencies, the military, healthcare, research, and nonprofits—that could benefit from improved intelligence.

- **Competing and conflicting versions of the truth:** Interdepartmental meetings turn contentious as participants argue whose spreadsheet has the correct figures and blame others for not providing the latest data.
- **Lagging reports:** IT cannot meet managers' requests for custom reports when they want them. Or accounting cannot do the reconciliations and financial reporting because sales can't figure out their numbers. Or, as in the case at Jamba Juice, store managers don't have access to the data they need for their reporting duties.
- **Can't perform in-depth analysis:** Management knows which of its retail outlets have the greatest sales volume but cannot identify which products have the highest sales.
- **Difficulty finding crucial data:** Managers recently heard that a report showing year-over-year growth for each customer has been posted to the intranet but have no idea how to find it.
- **Need simple-to-use production reporting technology:** Managers compile financial reports using spreadsheets from data they acquire via numerous e-mail and text messages.
- **Delay and difficulty consolidating data:** Reports that require data from multiple operational systems involve generating separate reports from each and then combining the results in a spreadsheet.
- **Not able to comply with government and regulatory reporting mandates:** Sarbanes-Oxley, Basel III, privacy legislation, or other regulatory agency mandates reliable and proper audit trails to attest to financial accuracy.

When companies get to the point where they can no longer perform their analyses with spreadsheets, they tend to migrate to more powerful BI tools. Now we discuss the components of BI.

**THE BUSINESS CASE
FOR BI**

In a tight economy with high interest and unemployment rates, any project requiring a large investment needs to be economically justified. Justifying an IT investment is also known as *making a business case* for it. A **business case** is required to document your initiative and to move it through the approval and funding process.

A successful business case must be well written, compelling, and able to withstand challenges from individuals who do not support, or oppose, your project. Convincing others that your IT project—or any project—should be funded is a challenging job. Typically, many projects are competing for limited organizational resources. Another challenge with justifying BI is that the implementation may start off small and then expand. At one large government agency, BI was first installed as a means for human resources (HR) to keep track of military personnel but then evolved into an enterprise-wide effort, including a build-out of a large Teradata data warehouse and the installation of SAP's Business Objects BI platform. Trying to justify the enterprise-wide BI was easier after the success of the HR BI system.

Three Key Business Goals. Building a business case for BI is the key step in obtaining business sponsorship, commitment, and involvement. The three key business goals used to sell a BI consolidation program are:

1. Lowering total cost of ownership (TCO).

2. Enabling businesspeople to analyze information rather than gathering and reconciling data.

3. Improving consistency of and trust in information and analytics.

Each of the above business goals has associated costs that need to be estimated in preparing a cost-benefit analysis. It would be great if you could just obtain a set of formulas to calculate the business ROI, but it is just not that simple. You need to quantify some benefits. In order to obtain a truly valid cost-benefit and ROI calculation, IT needs to work very closely with business decision makers.

Eliminating Blindspots. Justifying a BI project involves identifying key strategic, tactical, or operational decisions and business processes that affect performance, and would benefit from more comprehensive data and better reporting capabilities. For example, it's tough to identify costs that are saved by using real-time metrics instead of wait-and-see lagging metrics. Justification focuses on improving specific business processes that are hampered by lack of data, or blindspots. **Blindspots** are areas in which managers fail to notice or to understand important information—and as a result make bad decisions or do nothing when action is necessary.

Integrating Data Silos. Before the introduction of BI in the 1980s, managers often complained that they couldn't get the information they needed, at the right level of detail or precision, or at the time when they needed it. Many IT investments had not translated into more sales. And when it came to understanding customers and their buying decisions, there was much more data than there were answers. As a result, when trying to develop a complete view of each customer across all product lines, managers hit a brick wall. For many companies, years of data were, in effect, *locked up* in transactional data silos. Data silos, nonstandardized data, and disparate information systems made getting a unified view of individual customers impossible.

Data silos limit what companies can do, as AT&T's experience demonstrates. Each time a customer called in for service or to complain, AT&T wanted its customer service reps (CSRs) to up-sell the caller by offering a higher level of service, such as an upgraded plan, or to cross-sell by offering a complementary service. But up-selling or cross-selling cannot be done unless the CSR can access reports online showing all services and plans the caller already had and thus know what to try to up- or cross-sell. Customers are not going to wait for the CSR to read off a long list of extras to buy. Typically, CSRs get one chance to make an offer, so it has to be the right one.

OVERVIEW OF BI COMPONENTS AND CORE FUNCTIONS

When you examine the components of BI, you realize that it is not an entirely new set of ITs. BI capabilities depend on an integration of several ITs that you read about in earlier chapters. BI incorporates data warehousing, data mining, online analytical processing (OLAP), dashboards, the use of the Web, and, increasingly, social media. Other requirements are wired and wireless broadband networks.

Three core functions of BI are query, reporting, and analytics. Queries are one way to access a particular view of the data or to analyze what is happening or has happened. For operational BI, data is typically accessed or distributed via reports. Data mining and predictive analytic tools are used to find relationships that are hidden or not obvious, or to predict what is going to happen. For instance, data mining can identify correlations, such as which factors—a prospect's income, education, age, last purchase amount, and so forth—were most closely related to a successful response in a marketing campaign. Some data mining, predictive analytics, and other analytical tools can be used directly by users, but some are too complex for them to understand and use. Knowing how to interpret and act on the results of queries, reports, or analytics depends on human expertise.

The ability to quickly and easily access data that you couldn't trust would be a total waste. Therefore, BI also includes processes and tools to accurately and consistently consolidate data from multiple sources and to ensure data quality.

Other BI components include the following:

- **Search** is a familiar concept to you. Powerful search engines and indexing are needed to locate data, reports, schematics, messages, and other electronic records.
- **Data visualization tools,** such as dashboards and mashups, display data in summarized, easy-to-understand formats. **Dashboards** are user interfaces that enable managers and other workers to measure, monitor, and manage business performance effectively. The importance of data visualization cannot be overestimated.
- **Scorecards** and **performance management** help to monitor business metrics and key performance indicators (KPIs). Examples of KPIs are customer satisfaction, profitability, and sales per employee.

A **scorecard** is a methodology for measuring an organization's performance. A dashboard is a means of presenting measurements from whatever source. Thus, a dashboard could be used to present a scorecard. The two concepts are complementary, not competitive. Visit *iDashboards.com* to preview live dashboards by industry or by function. You read about these components throughout this chapter.

INTEGRATING DISPARATE DATA STORES

With constantly changing business environments, companies want to be responsive to competitors' actions, regulatory requirements, mergers and acquisitions, and the introduction of new channels for the business. As you've read, responsiveness requires intelligence, which in turn requires having trusted data and reporting systems. Like many companies, global securities firm J.P. Morgan Chase had suffered from a patchwork of legacy reporting systems that could not be easily integrated because of their lack of standardization. When data is not integrated into a unified reporting system, there is no trusted real-time view.

Product data for international retailers in particular is a problem. Countries use different barcodes, but they need to be linked so that retailers can optimize product availability and revenues. Other deficiencies that have frustrated decision makers because of disparate ISs are:

- Getting information too late
- Getting data at the wrong level of detail—either too detailed or too summarized

- Getting too many directionless data
- Not being able to coordinate with other departments across the enterprise
- Not being able to share data in a timely manner

Faced with those deficiencies, decision makers had to rely on the IT department to extract data to create a report, which usually took too long. Or they extracted data and created their own decision support spreadsheets, which were subject to data errors and calculation mistakes. Making matters worse, if spreadsheets were not shared or updated, then decisions were being made based on old or incomplete data. BI was the solution to many data problems.

POWER OF PREDICTIVE ANALYTICS, ALERTS, AND DECISION SUPPORT

BI technology evolved beyond being primarily a reporting system when the following features were added: sophisticated predictive analytics, event-driven (real-time) alerts, and operational decision support. Using a BI system for reporting alone was like driving a car looking through the rear-view mirror. The view was always of the past. The greatest strength of a company's predictive analytical technology is that it allows a company to react to things as they happen and to be proactive with respect to their future.

Predictive Analytics. **Predictive analytics** is the branch of data mining that focuses on forecasting trends (e.g., regression analysis) and estimating probabilities of future events. The top five business pressures driving the adoption of predictive analytics are shown in Figure 11.5. **Business analytics,** as it is also called, provides the models, which are formulas or algorithms, and procedures to BI. An **algorithm** is a set of rules or instructions for solving a problem in a finite number of steps. Algorithms can be represented with a flow chart, as in Figure 11.6. There are predictive analytic tools designed for hands-on use by managers who want to do their own forecasting and predicting. Demand for this capability to predict grew out of frustration with BI that helped only managers understand what had happened.

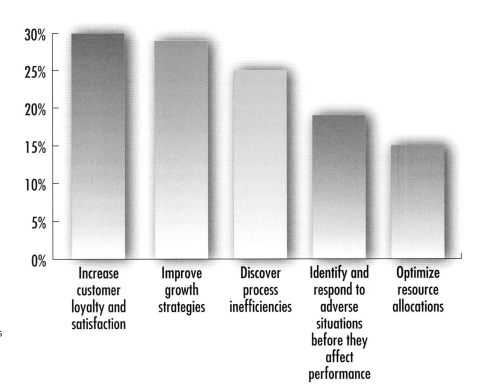

Figure 11.5 Top five business pressures driving the adoption of predictive analytics. (*Data from Aberdeen Group.*)

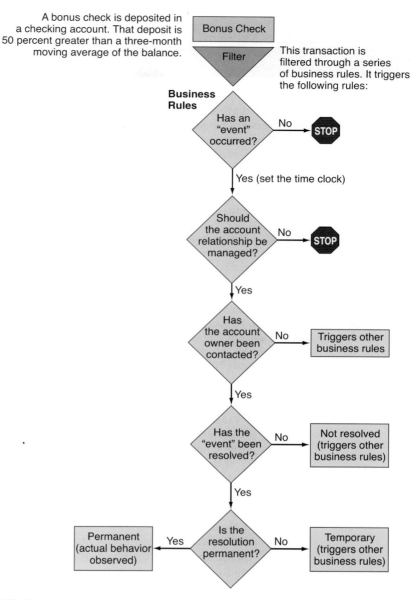

A bonus check is deposited in a checking account. That deposit is 50 percent greater than a three-month moving average of the balance.

This transaction is filtered through a series of business rules. It triggers the following rules:

Figure 11.6 Real-time alerts triggered by customer-driven events.

While there were many query, reporting, and analysis tools to view what had happened, managers wanted tools to predict what would happen and where their businesses were going. The value of predictive analytics at eHarmony is discussed in *IT at Work 11.1.*

Building predictive analytic capabilities requires computer software and human modeling experts. Experts in advanced mathematical modeling build and verify the integrity of the models and interpret the results. This work is done in two phases. The first phase involves identifying and understanding the business metrics that the enterprise wants to predict, such as compatibility matches, customer churn, or best cross-sell or up-sell marketing opportunities by customer segment. While an advanced degree is not needed to identify metrics, PhD-level expertise is necessary for the second phase—defining the predictors (variables) and analytical models to accurately predict future performance.

Event-Driven Alerts. As the name implies, **event-driven alerts** are real-time alerts or warnings that are broadcast when a predefined event, or unusual event, occurs. Figure 11.6 shows the processing that occurs when a predefined event occurs—in this case, an unusually large deposit. Since events need to be quantified, an unusually large deposit is considered a deposit that is 50 percent greater than a three-month moving

IT at Work 11.1

China's New Predictive Analytics Lab

SVR   MKT

IBM launched a new predictive analytics–software lab in Xi'an, China, in March 2011. The lab will help IBM's clients see patterns in vast amounts of data and forecast trends before they occur, to improve their decision making and competitive advantage.

The new lab is part of IBM's China Development Laboratory (CDL), IBM's largest network of labs with more than 5,000 software engineers. IBM had also opened an Energy & Utilities Solution Lab in Beijing that brought together analytics skills, industry-specific offering, and best practices to make energy and utility networks safer, more efficient, and smarter.

IBM has invested more than $12 billion to build an analytics portfolio. The company works with more than 250,000 clients worldwide on predictive analytics, including 22 of the top 24 global commercial banks.

According to IDC's China Business Analytics Software Market Forecast, the market opportunity for business analytics in China is expected to grow 10 percent annually through 2013, faster than the average IT market growth of 8 percent. Demand for predictive analytics is driven by risk management, compliance mandates, and wanting to integrate business analytics into operations.

Xi'an City Commercial Bank. Xi'an City Commercial Bank (XACB) is the first foreign-invested commercial bank in western China. It has 113 branches and more than 2,000 employees. XACB is becoming one of the most profitable domestic commercial banks in the region. To continue its growth, the bank has teamed up with experts at IBM's new predictive analytics lab to explore how it can transform its operations through improved insight into their business information and predict new outcomes for improved customer service.

Sources: Compiled from *IBM.com* (2011) and *PRNewsWire.com* (2011).

Discussion Questions:

1. Visit IBM's Web site at *ibm.com* and search for "press kits" or "press releases." Select one of the press releases discussing *business analytics and optimization*. Briefly describe what you learned.

2. Watch the *How it Works Video: Analytics* on YouTube at *youtube.com/watch?v=_HbjsNaUJ2A*. Discuss what you learned.

---

average of the balance. Notice that the deposit is the event that triggers an analysis of the event. The analysis is done according to predefined business rules to determine what type of action would improve profitability.

Of course, alerts require real-time monitoring to know when an event of interest has occurred and business rules to know what to monitor and what to do. In Figure 11.6, the business rules are in the diamonds. In this scenario, when a deposit is made that is more than double the amount of the average deposit over the past three months, it triggers a series of business rules. The bank may contact the customer with offers for a one-year CD, investment plan, insurance product, and so on. Based on the answers to the business rules, further processing may stop or other rules leading to an alert to take action may be triggered.

For a credit card company, a customer's sudden payoff of the entire balance might trigger a business rule that leads to an alert because the payoff could be a signal that the customer is planning to cancel the card. There may be intervention, such as a special, low interest rate offering, to reduce the risk of losing the customer.

Event-driven alerts can also be built into a business process or application. For example, the process could be programmed to predict the impact of events such as sales, orders, trades, shipments, and out-of-stock items on the company's performance. Typically, the results would be presented through a portal or Web-based dashboard. Figure 11.7 shows a sample performance dashboard, which includes KPIs. Note that the dashboard is configurable by using the drop-list controls to select period and product, and by using the tabs across the top of the dashboard. Dashboards are discussed later in the chapter. The software can be configured to alert staff to unusual events and to automatically trigger defined corrective actions.

Event-driven alerts are an alternative to more traditional (non-real-time) BI systems that extract data from applications, load it into databases or data warehouses, and then run analytics against the data stores. While demand for near-real-time information always existed in customer-facing departments like marketing, the costs and complexity of loading data in traditional BI systems several times per day kept data out of their reach. Those technological BI limitations have been resolved to a large extent.

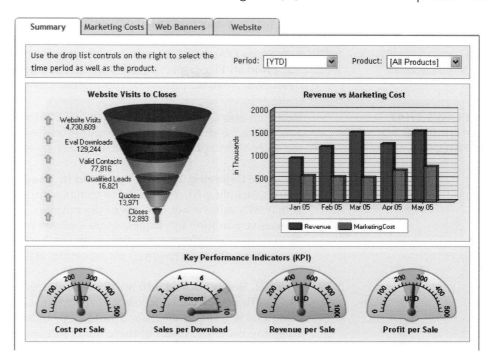

Figure 11.7 Sample performance dashboard.

Figure 11.8 shows how the components come together in a BI app. Consider a national retail chain that sells everything from grills and patio furniture to paper products. This company stores data about inventory, customers, past promotions, and sales numbers in various databases. Even though this data is scattered across multiple systems—and may seem unrelated—ETL tools can bring the data together to the data warehouse (DW). **ETL** stands for extraction, transformation, and load processes that are performed on the data. In the DW, tables can be linked, and *data cubes* (another

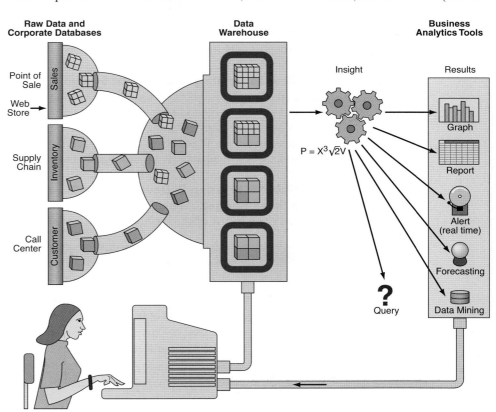

Figure 11.8 How a BI system works.

term for multidimensional databases) are formed. For instance, inventory data is linked to sales numbers and customer databases, allowing for extensive analysis of information. Some DWs have a dynamic link to the databases; others are static.

From an IT perspective, BI is a collection of software and tools, as we have just described. Next, we discuss BI flaws, mostly from a business perspective.

BI FLAWS THAT CONTRIBUTE TO BI FAILURES

Research firm Gartner says most failed BI efforts suffer from one or more fatal flaws, generally revolving around people and processes rather than technology. The following seven flaws apply not only to BI but also to other enterprise IT implementations.

Flaw #1. Believing That "If You Build It, They Will Come." Often IT implementations, including BI, are treated as technical projects. The danger with this approach is that BI's value is not obvious to the business, so all the hard work does not result in massive adoption by business users. Gartner recommends that the BI project team include significant representation from the business side. In addition, IT and communication skills are required for successful BI initiatives.

Flaw #2. Being Locked into an "Excel Culture." Microsoft Excel is the most widely used software for data analysis and reporting. Users extract data from internal systems, load it to spreadsheets, and perform their own calculations without sharing them company-wide. The result of these multiple, competing frames of reference is confusion and even risk from unmanaged and unsecured data held locally by individuals on their PCs. This *Excel culture* will interfere with the success of BI. Executive sponsorship is needed to motivate and transition users to believe in a transparent, fact-based approach to management and have the strength to cut through political barriers and change culture. Table 11.2 lists other BI-relevant organizational culture factors.

Flaw #3. Ignoring Data Quality and Relevance Issues. People won't use BI apps that are based on irrelevant, incomplete, or questionable data. To avoid this, firms should establish a process or set of automated controls to identify data quality issues in incoming data and block low-quality data from entering the data warehouse or BI platform. No matter how spectacular the dashboard interface is, it means little unless it is being fed with trusted data.

Flaw #4. Treating BI as a Static System. Many organizations treat BI as a series of departmental projects, focused on delivering a fixed set of requirements. However, BI is a moving target. During the first year of any BI implementation, as people use the system, they think of changes to suit their needs better or to improve underlying business processes. These changes can affect 35 percent to 50 percent of the application's functions. Organizations should expect and encourage changes to the BI portfolio.

Flaw #5. Pressing BI Developers to Buy or Build Dashboards Quickly and with a Small Budget. Managers don't want to fund expensive BI tools that they think are risky. Many of the dashboards delivered are of very little value because they are

TABLE 11.2	Organizational Culture Factors That Contribute to BI Success

These elements of organizational culture impact the degree of BI success.

- The enterprise is comfortable with fact-based analysis.
- Operational measures of transparency exist.
- Analysis and facts flow freely throughout the company.
- The enterprise is not limited by traditional hierarchal structures.
- Fact-based decision making is an integrated process that maximizes the ROI.
- Quantitative practitioners are considered by their leadership and peers to be sources of new insights.

TABLE 11.3	Defining KPIs

To report on key performance indicators (KPIs), those KPIs must be identified and agreed to. For example, managers typically need answers to the following questions. However, answers to these queries depend on how metrics are defined and measured.

1. Which of our customers are most profitable and least profitable?
2. Which products or services can be cross-sold and up-sold to which customers most profitably?
3. Which sales and distribution channels are most effective and least effective for which products?
4. What are the response rates and profit contributions of current marketing campaigns?
5. How can we improve customer loyalty?
6. What is the full cost of retaining a satisfied customer?

Some agreement as to how to define and measure customer profitability, costs to retain a customer, and so forth, is needed to define the benchmarks or metrics.

silo-specific and not founded on a connection to corporate objectives. Gartner recommends that IT organizations make reports as pictorial as possible.

Flaw #6. Trying to Create a "Single Version of the Truth" When One Doesn't Exist. This flaw seems contradictory because *single version of the truth* is one of the benefits most often mentioned. The "single version" concept is a flaw for organizations that haven't agreed on definitions of fundamentals, such as revenues and expenses. Achieving one version of the truth requires cross-departmental agreement on how business entities—customers, products, key performance indicators, metrics, and so on—are defined. Many organizations end up creating siloed BI implementations that perpetuate the disparate definitions of their current systems. See Table 11.3 for challenges in defining *one truth*.

Flaw #7. Lack of a BI Strategy. The biggest flaw is the lack of a documented BI strategy or the use of a poorly developed or implemented one. Gartner recommends creating a team tasked with writing or revising a BI strategy document, with members from the IT, other functions, and/or the BI project team (see Flaw #1).

BI Vendors. Until 2007, the BI market was dominated by Cognos and Business Objects. In 2008, three multibillion-dollar acquisitions helped consolidate the BI vendor market and intensified competition among the megavendors. SAP acquired Business Objects for $7 billion, IBM acquired Cognos for $4.9 billion, and Oracle acquired Hyperion for $3.3 billion. These acquisitions highlighted two important trends in modern business: (1) BI has evolved into one of the hottest segments in the software market, and (2) major software corporations are integrating BI capabilities into their product mix.

Although they're not pure-play BI vendors, in 2010, IBM, Microsoft, Oracle Corp., and SAP AG owned two-thirds of the $6 billion BI market. They've captured huge market share because they optimized their BI platforms to work well with their enterprise and information management applications. This integrated approach, as well as the fact that many enterprises already have these vendors' ERP and information management apps in place, is motivating customers to standardize on one of their BI platforms.

However, according to Gartner, these four vendors innovate slowly and are facing greater competition from newer companies, such as Tableau Software Inc. and QlikTech International AB, and from pure-play BI vendors, such as Information Builders and Microstrategy. To compete against the Big 4 in BI, the pure-play and niche vendors offer a better product mix and features (Torode, 2010). They offer newer interfaces with interactive visualization tools, scenario modeling, and data mashups, which are changing the way information is collected and analyzed. Also helping niche and pure-play vendors gain market share is the fact that enterprises usually introduce more than one BI platform to meet their varying business needs.

Review Questions

> 1. Explain how to recognize the need for BI.
> 2. Describe the components of BI.
> 3. Explain the cause of blindspots.
> 4. What is meant by a trusted view of data? Why wouldn't data be trusted?
> 5. Distinguish between traditional and operational BI.
> 6. Explain predictive analytics. List three business pressures driving adoption of predictive analytics.
> 7. Explain how an event-driven alert system functions.
> 8. Explain four BI flaws that contribute to BI failure.
> 9. Why is organizational culture important to BI success?

11.2 BI Architecture, Analytics, Reporting, and Data Visualization

The Data Warehousing Institute's (TDWI) definition of BI is *to gain insight from data for the purpose of taking action.* The ability to take action is closely tied to the topics in this section: analytics, reporting, alerts, dashboards, scorecards, and other visualization tools. Data visualization is often critical to conveying status and other information quickly so users know what action to take. For example, UPS uses data analysis and visualization as part of its tactical and strategic planning process. In an industry where delivery time is critical, UPS leverages BI tools that make it possible to make *game-time* decisions and quickly adjust operations as new information is received.

All types of organizations are using BI analytics, reporting, and visualization. It's not surprising that leading retailers, manufacturers, and finance and service companies, such as Sears, Walmart, Whirlpool, Ford Motors, Dow Chemical, UPS, and Citi, rely on these tools. BI tools are also used in much less known situations, such as transport of wounded soldiers to treatment facilities worldwide, as discussed in *IT at Work 11.2*, and in anti-HIV therapy research, which is discussed in the EuResist Nonprofit Case at the end of the chapter.

A CLOSER LOOK AT BI ARCHITECTURE

The IT architecture that is needed for BI depends on the number and type of data sources or ISs, the volume of data, how much data extraction and transformation needs to be done, and the reporting timeline that's needed. For example, near-real-time reporting that needs to capture POS data and integrate data from several data marts, as at Jamba Juice, is going to need a complex architecture.

In this section, you read about BI architecture in greater detail. This section describes data extraction and integration; reporting and user interfaces; query, data mining, and analysis tools; and then business performance management (BPM). Table 11.4 lists the elements of a BI strategic project plan.

Data Extraction and Integration. To begin, tools extract data of interest from various data sources such as ERP, CRM, SCM, legacy systems, data marts or warehouses, and/or the Web. Extracted data, particularly when it's extracted from multiple sources, is not in usable format. Another problem is that different systems use their own field names, for example, *CUST_NUMBER* vs. *CUSTOMER_NUM*. Data extraction tools have to map the field names of the same data types and then reformat the data itself into a standard format. It is impossible to integrate data until the data transformation process is done. The third process is to load the standardized data into a data warehouse, or other data store, where it can be analyzed or used as the source of data for reports.

To summarize, the three data integration processes, **extraction, transformation, and load (ETL),** move data from multiple sources, reformat it, and load it into a central data store. Standardized data can be analyzed, loaded into another operational

IT at Work 11.2

Soldiers Saved by Battlefield BI

When soldiers are wounded in battle, the military needs to quickly diagnose their condition and provide efficient medical transport. Such action depends on real-time data, pinpoint accuracy, and easy-to-understand visualizations. The Transportation Command (TRANSCOM), under the Department of Defense (DoD), uses Information Builders' WebFocus BI software to optimize patient-movement plans. These plans are based on key factors such as urgent medical needs and available facilities.

TRAC2ES for Patient Movement. TRAC2ES (TRANSCOM Regulating and Command and Control Evacuation System) supports patient movement from the battlefield to treatment facility or rehabilitative care. The BI architecture of TRAC2ES is shown in Figure 11.9. The comprehensive BI reporting and analysis system helps sick or injured personnel reach the optimal destination via the most expedient transport method.

Supporting Military Operations. TRAC2ES tracks and coordinates patient information throughout the U.S. military's worldwide network of healthcare facilities. Figure 11.9 presents an overview of TRAC2ES BI infrastructure. TRAC2ES' decision-support system supported the troops during operations Enduring Freedom and Iraqi Freedom by providing 100 percent patient-in-transit visibility for more than 73,000 patient movements.

Prior to TRAC2ES, the transport of wounded and sick soldiers was often wrong and delayed. Mistakes during Operation Desert Storm highlighted the need for improved coordination of medical care for injured soldiers. In some cases, wounded soldiers were directed to the wrong hospital or to facilities that didn't provide the necessary specialties and treatments. The need for a more efficient patient-movement process led to the implementation of TRAC2ES.

From Baghdad to Germany to U.S. TRAC2ES also provides critical patient safety metrics. For example, it insures that an injured person won't be adversely affected by a long flight. When a 21-year-old active duty army specialist sustained blast and burn injuries in a car bombing on the Iraqi battlefield, the system helped ensure he was rapidly evacuated. Using TRAC2ES, the military team transmitted vital patient information from the 31st Combat Support Hospital in Baghdad to surgeons at Landstuhl Regional Medical Center in Germany, then on to the USAISR Burn Center in San Antonio, Texas. Coordinated communication and evacuation insured the patient received critical care at each step of the process. The BI capabilities integrate data, giving decision makers a clear view of all the paths leading toward resolving resource allocation challenges.

Sources: Compiled from *cs.amedd.army.mil/, trac2es.transcom.mil/* and Information Builders (2009).

Discussion Questions: Explain the intelligence provided by TRAC2ES. Explain the resource allocation process—given that many of the resources do not move, but rather troops are moved to the resources. Describe the performance metrics. What inefficiencies has TRAC2ES minimized or eliminated? In your opinion, how important are the data visualization tools? Explain your answer.

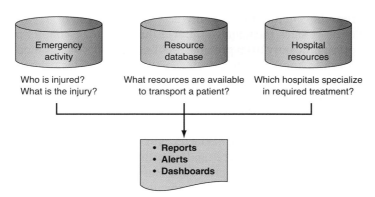

Figure 11.9 BI architecture of TRAC2ES.

TABLE 11.4	Elements of a BI Plan

Planning a BI implementation is a complex project and includes typical project management steps. Here is an overview of the steps of a BI project plan. Concepts mentioned, for instance *making a business case for BI*, are described in the chapter. It would be valuable to consider the seven flaws described in Section 11.1 as you read these steps.

1. Define the scope of the BI implementation. Specify what is included in the scope and what is not. Key questions to be answered:

    a. Is the BI just reporting, analytics, and dashboards?

    b. Or does the BI also require ETL, data warehousing, Web portals, broadband wireless networks, and other advanced IT?

    BI projects range from relatively simple if only (a) is *yes,* to enormous projects if both (a) and (b) are *yes*.

2. Obtain senior management commitment and a champion. No IT project can succeed without the financial support of top management. Getting commitment and a champion may require making the business case for BI or showing the ROI of other companies.

3. Organize a BI project team.

4. Document the current status of and problems with reporting, analysis, data quality, and other data-related issues.

5. Define the BI requirements, including who will be affected and supported, data latency tolerances, whether the BI will be traditional or operational, reporting and delivery (desktop, mobile, portal, extranet), and training needs.

6. Create a list of vendors and consultants that can meet the BI requirements. Review demos and case studies, and make use of free trials and downloads.

7. Select BI and data warehousing software vendors, consultants, and systems integrators, as needed.

Sources: Adapted from Evelson (2010) and *Teradata.com*.

system, or used for reporting or other business process. The central data repository, data security, and administrative tools form the **information infrastructure.**

Reporting. Enterprise reporting systems provide standard, ad hoc, or custom reports that are populated with data from trusted sources. Almost all companies that implement BI have installed self-service data delivery and reporting. Users access the information and reports they need directly. The self-service approach reduces costs, improves control, and reduces **data latency.** Technically, the speed with which data is captured is referred to as data latency.

Routine reports are generated automatically and distributed periodically to internal and external subscribers on mailing or distribution lists. Examples are weekly sales figures, units produced each day and each week, and monthly hours worked—and transport of wounded troops as described in *IT at Work 11.2.*

Here is an example of BI reporting: A store manager receives store performance reports generated weekly by the BI software. After a review of one weekly report on store sales, the manager notices that sales for computer peripherals have dropped off significantly from previous weeks. She clicks on her report and immediately drills down to another enterprise report for details, which shows her that the three best-selling hard drives are surprisingly underselling. Now the manager needs to investigate why. Further drill-down by individual day may reveal that bad weather on two days caused the drop in sales for that week.

User Interfaces: Dashboards and Scorecards. Dashboards and scorecards are interactive user interfaces and reporting tools. Dashboards, like a vehicle's dashboard, display easy-to-understand data. Business users like these tools for monitoring and analyzing critical information and metrics. Information is presented in graphs, charts, and tables that show actual performance vs. desired metrics for at-a-glance status reports. Table 11.5 lists capabilities of dashboards.

TABLE 11.5	Digital Dashboards Capabilities
Capability	**Description**
Drill-down	Ability to go to details at several levels; can be done by a series of menus or by query.
Critical success factors (CSFs)	The factors most critical for the success of business. These factors can be organizational, industry, departmental, etc.
Key performance indicators (KPIs)	The specific measures of CSFs.
Status access	The latest data available on KPI or some other metric, ideally in real time.
Trend analysis	Short-, medium-, and long-term trend of KPIs or metrics, which are projected using forecasting methods.
Ad hoc analysis	Analyses made any time, upon demand, and with any desired factors and relationships.
Exception reporting	Reports that highlight deviations larger than certain thresholds. Reports may include only deviations.

The more advanced dashboards present KPIs, trends, and exceptions using Adobe Flash animation. With Microstrategy Dynamic Enterprise Dashboards (*microstrategy.com/dashboards/*), dashboard designers can integrate data from various sources to provide performance feedback in multiple dimensions and optimize decision making in an interactive Flash mode. Figure 11.10 is an example of a multidimensional view of sales revenue data.

Dashboards are designed to support a specific function. For example, marketing dashboards report the traditional metrics—customer acquisition costs, customer retention rates, sales volume, channel margins, and the ROI of marketing campaigns. Accounting dashboards report on cash flows, accounts receivables and payables, and profitability metrics.

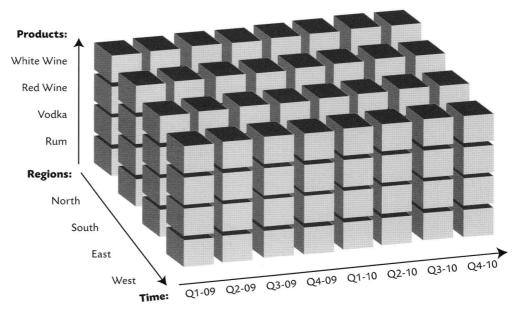

Figure 11.10 Multidimensional (3-D) view of sales revenue data.

Dashboards are also part of green IT initiatives. Because of demands from customers, employees, shareholders, and policymakers for environmentally friendly business practices, companies use dashboards instead of paper.

The **balanced scorecard methodology** is a framework for defining, implementing, and then managing an enterprise's business strategy by linking objectives with factual measures. In other words, it is a way to link top-level metrics, such as the financial information created by the chief financial officer (CFO), with actual performance.

DATA MINING, QUERY, AND ANALYSIS

Data mining, ad hoc and planned queries, and analysis tools help people "understand the numbers." These tools convert data to information and knowledge. The trend toward self-sufficiency applies to these tools also. BI prepares and provides the data for real-time reporting, decision support, and detailed analysis by end users. Users are able to explore the data to learn from it themselves.

To avoid confusion, here is the general difference between analysis and analytics: *Analysis* is the more general term referring to a process; *analytics* is a method that uses data to learn something. Analytics always involves historical or current data.

Query Example. An example of a multidimensional business query is: *For each of the four sales regions, what was the percent change in sales revenue for the top four products per quarter year compared to the same quarters for the past three years?*

This business question (query) identifies the data—*sales revenues*—that the user wants to examine. That data can be viewed in three dimensions: *sales regions, products*, and *time* in quarters. The results of this query would be shaped like the multidimensional cube shown in Figure 11.10.

Any query that's not predefined is an *ad hoc query*. Ad hoc queries allow users to request information that is not available in periodic reports, as well as to generate new queries or modify old ones with significant flexibility over content, layout, and calculations. These answers expedite decision making. Simple ad hoc query systems are often based on menus for self-service.

BUSINESS PERFORMANCE MANAGEMENT (BPM)

Business performance management (BPM) requires that managers have methods to quickly and easily determine how well the organization is achieving its goals and objectives, and whether or not the organization is aligned with the strategic direction. BPM relies on BI analysis reporting, queries, dashboards, and scorecards. The relationship between BPM and other components is shown in Figure 11.11.

The objective of BPM is strategic—to optimize the overall performance of an enterprise. By linking performance to corporate goals, decision makers can use the day-to-day data generated throughout their organization to monitor KPIs and make decisions that make a difference.

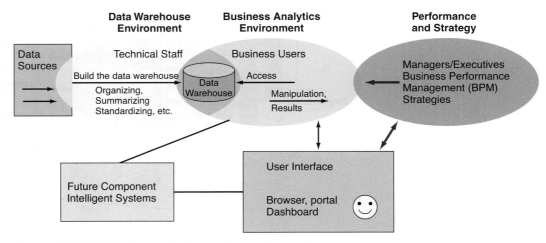

Figure 11.11 BPM for monitoring and assessing performance.

IT at Work 11.3

Bank Chain Relies on BI and DSS to Forecast Fashion Trends   OM   MKT

Fashion chain Bank (*bankfashion.co.uk/*), headquartered in the U.K. (see Figure 11.12), doubled the number of branches because of its excellent stock availability, faster replenishment, accurate forecasting and minimal merchandising and buying costs. Only an additional 7 merchandising and buying staff were needed to manage the extra volume of work. Warehousing staff had been reduced by 15 percent despite 15 more stores being added. These results were achieved from the use of sophisticated BI and DSS tools.

Figure 11.12 Bank Clothes store, Cambridge UK. (© *Kumar Sriskandan/Alamy*)

Decision Support and Forecasting. A key reason cited by Bank for its expansion is **real-time visibility**—the ability to consistently have the right customer sizes in stock. Bank's buyers have used BI tools to analyze which trends are taking off and to take full advantage of this knowledge to make sure the goods are in stock.

The system forecasts future buying patterns based on historical data. Buyers use *what-if* analysis to understand the effects of different buying ranges. For instance, when Bank analyzed its customers' size profiles, it found it was buying too many large sizes. The retailer altered its size ratios for appropriate styles, increasing sell-through by 5 percent.

Buyers and managers quickly see current stock levels, product performance, and profitability in real time on dashboards and, equally important, what customers are not buying. By comparing sales with previous years' figures, buyers can establish when sales patterns are different to determine price elasticity, so stock items can be priced correctly and mid-season promotions can be changed overnight when necessary. Merchandisers' minimum stock levels are predefined for each store. When new stock arrives in the warehouse, it is sorted quickly and dispatched in a very smooth operation. This allocation/replenishment method is extremely efficient. Management uses Futura's (*futurauk.com/*) performance management and analytical tools to model future sales, costs, cash and inventories, then define the top-level budget.

Sources: Compiled from *Futurauk.com*, Goulden (2006), and Perry (2007).

Discussion Questions: What is the impact of real-time visibility on managers' performance at Bank? What efficiencies have BI and DSS capabilities provided Bank? How do these efficiencies create a competitive advantage? Why was Bank able to increase the number of stores and reduce the number of employees?

BI PAYOFFS AND APPLICATIONS

BI has paid big dividends for companies in competitive marketplace environments, as illustrated in *IT at Work 11.3* at Bank, a retailer in the United Kingdom.

BI ranked near the top of many companies' IT purchase plans in 2010 and 2011. An underlying reason for this interest is that companies cannot afford mistakes or waste. At a time when inflation and energy prices are cutting into profit margins and consumers' disposable income, managers need to make smarter, more informed decisions. Exxon/Mobil and Cigna Insurance credit their profitability and explosive growth to BI. Using balanced scorecards, they precisely gauge their market opportunities and position their companies to become financial and performance leaders in their market niches. Examples of other common BI apps are listed in Table 11.6.

INDUSTRY-SPECIFIC BI

Because BI needs vary among business sectors, many BI tools are highly industry-specific. Using business analytics software, the user can make queries, request ad hoc reports, or conduct analyses. For example, because all of the databases are linked, you can search for which products are overstocked in a particular store. You can then determine which of these products commonly sell with popular items, based on previous sales. After planning a promotion to move the excess stock along with the popular products (e.g., bundling them together), you can dig deeper into the data to see where this promotion would be most popular and most profitable. The results of your request can be reports, predictions, alerts, and/or graphical presentations.

TABLE 11.6	Business Value of BI Analytical Apps	
Analytical Application	**Business Questions**	**Business Value**
Customer segmentation	What market segments do my customers fall into and what are their characteristics?	Personalize customer relationships for higher customer satisfaction and retention.
Propensity to buy	Which customers are most likely to respond to my promotion?	Target customers based on their need to increase their loyalty to your product line. Also, increase campaign profitability by focusing on those most likely to buy.
Customer profitability	What is the lifetime profitability of my customers?	Make business interaction decisions based on the overall profitability of customers or customer segments.
Fraud detection	How can I detect which transactions are likely to be fraudulent?	Quickly detect fraud and take immediate action to minimize cost.
Customer attrition	Which customers are at risk of leaving?	Prevent loss of high-value customers and let go of lower-value customers.
Channel optimization	What is the best channel to reach my customers in each segment?	Interact with customers based on their preference and your need to manage cost.

Review Questions

1. Define *data extraction* and *data integration*, and explain why they are needed.
2. What is data latency? How does giving users the ability to create their own reports reduce data latency? What is the age of fresh data?
3. Explain the capabilities of dashboards and scorecards. Why are they important BI tools?
4. What is the benefit to end users of having ad hoc query capabilities?
5. What is a multidimensional view of data? Sketch such a view in 3-D and label the multiple dimensions for a service company.
6. Define *business performance management* (BPM). What is the objective of BPM?

11.3 Data, Text, and Web Mining

Data is not the only type of content that can be mined for insights, although it is certainly the easiest. Textual information, or simply *text,* from documents, electronic communications, and e-commerce activities can be mined. Content that is mined includes unstructured data from documents, unstructured text from e-mail, and Web log data. Organizations recognize that a major source of competitive advantage is their unstructured knowledge. Text needs to be codified, typically with XML (eXtensible Markup Language), and extracted so that predictive data mining tools can be used to generate real value. Given that perhaps 80 percent of all collected/stored information is in text, or at least *nonnumeric,* format, text mining and Web mining are major growth areas. **Web mining,** or *Web-content mining,* is used to understand customer behavior, evaluate a Web site's effectiveness, and quantify the success of a marketing campaign. Text mining is not the same thing as a search engine on the Web. In a search, you are trying to find what others have prepared. With text mining, you are trying to discover new patterns that may not be obvious or known.

Documents containing unstructured data can contribute to the decision making of BI, but they cannot be used directly in data-driven reports and analyses unless facts discovered in unstructured data are extracted and transformed into structured data conducive to reporting and analysis. Tools to accomplish this are **text analytics.** Text analytics transforms unstructured text into structured "text data." This text data can then be searched, mined, or discovered. Text search, mining, and discovery address two of today's most pressing data management problems: customer and product data management.

BENEFITS OF DATA MINING

Data mining is a process that uses statistical, mathematical, artificial intelligence, and machine-learning techniques to extract and identify useful information and subsequent knowledge from large databases, including data warehouses. This information includes patterns usually extracted from large sets of data. These patterns can be rules, affinities, correlations, trends, or prediction models. The following are the major characteristics and objectives of data mining:

• Data is often buried deep within very large databases, which sometimes contain data from several years. In many cases, the data is cleaned and consolidated in a data warehouse.

• Sophisticated new tools, including advanced visualization tools, help to remove the information buried in corporate files or archival public records. Finding it involves massaging and synchronizing this data to get the right results.

• The miner is often an end user, empowered by data drills and other power query tools to ask ad hoc questions and obtain answers quickly with little or no programming skill.

• Striking it rich often involves finding an unexpected result and requires end users to think creatively.

• Data mining tools are readily combined with spreadsheets and other software development tools. Thus, the mined data can be analyzed and processed quickly and easily.

• Because of the large amounts of data and massive search efforts, it is sometimes necessary to use parallel processing or supercomputers to execute data mining.

• The data mining environment is usually a client/server architecture or a Web-based architecture.

POWER USERS OF DATA MINING TOOLS

Business sections that most extensively use data mining are finance, retail, and healthcare. For example, in the financial sector, data mining is used by banks, investment funds, hedge funds, and insurance companies as well as sophisticated private investors and traders. Financial data is structured and is often in time series, such as stock market prices, commodity prices, utility prices, or currency exchange rates observed over time. Data mining techniques are well suited to analyze financial time series data to find patterns, detect anomalies and outliers, recognize situations of chance and risk, and predict future demand, prices, and rates.

That's why data mining supports analysts, investors, and traders in their decisions when trading stocks, options, commodities, utilities, or currencies. Data mining is also important in detecting fraudulent behavior, especially in insurance claims and credit card use; identifying buying patterns of customers; reclaiming profitable customers; identifying trading rules from historical data; and aiding in market basket analysis.

DATA MINING APPS

The following examples of data mining apps can identify business opportunities in order to create a competitive advantage:

• **Retailing and sales.** Predicting sales, determining correct inventory levels and distribution schedules among outlets, and preventing loss.

• **Banking.** Forecasting levels of bad loans and fraudulent credit card use, credit card spending by new customers, and which kinds of customers will best respond to and qualify for new loan offers.

• **Manufacturing and production.** Predicting machinery failures; finding key factors that control optimization of manufacturing capacity.

• **Healthcare.** Correlating demographics of patients with critical illnesses; developing better insights into symptoms and their causes and how to provide proper treatments

• **Broadcasting.** Predicting which programs are best to air during prime time and how to maximize returns by interjecting advertisements.

• **Marketing.** Classifying customer demographics that can be used to predict which customers will respond to a mailing or Internet banners, or buy a particular product, as well as to predict other consumer behavior.

TEXT MINING AND WEB MINING

Text Mining. Documents are rarely structured, except for forms such as invoices or templates. **Text mining** helps organizations to do the following:

1. Find the meaningful content of documents, including additional useful relationships.

2. Relate documents across previously unnoticed divisions; for example, discover that customers in two different product divisions have the same characteristics.

3. Group documents by common themes; for example, find all of the customers of an insurance company who have similar complaints.

In biomedical research, text analytics and mining have the potential to reduce the time it takes researchers to find relevant documents and to find specific factual content within documents that can help researchers interpret experimental data, clinical record information, and BI data contained in patents.

Web Mining with Predictive Analysis. Each visitor to a Web site, each search on a search engine, each click on a link, and each transaction on an e-commerce site create data. Analysis of this data can help us make better use of Web sites and provide a better relationship and value to visitors to our own Web sites. Web mining is the application of data mining techniques to discover actionable and meaningful patterns, profiles, and trends from Web resources. The term Web mining is used to refer to both Web-content mining and Web-usage mining. *Web-content mining* is the process of mining Web sites for information. *Web-usage mining* involves analyzing Web access logs and other information connected to user browsing and access patterns on one or more Web localities.

Web mining is used in the following areas: information filtering of e-mails, magazines, newspapers, social media; surveillance of competitors, patents, technological development; mining of Web-access logs for analyzing usage, or *clickstream analysis*; assisted browsing; and services that fight crime on the Internet.

In e-commerce, Web-content mining is critical. For example, when you search for a certain book on *amazon.com,* the site uses mining tools to also present to you a list of books purchased by customers who had bought that book. Amazon has been extremely successful at cross-selling because it knows what to suggest to its customers at the critical point of purchase.

Predictive analytics is a component of Web mining that sifts through data to identify patterns of behavior that suggest, for example, what offers customers might respond to in the future or which customers you may be in danger of losing. For instance, when sifting through a bank's data warehouse, predictive analytics might *recognize* that customers who cancel an automatic bill payment or automatic deposit and are of a certain age often are relocating and will be moving to another bank within a certain period of time. Predictive analysis appears in many different formats, as illustrated in the following example and in *IT at Work 11.4.*

Example: Recognizing What Customers Want Even Before They Enter a Restaurant. HyperActive Technologies (*hyperactivetechnologies.com*) developed a system in which cameras mounted on the roof of a fast-food restaurant track vehicles pulling into the parking lot or drive-through. Other cameras track the progress of customers moving through the ordering queue. Using predictive analysis, the system predicts what arriving customers might order. A database includes historical car-ordering data, such as "20 percent of cars entering the lot will usually order at least one cheeseburger at lunchtime." Based on the camera's real-time input and the database, the system predicts what customers will order 1.5 to 5 minutes before they actually order. This alert gives cooks a head start in food preparation to minimize customers' wait times.

The *core element* of predictive analytics is the *predictor,* a variable that can be measured for an individual or entity to predict future behavior. For example, a credit card company could consider age, income, credit history, and other demographics as predictors determining an applicant's risk factor.

IT at Work 11.4

Enterprise Location Intelligence Apps

By combining information about location or geography with critical business data and geospatial technologies, organizations can create location intelligence, or LI. LI provides a new perspective on consumers and businesses to improve decision making. Examples of ways to use LI for competitive advantage are:

Public safety. A public works service rep receives a call from a resident who explains a light is out in front of her house. After receiving an address, the rep displays a map of the area, showing nearby streetlights. With a view of the intersection, the rep asks specific questions and determines that the nonfunctioning light is a traffic signal. By tying the geospatial data into the enterprise data warehouse (EDW), the agent is able to issue the correct repair request.

Store locations. A retail chain with plans to open 50 new stores uses geospatial technology to determine where those stores should be placed. Using LI, analysts identify relevant clientele demographics, such as who the most profitable customers are. Analysts combine that knowledge with information about potential sites' proximity to highways, public transportation, and competitors' stores to select the best location options.

Customer service. An insurance company represents customers in an area hit by a natural disaster. Geospatial data shows wind velocities in the vicinity of the storm. The company sends reps to affected customers to survey damage and offer payment for damages or repair services. Given the high risk of fraud in disaster areas, the insurance company uses data to identify potentially fraudulent claims.

Better intelligence can lead to improved insight, business-process efficiency, and reduced risk and fraud.

Bloomberg's LI Apps. Bloomberg provides services to investors based on their hourly or daily monitoring of world industries. Bloomberg has 30,000 sources of raw data, and their objective is to monitor everything, especially data related to infrastructure. Bloomberg uses enterprise LI to track every cargo vessel over 10,000 deadweight tons. It can tell where 127 bulk tankers are, where they are headed, and whether or not they are carrying cargo. To Bloomberg, data is a cost. Bloomberg's Equity BMap (mapping tool) turns raw data into value, which it then sells as a service.

How LI Works. LI can be created by integrating postal codes, maps, and other geographic data within an EDW. Locations are probably already in existing data stores, but not in a format needed for analytics. By using a geocoding process, postal addresses can be converted into geospatial data for LI. Decision makers can use this geospatial context to make data-driven and fact-based decisions, and respond to opportunities. The following are several scenarios:

* By merging location data with demographic and other business data, companies can create interactive maps that let users drill down to details about specific locations.
* Analysts can investigate new relationships to pinpoint the average income in areas where the highest-performing stores are located.
* Retailers can determine how store sales vary by population level or proximity to competitors.

Sources: Compiled from Krivda (2010) and Zeiss (2011).

Discussion Question: Visit YouTube to view the video *Bloomberg's BMAP Application for Energy & Commodity Traders*, which was uploaded on April 2, 2010. URL is *youtube.com/ watch?v= OqpevD4xFXU*. Describe what you learned.

Review Questions

1. What is text mining? Give three examples of text that would be mined for intelligence purposes.
2. How does text mining differ from search?
3. What is Web mining? Give three examples of Web content that would be mined for intelligence purposes.
4. Describe one advantage and one disadvantage of data mining tools.
5. List three data mining applications for identifying business opportunities.

11.4 Decision-Making Processes

To appreciate how and why ISs were designed to support managers, you need to understand what managers do. Managers' roles can be put into three categories based on Mintzberg (1973):

1. *Interpersonal role:* Leader, figurehead, liaison, or coach
2. *Informational role:* Monitor, disseminator, or spokesperson
3. *Decisional role:* Entrepreneur, problem solver, resource allocator, or negotiator

Early ISs mainly supported informational roles because they were the easiest roles to support. With the introduction of ISs in organizations, managers would receive an avalanche of data about issues and problems, which led to information overload. Managers lacked ISs that could adequately support doing something about those issues and problems. The situation created what we call the *inbox problem*, which is a metaphor for a growing inbox of problems that managers found out about but that remained in the inbox because they lacked tools for dealing with the problems and communicating results. Many new ITs emerge or are enhanced to solve problems of existing ITs. You can see that trend in BI as new features are added.

ISs have grown to support all managerial roles. In this section, we are mainly interested in IT that supports decisional roles. We divide the manager's work, as it relates to decisional roles, into two phases. Phase I is the identification of problems and/or opportunities. Phase II is the decision of what to do about them. Figure 11.13 provides a flowchart of this process and the flow of information in it.

DECISION PROCESS AND DECISION SUPPORT SYSTEMS (DSS)

Decision makers go through four systematic phases: *intelligence, design, choice*, and *implementation*, as diagrammed in Figure 11.14. Note that there is a continuous flow of information from intelligence to design to choice (bold lines), but at any time there may be a return to a prior phase (broken lines).

The decision-making process starts with the *intelligence phase*, in which managers examine a situation, then identify and define the problem. In the *design phase*, decision makers construct a model that represents and simplifies the problem or opportunity. This is done by making assumptions and expressing the relationships among all variables. The model is then validated, and decision makers set criteria for

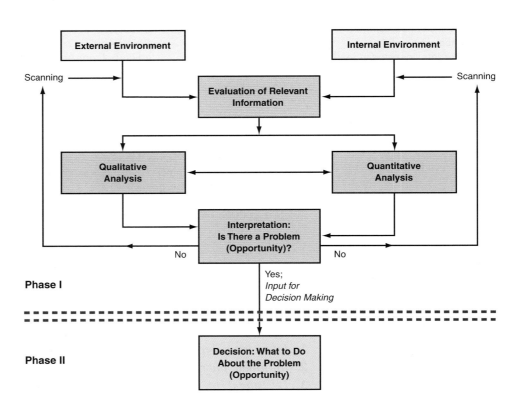

Figure 11.13 Manager's decision roles.

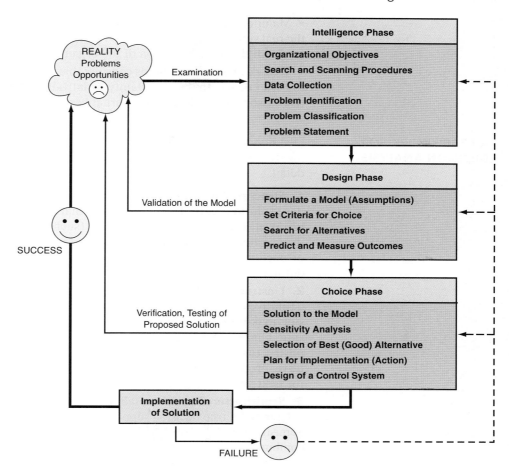

Figure 11.14 Phases in the decision-making process.

the evaluation of alternative potential solutions that are identified. The process is repeated for each sub-decision in complex situations. The output of each sub-decision is an input for the main decision. The *choice phase* involves selecting a solution, which is tested "on paper." Once this proposed solution seems to be feasible, we are ready for the last phase—implementation. Successful *implementation* results in resolving the original problem or opportunity. Failure leads to a return to the previous phases. A DSS automates several tasks in this process.

Decision Modeling and Models. A decision model is a simplified representation, or abstraction of reality. Simplicity is helpful because a lot of complexity may be irrelevant to a specific problem. One simplification method is making assumptions, such as assuming that growth in customer demand in the next quarter will be the same as the current quarter. The risk when using assumptions is if they are wrong, then the foundation for the analysis is flawed. For example, in July 2008, General Motors' (GM) sales of SUVs, minivans, and trucks had plunged due to very high gas prices that consumers knew were not going to drop. Since GM selected its models three years in advance, in 2005, GM's managers had assumed that the demand for large vehicles would remain at 2005 levels. That highly inaccurate assumption had a devastating influence on the company's sales and profits.

The benefits of modeling in decision making are as follows:

• The cost of virtual experimentation is much lower than the cost of experimentation conducted with a real system.
• Models allow for the simulated compression of time. Years of operation can be simulated in seconds of computer time.

- Manipulating the model by changing variables is much easier than manipulating the real system. Experimentation is therefore easier to conduct, and it does not interfere with the daily operation of the organization.
- Today's environment holds considerable uncertainty. Modeling allows a manager to better deal with the uncertainty by introducing many *what-ifs* and calculating the risks associated with various alternatives.

A FRAMEWORK FOR DECISION ANALYSIS

Decision-making activities fall along a continuum ranging from highly structured to highly unstructured, as you read in earlier chapters. Here we describe them in more detail.

1. **Structured decisions** involve routine and repetitive problems for which standard solutions exist. Examples are formal business procedures, cost minimization, profit maximization, and algorithms (such as those used by eHarmony to match its members). Whether the solution means finding an appropriate inventory level or deciding on an optimal investment strategy, the solution's criteria are clearly defined.

2. **Unstructured decisions** involve a lot of uncertainty, meaning that there are no definitive or clear-cut solutions. With unstructured decisions, for example, each decision maker may use different data, assumptions, and processes to reach a conclusion. Unstructured decisions rely on intuition, judgment, and experience. Typical unstructured problems include planning new services to be offered, hiring an executive, predicting markets, or choosing a set of research and development projects for next year.

3. **Semistructured decisions** fall between the polar positions. Most of what are considered to be true decision support systems are focused on semistructured decisions. Semistructured problems, in which only some of the phases are structured, require a combination of standard solution procedures and individual judgment. Examples of semistructured problems are trading bonds, setting marketing budgets for consumer products, and performing capital acquisition analysis. Here, a DSS is most suitable. It can provide not only a single solution but also a range of what-if scenarios.

Review Questions

1. What are the three roles of management?
2. What is meant by the inbox problem?
3. Identify and explain the three phases of decision making.
4. Why are models used in decision making? What is an inherent risk of using models in decision making?
5. Give an example of a structured, an unstructured, and a semistructured decision. Which of these types of decisions can be optimized? Why?

11.5 Decision Support Systems (DSS)

Decision support systems (DSS) are a class of ISs that combine models and data to solve semistructured and unstructured problems with intensive user involvement. A DSS is interactive, flexible, and adaptable—and supports the solution of unstructured or semistructured problems. DSSs have easy-to-use interfaces and allow for the decision maker' own insights.

Structured decisions are so well defined that they can be automated or become standard operating procedures (SOPs) that do not require a DSS to solve.

A properly designed DSS is an interactive application to help decision makers compile data and then analyze the data using business models. The central point is that the DSS should result in a better decision than was possible without it. The most popular software used to develop DSSs is Microsoft Excel.

Typical information that a decision support application might gather and present are:

- Comparative sales figures of a specific product between one week or month and the following week or month
- Projected revenue figures based on new product sales assumptions
- Projected consequences of different decision alternatives, given past experience and forecasted conditions.

SENSITIVITY ANALYSIS: WHAT-IF AND GOAL SEEKING

The mathematical models used in DSSs enable *sensitivity analysis*. **Sensitivity analysis** is the study of the impact that changes in one or more parts of a model have on other parts or the outcome. Usually, we check the impact that changes in input (*independent variables*) have on outcomes (*dependent variables*). For example, quantity demanded is a dependent variable, whereas price, advertising, disposable income, and competitor's price are four examples of the independent variables in the classic economic model. The dependent variable changes in response to changes in the independent variables. An easy way to remember the relationship between dependent and independent variables is this example: The number of umbrellas sold (dependent variable) is determined by the amount of rainfall (independent variable). It's obvious that the reverse is not true.

Consider this product demand example: The value of each controllable independent variable is varied—price and advertising—to determine how sensitive quantity demanded is to those adjustments. A *sensitive model* means that small changes in conditions (variables) suggest a different solution. In a *nonsensitive model*, changes in conditions do not significantly change the recommended solution.

Sensitivity analysis is extremely valuable in DSSs because it makes the system flexible and adaptable to changing conditions and to the varying requirements of different decision-making situations. It allows users to enter their own data, including the pessimistic data, or worst-case scenario, and to view how systems will behave under varying circumstances. It provides better understanding of the model and the problem it purports to describe. It may increase users' confidence in the model, especially when the model is not very sensitive to changes.

STRUCTURE AND COMPONENTS OF DSS

Basic components of a DSS are a database, model base, user interface, and the users. An additional component is a knowledge base.

Database. A DSS database system, like any database, contains data from multiple sources. Some DSSs do not have a separate database; data are entered into the DSS model as needed (e.g., as soon as they are collected by sensors).

Model Base. A model base contains completed models and sets of rules, which are the building blocks necessary to develop DSS applications. Types of models include financial, statistical, management science, or economic. Model-building software, such as Excel, have built-in mathematical and statistical functions. These models provide the system's analytical capabilities.

User Interface. The user interface covers all aspects of the communications between a user and the DSS. A well-designed user interface can greatly improve the productivity of the user and reduce errors.

Users. A DSS is a tool for the user, the decision maker. The user is considered to be a part of the highly interactive DSS system. A DSS has two broad classes of users: managers and staff specialists, such as financial analysts, production planners, and market researchers.

Knowledge Base. Many unstructured and semistructured problems are so complex that they require expertise for their solutions. Such expertise can be provided by a

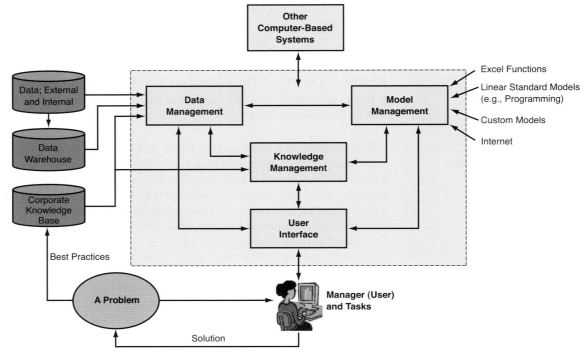

Figure 11.15 Conceptual model of DSS and its components.

knowledge-based system, such as an expert system. Therefore, the more advanced DSSs are equipped with a component called a knowledge base. A knowledge base provides the expertise to solve some part of the problem. For example, a knowledge base can estimate the cost of a massive construction job based on dimensions, materials, labor costs, weather delays, and numerous other cost factors. It is a complex process that requires models, a database, and judgment. Figure 11.15 shows how the components of a DSS interact.

DSS APPS

A large number of DSS apps can be found in any industry, including manufacturing and services, as shown in the following examples.

Example 1: Wells Fargo Targets Customers. Wells Fargo *(wellsfargo.com)* has become so good at predicting consumer behavior that it practically knows what customers want before they do. The bank developed a DSS in-house that collects data on every transaction—phone, ATM, bank branch, and online—and combines this data with personal data from the customer. The Wells Fargo DSS program then analyzes the data and models the customer's behavior to automatically come up with prospective offers, such as a home equity loan, just at the right time for the customer.

Example 2: Lowering Costs in Healthcare. Owens & Minor *(owens-minor.com/)*, a Fortune 500 company, is a leading distributor of medical and surgical supplies to the acute-care market and a healthcare supply chain management company. The company was the winner of the 2010 Distributor of the Year Service Excellence Award from the University Health System Consortium (UHC). UHC is an alliance representing 90 percent of the nation's nonprofit academic medical centers. The award is given to the distributor that provides exceptional support and commitment in helping hospital members meet their supply chain goals.

One of those goals is driving down the price of thousands of hospital supplies. Owens & Minor uses its DSS to help customers hunt for bargains among hundreds of competing medical suppliers. The DSS pinpoints lower pricing on similar items, helping customers take advantage of discounts already negotiated. Hospitals keep better tabs on their bills and cut costs an average of 2 to 3 percent. For Owens & Minor, the DSS attracts new customers, and when existing customers find lower prices, they order more.

These examples demonstrate the diversity of decisions that DSSs can support. In addition, many examples can be found at *sas.com* and *microstrategy.com*, where hundreds of apps and success stories are listed by industry.

Review Questions

> 1. Explain the two types of decisions that DSSs are used to solve. Why aren't DSSs used to support structured decisions?
> 2. Describe sensitivity analysis.
> 3. Explain the difference between what-if analysis and goal seeking.
> 4. Explain the difference between dependent and independent variables.
> 5. What are the components of a DSS?

11.6 Mobile Intelligence: Convergence of Mobile Computing and BI

Since the 1960s, there have been five major generations, or cycles, of computing: mainframes, miniframes, PCs, desktop Internet computing, and mobile Internet computing (or simply mobile computing), as shown in Figure 11.16. Mobile computing, the fifth computing generation, has already had a huge impact and adoption rate, as you read in Chapters 1, 7, and 8. Mobile devices are becoming the world's dominant computing platform.

Mobile computing is not just a U.S. phenomenon. Japan is leading the world in mobile computing, but the United States has the largest 3G subscriber base. China and other countries have broadband and 3G penetration equal to or greater than that in the United States, but those countries are deliberately encouraging deployment of new apps and services. Worldwide, cell coverage and more powerful wireless 3G and 4G technologies are expanding Internet connectivity.

MOBILE INTELLIGENCE INFRASTRUCTURE

The speed with which Apple's iPhone and iTouch have sold—roughly 57 million sold in 28 months—is an indicator that MI apps will be in high demand. According to Morgan Stanley's *Global Mobile Internet Report* (2009), mobile computing may be the fastest-growing and most disruptive technology launch we have ever seen because of the following:

- Scale of adoption—wireless global adoption was 4.1 billion subscriptions, compared to 1.6 billion Internet users.
- Accelerating rate of adoption.
- Confluence of powerful new technologies.
- New usage models that consumers and enterprises are enthusiastically adopting.

Redefining Hardware Functions. The functions of hardware are being redefined. For example, smartphones are becoming PCs, PCs are becoming servers, servers are becoming the cloud, and the cloud is the new app source. Your smartphone may be taking on more of the functions you used to do on your desktop or laptop, and you may be backing up content from smartphones onto your laptop or dropping it to the cloud. The cloud is the infrastructure for new generations of Web and mobile apps.

Figure 11.16 Five generations of computing from the 1960s to the 2010s.

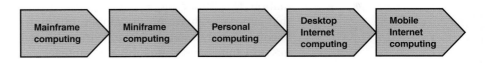

Vendor Incentives. Vendors have enormous incentives to develop mobile business apps. The Apple ecosystem composed of iPhone and iTouch devices, the iTunes easy-to-use payment/distribution system, and the App Store—a developer-friendly environment for new apps—creates a cycle of incentives for more and better mobile Internet usage. Expect to see changes in everything mobile—social networking, music, video, games, books, commerce, messaging, and location-based GPS apps.

Unifying Communications in the Cloud. The topology of the Internet itself is changing. Powerful devices using IP-based infrastructure, such as 4G networks, combined with easy-to-use software, are unifying communications. And always-on connectivity is increasing demand for cloud-based computing.

Smartphones and other Internet-enabled mobile devices change how people stay informed, communicate, and in general, manage their professional and personal lives. Accessing information at any time, in any location, on a handheld device on a regular basis has changed the way that managers and other workers expect to make decisions. Business apps that were fairly successful when used on a desktop become more successful and valuable when they can be used on the go, whenever and wherever business is conducted. Information access via mobiles may soon far exceed desktop or laptop information access in the near future, creating an era of **mobile intelligence (MI).** MI functionality is critical to companies that have a mobile workforce or teams of field representatives.

MOBILE INTELLIGENCE

Recall the discussion on interactivity in Chapter 1. Those interactive apps on mobile devices are revolutionizing information dissemination and consumption. And the alignment of business data, analytics, and mobile computing is transforming business processes.

MI is positioned to change how organizations deliver, consume, and act on information. Without 24/7 convenient access to business information, decisions and actions get postponed, causing bottlenecks and delays. These restrictions and delays are blown away with MI, which allows heuristic analysis and decision making wherever a decision is required.

Here are two concepts related to MI:

• **Decision sweet spots:** These spots are locations, such as a commuter train, an aisle in a store, a line in a factory, or a retail floor. Businesspeople need to be able to make data-driven decisions in the sweet spot, rather than delay due to a lack of information or analysis capabilities.

• **Decision windows of opportunity:** This window exists when a choice or action can be made to maximize an impact. The longer it takes someone to get to the information and completely evaluate the situation, the greater the chance of missing an opportunity. And delays risk the loss of a sale or customer.

Mobile technology makes it possible for people to make immediate decisions. Users can sift through enormous volumes of data on their handheld devices and convert this data into actionable insight. Within moments, information is accessible without sitting down and finding a place to plug in a laptop. And rapid decision making is key to accelerating the profitability of business. In today's fast-changing, competitive business environment, it is imperative to provide immediate answers to both internal and external customers. With MI, decision makers now have the power to make these decisions immediately. In the mobile intelligence era, businesses that don't yet exist may evolve into industry leaders. Moderately valuable apps that run on desktops may become hugely successful apps when fully applied to the mobile Internet.

The next Facebook, YouTube, or Twitter hasn't been invented yet, but it will be designed as a mobile app. Organizations that stay with today's desktop-based information distribution models may become obsolete, outpaced by those organizations that choose to thrive on the mobile Internet. Organizations that embrace MI will become leaner, faster, and be able to make smarter decisions resulting in more business, revenues, and competitive advantage.

1. What are the five computing generations?
2. How are hardware devices being redefined?
3. Explain the incentives to vendors to further develop mobile apps.
4. Explain the importance of people being able to make immediate decisions.
5. What might be the impact on organizations that exploit mobile intelligence?

Key Terms

algorithm *330*
balanced scorecard methodology *340*
blindspot *328*
business case *328*
business performance management (BPM) *340*
customer churn *323*
dashboard *329*
data latency *338*

data mining *343*
data visualization *329*
decision support system (DSS) *348*
ETL (extract, transform, and load) tools *333*
event-driven alert *331*
information infrastructure *338*
mobile intelligence (MI) *352*
operational BI *327*

performance management *329*
predictive analytics *330*
proper resource allocation *322*
real-time visibility *341*
sensitivity analysis *349*
text analytics *342*
text mining *344*
traditional BI *326*
Web mining *342*

Chapter Highlights and Insights

(Numbers refer to Learning Objectives)

1 Business intelligence is driven by the need to get accurate and timely information in an easy way, and to analyze it, sometimes in minutes, possibly by the end users.

1 BPM is an umbrella term covering methodologies, metrics, processes, and systems used to drive the performance of the enterprise. It encompasses a closed-loop set of processes such as strategize, plan, monitor, analyze, and act (adjust).

2 The major components of BI are data warehouses and/or marts, predictive analytics, data mining, data visualization software, and a business performance management system.

3 Predictive analysis uses different algorithms to forecast results and relationships among variables as well as to identify data patterns. Data mining is one of the tools.

3 Scorecards and dashboards are a common component of most, if not all, performance management systems, performance measurement systems, and BPM suites.

3 The fundamental challenge of dashboard design is to display all of the required information on a single screen, clearly and without distraction, in a manner that can be assimilated quickly.

3 Decision making involves four major phases: intelligence, design, choice, and implementation.

4 Models allow fast and inexpensive virtual experimentations with new or modified systems.

5 A DSS is an approach that can improve the effectiveness of decision making, decrease the need for training, improve management control, facilitate communication, reduce costs, and allow for more objective decision making. DSSs deal mostly with unstructured problems. Structured decisions are solved with management science models.

5 The major components of a DSS are a database and its management, the model base and its management, and the user-friendly interface.

6 Mobile intelligence (MI) is the result of the convergence of mobile computing, powerful smart mobile devices, and BI capabilities that are Web-accessible. MI and analytics *in the cloud* are expected to define the future of BI.

Questions for Discussion

1. Discuss what John Wanamaker meant by his remark: "Half the money I spend on advertising is wasted; the trouble is I don't know which half."
2. Discuss the meanings of intelligence and uncertainty.
3. Discuss how your experiences with customer service could have been better or more productive.
4. What are the trade-offs in terms of cost and service involved in deciding the allocation of resources?
5. Differentiate the three types of BI.
6. What are the key types of support provided by BI?
7. Differentiate predictive analysis from data mining. What do they have in common?
8. Describe the concepts underlying Web mining and Web analytics.
9. When is real-time BI critical?

10. What could be the biggest advantages of a mathematical model that supports a major investment decision?

11. How is the term *model* used in this chapter? What are the strengths and weaknesses of modeling?

12. What ITs have contributed to the emergence of data mashups for BI?

13. What ITs have contributed to the emergence of mobile intelligence?

Exercises and Projects

You need to register for exercises that involve the Teradata University Network at *http://academicprograms.teradata.com/tun/*. Also see directions on the textbook's companion Web site.

1. Visit Teradata University Network and find the Powerpoint presentation *Why is Data Quality Important,* by Lori Roets, Teradata, 6-5-2010. Download and read the presentation and answer the following questions:
    a. Why and to what extent is data quality important?
    b. How should companies address data quality?
    c. What are five other lessons you learned about data quality?

2. Visit Teradata University Network and find the research report *TDWI Best Practices Report: Transforming Finance*, by Wayne Eckerson, 5-28-2010.
    a. Describe current practices of how finance uses BI.
    b. In the report is a discussion on "Single Version of Truth." In this chapter, you learned that, in practice, managers or supervisors may not agree on a single version of the truth. Discuss how the author defines a single version of the truth. Do you agree?
    c. What are five other lessons you learned about the use of BI by finance?

3. Visit the textbook's Web site and download *Harrah's High Payoff from Customer Information,* by H.J. Watson and Linda Volonino. Answer the following:
    a. What were the objectives of the project?
    b. What was the role of the DW?
    c. What kinds of analyses were used?
    d. What strategic advantages does the BI provide?
    e. What are the role and importance of an executive innovator?

4. Visit Teradata University Network and search recent developments in the field of BI.
    a. Watch the Webinar on information visualization. What are the capabilities of Tableau Software's products?
    b. Find the assignment "AdVent Technology" and use the Microstrategy "Sales Analytical Model." Answer the three questions. Ask your instructor for directions.

5. West 88 (fictitious name) is an ice cream and yogurt dessert take-out or eat-in chain. There are 12 West 88 locations in busy tourist areas. Jen K, the CEO, asked that you research and make a recommendation for a BI reporting and visualization tool.
    a. Prepare a list of the BI reporting and visualization tools of three vendors to consider.
    b. Prepare a table that compares the key advantages and costs of each tool as it relates to this specific case.
    c. Make a recommendation based on available information.

6. Consider this perspective on BI and BPM. Conceptually, BI is simple: Data produced by an organization's transactional processing and operational IT systems can be collected and summarized into totals and reports that give managers an immediate view of how they are doing. Business performance management (BPM) is about people and culture, and it should involve every knowledge worker in an organization, but there are some behavioral hurdles that still need to be overcome.
    Respond to the following points:
    a. Prepare a table that lists the BI technologies involved in each step of the process, from data production to reports that give managers an immediate view of how they are doing. List the process (e.g., extraction from TPS) in the first column and the BI technology in the second column.
    b. Using the table produced in (a), search for two vendors that provide a BI tool for each process. Put the results of your research in the third column. Include the brand name of the BI tool, the vendor's name, and the URL to the BI tool.
    c. Find one vendor, white paper, or article that addresses potential behavioral problems associated with BI or BPM. How do they respond to or address such obstacles? (*intelligententerprise.com/* may be a good place to research.) Report what you learn.

7. Search and visit a blog focused on BI or predictive analytics. Verify that the blog has current content. What are the BI-related topics discussed in five of the posts?

Group Assignments and Projects

1. Data visualization tools are offered by major BI vendors and niche vendors. These vendors are listed in the *Chapter 11 Link Library* and mentioned in the chapter. Each group is assigned to one or two vendors to research its data visualization products. Each group summarizes those products and their capabilities.

2. Search the BI vendors listed in the *Chapter 11 Link Library*. Each group finds a demo related to BI. View the demo and report what you learned.

3. Visit *sas.com* and look for success stories related to BI. Find five that include an SAS video and prepare a summary of each for a class presentation.

4. Search for vendors in Web analytics and prepare a report on their products and capabilities. Each group presents the capabilities of two companies.

Internet Exercises

1. Visit *microstrategy.com/dashboards/* to see the kinds of better business insights possible, in the section Real-life Dashboards from Microstrategy Customers. Explain how the dashboards can lead to better business insights. What are the limitations dashboards?

2. Visit *microstrategy.com/dashboards/* to see how your organization can improve business operations, in the section Cutting-Edge Industry and Role-Based Dashboards. Explain how the dashboards can improve business operations.

3. Find a case study about the benefits of a DSS implementation at a nonprofit or government agency. Briefly describe the organizations, the reasons for the DSS, and the benefits.

4. Visit *informatica.com* or *accure.com* and identify their Internet analytics solutions. Compare and comment. Relate your findings to business performance measurement.

5. Access the Web and online journals to find at least three articles or white papers on the use of predictive analytics. Identify the vendor or enterprise, the predictive analytic software product, and the benefits gained.

6. Find two cases published after January 2011 of successful business analytics applications. Try BI vendors and look for cases or success stories. What do you find in common with their case stories? How do they differ?

BUSINESS CASE

Responding to "Need it Yesterday" Customers with BI Apps

McNICHOLS (*mcnichols.com/*) is a worldwide leader in the custom fabrication of a wide variety of perforated and mesh metal products. (Visit the Web site to better understand the business.) Its customers are universities, government agencies, municipalities, commercial construction, manufacturers, wholesalers, and retailers. Dino DePaolis, finance director at McNICHOLS, described the pressures the company was under by stating: "Customers want everything right now or they need things yesterday, and we have to ensure that we have the right inventory at the right time." Managers wanted information *right now* too. They needed real-time metrics showing profitability, sales success, and inventory availability because McNICHOLS guarantees 24-hour turnaround time.

Manual Planning and Budgeting

McNICHOLS's manual quarterly budget process was unmanageable. The manual budget method involved MS Access databases and spreadsheets scattered throughout the organization. DePaolis described the old budgeting life cycle as an octopus with long tentacles. The body was an Access database and the tentacles were Excel spreadsheets that reached throughout the organization's districts that were tasked with contributing daily sales data. Collecting sales data and moving it into other spreadsheets to feed into Access was very cumbersome and required constant review to ensure the accuracy of the data.

McNICHOLS needed a solution that could provide trusted forecast to senior managers, enabling them to make quick and effective decisions. DePaolis identified his requirements for a financial planning solution: data accuracy, data integrity, able to display complex financial scenarios, flexibility, and ease of use.

Cognos 8 BI

In 2008, McNICHOLS implemented IBM Cognos 8 BI. Cognos 8 BI integrates and consolidates transactional data into executive dashboards to deliver information to district managers, the CFO, CEO, and vice presidents. The BI helps them to quickly measure all key performance indicators (KPIs) including sales, gross profit, margins, customer inquiries, and invoice counts. BI reporting capabilities were later extended to the Finance department.

The budget process that had taken 7 to 10 days at the end of each quarter and several hours each month is now done in seconds. The CFO saves nearly two weeks every quarter just in labor hours. Other key benefits of their BI implementation are:

- Sales analytics that are linked budgeting modules, making it easier for managers to monitor KPIs.
- Integrated views of all business and financial data, provided in a single Web-based portal.
- Improved accuracy and quality of data.
- Marketing, production, and order dashboards that enable real-time tracking of the profitability of all aspects of the business.
- Managers that have a good handle on actual transactions, forecasts, and targets.

Every day, managers are challenged to do more and accomplish more with less. With BI, they can provide the highest level of service to customers internally and externally, and do so with greater functionality and fewer resources allocated to reporting and analytics.

Sources: Compiled from *mcnichols.com/* and IBM Cognos BI 8 (2010).

Questions

1. Describe McNICHOLS's data and reporting problems.
2. Why do you think the company was using Access and Excel for its intelligence and reporting requirements?
3. Describe McNICHOLS's business strategy, or how it defines its competitive advantage. How important is customer loyalty?

4. Were resources improperly allocated under the manual system? How has the BI system reallocated resources?
5. What might have been the business case for BI at McNICHOLS?

NONPROFIT CASE

EuResist Develops Disease-Resistant Research App

GLOBAL   SVR   HRM   IS

Development of antiretroviral drug resistance is a major cause of treatment failure in HIV-infected patients. When EuResist(*euresist.org/*), a European network dedicated to improving the success rate of HIV treatments, wanted to develop a smarter way to predict the most effective drug combinations for patients, they worked with IBM to create an integrated data analytics solution.

EuResist Network

EuResist Network GEIE wanted to help physicians determine the optimal combination of HIV treatment drugs that would help patients while limiting the evolution of drug resistance. Previously, physicians based much of their decision making on personal experience with HIV cases and limited prediction tools. But EuResist hoped to introduce a better modeling solution that would better reflect patient reactions.

Drug Interaction Modeling Tool

EuResist worked with IBM Research to develop a drug interaction modeling tool for users to predict the success rate and impact on virus evolution of various drug combinations via an online portal. The prediction engine, operating on an IBM WebSphere Application server, leverages medical data (e.g., viral gene sequences, patient histories) from seven sources hosted within a DB2 data server.

Based on DB2 and WebSphere, the solution processed and correlated clinical and genomic data from many sources, consolidating more than 39,000 patient records, 109,000 therapies, and 449,000 viral load measurements—predicting patient responses to therapy with over 75 percent accuracy. Additionally, in a head-on competition with human clinical experts, EuResist outperformed the experts nine out of 10 times. Other benefits included:

- Being able to compare patient details against 33,000 previous cases and treatment data to help choose a therapy with a high probability of success
- Reduced incidents of treatment-related toxicity by pulling data from seven sources to create more accurate patient models

EuResist Prediction Engine

The EuResist project had received a grant from the European Commission to develop an integrated European system for computer-based clinical management of antiretroviral drug resistance. The resulting system, the *EuResist prediction engine* (*engine.euresist.org/*), provides clinicians with Internet-based prediction of clinical response to antiretroviral treatment in HIV patients. This engine helps medical experts to choose the best drugs and drug combinations for any given HIV genetic variant. To this end, a large integrated data set has been created, uniting several of the largest existing resistance databases. Access to the database and prediction engine are provided at no cost.

Sources: Compiled from *euresist.org/*, *engine.euresist.org/*, IBM (2010), and IBM Cognos BI 8 (2010).

Questions

1. Predictive analytics can improve diagnosis and treatment in healthcare. Explain the need for a smarter way to predict the most effective drug combinations.
2. How can DSS and predictive analytics reduce the costs of healthcare treatments?
3. What have been the benefits of the DSS to the EuResist project?
4. What might be some types of resistance to the use of EuResist? From medical experts? From patients?
5. In your opinion, do you think that insurance companies that pay for drug treatments would be in favor of or against it? Explain your answer.
6. Visit the textbook's Web site to view the *Euresist_300k.wmv* audio/video (5.5 minutes). Explain the benefits of the prediction engine. Does EuResist's statistical approach replace or supplement the expertise of medical experts?

ANALYSIS USING SPREADSHEETS

Making the Business Case for BI

Refer to the McNICHOLS Business Case at the end of this chapter. You have been asked to calculate the one-year cost savings from the BI. That calculation will be used in the business case to extend the BI's capabilities and invest in mobile intelligence (MI). You need to calculate monthly cost savings for January through December 201X, and then show the one-year total cost savings per category.

Cost issues:

- As the case states, real-time metrics showing profitability, sales success, and inventory availability are critical to success because McNICHOLS guarantees 24-hour turnaround time. It costs the company an average of $1,000 for each guarantee that it does not keep.
- For managers, the average hourly salary is $110 per hour.
- The cost of each lost customer is estimated at $500 per month.
- The cost of missing the deadline for a quarterly financial report is $2,000 per quarter.

- The reduction in operations waste and errors due to improved data quality is $1,800 per month.

Base your analysis on the following cost reductions in each of the following categories.

1. Labor costs. Review the case for the hours saved by the BI. Explain how you estimated the number of hours in a note or comment on the spreadsheet.
2. Guarantee costs.
3. Customer attrition.
4. Timely quarterly financial reports.
5. Waste and errors in operations.

Format the spreadsheet so that it is easy to understand. Do not use decimal places. Include your name and the date of your analysis.

References

Briggs, L., "BI Case Study: DIRECTV Connects with Data Integration Solution," *Business Intelligence Journal,* Vol. 14, No. 1, March 2009.

DIRECTV, *investor.directv.com/overview.cfm,* 2010

Evelson, B., "10 Components of a Successful BI Strategy Plan," *Information Management Blogs,* June 4, 2010.

Gartner, "Gartner Indentifies Four Information Management Roles IT Departments Need to Remain Effective," January 18, 2010.

Gartner Research, "BI Failure? Technology Is Not the Culprit," *CXOtoday.com,* October 13, 2008, *cxotoday.com/*

Goulden, B., "Fashion Chain Store on the Way," *Coventry,* July 14, 2006.

IBM, "Why EuResist Uses IBM," 2010. *www-03.ibm.com/systems/smarter/questions/information-analytics.html*

IBM Cognos BI 8, "Leading Metal Supplier and Fabricator Introduces Efficiency, Ease of Use to Financial Planning with IBM Cognos 8 BI and TM1," May 26, 2010.

IBM.com (2011)

Imhoff, C, "Enterprise Business Intelligence," *Intelligent Solutions, Inc.,* May 2006.

Information Builders, "U.S. Transportation Command Saves Lives with BI Technology from Information Builders," April 13, 2009. *informationbuilders.com/news/press/release/8365*

Krivda, C.D. "Pinpoint Opportunity." *Teradata Magazine.* Q1 2001. *teradata-magazine.com/v10n01/Features/Pinpoint-opportunity/*

Mintzberg, H., *The Nature of the Managerial Work.* New York: Harper & Row, 1973.

Morgan Stanley, "Global Mobile Internet Report," December 2009. *Morganstanley.com*

Oracle, "Business Interest in Business Intelligence Solutions for JD Edwards EnterpriseOne," an Oracle White Paper, April 2007.

Perry, J., "All the Right Answers," *Retail Week,* June 1, 2007.

PRNewsWire.com (2011)

PRNewswire, "INRIX and WSI Partner to Make Commutes Easier with Traffic Forecasts for Broadcast and Cable Television Stations Across North America," *BNet,* April 14, 2008.

Torode, C., "Gartner Rates the Big Four Business Intelligence Vendors," *SearchCIO.com,* April 27, 2010.

Zeiss, G. "Between the Poles." March 2011. *geospatial.blogs.com/geospatial/2011/03/location-intelligence-enterprise-usa-benefiting-from-spatial-data-obesity.html*

Chapter

12

IT Strategic Planning

Learning Objectives

1 Explain the value of aligning the IT and business strategies and how this alignment can be achieved.

2 Recognize the importance, functions, and challenges of IT governance.

3 Describe the reasons and benefits of aligning IT strategy and business strategy.

4 Describe the IT strategic planning process.

5 Understand major types of outsourcing, reasons for outsourcing, and the risks and benefits.

Integrating *IT*

 ACC
 FIN
 MKT
 OM
 HRM
 IS

CHAPTER 12 LINK LIBRARY

Balanced Scorecard Institute *balancedscorecard.org/*

International Association of Outsourcing Professionals' best outsourcing service providers, *The Global Outsourcing 100* *outsourcingprofessional.org/content/23/152/1197/*

Visual Ark *virtualark.com/*

Windows Azure *microsoft.com/windowsazure/*

Rackspace Hosting *rackspace.com/*

CIO Insights and Strategy *IBM.com/CIO/*

Debate over Offshore Outsourcing *quality-web-solutions.com/offshore-outsourcing-debate.php*

Outsource Blog *theoutsourceblog.com/*

Bloomberg Real-Time Information Services *bloomberg.com/*

Debate over Offshore Outsourcing *quality-web-solutions.com/offshore-outsourcing-debate.php*

IT Governance Institute *itgi.org/*

Video interview on SaaS and Outsourcing Relationship Management *janeeva.com/blog/*

QUICK LOOK at Chapter 12, IT Strategic Planning

This section introduces you to the business issues, challenges, and IT solutions in Chapter 12. Topics and issues mentioned in the Quick Look are explained in the chapter.

Throughout this book, you read cases about organizations that have invested in real-time operational and reporting apps, networks, mobile computing, social media, enterprise systems and infrastructure, and other IT to solve problems, get work done, gain advantages, and other business purposes. Most likely, each investment was justified and approved through some budget process. Making IT investments on the basis of an immediate need or threat is sometimes necessary, but these reactive approaches won't maximize ROI—and can result in incompatible, redundant, or failed systems.

Two of the biggest risks and concerns of top management are (1) failing to align IT to real business needs and, as a result, (2) failing to deliver value to the business. Since IT can have a dramatic effect on business performance and competitiveness, the failure to manage IT effectively has a serious impact on the business as a whole. Conversely, payoffs from IT successes include substantial reductions in operating costs and improvements in agility. This strategic fit is inherently dynamic because IT strategy alignment is not an event, but an ongoing process that's summarized by the following principle: *ISs are never built—but are always being built.*

In this chapter, we discuss the issues, risks, and payoffs associated with aligning business and IT strategies. The two basic types of IT strategies are *in-house development,* often with help from a consulting firm and/or vendor, and *outsourcing* to a third-party that resides either in the same country or is offshore. Two other forms of outsourcing are cloud computing and software-as-a-service (SaaS). Outsourcing creates its own set of challenges. For example, companies that have multiple outsourcers face the challenges of managing all of those relationships as their operations grow increasingly complex. And as companies increase outsourcing activities, a gap is created in their organizational structures, management methods, and software tools. At that point, companies need to hire an **outsource relationship management (ORM)** company. ORMs can provide automated tools to monitor and manage outsourcing relationships, leading to more productive service-level agreements (SLAs), better alignment of business objectives, and streamlined communication.

AstraZeneca IT Outsourcing Strategy

British-Swedish company AstraZeneca (astrazeneca.com/) is one of the world's leading biopharmaceutical companies, with 2010 annual revenues of $21 billion and 62,700 employees worldwide. The company focuses on the discovery, development, and commercialization of prescription medicines for six healthcare areas. In 2010, AstraZeneca's widely used cholesterol-lowering drug *Crestor* was approved by U.S. regulators to prevent heart attacks and strokes for a broader group of patients, increasing its demand. Crestor was AstraZeneca's third largest-selling drug in 2010 with approximate sales of $5 billion.

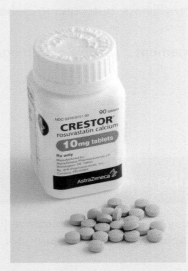

Figure 12.1 AstraZeneca's Crestor medication had sales of 1.3 billion in 2009. (© *Martin Shields/Alamy*)

AstraZeneca explains its forward-looking business strategy as follows:

> Each year, at the beginning of our business planning cycle, we assess the challenges and opportunities presented by the market, stress test our short and long-term planning assumptions, and critically assess our strengths and weaknesses as an organisation. We do so to assure ourselves that, whatever our past successes, the strategic path we are following is the right one for the future.

Preparing for Its Future

In 2007, management forecasted that the company was going to lose 38 percent of its revenues over the next five years because patents on its key drug were expiring. Once the patents had expired, competitors could legally produce and sell drugs that AstraZeneca had developed, cutting into its sales and profit. To counter that threat, management launched a radically new business strategy and began major restructuring. David Smith, executive vice president of operations, was responsible for restructuring to cut costs and improve profitability before the patents expired.

Business Restructuring Model

Smith, who previously worked for cosmetics group Estée Lauder and clothing group Timberland, wanted to follow the restructuring model set years ago in the fashion, electronics, and auto industries. Those industries had shifted away from the traditional, tightly bound model of a vertically integrated company. **Vertically integrated companies** control every part of their business from research and development (R&D) to manufacturing and logistics. Smith shifted AstraZeneca from a vertically integrated biopharmaceutical company to a loosely coupled organizational model connected by outsourced arrangements and relationships.

Looking to AstraZeneca's new strategy, Smith explained:

> We would own the IP [intellectual property], the research, branding and the quality and safety issues . . . but [everything else] would be outsourced. The idea is to take out as many stages as you can.

Because of its new business strategy, by 2014 AstraZeneca would have completed its shift toward outsourcing R&D, the manufacturing of active pharmaceutical ingredients, and the IT function. Outsourcing relationships would take several years to complete, largely because of complex regulatory hurdles.

Industry Shakeup

The R&D function is the heart of any pharmaceutical company. R&D leads to the discovery of breakthrough drugs that could generate huge profits. So when AstraZeneca cut 7,600 R&D jobs worldwide in 2010, it triggered one of the biggest shake-ups in the industry's history. Jobs were cut because of management's plan to outsource drug manufacturing activities within 10 years. Most of AstraZeneca's R&D work was offshored to pharmamerging markets, such as China. According to Smith:

> Manufacturing for AstraZeneca is not a core activity. AstraZeneca is about innovation and brand-building . . . . There are lots of people and organizations that can manufacture better than we can . . . . We are going to go through a model of outsourcing the back-end . . . we don't see manufacturing as core.

Later, the company planned to strip out and outsource more sophisticated manufacturing and supply chain operations, and logistics activities. These transformations are especially radical because the pharmaceutical industry had been among the most conservative global industries in its attitude toward manufacturing and the supply chain.

Outsourcing IT

AstraZeneca depends on its IT capabilities as much as it depends on its R&D—both are crucial. Outsourcing also became a major IT strategy, which was achieved by creating outsourcing relationships with several vendors. Infosys (*infosys.com/*) manages AstraZeneca's manufacturing, supply chain, finance, and human resources applications. Cognizant (*cognizant.com/*) runs the centralized data storage. And IBM (*ibm.com/*) hosts the e-mail and office infrastructure. In 2007, AstraZeneca had signed a seven-year global outsourcing agreement with IBM. Under the deal, IBM provides a single global technical infrastructure for AstraZeneca covering 60 countries. The contract includes server hosting and storage for scientific, network and communications, commercial, and supply chain operations. The former infrastructure was limited to major operations in the United States, United Kingdom, and Sweden. AstraZeneca retains control of its overall IT strategy and development and support of its application systems.

With these outsourcing relationships, AstraZeneca has a single infrastructure linking all functions, regions, and markets. Richard Williams, chief information officer (CIO) of AstraZeneca, said the outsourcing deal enables the company to provide greater value to the business by providing a consistent infrastructure across all its global sites. The consistent infrastructure enables it to roll out new technologies, reporting systems, and apps more quickly and efficiently. Williams added: "In allowing IBM greater autonomy on methods of delivery, the agreement will result in cost efficiencies when compared with running in-house systems."

Sources: Compiled from Boyle (2010), Lomas (2007), and Pagnamenta (2007).

For Class Discussion and Debate

1. Scenario for Brainstorming and Discussion: What will AstraZeneca look like in 2014 after its restructuring and outsourcing strategies have been completed? That is, which functions will be performed by the company and which ones won't be? What new types of management skills will be necessary? Do you think that this organizational model is the model of the future?

2. Debate: IT offshoring is a very controversial issue because it shifts jobs to other countries. At the same time, it has the potential to decrease the organization's costs significantly. Whether offshoring is good or bad for the people of affected countries is an issue of constant controversy. You might review at least one Web site that discusses the offshoring debate. For example, review Debate over Offshore Outsourcing at *quality-web-solutions.com/offshore-outsourcing-debate.php*.

Take one side of this controversy. One group takes the position of AstraZeneca's top management and debates the benefits of using offshoring as part of its business and IT strategy. Be sure to consider the threats the company is facing and its reasons for outsourcing. The other group takes the position of those opposed to offshoring on economic, ethical, and/or social grounds. Each group needs to argue its position using verifiable facts, not solely emotion.

12.1 IT Strategies

Organizations develop plans and IT strategies that support the business strategy and objectives. The four main points of **IT strategic plans** are to:

- Improve management's understanding of IT opportunities and limitations
- Assess current performance
- Identify capacity and human resource requirements
- Clarify the level of investment required

IT strategic plans should be made within the context of the business strategy that they need to support. Yet this is not always how IT planning is done. As you learn from the AstraZeneca case, manufacturing, R&D, and IT strategies require a forward-looking SWOT (strengths, weaknesses, opportunities, threats) analysis to prepare for the future instead of reacting to crises. And IT implementations that require new IT infrastructure or the merging of disparate ISs can take years. Long lead times and lack of expertise have prompted companies to explore a variety of IT strategies, which are discussed next.

IT STRATEGIES: IN-HOUSE AND OUTSOURCING

The IT strategy guides investment decisions and decisions on how ISs will be developed, acquired, and/or implemented. IT strategies can be divided into two broad categories:

1. In-house development occurs when systems are developed or other IT work is done in-house, possibly with the help of consulting companies or vendors. Typically, ITs that provide competitive advantages or that contain proprietary or confidential data are developed and maintained by the organization's own in-house IT function.

2. Outsource development, or **outsourcing,** occurs when systems are developed or IT work is done by a third party. There are many versions of outsourcing. Work or development can be outsourced to consulting companies or vendors that are in the same country, which is referred to as **onshore sourcing.** Or the work can be outsourced offshore to other countries. Outsourcing that is done offshore is also called **offshoring.** Other options are to lease or purchase IT as services. Cloud computing and software-as-a-service (SaaS) have expanded outsourcing options.

Organizations use combinations of these IT strategies—in-house, onshore (domestic) outsourcing, offshoring, cloud computing, and SaaS. You will read more about outsourcing in Section 12.5.

IT AND BUSINESS STRATEGY DISCONNECTS

According to a survey of business leaders by Diamond Management & Technology Consultants (*diamondconsultants.com/*), 87 percent believe that IT is critical to their companies' strategic success, but relatively few business leaders work with IT to achieve that success. Other key findings of the Diamond study are the following:

• Only 33 percent of business leaders reported that the IT division is very involved in the process of developing business strategy.

• Only 30 percent reported that the business executive responsible for strategy works closely with the IT division.

• When the IT strategy is not aligned with the business strategies, there is a high risk that the IT project will be abandoned before completion. About 75 percent of companies abandoned at least one IT project and 30 percent abandoned more than 10 percent of IT projects for this reason.

There are several possible reasons why a high percentage of IT projects are abandoned—the business strategy changed, technology changed, the project was not going to be completed on time or on budget, the project sponsors responsible did not work well together, or the IT strategy was changed to cloud or SaaS.

IT AND BUSINESS STRATEGY SUCCESS CASES

Companies that align their business strategy and IT strategy increase their revenues. Here are two cases as examples.

1. At Travelers Companies, Inc., a property and casualty insurance company, a 75 percent increase in new customer sales was realized with the use of a new IS (software) by its independent agents. The success of the software deployment was attributed to the CIO's extensive involvement in strategy development and the close working relationship between the IT division and the responsible business unit.

2. Kraft Foods Inc. launched a master data management (MDM) project to simplify and harmonize its global business processes and enable strategic enterprise information capabilities. Kraft had grown through acquisitions, resulting in ISs that could not share data because of differences in the way data was defined—referred to as the master data. For example, most ISs have lists of data that are shared and used by several of the applications that make up the system. A typical ERP system has a Customer Master, an Item Master, and an Account Master. These master data lists enable apps to share data. Because they are used by multiple apps, any errors or inconsistencies in master data cause errors or failures in apps that use them.

Kraft's assessment of its master data situation revealed problems that were negatively impacting its business strategies. According to IT director Marcelo De Santis: "Our master data management program is a key strategic enabler. It is viewed as foundational—data is critical to the business. We have executive sponsorship from the chief financial officer and executive vice president of operations and business services." The MDM project was undertaken for several business reasons; for example, to reduce the complexity of its product portfolio and thus lead to inventory reductions. BI initiatives are also being facilitated by this project—the ability to obtain an integrated sales view of customer and product; higher reliability when measuring and ranking partners; enhanced evaluations of product performance during launches; easily identified category/geographic business opportunities; robust analytics and reporting; and the ability to respond faster to business changes, such as acquisitions, regulatory changes, and customer requirements.

The fundamental principle to be learned is that when organizational strategies change, the IT strategies need to change with them. Both strategies are dynamic. And when people are resistant to change, they create risk because IS success depends on the skills and cooperation of people as well as the design of business processes and IT capabilities.

BUSINESS AND IT STRATEGIES DEFINED

Business strategy has its own terms that are important to know. Those key terms are defined in Table 12.1 and discussed next.

The **business strategy** sets the overall direction for the business. The **IT strategy** defines *what* information, information systems, and IT architecture are required to support the business and *how* the infrastructure and services are to be delivered.

IT–business alignment refers to the degree to which the IT division understands the priorities of the business and spends its resources, pursues projects, and provides information consistent with these priorities. IT–business alignment includes two facets.

1. One facet is aligning the IT function's strategy, structure, technology, and processes with those of the business units so that IT and business units are working toward the same goals. This facet is referred to as **IT alignment.**

2. Another type of alignment, referred to as **IT strategic alignment,** involves aligning IT strategy with organizational strategy. The goal of IT strategic alignment is to ensure that IS priorities, decisions, and projects are consistent with the needs of the entire business. Failure to properly align IT with the organizational strategy can result in making large investments in systems that have a low payoff or not investing in systems that potentially have a high payoff.

TABLE 12.1	Business Strategy Definitions

Definitions of key terms related to organizational strategy.

1. Strategy is how an organization intends to accomplish its vision. It's the overall game plan.

2. Objectives are the building blocks of strategy. Objectives set out what the business is trying to achieve. They are action-oriented statements (e.g., achieve an ROI of at least 10 percent in 201X) that define the continuous improvement activities that must be done to be successful. Objectives have the following "SMART" criteria:

- *Specific:* define what is to be achieved
- *Measurable:* are stated in measurable terms
- *Achievable:* are realistic given available resources and conditions
- *Relevant:* are relevant to the people who are responsible for achieving them
- *Timeframe:* include a time dimension

3. Targets are the desired levels of performance.

4. Vision statement is an organization's picture of where it wants to be in the future.

5. Mission statement defines why an organization exists.

Figure 12.2 Activists protest the BP oil spill at a BP Gas Station in the Soho section of New York City by spilling "oil" on themselves. May 28, 2010. (© Luay Bahoora/Alamy)

Business and IT strategies depend on shared IT ownership and shared IT governance among all senior managers (Shpilberg et al., 2007). When an IT or any type of failure causes harm to customers, business partners, employees, or the environment, then regulatory agencies—as well as the public—will hold the CEO accountable (see Figure 12.2). A high-profile example is BP CEO Tony Hayward, who was held accountable to Congress for the role of BP in the *Deepwater Horizon* explosion and oil spill; that is, the rig explosion that killed 11 workers and caused the subsea oil gusher that released 60,000+ barrels of crude oil per day into the Gulf of Mexico for approximately three months. Hayward's attempts to claim ignorance of the risks and use the SODDI defense ("some other dude did it") doesn't get him or any CEOs off the hook. *A company can outsource the work but not the responsibility for it.*

Because of the interrelationship between IT and business strategies, IT and other business managers share responsibility in developing IT strategic plans. Therefore, a governance structure needs to be in place that crosses organizational lines and makes senior management responsible for the success of key IT initiatives, which is discussed in the next section.

Review Questions

1. What are the four main points of IT strategic plans?
2. Explain the difference between in-house and outsourcing IT strategies.
3. What are the main types of outsourcing?
4. What are possible reasons why a high percentage of IT projects are abandoned?
5. Define *business strategy* and *IT strategy*.
6. What is the goal of IT–business alignment?

12.2 Corporate and IT Governance

IT governance is concerned with ensuring that organizational investments in IT deliver full value. As such, **IT performance management**—being able to predict and anticipate failures before it's too late—is a big part of IT governance. IT performance management functions include the following: verifying that strategic IT objectives are being achieved; reviewing IT performance; and assessing the contribution of IT to the business. For example, IT performance management assesses outcomes to answer the question: Did the IT investment deliver the promised business value?

In order for IT to deliver full value, three objectives must be met (the first objective you're already familiar with).

1. IT has to be fully aligned to business strategies and direction.

2. Key risks have to be identified and controlled.

3. Compliance with laws, industry rules, and regulatory agencies must be demonstrated.

In light of many corporate failures and scandals, corporate and IT governance have a higher profile today than ever before. Risk management, oversight, and clear communication are all parts of governance.

IT GOVERNANCE

IT governance is part of a wider corporate governance activity but has its own specific focus. The benefits of effective IT governance are reduced costs and damages caused by IT failures as well as more trust, teamwork, and confidence in the use of IT and the people providing IT services.

Issues Driving the Need for IT Governance. The IT Governance Institute (*itgi.org/*) publishes on its site the finding of the IMPACT Programme's IT Governance Specialist Development Group (SDG). SDG found that the following issues drive the need for IT governance (IMPACT, 2005):

1. There is a general lack of accountability and not enough shared ownership and clarity of responsibilities for IT services and projects. The communication between customers (namely, the IT users) and providers has to improve and be based on joint accountability for IT initiatives.

2. There is a potentially widening gap between what IT departments think the business requires and what the business thinks the IT department is able to deliver.

3. Organizations need to obtain a better understanding of the value delivered by IT, both internally and from external suppliers. Measures are required in business (the customer's) terms to achieve this end.

4. Top management wants to understand "how is my organization doing with IT in comparison with other peer groups?"

5. Management needs to understand whether the infrastructure underpinning today's and tomorrow's IT (technology, people, processes) is capable of supporting expected business needs.

6. Because organizations are relying more and more on IT, management needs to be more aware of critical IT risks and whether they are being managed.

Individuals Concerned About IT Governance. Those individuals who are concerned about IT governance are:

- Top-level business leaders, which are the board, executives, managers, and especially heads of finance, operations, and IT
- Public relations and investor relations managers
- Internal and external auditors and regulators
- Middle-level business and IT management
- Supply chain and business partners
- Customers and shareholders

As the preceding lists of issues and concerned individuals indicate, IT governance is not just an IT issue or only of interest to the IT function. It is an integral part of corporate governance focused on improving the management and control of IT. Ultimately, it is the duty of the board of directors (BOD) to ensure that IT and other critical activities are effectively governed.

IT plays a pivotal role in improving corporate governance practices because most critical business processes are automated; managers rely on information provided by these processes for their decision making.

The governance structure within an organization can either facilitate IT–business alignment or hinder that alignment. The CIO oversees the IT division and is responsible for the company's technology direction. The CIO is a member of the C-suite of "chief officers" in the company who share authority in their respective areas of responsibility, such as CEO, chief financial officer (CFO), chief marketing officer (CMO), or chief compliance officer (CCO). To whom the CIO reports is telling of

TABLE 12.2	Important Skill Set of the CIO

Skills of CIOs that have shown to improve the IT governance and IT–business alignment include:

- *Political savvy.* Effectively understand other workers and use that knowledge to influence others to support organizational objectives.
- *Influence, leadership, and power.* Able to inspire a shared vision and influence subordinates and superiors.
- *Relationship management.* Build and maintain working relationships with coworkers and those external to the organization. Negotiate problem solutions without alienating those impacted. Understand others and get their cooperation in nonauthority relationships.
- *Resourcefulness.* Think strategically and make good decisions under pressure. Can set up complex work systems and engage in flexible problem resolution.
- *Strategic planning.* Capable of developing long-term objectives and strategies and translating vision into realistic business strategies.
- *Doing what it takes.* Persevering in the face of obstacles.
- *Leading employees.* Delegating work to employees effectively, broadening employee opportunities, and interacting fairly with employees.

how IT is perceived within the company. For example, if IT is perceived as a strategic weapon to grow revenues and increase operational effectiveness, then the CIO likely reports to the CEO. If IT is perceived as a cost-cutting center, the CIO likely reports to the CFO. Table 12.2 lists the important skills of CIOs.

WHAT IT GOVERNANCE COVERS

IT governance covers IT management and controls across five key areas:

1. Supports the strategy: Provides for strategic direction of IT and the alignment of IT and the business.

2. Delivers value: Confirms that the IT/business organization is designed to derive maximum business value from IT. Oversees the delivery of value by IT to the business and assesses ROI.

3. Risk management: Confirms that processes are in place to ensure that risks have been adequately managed. Includes assessment of the risk of IT investments.

4. Resource management: Provides high-level direction for sourcing and use of IT resources. Oversees funding of IT at the enterprise level. Ensures that there is an adequate IT capability and infrastructure to support current and expected business requirements.

5. IT performance management: (Refer also to the beginning of Section 12.2.) Verifies strategic compliance, or the achievement of strategic IT objectives. Measures IT performance and the contribution of IT to the business, including delivery of promised business value (IMPACT, 2005).

IT governance, like security, is not a one-time exercise or something achieved by a mandate or setting of rules. It requires a commitment from the top of the organization to instill a better way of dealing with the management and control of IT. IT governance is an ongoing activity that requires a continuous improvement mentality and responsiveness to the fast-changing IT environment. When companies run into legal or regulatory challenges, IT governance is what saves or dooms them.

Review Questions

1. What is the concern of IT governance?
2. Why is IT performance management a key part of IT governance?
3. In order for IT to deliver full value, what three objectives must be met?
4. Identify four issues driving the need for IT governance.
5. Who is concerned about IT governance?
6. What does IT governance cover?

12.3 Aligning IT with Business Strategy

Alignment is a complex management activity, and its complexity increases with the increasing complexity of organizations as the pace of global competition and technological change increases. IT–business alignment can be improved by focusing on the following activities:

1. **Understanding IT and corporate planning.** A prerequisite for effective IT–business alignment is for the CIO to understand business planning and for the CEO and business planners to understand their company's IT planning.
2. **CIO is a member of senior management.** The key to achieving IT–business alignment is for the CIO to attain strategic influence. Rather than being narrow technologists, CIOs must be both business- and technology-savvy.
3. **Shared culture and good communication.** The CIO must understand and buy into the corporate culture so that IS planning does not occur in isolation. Frequent, open, and effective communication is essential to ensure a shared culture and keep everyone aware of planning activities and business dynamics.
4. **Commitment to IT planning by senior management.** Senior management commitment to IT planning is essential to success.
5. **Multilevel links.** Links between business and IT plans should be made at the strategic, tactical, and operational levels.

STRATEGIC ROLE OF IT

Companies must determine the use, value, and impact of IT to identify opportunities that create value and support the strategic vision. This requires that the CIO and other senior IT staff closely interact with the CEO and the senior management in functional areas or business units. And the CIO must be in a position to influence how IT can assume a strategic role in the firm.

For example, at Toyota Motor Sales USA, headquartered in California, the new CIO Barbra Cooper arrived to find that six enterprise-wide IT projects had so overwhelmed the workload of the IS group that there was little time for communication with the business units (Wailgum, 2008). IS was viewed as an *order taker* rather than as a partner with whom to build solutions. CIO Cooper radically changed the structure of Toyota's IS department within six months to build close communication with business operations. A year later, the IS and the business units were working closely together when planning and implementing IT projects.

COMPETITIVE ADVANTAGE THROUGH IT

Competitive advantage is gained by a company by providing real or perceived value to customers. To determine how IT can provide a competitive advantage, the firm must know its products and services, its customers and competitors, its industry and related industries, and environmental forces—and have insight about how IT can enhance value for each of these areas. To understand the relationship of IT in providing a competitive advantage, we next consider the potential of a firm's IT resources to add value to a company.

Three characteristics of resources give firms the potential to create a competitive advantage:

- **Value.** Resources are a source of competitive advantage only when they are valuable. A resource has value to the extent that it enables a firm to implement strategies that improve efficiency and effectiveness. But even if valuable, resources that are equitably distributed across organizations are only commodities.
- **Rarity.** Resources must also be rare in order to confer competitive advantages.
- **Appropriability.** Appropriability refers to the ability of the firm to generate earnings from the resource. Even if a resource is rare and valuable, if the firm expends

TABLE 12.3	Key Resource Attributes That Create Competitive Advantage
Resource Attributes	**Description**
Value	The degree to which a resource can help a firm improve efficiency or effectiveness
Rarity	The degree to which a resource is nonheterogeneously distributed across firms in an industry
Appropriability	The degree to which a firm can make use of a resource without incurring an expense that exceeds the value of the resource
Imitability	The degree to which a resource can be readily emulated
Mobility	The degree to which a resource is easy to transport
Substitutability	The degree to which another resource can be used in lieu of the original resource to achieve value

more effort or expense to obtain the resource than it generates through the resource, then the resource will not create a competitive advantage.

Many firms attempting to hire ERP-knowledgeable personnel in 1999–2000 discovered that they were unable to realize an ROI because of the higher salaries. Table 12.3 lists the three characteristics necessary to achieve competitive advantage and three additional factors needed to sustain it.

The first three characteristics described in Table 12.3 are used to characterize resources that can create an initial competitive advantage. In order for the competitive advantage to be sustained, however, the resources must be imitable, imperfectly mobile, and have low substitutability. **Imitability** is the feature that determines whether a competitor can imitate or copy the resource. **Mobility** (or *tradability*) refers to the degree to which a firm may easily acquire the resource necessary to imitate a rival's competitive advantage. Some resources, such as hardware and software, are easy to acquire and are thus highly mobile and unlikely to generate sustained competitive advantage. Even if a resource is rare, when it's possible to purchase or hire the resource, then the resource is mobile and incapable of contributing to a sustained advantage. Finally, **substitutability** refers to the ability of competing firms to utilize an alternative resource.

Information systems can contribute three types of resources to a firm: technology resources, technical capabilities, and IT managerial resources, as listed in Table 12.4.

Technology resources include the IT infrastructure, proprietary technology, hardware, and software. The creation of a successful infrastructure may take several years

TABLE 12.4	IS Resources and Capabilities	
IS Resource/Capability	**Description**	**Relationship to Resource Attributes**
Technology resources	Include infrastructure, proprietary technology, hardware, and software.	Not necessarily rare or valuable, but difficult to appropriate and imitate. Low mobility but a fair degree of substitutability.
IT skills	Include technical knowledge, development knowledge, and operational skills	Highly mobile, but less imitable or substitutable. Not necessarily rare but highly valuable.
Managerial IT resources	Include vendor and outsourcer relationship skills, market responsiveness, IS–business partnerships, IS planning, and management skills.	Somewhat more rare than the technology and IT skills resources. Also of higher value. High mobility given the short tenure of CIOs. Nonsubstitutable.

to achieve. Thus, even while competitors might readily purchase the same hardware and software, the combination of these resources to develop a flexible infrastructure is a complex task. It may take firms many years to catch up with the infrastructure capabilities of its competitors.

Technical capabilities include IS technical knowledge such as app development skills, IS development knowledge such as experience with social media or development platforms, and IS operations. Technical IT skills include the expertise needed to build and use IT apps.

Managerial resources include IS managerial resources such as vendor relationships, outsourcer relationship management, market responsiveness, IS–business partnerships, and IS planning and change management.

BUSINESS IMPROVEMENT OPPORTUNITY MATRIX

IT can improve many domains of business activity, as presented in the opportunity matrix shown in Table 12.5.

To ensure that business and IT executives have a common understanding of potential business improvements attainable through the use of IT, each of these benefits should be evaluated in terms of the value to be provided to the business. One or more improvements may be attained through IT. For example, if customer service, number 8 in Table 12.5, is expected to be improved through the use of IT in a package delivery service, such an improvement may be regarded as providing high impact value. The description of the business value of enhancing the customer service experience would state:

> *The currently high volume of customer complaints about late delivery of packages will be addressed with an automatically generated personalized e-mail message, to each customer experiencing late delivery, to provide notification of the revised delivery date. This e-mail communication also provides an opportunity for each customer to express any remaining concerns. The external focus on improving customer service will contribute to a positive image of the company.*

TABLE 12.5	Business Improvement Opportunity Matrix				
Business Improvement with IT	**High-Impact Value**	**Low-Impact Value**	**No Value**	**Description of the Business Value of the Improvement**
1. Improve process efficiencies				
2. Increase market share and global reach				
3. Reach new markets, audiences, and channels				
4. Improve external partnering capabilities				
5. Enable internal collaboration				
6. Launch innovative product and service offerings				
7. Improve time to market				
8. Enhance customer service experience				
9. Improve information access and effectiveness in decision-making processes				
10. Bring about new business models				
11. Enable a business to gain, or simply maintain, a competitive advantage				
12. Other				

Sources: Compiled from Kesner (2003) and Center for CIO Leadership (2007).

This process change to improve customer service may also improve process efficiencies, number 1 in the table, providing low-impact value to the business. The description of the business value of this process improvement would state:

> *Customer service agents will be freed from personally attending to all customer complaints, allowing them to focus on resolving the most serious complaints. This improved use of customer service agents' time is expected to improve operational efficiencies and costs.*

Being able to explain how IT adds business value can be facilitated with this matrix. To provide a common understanding, this matrix serves as a tool for discussing and clarifying expectations concerning the potential impact of the improvements to the business. Clear, frequent, and effective communication is critical to achieving this potential.

IT DIVISION AND BUSINESS MANAGEMENT PARTNERSHIP

Including the CIO on the CEO's senior management team promotes a partnership between them. For example, at Walgreen Company, a leading drugstore chain, the CIO has been on the top-management team since the late 1990s (Worthen, 2007). This arrangement facilitated the delivery of a single IS to connect all Walgreen pharmacies, with continual improvements based on feedback and suggestions from both employees and customers. The CEO recognizes that including the CIO in strategy meetings encourages teamwork. To maintain this mutually beneficial relationship, the CIO must continually educate and update the other executives in the C-suite (chief executive) team about technological advances and capabilities relevant to the business needs.

The partnership between the IT division and business management can extend to fuse with the business, as you will read in *IT at Work 12.1*. Such a fusion could be achieved with a new organizational structure, wherein the CIO becomes responsible for managing some core business functions. For example, the CIO at Hess Corporation, a leading energy company based in New York City, is part of a new organizational structure (Hoffman and Stedman, 2008). The CIO began managing several core business functions. Additionally, Hess Corporation is creating a joint IT and business group to develop new operating processes and advanced technologies. Comprised of IT workers, geologists, scientists, and other employees, this unit will report to the senior vice president of oil exploration and production.

IT at Work 12.1

CIO's Strategic Direction and Initiative

ACC   IS   FIN

The strategic CIO is a business leader who leverages IT to add value and gain a competitive advantage. The strategist's focus is on how a company creates shareholder value and serves its customers. Rather than being focused primarily on internal operations, the strategic CIO looks at the company from the outside-in by asking how the company is perceived by customers and how competitors apply IT to compete. The role of strategic CIO is focused on business strategy and innovation. This broader, more business-oriented, and strategic focus is the direction for the CIO role.

Building a resilient enterprise is (or should be) a strategic initiative for CIOs. Reducing vulnerability means reducing the probability of a disruption and increasing the ability to recover (resilience) from a disruption. CIOs achieve resilience through redundancy and flexibility in IT infrastructure and support systems, which can be done through outsourcing arrangements.

Discussion Questions: Why has the role of CIO expanded? What are the benefits of this strategic CIO role to the company?

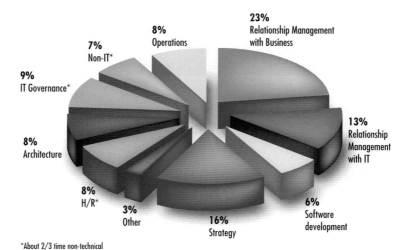

Figure 12.3 How CIOs spend their time. (*Source: Luftman, 2007.*)

*About 2/3 time non-technical

Alternatively, the CIO could work directly with other top executives to influence strategic directions, suggest changes in internal business processes, and lead a diversity of initiatives that encompass more than just technology projects. For example, the vice president of IT at PHH Mortgage, in Mount Laurel, New Jersey, works alongside the sales managers (Hoffman and Stedman, 2008). This working relationship has fostered a rapport between the CIO and sales executives. In discussions with the sales team about potential changes in some of the mortgage application processes, the CIO is able to take the lead on business improvement opportunities by communicating his understanding of concerns and offering insightful recommendations.

The CIO's focus on managing business activities is revealed by looking at how CIOs spend their time. As shown in Figure 12.3, about two-thirds of a CIO's time is spent on nontechnical duties, including relationship management with the business, strategy-related activities, non-IT activities, and other. The largest percentage among nontechnical duties (23 percent) is spent on managing relationships with business functional areas and business units (Luftman, 2007).

To realize the greatest potential from IT, the business strategy must include the IT strategy and the use of IT must support the business strategy. The next largest slice of the CIO's time (16 percent) is spent on business and IT strategy. Critical in addressing strategy is the alignment of business and IT strategies. To achieve this alignment, a firm must carefully plan its IT investments. We therefore now turn to the topic of the IT planning process.

Review Questions

1. How can the IT–business alignment be improved?
2. What are three characteristics of resources that give firms the potential to create a competitive advantage?
3. Describe the three types of resources that information systems can contribute to a firm.
4. Why is it important for the CIO to be included as a member of the CEO's senior management team?

12.4 IT Strategic Planning Process

CIOs undertake IT strategic planning on a yearly, quarterly, or monthly basis. A good IT planning process can help ensure that IT aligns, and stays aligned, within an organization. Because organizational goals change over time, it is not sufficient to develop a long-term IT strategy and not reexamine the strategy on a regular basis. For this reason, IT planning is an ongoing process.

IT at Work 12.2

IT Steering Committees

The corporate steering committee is a group of managers and staff representing various organizational units that is set up to establish IT priorities and to ensure that the IS department is meeting the needs of the enterprise. The committee's major tasks are:

- **Direction setting.** In linking the corporate strategy with the IT strategy, planning is the key activity.
- **Rationing.** The committee approves the allocation of resources for and within the information systems organization. This includes outsourcing policy.
- **Structuring.** The committee deals with how the IS department is positioned in the organization. The issue of centralization–decentralization of IT resources is resolved by the committee.

- **Staffing.** Key IT personnel decisions involve a consultation-and-approval process made by the committee, including outsourcing decisions.
- **Communicating.** Information regarding IT activities should flow freely.
- **Evaluating.** The committee should establish performance measures for the IS department and see that they are met. This includes the initiation of *service-level agreements* (SLAs).

The success of steering committees largely depends on the establishment of IT *governance*, formally established statements that direct the policies regarding IT alignment with organizational goals and allocation of resources.

The IT planning process results in a formal IT strategy or a reassessment each year or each quarter of the existing portfolio of IT resources.

IT STRATEGIC PLANNING PROCESS

Recall that the focus of IT strategy is on how IT creates business value. Typically, annual planning cycles are established to identify potentially beneficial IT services, to perform cost-benefit analyses, and to subject the list of potential projects to resource-allocation analysis. Often the entire process is conducted by an IT *steering committee*. See *IT at Work 12.2* for the duties of an IT steering committee.

Figure 12.4 presents the IT strategic planning process. The entire planning process begins with the creation of a strategic business plan. The *long-range IT plan*, sometimes referred to as the *strategic IT plan*, is then based on the strategic business

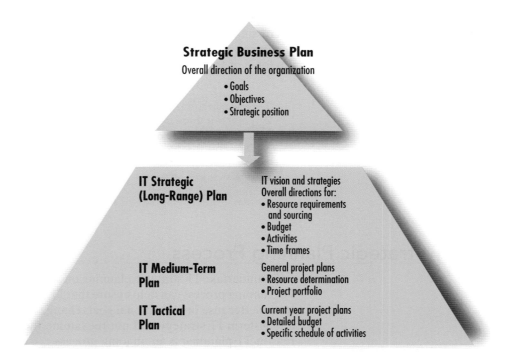

Figure 12.4 IT strategic planning process.

plan. The IT strategic plan starts with the IT vision and strategy, which defines the future concept of what IT should do to achieve the goals, objectives, and strategic position of the firm and how this will be achieved. The overall direction, requirements, and **sourcing** (i.e., outsourcing or insourcing) of resources—such as infrastructure, application services, data services, security services, IT governance, management architecture, budget, activities, and timeframes—are set for three to five years into the future. The planning process continues by addressing lower-level activities with a shorter timeframe.

The next level down is a *medium-term IT plan*, which identifies general project plans in terms of the specific requirements and sourcing of resources, as well as the **project portfolio.** The project portfolio lists major resource projects, including infrastructure, application services, data services, and security services that are consistent with the long-range plan. Some companies may define their portfolio in terms of applications. The **applications portfolio** is a list of major approved IS projects that are also consistent with the long-range plan. Expectations for sourcing of resources in the project or applications portfolio should be driven by the business strategy. Since some of these projects will take more than a year to complete and others will not start in the current year, this plan extends over several years.

The third level is a *tactical plan*, which details budgets and schedules for current-year projects and activities. In reality, because of the rapid pace of change in technology and the environment, short-term plans may include major items not anticipated in the other plans.

The planning process just described is currently practiced by many organizations. Specifics of the IT planning process, of course, vary among organizations. For example, not all organizations have a high-level IT steering committee. Project priorities may be determined by the IT director, by his or her superior, by company politics, or even on a first-come, first-served basis.

The deliverables from the IT planning process should include the following: an evaluation of the strategic goals and directions of the organization and how IT is aligned; a new or revised IT vision and assessment of the state of the IT division; a statement of the strategies, objectives, and policies for the IT division; and the overall direction, requirements, and sourcing of resources.

TOOLS AND METHODOLOGIES OF IT STRATEGIC PLANNING

Several tools and methodologies are used to facilitate IT strategic planning. Most of these methodologies start with some investigation of strategy that checks the industry, competition, and competitiveness, and relates them to technology (*alignment*). Others help create and justify new uses of IT (*impact*). In the next section, we look briefly at some of these methodologies.

Business Service Management. Business service management is an approach for linking key performance indicators (KPIs) of IT to business goals to determine the impact on the business. KPIs are metrics that measure the actual performance of critical aspects of IT, such as essential projects and applications, servers, the network, and so forth, against predefined business goals, such as revenue growth, reduced costs, and lower risk. For a critical project, for example, performance metrics include the status of the project, the ability to track milestones to budget, and a view of how the IT staff spends its time (Biddick, 2008).

KPIs can be classified into two types. The first type includes those that measure *real-time performance or predict future results*. These KPIs assist in proactive, rather than reactive, responses to potential user and customer problems. For example, 80 percent of IT staff may be needed to work on active projects. An evaluation of KPIs may predict that the following month a projected slowdown of project activity will reduce the utilization rate to 70 percent, allowing time to adjust staffing or add more projects. The second type of KPI measures *results of past activity*. For example, an IT organization may have committed to an application availability rate of 99 percent for certain applications, such as a Web-based customer order entry system (Biddick, 2008).

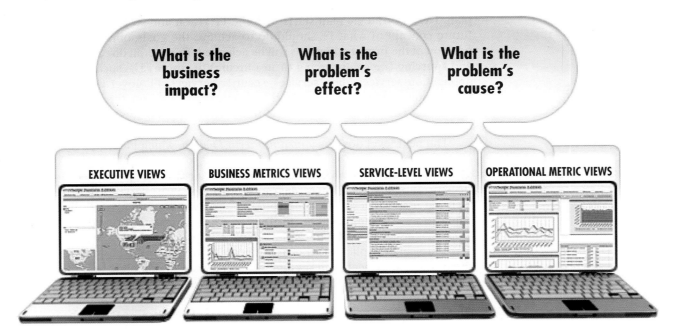

Figure 12.5 Business service management (from FireScope). FireScope delivers a single view into the business impact of IT operations by aggregating all IT and business metrics into real-time dashboards, customizable for the needs of each member of IT. (Used with permission.)

As shown in Figure 12.5, business service management software tools provide real-time dashboard views for tracking KPIs at the executive, functional business areas, services, and operations levels. Dashboards make it easier to understand and predict how IT impacts the business and how business impacts the IT architecture.

Business Systems Planning Model. The business systems planning (BSP) model was developed by IBM and has influenced other planning efforts such as Accenture's method/1. BSP is a top-down approach that starts with business strategies. It deals with two main building blocks—business processes and data classes—which become the basis of an information architecture. From this architecture, planners can define organizational databases and identify applications that support business strategies, as shown in Figure 12.6. BSP relies heavily on the use of metrics in the analysis of processes and data, with the ultimate goal of developing the information architecture.

Balanced Scorecard. Described by Robert Kaplan and David Norton in a number of articles published in the *Harvard Business Review* between 1992 and 1996, the **balanced scorecard** is a business management concept that transforms both financial

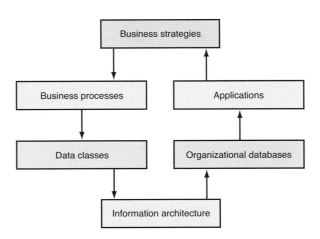

Figure 12.6 Business systems planning (BSP) approach.

and nonfinancial data into a detailed roadmap that helps the company measure performance.

Kaplan and Norton introduced the balanced scorecard as a way of measuring performance in companies. The major difference with Kaplan and Norton's scorecard was that it measured a company's performance in other than strictly financial terms. For example, it measures performance from any of the following perspectives:

- Customer perspective
- Internal business process perspective
- Learning and growth perspective
- Financial perspective

The balanced scorecard framework supplements traditional tangible financial measures with criteria that measure four intangible perspectives and address important questions, including the following (Kaplan and Norton, 2007):

1. How do customers see the company?
2. At what must the company excel?
3. Can the company continue to improve and create value?
4. How does the company appear to shareholders?

The balanced scorecard can be applied to link KPIs of IT to business goals to determine the impact on the business. The focus for the assessment could be, for example, the project portfolio or the applications portfolio. As shown in Table 12.6, the balanced scorecard can be used to assess the IT project portfolio of a retail department store chain. Projects are listed along the vertical dimension, and specific measures, critical to what the organization needs to track, are presented horizontally. The balanced scorecard helps managers to clarify and update strategy, align IT strategy with business strategy, link strategic objectives to long-term goals and annual budgets, identify and align strategic initiatives, and conduct periodic performance reviews to improve strategy (Kaplan and Norton, 2007).

Critical Success Factors Model. **Critical success factors (CSFs)** are the most essential things (factors) that must go right or be closely tracked in order to ensure the organization's survival and success. For companies dependent on the price of oil, oil prices would be a CSF. The *CSF approach* to IT planning was developed to help identify the information needs of managers. The fundamental assumption is that in every organization there are three to six key factors that, if done well, will result in the organization's success. The reverse is also true. The failure of these factors will result in some degree of failure. Therefore, organizations continuously measure performance in these areas, taking corrective action whenever necessary. CSFs also exist in business units, departments, and other organizational units.

TABLE 12.6	IT Project Balanced Scorecard					
IT Project	**Project's Role in Strategic Business Plan**	**Project's Evolving Versus Stable Knowledge**	**Degree of Change Needed in the Project**	**Where the Project Gets Sourced**	**Data's Public or Proprietary Nature**	**Project Budget**
Infrastructure	Efficiency	Stable	Low	Outsourced	Proprietary	Small
Application services	Customer focus	Evolving	High	ERP software	Proprietary	High
Data services	Innovation	Evolving	High	Business intelligence software	Proprietary	High
Security services	Compliance requirement	Evolving	Low	Outsourced	Proprietary	Small

CSFs vary by sector—manufacturing, service, or government—and by specific industries within these categories. For organizations in the same industry, CSFs vary depending on whether the firms are market leaders or weaker competitors, where they are located, and what competitive strategies they follow. Environmental issues, such as the degree of regulation or amount of technology used, influence CSFs. In addition, CSFs change over time, based on temporary conditions, such as high interest rates or long-term trends.

IT planners identify CSFs by interviewing managers in an initial session and then refining CSFs in one or two additional sessions. Sample questions asked in the CSF approach are:

- What objectives are central to your organization?
- What are the critical factors that are essential to meeting these objectives?
- What decisions or actions are key to these critical factors?
- What variables underlie these decisions, and how are they measured?
- What information systems can supply these measures?

The first step following the interviews is to determine the organizational objectives for which the manager is responsible and then the factors that are critical to attaining these objectives. The second step is to select a small number of CSFs. The final step is to determine the information requirements for those CSFs and measure to see whether the CSFs are met. If they are not met, it is necessary to build appropriate applications. See Figure 12.7.

The critical success factors approach encourages managers to identify what is most important to their performance and then develop good indicators of performance in these areas.

Scenario Planning. **Scenario planning** is a methodology in which planners first create several scenarios; then a team compiles as many future events as possible that may influence the outcome of each scenario. This approach is used in planning situations that involve much uncertainty, like that of IT in general and e-commerce in particular. Five reasons to do scenario planning are:

1. To ensure that you are not focusing on catastrophe to the exclusion of opportunity.
2. To help you allocate resources more prudently.
3. To preserve your options.
4. To ensure that you are not still "fighting the last war."
5. To give you the opportunity to rehearse testing and training of people to go through the process.

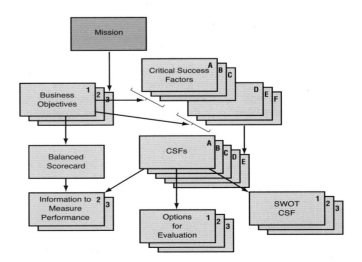

Figure 12.7 Critical success factors—basic processes.

TABLE 12.7	Essential Steps of Scenario Planning

- Determine the scope and timeframe of the scenario you are flashing out.
- Identify the current assumptions and mental models of individuals who influence these decisions.
- Create a manageable number of divergent, yet plausible, scenarios. Spell out the underlying assumptions of how each of these imagined futures might evolve.
- Test the impact of key variables in each scenario.
- Develop action plans based on either (1) the solutions that play most robustly across scenarios or (2) the most desirable outcome toward which a company can direct its efforts.
- Monitor events as they unfold to test the corporate direction; be prepared to modify it as required.

The educational experience that results from this process includes

- Stretching your mind beyond the groupthink that can slowly and imperceptibly produce a sameness of minds among top team members in any organization.
- Learning the ways in which seemingly remote potential developments may have repercussions that hit close to home.
- Learning how you and your colleagues might respond under both adverse and favorable circumstances.

Scenario planning follows a rigorous process; the essential steps are summarized in Table 12.7. Scenario planning has been widely used by major corporations to facilitate IT planning (e.g., *ncri.com* and *gbn.com*). It has also been particularly important to e-commerce planning. For instance, creating customer scenarios helps the company better fit the products and services into the real lives of the customers, resulting in sales expansion and customer loyalty. National Semiconductor, Tesco, and *Buzzsaw.com*, for example, have used customer scenarios to strengthen customer relationships, to guide business strategy, and to deliver business value.

A major aspect of IT planning is properly allocating IT resources to the right set of projects. Organizations simply cannot afford to develop or purchase each application or undertake each application enhancement that business units and end users might like. The IT steering committee has an important responsibility in deciding how IT resources will be allocated.

Resource Allocation. Resource allocation consists of developing the plans for hardware, software, data communications and networks, facilities, personnel, and financial resources needed to execute the master development plan, as defined in the requirements analysis. Resource allocation, as you read in Chapter 6, is a contentious process in most organizations because opportunities and requests for spending far exceed the available funds. This can lead to intense, highly political competition among organizational units, which makes it difficult to objectively identify the most desirable investments.

Requests for funding approval from the steering committee fall into two categories. The first category consists of projects and infrastructure that are critical for the organization to stay in business. For example, it may be imperative to purchase or upgrade hardware if the network, disk drives, or processor on the main computer is approaching capacity limits. Obtaining approval for this type of spending is largely a matter of communicating the gravity of the problems to decision makers.

The second category includes less critical items, such as new projects, maintenance or upgrades of existing systems, and infrastructure to support these systems and future needs. Approval for projects in this category may become more difficult to obtain because the IS department is already receiving funding for the critical projects. Generally speaking, organizations set aside funds for the first category of projects and then use the remainder of the IT budget for the second category.

1. Why must IT strategic planning be revisited on a regular basis?
2. Describe the committee that usually conducts the IT strategic planning process. Who is included on this committee? What are the major tasks of this committee? On what is this committee's success dependent?
3. What is the focus of IT strategy?
4. Describe the IT strategic planning process.
5. Describe the project portfolio. Describe the applications portfolio. When are these portfolios developed?
6. What tools and methodologies are available to assist in the IT strategic planning process? How are these methods used to help organizations?
7. What is resource allocation? What are the two types of funding requests?

12.5 IT Outsourcing Strategies

The core competencies of many organizations—the things they do best and that represent their competitive strengths—are in retailing, services, manufacturing, or some other function. IT is an *enabler* only, and it is complex, expensive, and constantly changing. IT is difficult to manage, even for organizations with above-average IT management skills. Therefore, many organizations have implemented outsourcing as an IT strategy. Outsourcing can be done domestically or offshore, or via cloud computing or SaaS. Those topics are covered in other chapters but are mentioned here because they are examples of IT outsourcing strategies.

Cloud computing is not simply about outsourcing the routine computing tasks. It's about the delivery of real business services, enabled by the applications needed to support them, and then powered by computing and network infrastructure to host and deliver them.

SaaS provides an ability to easily extend internal processes outside the organizational boundary to support **business processing outsourcing (BPO)** arrangements and can become a strong competitive advantage for an organization today and in the future. BPO is the process of hiring another company to handle business activities for you.

BPO AND ITES

BPO is distinct from IT outsourcing, which focuses on hiring a third-party company or service provider to do IT-related activities, such as application management and application development, data center operations, or testing and quality assurance.

Originally, BPO consisted of outsourcing standard processes, such as payroll; it then expanded to employee benefits management. Currently, BPO includes many functions that are considered noncore to the primary business strategy, such as financial and administration processes, human resource functions, call center and customer service activities, and accounting.

These outsourcing deals are multiyear contracts that can run into hundreds of millions of dollars. Often, the people performing the work internally for the client firm are transferred and become employees of the service provider. Dominant outsourcing service providers in the BPO fields—some of which also dominate the IT outsourcing business—are IBM, Accenture, and Hewitt Associates in the United States and European and Asian companies Capgemini, Genpact, TCS, Wipro, and Infosys. Many of these BPO efforts involve offshoring, with India one of the most popular locations for BPO activities.

BPO is also referred to as **ITES,** or **information technology-enabled services.** Since most business processes include some form of automation, IT "enables" these services to be performed.

Andrew Pery, chief marketing officer for document management company Kofax (*kofax.com/*), predicts the BPO market "will likely outgrow all segments of the IT industry. There is increased competition and increased choice."

IT at Work 12.3

eBay's Rapid Growth Pains

Since its 1998 IPO, eBay has gone from being an online experiment in consumer-to-consumer e-commerce to a Fortune 500 enterprise that sells $60 billion in goods annually. It supports 88 million individual buyers and sellers, plus an expanding list of small businesses. This metamorphosis was not without growing pains. Exploding demand for eBay's services created enviable, but staggering, challenges. By 2004, eBay's annual revenues had exceeded $3 billion. Up to then, its accounts payable (AP) function had been able to keep up with the exponentially growing workload. The AP function was a critical system because sellers expected to get paid instantaneously. It was foreseeable that a much larger transaction accounting capacity would be needed than the current IT structure could deliver quickly. eBay's acquisition of several companies with disparate AP processes created additional integration challenges.

Outsourcing Challenges and Lessons Learned. eBay turned to outsourcing for a solution for transaction processing of accounts. In early 2005, eBay migrated all of its AP operations to Genpact. Genpact (*genpact.com/*) is a global leader in business process and technology management. The migration of AP and other business processes to BPO provider Genpact was not without challenges but was ultimately a success. Six lessons that eBay and Genpact learned from the BPO implementation are the following:

1. **Manage change** by securing the commitment of senior leaders in an overt fashion and by recognizing subtle cultural differences that can undermine initial transition efforts.

2. **Assess organizational readiness** for a BPO transition from a mental and technical standpoint, and set realistic expectations and manage them actively.

3. **Anticipate risks and formulate a plan for mitigating them,** beginning with a strategy for dealing with "loss of control" threats, both real and imagined.

4. **Build project-management infrastructure** that recognizes that the "process of transition" needs to be managed as carefully as processes being transitioned. Mapping how the AP process should look post-transition, and how it will be managed end-to-end, and by whom, are important.

5. **Create a governance mechanism** that can discreetly collect feedback from the transition project manager and provide formal executive oversight and guidance. Form an executive steering committee that includes two senior managers from each organization and representation from all business units impacted by BPO.

6. **Properly define how success will be measured,** both qualitatively and quantitatively. Identifying the right benchmarks for success and vigilantly measuring efforts against them over time are critical.

Performance Improvements. The transition was far from perfect at first, but hard lessons learned early helped achieve impressive results in time. Year-end 2009 revenues were triple 2004 revenues, and AP transaction volume and headcount doubled, but at a much low cost per volume. On-time payments grew to 30 percent. In other words, more volume is now being handled and being handled more effectively per AP person. This success paved the way for migration of other eBay transaction accounting processes. From 2006 to early 2008, eBay outsourced its global vendor/supplier maintenance and general ledger (GL) activities.

Discussion Questions: Why is the ability to process AP a critical success factor for eBay? Why did eBay choose outsourcing as its IT strategy instead of in-house development? Why did eBay rely on Genpact for its BPO transition? Given that Genpact is a global leader in business process and technology management, why did eBay encounter challenges?

Sources: Compiled from Genpact (2010) and *OutsourcingPapers.com* (2010).

Why is the BPO industry changing? Don Schulman, general Manager for finance and administration at IBM, gives two reasons (Rosenthal, 2010).

- The economy has triggered a broader group of buyers to consider BPO as a viable option. In an era where companies are challenged to do more with less, buyers are seeking strategic partnerships that enable them to accelerate transformation.

- The industry has matured. It's no longer about price, cost, and labor arbitrage. The future will be about enterprise business outcomes, process optimization, and cloud computing.

eBay relies on BPO, as you have read in *IT at Work 12.3.*

FACTORS DRIVING GROWTH IN OUTSOURCING AS AN IT STRATEGY

Since the late 1980s, many organizations have outsourced the *majority of their IT functions*, rather than just incidental parts. The trend became classic in 1989 when Eastman Kodak transferred its data centers to IBM under a 10-year, $500 million contract. This example, at a prominent multibillion-dollar company, gave a clear signal that outsourcing was a legitimate IT strategy. Since then, many mega out-sourcing deals have been announced, some for several billion dollars. The trend, however, has turned away from the megadeal in favor of the *multivendor approach,* incorporating the services of several best-of-breed vendors to meet IT demands.

The major reasons why organizations are increasingly outsourcing are:

• It allows a focus on core competency, as you read in the AstraZeneca opening case.
• It's a cheaper and/or faster way to gain or enhance IT capabilities.
• Doing so cuts operational costs.
• Offshoring has become a more accepted IT strategy.
• Cloud computing and SaaS have proven to be effective IT strategies.

Increasingly, organizations are leveraging existing *global cloud infrastructures* from companies like Amazon, Google, Rackspace, and Windows Azure. Established companies are more willing to outsource company-critical functions in an effort to reduce costs. And new start-up companies typically outsource and rely on SaaS to avoid upfront IT costs. For example, S3, one of Amazon's Web services, lets busi-nesses store their data in the cloud, avoiding the need to operate their own servers. S3 is part of the same online infrastructure that Amazon uses to run its own busi-ness. Twitter uses S3, as does *The New York Times* to store and deliver articles from its historical archives. Outsourcing companies have started to offer some interest-ing new business models and services around cloud computing. These innovative, new IT models have added to the number of options to be considered in IT strate-gic planning.

CIOs are focusing more on outsourcing to deliver business value, beyond the tra-ditional areas of cost savings and operational efficiencies, in response to an increas-ingly dynamic environment (IBM, 2008). The environment is characterized by rapid developments in IT; firms that are being transformed by global expansion, mergers, and acquisitions; and new disruptive business models and mobile capabilities. Benefits of outsourcing are listed in Table 12.8.

RISK CONCERNS AND HIDDEN COSTS

As companies find that as their business strategy is increasingly tied to IT solu-tions, the concerns about outsourcing risks increase. Risks associated with out-sourcing are:

• *Shirking:* The vendor deliberately underperforms while claiming full payment; for example, billing for more hours than were worked and/or providing excellent staff at first and later replacing them with less qualified ones.
• *Poaching:* The vendor develops a strategic application for a client and then uses it for other clients.
• *Opportunistic repricing:* When a client enters into a long-term contract with a ven-dor, the vendor changes financial terms at some point or overcharges for unantici-pated enhancements and contract extensions.

Other risks are possible breach of contract by the vendor or its inability to deliver, vendor lock-in, loss of control over data, and loss of employee morale.

Depending on what is outsourced and to whom, an organization might end up spending 10 percent above the budgeted amount to set up the relationship and man-age it over time. The budgeted amount may increase anywhere from 15 to 65 per-cent when outsourcing is sent offshore and the costs of travel and cultural differences are added in.

OFFSHORING

Offshoring (or offshore outsourcing) of software development has become a com-mon practice due to global markets, lower costs, and increased access to skilled labor.

TABLE 12.8	Benefits of Outsourcing

Financial
- Avoidance of heavy capital investment, thereby releasing funds for other uses
- Improved cash flow and cost accountability
- Improved cost benefits from economies of scale and from sharing hardware, software, and personnel
- Less need for expensive office space

Technical
- Access to new information technologies
- Ability to achieve technological improvements more easily
- Faster application development and placement of IT apps into service

Management
- Concentration on developing and running core business activity; improved company focus
- Delegation of IT development (design, production, and acquisition) and operational responsibility to suppliers
- Elimination of need to recruit and retain competent IT staff
- Reduced risk of bad software

Human Resources
- Opportunity to draw on specialist skills available from a pool of expertise, when needed
- Enriched career development and opportunities for remaining staff

Quality
- Clearly defined *service levels*
- Improved performance accountability

Flexibility
- Quick response to business demands (agility)
- Ability to handle IT peaks and valleys more effectively (flexibility)

About one-third of Fortune 500 companies outsource software development to software companies in India.

It is not only the cost and the technical capabilities that matter. Several other factors to consider are the business and political climates in the selected country; the quality of the infrastructure; and risks involving such things as IT competency, human capital, the economy, the legal environment, and cultural differences.

Duke University's *Center for International Business Education and Research* studied actual offshoring results. According to this study, Fortune 500 companies reduced costs by offshoring—63 percent of the companies achieved over 30 percent annual savings and 14 percent of them achieved savings over 50 percent. The respondents were overwhelmingly satisfied with their offshore operations. Three-quarters (72 percent) said their offshore implementations met or exceeded their expected cost savings. Almost one-third of the respondents (31 percent) achieved their service-level goals within the first five months of their contracts, while 75 percent did so within 12 months. The study concluded that "offshoring delivers faster results than average domestic improvement efforts." Even though these are very general results, offshoring success stories ease the fears about the risks of offshoring.

According to a mid-2009 report by AMR Research Inc. on the state of IT outsourcing, roughly 80 percent of enterprises planned to increase their amount of IT offshoring or keep it the same.

Based on case studies, the types of work that are not readily offshored include the following:

- Work that has not been routinized
- Work that if offshored would result in the client company losing too much control over critical operations
- Situations in which offshoring would place the client company at too great a risk to its data security, data privacy, or intellectual property and proprietary information
- Business activities that rely on an uncommon combination of specific application-domain knowledge and IT knowledge in order to do the work properly.

IT at Work 12.4 gives an example of when insourcing becomes preferable to outsourcing.

THE OUTSOURCING LIFE CYCLE

The International Association of Outsourcing Professionals (IAOP) has defined 9 critical stages in the outsourcing life cycle that managers need to understand prior to outsourcing (IAOP, 2009).

1. Strategy: Outsourcing is a strategic decision that is typically developed at senior levels within a business. It may be part of a larger strategy to move the company to a leveraged business model and to focus on core competencies. Or it may be done to save net costs or due to a lack of internal resources. Outsourcing may act as a key differentiator that will give a business a competitive advantage over its competitors. Too few businesses consider taking legal counsel at this stage, but they should. For example, difficulties about licensing, intellectual property rights, or a preexisting contractual or leasing arrangement require legal expertise.

IT at Work 12.4

CIO Discusses J.P. Morgan Chase Sourcing Strategy

J.P. Morgan Chase & Co. is a leading global financial services firm with assets of $2 trillion in 2011 and operations in more than 60 countries. Two years into a seven-year $5 billion IT outsourcing contract with IBM, Chase canceled the remainder of the contract after its $58 billion acquisition of Bank One. J.P. Morgan said the addition of Bank One created a larger company with the capacity to manage the IT infrastructure on its own, a strategy known as **insourcing.**

People who oppose outsourcing, especially offshoring, declared it the "end of outsourcing." But CIO Austin Adams, who pushed to end the outsourcing contract, said that his move was greatly misunderstood by the media who incorrectly described him as a patriot trying to keep IT jobs in the United States. Austin clarified, saying: "I am clearly an advocate of offshoring." Chase had good reason for insourcing, mainly to get a better competitive advantage from IT. However, Adams believes that in smaller organizations, large-scale outsourcing is logical. Further, Adams manages over 3,000 offshore employees in India, who work in the bank's call center and do basic operations and accounting functions. This offshoring is expected to grow rapidly.

Adams was key in the decision to insource IT at JP Morgan Chase and offers his observations:

- Outsourcing of major parts of mission-critical technologies is not a best solution for a large firm. Technology development should be in-house; support services can be outsourced.
- Four criteria were used to determine what and how much to outsource: (1) the size of the company (should be large enough to attract good IS employees), (2) the cost of outsourcing vs. the cost of insourcing, (3) the interest level of top management in having and properly managing IT assets, and (4) the financial arrangements of the outsourcing.
- It may be difficult to align business and technology objectives when large-scale outsourcing exists.
- Insourcing requires developing and maintaining data centers, help desks, data processing networks, and systems development.

Sources: Compiled from Adams (2006) and Barrett (2006).

Discussion Questions: How can one determine when a company is large enough for insourcing? How important is the financial consideration? How accurate is it?

2. Reassessment: This stage is not given enough consideration. But organizations should look again at their business processes, IT capabilities, internal supply, or other problems to see if they could be reengineered to meet the requirements so that outsourcing is not needed.

3. Selection: This stage involves identifying and defining the work to be outsourced, as well as the selection of the vendors using RFI (request for information) or RFP (request for proposals) processes. The best-value outsourcer is selected.

4. Negotiation: In this phase, contracts, schedules, and agreements are negotiated by someone experienced in these issues. Then the final contract is reviewed extensively before signing. This negotiation process must involve adequate resources and senior executives from both sides—the key issues in a long-term relationship, such as outsourcing, are too important not to justify executive engagement from supplier and customer.

5. Implementation: This phase involves the start-up activities of planning the transition and the implementation of the outsourced agreement, as well as establishing the detailed budget and administrative functions needed for its management and formal launching of the program.

6. Oversight management: This phase encompasses all ongoing activities required to manage the program and achieve the contracted results. Specifically, this includes liaison between the customers and the supplier, performance monitoring, contract administration, vendor/partnership management, delivery integration, and vendor transition. Inevitably, stresses will develop in a contract, and it is important for both sides to take an adult approach to contract interpretation. Remember that these are long-term relationships that need to flex with time.

7. Build completion: This phase covers all completion activities of the build phase, including any development program, and then acceptance and the introduction of new services.

8. Change: All complex outsourcing contracts will be subject to change and alteration. These are either run as minor changes to the outsourcing contract or major changes, which might involve a retendering process. The contract will—or should—have built into it a contract change procedure to deal with changes that are in the broad scope of the original procurement.

9. Exit: All outsourcing relationships end either because the contract has expired, by mutual agreement, or because the outsourcing relationship has failed. The terms of the contract become very important at this time.

Review Questions

1. What is outsourcing?
2. What are some of the major reasons for outsourcing?
3. What IT functions are outsourced?
4. Distinguish between mega outsourcing and the multivendor approach to outsourcing.
5. What are the benefits of outsourcing? What are the risks of outsourcing?
6. Discuss the strategies organizations should consider in managing the risks associated with outsourcing contracts.
7. Distinguish between outsourcing and offshore outsourcing.
8. What types of work are not readily outsourced offshore?
9. Describe a tool useful in measuring the business value of outsourcing relationships.

Key Terms

applications portfolio *373*
balanced scorecard *374*
business processing outsourcing (BPO) *378*
business strategy *363*

critical success factors (CSFs) *375*
in-house development *362*
IT–business alignment *363*
ITES (information technology-enabled services) *378*

IT governance *364*
IT performance management *364*
IT strategic planning *361*
IT strategy *363*
mission statement *363*

Chapter Highlights and Insights

(Numbers refer to Learning Objectives)

❶ Because of the close alignment between IT and business strategies, IT and other business managers need to share responsibility in developing IT strategic plans.

❶ IT strategic alignment ensures that IS priorities, decisions, and projects are consistent with the needs of the entire business.

❶ The business strategy and IT strategy must be aligned, with shared ownership and shared governance of IT among all members of the senior executive team.

❷ The benefits of effective IT governance are reduced costs and damages caused by IT failures as well as more trust, teamwork, and confidence in the use of IT and the people providing IT services.

❸ IT can add value to a company in one of two general ways — either *directly* by *reducing costs* or *indirectly* by *increasing revenues.*

❹ The focus of IT strategy is on how IT creates business value.

❹ The entire planning process begins with the creation of a strategic business plan. The *long-range IT plan,* or *strategic IT plan,* is then based on the strategic business plan. The IT strategic plan starts with the IT vision and strategy.

❹ The planning process also addresses lower-level activities with a shorter timeframe. A *medium-term IT plan* identifies

general project plans in terms of the specific requirements and sourcing of resources as well as the project portfolio. Some companies may also define their application portfolio.

❹ Several tools and methodologies facilitate IT strategic planning, including business service management, the business systems planning (BSP) model, the balanced scorecard, critical success factors (CSFs), and scenario planning.

❺ The major reasons for outsourcing include a desire to focus on core competency, cost reduction, improved quality, increased speed to market, and faster innovation.

❺ Outsourcing may reduce IT costs and can make it possible for organizations to concentrate on their core competencies. However, outsourcing may reduce the company's flexibility to find the best IT fit for the business, and it may also pose a security risk. In making a decision to outsource, executives should consider major risk areas.

❺ Outsourcing is a viable option for many organizations, providing services at a lower cost, transferring risk to a third party, and easing the burden of providing routine services. However, outsourcing can also require more up-front effort during initial contract negotiations to develop service-level agreements (SLAs) that ensure the outsourcer will adhere to public sector requirements and government regulations.

Questions for Discussion

1. Vinay Gupta, president and CEO of Janeeva, which sells software to help companies manage outsourcing relationships, gave this advice: "I would strongly encourage business owners to visit the vendor's facilities. There are a lot of fly-by-night operators, so you want to make sure you have touched and seen the facility before you hand them your business. And I would do at least a 30-day free pilot with the provider. You want to see if it is a good fit and find out who you will be interacting with on a day-to-day basis." Not all companies follow this advice. Discuss why companies would or would not take these precautions when setting up an outsourcing relationship.

2. What might be some reasons why companies consider outsourcing?

3. What are the benefits and disadvantages of outsourcing work/jobs to other companies within the country?

4. What are the benefits and disadvantages of offshoring work/jobs to other countries, for example, to China or India? Compare your answers here to your answers to questions 1 and 2 about outsourcing and offshoring.

5. What issues does IT governance cover?

6. Why is IT governance the responsibility of the BOD?

7. What does failure to properly align IT with the organizational strategy result in?

8. Why does IT–business alignment continue to be an important issue for CIOs?

9. What does successful IT–business alignment require?

10. Discuss how a CIO might interact with executive management as technology becomes increasingly central to a business.

11. Three characteristics of resources give firms the potential to create a competitive advantage. Discuss the potential of a firm's IT resources to add value to a company.

12. Discuss how the partnership between the IT division and business management can extend to fuse with the business.

13. Describe the IT strategic planning process.

14. What tools facilitate IT strategic planning?

15. Describe strategies for outsourcing.

16. Describe how a company might assess the business value delivered by an outsourcing relationship.

Exercises and Projects

1. Read the *Business Case* at the end of the chapter. Apply the balanced scorecard method to address the four important questions within the balanced scorecard framework.

2. Visit the Web site of *amazon.com*. Click on "Careers at Amazon" and read "About Amazon." Begin applying the business systems planning (BSP) approach by identifying Amazon's business strategies and what applications support these strategies.

3. Consider the airline industry. Identify how IT adds business value in this industry. Be sure to address value added both directly and indirectly by IT.

4. Visit *teradatastudentnetwork.com*. Read and answer the questions to the case "Data Warehousing Supports Corporate Strategy at First American Corporation." Describe the customer relationship–oriented strategy of First American Corporation and how it is supported by IT. Contrast this strategy with that of other financial service companies.

5. Select two companies with which you are familiar. Find their mission statement and current goals (plans). Explain how IT adds value in achieving each of these goals.

6. Identify reasons why the alignment of business strategy and IT strategy might not be achieved.

Group Assignments and Projects

1. Innovative use of IT has become increasingly important in the global economy. Choose multiple industries and provide an example company for each industry in which IT plays a strategic role by adding value and providing a competitive advantage through innovative application of IT. Now identify competitive counterpart companies for which IT does not play a strategic role. Report on the successes/failures of each pair of companies.

2. Considerable discussions and disagreements occur among IT professionals regarding outsourcing. Divide the group into two parts: One will defend the strategy of large-scale outsourcing. One will oppose it. Start by collecting recent material at *google.com* and *cio.com*. Consider the issue of offshore outsourcing.

3. Each group searches nonvendor blogs or Web sites for opinions, risks, successes, and failures on outsourcing. Compare results.

Internet Exercises

1. Visit *cio.com* to find articles addressing the changing role of the CIO. Read these articles and write a report highlighting the changes.

2. Visit the IBM CIO Interaction Channel at *http://www-935.ibm.com/services/ie/cio*. This site showcases insights and perspectives on the issues that matter most to CIOs, including the most important one of all—aligning IT with overall business goals. Select a topic that interests you, read a report on that topic, and summarize the main points of the report.

3. Visit *Amazon.com*. Discuss how IT adds value to the customer's purchase experience at *Amazon.com*.

4. Visit Cognos at *cognos.com* and do a search on balanced scorecard software. Identify and describe their balanced scorecard software product.

5. Visit FireScope at *firescope.com*. Discuss how business service management software tools provide real-time

dashboard views for tracking key performance indicators at the executive, functional business areas, services, and operations levels.

6. Visit *accenture.com* and do a search on outsourcing. Prepare a report that overviews the IT outsourcing services offered by Accenture. Do the same for one other large international accountancy and professional services firms such as Deloitte at *deloitte.com*, Ernst & Young at *ey.com*, KPMG at *kpmg.com*, or PricewaterhouseCoopers at *pwc.com*.

7. Visit the Web site for the Association for Computing Machinery (ACM) and access its report on "Globalization and Offshoring of Software" at *acm.org/globalizationreport*. Select two of the case studies presented in Section 4.2 on pages 136–152. Write a report comparing and contrasting the two companies.

BUSINESS CASE

Kimberly-Clark's Outsourcing Partnership

ETHIC   FIN   GOV   ACC   HRM   IS   OM

Kimberly-Clark (K-C) Corporation (*kimberly-clark.com*) is a multinational consumer health and hygiene products manufacturer with operations in 37 countries and more than 55,000 employees worldwide. K-C brands are sold in more than 150 countries.

Global Business Plan

In 2010, K-C updated its *Global Business Plan*, which was aimed at achieving sustainable growth and improving shareholder returns through 2015. Thomas J. Falk, chairman and

CEO, said, "We have strengthened our brands, increased our exposure to faster-growing, higher-margin businesses and markets, generated significant cost savings, improved our capital efficiency and returned cash to shareholders. Our updated Global Business Plan represents our strategies and plans to achieve our existing top- and bottom-line growth objectives. We will manage our portfolio to drive growth, margin and cash flow."

Through its Global Business Plan, K-C sought to accelerate growth, reinvent its approach to innovation, be a market leader, and build strong customer loyalty. In particular, management wanted to increase the pace at which it converted customer needs into innovative products while holding costs down.

IT Adds Business Value

Central to that plan, K-C began outsourcing IT application development and maintenance to Cognizant (*cognizant.com*). Doing so helped K-C reduce IT costs and transform its IT function into an organization that proactively adds business value. IT adds business value by delivering a wide range of innovative services to external and internal customers.

According to Ramon Baez, CIO and vice president of IT, "We wanted to focus on providing more service and value to our internal and external clients and partners, and outsourcing allows us to do that because we're not spending our time doing IT application development and maintenance. We now have the capability within our company to be focused on value creation."

Virtual Reality

K-C recognizes that IT can improve relationships with retailers by helping them sell more products. For instance, IT worked with the marketing and engineering organizations to develop a virtual reality lab, called the *Innovation Design Studio*, so retail customers could visualize in 3D, virtual store layouts and merchandising options without moving a single package of product. With virtual reality, K-C helps its retail customers be more successful by improving how they position, market, and sell merchandise.

Innovation Design Studio

Customers are surrounded by full-length rear-projection screens, creating a virtual store powered by applications running on eight Hewlett-Packard PCs. In this simulated shopping experience, the virtual store takes on the look and feel of a specific retail store. People "walk through the aisles" and "shop" via a touch screen panel. As they react to different shopping environments or product packaging, sensors embedded in the floors, walls, and ceilings, along with eye-tracking technology, measure the level of engagement to assess influencing factors on purchase decisions. K-C and its customers test and explore various in-store designs and merchandising concepts without

the time and cost of physically constructing alternative layouts, displays, and shelving mockups. K-C is also using the new simulation tools to elicit immediate customer feedback on new product initiatives.

The Studio helps K-C develop new products based on immediate customer feedback, decreasing the time-to-market for introducing new products by 50 percent. Retail customers are able to create the most effective display designs that sell more K-C products. The introduction of a new line of K-C sun care products, Huggies® Little Swimmers®, was prompted by feedback to make the baby-care aisle a one-stop shop for moms.

This virtual reality technology, however, is delivering even more by providing retailers with ideas on how to better sell other merchandise not offered by K-C, such as clothing. The benefit to K-C is in image-building as an IT innovator.

K-C also partners with large customers on RFID technology to more efficiently track merchandise through the supply chain. Supermarket chains sought better ideas for shelving, which led them to team with K-C to explore using RFID to improve the process of moving products from delivery trucks to store shelves.

It's Not the IT, It's How You Use IT

CIO Baez explained, "It's not just the technology; it's how you use it. We're actually embedded with our largest customers, co-located there so we can understand their pain points and partner with them to solve some of their technology issues."

Doing so offers the IT staff, who are now more business-focused than in the past, a way to inject innovation into the company, which gives it an advantage in the fiercely competitive consumer goods industry.

In December 2007, Forrester research wrote that "CIOs should learn from the Kimberly-Clark example to make sure they are structured to stay close to business idea creation and execution, including assigning staff to work with R&D organizations, cultivating a broad pool of talent, engaging in cross-functional teams and actively seeking and participating in innovation networks beyond the walls of the firm."

Sources: Compiled from DiCarlo (2010), Jusko (2007), McGee (2007), Wailgum (2008), and *kimberly-clark.com*

Questions

1. Explain how K-C is managing its products at the retail level—in stores that they don't own.
2. How does collaborating with its customers—the retail stores—improve its financial performance? Contrast this collaborative approach to one in which K-C seeks to maximize its profits at the expense of the retailers.
3. Why do retailers want to do business with K-C?
4. Consider Porter's five competitive forces model, which includes bargaining power of customers and suppliers. In your opinion, does K-C ignore that competitive model in favor of collaboration?

NONPROFIT CASE

Health Information Exchange

GLOBAL   SRV   HEALTHCARE   IS

For this case, you should view the YouTube video *Connected HIE with UMass Memorial Health Care*, available on the IBM Healthcare channel at *youtube.com/watch?v=tUwm4zZxNy0*. In this video, Richard Cramer, Associate CIO of operations, UMass Memorial Health Care, discusses the need to help patients and health care providers share and manage information appropriately and easily.

Managing Data Privacy and Sharing

UMass Memorial Health Care (*umassmemorial.org/*) is an academic medical center and the largest healthcare hospital system in central and western Massachusetts. UMass Memorial is using *health information exchange (HIE)* to facilitate patient-centered care. That is, it has aligned its IT with its business strategy to be responsive to the need to share information.

One of the critical components of the HIE is the ability to manage and answer questions about a patient's identity and discover what patient information is shareable, no matter where it is stored, and what information is privacy protected.

HIE Use Depends on Trust

All of this is well and good, but if patients, physicians, or anyone else involved with the healthcare system doesn't trust the system or have confidence that the data is protected, it won't be used.

Security isn't just about protecting an individual's personal information from hackers and fraud, nor is it merely about complying with new regulations. Security is about ensuring the proper privacy of patients' data while improving the quality and accuracy of care.

This really means that not only should the right patient data be available to the right caregiver or care system at the right time, but the system must reliably and continuously build trust among all parties involved.

Master Data Management Eases Data Sharing

With seven hospitals and over 1,100 beds, 13,500 employees, and $1.4 billion in annual revenue, UMass Memorial faced many of the problems plaguing other industries. The lack of information sharing adversely impacted quality, costs, and efficiency—not to mention patient safety. UMass Memorial turned to master data management (MDM) with a number of objectives, including:

- Knowing a patient wherever they are seen in the system
- Enabling seamless interoperability with community healthcare providers
- Meeting government regulations
- Facing competitive pressures from other healthcare systems

The HIE architecture had to enable information sharing across numerous legacy systems while also ensuring data privacy and security. With the right architectural approach and a shared vision, UMass Memorial is overcoming data governance challenges and being seen by others as an innovator.

By modernizing its IT infrastructure, UMass Memorial has improved quality and patient safety, increased efficiency, and enhanced patient satisfaction—all essential for success in today's competitive healthcare market. With its new patient-centric information architecture, UMass Memorial delivers a comprehensive view of a patient's entire clinical history to physicians and care providers across the healthcare community, irrespective of the care setting or clinical application being used.

Questions

1. What role does information play in the reputation of UMass Memorial?
2. In the case of healthcare, what are the consequences of not having data that can be trusted—or one version of the truth?
3. How has UMass Memorial aligned its IT and business strategies?
4. Compare the importance of MDM at UMass Memorial and at Kraft Foods Inc., discussed in Section 12.1. Why do disparate or legacy systems create the need for MDM?

ANALYSIS USING SPREADSHEETS

Total Cost of Ownership (TCO): Comparison of Third-Party Offshoring to Company-Owned Offshoring

FIN   IS   ACC

Major companies, such as Citigroup, had wholly owned offshore service centers. Those types of company-owned offshore centers are called captive models. Captive offshoring models reduce the risk of offshoring. A recent study from the Everest Research Institute estimated the costs of third-party

offshoring and captive offshoring. The estimates are shown in the accompanying table.

Create a spreadsheet that totals the average cost of each model for each cost item. For example, average the annual salary based on the range for third parties and also for captives. Then calculate the TCO of each model. The difference is the cost of risk.

Full-time equivalents (FTE) are used to standardize labor costs since workers may be part time or full time. For example, two part-time workers equal one FTE. The estimates are given in terms of FTE, so the conversion is already done.

Based on your results, how much does the captive offshoring model allow for risk? The answer is the difference between the TCOs of the two models.

	Third-Party Offshoring Mode	Captive Offshoring Model
Office space: Annual rental cost per square foot (assume 10,000 square feet of office space)	$11 to $13	$14 to $16
Base salary costs of workers (assume 1,000 FTEs)	$7,770 to $8,200	$9,500 to $10,300
General management staff for every 1,000 FTEs	12 to 14	16 to 18
General management salary	$55,000 to $65,000	$70,000 to $90,000
Travel and housing costs per FTE	$280 to $320	$900 to $1,060

References

Adams, A. "Mistaken Identity," *CIO Insight*, March 2006.

Barrett, L. "A Return Home," *Baseline* January 2006.

Biddick, M., "Hunting the Elusive CIO Dashboard," *InformationWeek*, March 3, 2008.

Boyle, C., "AstraZeneca to Axe 8,000 Jobs in Global Cull," *Times Online*, January 28, 2010. *business.timesonline.co.uk/tol/business/industry_sectors/health/article7006615.ece*

Center for CIO Leadership, "The CIO Profession: Driving Innovation and Competitive Advantage," October 2007.

DiCarlo, L. An Innovative Partnership." *Cognizant.com*. 2010. *cognizant.com/InsightsCasestudies/Innovative_Partnership.pdf*

Genpact White Paper, "Six Keys to a Successful BPO Transition," 2010.

Höffman, T., and C. Stedman, "Forget IT–Business Alignment—It's All About Fusion Now, CIOs Say," *Computerworld*, March 12, 2008.

IAOP, "The Outsourcing Life-Cycle—9 Stages," 2009. *outsourcingprofessional.org/firmbuilder/articles/34/200/945/*

IBM, "The Outsourcing Decision for a Globally Integrated Enterprise: From Commodity Outsourcing to Value Creation," January 2008.

IMPACT Programme, *IT Governance: Developing a Successful Governance Strategy,* Published by the U.K. National Computing Centre, 2005.

Jusko, J., "Kimberly-Clark Embraces Virtual Reality," *IndustryWeek.com*, December 1, 2007.

Kaplan, R. S., and D. P. Norton, "Using the Balanced Scorecard as a Strategic Management System," *Harvard Business Review*, 85(7, 8), July/August 2007.

Kesner, R. M., "Running Information Services as a Business," *IS Management Handbook*, 8th ed., C. V. Brown and H. Topi (eds.), CRC Press, 2003.

Lomas, N., "AstraZeneca Signs IBM Outsourcing Deal," *ZDNet UK*, July 18, 2007.

Luftman, J., "SIM 2007 Survey Findings," *SIMposium 07*, October 7–12, 2007, *simposium.simnet.org*.

McGee, M. K., "Kimberly-Clark—Virtual Product Center Yields Real Ideas," *InformationWeek*, September 17, 2007.

OutsourcingPapers.com, 2010.

Pagnamenta, R, "AstraZeneca to Outsource Manufacturing," *Times Online*, September 17, 2007. *business.timesonline.co.uk/tol/business/industry_sectors/health/article2468741.ece*

Rosenthal, B. E., "Changes in BPO: How Technology Is Changing the Landscape," *Outsourcing Center*, January 2010. *outsourcing-bpo.com/jan2010-bpo.html*

Wailgum, T., "How to Stay Close to the Business," January 10, 2008. *cio.com/article/171150/How_to_Stay_Close_to_the_Business*

Worthen, B., "Business Technology: The IT Factor: Tech Staff's Bigger Role; Increased Input Helps Products Debut Faster, Deals Become Successful," *Wall Street Journal*, December 4, 2007.

Chapter 13

Business Process Management and Systems Development

Learning Objectives

❶ Understand business process management (BPM), BPM tools, and service-oriented architecture (SOA)—and their role in business agility and process optimization.

❷ Understand the importance of software architecture design to the maintenance and agility of business processes.

❸ Describe IT project identification, justification, and planning; understand the triple constraints.

❹ Describe the systems development lifecycle (SDLC).

Integrating *IT*

 ACC   **FIN**   **MKT**   **OM**   **HRM**   **IS**

ARIS Express, free business process modeling software.   *ariscommunity.com/aris-express*

Oracle BPM Suite 11g   *oracle.com/us/technologies/bpm/*

Oracle SOA Suite 11g   *oracle.com/us/technologies/soa/*

Project Management Institute   *pmi.org/*

Fastforward BPM blog   *fastforwardblog.com/2010/06/26/social-bpm-business-process-management-enters-the-21st-century/*

Open source BPM and workflow   *processmaker.com/*

BPM/SOA Community Insights   *blog.soa-consortium.org/*

Adaptive Planning demo for budgeting, forecasting, reporting, and analysis   *adaptiveplanning.com/*

IBM BPM   *www-01.ibm.com/software/info/bpm/*

IBM BPM Blueprint demo (download the demo)   *www-01.ibm.com/software/integration/bpm-blueprint/*

ITBusinessEdge BPM   *itbusinessedge.com/topics/show.aspx?t=482*

Oracle Business Activity Monitoring (BAM), integral part of the BPM suite   *oracle.com/appserver/business-activity-monitoring.html*

InfoSys Research BPM, SOA, and enterprise architecture; Centers of Excellence   *infosys.com/research/*
infosys.com/research/centers-of-excellence/

QUICK LOOK at Chapter 13, Business Process Management and Systems Development

This section introduces you to the business issues, challenges, and IT solutions in Chapter 13. Topics and issues mentioned in the Quick Look are explained in the chapter.

Ever-changing ITs, company mergers, industry consolidations, regulatory requirements, financial conditions, customer expectations, and global competition—what are these forces doing to organizations and the business climate? The simple and obvious answer is that they are causing rapid changes. Being able to redesign business processes to respond to those changes can be extremely complex, as you read in this chapter.

Business leaders know that each type of change—whether in the form of an opportunity or a threat—demands a smart (informed) response. Those demands trickle down to the business process level—the building blocks of each functional area. A **business process** is any system or procedure that an organization uses to achieve a larger business goal. Examples of business processes are:

- Accounting business processes
  - Accounts receivable (A/R) and accounts payable (A/P)
- Bank account reconciliations
- Cash receipts
- Finance business processes
  - Business forecasting
  - Financial cash flow reports
  - Credit approval and terms
- Human resources (HR) business processes
  - Employee hiring, screening, and training
  - Occupational health and workplace safety
  - Payroll
- Marketing business processes
  - Sales forecasting
  - Media campaigns
  - Customer service
- Management information systems (MIS) business processes
  - Network design and implementation
  - Data management
  - Information security and incident response
- Production and operations management business processes
  - Product design and development

- Quality control and assurance
- Shipping, receiving, and inventory management

Common to all business processes is that they *change*—and the management of those changes is the key topic of this chapter: business process management (BPM). To manage and redesign processes successfully, companies need a sound BPM strategy and the right set of tools.

Closely related to, but distinct from, BPM is **service-oriented architecture** (SOA). BPM is about modeling, implementing, and monitoring business processes; and most business processes entail several functions and/or services. SOA is a technology approach to implementing a business process, but it's only part of the technology required to implement business processes. Also in this chapter, we discuss IT project management—a disciplined approach to developing systems that meet specifications and are completed on time and within budget. Then you learn about the systems development process.

HR Business Processes at Microsoft International

GLOBAL

HRIS

IS

Microsoft International provides sales, marketing, and services for Microsoft Corporation's locations outside of North America. The human resources (HR) team within Microsoft International is made up of approximately 600 employees and provides support for HR management in more than 100 countries. HR performs many legal and staffing functions; key among them are recruiting, training, and employee development as well as compliance with regulations and health and safety laws, such as the U.K. Employment Law, U.K. health and safety regulations (*direct.gov.uk/*), and OSHA (Occupational Safety and Health Administration, *osha.gov/*) in the U.S. HR functions also include managing employee benefits, compensation, employee records, and personnel policies. Policies are often in the form of employee manuals, which are posted on the companies' intranets.

Standardizing HR Business Processes

The HR team uses many global systems and tools across each of the international Microsoft subsidiaries. One key HR objective was to standardize common business processes of all subsidiaries across all Microsoft locations. As each subsidiary developed its own unique business processes, such as training new hires, there was no standardized way to compare, manage, or evaluate the efficiency or effectiveness of the business processes. (As you have read, *you can't manage what you can't measure.*) HR believed that the costs and time required to perform its common activities and train new employees were much higher than they should be. Jean O'Connor, HR project manager for Microsoft International, explained:

> *Experience with different HR business processes would vary significantly from one location to the next. Without documentation, each new HR employee will need to be trained by someone who may or may not know the process. Teaching new hires an inefficient process can introduce repeatable errors and decreases our overall effectiveness.*

HR Inefficiencies

The lack of standardized business processes and process documentation had a number of adverse impacts on the HR team:

- Increased the time and cost to train new employees because there was no simple way to describe critical HR processes
- Limited ability to review its business processes and make informed decision regarding the sequencing of steps, and roles and responsibilities involved
- Decreased business process efficiency, with wide ranges in time to complete tasks across subsidiaries.

Business Processes Modeling

The team wanted to find ways to improve process efficiency and effectiveness across subsidiaries. To start, the HR team needed to understand current business processes at each subsidiary and be able to discuss them, which they achieved by diagramming them using Visio modeling software (*visiotoolbox.com/2010/home.aspx*). An example of a diagram of a business process is shown in Figure 13.1. (Visit the Microsoft Visio 2010 Web site at *visiotoolbox.com/2010/home.aspx* for more examples of business process modeling.)

After the workflows and information processing involved in a business process are accurately mapped out using standard notation, that process is ready to be analyzed so as to identify how to improve it. Equally important, these maps (or models) provide the starting point for standardizing the language used to describe their tasks.

Benefits of Business Process Modeling

The HR team used Microsoft Visio Premium 2010—a business process modeling tool—to design templates (also called models) that define and describe the steps in each process. The templates help HR staff understand Microsoft's standardized processes and are used in staff training. Benefits that the HR teams achieved were:

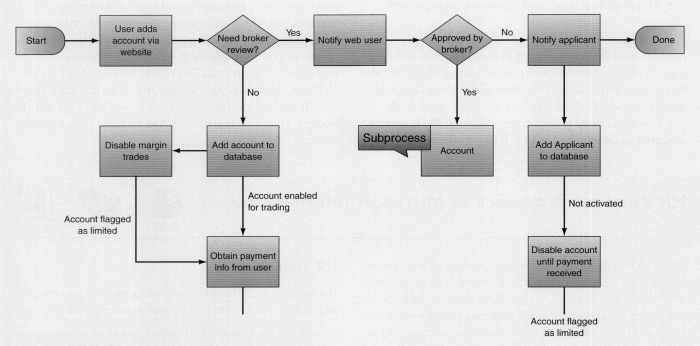

Figure 13.1 Business process model diagrammed using Visio (*Source: visiotoolbox.com/2010/*).

- **Significant savings in labor hours through increased process efficiency.** The models significantly reduced the time required to execute HR processes in all subsidiaries. According to O'Connor, "The key benefit for the HR organization is increased productivity through the creation of standardized process documentation across all of our sales, marketing, and services processes." The increased standardization helps clarify roles and responsibilities across HR employees and reduces the time HR teams spend on administrative tasks. As a result, "the right people are doing the right work at the right time across our business processes," said O'Connor.

- **Decrease in the training time of newly hired employees.** As HR processes are standardized from one subsidiary to the next, it's easier for an HR member from one country to move to another because roles, responsibilities, and process steps are similar in all locations. This further reduces the time and cost associated with training.

- **Improved decision making through visual process analysis.** Visual displays make it easier to understand and communicate about processes than using text.

Sources: Compiled from *Microsoft.com* (2010), Visio 2010, and *visimation.com/*.

For Class Discussion and Debate

1. *Scenario for Brainstorming and Discussion:* Why did Microsoft International have inefficient HR business processes until this HR initiative was completed in 2010? Does it seem strange that a mega-multinational computer software and services company had not been able to ensure that "the right people are doing the right work at the right time across our business processes" until 2010? What may have motivated or pressured Microsoft International to standardize its HR processes?

2. *Debate:* Select a process that you are familiar with, such as withdrawing cash from an ATM, registering for courses for the semester, or applying for a new job. Selecting a business process that everyone understands would be best. Working individually or in small teams of two or three, diagram all of the tasks needed to perform the process, making sure that you show the physical flows and the information flows in your model. After everyone or every team has completed their model diagrams, debate the tasks and flows until you have agreed to a standard (single) model to represent the process. Then continue to work on the model to improve the efficiency of the process. (You can expect to learn how difficult it is for people to agree on how a complex process is performed and how to improve it. You learn that modeling a business process is a series of debates over disagreements until agreement is reached.)

13.1 Business Process Management (BPM) and Service-Oriented Architecture (SOA)

BUSINESS PROCESSES AND TASKS

A **business process** accomplishes or produces something of value to the organization. A business process consists of a collection of tasks or activities that are executed according to certain rules and with respect to certain goals. For example, the credit approval process follows rules that take into consideration credit scores, debt, and annual salary to estimate the borrower's risk. The goal is to extend credit to those who are below some risk level.

When you break it down, you see that a business process is actually a series of individual tasks, and each task is executed in a specific order. A **task** is the smallest unit of work and management accountability that is not split into more detailed steps. The order of tasks/activities may be fully or only vaguely defined. Tasks can be automated, semiautomated, or performed manually.

A process has inputs and outputs that are *measurable* and therefore can be managed. Most processes cut across functional areas. For example, a product development process cuts across marketing, research and development, production, and finance (product development needs to be financed). Business processes are becoming more and more complex—composed of interactions across systems and dependent on collaborative activities between business users and IT. Complex processes often need to be broken into a number of subprocesses for easier management. When processes are designed for maximum efficiency, they said to be *optimized*.

Business Process Life Cycle. Business processes integrate ISs and people. Purchase order processing, staff recruitment, patient billing, order fulfillment, and everything else an organization does consist of processes that are performed by employees using ISs. Management of business processes boils down to the management of their life cycles, as shown in Figure 13.2. Business processes are introduced, modified to the extent possible, and get replaced—the standard format of a *life cycle*. Changes may require only simple adjustments to the tasks or rules of the process, such as changing the sales commission percent, or may be reengineered, such as changing the HR function, as you read in the Microsoft International opening case.

Design Stage. The cycle starts with process design. Process design is typically mapped and documented using a modeling tool, such as IBM BPM Blueprint or Microsoft Visio. This model plays a key role and, once finalized, serves as documentation of the entire process.

During the design stage, the team of business analysts and technology experts brainstorm possible solutions to current problem areas or opportunities. The design and functional specifications (specs) are completed at this phase. The *design spec*, also called the *technical spec*, identifies how the business process will be implemented in as much detail as possible. This spec identifies which systems are involved in the process, how they integrate, and the technical details of the implementation.

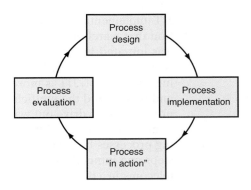

Figure 13.2 Business process life cycle.

Functional and technical specs can be hundreds of page long, which explains why specialized modeling tools are essential. The deliverables from the design stage are not all technical. The design spec also identifies how process users interact and complete tasks.

Implementation Stage. The business process agreed to in the design stage is delivered. Implementation includes integrating the process with other processes that share inputs or outputs, testing, and verifying that it works correctly and reliably. Problems may require going back to the process design stage.

Not only is the development of the process important, the testing of the process is equally as critical. The three tests are:

- **User acceptance:** Users tests whether the process is designed well from their perspective.
- **Functional acceptance:** Process analysts test whether the process performs its functions.
- **System acceptance:** Technical experts attest that the process is integrated correctly with inputs and outputs of other processes, data sources, and data stores.

After tests and refinements are completed, the process is ready to *go live*, and be put into action. After being put into action, the process is said to be "in production."

Process "In Production" and Evaluation Stages. As new processes are added, or as processes are redesigned or removed, processes that are in production may become problematic or unstable. Therefore, during this stage, the processes are monitored. Many software vendors that implement business processes, such as Oracle, Microsoft, Cordys, and IBM, include tools with **business activity monitoring (BAM)** functionality. For example, Oracle BAM is an integral part of the BPM suite (*oracle.com/appserver/business-activity-monitoring.html*). It is a message-based, event-driven tool that allows business users to link KPIs (key performance indicators) associated to the process being monitored on a real-time basis and provides relevant information via dashboards.

BUSINESS PROCESS MANAGEMENT

Business process management (BPM) is a fundamental management technique that includes methods and tools to support the stages of the business process life cycle. In the short term, BPM helps companies improve profitability by reducing waste and costs; in the long run, BPM helps keep companies responsive to business changes.

The BPM approach has its roots in **business process reengineering (BPR).** BPR is the radical redesign of an organization's business processes. BPR first attempts to *eliminate* processes that no longer have any purpose, often because of new mobile apps, Web services, or other IT. The processes that remain are redesigned and automated to the extent possible.

BPR quickly became a management fad, similar to just-in-time (JIT) inventory management. BPR and JIT were both based on assumptions. And if those assumptions were not met, then they failed to achieve the great expected results. That is, BPR was not understood enough and was applied incorrectly, with terrible results. Many JIT implementations increased inventory costs because JIT was based on the assumption that warehousing costs were extremely high, as they were in Japan, where JIT was initiated by Toyota. Why? Because JIT increases transportation and ordering costs. The increase in the costs must be offset by an even larger drop in warehousing costs. If not, JIT is more expensive. With BPR, companies first have to analyze and understand the inefficiencies in their business processes. They then have to figure out how to drive out waste and streamline processes and design those processes to minimize the risk of errors that led to rework. Then, and only then, should remaining processes be designed and automated. Many companies skipped the beginning steps and jumped to downsizing—firing employees. A manager at one of the major telecoms, in a discussion with one of the authors, lamented that "we amputated before we diagnosed." In addition to business disruptions, labor costs increased sharply as companies rehired employees. Therefore, in the 1990s most organizations failed to achieve fundamental process improvement because they attended a BPR seminar and then made mistakes in the implementation.

Despite decades of reengineering attempts, organizations still have problems with their business operations. They duplicate processes. They perform hundreds of noncore tasks that should be outsourced, and they spend vast amounts on proprietary process-management software that's difficult to update. To address these issues, BPM has evolved as a technique that ties people, processes, and technology to strategic performance improvement goals. To properly address process improvement, organizations must develop a carefully crafted BPM strategy.

BPM Strategy Considerations. Specifically, a well-implemented BPM strategy enables an organization to

- Gain greater visibility into processes
- Identify root causes of bottlenecks within processes
- Pinpoint the time and conditions when data from a process is handed-off (transferred) to other processes.

Done correctly, BPM helps an organization cut costs, improve service, achieve growth, or comply with regulations. For example, a manufacturer with a strategic goal of improving product quality and reliability must look at its manufacturing processes and see how they link to this business objective. If organizations focus exclusively on automation and cost savings, they might achieve significant operational efficiencies but lose their competitive edge and fall short of their performance targets, as British Telecom (BT) and United Airlines did when they failed to link strategic goals with their BPM initiatives.

Once the assessment is complete, it is necessary to develop a process performance plan that documents the ways in which the identified operational processes contribute to strategic goals. If a strategic goal is customer satisfaction, for example, appropriate process benchmarks should be established to accurately and consistently analyze progress of a BPM initiative. In improving an order-to-fulfillment process, although order throughput and on-time delivery are important, other measures might have a direct impact on customer satisfaction, such as fulfillment accuracy.

Finally, processes must be prioritized, with highest priority given to those processes that are determined to have the greatest potential impact on strategic objectives.

SERVICE-ORIENTED ARCHITECTURE (SOA)

SOA is a confusing concept, even for practitioners, for one of two reasons—either because SOA is mistakenly described like BPM or the definition of SOA is incomprehensible. To illustrate the latter, this is how IBM defines SOA on its Web site *http://www-01.ibm.com/software/solutions/soa/*:

> *Service Oriented Architecture (SOA) is a business-centric IT architectural approach that supports integrating your business as linked, repeatable business tasks, or services. With the Smart SOA approach, you can find value at every stage of the SOA continuum, from departmental projects to enterprise-wide initiatives.*

It's as if someone in the legal department wrote that IT definition in language few others could understand. Another definition of SOA was: "SOA is essentially a collection of services." Clearly that definition does not help either.

Services are like reusable software programs, or modules. You might even compare them to a macro in Excel. You can use and reuse them instead of writing code to perform common functions.

Oracle offers a technical explanation of SOA, which you find in Table 13.1.

TABLE 13.1	SOA Defined

SOA is an architectural style for building software applications that use services available in a network such as the Web. It promotes loose coupling between software components so that they can be reused. Applications in SOA are built based on services. A service is an implementation of well-defined business functionality, and such services can then be used by clients in different applications or business processes.

SOA allows for the reuse of existing assets where new services can be created from an existing IT infrastructure of systems. In other words, it enables businesses to leverage existing investments by allowing them to reuse existing applications, and promises interoperability between heterogeneous applications and technologies. SOA provides a level of flexibility that wasn't possible before in the sense that:

- Services are software components with well-defined interfaces that are implementation-independent. An important aspect of SOA is the separation of the service interface (the what) from its implementation (the how). Such services are consumed by clients that are not concerned with how these services will execute their requests.
- Services are self-contained (perform predetermined tasks) and loosely coupled (for independence).
- Services can be dynamically discovered.
- Composite services can be built from aggregates of other services.

See *java.sun.com/developer/technicalArticles/WebServices/soa/*

BPM and SOA: Business Optimization. BPM and SOA are two of the most talked-about business initiatives. Both promise to help companies create new value from existing IT investments. They reuse IT programming efforts (think macros or modules) across many other processes. They also promise to enable agility through greater flexibility and lower cost structures.

The two are often confused because they confer many of the same benefits. SOA focuses on creating a more flexible IT architecture, while BPM has a pure focus on optimizing the way actual work gets done. SOA has delivered business value to very large corporations, but almost all SOAs in practice are used only in Web services, application integration as middleware, and B2B solutions.

BPM Mashups Through Web Services. Business processes are not self-contained. They need information from people and ISs (data stores) across departments and business areas. Many business processes even require information to be shared with external partners, clients, and providers. Web services can expand the functionality of the BPM system. A **Web service** is a set of technologies used for exchanging data between applications. Web services can connect processes with other systems across the organization and with business partners. The resulting integrated BPM systems are called **BPM mashups.**

Mashups are preconfigured, ready-to-go integrations between different business software packages. They streamline information sharing among systems. For example, a BPM system can leverage Web services to share customer data with CRM (customer relationship management). Budget and cost data from an ERP (enterprise resource planning) can be shared with the BPM, either to approve or deny an expense report filed using the BPM and subsequently, to update the ERP once the expense report is complete. Web services can be used to share information with any other system that uses Web services. Mashups make the sharing process easier by providing the systems integration and streamlining the way that the two systems work together.

Review Questions

1. What is a business process? Give three examples.
2. What are the stages in the business process life cycle?
3. Define *business process management.*
4. Why is BPM important?
5. What is a BPM mashup?

13.2 Software Architecture and IS Design

An organization's software architecture refers to the structure of its applications. As with roads and bridges, architecture determines what is possible and the ease with which changes can be made to systems and processes.

AN OVERVIEW OF COUPLING IN SOFTWARE APPS

Long ago, business applications were written in COBOL software. These apps were one large piece or tightly coupled programs that performed many functions. *Tightly coupled* means that the programs and the data they processed and reports they generated were hardwired. Changes to these apps were tedious and time-consuming, as the Y2K problem demonstrated. For an explanation of the Y2K, or millennium bug, see *cybergeo.com/y2k/fulldetails*.html or search for online articles.

The preferred software design is loosely coupled and performs a single function or very few functions. What does *loose coupling* mean?

Loosely Coupled. Loose coupling refers to the way in which components in a system or network are connected. Loosely connected components have minimal dependence on one another. This simplifies testing, maintenance, and troubleshooting procedures because problems are easy to isolate and unlikely to spread or propagate. The extent, or "tightness," to which the components in a system are coupled is a relative term. A loosely coupled system can be easily broken down into definable elements.

The goal of loose coupling is to reduce dependencies between systems. Benefits of loose coupling include flexibility and agility. A loosely coupled approach offers unparalleled flexibility for adaptations to changing landscapes. Since there are no assumptions about the landscape your application is running against, you can easily adapt the composite application as needed.

Another aspect to consider is the probability of landscape changes during the lifetime of the application. Due to mergers and acquisitions and system consolidations, the landscape underneath the application is constantly changing. Without loose coupling, organizations are forced to adapt or rewrite their apps again and again.

Maximizing Architecture Flexibility. An organization's software architecture can also be designed for greater flexibility by using a tiered model. An example of a three-tier architecture model is shown in Figure 13.3.

Notice the modular architecture. The three-tier architecture is intended to allow any of the three tiers to be upgraded or replaced independently as business requirements or technologies change. For example, a change of OS (operating system) in the presentation tier would only affect the user interface code.

Typically, the user interface runs on a PC, laptop, or handheld and displays a standard graphical user interface (GUI). The middle tier does the processing and coordinating of the data. The middle tier may be multitiered itself, which is called an n-tier architecture.

Three-tier architecture has the following three tiers:

1. Presentation or client tier. This is the topmost level of the application, an example of which is your Web browser. The presentation tier displays information related to such services as browsing merchandise, purchasing, and showing shopping cart contents. It communicates with other tiers by outputting results to the browser/client tier and all other tiers in the network.

2. Application or business logic tier. Detailed processing is performed in this tier. This middle tier consists of **middleware.** Middleware refers to a broad range of software or services that enable communication or data exchange between applications across networks. Specifically, middleware enables the data exchange by translating data requests and responses between clients and servers. This type of software is often described as "glue" because it connects or integrates business-critical software

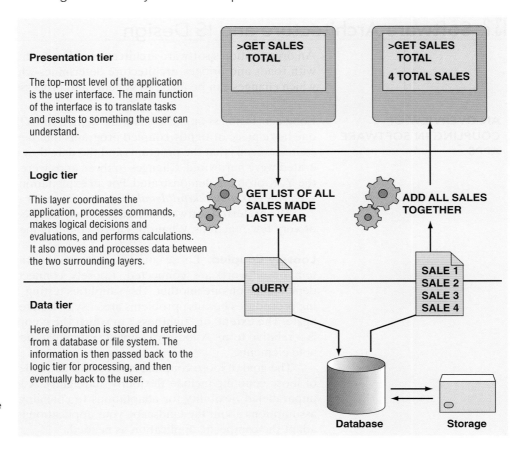

Presentation tier

The top-most level of the application is the user interface. The main function of the interface is to translate tasks and results to something the user can understand.

Logic tier

This layer coordinates the application, processes commands, makes logical decisions and evaluations, and performs calculations. It also moves and processes data between the two surrounding layers.

Data tier

Here information is stored and retrieved from a database or file system. The information is then passed back to the logic tier for processing, and then eventually back to the user.

>GET SALES TOTAL

>GET SALES TOTAL
4 TOTAL SALES

GET LIST OF ALL SALES MADE LAST YEAR

ADD ALL SALES TOGETHER

QUERY

SALE 1
SALE 2
SALE 3
SALE 4

Database   Storage

Figure 13.3 Overview of a three-tier software architecture design. (*Courtesy of Bartledan (Wikipedia, 2009).*)

applications to other applications. By performing some of the tasks that an application would have performed, middleware eliminates the need for an application that is shared by multiple clients to function differently for each different type of client.

With today's network-based applications—especially ERP, SCM, CRM, B2B, and B2C e-commerce—business operations depend on middleware to provide secure data transfers between these applications.

3. Data tier. This tier consists of the data sources, such as the database and data warehouse servers. Here information is stored and retrieved. This tier keeps data neutral and independent from application servers or business logic. Giving data its own tier also improves scalability and performance.

Conceptually the three-tier architecture is linear. A fundamental rule in a three-tier architecture is that the presentation tier never communicates directly with the data tier; all communication must pass through the middleware tier.

With this understanding of tiered architecture, we now discuss the IT acquisition process. Recall from Chapter 12, which focused on outsourcing strategies, that developing ISs in-house was the alternative option. We examine that option for developing business processes next.

THE IT ACQUISITION PROCESS

The acquisition process of an IT application has five major steps, which are shown in Figure 13.4 and discussed next.

Step 1: Planning, identifying, and justifying IT-based systems. IT systems are usually built as *enablers* of some business processes. Therefore, their planning must be aligned with the organization's overall business plan and the specific tasks they intend to support. Often processes may need to be redesigned or restructured to fully reap

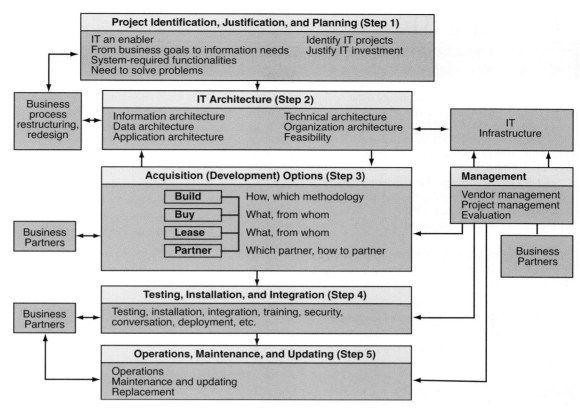

Figure 13.4 The process of IT application acquisition.

the benefits of the supporting IT applications. Also, the systems may need to be justified, for example, by cost-benefit analysis. Both of these activities may be complex, especially for systems that require a significant investment to acquire, operate, and maintain—or that are cutting-edge.

The output of this step is the decision to invest or not invest in a specific application and a timetable, budget, and assigned responsibility. This step is usually done in-house, with consultants as needed. All other steps can be done in-house or outsourced.

The importance of a realistic evaluation cannot be overstated. Many projects pass this stage because of political reasons or fear of taking an unpopular position. Managers may hope that the system will work out. *Hope is not a plan*—it's a risk.

Step 2: Creating IT architecture. IT architecture is a plan for organizing the underlying infrastructure and applications of the IT project. The architecture plan includes the following:

• Data required to fulfill the business goals and vision
• Application modules that will deliver and manage the information and data
• Specific hardware and software on which the application modules will run
• Security, scalability, and reliability required by the applications
• Human resources and procedures for implementing the IT project

Various IT tools and methodologies are used to support the creation of an IT application architecture. The results obtained from Step 2 are routed to the strategic planning level; for example, to a steering committee. Based on the results of

IT at Work 13.1

FINRA SOA Approach to System Integration

IS   ACCT   FIN

Financial Industry Regulatory Authority (FINRA; *finra.org/*) is the largest independent regulator for all securities firms doing business in the United States. FINRA was created in July 2007 through the consolidation of NASD (National Association of Securities Dealers) and the regulatory and enforcement functions of the New York Stock Exchange (NYSE).

FINRA protects investors and market integrity through effective and efficient regulation, and complementary compliance and technology-based services. FINRA oversees 4,700 brokerage firms and over 600,000 registered securities representatives.

FINRA SOA Project: Consolidate Information Systems. The FINRA SOA project consolidated the information systems of the NASD and NYSE. The primary challenges were:

- Consolidation of the two organizations' application portfolios that supported the member regulation business.
- Reconciliation of two sets of legacy business processes into updated business processes called the *final-state business processes*.

Benefits of SOA approach. FINRA (the new merged regulator) benefited greatly from the SOA approach in the following ways:

1. Fast time to Market—Project delivery was faster. The SOA approach allowed each team to rapidly deliver individual services that were later integrated and tested.
2. Reduced Risk—The SOA approach reduced or eliminated many of the risks associated with large development teams (100+ staff) by facilitating development in parallel and reducing team interdependencies.
3. Cost Savings—The modular SOA architecture of the new system consolidated business functions into a common set of business services that are leveraged across many business processes, which cut costs.
4. Improved Agility—The design and modularity of the SOA could be easily changed to support future business processes.
5. Process Optimization—IT duplication is eliminated by consolidating processes into standardized business services.

The single, most important lesson from this SOA project is that extremely large and time-critical apps can benefit from a SOA approach. SOA isolates common services so that independent teams can work on them at the same time (that is, teams can work in parallel). The SOA approach increases productivity and removes some of the risks characteristic of large projects.

Sources: Compiled from FINRA (*finra.org/AboutFINRA/*, 2010), SOA Consortium (*blog.soa-consortium.org/*, 2009), and CIO Magazine (*cio.com*).

Discussion Questions: How tolerant of business disruption or errors do you think FINRA would be? Explain. Do you think that cost was one of the most important concerns for using the SOA approach? Explain why or why not. Assuming that it was not cost, what do you think was the most important criteria during the implementation?

Step 2, the application portfolio (a portfolio is *a set of applications*) or a specific project may be changed. For example, the steering committee may scale down a specific project because it is too risky at that time. Once the architecture is compiled and the project gets final approval, a decision about *how* to acquire the specific IT application must be made.

Step 3: Selecting an acquisition option. IT applications can be:

- Built in-house. In-house development using the systems development life cycle (SDLC) approach is covered in Section 13.4.
- Custom-made by a vendor.
- Bought and customized, in-house or through a vendor. See Table 13.2 for a list of advantages and limitations of the *buy option*.
- Leased from an application service provider (ASP) or leased through a software-as-a-service (SaaS) arrangement, as you read in Chapter 12.
- Acquired via a partnership or alliance that will enable the company to use someone else's application.

TABLE 13.2	Advantages and Limitations of the Buy Option
Advantages of the Buy Option	**Disadvantages of the Buy Option**
• Many different types of off-the-shelf software are available. • Much time can be saved by buying rather than building. • The company can know what it is getting before it invests in the software. • The company is not the first and only user. • Purchased software may preclude the need to hire personnel specifically dedicated to a project. • The vendor updates the software frequently. • The price is usually much lower for a buy option.	• Software may not exactly meet the company's needs. • Software may be difficult or impossible to modify, or it may require huge business process changes to implement. • The company will not have control over software improvements and new versions. (Usually it may only recommend.) • Purchased software can be difficult to integrate with existing systems. • Vendors may drop a product or go out of business.

Once an option is chosen, the system can be acquired. At the end of this step, an application is ready to be installed and deployed. No matter what option is chosen, you most likely will have to select one or more vendors and consulting companies.

Step 4: Testing, installing, integrating, and deploying IT applications. Once an acquisition option has been selected, the next step involves getting the application up and running on the selected hardware and network environment. One of the steps in installing an application is connecting it to back-end databases, to other applications, and often to partners' information systems. This step can be done in-house or outsourced. During this step, the modules that have been installed need to be tested. A series of tests are required:

• *Unit testing*: Testing the modules one at a time

• *Integration testing*: Testing the combination of modules interacting with other applications

• *Usability testing*: Testing the quality of the user's experience when interacting with the portal or Web site

• *Acceptance testing*: Determining whether the application meets the original business objectives and vision.

After the applications pass all of the tests, they can be rolled out to the end users. Here developers have to deal with issues such as conversion from the old to the new system, training, changes in priorities affecting acceptance of the application, and resistance to changing processes to maximize the benefit from the application.

Step 5: Operations, maintenance, and updating. It usually takes as much time, effort, and money to operate and maintain an application as it does to acquire and install it in the first place. For the maximizing of its continual usage, an application needs to be continually updated. Software maintenance can be a big problem due to rapid changes in the IT field. Operation and maintenance can be done in-house and/or outsourced.

Managing the IT Acquisition Process. The IT acquisition process most likely will be a complex project that must be managed properly. Except for small applications, an IT project team is usually created to manage the process, budget, costs, and vendors. Projects can be managed with *project management* software, such as Microsoft Project (*office.microsoft.com/project*). Three criteria that are used to evaluate the effectiveness of IT project management are performance, time, and cost. That is, was the IT project done right, on budget, and on time?

Standard project management techniques and tools are used by project managers to manage project resources to keep them on time, on budget, and within performance specifications. Finally, implementing an IT project may require restructuring one or more business processes.

IN-HOUSE DEVELOPMENT: INSOURCING

A third development strategy is to develop or build applications in-house. Although in-house development—*insourcing*—can be time-consuming and costly, it may lead to IT applications that better fit an enterprise's strategy and vision and differentiate it from competitors. The in-house development of IT applications, however, is a challenging task, as most applications are novel and may involve multiple organizations.

Options for In-House Development. Three major options exist for in-house development:

- **Build from scratch.** This option should be considered only for specialized IT applications for which components are not available. This option is expensive and slow, but it will provide the best fit to the organization's needs.
- **Build from components.** The required applications are often built from standard components (e.g., random number generators or Web servers such as Microsoft's IIS). Commercially packaged and homegrown components must integrate correctly and reliably or the system will fail. This is especially critical for real-time applications and for e-business systems. The scope of component integration and code reuse is broadening, too.
- **Integrating applications.** The application integration option is similar to the build-from-components option, but instead of components being used, entire applications are employed. This is an especially attractive option when IT applications from several business partners need to be integrated. Integration methods such as Web services or enterprise application integration (EAI) can be used.

Insourcing is a challenging task that requires specialized IT procedures and resources. For this reason, most organizations usually rely on packaged applications or outsource the development and maintenance of their IT applications.

Methods Used in In-House Development. Several methods can be used when developing IT applications in-house. Two major development methods are:

- **Systems development life cycle (SDLC).** Large IT projects, especially ones that involve infrastructure, are developed according to the SDLC methodology using several tools. Details about this approach are provided in Section 13.4.
- **Prototyping methodology.** With a prototyping methodology, an initial list of basic system requirements is defined and used to build a prototype. The prototype is then improved in several iterations, based on users' feedback. This approach can be very rapid. The prototype is then tested and improved, tested again, and developed further, based on the users' feedback. The prototyping approach, however, is not without drawbacks. There is a risk of getting into an endless loop of prototype revisions, as users may never be fully satisfied. Such a risk should be planned for because of the rapid changes in IT and business models.
- **Web 2.0 or Application 2.0 methodology.** This development approach involves quick, incremental updates with close user involvement. For new application developments, a beta (prototype) version is developed and then refined—also in very close collaboration with users.

End-User Development. End-user development (also known as **end-user-computing**) is the development and use of ISs by people outside the IS department. This includes users in all functional areas at all skill levels and organizational levels: managers, executives, staff, secretaries, and others. End-user development has risks and limitations. End users may not be skilled enough in computers, so quality and cost may be jeopardized unless proper controls are installed. Also, many end users do not take time to document their work and may neglect proper security measures.

Review Questions

1. What is the advantage of loosely coupled software design?
2. Explain the three-tier software architecture design.
3. Explain the functions of middleware.
4. What is IT architecture?
5. What testing needs to be done on an application?
6. List the major acquisition and development strategies.
7. Compare the buy option against the lease option.
8. List the in-house development approaches.
9. What are the risks and limitations of end-user development?

13.3 IT Project Management

Successful organizations perform projects that produce desired results in established timeframes, with assigned resources. Projects are not limited to IT, but can apply to most all functions of the organization. The project management principles and practices discussed in this section apply to any type of project.

Projects are managed by managing the triple constraints, which are:

1. Scope: The project scope is the definition of what the project is supposed to accomplish—its outcomes or deliverables. Scope is measured in terms of the project size, goals, and requirements.

2. Time: A project is made of up *tasks*. Definitions of the tasks should start with active verbs, such as *purchase* servers, *apply for* permits, and *interview* vendors. Each task is assigned a duration, which is the difference between the task's start date and its end date. The project's time is determined by task durations and task dependencies. Some tasks are dependent on other tasks being completed before they can begin. For example, in construction, a hole must be dug before the pouring of concrete can start. Task durations and task dependencies determine the time required to complete the project.

3. Budget: Projects are approved subject to their costs.

These constraints are interrelated, so they must be managed together for the project to be completed on time, within budget, and to specification (spec).

After the project scope has been defined, it is used to estimate a realistic timeline and budget based on the availability of necessary resources. Resources include the people, equipment, and material needed to complete the project. The result is a project plan that is specified in a **Work Breakdown Structure (WBS).** Figure 13.5 shows a screen shot of Microsoft Project, with a WBS on the left side and a Gantt chart on the right side. A **Gantt chart** is a type of bar chart that illustrates a project schedule. Gantt charts illustrate the start and finish dates of the terminal elements and summary elements of a project. Terminal elements and summary elements comprise the Work Breakdown Structure of the project. Project resources must be managed according to the WBS.

Scope Creep. It is absolutely imperative that any change to the scope of the project explicitly include compensating changes in the budget, the deadline, and/or resources. **Scope creep,** which refers to the growth of the project after the scope has been defined, is a serious issue. Scope creep is the piling up of small changes that by themselves are manageable but in aggregate are significant. IT projects, particularly one as complex as implementing an ERP or CRM, can take a long time to complete.

During the project, it's almost guaranteed that requests will be made that change the scope. If the project scope is to build an accounting app for processing expense

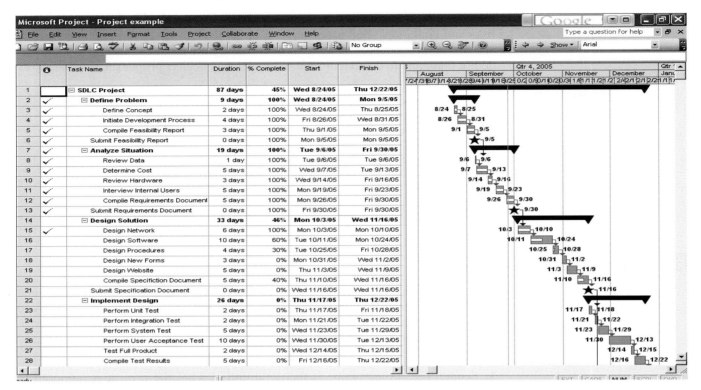

Figure 13.5 Microsoft Project screenshot of WBS (left side) and Gantt chart (right side).

reports with a budget of $100,000 and a four-month duration, the project manager is expected to do that. However, if the scope is changed to also include processing of sales commissions, the project manager must obtain an appropriate change in budgeted resources and time. If the budget is not adjusted, the smart project manager will refuse to agree to the change in scope. Make sure any requested change, no matter how small, is accompanied by approval for a change in budget or schedule, or both.

WHAT DO PROJECT MANAGERS DO?

Project management is the process of guiding a project from its beginning through its performance to its closure. Project management includes three basic operations:

1. Planning: Specifying the desired results, determining the schedules, and estimating the resources.

2. Organizing: Defining people's roles and responsibilities.

3. Controlling: Tracking the planned performance and budget against the actual performance; also, managing people's performances, addressing problems, putting out fires, and keeping priorities well known.

Managing the Critical Path. Tasks must be completed in a specific order to get the job done. Certain tasks make up what is called the critical path, which is an important principle of project management. Project managers must manage the critical path. The **critical path** consists of activities or tasks that must start and finish on schedule or else the project completion will be delayed—unless action is taken to expedite one or more critical tasks. The critical path is the length of the project. Each task on the critical path is a **critical task.**

There are non-critical paths composed of tasks that are not critical, but since their status could easily change to critical, you need to monitor and manage the critical and non-critical paths.

The purpose of the **critical path method (CPM)** is to recognize which activities are on the critical path so that you know where to focus your efforts. You use critical tasks to identify or prioritize trade-offs.

Project Manager Success Skills. The success of a project manager depends on:

• **Communication:** Clear, open, and timely sharing of information with appropriate individuals and groups is necessary. Since people tend to want to admit bad news, extra effort is needed to ensure that news about anything that will delay or compromise the project is reported promptly. Without truthful and complete communication during the project, it will fail.

• **Information:** There should be no surprises. Accurate, timely, and complete data for the planning, performance monitoring, and final assessment is necessary.

• **Commitment:** Team members should personally promise to produce the agreed-upon results on time and within budget.

Review Questions

1. Define *triple constraint*.
2. What is the project scope?
3. What is scope creep? Why does it pose such a risk to the project and project manager?
4. What is the critical path?
5. What do project managers do?

13.4 Systems Development

The **systems development life cycle (SDLC)** is the traditional systems development method used by organizations for large IT projects such as IT infrastructure. The SDLC is a structured framework that consists of sequential processes by which information systems are developed. As shown in Figure 13.6, these processes are investigation, analysis, design, programming, testing, implementation, operation, and maintenance. The processes, in turn, consist of well-defined tasks. Large projects typically require all of the tasks, whereas smaller development projects may require only a subset of the tasks.

Within the SDLC, there is an iterative feature. *Iteration* is the revising of the results of any development process when new information makes this revision the smart thing to do. Iteration does not mean that developments should be subjected to infinite revisions, but it does mean that developers should adjust to new relevant information. Recall the scope creep that tends to happen to projects. IS design is highly susceptible

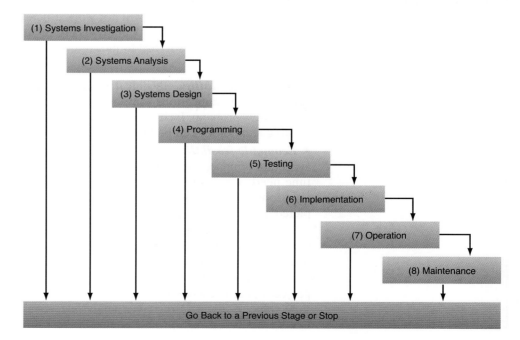

Figure 13.6 An eight-stage system development life cycle (SDLC).

(1) Systems Investigation
(2) Systems Analysis
(3) Systems Design
(4) Programming
(5) Testing
(6) Implementation
(7) Operation
(8) Maintenance

Go Back to a Previous Stage or Stop

to scope creep as users ask for additional features or try to keep up with the latest mobile technologies. It is especially important for social media, viral marketing, and e-commerce development because those systems must constantly evolve.

Systems development projects produce desired results through team efforts. Development teams typically include users, systems analysts, programmers, and technical specialists. *Users* are employees from all functional areas and levels of the organization who will interact with the system, either directly or indirectly. **Systems analysts** are information systems professionals who specialize in analyzing and designing information systems. Programmers are information systems professionals who modify existing computer programs or write new computer programs to satisfy user requirements. Technical specialists are experts on a certain type of technology, such as databases or telecommunications. All people who are affected by changes in information systems (e.g., users and managers) are known as systems stakeholders and are typically involved in varying degrees and at various times in the systems development.

SDLC STAGE 1: SYSTEMS INVESTIGATION

Systems development practitioners agree that the more time invested in understanding the business problem or opportunity, in understanding technical options for systems, and in understanding problems that are likely to occur during development, the greater the probability that the IS will be a success. For these reasons, systems investigation begins with the *business problem* or *opportunity*.

Problems and opportunities often require not only understanding them from the internal point of view, but also seeing them as organizational partners—suppliers or customers—would see them. Another useful perspective is that of competitors. How have they responded to similar situations, and what outcomes and additional opportunities have materialized? Creativity and out-of-the-box thinking can pay big dividends when isolated problems can be recognized as systemic failures, whose causes cross organizational boundaries. Once these perspectives can be gained, those involved can also begin to better see the true scope of the project and propose possible solutions. Then an initial assessment of these proposed system solutions can begin.

Feasibility Studies. The next task in the systems investigation stage is the feasibility study. The feasibility study determines the probability of success of the proposed project and provides a rough assessment of the project's technical, economic, organizational, and behavioral feasibility. The feasibility study is critically important to the systems development process because, done properly, the study can prevent organizations from making costly mistakes, such as creating systems that will not work, that will not work efficiently, or that people cannot or will not use. The various feasibility analyses also give the stakeholders an opportunity to decide what metrics to use to measure how a proposed system meets their various objectives.

- *Technical feasibility.* Technical feasibility determines whether the hardware, software, and communications components can be developed and/or acquired to solve the business problem. Technical feasibility also determines whether the organization's existing technology can be used to achieve the project's performance objectives.
- *Economic feasibility.* Economic feasibility determines whether the project is an acceptable financial risk and whether the organization can afford the expense and time needed to complete the project. Economic feasibility addresses two primary questions: Do the benefits outweigh the costs of the project? Can the project be completed as scheduled?

Three commonly used methods to determine economic feasibility are return on investment (ROI), net present value (NPV), and breakeven analysis. Return on investment is the ratio of the net income attributable to a project divided by the average assets invested in the project. The net present value is the net amount by which project benefits exceed project costs, after allowing for the cost of capital and the time value of money. Breakeven analysis determines the point at which the cumulative cash flow from a project equals the investment made in the project.

Determining economic feasibility in IT projects is rarely straightforward, but it often is essential. Part of the difficulty stems from the fact that benefits are often intangible. Another potential difficulty is that the proposed system or technology may be "cutting edge," and there may be no previous evidence of what sort of financial payback is to be expected.

- *Organizational feasibility.* Organizational feasibility has to do with an organization's ability to accept the proposed project. Sometimes, for example, organizations cannot accept a financially acceptable project due to legal or other constraints. In checking organizational feasibility, one should consider the organization's policies and politics, including impacts on power distribution, business relationships, and internal resources availability.

- *Behavioral feasibility.* Behavioral feasibility addresses the human issues of the project. All systems development projects introduce change into the organization, and people generally fear change. Overt resistance from employees may take the form of sabotaging the new system (e.g., entering data incorrectly) or deriding the new system to anyone who will listen. Covert resistance typically occurs when employees simply do their jobs using their old methods.

Behavioral feasibility is concerned with assessing the skills and the training needed to use the new IS. In some organizations, a proposed system may require mathematical or linguistic skills beyond what the workforce currently possesses. In others, the workforce may simply need to improve their skills. Behavioral feasibility is as much about "can they use it" as it is about "will they use it."

After the feasibility analysis, a "go/no-go" decision is reached. The functional area manager for whom the system is to be developed and the project manager sign off on the decision. If the decision is "no-go," the project is put on the shelf until conditions are more favorable or the project is discarded. If the decision is "go," then the systems development project proceeds and the systems analysis phase begins.

SDLC STAGE 2: SYSTEMS ANALYSIS

The systems analysis stage produces the following information: (1) strengths and weaknesses of the existing system, (2) functions that the new system must have to solve the business problem, and (3) user information requirements for the new system. Armed with this information, systems developers can proceed to the systems design stage.

There are two main approaches in systems analysis: the traditional (structured) approach and the object-oriented approach. The traditional approach emphasizes *how*, whereas the object-oriented approach emphasizes *what*.

SDLC STAGE 3: SYSTEM DESIGN

Systems analysis describes what a system must do to solve the business problem, and *systems design* describes *how* the system will accomplish this task. The deliverable of the systems design phase is the technical design that specifies the following:

- System outputs, inputs, and user interfaces
- Hardware, software, databases, telecommunications, personnel, and procedures
- How these components are integrated

This output represents the set of *system specifications*. Systems design encompasses two major aspects of the new system: **Logical system design** states what the system will do, using abstract specifications. **Physical system design** states how the system will perform its functions, with actual physical specifications. Logical design specifications include the design of outputs, inputs, processing, databases, telecommunications, controls, security, and IS jobs. Physical design specifications include the design of hardware, software, database, telecommunications, and procedures. For example, the logical telecommunications design may call for a wide area network connecting the company's plants. The physical telecommunications design will specify the types of communications hardware (computers and routers), software (network operating system), media (fiber optics and satellite), and bandwidth (e.g., 100 Mbps).

When both of these aspects of system specifications are approved by all participants, they are "frozen." That is, once the specifications are agreed upon, they should not be changed. However, users typically ask for added functionality in the system (called *scope creep*). This occurs for several reasons: First, as users more clearly understand how the system will work and what their information and processing needs are, they see additional functions that they would like the system to have. Also, as time passes after the design specifications are frozen, business conditions often change, and users ask for added functionality. Finally, because scope creep is expensive, project managers place controls on changes requested by users. These controls help to prevent *runaway projects* — systems development projects that are so far over budget and past deadline that they must be abandoned, typically with large monetary loss.

SDLC STAGE 4: PROGRAMMING

Systems developers utilize the design specifications to acquire the software needed for the system to meet its functional objectives and solve the business problem. Organizations may buy the software or construct it in-house.

Although many organizations tend to purchase packaged software, many other firms continue to develop custom software in-house. For example, Walmart and Eli Lilly build practically all of their software in-house. The chief benefit of custom development is systems that are better suited than packaged applications to an organization's new and existing business processes. For many organizations, custom software is more expensive than packaged applications. However, if a package does not closely fit the company's needs, the savings are often diluted when the information systems staff or consultants must extend the functionality of the purchased packages.

If the organization decides to construct the software in-house, then programming begins. **Programming** involves the translation of the design specifications into computer code. This process can be lengthy and time-consuming because writing computer code remains as much an art as a science. Large systems development projects can require hundreds of thousands of lines of computer code and hundreds of computer programmers. In such projects, programming teams are used. These teams often include functional area users to help the programmers focus on the business problem at hand.

In an attempt to add rigor (and some uniformity) to the programming process, programmers use structured programming techniques. These techniques improve the logical flow of the program by decomposing the computer code into *modules*, which are sections of code (subsets of the entire program). This modular structure allows for more efficient and effective testing because each module can be tested by itself. The structured programming techniques include the following restrictions:

• Each module has one, and only one, function.
• Each module has only one entrance and one exit. That is, the logic in the computer program enters a module in only one place and exits in only one place.
• GO TO statements are not allowed.

For example, a flowchart for a simple payroll application might look like the one shown in Figure 13.7. The figure shows the only three types of structures that are used in structured programming: sequence, decision, and loop. In the *sequence* structure, program statements are executed one after another until all of the statements in the sequence have been executed. The *decision* structure allows the logic flow to branch, depending on certain conditions being met. The *loop* structure enables the software to execute the same program, or parts of a program, until certain conditions are met (e.g., until the end of the file is reached or until all records have been processed).

As already noted, structured programming enforces some standards about how program code is written. This approach and some others were developed not only

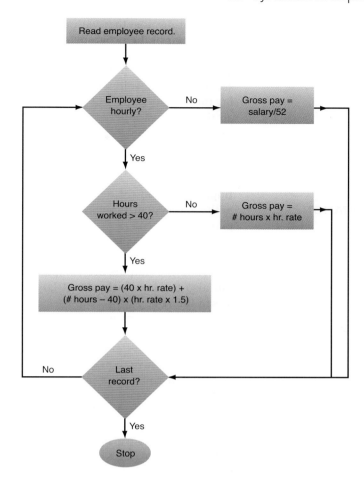

Figure 13.7 Flowchart of a payroll application.

to improve programming, but also to standardize how a firm's various programmers do their work. This uniform approach helps ensure that all of the code developed by different programmers will work together. Even with these advances, however, programming can be difficult to manage.

SDLC STAGE 5: TESTING

Thorough and continuous testing occurs throughout the programming stage. Testing verifies that computer code works correctly under various conditions. Testing requires a lot of time, effort, and expense to do properly. However, the costs of improper testing, which could possibly lead to a system that does not meet its objectives, are enormous.

Testing is designed to detect errors (bugs) in the computer code. These errors are of two types: syntax errors and logic errors.

- *Syntax errors* (e.g., a misspelled word or a misplaced comma) are easier to find and will not permit the program to run.
- *Logic errors* permit the program to run but result in incorrect output. Logic errors are more difficult to detect because the cause is not obvious. The programmer must follow the flow of logic in the program to determine the source of the error in the output.

To have a systematic testing of the system, we must start with a comprehensive *test plan*. There are several types of testing: In *unit testing,* each module is tested alone in an attempt to discover any errors in its code. *String testing* puts together several modules to check the logical connection among them. The next level, *integration testing,* brings together various programs for testing purposes. *System testing* brings together *all* of the programs that comprise the system.

As software increases in complexity, the number of errors increases, making it almost impossible to find them all. This situation has led to *"good-enough" software,* software that developers release knowing that errors remain in the code but believing that the software will still meet its functional objectives. That is, they have found all the "show-stopper" bugs, errors that will cause the system to shut down or will cause catastrophic loss of data.

SDLC STAGE 6: IMPLEMENTATION

Implementation (or deployment) is the process of converting from the old system to the new system. Organizations use four major conversion strategies: parallel, direct, pilot, and phased.

In a **parallel conversion,** the old system and the new system operate simultaneously for a period of time. That is, both systems process the same data at the same time, and the outputs are compared. This type of conversion is the most expensive but also the least risky. Most large systems have a parallel conversion process to lessen the risk.

In a **direct conversion,** the old system is cut off and the new system is turned on at a certain point in time. This type of conversion is the least expensive but the most risky if the new system doesn't work as planned. Few systems are implemented using this type of conversion, due to the risk involved.

A **pilot conversion** introduces the new system in one part of the organization, such as in one plant or in one functional area. The new system runs for a period of time and is assessed. After the new system works properly, it is introduced in other parts of the organization.

A **phased conversion** introduces components of the new system, such as individual modules, in stages. Each module is assessed, and when it works properly, other modules are introduced until the entire new system is operational.

Enterprise application integration (EAI) is often called the *middleware,* which you read about in Section 13.2. Interfaces were developed to map the major packages to a single conceptual framework that guides what all these packages do and the kinds of information they normally need to share. This conceptual framework could be used to translate the data and processes from each vendor's package to a common language. It is the only way to implement collaborative supply chain sharing of information.

XML is the technology that is being used by many EAI vendors in their cross-enterprise applications development. It can be thought of as a way of providing variable format messages that can be shared between any two computer systems, as long as they both understand the format (tags) that is (are) being used.

SDLC STAGES 7 AND 8: OPERATION AND MAINTENANCE

After conversion, the new system will operate for a period of time, until it no longer meets its objectives. Once the new system's operations are stabilized, *audits* are performed during operation to assess the system's capabilities and determine if it is being used correctly.

Systems need several types of maintenance. The first type is *debugging* the program, a process that continues throughout the life of the system. The second type is *updating* the system to accommodate changes in business conditions. An example would be adjusting to new governmental regulations (such as tax rate changes). These corrections and upgrades usually do not add any new functionality; they are necessary simply in order for the system to continue meeting its objectives. The third type of maintenance *adds new functionality* to the system—adding new features to the existing system without disturbing its operation.

1. Define the eight stages of the SDLC.
2. What is the difference between logical and physical design?
3. Explain logic errors and syntax errors.
4. Explain the feasibility tests and their importance.
5. Discuss the four conversion methods.

Key Terms

BPM mashup *396*

business activity monitoring
  (BAM) *394*

business process *390*

business process management
  (BPM) *394*

business process reengineering
  (BPR) *394*

critical path *404*

critical path method (CPM) *404*

critical task *404*

end-user development
  (computing) *402*

Gantt chart *403*

IT architecture *399*

logical system design *407*

physical system design *407*

prototyping *402*

service-oriented
  architecture (SOA) *391*

systems development
  lifecycle (SDLC) *405*

Web services *396*

Work Breakdown Structure
  (WBS) *403*

Chapter Highlights and Insights

(Numbers refer to Learning Objectives)

❶ New applications need to be connected to databases, other enterprise systems, and so on inside the organization. They may also be connected to partners' information systems. Web Services and service-oriented architecture (SOA) provide a way to reuse an organization's IT assets. Introducing new technology may require restructure or redesign of processes. Also, processes may need to be redesigned to fit standard software. Several methodologies exist for redesigning processes, notably BPR and BPM. IT can help in analyzing, combining, improving, and simplifying business processes.

❷ The three-tier architecture simplifies application development and BPM. An organization's software architecture can also be designed for greater flexibility by using a tiered model.

❸ Projects are managed by managing the triple constraints. The project scope is the definition of what the project is supposed to accomplish—its outcomes or deliverables. A project is made up of *tasks.*. Each task is assigned a duration, which is the difference between the task's start date and its end date. The project's time is determined by task durations and task dependencies. Some tasks are dependent on other tasks being completed before they can begin. For example, in construction, a hole must be dug before the pouring of concrete can start. Task durations and task dependencies determine the time required to complete the project. Projects have budgets that typically are exceeded due to scope creep.

❹ Building ISs in-house can be done by using the SDLC or by using prototyping or other methodologies, and it can be done by outsourcers, the IS department employees, or end users.

Questions for Discussion

1. What is a business process and how does it differ from an information system?
2. Why is it important for all business managers to understand business processes?
3. Review the Microsoft International opening case. Why was it necessary to standardize common HR business processes?
4. Why did many early BPR efforts fail?
5. Explain the relationship between BPM and SOA.
6. Why is there confusion among IT practitioners as to what SOA is?
7. Why does BPM begin with understanding current processes?
8. Discuss the reasons why end-user-developed IT systems can be of poor quality. What can be done to improve the situation?
9. Explain the three-tier IT architecture.
10. Explain why IT is an important enabler of business process redesign.
11. What is the critical path?
12. Explain the triple constraint.
13. Explain the stages of the SDLC.
14. Why are feasibility tests done?

Exercises and Projects

1. Visit *www-01.IBM.com/software/info/bpm/* and download the IBM BPM eKit. After reviewing the eKit, explain how BPM and enterprise architecture improve business outcomes.

2. Research open-source BPM software vendors. Create a table that lists five of these vendors, the software applications they provide, and their features.

3. Refer to the prior exercise. Redo the research but on proprietary BPM vendors. In the table, list the pricing options if they are available.

4. Examine some business processes at your university or in your company. Identify one process that needs to be redesigned to eliminate waste or inefficiencies. Diagram the existing tasks/activities in the process, and then diagram an improved process. Use modeling tools in Microsoft Word or one of the free BPM or workflow software tools.

5. Explore project management software on vendors' Web sites. Select a single project management package, download the demo, and try it. Make a list of the important features of the package. Be sure to investigate its Web, repository, and collaboration features. Report your findings to the class.

Group Assignments and Projects

1. As a group, design an information system for a start-up business of your choice. Describe your chosen IT resource acquisition strategy, and justify your choices of hardware, software, telecommunications support, and other aspects of a proposed system.

Internet Exercises

1. Visit Gartner at *gartner.com/technology/research/content/business_process_improvement.jsp*. Listen to the podcast "Tying BPM to Other IT Disciplines." The podcast is 11.5 minutes. Why is it important to link BPM to other IT disciplines?

2. Visit *ehow.com/how_4460942_use-excel-project-manage-ment.html* and read the four steps on "How to Use Excel for Project Management." You can also go to *ehow.com* and then search for this title. Then visit *ehow.com/video_2324033_plan-large-project.html* and read "How to Plan a Large Project" and watch the video. *Review* the capabilities of MS-Project for managing large projects. Prepare a report comparing the advantages and disadvantages of using Excel and MS-Project to manage a large IT project. In your comparison, assume that the IT project management team will consist of 10 users, each user has Excel 2007 or 2010 and Internet access, and no one has MS-Project.

3. Search the Internet to find recent material on the role BPM software plays in support of BPM. Select two vendors' software products and download/view their demos. In your opinion, how useful were the software products? For example, would they be helpful for both simple processes and complex processes? What skill level was needed to use the tools? Were they easy to learn *how to use*?

BUSINESS CASE

Mitsui Norin Balances Production and Inventory with BPM Analytics   POM

Mitsui Norin is one of Japan's largest tea manufacturers. At Mitsui Norin, production and inventory optimization are top priorities. Mr. Masahiko Iwasawa, the director of Production Management, explained that "sales of tea products and the amount of tea leaf procurement vary significantly by seasons. As we deal with foods, production volume optimization is strictly required to maintain quality. This is always quite a challenge. Keeping an *optimized balance between production and inventory* is essential to product quality."

Siloed Information Causes Production Inefficiency

Mitsui Norin were determining the optimal volume of tea production volume by collecting sales forecasts, shipment records, inventory level data, and production plans from different departments.

The tedious, manual process of data collection from different systems began with the production management team gathering data from each system, cross-referencing the data, and then analyzing them in spreadsheets. The team tracked between 600 and 1,000 parameters annually, and each spreadsheet had over 5,000 cells. Seven additional people were hired during peak periods to do the work, but the data analysis could not get done on time. The manual process made it impossible to predict inventory shortage accurately and make adjustments quickly. Production-adjustment decisions were based on staff's personal experiences, according to Mr. Iwasawa. Mr. Jyunetsu Sasaki, the director of Information System Department, explained that it was impossible to monitor the data in real-time because of the data silos and the time that it took to manually collect data for analysis.

Fujitsu's Interstage Business Process Manager

In April 2008, Mitsui Norin began implementing Fujitsu's Interstage Business Process Manager (BPM). The implementation was completed in three months. Interstage BPM (*fujitsu.com/global/services/software/interstage/solutions/bpm/*) provides managers and workers with the ability to monitor and analyze business in real-time, and detect and correct business issues early and quickly. The IT solution was implemented without modification to the existing systems and it helped users collect and analyze data to optimize their production processes.

Data-Driven Production Management

The team started by tracking 50 items and expanded the number of items gradually. Interstage BPM was used to build apps that tracked inventory levels for products and then alerted the group to restock when the levels hit a predefined reorder point. This solution helps remove delays in responding to inventory shortages or overstocks. "We now have an environment that lets us predict issues and respond to them before they actually happen. Moreover, our staff can concentrate on our core business processes such as improving production planning and preventing production mishaps," said Mr. Kitamura, manager of the Production Management Office. Mitsui Norin has successfully created the IT infrastructure that supports production-volume optimization and inventory-level optimization, and which can zero in on areas for process improvement.

Sources: Compiled from fujitsu.com/ and Interstage BPM Analytics (2009).

Questions

1. Explain the impact of data silos on business performance.
2. Why were adjustment decisions based on the staff's personal experiences? What problems would that create for Mitsui Norin?
3. What is needed for any type of optimization, such as volume optimization or inventory level optimization?

PUBLIC SECTOR CASE

SRV

Chilean Government Builds Four Soccer Stadiums for FIFA World Cup

In 1990 democracy returned to Chile. Sustained growth and economic development depended on rebuilding its decaying public infrastructure. Chile's Ministerio de Obras Publicas (Ministry of Public Infrastructure, or MOP) made substantial internal changes and adopted a new development model. The model focused on private concessions and a close working relationship with local city governments, which allowed for major upgrades of Chile's airports, seaports, roads, water systems and public buildings.

World Cup Becomes a National Project and Priority

The goal of President Michelle Bachelet and the Chilean government was to attract major sporting events. Chile won the right to host the 2008 Federation Internationale de Football Association (FIFA) Under-20 Women's World Cup. Preparing for the World Cup was identified as a national project sponsored by the Presidency of the Republic. This project had

presidential priority, and was embraced enthusiastically by Chile's residents.

Time and Resource Constraints on the Projects

Temuco, La Florida, Coquimbo, and Chillan were the four cities selected as venues for FIFA. Because none of the cities had soccer stadiums that met FIFA's strict regulations, Chile needed to build four new stadiums in only nine months. In addition to this time constraint, Chile also faced a resource shortage—not enough qualified people available to plan and execute the stadium projects.

MOP could not build four stadiums in nine months using the informal, decentralized methods of planning, managing, and executing projects that they had for projects in the past. Project timelines, costs, and requirements were too complex for outmoded project management principles and practices. MOP had to update project management techniques and practices.

Adopting Best Practices and Integrated Project Management Model

By adopting the latest standards from the Project Management Institute (PMI, *pmi.org/*), MOB was able to implement the structure it needed. Chile partnered with PMI Santiago de Chile chapter to develop what it called the *GIP model,* Gestión Integrada de Proyectos (Integrated Project Management). The approach was composed of the following:

- Extensive training program for its project managers
- Development of standardized project management processes based on the *Guide to the Project Management Body of Knowledge* (PMBOK® Guide)
- New organizational structure based on flexible project teams
- Implementation of a new IT platform for centralized coordination and virtual-team collaboration.

Using PMI standards, MOP created a small command team with a single project manager. In addition, each host city had its own team of three people who supervised stadium engineering and construction. In total there were 250 workers in each stadium for a total of 1,000 workers for the entire project.

Following PMI's standards, MOP aligned its staff at all levels of the organization, from the president to field workers, so that everyone would be committed to the project goal. If any level was not in alignment, the project would fail. Therefore, having a common vision and understanding of the plan, procedures, and ultimate goals were critical success factors.

Since a project's success depends largely on the tools that are available to the team, MOP implemented collaboration tools, monitoring and controlling tools, communication tools, and supervisory and reporting tools at each stadium. These technologies included collaborative technology platforms based on Microsoft® SharePoint, online communications, and document management tools. Virtual collaboration was a necessity because the distance between the farthest two stadiums was 2,000 km.

Successful Project Completion

The four-stadium project began in January 2008 with a $100 million budget. The stadiums were completed on time and on budget in late October 2008. The 2008 FIFA U-20 Women's World Cup was held in Chile from November 19 to December 7, 2008.

Based on the project's success, MOP is planning a new phase; to have one soccer stadium that meets FIFA standards in each Chilean city that has more than 200,000 residents—a commitment that requires an investment of more than $150 million by 2012.

Sources: Compiled from PMI.org (2009), *ThisisChile.cl,* and *Wikipedia.org.*

Questions

1. Identify the types of problems and challenges that Chile faced after winning the bid to host the 2008 FIFA U-20 Women's World Cup.
2. What type of commitment and support was critical to the success of this project? Explain why.
3. What were the project constraints?
4. Why was virtual teamwork needed?
5. Describe the IT infrastructure supporting the project.
6. Why was the project a success?

MODELING USING ARIS EXPRESS AND BLUEPRINT

Modeling a Business Process and Brainstorming a Business Strategy

ARIS Express is a BPM modeling tool based on industry standards. A free, downloadable feature-rich version is available from *http://www.ariscommunity.com/aris-express/how-to-start.* Support features on the Web site are installation instructions, quick reference, and video tutorials.

1. To get started with ARIS, download and install ARIS Express.
2. View the video tutorial "How to Model Business Processes" to learn how to model process steps in ARIS Express and understand the meaning of symbols used in the "business process" model type. View other tutorials, as needed.
3. Create a new model type. Select business process as the model type.
4. Design and develop a model of a business process. Review your model for any missed steps or other omissions. Edit as needed.

5. Download the BPM Blueprint 30-day trial and the demo from *http://www-01.ibm.com/software/integration/bpm-blueprint/.* Model the process you've completed in #4 with this software tool.
6. Which BPM modeling tool did you prefer? Why?
7. View the ARIS Express video tutorial "How to Model a Whiteboard" to learn how to structure ideas and tasks with a Whiteboard model. Then use the Whiteboard to model a brainstorming session related to a business plan. For example, you could brainstorm ideas about how to manage a new project to use social media and 2D tags to market a new product or service. To what extent did the Whiteboard tool make planning the project easier? Explain.

References

ARIS Express, *ariscommunity.com/aris-express/how-to-start/*

CIO Magazine, "SOA Consortium and CIO Magazine Announce Winners of SOA Case Study Competition," 2009. *soa-consortium.org/*

Financial Industry Regulatory Authority (FINRA), 2010. *finra.org/About FINRA*

Fujitsu.com/

Hogue, F., "Handling the Census Handheld Debacle," *Baseline.com,* April 15, 2008.

Holmes, A., "Census Program to Use Handheld Computers Said to Be in 'Serious Trouble,'" *GovernmentExecutive.com,* January 2, 2008. *govexec.com/dailyfed/0108/010208h1.htm/*

Interstage BPM Analytics, "Mitsui Norin optimizes production and inventory with Interstage BPM Analytics," November 2009. *fujitsu.com/downloads/EU/uk/pdf/industries/manufacturingservices/mitsui-norin.pdf*

Microsoft.com, 2010.

Oracle BAM, 2010. *oracle.com/appserver/business-activity-monitoring.html*

PMI.org, "Game On," 2009. *pmi.org/Business-Solutions/OPM3-Case-Study-Library.aspx*

SOA Consortium, 2010. *blog.soa-consortium.org/*

U.S Census Bureau, Press Release 2008. *census.gov/*

Visio 2010, microsoft.com

Chapter 14

Global Ecology, Ethics, and Social Responsibility

Learning Objectives

❶ Understand how IT and users can reduce carbon emissions and hence global warming, which harms the planet, through green business practices and data center designs that conserve natural resources.

❷ Understand the trade-offs associated with the conveniences and competitive advantages that IT offers.

❸ Recognize the impacts of *constant connectivity* and distractions on quality of life, business, safety, and interpersonal relationships.

❹ Understand the key trends and forecasts for IT.

Integrating *IT*

 ACC
 FIN
 MKT
 OM
 HRM
IS

CHAPTER 14 LINK LIBRARY

QUICK LOOK at Chapter 14, Global Ecology, Ethics, and Social Responsibility

This section introduces you to the business issues, challenges, and IT solutions in Chapter 14. Topics and issues mentioned in the Quick Look are explained in the chapter.

Tackling global warming by reducing emissions of carbon dioxide (CO_2) and other greenhouse gases (GHGs) is high on the list of global challenges. **Carbon footprint** refers to the amount of CO_2 and other GHGs emitted by a particular activity (e.g., driving cars), industry (e.g., auto manufacturing), or value chain (e.g., telecom value chain). Roughly 72 percent of GHGs are made up of CO_2. A carbon footprint is typically measured in **MtCO2e,** which stands for **metric tonne (ton) carbon dioxide equivalent.** Annual emissions are generally measured in gigatonnes (billions of tonnes) of carbon dioxide equivalent per year (GtCO2e/y).

A carbon footprint is a way to measure the impact of the carbon-producing activities of an individual, organization, or industry sector on the environment via climate change and global warming. All carbon emissions worldwide make up the *global carbon footprint.*

The IT sector, including computing and telecommunications, is responsible for an estimated 2 to 3 percent of the global carbon footprint as a result of emissions from the energy used to run servers, computers, and other hardware. That 2 to 3 percent can be cut in half by switching to low-emission data centers, placing them in cold climates to reduce the energy needed to cool the heat-generating hardware, and buying ecofriendly hard drives with considerably reduced power consumption, as shown in Figure 14.1.

Figure 14.1 Ecofriendly computing. Computer hard drive with considerably reduced power consumption by manufacturer Western Digital. (© *Olaf Kowalzik-editorial collection/Alamy*)

IT can play a greater role by helping reduce the remaining 97 to 98 percent of the GtCO2e/y from other industries. One example is replacing commuting and long-distance travel, when feasible, with collaboration and telework tools, Web-based meetings, and other IT applications to significantly reduce transportation carbon emissions. Innovative IT solutions can both provide a better quality of life and contribute to dramatically reduced emissions. That is, quality of life and reduced emissions do not involve a trade-off.

Governments and industry associations have introduced a range of programs on IT and the environment to address global warming and energy use. And business associations continue to develop initiatives to reduce energy consumption and to demonstrate corporate social responsibility.

In this chapter, we examine the greening of computing and IT's role in reducing global warming. We take a closer look at IT ethical responsibilities and impacts on people's lives. Social media has negative consequences, as "reporting" of personal text messages and activities becomes more invasive, abusive, engineered (faked), and sensational. The Internet, real-time data analysis, mobile communications, automated decision making, and social media create capabilities, which carry ethical responsibilities.

GOV   ETHICS   IS

IT Carbon Footprint

Global warming is the upward trend in global mean temperature (GMT) and one of the most complicated issues facing world leaders. Warnings from the scientific community point to dangers from the ongoing buildup of CO_2 and greenhouse gases, mostly from the burning of fossil fuels and forests (U.S. Global Change Research Program, *globalchange.gov/*). Global warming is the theory that the earth's atmosphere is warming because of the release of greenhouse gases (GHGs) from burning gas, oil, coal, wood, and other resources, which then holds heat in, similar to the walls of a greenhouse. The **greenhouse effect** refers to the holding of heat within the earth's atmosphere by certain GHGs—such as CO_2, methane (CH_4), and nitrous oxide (N_2O)—that absorb infrared radiation (IR), as diagrammed in Figure 14.2. Scientists predict that the increased temperature and sea level rise from global warming will adversely affect the earth's biodiversity.

Keeling Curve

The rise of CO_2 gas in our atmosphere has been measured continuously since 1958 and follows an oscillating (squiggle) and upward line known as the **Keeling curve,** named after Dr. Charles David Keeling, professor at Scripps Institution of Oceanography. An expert on the way carbon moves through the ecosystem, Keeling was the first to measure CO_2 in the atmosphere on a continuous basis, rather than on a monthly or yearly basis. Figure 14.3 shows the upward movement of the Keeling curve of increasing CO_2 concentration. The measurements are made at a station on top of Mauna Loa in Hawaii. Note carefully the magnitude of the increase from 1958 through 2010. The most recent data can be found at

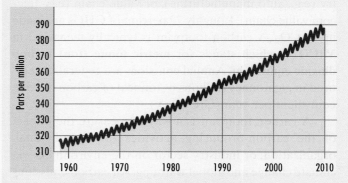

Figure 14.3 The Keeling curve tracks changes in the concentration of CO_2 in the earth's atmosphere at a Mauna Loa research station. (*Courtesy of Scripps CO_2 Program, 2010, and National Oceanic and Atmospheric Administration (Source: NOAA.gov/).*

Figure 14.2 Earth's greenhouse effect. Greenhouse gases absorb infrared radiation (IR) emitted from the earth and reradiate it back, thus contributing to the greenhouse effect.

scrippsco2.ucsd.edu. The Keeling curve has become the symbol of the ever-changing chemistry of the earth's atmosphere and the associated warming of the planet.

Scientists have determined that we should aim to stabilize the concentration of GHGs in the atmosphere in the range of 450 to 550 parts per million (ppm). This is higher than the present level of roughly 400 ppm, which in turn is higher than the level of only 228 ppm before the Industrial Revolution. To stabilize, emissions per year must peak within the next 10 to 20 years and then fall at a rate of 2 percent a year. By 2050, GHG emissions must be about a quarter less than they are now. What is more, because the world economy is expected to expand, the rate per unit of GDP (gross domestic product) will have to be much lower, perhaps only a quarter of the current level.

For Class Discussion and Debate

1. Scenario for Brainstorming and Discussion: Investments in energy-conserving data centers or other computing facilities can reduce the long-term costs of ownership and maintenance. But organizations need to pay upfront premiums to invest in green computers that are both energy efficient and environmentally responsible. Organizations that have invested in green hardware find that the energy savings, extended product life cycle, positive public image, and other benefits have exceeded the additional costs of that hardware—improving net profit.

a. Given this situation, in your opinion, why wouldn't companies invest in energy-saving IT and business practices?

b. In your opinion, why aren't managers more concerned with global warming and the greenhouse effect? That is, why aren't all levels of management concerned enough about the health of current and future generations and the planet to make investments to reduce GHGs?

c. What can you do to reduce your carbon footprint and still meet your responsibilities? (Skipping class to reduce driving would not meet both those criteria.) What would motivate you to take those actions? Why is reducing your carbon footprint so difficult?

2. Debate: To increase payback from its green initiatives, customers would have to learn that the company was *green*, and they'd also need to be concerned about the dangers of global warming. Debate the most effective and cost-effective ways for companies to promote their green public image and convince customers of the value of green efforts.

14.1 IT's Role in Reducing the Global Carbon Footprint

The IT industry sector (called *information and communications technology*, or ICT, in emission reports) has supported economic growth in developed and developing countries. But what impact does our expanding IT dependence have on global warming? And how can business processes be changed to make use of IT to reduce greenhouse gases? And what alternative energy sources can be used to power the increasing demands for telecommunications (telecom)? We examine several reports and initiatives to help answer these important questions.

GLOBAL E-SUSTAINABILITY INITIATIVE AND THE SMART 2020 REPORT

The Climate Group's **SMART 2020 Report** (*theclimategroup.org/programs/ict/*) is the world's first comprehensive global study of the IT sector's growing significance for the world's climate.

In 2008, **The Climate Group,** on behalf of the **Global e-Sustainability Initiative** (GeSI, *gesi.org/*), found that ICT is a key sector in the struggle to reduce climate warming. Transforming the way people and businesses use IT could reduce annual human-caused global emissions by 15 percent by 2020 and deliver energy-efficiency savings to global businesses of over 500 billion euros, or US $800 billion. And using social media, for example, to inform consumers of the grams (g) of carbon emissions associated with the products they buy could change buyer behavior and, ultimately, have a positive environmental effect. Like food items that display calories and grams of fat to help consumers make healthier food choices, product labels display grams of CO_2 emissions, as shown in Figure 14.4.

Figure 14.4 Label showing the amount of CO_2 emissions produced in the making of a bag of Walkers crisps in the United Kingdom.(© Alex Segre/Alamy)

According to analysis conducted by international management consultants McKinsey & Company, which were listed in the SMART 2020 Report:

• The IT sector's own footprint of 2 percent of global emissions could double by 2020 because of increased demand for smartphones and other hardware, software, and services. To help, rather than worsen, the fight against climate change, the IT sector must manage its own growing impact and continue to reduce emissions from data centers, telecom networks, and the manufacture and use of its products.

• IT has the unique ability to monitor and maximize energy efficiency both within and outside of its own industry sector and cut CO_2 emissions by 7.8 GtCO2e/y by 2020, which is greater than the 2010 annual emissions of either the United States or China.

TOWARD A LOW-CARBON ECONOMY IN THE INFORMATION AGE

At least 4 billion people are mobile phone users. By 2020, the number of users is expected to double to 8 billion. Not only will more people get connected, but things will, too: There could be 50 billion machine-to-machine connections in 2020. The good news is that information from these machines could help monitor our environmental impacts and emissions.

From smart meters to smart grids, The Climate Group is working with members and partners, such as Google and Cisco, to build on the enormous potential and economic opportunities of IT in the low-carbon economy. Fortunately, the IT industry has the potential to reduce global GHG emissions by up to 30 percent. Many industries can make use of the latest IT to move into higher-efficiency low-carbon markets. But better use of IT to shift away from existing energy-intensive work habits and lifestyles will depend on government policy innovations, incentives for companies, and the active participation of consumers.

The SMART 2020 Report gives a clear picture of the key role that the IT industry plays in addressing climate change globally and facilitating efficient and low-carbon development. The role of IT includes emission reduction and energy savings not only in the IT sector itself, but also in transforming how and where people work. The most obvious ways are by substituting digital formats—telework, videoconferencing, e-paper, and mobile and e-commerce—for physical formats. Researchers estimate that replacing physical products/services with their digital equivalents would provide about 6 percent of the benefits the IT sector can deliver. But if IT is applied to other industries, then the benefits in terms of lower GHG emissions would be even greater. Examples of those industries include smart building design and use, smart logistics, smart electricity grids, and smart industrial motor systems.

"Smart" means that wasted energy and materials are minimized and that procurement, manufacturing, distribution, service, and recycling are done in an environmentally friendly manner.

GREEN IT AND MOBILE SOLUTIONS IN DEVELOPED AND DEVELOPING NATIONS

In this section, you read of several impressive green power initiatives and efforts at sustainability. **Sustainability,** whether applied to energy, technology, or consumption of resources in general, refers to the concept of using things at a rate that does not deplete their availability in future generations. In environmental terms, a process or industry is *unsustainable* when it uses up natural resources faster than they can be replenished.

These examples give you a wider perspective on how mobile initiatives and changes in behavior and business processes are reducing GHG and soot emissions worldwide, including on Vanuatu, a volcanic archipelago of 82 islands in the South Pacific.

• Isotrak's (*isotrak.com/*) fleet management system is designed to help U.K. businesses cut fuel costs and CO2e emissions, reduce fleet size, and save staff time. Isotrak's fleet management system combines satellite tracking and onboard telematics data sent over the Vodafone mobile network using standard SIM cards. This IS enables businesses to monitor their fleets remotely and plan more efficient logistics based on where vehicles travel, what they carry, and how they are driven. Isotrak estimates that by changing driving styles, for example, fuel efficiency is improved by up to 15 percent.

• Using Isotrak's system, the U.K. supermarket chain Asda's fleet saved 29 million kilometers, or 28 KtCO2e, and cut fuel costs by 23 percent over three years. Asda drivers have changed their behavior to improve fuel efficiency by 6.6 percent, and the system is also enabling Asda to haul more waste and recyclable materials between stores and distribution centers, minimizing the number of trucks running without full loads.

• The **GSMA *Green Power for Mobile* (GPM) program** (*wirelessintelligence.com/green-power/*) was launched in 2008 to advance the use of renewable energy sources by the mobile industry. Achieving this target will cut diesel fuel costs by $2.5 billion, cut carbon emissions by up to 6.8 million tons per year, and connect 118 million people in developing countries to mobile networks using green power. Using the Google Earth plugin (*earth.google.com/plugin/*), you can search and view in 3D the global mobile deployments at *wirelessintelligence.com/green-power/*.

The *GSMA Development Fund* (*gsmworld.com/*) has delivered mobile green projects in Namibia (Africa) and on Vanuatu through its GPM program, which has been established to promote the use of green power to achieve two commercial objectives.

1. To expand mobile networks into regions currently lacking coverage. The GSMA's Green Power for Mobile (GPM) program has the goal of helping the mobile industry use renewable energy sources, such as solar, wind, and sustainable biofuels to power 118,000 new and existing off-grid base stations in developing countries by 2012. Figure 14.5 shows a GSM base station.

2. To reduce diesel fuel consumption by telecom (telecommunications) operators. Solar, wind, and **sustainable biofuels** would replace diesel fuel. Although diesel emits less carbon dioxide than gasoline, diesel can emit 25 to 400 times more mass of particulate black carbon and associated organic matter (soot) per kilometer or mile. *IT at Work 14.1* explains biofuels.

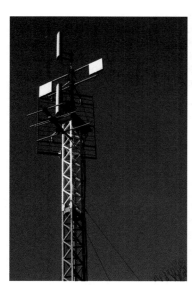

Figure 14.5 GSM cellular base station. (© *Tomislav Stajduhar/ iStockphoto*)

IT at Work 14.1

South Africa Use of Biofuels Cuts Energy and Creates Local Employment

South Africa's MTN Group (*mtn.com/*) is the leading mobile telecommunications company operating in Africa and the Middle East. As part of its network rollout, MTN has installed more power-efficient base stations. The new-generation network also uses 40 to 60 percent less power than its predecessor, helping reduce the cost of provisioning, while increasing the capacity of the network.

In Nigeria, MTN conducted research on biofuel-powered generators. Tests were completed using locally produced biofuels. Three base stations in the Badagry region have been running on biodiesel produced from locally grown soybeans. The project has forged many local partnerships in preparation for the local growth and processing of crops, for the long-term solution. The use of soybean biofuel has, in turn, created local employment.

Karel Pienaar, chief technology and information officer of MTN Group, commented on the value of the program to the company, the local community, and the environment:

> MTN regards the Biofuels Programme to be of great importance. We are working with our partners the

GSMA and Ericsson to develop an environmentally friendly, self-sustainable, cost effective solution to extending mobile coverage into remote and rural parts of Nigeria, and potentially the rest of Africa where MTN is operating. I am personally excited that the Biofuels Programme could create employment for tens of thousands of agricultural workers, whose labour will bring communications to their villages for the first time, placing the mobile industry at the forefront of social development.

Sources: Compiled from MTN Group (2010), Biofuels Programme (2007), and GSMWorld.com.

Discussion Questions: What factors contributed to the success of the biofuels program in Nigeria? What payback did MTM expect and achieve from this program?

The ecological importance of the vendor-neutral GPM program is not evident until you understand that many regions of the world don't have access to electricity grids. Since electricity is needed to power mobile networks, off-grid base stations are built to generate their own power. In Nigeria, for example, only 25 percent of mobile base stations are connected to the electricity grid, which means that telecom operators generate power using ecologically damaging diesel fuel to run the other 75 percent of the base stations. Africa alone consumes over 30 million liters of diesel fuel per year to power off-grid base stations. That's an average of 18,000 liters of diesel fuel per base station per year. As such, use of alternative energy sources (solar, wind, and sustainable biofuels) has successfully reduced harmful emissions and global warming. Note that these are commercial ventures of telecoms, which have improved the profitability of telecoms in the long run. There are also green initiatives that companies can undertake, as well as partnerships sponsored by local, regional, and national government, which are discussed next.

WORLDWIDE TELECOM INDUSTRY CAN LEAD THE LOW-CARBON REVOLUTION

In 2010, the worldwide telecoms industry was responsible for 183 million MtCO2e/y, or 0.7 percent, a reasonable amount considering that it represents 2 percent of global GDP. The average European mobile phone user is responsible for around 17 kg of CO_2 emissions per year. The average fixed and Internet user will emit 44 kg. These performance statistics are only slightly influenced by the desire to be green because mobile phones are already very power-efficient in order to have longer battery life, and power savings in fixed networks are mainly driven by the desire to control costs. Given these levels of CO_2 emissions, the telecoms industry is relatively ecofriendly.

Distribution of the carbon (CO_2) footprint across the Telecom value chain, 2008–2009

| Chipsets 8.4% | Components 9.4% | Network infrastructure 4.2% | Telecom services 54.5% | Terminal equipment 5.0% | End user 16.0% | Disposal & recycling 2.6% |

Figure 14.6 Telecom value chain's carbon footprint.

Each part of the telecom value chain, shown in Figure 14.6, is responsible for important CO_2 emissions, and reductions are possible in each part of that value chain. As the telecoms market grows, so will its emissions, unless specific measures are implemented by all players in the carbon chain.

There are four carbon hotspots where significant CO_2 savings can be achieved. The first two hotspots are under the control of telecom operators and vendors. The other two hotspots are under the control of users—and hopefully will motivate you to reduce your carbon emissions. End users account for a substantial 16 percent of the telecom footprint (see Figure 14.6).

1. Data centers. The numerous pieces of IT equipment needed to run networks effectively and manage their client bases are energy guzzlers. IT equipment vendors now offer much greener equipment; overall, data center management, cooling, and recycling can significantly reduce costs and CO_2 emissions. Data centers are discussed later in this chapter.

2. Radio base stations. Millions of mobile radio base stations have to run at full power 24/7/365 worldwide. Equipment vendors are developing smart solutions to reduce power consumption. As you read, off-grid solutions are using alternative fuels.

3. Fixed network access equipment. Routers, switches, and modems operated by end users are inefficient machines that could be significantly greener. Household broadband modems, built at the lowest possible cost, are power guzzlers. Users can invest in ecofriendly equipment and take the responsibility to manually switch off their equipment when not in use.

4. Mobile handsets. Mobiles consume very little electric power, but are a threat to the environment because millions of phones are being produced and disposed of. Recycling practices are very poor, with only 5 percent of discarded handsets properly disposed of. If users slowed their renewal rates (tough with new iPhones and Sprint's 4G phones) or ensured that their old equipment was properly recycled, this carbon hotspot could be reduced.

FINANCIAL BENEFITS OF REDUCING IT POWER CONSUMPTION

The Internet is composed of huge numbers of power-consuming, heat-generating *servers* running 24/7/365 worldwide, and *routers* that direct data packets over *networks* to their destination IP (Internet Protocol) addresses on *client machines*—computers and mobiles. Most servers are housed in data centers that must be cooled continuously. Harvard University physicist Alex Wissner-Gross (*CO2stats.com*) studied the Web overall and reported in 2009 that it takes on average about 20 milligrams of CO_2 per second to visit a Web site. Google's massive data centers around the world handle over 200 million searches daily; this power consumption has a definite environmental impact. And as you have read, the global IT industry generates about 2 to 3 percent of global CO_2 emissions, or about as much greenhouse gases as the world's airlines.

Bottom Line of Green Computing High energy costs together with the growing power consumption of computing and communications technologies are having a direct, negative impact on many businesses' bottom lines. There is also a growing desire among consumers to shrink their carbon consumption (like switching to vehicles that get more miles per gallon or kilometers per liter) and increase the use of recycled and recyclable materials. But the business case for green computing is not always compelling enough for companies to invest in it and make the necessary process changes. *IT at Work 14.2* discusses the three biggest myths about green IT.

IT at Work 14.2

Green IT Myths

All hardware manufacturers offer systems that meet stringent standards for efficiency and sustainable manufacturing. Lead and toxic materials are eliminated or minimized, and data centers are consuming less energy. While it may seem that going green is a common goal, it's the actual execution that matters. Here are three green IT myths managers need to understand.

Myth #1: The business case for green IT is clear. Trying to quantify the cost savings of green IT may be impossible or non-applicable if cloud computing is used. The beneficiary of energy-efficient servers is not the company, but its outsourcer. For in-house servers and other hardware, energy costs may not be broken down enough for anyone to know what the savings would be. So the issue of who realizes the cost benefits is unclear, and that makes it tricky to pinpoint the real payback drivers for a given green project. Once a company can track the energy use of specific equipment, and break it down by business units, it becomes possible to incentivize and recognize those departments (like IT) that drive improvements.

Myth #2: Green IT is an achievable outcome. Green IT is an ongoing process and includes policies that define a way of operating over the long term. Companies don't achieve green and then quit. Energy efficiency and environmentally responsible manufacturing need to be made a part of hardware procurement policy. Industry standards like EPEAT and ENERGY STAR (discussed

in this chapter) change. We're now on ENERGY STAR 5.0, which means the standards keep ramping up and will again. As green technology evolves, so do the standards, making green IT a continuous improvement process.

Myth #3: Everyone cares about green IT. The Society for Information Management (SIM) surveyed CIOs and IT executive leaders about their top priorities for 2010, based on a list of 20 IT and business concerns. Green IT wasn't one of them. The two top priorities were *cost reduction* because of the recession and alignment of IT and the business. Companies are concerned with costs—and so are the public and nonprofit sectors. To get management's attention, green IT initiatives should be described in terms of reducing waste and inefficiency. But even that tactic may be a tough sell if prior IT investments touted as reducing waste and inefficiency did not achieve those objectives.

Sources: Compiled from Alvares (2010) and Chickowski (2009).

Discussion Questions: Discuss the implications of these three myths. If you can't sell *green IT* as a concept to management, identify a way to package and present the concept. Viewing the slideshow *CIO Priorities for 2010* on *Baseline.com* at *baselinemag.com/c/a/IT-Management/CIO-Priorities-for-2010-706071/* may be helpful.

While not often recognized, there are financial benefits associated with becoming a sustainable company. Three leading benefits are:

- Cost savings by limiting waste and consumption of natural resources
- New business opportunities through environmentally friendly product innovations
- Enhanced brand value and reputation with customers, partners, and others.

Green computing, the study and practice of ecofriendly computing resources, may be in companies' best financial interests, as you will read next.

VIRTUALIZATION IN DATA CENTERS

At the heart of the "Next Generation Data Center" strategy is the ability to deliver and support secure IT applications through **virtualization.** Virtualization is about efficient use of available resources. With energy and power costs increasing as the size of IT infrastructures grow, holding expenses to a minimum is a top priority for many CIOs. Data center virtualization means that servers are consolidated (integrated) so that they can be shared. Most stand-alone servers are highly underutilized. Virtualization technology optimizes the capacity and processing power of servers so that fewer servers are needed to provide the necessary processing power. Two examples are provided here:

1. Microsoft's commitment to green technology heavily leverages virtualization because of its massive data centers. Data centers are where virtualization can have the greatest impact, and that's where leading companies in the virtualization market are investing their resources. Virtualized, dynamic data centers lower energy consumption, reduce the number of servers needed, and extend server life. The benefits of longer server life are less manufacturing and less toxic materials in landfills.

2. By consolidating and moving to more efficient data centers, Sun increased processing power by over 450 percent with about one-half the servers, and achieved an increase in storage capacity of over 240 percent with about one-third the storage devices.

GLOBAL GREEN
REGULATIONS

Global regulations also are influencing green business practices. Sustainability regulations such as RoHS (*rohs.eu* and *rohs.gov.uk*) in the European Union (EU) will increasingly impact how supply chains function regardless of location. The RoHS directive stands for "the restriction of the use of certain hazardous substances in electrical and electronic equipment." For example, EU member states ensured that beginning in July 2006, new electrical and electronic equipment put on the market would not contain any of six banned substances—lead, mercury, cadmium, hexavalent chromium, polybrominated biphenyls (PBB), and polybrominated diphenyl ethers (PBDE)—in quantities exceeding maximum concentration values. Moreover, China has passed its own RoHS legislation.

Similar legislation is developing elsewhere. For example, California's Electronic Waste Recycling Act (EWRA) prohibits the sale of electronic devices banned by the EU's RoHS, including CRTs, LCDs, and other products that contain the four heavy metals restricted by RoHS. In addition, many states have enacted mercury and PBDE bans, and several are considering bills similar to EWRA. For example, Seattle has issued many regulations related to eliminating paper-based manuals and mandating recycling.

Ecofriendly practices reduce costs and improve public relations in the long run. Not surprisingly, demand for green computers is on the rise. A tool to help companies find such hardware is the Electronic Product Environmental Assessment Tool, or EPEAT.

EPEAT and ENERGY STAR. Maintained by the Green Electronics Council (GEC), the **Electronic Product Environmental Assessment Tool (EPEAT)** is a searchable database of computer hardware that meets a strict set of environmental criteria. Among other criteria, products registered with EPEAT comply with the U.S. government's ENERGY STAR 5.0 rating (see *energystar.gov*); have reduced levels of cadmium, lead, and mercury; and are easier to upgrade and recycle. ENERGY STAR products use less energy. Depending on how many criteria they meet, products receive a gold, silver, or bronze certification rating.

The EPEAT rates computers and monitors on a number of environmental criteria, including energy efficiency, materials used, product longevity, takeback programs, and packaging.

Stand-alone data centers and buildings that house large data centers can now earn the ENERGY STAR label (see Figure 14.7). To earn the label, data centers must be in the top 25 percent of their peers in energy efficiency according to the EPA's energy performance scale. By improving efficiency, centers can save energy and money and help fight climate change.

Traveling this summer? Check Into an ENERGY STAR Labeled Hotel. In May 2010, the EPA began this campaign to encourage travelers to bring their green on the road and choose hotels that have earned EPA's ENERGY STAR. Hotels that have earned the ENERGY STAR perform in the top 25 percent of hotels nationwide, use at least 35 percent less energy, and emit at least 35 percent less greenhouse gas emissions than their peers, making an environmentally friendly lodging choice a snap when planning a summer vacation.

Figure 14.7 ENERGY STAR label. (© *Art Directors & TRIP/Alamy*)

TELEWORK

Telework can minimize damaging the environment or depleting natural resources by reducing pollution. Also called telecommuting or virtual work, it offers many green benefits, including reducing rush-hour traffic, improving air quality, improving highway safety, and even improving healthcare. See Table 14.1 for a list of potential benefits.

TABLE 14.1	Benefits of Telework	
Individuals	**Organizations**	**Community and Society**
• Reduces or eliminates travel-related time and expenses • Improves health by reducing stress related to compromises made between family and work responsibilities • Allows closer proximity to and involvement with family • Allows closer bonds with the family and the community • Decreases involvement in office politics • Increases productivity despite distractions	• Reduces office space needed • Increases labor pool and competitive advantage in recruitment • Provides compliance with Americans with Disabilities Act • Decreases employee turnover, absenteeism, and sick leave usage • Improves job satisfaction and productivity	• Conserves energy and lessens dependence on foreign oil • Preserves the environment by reducing traffic-related pollution and congestion • Reduces traffic accidents and resulting injuries or deaths • Reduces the incidence of disrupted families because people do not have to quit their jobs if they need to move because of a spouse's new job or family obligations • Increases employment opportunities for the homebound • Allows the movement of job opportunities to areas of high unemployment

Review Questions

1. What is green computing?
2. Explain global warming and the greenhouse effect.
3. What does the Keeling curve track?
4. What are some low-carbon alternatives to fossil fuels, such as diesel?
5. What is the role of virtualization in green data centers?
6. How does RoHS in the European Union help protect the environment?
7. What are EPEAT and ENERGY STAR?
8. What are the benefits of telework?

14.2 IT Ethical Issues and Responsibility

Does the availability of information justify its use? Can shoppers keep their buying habits, online gaming, and other legal activities private? Does the media have the right to publish or post highly private text messages of politicians, celebrities, or others in the news?

Questions about data access and capture, tracking and monitoring, privacy and profiling are examples of IT capabilities that have ethical considerations. And there are no easy or agreed-upon answers to these dilemmas. We look at a few of the most contentious ethical issues and what, if any, responsibility is associated with the use of information.

SOCIAL MEDIA MONITORING

Social media monitoring may be considered an integral component of social media strategies because it gives marketers the ability to discover public conversations about their brands and, if necessary, respond to posters directly or to their posts. Opponents of monitoring define it as spying and an intolerable invasion of privacy.

In mid-2010, the use of social media monitoring came under fire from the U.K.'s national *Daily Mail* newspaper over revelations that a number of large brands, including networking retailer BT, budget airline easyJet, mobile phone retailer Carphone Warehouse, and Lloyds TSB bank, were using specialized software to spy on customers. These companies used specially developed software to scan for negative comments about their brands on the social media sites Twitter, Facebook, and YouTube. The companies then contacted some of the complainants in an attempt to solve their problems. While some customers and others were outraged, not all those contacted were offended. Companies defended their use of monitoring software by explaining that there was nothing sinister about the practice.

Why did companies risk angering customers by letting them know of the monitoring? Because research has found that negative comments by a frustrated customer on social media sites can lose a company as many as 30 other customers. Given that situation, you can see that the risk of not contacting the complaining customer to resolve the problem may be higher. General Motors, for example, doubled its team of social media agents in March 2010 to become more proactive in responding to customers' online complaints and repair its tarnished post-bankruptcy image. Privacy advocates were angered by the "outright spying," while legal experts claimed that firms making unsolicited approaches to customers could be violating the U.K.'s data protection laws. There are also fears that the software will be used to spam customers with sales pitches and advertising, or be used by political parties to exert pressure or control.

Privacy Sensitivity. Because of privacy scandals in 2010 surrounding **Facebook** and **Google,** the public in general is extremely sensitive to the issue of privacy. The *Daily Mail* has a history of attacks on social media and a reputation for stirring up moral outrage, for example, by publishing an article titled "How Using Facebook Could Raise Your Risk of Cancer" in February 2009. Campaigns against social media monitoring that incite privacy concerns could have huge implications for social media strategies.

Competing Responsibilities. There are competing interests and trade-offs at work when the issue is privacy. And there's not a clear-cut framework for deciding what is ethical and what's not. The personal privacy vs. public's security debate is a prime example. Typically, invasion of privacy is considered unethical. An ethically conscious corporate attitude sounds politically correct, but managers also have responsibility to stakeholders. Monitoring may be the responsible thing to do. And with intense competition, marketers naturally want to use every tool or technique to gain an edge or nullify a risk.

Globalization, the Internet, and connectivity have the power to undermine moral responsibility because it becomes relatively easy to ignore the harm that might be done to others. Despite the challenges and lack of clear answers, ethics is important because it has become clear that relying on the law alone to safeguard the community is insufficient. The law has its limits in large part because it changes so slowly.

URBAN PLANNING WITH WIRELESS SENSOR NETWORKS

Should IT be applied to social situations when it has the ability to provide benefits? If the answer is yes, the next question is: Who pays for it? The answer to the second question is tougher. In this section, we point out challenges more than we recommend solutions.

Traffic jams and parking problems in congested cities cause air and noise pollution, wasted fuel, stress, delays, and lost revenues. Studies of traffic congestion in New York and Los Angeles have found that drivers cruising for a parking space are a major source of gridlock. Disturbing results from studies conducted on behalf of urban planning efforts include the following:

• A study released in June 2008 by Transportation Alternatives *(transalt.org)*, a public transit advocacy group, reported that 28 to 45 percent of traffic on some streets in New York City is generated by people circling the block searching for parking. Drivers searching for parking within a 15-block area on Manhattan's Upper West Side drove 366,000 miles a year. Traffic congestion costs $13 billion in lost revenue and 50,000 jobs in the city annually for workers who are late for work once too often.

• Analysis conducted in Los Angeles by Donald Shoup, an urban planning professor at UCLA, found that over the course of a year, the search for curbside parking in a 15-block business district resulted in 950,000 excess vehicle miles of travel. Those wasted miles are the equivalent to 38 trips around the earth, and they consume

47,000 gallons of gas and produce 730 tons of the greenhouse gas carbon dioxide (CO_2) (Markoff, 2008).

These adverse effects can be reduced by implementing sensors and wireless networks—paid for by taxpayers who may not drive. In late 2008, the city of San Francisco initiated the most ambitious trial to date of a wireless sensor network that announces which parking spaces are free at any moment. The trial involved 6,000 of its 24,000 metered parking spaces. The system alerts drivers of empty parking places either by displays on street signs or via maps on their smartphone screens. In addition, the system can be extended so that drivers may even be able to pay for parking by cell phones and add funds to their parking meters from their phones without having to return to the meter. Solving the parking crisis takes on greater significance in San Francisco when you consider that a 19-year-old man was stabbed to death during a fight over a parking space—and calculate the GHG emissions due to all the excess driving around looking for parking.

Streetline (*streetlinenetworks.com*) is a company that provides city infrastructure technologies to improve urban operations through reliable information. Over the years, parking operations have become increasingly complex, and parking management has assumed a central role in the economic health of cities. But the quality of information to reduce their impacts has not kept up.

Streetline's product line includes *congestion management systems* that consist of parking sensors and wireless networked meters. The sensors, engineered using the same principles that make a compass operate, create a unique parking signature for each vehicle; they can determine, based on variations in parking angles and size of vehicles, when a parking space is filled, when a vehicle departs, and when a new vehicle replaces it. Wireless networked meters enable parking officials to instantly identify who has or has not paid, as well as the total revenue for parking by meter and street, based on the time of day or the day of the week.

Presence, Location, and Privacy. Facebook enables users to know when friends are online. IBM Lotus also supports presence capabilities tied into "Connections," while Microsoft offers similar capabilities for SharePoint. iPhone has built-in location awareness capabilities.

What happens when LinkedIn, Facebook, or MySpace provides the ability for a GPS-enabled mobile device or iPhone to dynamically share its location status with others? Will—or how will—businesses begin to take advantage of these same capabilities to build applications to enable the tracking of field sales and support personnel by leveraging the location status capabilities already present in their mobile devices? With logs of location and presence, there will be an audit trail literally tracking people's movements. What are the privacy implications, assuming there would be any privacy remaining? Who will be held responsible or legally liable for unforeseen harm resulting from so much awareness and connectivity?

Free Speech via Wikis and Social Networks. Free speech and privacy rights collide in a world populated by anonymous critics, vengeful people, individuals with personal agendas, and malcontents. But the attacks are not always from competitors or others outside the company. The nature of the Internet ensures that we, at times, may become our own worst enemies personally and professionally, based on the content or images we post on blogs or the friends we keep on social networking pages. *IT at Work 14.3* describes the insensitive tweets made by designer Kenneth Cole and the resultant backlash. The lesson to be learned from this case is that companies need to make sure that when employees post in the blogosphere, they know what they can and cannot say about business information.

Companies victimized by online gossip and rumors have legal recourse, but against whom? What if the identity of the sender or poster is not known? Who is responsible for restricting troublesome content? Furthermore, companies face legal actions if they are found to be negligent for not restricting harmful content.

IT at Work 14.3

Kenneth Cole Faces Backlash for Insensitive Tweet and Lack of Integrity

FIN   ETHICS

In February 2011, designer Kenneth Cole and his company faced fierce backlash after making one of the worst social media mistakes. @KennethCole, actually the CEO himself, tried to joke on Twitter about the political unrest in Egypt and use it to promote the company's new spring clothing collection with the tweet:

> *"Millions are in uproar in #Cairo. Rumor is they heard our new spring collection is now available online at http://bit.ly/KCairo – KC"*

Within a few hours, the post was deleted. An apology was posted by KC on Facebook, but that did not arrest damages resulting from the insensitive tweet. Two hours after trying to profit from the #Cairo hashtag, @KennethCole said:

> *"We weren't intending to make light of a serious situation. We understand the sensitivity of this historic moment – KC"*

The arrogant format of the Facebook apology sparked another outrage.

Two Hours is Very Long in Social Media Time. The tweet was personally signed with Kenneth Cole's initials, an indication that it was from the designer himself—as noted in the @KennethCole Twitter profile. That and the bit.ly URL that was modified to specifically include the word "Cairo" (actually playing on the KC initials) were further signs of extremely poor judgment.

Socially Irresponsible Use of Social Media. The negative reactions to socially irresponsible acts serve as a warning. Every use of social media has potential for either attracting followers to a brand or damaging it. Using social media to connect with customers needs to be done with integrity.

Kenneth Cole's failure shows the danger of exploiting an unrelated and highly charged topic to promote a product, which is known as **hashtag hijacking.** When damage control is needed, acknowledge the mistake and offer a sincere apology immediately. Offering a non-apology that says "this whole uproar isn't what we intended" is likely to intensify damages.

Review Questions

1. Why would a company engage in social media monitoring? What are objections to the monitoring?
2. How can wireless sensors improve urban planning efforts?
3. Distinguish between presence and location. Give an example of each.
4. Where and why do free speech and privacy rights collide?

14.3 Connectivity Overload and the Culture of Distraction

Consider your daily sources of information and what you check on your mobile or the Internet: tweets, texts, feeds, posts, voice messages, Facebook, LinkedIn, sport sites, Web cams, Skype, and dozens of apps. You probably haven't noticed the increase in the amount of information that you receive or check routinely. How many more things do you check today compared to a year ago? How long can you go without checking your mobile or computer without experiencing some anxiety? How many browser tabs do you have open right now, as you read? When do you put down your mobile and concentrate on one thing at a time? Your answers indicate information or connectivity overload and your tolerance for distractions, even if you're not aware of it.

People adapt to new ITs, many of which become *must have* and *can't function without* gadgets rather quickly. This situation is not limited to millennials or members of Generation Y—those born after 1982. Studies show that older adults are just as distracted as teenagers and 20-somethings, which can also be confirmed with a casual glance at offices, airports, cafes, and so on.

OVERLOADS AND DISTRACTIONS

IT's capability to introduce ever-growing amounts of data into our lives can exceed our capacity to keep up with the data, leading to **information overload.** Business users are more likely to suffer from too much data than from data scarcity. Finding the information they need in massive collections of documents can be complicated, time-consuming, frustrating, and expensive.

Maggie Jackson, author of *Distracted: The Erosion of Attention and the Coming Dark Age* (2009), suggested that: "We're really facing the limit of human ability to cope with stimuli in our environment." University of California–San Diego researchers found that on average, Americans hear, see, or read 34 gigabytes worth of information a day—about 100,000 words from TV, the Internet, books, radio, newspapers, and other sources. And Bloomberg BusinessWeek (2008) reported that knowledge workers are distracted every three minutes at work—answering the phone, checking e-mail, responding to a text, or checking YouTube or Facebook. The consequence is that people are continuously paying *partial attention* to everything—skimming instead of being fully engaged. But there are also financial costs. According to Basex, a business research company in New York City, distractions take up to 28 percent of the average U.S. worker's day, including recovery time, and sap productivity to the cost of $650 billion a year.

To be effective at solving the problem of information overload, information systems must differentiate between the data that can be safely summarized and the data that should be viewed in its original form. This is a difficult problem to solve.

INFORMATION QUALITY

As organizations and societies continue to generate, process, and rely on rapidly increasing amounts of information, they begin to realize the importance of information quality. **Information quality** is a somewhat subjective measure of the utility, objectivity, and integrity of gathered information. To be valuable, both data and information must possess a number of essential characteristics, such as being complete, accurate, up-to-date, and consistent with the purpose for which they are used. The value and usability of data and information that do not satisfy these requirements are severely limited.

Information quality is mandated by several laws. The Data Quality Act of 2001 and the Sarbanes-Oxley Act of 2002 impose strict information quality requirements on government agencies and companies. For example, one of the provisions of the Sarbanes-Oxley Act makes CEOs and CFOs personally responsible and liable for the quality of financial information that firms release to stockholders or file with the Securities and Exchange Commission. This provision emphasizes the importance of controlling and measuring data quality and information quality in BI, corporate performance management, and record management systems.

Problems with information quality are not limited to corporate data. Millions of individuals face information quality issues on a daily basis as they try to find information online, whether on publicly available Web pages or in specialized research databases, wikis, blogs, and newsfeeds.

Among the most common problems that plague online information sources is omission of materials. A number of online "full-text" periodicals databases may omit certain items that appeared in the printed versions of their publications. In addition, online sources of information leave out older documents, which are not available in digital form. Thus, one cannot be assured of having access to a complete set of relevant materials. Even materials that are available from seemingly reputable sources present information quality concerns. Information may have been incorrectly reported, whether intentionally or unintentionally, or it may have become out of date. These and other information quality issues are contributing to the frustration and anxiety that for some people have become the unfortunate side effect of the information age.

IMPACTS ON INDIVIDUALS

Pervasive IT has caused changes in structure, authority, power, and job content, as well as personnel management and human resources management. Details of these changes are shown in Table 14.2. Together, the increasing amounts of information and IT use impact job satisfaction, dehumanization, and information anxiety, as well as health and safety. Although many jobs may become substantially more enriched with IT, other jobs may become more routine and less satisfying.

Review Questions

1. What is information overload?
2. What are the consequences of connectivity or information overload?
3. What are the consequences of constant distractions?
4. What is information quality? Name one law that requires companies to ensure their information quality.
5. What are the impacts of pervasive IT?

TABLE 14.2	Impacts of IT on Structure, Authority, Power, and Job Content
Impact	**Effect of IT**
Flatter organizational hierarchies	IT increases *span of control* (more employees per supervisor), increases productivity, and reduces the need for technical experts (due to expert systems). Fewer managerial levels will result, with fewer staff and line managers. Reduction in the total number of employees, reengineering of business processes, and the ability of lower-level employees to perform higher-level jobs may result in flatter organizational hierarchies.
Change in blue-collar-to-white-collar staff ratio	The ratio of white- to blue-collar workers increases as computers replace clerical jobs and as the need for information systems specialists increases. However, the number of professionals and specialists could *decline* in relation to the total number of employees in some organizations as intelligent and knowledge-based systems grow.
Growth in number of special units	IT makes possible technology centers, e-commerce centers, decision support systems departments, and/or intelligent systems departments. Such units may have a major impact on organizational structure, especially when they are supported by or report directly to top management.
Centralization of authority	Centralization may become more popular because of the trend toward smaller and flatter organizations and the use of expert systems. On the other hand, the Web permits greater empowerment, allowing for more decentralization. Whether use of IT results in more centralization or in decentralization may depend on top management's philosophy.
Changes in power and status	Knowledge is power, and those who control information and knowledge are likely to gain power. The struggle over who controls the information resources has become a conflict in many organizations. In some countries, the fight may be between corporations that seek to use information for competitive advantage and the government (e.g., Microsoft vs. the Justice Department). Elsewhere, governments may seek to hold onto the reins of power by not letting private citizens access some information.
Changes in job content and skill sets	*Job content* is interrelated with employee satisfaction, compensation, status, and productivity. Resistance to changes in job skills is common and can lead to unpleasant confrontations between employees and management.

14.4 Future of IT in Business

The slideshow "Microsoft's Home of the Future: A Visual Tour" (*cio.com/article/597693/Microsoft_s_Home_of_the_Future_A_Visual_Tour*) shows a full-scale model home of the future. The Microsoft home seems like science fiction because of its interactive bedrooms, dishes that charge cell phones, sensors that notify you when plants need water, and kitchen counters that read your recipes. No wall or table in the home is safe from being a digital or information device. It's an exciting view of what homes could look like.

The future of IT in the organization may also bring about exciting changes. Here are seven IT trends that help define how the organization and business world are developing, as described in the report *Everything Elastic* from Accenture Technology Labs (Swaminathan, 2010).

1. Computing forecast: Into the clouds. *A more flexible model that aligns better with business objectives.* Cloud computing allows any part of the IT to be sourced from the Internet, ultimately offering a more flexible model that aligns better with business objectives. This new, adaptable IT framework may make it much easier to manage issues of cost, scale, and agility.

2. The new Web: *The Web as a turning point.* The Web is undergoing its most significant overhaul since the emergence of browsers and will emerge as an increasingly attractive enterprise platform. Because of the Web's reach (1.6 billion devices connected, with this number expected to reach 2.7 billion by 2013), even small changes to its basic capabilities can have enormous potential—changing how people socialize, changing how societies link together, and changing how businesses operate. Right now, the Web is in the midst of its most significant overhaul since the first browsers emerged 15 years ago. Low-level engineering work—from networking protocols to browser optimization—is making the Web faster and more robust. New capabilities—such as location-awareness, online/offline modes, and social connectivity—are paving the way for new classes of Web apps. And a growing set of productivity, communication, and integration capabilities are making the Web increasingly attractive as an enterprise platform. It is a world that presents a new set of challenges—privacy, security, control of standards, interoperability—and requires a new set of technical and strategic skills.

3. Devices as doorways. *User experience integrates over devices.* With more data residing on the Web (cloud), users will increasingly access and manipulate this data using the devices that most suit their needs. Corporate IT will move away from hardware support to providing the secure transport layer for workers to access the information they need—using their own devices. We are now entering a world where any device can deliver any content.

4. Fluid collaboration. *Seeking collaboration technology that pulls its weight.* Collaboration across time zones and geographies is the new business norm. Given the realities of global workforces, carbon-reduction efforts, and the drive for greater productivity, these numbers are going up. Global—and thus virtual—collaboration will increasingly become the way business is done. Expect a wave of innovation to provide the technologies to enable collaboration across time zones and geographies.

5. The conversation economy. *Social computing creates discontinuities in how we communicate and consume information.* The rise of social networks is creating new ways of connecting with customers. Social computing has brought about change in how people connect, how they converse, and how they get and share information. The social network itself is fast becoming a primary information channel for many people. Any object of attention—rumors, novels, recipes, petitions—can explode in importance and visibility if it taps into the right social channels at the right time. But information can also travel in the opposite direction: Social networks are emerging as a rich source of information about consumer sentiment, preferences, and desires.

6. Fourth-generation system development. *New architectures and new approaches.* Technological and economic forces are prompting fresh approaches to systems development—as always, competitive advantage will go to those with the ability to spot technology hotspots and the skills to exploit them.

7. Data + decisions = differentiation. As analytics become a commodity, the real differentiators are the quality of the data—and the ability to use it to make productive decisions. Insightful analytics can help organizations discover patterns, detect anomalies, improve data quality, and ultimately, take effective action. But as analytics tools have been incorporated into standard offerings from software vendors, it is becoming clear that the real advantage in analytics is gained before the analysis begins (in data collection) and after it ends (in decision making).

With IT creating organizations that have the characteristics of elasticity—scalable, infinitely flexible, and adaptive—companies and your job will be defined by IT.

Review Questions

1. Describe Microsoft's home of the future.
2. Describe the major IT trends influencing organizations.
3. What are the characteristics of elasticity as they apply to organizations?

Key Terms

computer cluster *435*

Electronic Product Environmental
   Assessment Tool (EPEAT) *425*

global warming *418*

green computing *424*

greenhouse effect *418*

information overload *429*

information quality *430*

Keeling curve *418*

MtCO2e, metric tonne (ton) carbon
   dioxide equivalent *417*

SMART 2020 Report *419*

social media monitoring *426*

sustainability *421*

sustainable biofuels *421*

virtualization *424*

Chapter Highlights and Insights

(Numbers refer to Learning Objectives)

❶ Global warming is the upward trend in global mean temperature (GMT) and one of the most complicated issues facing world leaders.

❶ The role of IT includes emission reduction and energy savings not only in the IT sector itself but also by transforming how and where people work. The most obvious ways are by substituting digital formats—telework, videoconferencing, e-paper, and mobile and e-commerce—for physical formats.

❶ Organizations are paying premiums to invest in green computers that are both energy efficient and environmentally responsible. Organizations that invest in green hardware find that the energy savings, extended product life cycle, positive public image, and other benefits exceed the additional costs of that hardware.

❶ Green computing is the study and practice of ecofriendly computing resources that is now a key concern of businesses in all industries and organizations. Now companies worry about their power consumption as well as the demand of physical space.

❷ Social media monitoring may be considered an integral component of social media strategies because it gives marketers the ability to discover public conversations about their brands and, if necessary, respond to posters directly or to their posts. Opponents of monitoring define it as spying and an intolerable invasion of privacy.

❷ Globalization, the Internet, and connectivity have the power to undermine moral responsibility because it becomes relatively easy to ignore the harm that might be done to others. Despite the challenges and lack of clear answers, ethics is important because it has become clear that relying on the law alone to safeguard the community is insufficient.

❸ IT's capability to introduce ever-growing amounts of data into our lives can exceed our capacity to keep up with the data, leading to information overload. Business users are more likely to suffer from too much data than from data scarcity. Finding the information they need in massive collections of documents can be complicated, time-consuming, frustrating, and expensive.

❹ Business executives and CIOs should consider reshaping their thinking in line with this concept. The idea of elasticity—scalable, infinitely flexible, adaptive—may be integrated into the very fabric of the business. Only then will high performance be achievable in this new marketplace.

Questions for Discussion

1. What is the relationship between GHG emissions and global warming?

2. How can carbon footprints be reduced by users and by organizations?

3. In your opinion, have mobiles, the Internet, and social media changed the way we communicate with each other and get news about our friends and family?

4. How has IT changed the way you communicate?

5. What changes do you predict in the way we communicate with each other in the future?

6. What are some communication casualties of IT?

7. If you were an employee in a company that offered telecommuting options, would you prefer to work from home, from the office, or some combination of both? Explain your answer.

8. Clerks at 7-Eleven stores enter data regarding customers' gender, approximate age, and so on into a computer system. However, names are not keyed in. These data are then aggregated and analyzed to improve corporate decision making. Customers are not informed about this, nor are they asked for permission. What problems do you see with this practice?

9. Discuss whether information overload is a problem in your work or education. Based on your experience, what personal and organizational solutions can you recommend for this problem?

10. Discuss how IT is expected to influence organizations in the future.

Exercises and Projects

1. List five opportunities to work remotely that are available at your workplace or educational institution. If you were to take advantage of these opportunities to telework, describe what potential impacts they could have on your life.

2. List three business applications or support for business activities available on the iPhone 3G or Sprint 4G phone.

3. Visit *wirelessintelligence.com/green-power/* and download the Google Earth plugin at *earth.google.com/plugin/*. Then look at the 3D view of mobile green power deployments/solutions. Report what you learned.

4. Read *IT at Work 14.1*. Answer the questions at the end.

Group Assignments and Projects

1. The news that the U.S. Department of Justice (DOJ) has been seeking search data from Google, Yahoo, MSN, and America Online to track activities of "people or groups of interest" has struck fear into the hearts of Web surfers. Many users are concerned, not because they've done anything wrong, but because they wonder just how much personal information can be gleaned from their online searches. With the class divided into groups, debate the issues involved.

2. The state of California maintains a database of people who allegedly abuse children. (The database also includes names of the alleged victims.) The list is made available to dozens of public agencies, and it is consid-

ered in cases of child adoption and in employment decisions. Because so many people have access to the list, its content is easily disclosed to outsiders. An alleged abuser and her child, whose case was dropped but whose names had remained on the list, sued the state of California for invasion of privacy. With the class divided into groups, debate the issues involved. Specifically:

a. Who should make the decision or what criteria should guide the decision about what names should be included and what the criteria should be?
b. What is the potential damage to the abusers (if any)?
c. Should the state of California abolish the list? Why or why not?

Internet Exercises

1. Visit the U.S. Green Building Council at *usgbc.org/*. From the menu bar, select the Quick Link for *Case for Green Building (PowerPoint)*. Download the file about LEEDS and view the slides. Identify three buildings and their ecofriendly characteristics.

2. Assume that you read about a new nonprescription drug discovery called "Ace-the-Exam." This remarkable drug,

being marketed to students for $19.99 plus shipping and handling, would keep the person awake and with perfect recall of what he or she had read in the textbook in preparation for the exam. How would you verify the truth about this drug—or any new drug treatment—before ordering it or ingesting it? Identify five sources of trusted health, medical, or drug information.

BUSINESS CASE
Auto Industry Worldwide Forms a Program for Fuel Economy and GHG Emissions GLOBAL ETHICS

Visit *epa.gov/oms/climate/regulations.htm* to read the *Commitment Letters* from the CEOs and presidents of Porsche, Toyota, GM, Honda, Hyundai, Jaguar Land Rover, Chrysler, Mazda, Mitsubishi, Daimler, Ford, and Volkswagen. You will read of the auto manufacturers agreement and commitment to reduce dependency on fossil fuel and cut GHG emissions. The sections that follow discuss what the EPA is doing to help preserve the environment.

ENERGY STAR Program

The Environmental Protection Agency's ENERGY STAR program in the U.S. has helped the auto manufacturing industry increase its energy efficiency. As of mid-2010, the auto manufacturers cut fossil fuel use by 12 percent and GHG emissions by more than 700,000 MtCO2e/y (metric tons of carbon dioxide equivalent annually), according to the June 2010 report by the Nicholas Institute for Environmental Policy Solutions at

Duke University (Boyd, 2010). You can read the report at *nicholas.duke. edu/institute/Duke_EE_WP_10-01.pdf*.

The GHG emissions reductions, which help to fight climate change, equal the emissions from the electricity use of more than 80,000 homes for a year.

Central to this energy management approach is the ENERGY STAR Energy Performance Indicator (EPI) for auto assembly plants, which enables industry to benchmark plant energy performance against peers and over time. ENERGY STAR EPIs exist or are under development for more than 20 other industries. Across these industries, the EPA has recognized nearly 60 manufacturing plants with the ENERGY STAR label, representing savings of more than $500 million and more than 6 million MtCO2e/y.

The U.S. industrial sector accounts for more than 30 percent of energy use in the United States. If the energy efficiency of industrial facilities improved by 10 percent, the EPA estimates that Americans would save nearly $20 billion and reduce GHG emissions equal to the emissions from the electricity use of more than 22 million homes for an entire year.

Hundreds of industrial companies across more than a dozen manufacturing industries are working with the EPA's ENERGY STAR program to develop strong energy management programs, earn the ENERGY STAR for their plants, and achieve breakthrough improvements in energy efficiency. http://www.epa.gov/oms/climate/regulations.htm

Sources: Compiled from Boyd (2010), EPA, ENERGY STAR (2010), and Nicholas Institute for Environmental Policy Solutions at Duke University.

Questions

1. Explain ENERGY STAR Energy Performance Indicators (EPIs).
2. What is the importance of cutting carbon emissions?
3. Why are companies in many industries motivated to earn the ENERGY STAR label?
4. What is energy management?
5. Global warming has been a known problem for over a decade. Why didn't the auto manufacturers undertake the ENERGY STAR program years ago?

PUBLIC SECTOR CASE

Understanding Energy Technologies to Cut Carbon Footprint

Argonne's Center for Nanoscale Materials (CNM) studies the behavior of nanoscale materials (*nano.anl.gov*). Nanoscale materials are slightly larger than the size of atoms and can only be studied with the CNM's nanoscope, shown in Figure 14.8, the world's most powerful X-ray microscope. CNM's mission is to find new energy technologies and to understand and lessen the environmental impacts of energy use. Researchers study nanoscale materials and devices to learn how to harvest solar energy more efficiently.

Conserving Energy, Space, and the Environment

To achieve its mission, the CNM needed lab and computing facilities that could provide or accommodate extensive processing power, which would typically take up a lot of space—in other words, have a large **carbon footprint**—consume a huge amount of energy, and generate extreme heat that had to be controlled with air conditioning. The CNM had to be designed to conserve energy, space, and the environment and support future research missions.

Therefore, when research was just beginning at the CNM, the Department of Energy wanted to be sure that the center's infrastructure could accommodate not only current requirements, but also future needs. Its ecofriendly plan was to deliver the computer processing performance required to support world-class scientific research on nanoscale materials in such a way that it would reduce the physical footprint of hardware while minimizing power consumption, cooling costs, and real estate costs.

High-Performance Computer Cluster

The CNM team built a high-performance computer cluster with Intel processors that delivered the extreme performance required with low power consumption and a small physical footprint. A **computer cluster** is a group of computers linked via a LAN (local area network) that work together to form the equivalent of a single computer. Using Intel software tools, CNM application developers have improved the efficiency of their research applications by 20 to 30 percent.

Figure 14.8 *Nanoscope,* powerful X-ray microscope to view nanoscale materials. (*Courtesy of U. S. Department of Energy's Argonne National Laboratory.*)

Built from the ground up, the new CNM facility enables scientists and engineers to conduct a wide variety of projects in a single location. The computing infrastructure delivers the computing power and data transfer rate required to capture and analyze large amounts of data in real time. Some experiments produce enormous amounts of data. Researchers are able to analyze those data in real time so they can reposition samples, adjust instruments, and fine-tune their experiments. Research performed at the facility is contributing to advances in medicine, electronics, manufacturing, and alternative energy sources.

By providing a way to achieve fast results within a single facility, the CNM can accommodate more researchers in less time. Overall, it achieved its mission of providing a powerful computing infrastructure that enables researchers to produce better science while simultaneously protecting the environment.

Sources: Compiled from Argonne National Laboratory (2008), Center for Nanoscale materials, (2010) and Intel multi-care performance. Accelerates Nanoscience Research (2008).

Questions

1. Explain the importance of nanoscale research.
2. Why is nanoscale research so power-intensive?
3. What is the advantage of a computer cluster over a single computer of comparable computing power?
4. In this chapter, you read many examples of companies, industry groups, and government agencies investing in IT infrastructure that ultimately reduced GHGs and CO_2 emissions. Compare and contrast the green initiatives at Argonne's CNM to the biofuel initiative in Nigeria discussed in *IT at Work 14.1.*

SIMULATION USING SPREADSHEETS

Global Warming Calculator

Visit *http://timeforchange.org/mitigation-global-warming-calculator* to download the Excel file attachment *Global-warming-calculator-Excel.xls.* The Global Warming Calculator is an Excel-based interactive simulation. Input data for three different scenarios in the section: *What would happen if everyone was like you?* Explain what you learned.

References

Alvares, M., "The Three Biggest Myths About Green IT," Greenbiz.blog, June 22, 2010. *greenbiz.com/blog/2010/06/22/three-biggest-myths-about-green-it*

Argonne National Laboratory, 2008. *anl.gov*

Biofuels Programme, GSMA Development Fund, January 2007, *businessaction for africa.org*

Boyd, G., "Assessing Improvement in the Energy Efficiency of U.S. Auto Assembly Plants," *Duke University Environmental Economics Working Paper Series,* Working Paper EE 10-01, June 2010. *nicholas.duke.edu/institute/Duke_EE_WP_10-01.pdf*

Center for Nanoscale Materials 2010, *nano.anl.gov/index.html*

Chickowski, E., "CIO Priorities for 2010," *Baseline,* September 28, 2009. *baselinemag.com/c/a/IT-Management/CIO-Priorities-for-2010-706071/*

EPA, *epa.gov*

ENERGY STAR, *energystar.gov*

GSM World.com

"Intel® Multi-Core Performance Accelerates Nanoscience Research," April 9, 2008. *communities.intel.com/servlet/JiveServlet/previewBody/1489-102-1-1705/Intel_ESS_Argonne_LR.pdf*

Jackson, M., *Distracted: The Erosion of Attention and the Coming Dark Age,* Prometheus Books, 2009.

Markoff, J., "Can't Find a Parking Spot? Check Smartphone," *The New York Times,* July 12, 2008.

MTN Group, 2010. *mtn.com/*

Nicholas Institute for Environmental Policy Solutions, *nicholasinstitute.duke.edu*

Swaminathan, K. S., "Everything Elastic," 2010. a *ccenture.com*

U.S. Global Change Research Program, *globalchange.gov/*

Glossary

2D tag Technology that makes it possible to interact with individuals via the devices closest to them and when they'd be most interested or responsive.

2G Second-generation mobile network standard.

3G Third-generation mobile network standard.

4G Fourth-generation mobile network standard.

3GSM Third-generation Global System for Mobile Communications Services.

Acceptable use policy (AUP) Policy that informs users of their responsibilities, acceptable and unacceptable actions, and consequences of noncompliance.

Access control Management of who is allowed access and who is not allowed access to networks, data files, applications, or other digital resources.

Adaptability The ability to adjust the design of the supply chain to meet structural shifts in markets and modify supply network strategies, products, and technologies.

Adaptive enterprise An organization that can respond properly and in a timely manner to changes in the business environment.

Ad hoc report Unplanned reports generated on request to provide more information about a situation, problem, or opportunity.

Administrative controls Deal with issuing guidelines and monitoring compliance with the guidelines, policies, and procedures.

Adoption process A process that occurs over time and passes through five stages: (1) acquire knowledge, (2) persuade, (3) decide, (4) implement, and (5) confirm.

Advergaming The practice of using computer games to advertise a product, an organization, or a viewpoint.

Adware Software that automatically displays advertisements while running a program.

Affiliate marketing An arrangement whereby a marketing partner (a business, an organization, or even an individual) refers consumers to the selling company's Web site.

Agile enterprise A firm that can identify and capture opportunities more quickly than its rivals.

Agility An EC firm's ability to capture, report, and quickly respond to changes happening in the marketplace.

AJAX (Asynchronous JavaScript) A group of technologies that create Web pages that respond to users' actions without requiring the entire page to reload.

Algorithm A mathematical rule for solving a problem; a predetermined set of rules used to solve a problem in a finite number of steps.

Alignment The ability to create shared incentives that align the interests of businesses across the supply chain.

Android OS. Google/Open Hardset Alliance mobile OS.

Anti-malware technology Tool that detects malicious code and prevents users from downloading them.

Application controls Safeguards that are intended to protect specific applications.

Application development 2.0. A new application development process that involves constant interaction with users and provides developers with almost immediate notification of bugs and users' desires.

Applications portfolio Major information systems applications, such as customer order processing, human resource management, or procurement, that have been or are to be developed.

Application program A set of computer instructions written in a programming language, the purpose of which is to support a specific task or business process or another application program.

Application Programming Interfaces (APIs) A toll that allows programs to talk to or interact with one another.

Artificial intelligence (AI) The branch of computer science that is concerned with making computers behave and "think" like humans.

Asset Resource with recognized value that is under control of an individual or organization.

Attribute Characteristic describing an entity. Also known as a *field*.

Auction A competitive process in which either a seller solicits consecutive bids from buyers or a buyer solicits bids from sellers, and prices are determined dynamically by competitive bidding.

Audit or Auditing Investigation that is an important part of any control system.

Augmented reality An app that involves computer-generated graphic images superimposed over photos of real things.

Automated decision support (ADS) Rule-based systems that automatically provide solutions to repetitive managerial problems.

Automatic crash notification (ACN) Still-experimental device that would automatically notify police of the location of an ACN-equipped car involved in an accident.

Available-to-promise (ATP) A business function that provides data about resource availability and delivery dates to keep customers informed of their orders' status.

Avatar A cyberbody that a user creates when using an online 3-D virtual world.

B2B gateway A Suite of software products that support internal and external integration and business processes.

Back-end (or back-office) operations The activities that support fulfillment of sales, such as accounting and logistics.

Balanced scorecard A performance measurement approach that links business goals to performance metrics.

Balanced scorecard methodology Framework for defining, implementing, and managing an enterprise's business strategy by linking objectives with factual measures.

Bandwidth A measure of the speed at which data is transmitted.

Barriers to entry How easy or difficult it is to enter an industry.

Batch processing Processing system that processes inputs at fixed intervals as a file and operates on it all at once; contrasts with *online* (or *interactive*) processing.

Behavior-oriented chargeback Accounting system that sets IT service costs in a way that encourages usage consistent with organizational objectives, even though the charges may not correspond to actual costs.

Benchmarks Objective measures of performance, often available from industry trade associations.

Biometric control Automated method of verifying the identity of a person, based on physical or behavioral characteristics.

Bit The smallest unit of data a computer can process. Either a 0 or a 1.

BitTorrent tracker Server used in the communication, usually of very large files, between peers using the BitTorrent protocol.

Blackberry OS Made by Research in Motion. This is currently the dominant smart phone OS in the U.S.

Blindspot Areas in which managers fail to notice or to understand important information.

Blog Web log where users post information for others to read.

Blogosphere Blogs that exist together with similar interests as a connected community.

Bluetooth Chip technology that enables voice and data communications between many wireless devices through low power, short-range, digital two-way radio frequency.

Botnet Collection of computers infected by software robots, or bots.

BPM mashup Preconfigured, ready-to-go integrations between different business software packages.

Brick-and-mortar organizations Organizations in which the product, the process, and the delivery agent are all physical.

Broadband Short for broad bandwidth. A measure of a network's capacity or throughput.

Buffer stock Extra inventory in case of unexpected events. Also called *safety stock*.

Bullwhip effect Phenomenon that occurs when companies significantly cut or add inventories.

Business activity monitoring (BAM) A message-based, event-driven tool that allows business users to link KPIs (key performance indicators) associated to the process being monitored on a real-time basis and provides relevant information via dashboards.

Business analytics Provides models, which are formulas or algorithms and procedures to BI.

Business architecture Organizational plans, visions, objectives, and problems, and the information required to support them.

Business case A written document that is used by managers to justify funding for a specific investment and also to provide the bridge between the initial plan and its execution.

Business continuity plan Plan that outlines the process by which businesses should recover from a major disaster. Also known as a *disaster recovery plan*.

Business impact analysis (BIA) A method or exercise to determine the impact of losing the support or availability of a resource.

Business intelligence (BI) Category of applications for gathering, storing, analyzing, and providing access to data to help enterprise users make better decisions.

Business record A document that records business dealings such as contracts, research and development, accounting source documents, memos, customer/client communications, and meeting minutes.

Business model A method by which a company generates revenue to sustain itself.

Business network A group of people who have some kind of commercial relationship. For example, the relationships between sellers and buyers, buyers among themselves, buyers and suppliers, and colleagues and other colleagues.

Business performance management (BPM) A methodology for measuring organizational performance, analyzing it through comparison to standards, and planning how to improve it.

Business process A collection of activities performed to accomplish a clearly defined goal.

Business process management (BPM) A popular management technique that includes methods and tools to support the design, analysis, implementation, management, and optimization of operational business processes.

Business process management suites BPM software where you can graphically *compose* a process model, *optimize* it through simulation and analysis, and *execute* it on a built-in process engine.

Business process modeling An activity similar to drafting a blueprint for a house; it includes techniques and activities used as part of the larger business process management discipline.

Business process outsourcing (BPO) The process of hiring another company to handle business activities.

Business process reengineering The radical redesign of an organization's business, where one takes a current process and makes changes to increase its efficiency and create new processes.

Business process reengineering (BPR) A methodology in which an organization fundamentally and radically changes its business processes to achieve dramatic improvement.

Business process utilities (BPUs) Outsourced business process services for standardized processes.

Business records Records of business dealings, such as contracts, research and development, accounting source documents, memos, customer/client communications, and meeting minutes.

Business service management (BSM) A strategy and an approach for linking key IT components to the goals of the business. It enables you to understand and predict how technology impacts the business and how business impacts the IT infrastructure.

Business strategy Defines the business objectives and long-term direction of an organization.

Business-to-business EC (B2B) E-commerce in which both the sellers and the buyers are business organizations.

Business-to-business-to-consumers (B2B2C) EC E-commerce in which a business sells to a business but delivers the product or service to an individual consumer.

Business-to-consumers (B2C) EC E-commerce in which the sellers are organizations and the buyers are individuals; also known as *e-tailing*.

Business-to-employees (B2E) EC A special type of intrabusiness e-commerce in which an organization delivers products or services to its employees.

Buy-side marketplace B2B model in which organizations buy needed products or services from other organizations electronically, often through a reverse auction.

Byte A group of eight bits. Represents a single character.

Champion The person who will promote the benefits of the new system across different levels of the organization on an ongoing basis.

Change management A structured approach to transition individuals, teams, and organizations from a current state to a desired future state, which includes managing change as part of systems development to avoid user resistance to business and system changes.

Change process A structured technique to effectively transition groups or organizations through change.

Channel conflict Possible conflicts between the online selling channel and the traditional physical channel may be internal (e.g., regarding pricing or advertisement), or between a company that wants to sell direct to customers and its existing distributors.

Channel systems (in marketing) A network of the materials and product distribution systems involved in the process of getting a product or service to customers.

Chargeback System that treats the IT function as a service bureau or utility, charging organizational subunits for IT services with the objective of recovering IT expenditures.

Chief technology officer (CTO) One who evaluates the newest and most innovative technologies and determines how they can be applied for competitive advantage.

Circuit switching Older technology that was used for telephone calls. A circuit cannot be used by any other call unti the connection has ended.

Click-and-mortar organizations Organizations that do business in both the physical and digital dimensions.

Clickstream data Data generated by visitors' behavior on a company's Web site.

Client/server network Consists of user PCs, called *clients*, linked to high-performance computers, called *servers*, which provide software, data, or computing services over a network.

Cloud computing Technology that is rented or leased on a regular, or as-needed basis.

COBIT (Control Objectives for Information and Related Technologies) An internationally accepted IT governance and control framework that aligns IT business objectives, delivering value and managing associated risks.

Collaborative commerce (c-commerce) E-commerce in which business partners collaborate electronically.

Collaborative planning, forecasting, and replenishment (CPFR) Project in which suppliers and retailers collaborate in their planning and demand forecasting to optimize flow of materials along the supply chain.

Commodity Basic things that companies need in order to function, like electricity and buildings.

Comparison shopping engine Search engine that compares prices and finds great deals for certain brands and products.

Compatibility The degree to which the new system is perceived to fit with the existing values, past experiences, and needs of potential adopters.

Competitive advantage An advantage a company has over its competitors, which is gained by providing consumers with greater value through product or service offerings.

Competitive forces model A business framework devised by Michael Porter, depicting five forces in a market (e.g., bargaining power of customers), used for analyzing competitiveness.

Complexity The degree to which the new system is perceived to be difficult to understand and use, measured on a continuum from easy to difficult.

Computer-based information system (CBIS) Information system that includes a computer for some or all of its operation.

Computer cluster A group of computers linked via a LAN and working together to form the equivalent of a single computer.

Computer-integrated manufacturing (CIM) Integrates several computerized systems, such as CAD, CAM, MRP, and JIT, into a whole, in a factory.

Computer systems failures Failures due to poor manufacturing, defects, or outdated or poorly maintained networks.

Consumer-to-business (C2B) EC E-commerce in which consumers make known a particular need for a product or service, and suppliers compete to provide the product or service to consumers; an example is Priceline.com.

Consumer-to-consumer (C2C) EC E-commerce in which an individual sells products or services to other individuals (not businesses).

Content indexing A searchable index of all content.

Content marketing A type of marketing where valuable information is shared with current or prospective clients. Blogs are a key tool of this.

Context Defines the intent of the user; for example, trying to purchase music, find a job, or share memories with friends and family.

Context awareness Capturing a broad range of contextual attributes to better understand what the consumer needs, and what products or services he or she might possibly be interested in.

Contextual computing Enhancement of the computational environment for each user at each point of computing.

Converged network Powerful network architecture that enables enterprisewide integration of voice, data, video, and other communication applications.

Corporate governance Rules and processses ensuring that the enterprise adheres to accepted ethical standards, best practices, and laws.

Corporate procurement Buying products and services for operational and functional needs. Also called *corporate purchasing*.

Cost-benefit analysis Study that helps in decisions on IT investments by determining if the benefits (possibly including intangible ones) exceed the costs.

Cracker A *malicious hacker* who may represent a serious problem for a corporation.

Crime server Server used to store stolen data for use in committing crimes.

Critical path Activities or tasks that must start and finish on schedule or else the project completion will be delayed unless action is taken to expedite one or more critical tasks.

Critical path method (CPM) The purpose of this method of project management is to recognize which activities are on the critical path so that you know where to focus your efforts.

Critical response activities The major activities used by organizations to counter *business pressures*.

Critical success factors (CSFs) The most essential factors that must go right or be closely tracked in order to ensure an organization's survival and success.

Critical task Each task on the critical path.

Cross-border data transfer The flow of corporate data across nations' borders.

Crowdsourcing A model of problem solving and idea generation that marshals the collective talents of a large group of people.

CSS (Cascading Style Sheets) A style sheet language used to enhance the appearance of Web Pages written in a markup language.

Customer churn A customer switches to a competitor's service.

Customer relationship management (CRM) The entire process of maximizing the value proposition to the customer through all interactions, both online and traditional. Effective CRM advocates one-to-one relationships and participation of customers in related business decisions.

Customization Creation of a product or service according to the buyer's specifications.

Cybercriminals People who commit crimes using the Internet.

Cyberbanking Various banking activities conducted electronically from home, a business, or on the road instead of at a physical bank location.

Dashboard A BI tool that provides a comprehensive, at-a-glance view of corporate performance with graphical presentations, resembling a dashboard of a car. These graphical presentations show performance measures, trends, and exceptions, and integrate information from multiple business areas.

Data The raw material from which information is produced.

Database Repository of enterprise data that business applications create or generate, such as sales, accounting, and employee data. An organized logical grouping of related files.

Database management systems (DBMS) Programs used to create, manage, and access databases.

Data centers Facilities containing mission-critical ISs and components that deliver data and IT services to the enterprise.

Data entity Anything real or abstract about which a company wants to collect and store data, such as customer, vendor, product, or employee.

Data infrastructure Fundamental structure of a system that determines how it functions and how flexible it is to meet future requirements.

Data item An elementary description of things, events, activities, and transactions that are recorded, classified, and stored, but not organized to convey any specific meaning; can be numeric, alphanumeric, figures, sounds, or images.

Data latency Technically, the speed in which data is captured is referred to as data latency. It is a measure of data "freshness," specifically data that are less than 24 hours old.

Data management Structured approach for capturing, storing, processing, integrating, distributing, securing, and archiving data effectively throughout their life cycle.

Data mart Small data warehouse designed to support a department or SBU.

Data mining Process of analyzing data from different perspectives and summarizing it into useful information (e.g., information that can be used to increase revenue, cuts costs, or both).

Data quality The degree of data accuracy, accessibility, relevance, timeliness, and completeness.

Data silo An IS that is incapable of exchanging information with other related systems within an organization.

Data synchronization Integrating, matching, or linking data from disparate sources.

Data tampering An attack wherein someone enters false, fabricated, or fraudulent data into a computer, or changes or deletes existing data.

Data visualization Ways to depict data to make it easier for users to understand data.

Data warehouse A specialized type of database that is used to aggregate data from transaction databases for data analysis purposes, such as identifying and examining business trends, to support planning and decision making. See *enterprise data warehouse.*

Data workers Clerical workers who use, manipulate, or disseminate information, typically using document management, workflow, e-mail, and coordination software to do so.

Decision support system (DSS) Computer-based information system that combines models and data to solve semistructured and some unstructured problems with intensive user involvement.

Dehumanization Feeling a loss of identity because of computerization.

Demand-driven supply networks (DDSNs) Networks driven from the front by customer demand. Instead of products being pushed to market, they are pulled to market by customers.

Demand management Knowing or predicting what to buy, when, and how much.

Denial of Service (DoS) attack Occurs when a server or Web site receives a flood of traffic—much more traffic or requests for service than it can handle, causing it to crash.

Deploy To install, test, and implement an IS or application.

Desktop purchasing E-procurement method in which suppliers' catalogs are aggregated into an internal master catalog on the buyer's server for use by the company's purchasing agents.

Digital economy Another name for today's Web-based, or Internet, economy.

Digital enterprise A new business model that uses IT in a fundamental way to accomplish one or more of three basic objectives: reach and engage customers more effectively, boost employee productivity, and improve operating efficiency. It uses converged communication and computing technology in a way that improves business processes.

Digital supply chain A supply chain that is managed electronically, usually with Web-based software (also known as E-supply chain).

Direct file access method Uses the key field to locate the physical address of a record. The most appropriate access method when individual records must be located directly and rapidly for immediate processing, when a few records in the file need to be retrieved at one time, and when the required records are found in no particular order.

Direct file organization Records can be accessed directly regardless of their location on the storage medium.

Direct procurement Procuring materials to produce finished goods.

Dirty data Poor quality data.

Disaster avoidance Approach oriented toward prevention of a problem or crisis.

Discovery Process of gathering information in preparation for trial, legal or regulatory investigation, or administrative action as required by law.

Disintermediation The elimination of intermediaries in EC; removing the layers of intermediaries between sellers and buyers. Effective for technological forecasting and for forecasting involving sensitive issues.

Disruptors Companies that introduce a significant change in their industries, thus causing disruption in business operations.

Document management Automated control of imaged and electronic documents, page images, spreadsheets, voice and e-mail messages, word processing documents, and other documents through their life cycle within an organization, from initial creation to final archiving or destruction.

Document management systems (DMS) Hardware and software to manage and archive electronic documents and to convert paper documents into e-documents, and then to index and store them in an organized way.

Dot-com era (bubble) Period from 1995–2005 when number of Internet users sharply increased and during which countless Internet companies rode an enormous wave of enthusiasm.

Download speed How quickly data can be received from the Internet or other network, or how fast a connection can deliver data to a computer or mobile device.

Drawing tools A way to help demonstrate a business process using diagrams or charts, which works best in conjunction with text-based tools.

DWY (Driving While Yakking) Risky cell phone usage while driving.

E-commerce Process of buying, selling, transferring, or exchanging products or services or information via the public Internet or private corporate networks.

E-community Citizens, audiences, and business partners.

E-content Supplied by content providers.

Economic order quantity (EOQ) Inventory model that is used to determine when and how much to order of stock.

e-CRM (electronic CRM) The use of Web browsers and other electronic touch points to manage customer relationships. E-CRM covers a broad range of topics, tools, and methods, ranging from the proper design of digital products and services to pricing and to loyalty programs.

EDGE (Enhanced Data for Global Evolution) A type of network standard (3G).

E-government The use of e-commerce to deliver information and public services to citizens, business partners, and suppliers of government entities, and those working in the public sector.

E-infrastructure Technical consultants, system developers, integrators, hosting, security, wireless, and networks.

Electronic bartering The electronically supported exchange of goods or services without a monetary transaction.

Electronic commerce (e-commerce, EC) The process of buying, selling, transferring, or exchanging products, services, or information via computer networks, including the Internet; business conducted online.

Electronic data interchange (EDI) The electronic transfer of specially formatted standard business documents, such as bills, orders, and confirmations, sent between business partners.

Electronic funds transfer (EFT) Electronic payments and collections.

Electronic mall A collection of individual shops under one Internet address.

Electronic market (e-market) A network of interactions and relationships over which products, services, information, and payments are exchanged.

Electronic Product Environmental Assessment Tool (EPEAT) A searchable database of computer hardware that meets a strict set of environmental criteria.

Electronic records Archived electronic documents that are not subject to alteration.

Electronic records management (ERM) An infrastructure that helps reduce automated expensive time-intensive and manual processes, and consolidates multiple Web sites onto a single platform.

Electronic retailing (e-tailing) The direct sale of products and services through electronic storefronts or electronic malls, usually designed around an electronic catalog format and/or auctions.

Electronic storefront The Web site of a single company, with its own Internet address, at which orders can be placed.

E-market An online marketplace where buyers and sellers meet to exchange goods, services, money, or information.

Employee relationship management (ERM) The use of Web-based applications to streamline the human resources process and to better manage employees.

End-user development (also known as **end-user computing**) The development and use of ISs by people outside the IS department.

Enhanced messaging service (EMS) An extension of SMS capable of simple animation, tiny pictures, and short tunes.

Enterprise 2.0 Technologies and business practices that free the workforce from the constraints of legacy communication and productivity tools such as e-mail. It provides business managers with access to the right information at the right time through a web of interconnected applications, services, and devices.

Enterprise 2.0 The strategic integration of social computing tools (e.g., blogs, wikis) into enterprise business processes.

Enterprise application integration (EAI) A middleware that connects and acts as a go-between for applications and their business processes.

Enterprise content management (ECM) ECM is a comprehensive approach to electronic document management, Web content management, digital asset management, and electronic records management (ERM).

Enterprise data warehouse (EDW) A data repository of organizational data that is organized, analyzed, and used to enable more informed decision making and planning. See *data warehouse*.

Enterprise portal Set of software applications that consolidate, manage, analyze, and transmit information to users through a standardized Web-based interface.

Enterprise reporting systems Provide standard, ad hoc, or custom reports that are populated with data from a single trusted source to get a *single version of the truth*.

Enterprise resource planning (ERP) Software that integrates the planning, management, and use of all resources in the entire enterprise; also called *enterprise systems*.

Enterprise risk management (ERM) A model for IT governance that is risk-based integrating internal control, the Sarbanes-Oxley Act mandates, and strategic planning.

Enterprise search Offers the potential of cutting much of the complexity accumulated in applications and intranet sites throughout an organization.

Enterprise social network A social network within an enterprise that allows employees to communicate, collaborate, and set up virtual worlds in which they can meet like-minded colleagues within the company and exchange ideas with them to improve productivity.

Enterprise Web 2.0 (Enterprise 2.0, or E 2.0) The application of Web 2.0 technologies in the enterprise.

Environmental hazard Hazards such as volcanoes, earthquakes, blizzards, flood, power failures or strong fluctuations, fires, defective air conditioning, explosions, radioactive fall-out, and water cooling system failures.

E-process Payments and logistics.

E-procurement Purchasing by using electronic support.

E-reader Device that looks similar to slate tablet computers, but is used primarily as a way for users to read electronic books.

Ergonomics The science of adapting machines and work environments to people.

E-services CRM, PRM, and directory services.

E-sourcing Electronic procurement of products.

Ethics A branch of philosophy that deals with what is considered to be right and wrong.

ETL (Extract, Transform, and Load) Extraction, transformation, and loading of data from a database into a data warehouse.

ETL tools Tools that extract relevant customer data from the various data silos, transform the data into standardized formats, and then load and integrate the data into an operational data store or system.

EV-DO (Evolution, Data Only) A type of network standard (3G). Third upgrade to CDMA.

EV-DV (Evolution, Data and Voice) A type of network standard (3G). Most advanced CDMA upgrade.

Event-driven alerts Real-time alerts or warnings that are broadcast when a predefined event, or unusual event, occurs.

E-wallets (digital wallets) A software component in which a user stores secured personal and credit card information for one-click reuse.

Exception report Report generated only when some unusual event or deviation has occurred.

Expected value (EV) A weighted average, computed by multiplying the size of a possible future benefit by the probability of its occurrence.

Expense management automation (EMA) Systems that automate data entry and processing of travel and entertainment expenses.

Expert (or expertise) location systems (ELSs) Interactive computerized systems that help employees find and connect with colleagues who have expertise required for specific problems—whether they are across the country or across the room—in order to solve specific, critical business problems in seconds.

Explicit knowledge The knowledge that deals with objective, rational, and technical knowledge (data, policies, procedures, software, documents, etc.).

External supply chain Business or supply chain partners, such as customers or suppliers.

Extract, transform, and load (ETL) Process that moves data from multiple sources, reformats, cleanses, and loads them into another data warehouse or data mart for analysis or another operational system to support a business process.

Extranet Private, company-owned network that uses IP technology to securely share part of a business's information or operations with suppliers, vendors, partners, customers, or other businesses.

Fiduciary responsibility Legal and ethical obligation.

Field Characteristic describing an entity. Also known as an attribute.

File A collection of related records. Also called *data file*.

Financial flow The transfer of payments and financial arrangements, for example, billing payment schedules, credit terms, and payment via electronic funds transfer (EFT).

Financial value chain management (FVCM) The combination of financial analysis with operations analysis, which analyzes all financial functions in order to provide better financial control.

Firewall System or group of systems that enforces an access-control policy between two networks.

Fixed-line broadband. Either cable or DSL Internet connection.

Foreign key Field whose purpose is to link two or more tables together.

Forward auction An auction that sellers use as a selling channel to many potential buyers; the highest bidder wins the items.

Four P's of implementation Four widely accepted approaches that are usually used to implement an IT-based system; plunge, parallel, phased, and pilot.

Front-office operations The business processes, such as sales and advertising, that are visible to customers.

Functionality Entire set of capabilities of an IS or application.

Gantt chart A type of bar chart that illustrates a project schedule.

Gateway An entrance point that allows users to connect from one network to another.

General controls Protects the system regardless of the specific application.

Geocoding Process of finding geographic coordinates from other data, such as zip codes or addresses.

Geographic information system (GIS) Computer-based system that integrates GPS data onto digitized map displays.

Giant global graph Concept that illustrates the connections between people and/or documents and pages online.

Global information systems Interorganizational systems that connect companies located in two or more countries.

Global positioning systems (GPS) Wireless devices that use satellites to enable users to detect the position on earth of items (e.g., cars or people) the devices are attached to, with reasonable precision.

Global sourcing Occurs when companies purchase goods or services from sellers located anywhere in the world.

Global warming The upward trend in global mean temperature (GMT).

Google Wave A new type of platform consisting of e-mail, instant messaging, and documents.

GSM (Global System for Mobile Communcations) Type of network standard (2G). Upgrades include GPRS, EDGE, UMTS, HSDPA.

Government-to-business (G2B) EC E-commerce in which a government does business with other governments as well as with businesses.

Government-to-citizens (G2C) EC E-commerce in which a government provides services to its citizens via EC technologies.

Government-to-government (G2G) EC E-commerce in which government units do business with other government units.

Green computing Initiative to conserve valuable natural resources by reducing the effect computer usage has on the environment.

Green computing Study and practice of eco-friendly computing resources; now a key concern of businesses in all industries—not just environmental organizations.

Greenhouse effect The holding of heat within the earth's atmosphere by certain GSGs—such as CO_2, methane, and nitrous oxide—that absorb infrared radiation (IR).

Green IT The development of effective programs for IT eco-efficiency and IT eco-innovation that drive improved financial results and measurable environmental sustainable information and communications technology systems.

Green software Software products that help cut fuel bills, save energy, or help comply with EPA requirements.

Grid computing The use of networks to harness the unused processing cycles of all computers in a given network to create powerful computing capabilities.

Groundswell A spontaneous movement of people using online tools to connect, take charge of their own experience, and get what they need from each other.

Group decision support system (GDSS) An interactive computer-based system that facilitates the solution of semistructured and unstructured problems when made by a group of decision makers by concentrating on the *process* and procedures during meetings.

Group purchasing The aggregation of purchasing orders from many buyers so that a volume discount can be obtained.

Group work Work done together by two or more people.

Hacker Someone who gains unauthorized access to a computer system. A criminal.

Hotspot A specific geographic location in which an access point provides public wireless service to mobile users.

Hard ROI metric A method for businesses to measure the hard return on investment by evaluating various data.

HSDPA High-speed downlink (or data) packet access that allows for data speeds up to 10 Mbps (megabits per second).

HTML (Hypertext Markup Language) Predominant language for Web pages. Provides a means to create structured documents by denoting structural semantics for text, such as headings, paragraphs, and lists, as well as for links, quotes, and other items.

Human errors Mistakes made due to untrained or unaware users.

Hype-cycle A useful tool developed by Gartner, Inc in 1995 that is used widely by organizations to identify and assess fruitful emerging technologies and help them decide when to adopt. It assesses the maturity, impact, and adoption speed of hundreds of technologies across a broad range of technology, application, and industry areas.

Implementation All organizational activities involved in the introduction, management, and acceptance of technology to support one or more organizational processes.

Inbound logistics Incoming materials are processed in this activity.

Indexed sequential access method (ISAM) File organization method that uses an index of key fields to locate individual records.

Indirect procurement Procuring materials and products for daily operational needs.

Information Data that have been organized so they have meaning and value to the recipient.

Information flow The movement of detailed data among members of the supply chain, for example, order information, customer information, order fulfillment, delivery status, and proof-of-delivery confirmation.

Information infrastructure The physical arrangement of hardware, software, databases, networks, and information management personnel.

Information overload The inability to cope with or process evergrowing amounts of data into our lives.

Information quality A subjective measure of the utility, objectivity, and integrity of gathered information based on its being complete, accurate, up-to-date, and fit for the purpose for which it is used.

Information system (IS) A physical process that supports an organization by collecting, processing, storing, and analyzing data, and disseminating information to achieve organizational goals.

Information systems (IS) strategy Defines *what* information, information systems, and IT architecture is required to support the business.

Information technology (IT) The technology component of an information system (a narrow definition); or the collection of the computing systems in an organization (the broad definition used in this book).

Information technology architecture High-level map or plan of the information assets in an organization; on the Web, it includes the content and architecture of the site.

Information technology (IT)-business alignment Degree to which the IT group understands the priorities of the business and expends its resources, pursues projects, and provides information consistent with these priorities.

Information technology (IT) governance Formally established statements that direct the policies regarding IT alignment with organizational goals and allocation of resources.

Information technology (IT) strategic planning Defines the IT (long-range) strategic plan, the IT medium-term plan, and the IT tactical plan.

Information technology (IT) strategy Defines the IT vision, *how* the infrastructure and services are to be delivered.

Information technology (IT) vision The longer-term direction for IT; defines the future concept of what IT should do to achieve the goals, objectives, and strategic position of the firm.

In-house development When systems are developed or other IT work is done in-house.

Insourcing Development and management of IT services within the organization.

Intangible benefits Benefits that are hard to place a monetary value on (e.g., greater design flexibility).

Integrated Social Media (ISM) Social media services that are integrated into social networks.

Intellectual capital (intellectual assets) The valuable knowledge of employees.

Intelligent agents Applications that have some degree of reactivity, autonomy, and adaptability to react to unpredictable attack situations. Also referred to as softbots or knowbots.

Interactive marketing Online marketing, facilitated by the Internet, by which marketers and advertisers can interact directly with customers, and consumers can interact with advertisers/vendors.

Interactivity application Applications connect, communicate, collaborate, and do commerce on-demand, in real-time, and at a distance.

Internal control Process designed to provide reasonable assurance of effective operations and reliable financial reporting.

Internal control environment Work atmosphere that a company sets for its employees.

Internal supply chain Internal functions that take place within a company.

Internal threats Threats from those within the organization, such as employees, contractors, and temporary workers.

Internet protocol suite Standard used with almost any network service consisting of the **Internet Protocol** (IP) and **Transport Control Protocol** (TCP), or TCP/IP.

Interoperability Connectivity between devices. Refers to the ability to provide services to and accept services from other systems or devices.

Interorganizational information systems (IOSs) Communications systems that allow routine transaction processing and information flow between two or more organizations.

Intrabusiness (intraorganizational) commerce E-commerce in which an organization uses EC internally to improve its operations.

Intranet Network designed to serve the internal informational needs of a company, using Internet tools.

Intrusion Detection System (IDS) Technology tool that scans for unusual or suspicious traffic.

Intrusion Prevention Systems (IPS) Technology tool designed to take immediate action—such as blocking specific IP addresses—whenever a traffic-flow anomaly is detected.

Inventory control Maintaining optimal inventory levels by reordering the correct quantity at the right time.

iOS Apple's mobile OS.

iPhone 3G Apple's 3G version of the iPhone.

IP network Internet Protocol-based network that forms the backbone that is driving the merger of voice, data, video, and radio waves by digitizing content into packets that can be sent via digital networks.

IP telephony Voice communication over a network using the Internet Protocol. Also called VoIP.

ISO 9000 Developed as a standard for business quality systems by the International Organization for Standardization (ISO). A key element of ISO 9000 is the identification of nonconforming processes and the development of a plan to prevent nonconforming processes from being repeated.

IT applications Specific systems and programs for achieving certain objectives.

IT-business alignment Refers to the degree to which the IT division understands the priorities of the business and spends its resources, pursues projects, and provides information consistent with these priorities.

ITES (information technology-enabled services) See *Business process outsourcing (BPO).*

IT governance Supervision monitoring and control of an organization's IT assets.

IT infrastructure Provides the foundations for IT applications in the enterprise. It is shared by many applications throughout the enterprise and made to exist for a long time.

IT performance management Being able to predict and anticipate failures before it's too late.

IT security Protection of information, communication networks, and traditional and e-commerce operations to assure their confidentiality, integrity, availability, and authorized use.

IT strategy Defines what information, information systems, and IT architecture are required to support the business and how the infrastructure and services are to be delivered.

IT strategic planning Plans and strategies that support the business strategy and objective.

JavaScript An object-oriented language used to create apps and functionality on Web sites.

Just-in-time (JIT) An inventory scheduling system in which material and parts arrive at a work place when needed, minimizing inventory, waste, and interruptions.

Keeling curve The oscillating and upward line on a graph indicating the measurement of CO_2 gas in our atmosphere.

Key performance indicators (KPIs) Metrics that measure the actual performance of critical aspects of IT, such as critical projects and applications, servers, the network, and so forth, against predefined goals and objectives.

Key performance indicators (KPI) The quantitative expression of critically important metrics.

Knowledge Data and/or information that have been organized and processed to convey understanding, experience, accumulated learning, and expertise.

Knowledge management (KM) The process that helps organizations identify, select, organize, disseminate, and transfer important information and expertise that are part of the organization's memory and that may reside in unstructured form within the organization.

Knowledge management system (KMS) A system that organizes, enhances, and expedites intra- and inter-firm knowledge management; centered around a corporate knowledge base or depository.

Knowledge workers People who create and use knowledge as a significant part of their work responsibilities.

Kotter's organizational transformation model An eight-step process that organizations should follow in order to successfully transform an organization.

Law of accelerating returns This law suggests that the time interval between significant events grows shorter as time passes because technological change is exponential, not linear.

Lean manufacturing Demand-driven manufacturing, the objective of which is to remove waste of any kind from production.

Legacy system Application that has been used for a long period of time and that has been inherited from languages, platforms, and techniques used in earlier technologies.

Lessons learned An important step in wrapping up management of any implementation process, this step documents successes and failures in each systems development phase as well as the project as a whole.

Lewin's three-stage change model A simple change process model that consists of three stages of change; *unfreezing, change, (re)freezing.*

Linux OS. Linux mobile OS.

Local area network (LAN) Connects network devices over a relatively short distance. Capable of transmitting data at very fast rates, but operates in a limited area, such as an office building, campus, or home.

Location-based commerce (l-commerce) M-commerce transactions targeted to individuals in specific locations at specific times.

Logistical system design States what the system will do, using abstract specifications.

Logistics The operations involved in the efficient and effective flow and storage of goods, services, and related information from point of origin to point of consumption.

Loyalty programs Programs that recognize customers who repeatedly use the services (products) offered by a company (e.g., frequent flyers).

LTE (Long-Term Evolution) Type of network standard (4G). Developed by the Third Generation Partnership Project (3GPP).

Malvertisement Ads that when clicked redirect the user to a malicious Web site.

Malware Any unwanted software that exploits flaws in other software to gain illicit access.

Management information systems (MISs) Systems designed to provide past, present, and future routine information appropriate for planning, organizing, and controlling the operations of functional areas in an organization.

Mashup An application or Web page that pulls information from multiple sources, creating a new functionality.

Mass Web attack Web sites attacked by a malicious code.

Master data entity Main entities of a company, such as customers, products, suppliers, employees, and assets.

Master data management (MDM) The integration of data from various sources or enterprise applications to provide a more unified view of data.

Master reference file File that stores consolidated data from various data sources, which then feeds data back to the applications to create accurate and consistent data across the enterprise.

Maverick buying Buying done outside the established system.

Mesh network A type of wireless sensor network composed of motes, where each mote "wakes up" or activates for a fraction of a second when it has data to transmit and then relays those data to its nearest neighbor. So, instead of every mote transmitting its information to a remote computer at a base station, an "electronic bucket brigade" moves the data mote by mote until it reaches a central computer where it can be stored and analyzed.

Metadata Way of describing data so that it can be used by a wide variety of applications.

Metric A specific, measurable standard against which actual performance is compared.

Micro-blogging Sending messages up to 140 characters.

Micropayments Payment of small sums using a mobile device.

Mission-critical When business will grind to a halt if a company's legacy systems crash or stop working.

Mission statement Defines why an organization exists.

Mobile banking Carrying out banking transactions using mobile devices.

Mobile broadband Various types of wireless high-speed Internet access through a portable modem, telephone, or other device.

Mobile commerce (m-commerce, m-business) Any e-commerce done in a wireless environment, especially via the Internet.

Mobile electronic payment system. The various systems mobile devices use to purchase goods or services.

Mobile enterprise Enterprise that has the ability to connect and control suppliers, partners, employees, products, and customers from any location.

Mobile government (m-government) The wireless implementation of e-government applications mostly to citizens, but also to businesses.

Mobile intelligence (MI) Information access via mobiles that far exceed desktop or laptop information access.

Mobile portal A gateway to the Internet accessible from mobile devices; aggregates content and services for mobile users.

Mobile social networking Social networking where one or more individuals of similar interests or commonalities, conversing and connecting with one another, use mobile devices, usually with cell phones, and in virtual communities.

Mobile supply chain management (MSCM) Technology that monitors supply networks by observing specific events, disruptions, and exceptions in real-time alerts if problems occur and offers solutions.

Model Simplified representation or abstraction of reality. Models are often formulas.

MRO Products used for maintenance, repair, and operations.

MtCO2e (Metric tonne (ton) carbon dioxide equivalent)

Multichanneling Integrating online and offline channels for maximum reach and effectiveness.

Multidimensional database Specialized data store that organizes facts by dimensions, such as geographical region, product line, salesperson, or time.

Multimedia messaging service (MMS) The next generation of wireless messaging, which will be able to deliver rich media.

M-wallet (mobile wallet) Technology that enables cardholders to make purchases with a single click from their mobile devices; also known as *wireless wallet.*

MySpace Social network that started as a site for fans of independent rock music in Los Angeles.

Net earnings Net income, net profit, or the "bottom line," which is calculated as revenues minus expenses.

Net neutrality The absence of restrictions or priorities placed on the type of content carried over the Internet by carriers.

Network port Physical interface for communication between a computer and other devices on a network.

Networked computing A corporate information infrastructure that provides the necessary networks for distributed computing. Users can easily contact each other or databases and communicate with external entities.

Newgroups An area on a computer network devoted to the discussion of a specific topic.

Objective Building blocks of strategy. They set out what the business is trying to achieve. They are action-oriented statements that define the continuous improvement activities that must be done to be successful.

Occupational fraud Abuse of a person's influence in the workplace or deliberate misuse of the organization's resources or assets for personal gain.

Offshoring See *offshore outsourcing.*

Offshore outsourcing Contracting with a vendor, who is located outside of the organization's own country, to develop and manage IT services.

On-demand CRM CRM *hosted* by an ASP or other vendor on the vendor's premise; in contrast to the traditional practice of buying the software and using it *on-premise.*

One-back For any location on the supply chain, this is the immediate previous source.

One-up   For any location on the supply chain, this is the immediate subsequent recipient.

Online analytical processing (OLAP)   Systems that contain *read-only data* that can be queried and analyzed much more efficiently than OLTP application databases.

Online communities   Social networks of individuals who interact through specific media.

Online processing   Processing system that operates on a transaction as soon as it occurs, possibly even in real time.

Online transaction processing (OLTP)   A transaction processing system where transactions are executed as soon as they occur.

Onshore sourcing   Using vendors who are in the same country.

Open graph   An initiative proposed by Facebook that will link other Web sites to Facebook.

Open-source software   A software for which the source code (how the software was actually written) is available for anyone free of charge.

Operational awareness   The ability to see at any given time what is happening in the department or functional area of a business.

Operational BI   A relatively new operation. Used to manage day-to-day operations.

Operational data store   Database for transaction processing systems that uses data warehouse concepts to provide clean data.

Operational decisions   Ensure that day-to-day operations are running correctly and efficiently.

Operational-level information systems (or operational ISs)   System that captures and records all a company's data from operations and performs routine transactions needed to conduct business on an ongoing day-to-day basis.

Operational responsiveness   The ability to respond to unexpected changes in conditions and customer demands as they occur.

Operational risk   The risk of a loss due to inadequate or failed internal processes, people, and systems or from external events.

Operational systems   Systems designed to store data required by an organization (e.g., sales orders, customer deposits) and are optimized to capture and handle large volumes of transactions.

Optimization   Finding the best possible solution.

Order fulfillment   All of the activities needed to provide customers with ordered goods and services, including related customer services.

Organizational transformation   A major change in the way that an organization does business, often enabled by the application of information technology.

Outbound logistics   Products are prepared for delivery (packing, storing, and shipping).

Outsource relationship management (ORM)   Provides automated tools to monitor and manage outsource relationships.

Outsourcing   Contracting with a vendor, who is outside of the organization, to develop and manage IT services.

OWL (Web Ontology Language)   A type of language that was developed by the W3C to categorize and accurately identify the nature of things found on the Internet.

Packet   A small unit of data.

Packet switching   The path of the signal is digital and is neither dedicated nor exclusive.

Palm OS   Palm, Inc. mobile OS.

Parallel approach   An implementation approach where both new and old systems operate simultaneously for a designated period of time.

Partner relationship management (PRM)   Business strategy that focuses on providing comprehensive quality service to business partners.

Payment Card Industry Data Security Standard (PCI DSS)   Data security standard created by Visa, MasterCard, American Express, and Discover that is required for all members, merchants, or service providers who store, process, or transmit cardholder data.

Payment Card Industry Security Standards Council (PCI SSC)   Organization founded by American Express, Discover Financial Services, JCB International, MasterCard Worldwide, and Visa, Inc.

Performance management   These help to monitor business metrics and key performance indicators (KPIs).

Periodic report   Report created or run according to a preset schedule (daily, weekly, or quarterly).

Personal data assistant (PDA)   A small, handheld wireless computer.

Personal information management (PIM)   A system that supports the activities performed by individuals in their work or life through the acquisition, organization, maintenance, retrieval, and sharing of information.

Personalization   The user's personal characteristics that impact how relevant the 3Cs—content, commerce, and community—are to the individual.

Pervasive computing   Invisible, everywhere computing that is embedded in the objects around us.

Phased approach   An implementation approach that is based on the module or version concept, where each module or version of the system is implemented as it is developed and tested.

Phishing   Deceptive attempt to steal a person's confidential information by pretending to be a legitimate organization.

Physical controls   Protection of physical computer facilities and resources.

Physical system design   States how the system will perform its functions, with actual physical specifications.

Pilot approach   An implementation approach that is "pilot tested" at one site first, using either the plunge or the parallel approach, and later rolled out to other sites using the plunge approach.

Planners Lab   Software for building a DVD. It is free to academic institutions.

Plunge approach   An implementation system where the old system is turned off at the end of business on Day 0 and the new system is put into operation at the beginning of Day 1.

Pod or podcast   Video file transferred over a network.

Podcaster   Creator of pods.

Podcasting   Distributing or receiving audio and video files called pods or podcasts over the Internet.

Portal   Web-based gateway to files, information, and knowledge on a network.

Predictive analysis   A tool that helps determine the probable future outcome for an event or the likelihood of a situation occurring. It also identifies relationships and patterns.

Predictive analytics   The branch of data mining that focuses on forecasting trends (e.g., regression analysis) and estimating probabilities of future events. Business analytics, as it is also called, provides the models, which are formulas or algorithms, and procedures to BI.

Price-to-performance ratio   The relative cost, usually on a per-mips (millions of instructions per second) basis, of the processing power of a computer.

Primary activities   In Porter's value chain model, those activities in which materials are purchased and processed to products, which are then delivered to customers. Secondary activities, such as accounting, support the primary ones.

Primary key   Field or attribute that uniquely identifies a record in a database.

Priority matrix   A simple diagramming technique that assesses a technology's potential impact—from transformational to low—against the number of years it will take before it reaches mainstream adoption.

Private cloud   Cloud owned by a large company or government agency with multiple locations when data confidentiality is required.

Process improvement teams   Eliminates the non-value-adding steps and resolves quality problems in order to reduce the time needed to complete a process by adding new processes and/or deleting, splitting, combining, expanding, or reducing existing processes.

Productivity paradox   The seeming discrepancy between extremely large IT investments in the economy and relatively low measures of productivity output.

Produce-to-stock   The manufacture of products to stockpile inventory so the company is ready to respond to future demand.

Programming attacks   Attack that involves programming techniques to modify other computer programs, such as a virus or worm.

Project portfolio   IT resources, such as infrastructure, application services, data services, security services, to be developed.

Proper resource allocation   The optimal distribution of resources to a specific place at a specific time to achieve a specific purpose.

Protocol   The standard or set of rules that govern how devices on a network exchange and how they need to function in order to "talk" to each other.

Public exchange (exchange)   E-marketplace in which there are many sellers and many buyers, and entry is open to all; frequently owned and operated by a third party.

"Pure Play" BPM tools   Software tools that combine text and graphics and offer more advanced features such as a repository that allows reuse of resources and simulations. Using these, the process can be captured in greater detail, with a higher degree of accuracy.

Radio frequency identification (RFID)   Generic term for technologies that use radio waves to automatically identify individual items.

Random file organization   Records can be accessed directly regardless of their location on the storage medium. Also called direct file organization.

Reach and richness   An economic impact of EC: the trade-off between the number of customers a company can reach (called *reach*) and the amount of interactions and information services it can provide to them (*richness*).

Real-time system   An information system that provides real-time access to information or data.

Real-time visibility   The ability to consistently have the right customer sizes in stock.

Record   Related characters combined into a field or related fields, such as vendor name, address, and account data.

Reintermediation   Occurs where intermediaries such as brokers provide value-added services and expertise that cannot be eliminated when EC is used.

Relative advantage   The degree to which the new system is perceived as being better than the system it replaces, often expressed in the economic or social status terms that will result from its adoption.

Reliability   The degree to which the new system is perceived as being better than the system it replaces, often expressed in the economic or social status terms that will result from its adoption.

Remote Administration Trojan (RAT)   Malicious code that is a type of backdoor used to enable remote control over a compromised (infected) machine.

Requests for quotes (RFQ)   Listing an item or service on an auction site.

Resource allocation   Consists of developing the plans for hardware, software, data communications and networks, facilities, personnel, and financial resources needed to execute the master development plan, as defined in the requirements analysis.

Response hierarchies   Model that business use to set measurable objectives. Stages include: awareness, knowledge, liking, preference, and purchase.

Retinal scan   A biometric control that matches a user to the pattern of blood vessels in their retina.

Reverse auction   Auction in which the buyer places an item for bid (*tender*) on a request for quote (RFQ) system, potential suppliers bid on the job, with the price reducing sequentially, and the lowest bid wins; primarily a B2B or G2B mechanism.

Reverse logistics   A flow of material or finished goods back to the source; for example, the return of defective products by customers.

Reverse supply chain   Products that are returned.

Robot   Programmable machines.

Rootkit   Set of network administration tools to take control of the network.

RSS (Really Simply Syndication)   A standard of Web feed formats, usually Really Simple Syndication, that automate the delivery of Internet content.

RSS reader   A place where RSS feeds allow users to aggregate regularly changing data, such as blog entries, news stories, audio, and video.

Safety stock   Extra inventory kept in case of unexpected events. Also called *buffer stock*.

Sales automation software   Productivity software used to automate the work of salespeople.

SAP R/3   The leading EPR software (from SAP AG Corp.); a highly integrated package containing more than 70 business activities modules.

SAR (specific absorption rate)   A way of measuring the quantity of radio frequency energy absorbed by the body.

SCM 2.0   The use of social media tools to increase effectiveness of this communication, and enhancement of the acquisition of information necessary to make optimal decisions.

SCM software   Applications programs specifically designed to improve decision making in segments of the supply chain.

Scalability   Being able to add additional capacity incrementally, quickly and as needed.

Scenario planning   A methodology in which planners first create several scenarios; then a team compiles as many future events as possible that may influence the outcome of each scenario.

Search engines   Web sites designed to help people find information stored on other sites.

Search engine optimization (SEO)   The process of improving the volume or quality of traffic to a Web site from search engines via unpaid search results.

Secondary key   Nonunique field that has some identifying information (e.g., country of manufacture).

Sell-side marketplace   B2B model in which organizations sell to other organizations from their own private e-marketplace and/or from a third-party site.

Semantic Web   An evolving extension of the Web in which Web content can be expressed not only in natural language but also in a form that can be understood, interpreted, and used by intelligent computer software agents, permitting them to find, share, and integrate information more easily.

Semistructured decisions   Decisions in which only some of the phases are structured; require a combination of standard solution procedures and individual judgment.

Sensitivity analysis   Study of the impact that changes in one or more parts of a model have on other parts or the outcome.

Sequential file organization   Way in which data records are organized on tape requiring that they be retrieved in the same physical sequence in which they are stored.

Service-level agreement (SLA)   A written legal contract between a service provider and client wherein the service provider guarantees a minimum level of service.

Service-oriented architecture (SOA) An architectural concept that defines the use of services to support a variety of business needs. In SOA, existing IT assets (called services) are *reused* and *reconnected* rather than the more time consuming and costly reinvention of new systems.

Service packs Microsoft's releases to update and patch vulnerabilities in its operating systems or other software.

Session Initiation Protocol (SIP) Standardizes the signaling of calls or communications between different types of devices/end points from different vendors such as IP phones, instant messaging clients, softphones, and smartphones.

SharePoint An integrated suite of capabilities that provides content management and enterprise search to support collaboration.

Sharing site A Web site that allows users to share photos, videos, or other ideas/media.

Short codes A code of only five or six characters.

Shortage The absence of inventory.

Short messaging service (SMS) Technology that allows for sending of short text messages on some cell phones.

Signature A biometric control that matches a user to their signature.

Single sign-on Needing only one password, entered one time, to enter a Web site.

Six sigma A methodology to manage process variations that cause defects, defined as unacceptable deviation from the mean or target, and to systematically work toward managing variation to prevent those defects.

Smart phone Internet-enabled cell phones that can support mobile applications.

SMART 2020 Report The world's first comprehensive global study of the IT sector's growing significance for the world's climate.

Social bookmarking A method for Internet users to share, organize, search, and manage bookmarks of Web pages.

Social computing An approach aimed at making the human–computer interface more natural.

Social engineering Collection of tactics used to manipulate people into performing actions or divulging confidential information.

Social graph The global social network that reflects how we are all connected to one another through relationships.

Social marketplace The term social marketplace is derived from the combination of social networking and marketplaces, such that a social marketplace acts like an online community, harnessing the power of one's social networks for the introduction, buying, and selling of products, services, and resources, including people's own creations. A social marketplace can also be referred to as a structure that resembles a social network but has a focus on its individual members.

Social media The online platforms and tools that people use to share opinions and experiences, including photos, videos, music, insights, and perceptions, with each other.

Social media metrics The data-driving measurements that evaluate the effectiveness of social media efforts.

Social media monitoring Gives marketers the ability to discover public conversations about their brands and allows them to respond directly to their posts.

Social media monitoring services Services that use IT to track online content and then feed summary statistics into dashboards that can be used by their clients.

Social media ROI. This approach attempts to monetize the return on the cost of implementing social media strategies.

Social network Web sites that connect people with specified interests by providing free services such as photo and video sharing, instant messaging, blogging, and wikis.

Social network analysis (SNA) The mapping and measuring of relationships and flows between people, groups, organizations, animals, computers, or other information or knowledge processing entities. The nodes in the network are the people and groups, whereas the links show relationships or flows between the nodes. SNA provides both a visual and a mathematical analysis of relationships.

Social network service (SNS) A primarily Web-based service that uses software to build online social networks for communities of people who share interests and activities or who are interested in exploring the interests and activities of others. These services provide a collection of various ways for users to interact, such as chat, messaging, email, video, voice chat, file sharing, blogging, discussion groups, and so on.

Social network services (SNSs) Web sites that allow people to build their home pages for free and provide basic communication and other support tools to conduct different activities in the social network.

Softphone Computer that functions as a telephone via VoIP.

Software-as-a Service (SaaS) Also referred to as *on-demand computing*, *utility computing*, or *hosted services*. Instead of buying and installing expensive packaged enterprise applications, users access applications over a network, with an Internet browser being the only absolute necessity.

Sourcing Organizational arrangement instituted for obtaining IT products and services, and the management of resources and activities required for producing these services. These arrangements include insourcing, outsourcing, and offshore outsourcing.

Sourcing strategy Strategy to reduce cost of goods, increase speed to market, and improve quality of products.

Spam Use of e-mail to send unsolicited bulk messages.

SPRQL Language developed by the W3C that is a Protocol and RDF Query Language. It is used to write language programs that can retrieve and manipulate data stored in RDF format.

Spend management The way in which companies control and optimize the money they spend. It involves cutting operating and other costs associated with doing business. These costs typically show up as operating costs, but can also be found in other areas and in other members of the supply chain.

Spot sourcing Purchasing indirect materials on an as-needed basis.

Spyware Software that obtains information from a user's computer without the user's knowledge or consent.

Standard Operating Procedure (SOP) A clearly defined and mandatory procedure to be followed without deviation to complete a process or function.

Storage as a Service Storage capacity offered on a per usage basis, similar to SaaS.

Strategic decisions Decisions for sustained enterprise success and business growth.

Strategic planning A series of processes in which an organization selects and arranges its businesses or services to keep the organization viable even when unexpected events disrupt one or more of its business's markets, products, or services.

Strategy A broad-based formula for how a business is going to accomplish its mission, what its goals should be, and what plans and policies will be needed to carry out those goals.

Structured decisions Decisions that are routine and repetitive problems for which standard solutions exist.

Supplier relationship management (SRM) A comprehensive approach to managing an enterprise's interactions with the organizations that supply the goods and services it uses.

Supply chain A pipeline composed of multiple companies that perform any of the following functions: procurement of materials, transformation of materials into intermediate or finished products, distribution of finished products to retailers or customers, recycling or disposal in a landfill.

Supply chain management (SCM)   The management of all of the activities along the supply chain, from suppliers, to internal logistics within a company, to distribution, to customers. This includes ordering, monitoring, and billing.

Supply chain team   A group of tightly coordinated employees who work together to serve the customer; each task is done by the member of the team who is best capable of doing the task.

Support activities   Business activities that do not add value directly to a firm's product or service under consideration but support the primary activities that do add value.

Sustainability   Refers to the concept of using things at a rate that does not deplete their availability in future generations.

Sustainable biofuels   Energy source that will not be depleted in future generations.

SWOT analysis   Involves the evaluation of strengths and weaknesses, which are internal factors, and opportunities and threats, which are external factors.

Symbian OS   Symbian Foundation mobile OS.

Systematic sourcing   Direct materials are traded in large quantities in an environment of a long-term relationship.

Systems development life cycle (SDLC)   Large IT projects, especially those that involve infrastructure, are developed according to this methodology.

Tacit knowledge   The domain of subjective, cognitive, and experimental knowledge that is highly personal and difficult to formalize.

Tactical decisions   Decisions ensuring that existing operations and processes are in alignment with business objectives and strategies.

Tactical metrics   A way an organization can define and measure their objectives.

Tags   Identifier to describe various aspecsts of a Web page.

Tag clouds   Graphic representations of all the tags people have attached to a particular page.

Target   Desired levels of performance.

TCP/IP (Transmission Control Protocol/Internet Protocol)   Internet protocols created by U.S. Department of Defense to ensure and preserve data integrity and maintain communications in the event of catastrophic war.

Task–technology dependency   The ability of a technology to efficiently and effectively execute a task.

Technical resource strategy   Defines how IT is used internally within the company to improve operational efficiencies, with associated bottom line cost savings.

Technology acceptance model (TAM)   A robust, powerful, and simple model that measures an individual's intention to use technology by measuring two basic concepts: "perceived ease of use" and "perceived usefulness." The TAM is a good indicator of the success or failure of system implementation. It was originally developed by Fred Davis in 1989.

Technology adoption lifecycle   A technique developed in 1957 at Iowa State College to track the purchase patterns of hybrid seed corn by farmers, and currently used to explain how innovations are adopted for use in organizations.

Telematics   The integration of computers and wireless communications to improve information flow using the principles of telemetry.

Text   Unstructured data and an asset that can be managed.

Text analytics   Transforms unstructured text into structured "text data" that can then be searched, mined, or discovered.

Text mining   The application of data mining techniques to discover actionable and meaningful patterns, profiles, and trends from documents or other text data.

Thumbprint or fingerprint   A biometric control that matches a thumb or fingerprint to the user.

Time-to-exploitation   Elapsed time between when a vulnerability is discovered and the time it is exploited.

Tool-based metrics   Measurements designed to identify information about specific applications.

Total benefits of ownership (TBO)   An approach for calculating the payoff of an IT investment by calculating both the tangible and the intangible benefits and subtracting the costs of ownership: TBO–TCO=Payoff.

Total cost of ownership (TCO)   A formula for calculating the cost of owning and operating an IT system; includes acquisition cost, operations cost, and control cost.

Total quality management (TQM)   A management strategy aimed at embedding awareness of quality in all organizational processes.

Trackback   A type of hyperlink that is inserted into one's blog.

Traditional BI   Strategic and tactical BI.

Transaction costs   Costs that are associated with the distribution (sale) and/or exchange of products and services, including the cost of searching for buyers and sellers, gathering information, negotiating, decision making, monitoring the exchange of goods, and legal fees.

Transaction processing system (TPS)   An information system that processes an organization's basic business transactions such as purchasing, billing, and payroll.

Transport Control Protocol (TCP)   Network standard that provides a reliable, error-checking, connection-oriented delivery method.

Trojan horse   Malicious code that creates backdoors, giving an attacker illegal access to a network or account through a network port.

Tweets   Text posts to the Twitter Web site using the Web, phone, or IM. Tweets are delivered immediately to those signed up to receive them via the same methods.

Two-factor authentication   System to verify a user's identity based on two pieces of information, such as a password and smart card.

Unified messaging (UM)   Bringing together all messaging media such as e-mail, voice, mobile text, SMS, and fax into a combined communications medium.

Unstructured decisions   Decisions that involve a lot of uncertainty for which there are no definitive or clear-cut solutions.

Upload speed   How quickly data can be sent to a network or how fast a connection can transfer data from source computer or mobile device.

URI (uniform resource identifier)   One of the features that allow data to be used by multiple applications.

Usenet   Network that provided initial platform for online communities to make it possible for users to exchange messages on various topics.

User acceptance   The extent to which a new system is perceived as being useful and easy to use by the system users. Acceptance of a system will be higher if users are involved in systems design.

User Datagram Protocol (UDP)   Network standard that does not check for errors, and as a result, has less overhead and is faster than a connection-oriented protocol such as TCP. With UDP, the quality of the transmission is sacrificed for speed.

Utility computing   Unlimited computing power and storage capacity that, like electricity, water, and telephone services, can be obtained on demand, used and reallocated for any application, and billed on a pay-per-use basis.

Value chain model   Model developed by Michael Porter that shows the primary activities that sequentially add value to the profit margin; also shows the support activities.

Value proposition   The analysis of the benefits of using the specific model (tangible and intangible), including the customers' value proposition.

Vendor-managed inventory (VMI) Strategy used by retailers of allowing suppliers to monitor the inventory levels and replenish inventory when needed, eliminating the need for purchasing orders.

Vertical search A search strategy that focuses on finding information in a particular content area, such as travel, finance, legal, and medical.

Vertically integrated companies Companies that control every part of their business from research and development to manufacturing and logistics.

Viral blogging Viral marketing done by bloggers.

Viral marketing Word-of-mouth marketing by which customers promote a product or service by telling others about it.

Virtual community A group of people with similar interests who interact with one another using the Internet.

Virtual credit card A payment mechanism that allows a buyer to shop with an ID number and a password instead of with a credit card number, yet the charges are made to the credit card.

Virtual factory Collaborative enterprise application that provides a computerized model of a factory.

Virtualization A concept that separates business applications and data from hardware resources, allowing companies to pool hardware resources, rather than dedicate servers to application and assign those resources to applications as needed.

Virtual organizations Organizations in which the product, the process, and the delivery agent are all digital; also called *pure-play organizations.*

Virtual private network (VPN) Connects remote sites or users together privately using "virtual" connections routed through the Internet from the company's private network to the remote site or employee.

Virtual teams Groups of people who work interdependently with a shared purpose across space, time, and organization boundaries using technology to communicate and collaborate.

Virtual world A computer-based simulated environment intended for its users to inhabit virtual spaces and interact via avatars.

Virtual world A user-defined 3D world in which people can interact, play, and do business with the help of avatars.

Virus Malicious code that attaches itself and infects other computer programs, without the owner of the program being aware of the infection.

Vision statement An organization's picture of where it wants to be in the future.

VoIP (Voice over Internet Protocol) Voice communication over a network using the Internet Protocol. Also called IP telephony.

Voice commerce (v-commerce) An umbrella term for the use of speech recognition to allow voice-activated services including Internet browsing and e-mail retrieval.

Voice portal A Web site that can be accessed by voice (e.g., via cell phone), and not via a computer.

Voice scan A biometric control that matches a user to their voice pattern.

WAN (wide area network) Network that covers a large geographic area, such as a state, province, or county.

War driving Stealth search for wireless local area networks by driving around a city or elsewhere.

Warehouse management system (WMS) A software system that helps in managing warehouses.

Wearable devices Mobile wireless computing devices for employees who work on buildings and other difficult-to-climb places.

Web 2.0 The second generation of Internet-based services that let people collaborate and create information online in perceived new ways—such as social networking sites, wikis, and blogs.

Web 3.0 A term used to describe the future of the World Wide Web. It consists of the creation of high-quality content and services produced by gifted individuals using Web 2.0 technology as an enabling platform.

Web (or WWW) Application that runs on the Internet, as does e-mail, IM, and VoIP. A system with universally accepted standards or protocols for storing, retrieving, formatting, and displaying information via client/server architecture.

Web analytics The analysis of clickstream data to understand visitor behavior on a Web site.

Web-based system An application delivered on the Internet or intranet using Web tools, such as a search engine.

Web mining The application of data mining techniques to discover actionable and meaningful patterns, profiles, and trends from Web resources.

Web Services Modular business and consumer applications, delivered over the Internet, that users can select and combine through almost any device, enabling disparate systems to share data and services. These are software systems designed to support machine-to-machine interactions over a network.

Widget A small application that can be installed and executed within a Web page by an end user.

Wi-Fi Technology that allows computers to share a network or Internet connection wirelessly without the need to connect to a commercial network.

Wiki Software program, discovery tool, collaboration site, and social network.

WiMax A wireless standard (IEEE 802.16) for making broadband network connections over a large area.

Windows Mobile OS Microsoft mobile OS.

Wired equivalent privacy (WEP) Weak cryptographic technique used for encryption.

Wireless 911 (e-911) Calls from cellular phones to providers of emergency services.

Wireless access point (WAP Device that allows wireless communication devices to connect to a wireless network.

Wireless application protocol (WAP) A set of communications protocols designed to enable different kinds of wireless devices to talk to a server installed on a mobile network, so users can access the Internet.

Wireless encryption protocol (WEP) Built-in security system in wireless devices, which encrypts communications between the device and a wireless access point.

Wireless fidelity (Wi-Fi) The standard on which most of today's WLANs run, developed by the IEEE (Institute of Electrical and Electronic Engineers). Also known as *802.11b.*

Wireless mobile computing (mobile computing) Computing that connects a mobile device to a network or another computing device, anytime, anywhere.

Wireless sensor networks (WSNs) Networks of interconnected, battery-powered, wireless sensors called *motes* (analogous to nodes) that are placed into specific physical environments. Each mote collects data and contains processing, storage, and radio frequency sensors and antennas. The motes provide information that enables a central computer to integrate reports of the same activity from different angles within the network. Therefore, the network can determine information such as the direction a person is moving, the weight of a vehicle, or the amount of rainfall over a field of crops with great accuracy.

WLAN (Wireless Local Area Network) Type of local area network that uses high-frequency radio waves rather than wires to communicate between computers or devices such as printers, which are referred to as nodes on the network.

Wireless LAN (WLAN) LAN without the cables; used to transmit and receive data over the airwaves, but only from short distances.

Word processors A text-based document processor that is one of the simplest ways to document a process.

Work Breakdown Structure (WBS) A project plan where the project scope is defined, and is used to estimate a realistic timeline and budget based on the availability of necessary resources.

Workflow management (WFM) A technique where documents, information, and activities flow between participants according to existing process models and rules; refers to activities performed by businesses to optimize and adapt their processes.

World Wide Web Consortium (W3C) Group working on programming standards to make it possible for data, information, and knowledge to be shared even more widely across the Internet.

Worm Malicious code that uses networks to propagate and infect anything attached to it—including computers, handheld devices, Web sites, and servers.

WWWANs (wireless wide area networks) WAN for mobile computing.

XBRL (eXtensible Business Reporting Language) Version of XML for capturing financial information throughout a business's information processes.

XML (eXtensible Markup Language) Meta-language for describing markup languages for documents containing structured information. XML-based systems facilitate data sharing across different systems and particularly systems connected via the Internet.

Zombies Computers that are infected.